The World Community between Hegemony and Constitutionalism

The World Community between Hegemony and Constitutionalism

Andraž Zidar

eleven
international publishing

Published, sold and distributed by Eleven International Publishing
P.O. Box 85576
2508 CG The Hague
The Netherlands
Tel.: +31 70 33 070 33
Fax: +31 70 33 070 30
e-mail: sales@elevenpub.nl
www.elevenpub.com

Sold and distributed in USA and Canada
Independent Publishers Group
814 N. Franklin Street
Chicago, IL 60610
USA
Order Placement: (800) 888-4741
Fax: (312) 337-5985
orders@ipgbook.com
www.ipgbook.com

Eleven International Publishing is an imprint of Boom uitgevers Den Haag.

ISBN 978-94-6236-924-5
ISBN 978-94-6274-558-2 (E-book)

To my family – present, past and future

Table of Contents

Part II Power, Hegemony and Constitutionalism in International Law

List of Abbreviations

ADIZ	China's air defense identification zone
AJIL	American Journal of International Law
ASILP	American Society of International Law Proceedings
BaYBIL	Baltic Yearbook of International Law
BIT	Bilateral investment treaty
BRI	Belt and Road initiative
BYIL	British Yearbook of International Law
CAT	UN Convention against Torture and Other Cruel, Inhuman or Degrading Treatment or Punishment
COE	Council of Europe
CTC	UN Counter-Terrorism Committee
CTCED	UN Counter-Terrorism Committee Executive Directorate
CUP	Cambridge University Press
DDA	Doha Development Agenda
DSM	Dispute Settlement Mechanism
DSU	Dispute Settlement Understanding
EC	European Commission
ECHR	European Convention on Human Rights
ECtHR	European Court of Human Rights
ECJ	European Court of Justice/Court of Justice of the European Union
EEAS	European External Action Service
EEZ	Exclusive Economic Zone
EJIL	European Journal of International Law
ENP	European Neighbourhood Policy
FRY	Federal Republic of Yugoslavia (Serbia and Montenegro)
GA	UN General Assembly
GATS	General Agreement on Trade in Services
GATT	General Agreement on Tariffs and Trade
GYIL	German Yearbook of International Law
HIL	Hegemonic International Law
HRC	Human Rights Committee
IACHR	Inter-American Convention on Human Rights
ICC	International Criminal Court
ICCPR	International Covenant on Civil and Political Rights
ICISS	International Commission on Intervention of State Sovereignty
ICL	International Constitutional Law
ICLQ	International and Comparative Law Quarterly
ICJ	International Court of Justice
ICTY	International Tribunal for Former Yugoslavia
IGC	Intergovernmental conference
ILC	International Law Commission
INF	Intermediate-Range Nuclear Forces
ITLOS	International Tribunal on the Law of the Sea
LAS	League of Arab States
LDCs	Least developed countries

LJIL	Leiden Journal of International Law
MFN	Most favored nation
MOU	Memorandum of Understanding
NAFTA	North American Free Trade Agreement
NATO	North Atlantic Treaty Alliance
NSS	US National Security Strategy
OSPAR	Convention for the Protection of the Marine Environment of the North-East Atlantic
OUP	Oxford University Press
P5	Five permanent members of the UN Security Council
PCA	Permanent Court of Arbitration
PNAC	Project for the New American Century
PPNS	Princeton Project on National Security
PUF	Presses Universitaires de France
R2P	Responsibility to Protect
RCADI	Recueil des Cours de l'Academie de Droit International de la Haye
RGDIP	Revue générale de droit international public
RT	Russia Today
QMV	Qualified majority voting
SC	UN Security Council
TEU	Treaty on European Union
TFEU	Treaty on the Functioning of the European Union
TRIPS	Agreement on Trade-Related Aspect of Intellectual Property Rights
UDHR	Universal Declaration of Human Rights
UN	United Nations
UNCITRAL	United Nations Commission on International Trade Law
UNCLOS	United Nations Convention on the Law of the Sea
UNMIS	United Nations Mission in Sudan
UNOCI	United Nations Operation in Côte d'Ivoire
UNTS	United Nations Treaty Series
USTR	United States Trade Representative
VCCR	Vienna Convention on Consular Relations
VCLT	Vienna Convention on the Law of the Treaties
VRS	Republika Srpska armed forces
WMD	Weapons of mass destruction
WSO	World Summit Outcome
WTO	World Trade Organization
WWII	World War II

Introduction

Introduction

Two dominant global trends of today's world are hegemony and constitutionalism. Although the structure of the world community still revolves around the inter-state Westphalian logic, practical developments attest to a move away from the increasingly dysfunctional premise of 'effective multilateralism'. It is true that the main portion of global political, social and economic processes occurs within the post WWII architectural setup, embodying the horizontal framework of relations between states and international organizations.[1] But ever since the attacks of 9/11, the world dynamic has been developing in the direction of two potent and seemingly distinct global currents. Greater states or regional blocks, such as the United States, Russia, China, and the European Union have become more assertive in pursuing their interests in the international arena. Their attitude represents hegemony. In parallel, the process of constitutionalism is getting stronger. In this vein, international organizations are extending the scope of their actions, international adjudicatory bodies are expanding their judicial powers and 'higher norms' of international law resonate more profoundly in the international legal reality.

At first sight, hegemony and constitutionalism seem unrelated. But a detailed look reveals that the two phenomena are intertwined. Even though the great powers tend to resort to unilateral measures when confronted with the international reality, they are unable to manage complex global problems without the assistance of international norms, mechanisms and processes. On the other hand, there is a clear tendency of the international community to establish constitutional supranational structures that will have normative and institutional powers to regulate problems on the global scale. However, these institutions cannot be efficient without the support of states, including the powerful ones. The purpose of this work is to shed more light on the relationship between hegemony and constitutionalism.

The reason behind these developments is the power shift from the state level to the international level.[2] In the domain of international law, some authors speak of the disaggregation of the state power.[3] The process of power migration beyond national borders is generally described as globalization, which is primarily an economic phenomenon

1 *See* M. Mazower, *Governing the World: The History of an Idea*, The Penguin Press, New York, 2012, pp. 415-427.

2 *See, e.g.*, R. Falk, *Power Shift: On the New Global Order*, Zed Books, London, 2016 and A. Etzioni, *From Empire to Community: A New Approach to International Relations*, Palgrave Macmillan, New York, 2004.

3 *See* A.-M. Slaughter, *A New World Order*, Princeton University Press, Princeton (NJ)-Oxford, 2005, S. Sur, 'The State between Fragmentation and Globalization', 8 *EJIL* 1997, pp. 421-434 and T.S. Volgy, L. Imwalle & J.E. Schwarz, 'Where is the New World Order? Hegemony, State Strength, and Architectural Construction in International Politics', 2 *Journal of International Relations and Development* 1999, pp. 246-247.

although it affects many other fields, such as politics, culture, science, technology, and law.[4] Globalization can be defined as

> a process (or set of processes) which embodies a transformation in the spatial organization of social relations and transactions – assessed in terms of their extensity, intensity, velocity and impact – generating transcontinental or inter-regional flows and networks of activity, interaction, and the exercise of power.[5]

In the first decade of globalization (1990s), authors mainly underscored positive attributes of globalization: extension of the liberal democracy, more efficient protection for human rights, better international division of work, liberalization of capital flows, development of information technologies, and so on.[6] On this basis, Francis Fukuyama proclaimed 'The End of History' or, in other words, the world triumph of Western democratic liberalism.[7] At the beginning of the new Millennium, however, came the second decade of globalization, which brought to the forefront negative consequences of globalization. The disruptions due to globalization returned as a boomerang[8] and instead of the end of history, Joseph Stiglitz rather speaks of the discontents of globalization.[9] The world of today faces problems of extreme poverty, massive migrations, abrupt changes in the global climate, destruction of biodiversity, poisoning of nature with pesticides and other chemicals, the deterioration of human health and other negative occurrences.[10] All this induces a feeling that humankind is on the verge of a great catastrophe and the spirit of 'catastrophism' has become a regular component of daily life.[11] Scholars who deal with

4 *See* A. Giddens, *Runaway World – How Globalisation is Reshaping Our Lives*, Profile Books, London, 1999, pp. 10, 13, 14, S. Marks & A. Clapham, *International Human Rights Lexicon*, OUP, Oxford, 2005., *s.v. globalisation*, p. 179 and G. Ziccardi Capaldo, *Global Law: The Pillars*, Ashgate Publishing, Aldershot, 2008, p. xv. (Giddens also points that globalization implies migration of power downwards – to the local level. The main dynamic, however, occurs at the international level.)

5 D. Held *et al.*, 'Rethinking Globalization', *in* D. Held & A. McGrew (Eds.), *The Global Transformations Reader: An Introduction to the Globalization Debate*, Polity Press, Cambridge, 1999, p. 16.

6 *See* P. de Senarclens, *Critique de la mondialisation*, Presses de Sciences Po, Paris, 2003, pp. 53-56, Giddens, *Runaway World*, pp. 5, 43, 67-82 and Marks & Clapham, *International Human Rights Lexicon*, pp. 181, 185-186.

7 *See* F. Fukuyama, *The End of History and the Last Man*, Free Press, New York, 2006 and S. Marks, *The Riddle of All Constitutions: International Law, Democracy and the Critique of Ideology*, OUP, Oxford, 2000, p. 32.

8 I. Ramonet, *Géopolitique du chaos*, Galilée, Paris, 1997, p. 58.

9 This is the title of Stiglitz's book in English ('Globalization and Its Discontents'). The French version bears even a more pessimistic title 'La grande désillusion'. (*See* J.E. Stiglitz, *Globalization and its Discontents*, W.W. Norton & Company, New York, 2002.)

10 *See* G.J. Ikenberry, 'The End of Liberal International Order?', 94 *International Affairs* 2018, p. 19, de Senarclens, *Critique de la mondialisation*, pp. 8, 132 and Ramonet, *Géopolitique du chaos*, pp. 11-13.

11 J.-P. Dupuy, *Pour un catastrophisme éclairé*, Editions du Seuil, Paris, 2002, pp. 84-85.

globalization point to the fact that we are living in a period of historical transition, global transformation or even great perturbation.[12]

A closer look at the dynamic of the international community reveals that the world is going through a major paradigm shift.[13] The Westphalian structure of the international community and international law are slowly changing their nature. However, the new paradigm is not yet on the rise.[14] Furthermore, it is becoming increasingly evident that the international community is not capable of confronting and resolving problems, which arise precisely because of globalization.[15] While it is true that the international community is going through transformation, these changes materialize in bits and pieces and at best represent ad hoc responses to burning issues.[16]

As these developments transgress the horizontal logic of the international community, it is more appropriate to use the expression the 'world community'. Changes in the world include other actors and processes going beyond states and international organizations such as individuals, nongovernmental organizations, transnational corporations, transboundary networks and self-generative global processes. The term *world community* in the context of this book is even more appropriate given that the first part surveys the meanings of power, hegemony and constitutionalism through various temporal, historical, geographical and intellectual contexts. Nonetheless, the thrust of the contemporary world still revolves around the concept of the international community, with states and international organizations as main building blocks. Therefore, the international community shall serve as the main reference point throughout this work.

Generally, the community is a social entity, characterized by a high degree of cohesion, which originates in the solidarity between its members to act together for the pursuit of collective interests or common good.[17] As an extension of this logic, the world

12 *See* Ikenberry, 'The End of Liberal International Order?', pp. 8, 18, Giddens, *Runaway World*, p. 1, Ramonet, *Géopolitique du chaos*, p. 15, Z. Laïdi, *La grande perturbation*, Flammarion, Paris, 2004, p. i, Z. Laïdi, *Un monde privé de sens*, Hachette, Paris, 2004, p. iv, de Senarclens, pp. 76, 136 and Y. Sakamoto, 'Editor's Introduction', *in* Y. Sakamoto (Ed.), *Global Transformation: Challenges to the State System*, United Nations University Press, Tokyo-New York-Paris, 1994, p. 1.

13 For the concept of paradigm shifts, particularly in science, *see* T. Kuhn, *La structure des révolutions scientifiques*, Flammarion, Paris, 1983, trans. L. Meyer.

14 *See* contributions in two thematic issues of the *Foreign Affairs* magazine: 'Which World Are We Living in?', 97 *Foreign Affairs* July/August 2018 and 'Out of Order? The Future of the International System', 96 *Foreign Affairs* January/February 2017.

15 R. Haass, 'How a World Order Ends: And What Comes in Its Wake', 98 *Foreign Affairs* 2019, pp. 27-30.

16 *See* A. Bianchi, 'Ad-hocism and the Rule of Law', 13 *EJIL* 2002, pp. 263-272.

17 *See* C.H. McIlwain, *The Growth of Political Thought: From the Greeks to the End of the Middle Ages*, The MacMillan Company, New York, 1955 p. 64, E. Durkheim, *De la division du travail social*, PUF, Paris, 2004, pp. 24-15, 28, 74, F. Tönnies, *Communauté et société : categories fondamentales de la sociologie pure*, PUF, Paris, 1946, trans. J. Leif, pp. 19-21 and Aristotle, *Nicomachean Ethics*, Dover Publications Inc., Mineola (NY), trans. D.P. Chase, pp. 138-139.

community presupposes world actors in the wider landscape of humankind,[18] while the international community focuses on international actors in the essentially horizontal international architecture of sovereign states.[19]

Processes of international hegemony and international constitutionalism are innovative in that they both represent expressions of political power, which rise above the horizontal structure of international level.[20] In this way, the two phenomena proffer answers to contemporary international problems. A detailed look at hegemony and constitutionalism reveals that a concordant appearance of the two phenomena at the international level is not accidental. Hegemony and constitutionalism represent an antinomy. The antinomy stands for a dialectical relationship between the two notions, which simultaneously reaffirm and oppose each other.[21] In terms of dialectical philosophy, antinomy represents a force of progress as it leads to the next, 'higher' stage of historical development.[22] Nonetheless, before a new paradigm arises, antinomic dynamic between the two opposites generates numerous materializations of concrete and empirical reality based on syntheses of both the phenomena. The sequence of progress is therefore not a sudden shift to a new metaparadigm. Rather, it is a process of accumulation of hybrid formations at the intersection of hegemony and constitutionalism. These hegemo-constitutional crystallizations pave the way to a new social finality, that is, to a paradigm shift.[23]

Antinomic dynamic between hegemony and constitutionalism runs as follows. Hegemony represents an expansion of power in which the center dominates the periphery. Hegemony serves the interests of the hegemon. On the other hand, constitutionalism is a process of agglomeration of power, which is followed by the limits put on that power. Constitutionalism serves all entities equally and works in pursuit of the common interest. Conceptually, hegemony (perceived as dominance) is in direct opposition to constitutionalism (illustrated by egalitarianism). And yet, hegemony and constitutionalism cannot exist without each other. Hegemony cannot persist without the stability offered by constitutionalism, while constitutionalism cannot function without the dynamism of hegemony. Thus, there is a recurrent movement from hegemony to constitutionalism and

---

18 *See* J. Bartelson, *Visions of World Community*, CUP, Cambridge, 2009, pp. 11-12 and W.C. Jenks, 'The Will of the World Community as the Basis of Obligation in International Law', *in Hommage d'une generation de jurists au Président Basdevant*, Editions A. Pedone, Paris, 1960, pp. 287-288, 298-299.

19 *See* S. Villalpando, *L'émergence de la communauté internationale dans la responsabilité des Etats*, PUF, Paris, 2005, pp. 26, 40-41.

20 A. Peters, 'The Growth of International Law between Globalization and the Great Power', 8 *Austrian Review of International and European Law* 2003, p. 139.

21 According to Hegel, the world "gets involved in *antinomies*, i.e., in the assertion of two *opposed* propositions about *the same* ob-ject; and it finds, moreover, that each of the propositions must be affirmed with equal necessity." (G.W.F. Hegel, *The Encyclopaedia Logic (with Zusätze)*, Hackett Publishing Company, Indianapolis, 1991, trans. T.F. Gerates, W.A. Suchting & H.S. Harris, p. 91 (§48).)

22 B.M. Zupančič, *The Owl of Minerva: Essays on Human Rights*, Eleven International Publishing, Utrecht, 2008, pp. 6, 34.

23 On understanding the dialectical dynamic as a process *see* L. Sturzo, *Inner Laws of Society: A New Sociology*, P.J. Kennedy & Sons, New York, 1944, in particular Introduction and Chapters 1 and 10.

vice versa. Until a new world paradigm still in the making is established, the most apt description of the contemporaneous reality is the hegemo-constitutional world.

This work is interdisciplinary in combining international law with other social science disciplines, such as history, philosophy, sociology and political science. The interdisciplinary approach is characteristic for the first part of the book. The subsequent parts are, however, anchored in international law. The articulation of the relationship between power and international law enables the fluid communication between social sciences and international law throughout this work.

Part One deals with the topics of power, hegemony and constitutionalism. Chapter 1 focuses on power and surveys the omnipresent, agglomerated, diffused and systematic approaches to the understanding of power. It concludes with an overview of the characteristics of power. Power is fluid, immaterial and spontaneous. It tends towards a further expansion, which leads to agglomeration. When power reaches an aggregated form it opts for diffusion. Power is also a plural phenomenon, which can lead to a coexistence of plural centers of power. Another attribute of power is that it is a structure-forming phenomenon.

The next stage is a thorough analysis of the phenomena of hegemony in Chapter 2 and constitutionalism in Chapter 3. In the generic sense, hegemony stands for an expansion of power, which stabilizes a given structure of interactions through the relation of dominance of the commanding center over the asymmetric periphery. On the other hand, constitutionalism in the broadest sense denotes an agglomeration of power in the form of a structural framework, followed by the exigency of putting limitations on the power so constituted. A confrontation of hegemony and constitutionalism reveals that the two phenomena stand for antinomy, which is inherent in any body politic.

To get a better insight into this antinomy, the logical step is to deconstruct it, which is the topic of Chapter 4. The process of deconstruction goes in two ways. The first approach is to collapse the antinomy to the level of equally plausible premises. This general mode of deconstruction reveals power as the defining element of the two phenomena. The second, empirical approach is to disintegrate it to the level of concrete and pragmatic solutions. Disintegration of the two phenomena leads to the hybrid notion of in-betweenness accommodating a blend of elements belonging to both phenomena (the so-called hegemo-constitutional space). As incomplete as these two modes of deconstruction are, they are important because they provide some valuable insights on the origins of antinomy and on the possible course of future developments.

After determining the meanings of power, hegemony and constitutionalism, Part Two explores the interactions between these concepts and international law. Chapter 5 considers the relationship between power and international law. Social power aims at forming the normative structure in order to secure its peaceful existence (power on the law). Power partly becomes a constituent part of a legal system and serves purposes of law (power in the law). Law, on the other hand, needs power to transform its normative prescriptions into reality on the basis of coercion or legal power and legitimacy (power by the law). Legal power puts constraints on the functioning of social power. In the end, a legal system represents an inherent part of social power, whereas power makes an intrinsic component of law. Power and law are thus interrelated.[24]

Part Two goes on to deal with hegemony and constitutionalism in the international community. The accelerating pace of globalization leads to a situation in which horizontal international law is not able to cope with global processes. A partial response to these socioeconomic processes emerged through power structures of international hegemony and international constitutionalism. The work follows this dynamic through the articulation of the two phenomena in international law: hegemonic international law in Chapter 6 and international constitutional law in Chapter 7. In general, these two expressions of international law perform four functions: (i) they follow the growth of a power structure at the international level; (ii) they put a check on the excessive flow of power at the international level; (iii) they put a check on the opposite phenomenon (hegemony or constitutionalism); and (iv) they transform into the opposite phenomenon (hegemony or constitutionalism).

The chapter on hegemonic international law takes into account the main element of hegemony – dominance of the center over the international periphery – and surveys its application in the field of international law. Hegemonic international law comprises three models: the nationalist, the rational choice and the interventionist. All three models are premised upon three constituent elements: the center, the periphery and the sovereign border between the two. The nationalist model puts a larger emphasis on the self-oriented center that nearly completely overlooks the international periphery. The sovereign border is impermeable and practically allows for no feedback from the periphery. The rational choice theory model operates on the basis of the cost-benefit analysis of exchange between the center and international periphery. This model allows for some interaction between the center and periphery, with the main thrust coming from the hegemon. Finally, the interventionist model seeks its mission in projecting characteristics of the center to the international periphery. While the hegemon is ready to intervene abroad, this dynamic goes in one direction only. Examples by principal international hegemons, such as the United States, Russia, China and the European Union, are illustrated in more detail in the three models.

On the other hand, international constitutional law builds upon the egalitarian treatment of all entities under its province. The chapter on international constitutional law follows the growth of international constitutionalism through five functions: the normative, the institutional, the judicial, the coordinative and the self-referential. The normative component develops norms that have a heightened axiological meaning in the sense that

24 For an excellent analysis of the interrelation between power and law *see* M. Reale, 'Law and Power and Their Correlation', *in* R.A. Newman (Ed.), *Essays in Jurisprudence in Honor of Roscoe Pound*, The Bobbs-Merrill Co., Indianapolis, 1962, pp. 238-270.

they represent fundamental norms of the international community. The institutional component provides the international community with the necessary institutional machinery to put these norms into practice. The judicial component provides a tool for the resolution of disputes through the expansion of judicial powers at the international level. Under the coordinative component, international actors meet through regulatory networks to contribute to and participate in global governance. Finally, the self-referential component takes account of self-generative social processes that contribute to the formation of the global community through the pursuit of their intrinsic functions.

The last, third part of the book studies concrete instances when hegemonic international law and international constitutional law meet, metamorphose into each other and form a hybrid space accommodating elements of both phenomena. This dynamic, which originates in the empirical approach to deconstruction, confirms the existence of antinomy between hegemony and constitutionalism in the international community and shows their coexistence in numerous practical examples of the hegemo-constitutional space. Part Three surveys instances of the hegemo-constitutional space in three wider areas of international law: (i) the functioning of international organizations; (ii) the intervention on humanitarian grounds; and (iii) international adjudication.

Chapter 8 on international organizations deals with the convergence between common interests of international organizations and particular interests of leading member states. More specifically, it analyzes the role of the Security Council as a global legislator, the mechanism of enhanced cooperation in the European Union and the viability of plurilateral agreements in the WTO. The intervention on humanitarian grounds is the topic of Chapter 9, which surveys the tension between the hegemonic use of force for humanitarian purposes and the constitutional features of the international community. As concrete examples, it takes the military intervention in Kosovo and the emerging doctrine of the responsibility to protect. Chapter 10 surveys the field of international adjudication with a focus on the interplay between the judicial tendency to expand its jurisdictional reach and the increasing use of constitutional judicial reasoning and techniques. The chapter analyzes judicial 'battles for meaning' concerning the substantive issue of state responsibility, the procedural issue of jurisdiction and the protection of human rights.

Finally, the following question arises: is the juxtaposition between hegemony and constitutionalism useful for the reflections about the future paradigm of the world community? The general mode of deconstruction sees the origin of antinomy between the two phenomena in the factor of power. This likewise applies to hegemony and constitutionalism at the international level with their extensions in areas of hegemonic international law and international constitutional law. The deconstruction of these two phenomena in the context of underlying premises points to the relevance of the rearrangement of power structures for the novel shape of the world community. The empirical mode of deconstruction procures numerous examples of the hegemo-constitutional space. Although these examples are concrete and pragmatic, they represent accommodation between instances of hegemony and constitutionalism in practice. Taking into account that the dialectical dynamic elevates to a higher stage of progress, they may embed possible elements of the future world community.

These insights point in the direction of the development of the greater agglomeration of power in the form of a new global system that would represent a move away from the horizontal structure of international law. The conclusion of the book surveys some articulations of a possible new paradigm of the world community, such as in the form of the universal and homogeneous state (Alexandre Kojève), the community of universal universalism (Immanuel Wallerstein) and the global community with the rule of the global law at its core (Rafael Domingo).[25]

25 *See* A. Kojève, *Esquisse d'une phenomenologie du droit*, Gallimard, Paris, 1981, pp. 376, 389, I. Wallerstein, *European Universalism: The Rhetoric of Power*, New York-London, New Press, 2006, p. 84 and R. Domingo, *The New Global Law*, CUP, Cambridge, 2011.

Part I
Power, Hegemony and Constitutionalism

1 The Meaning of Power

Hegemony and constitutionalism have their source in the phenomenon of power, which is a key concept in the Western tradition of political thought.[1] However, there is a lack of agreement on its specific definition at the analytical level.[2] The conventional definition stands for a capacity of one actor in a given society to compel the other actor to do something, if necessary, against the latter's will.[3] Yet this is a simplified view, which focuses solely on one of its components; namely, the relation within the social setting. In many older traditions, power was understood as an *omnipresent* phenomenon that was not limited to the social reality. With the advent of humanism and the Renaissance, the concept of power evolved into a social phenomenon destined to form a larger body politic – a state (*agglomerated* power). Subsequently, this notion encountered criticism because of its preoccupation with the political dimension. Scholars of late modernity and post-modernism began to deconstruct the meaning of power and apply it to other areas of social life: for example, the economy, knowledge, sexuality, the health system, the legal field and communications (*diffused* power). Finally, contemporary authors of the twentieth century analyzed the issue of power in a comprehensive way from the perspective of social sciences, such as history, sociology and political science (*systematic* approaches to power).

1.1 Power as an Omnipresent Phenomenon

The conceptualization of power in antiquity started with accounts of its coercive capacity as seen in, for example, Homer's works.[4] Through the practice of the medicine school and the Sophists, the notion of power morphed to include the dynamic component through manifestation of substances.[5] However, it was Plato who first analyzed the concept of power (*dunamis*), though he did not develop it into a systematic doctrine. Plato's *duna-*

---

1 Similar concepts can be found in other cultures worldwide as well (in Africa, Asia, South America and the Pacific region). *See* the following notions in A. Jacob & S. Auroux (Eds.), *Encyclopédie philosophique universelle, II, Les notions philosophiques*, vol. 2, PUF, Paris, 1990: *t'un* (p. 3207), *pule* (p. 3174), *mana* (p. 3134), *komba* (p. 3124), *kuang* (p. 3125), *khuam* (p. 3120), *tenno* (pp. 3040-3041), *san cai* (p. 2974), *sanda* (pp. 2974-2975) and *śakti* (p. 2894).

2 T. Parsons, 'Power and the Social System', *in* S. Lukes (Ed.), *Power*, Basil Blackwell, London, 1987, p. 94.

3 The above definition draws upon Weber's definition of power.

4 *See* Homer, *The Iliad*, William Heinemann Ltd-Harvard University Press, London-Cambridge (MA), 1960, 1963, trans. A.T. Murray, and Homer, *The Odyssey*, Harvard University Press-William Heinemann Ltd, Cambridge (MA)-London, 1960, trans. A.T. Murray.

5 J. Souilhé, *Etude sur le terme dunamis dans les dialogues de Platon*, Librairie Félix Alcan, Paris, 1919, pp. 36, 70.

mis has a philosophical meaning through the revelatory quality of beings, which can be seen in an active and a passive sense. In the active sense, it affirms itself as an active attribute that resides in different entities and, through its exercise in the form of an expansive force, contributes to the manifestations and definition of those entities.[6] In the passive sense, power means that things undergo modifications through interactions that subsequently bear impressions on their essence. Their state of being or their attitude represents for them a way to manifest themselves.[7] Power in Plato therefore, has two components: the active one in the form of expansive force: and the passive one in the sense of internalizing the interaction. Plato's *dunamis* is important because it is dynamic in a sense that it hints at finality.

The conceptualization of *dunamis* as a principle of motion prompted Aristotle to elaborate a coherent doctrine around potency, and to link it to the category of finality in the form of actuality.[8] Aristotle follows Plato to define potency through its active and passive components. Therefore,

> the authoritative definition of potency in the primary sense will be "a principle producing change, which is in something other than that in which the change takes place, or in the same thing *qua* other".[9]

This use of potency comprises both, the factual aspect of power and the component of capacity that demonstrates potentiality. Aristotle breaks down this general definition into subcomponents encompassing:

a. a principle of change in something other than the thing changed or in it *qua* other;
b. a principle enabling a thing to be changed, by another or by itself *qua* other;
c. the power of producing change successfully;
d. the power of being changed successfully; and
e. a state in virtue of which a thing cannot be changed, or cannot be easily changed, for the worse.[10]

---

6 Ibid., pp. 149, 154. *See* Plato, *Lysis, Symposium, Gorgias*, William Heinemann Ltd-Harvard University Press, London-Cambridge (MA), 1961, trans. W.R.M. Lamb, 188 D, pp. 131, 133.

7 Souilhé, *Etude sur le terme dunamis dans les dialogues de Platon*, p. 152.

8 *Cf.* ibid., pp. 70, 168-170, 183. A caveat should be added that the consideration of the dichotomy between potency and actuality should be always placed in the context of the whole of Aristotle's teaching and related to other fundamental concepts in it, such as the prime mover, the doctrine of causes, the kinds of motion, the finiteness of the universe, the ultimate deduction of a primer mover etc. (*Cf.* I.E. Drabkin, 'Notes of the Laws of Motion in Aristotle', 59 *The American Journal of Philology* 1938, p. 61.)

9 Aristotle, *Metaphysics, Books I-IX*, William Heinemann Ltd-Harvard University Press, London-Cambridge (MA), 1961, trans. H. Tredennick, 1020a, p. 255.

10 W.D. Ross, *Aristotle's Metaphysics: A Revised Text with Introduction and Commentary*, Clarendon Press, Oxford, 1924, vol. I, pp. 318-319.

In each of these subcomponents, potency requires at least two entities and a motion between them. In other words, potency presupposes a relation between entities. Motion can be understood as "the progress of the realizing of a potentiality, *qua* potentiality".[11] Motion serves as a bridge between potency and actuality.[12]

Actuality (*energeia* and *entelexeia*)[13] is the point where potency reaches out into a new, higher qualitative stage. Potency is inconceivable without considering actuality, and can arrive at an apprehension of potency only due to its actuality.[14] The potency-actuality pair is strongly interrelated. Potency always gravitates towards a specific actuality while actuality contains traces of the preceding process which enabled it to come into being. However, since actuality always represents a new qualitative achievement, it is in every respect superior to potency. Actuality and potency are two notions that mutually presuppose and explain each other.[15]

The doctrine of power in antiquity presupposes a relation between potency and actuality. Potency implies power and potentiality of an entity, which can lead either to the subsequent change in another entity or to the process of that entity being subject to a change. This process is dynamic and has an aim to produce a final result in the sense of actuality, which represents a new qualitative achievement. The doctrine of power in antiquity therefore includes potency, the process of motion and the final result in the form of actuality. As this doctrine can be applied to virtually every discipline or field, it has an *omnipresent* character.[16]

1.2 Power as an Agglomerated Phenomenon

During the sixteenth century, 'modernists' abandoned the metaphysical notions of power and instead turned to reason and the empirical method. Their analysis of power was based on their experience of war and civil unrest as a part of everyday life. They concluded that the remedy for the unstable sociopolitical situation of that time was the ag-

---

11 Aristotle, *The Physics I, Books I-IV*, William Heinemann Ltd-Harvard University Press, London-Cambridge (MA), 1962, trans. P.H. Wicksteed & F.M. Cornford, 201a, p. 195.

12 *Cf.* Drabkin, 'Notes of the Laws of Motion in Aristotle', p. 61.

13 Although not essential in this context, the difference between *energeia* (energy) and *entelexeia* (entelechy) is important in Aristotle's doctrine. Both phenomena fall in the category of actuality. Nevertheless, energy still embodies a dynamic component and reflects the process leading to the realization. Entelechy, on the other hand, is a finite and perfected form of actuality and as such completely emancipated from the preceding process. *See* Aristotle, *Metaphysics*, Penguin Books, London, 2004, trans. H. Lawson-Tancred, pp. 26, 274, C.-H. Chen, 'Different Meanings of the Term Energeia in the Philosophy of Aristotle', 17 *Philosophy and Phenomenological Research* 1956, pp. 56-65 and C.-H. Chen, 'The Relation between the Terms Energeia and Entelexeia in the Philosophy of Aristotle', 8 *The Classical Quarterly, New Series* 1958, pp. 12-17.

14 A. Rivaud, *Le problème du devenir et la notion de la matière*, Félix Alcan, Paris, 1905, p. 389.

15 Souilhé, *Etude sur le terme dunamis dans les dialogues de Platon*, p. 183.

16 *Cf.* W. Morrison, *Jurisprudence: from the Greeks to Post-modernism*, Cavendish Publishing Limited, London-Sydney, 2000, pp. 41-43.

glomeration of power within a common body politic that would be powerful enough to prevent violent clashes amongst smaller entities. In this respect, we can speak of the creation of an absolutist state. Interestingly, however, 'modernists' did not envision the agglomerated entity in an abstract fashion, but gave it a personified component.

Niccolò Machiavelli, Jean Bodin and Thomas Hobbes each pursued the same basic idea: in order to transcend the 'state of war' there is a need to neutralize competing and damaging powers and construct a greater agglomeration of power. This agglomeration results in a political concept of sovereignty and in the formation of an absolutist state. The apparatus it erects is also a tool for the construction of a new legal and political community.

The inventor of the modern political orientation was Machiavelli. He was not interested in considering how people should behave. Rather, he based his approach on observing how people *do* behave.[17] The starting point for Machiavelli's reaction was the corruption that permeated the Florentine anomic reality in the period of *cinquecento*.[18] Another factor that preoccupied Machiavelli was that small city-states of the then Italy had fallen prey to invading armies, coming from much greater and powerful political formations such as France and Spain.

In order to resolve these problems, Machiavelli recommended the following:

> where there is so much corrupt matter that the laws are not enough to check it, together with them greater force is needed to give order there – a kingly hand that with absolute and excessive power puts a check on the excessive ambition and corruption of the powerful.[19]

Arriving at this agglomeration of 'absolute and excessive power', the vigorous undertaking of a talented individual, 'a kingly hand' of the Prince is needed. For Machiavelli, the Prince is a person who possesses a particular characteristic, which he calls *virtù*. In English this term stands for a variety of meanings, such as ambition, willpower, ability, skill, energy, determination, strength, shrewdness, spiritedness, courage and prowess.[20] Apart from relying on *virtù*, the success of the Prince depends also on *fortuna* (luck or favor).[21] *Fortuna* grants her favors to a man of *virtù*, a man of courage and audacity.

---

17 W. Winiarski, 'Niccolo Machiavelli', *in* L. Strauss & J. Cropsey (Eds.), *History of Political Philosophy*, Rand McNally & Company, Chicago, 1966, p. 247. This observation comes from an English philosopher Francis Bacon.

18 On the issue of corruption *see* A. Bonadeo, *Corruption, Conflict, and Power in the Works and Times of Niccolò Machiavelli*, University of California Press, Berkeley-Los Angeles-London, 1973, pp. 1-35.

19 N. Machiavelli, *Discourses on Livy*, The University of Chicago Press, Chicago-London, 1996, trans. H.C. Mansfield & N. Tarcov, I, 55, 4, pp. 111-112.

20 *See* 'Appendix B', *in* N. Machiavelli, *The Prince*, CUP, Cambridge, 1988, Q. Skinner & R. Price (Eds.), pp. 103-104. *See also* J.V. Femia, *Machiavelli Revisited*, University of Wales Press, Cardiff, 2004, p. 32.

21 *See* Machiavelli, *The Prince*, pp. 19-37.

The essence of Machiavelli's doctrine lies in connecting the individual's subjective ability, *virtù*, with an objective of agglomerated power leading to the new social order (*nuovo ordine*). In this regard, *virtù* "might be thought of as the formative principle that shaped the end, or as the very end itself."[22]

Machiavelli's approach to agglomeration of power enabled his successors to develop it into more coherent theoretical concepts. Bodin was the first to describe the form of an agglomerated power as an idea of sovereignty, which is the most important component of his political philosophy.[23] It is reasonable to assume that clashes between different religious groupings (*e.g.*, the St. Bartholomew's Day massacre) influenced Bodin to develop the absolutist vision of sovereignty.[24] In his major work *Les six livres de la République*, Bodin defines sovereignty as "the absolute and perpetual power of a commonwealth," which "is not limited either in power, charge or certain time."[25] It is a force of cohesion, unity in a community without which the body politic would disintegrate.[26] Like Machiavelli, Bodin projects sovereignty into an individual, the Prince.

Though the sovereign is not bound by the laws of his predecessors nor by laws that he proclaims himself,[27] he is bound by the laws of God and nature. According to *Les six livres de la République*, natural law is derived from ancient rituals whereby ordinary people ceded their sovereign power to a single nobleman. Among other examples, Bodin explicitly points to the ancient Slovenian custom of the enthronement of Dukes by peasants in Carinthia, originating in the ancient entity of Carantania.[28]

The tradition described above represents a foundation of the contractual theory of transfer of sovereign power from people to an individual. The Duke assumes his place on the basis of a hereditary right which reflects the perpetual power in the abstract position of a Duke. After he is appointed the Duke, no person can contest his activities which points to the absolute power of sovereignty. However, before his appointment, every would-be Duke has to submit himself to the will and scrutiny of the people. Symbolically,

---

22 J.G.A. Pocock, *The Machiavellian Moment: Florentine Political Thought and the Atlantic Republican Tradition*, Princeton University Press, Princeton-London, 1975, p. 41.

23 G.H. Sabine, *A History of Political Theory: Fourth Edition*, Dryden Press, Hinsdale (IL), 1973, rev. T.L. Thorson, p. 377.

24 *See* J.H. Franklin, *Jean Bodin et la naissance de la théorie absolutiste*, PUF, 1993, pp. 39, 63, 66 and Q. Skinner, *The Foundations of Modern Political Thought: Volume 2, The Age of Reformation*, CUP, Cambridge, 2000, p. 284.

25 J. Bodin, *Les six livres de la République: livre premier*, Fayard, Paris, 1986, p. 181 (trans. A.Z.).

26 J.-J. Chevallier, *Les grandes œuvres politiques de Machiavel à nos jours*, Armand Colin, Paris, 1996, p. 38.

27 M.C. Jacobsen, *Jean Bodin et le dilemme de la philosophie politique moderne*, Museum Tusculanum Press-University of Copenhagen, Copenhagen, 2000, p. 145.

28 *See* Bodin, *Les six livres de la République*, pp. 187-190, in particular p.188. Carantania was one of the early Middle Ages political entities of the Slovenian ancestors. It existed in different forms from the seventh to eleventh centuries and encompased what are today Austrian provinces of Carinthia and Styria, and the territory of north-eastern Slovenia. Inhabitants were called Carantanians. Gradually, Carantanians were pushed south, to the territory of the present day Slovenia. (*See, e.g.*, A. Bernard, *Petite histoire de la Slovénie*, Institut d'études slaves, Paris, 1996, pp. 16-26 and J. Prunk, *A Brief History of Slovenia*, Založba Grad, Ljubljana, 2000, pp. 16-23).

it is a representative of the people, a peasant, who approves the would-be Duke dressed in garments of a poor shepherd. Perpetual and absolute sovereign power in the form of the Duke is thus submitted to the natural law in the form of a lasting tradition.[29]

Hobbes's doctrine of political representation is a logical continuation of the intellectual efforts of Machiavelli and Bodin.[30] Also writing during a time of civil war, he argued that sovereignty was the solution to situations of social unrest. Hobbes conceived power essentially as a phenomenon that produces effects. He distinguished between the power motive of the body and power motive of the mind. The former, which may be called strength, moves other bodies; while the latter gives the 'animal motion' to the body, which results in man's affections and passions.[31]

However, powers of different individuals compete with men who have acquired more power exercising dominance or command over the power of other men.[32] Thus, man's life before social structure was characterized by the continuous and chaotic competition over power. The danger, according to Hobbes, lies in the fact that some men's desires are without limit.[33] This leads us to Hobbes' famous state of nature. If all restraint is removed, civilized life is impossible and any life is risky.[34] The natural condition of men "is a condition of Warre of every one against every one; in which ... every man has a Right to every thing; even to one another's body."[35] This state of nature is really a state of total war inundated by the "continual fear and danger of violent death, and the life of man [is] solitary, poor, nasty, brutish, and short."[36]

Therefore, in the state of nature the most reasonable thing to do is to give up the right to invade anybody, provided that everyone would simultaneously do the same.[37] The only plausible way to effectuate this would be to conclude a covenant by which all men would transfer all their rights and powers to some person or body. The transfer is not solely quantitative, but also includes a qualitative dimension. The newly established person in whom such powers are vested is more than a sum of all the transferred powers.[38] He *is* a power himself, or in other words, a Sovereign or, according to Hobbes, a Leviathan.[39] The Sovereign is able to enforce an agreement because he is authorized by

29 Sabine, *A History of Political Theory*, p. 384.
30 *Cf.* ibid., pp. 322-323, 435.
31 T. Hobbes, *The Elements of Law: Natural and Politic*, Frank Cass & Co. Ltd., London, 1969, F. Tönnies (Ed.), pp. 27-28.
32 Ibid., p. 34.
33 *See* C.B. MacPherson, 'Introduction', *in* T. Hobbes, *Leviathan*, Penguin Classics, London, 1985, pp. 35-37.
34 Ibid., pp. 40-41.
35 Hobbes, *Leviathan*, pp. 189-190.
36 Ibid., p. 186.
37 MacPherson, 'Introduction', p. 43.
38 *See* Hobbes, *Leviathan*, p. 227.
39 *See* R. Polin, *Politique et philosophie chez Hobbes*, Librairie philosophique J. Vrin, Paris, 1977, p. 72 and L. Jaume, *Hobbes et l'Etat représentatif moderne*, PUF, Paris, 1986, pp. 108-110.

the covenant to use the entire combined force of all the contractors.[40] The Leviathan is, therefore, not just a contract among individuals, but also a union among them.[41]

In contradistinction to Bodin, however, Hobbes complemented the concept of sovereignty with a coherent institutional framework.[42] The Sovereign disposes of all the necessary powers of government, such as legislation, the administration of justice, the enforcement of laws and the organization of inferior magistracies.[43] The Sovereign alone possesses the coercive power which he also uses to develop the institutional and legal framework for the service to the Common Benefit.[44] The development of Hobbes's argument with regard to the sovereign's duties in fact opens a way towards a bourgeois state and the market society.[45]

Thus, Machiavelli, Bodin and Hobbes each pursued the same basic idea; in order to transcend the 'state of war' there is a need to neutralize competing and damaging powers and construct a greater agglomeration of power. This agglomeration results in a political concept of sovereignty and in the formation of an absolutist state. The apparatus it erects is also a tool for the construction of a new legal and political community.

1.3 Power as a Diffuse Phenomenon

The writers in this section were critical of the perception that power is an agglomerated and preponderantly political phenomenon. Max Weber started with the premise of a concentrated power in bureaucratic states. However, by emphasizing the role of the bureaucratic apparatus, he began to diffuse power through the capacities of individuals comprising that apparatus. Hannah Arendt continued this dispersion outside the concentrated locus of political life. Finally, Michel Foucault extended and perfected the diffusion of power throughout the social environment.

Applying a sociological perspective, Weber defines power in relation to domination and applied both concepts to the wider political context. Power is the "opportunity existing within a social relationship which permits one to carry out one's own will even against resistance and regardless of the basis on which this opportunity rests."[46] Domina-

40 MacPherson, 'Introduction', p. 44.

41 Sabine, *A History of Political Theory*, p. 434.

42 *Cf.* ibid., p. 435.

43 Id.

44 Hobbes, *Leviathan*, pp. 226-227.

45 MacPherson, 'Introduction', pp. 48, 58. For more on this issue, *see* C.B. MacPherson, *The Political Theory of Possessive Individualism: Hobbes to Locke*, Clarendon Press, Oxford, 1964, pp. 46-106.

46 M. Weber, *Basic Concepts in Sociology*, Greenwood Press Publishers, Westport (CT), 1977, trans. H.P. Secher, p. 117. In English there are different translations of Weber's definition of power. For the debate on how to translate the definition of power, *see* I. Walliman *et al.*, 'On Many Weber's Definition of Power', *in* P. Hamilton (Ed.), *MAX WEBER: Critical Assessments 2*, Routledge, London-New York, 1991, vol. 1, pp. 232-239.

tion, on the other hand, is the probability that a command will be obeyed.[47] Thus, Weber understood power in terms of the relationship between two subjects.[48] For Weber, the concept of power is sociologically amorphous because every conceivable combination of circumstance can put an individual into a position where he or she could demand compliance with his or her will.[49] Herein lies the germ of the rationale behind the expansion of power beyond that which exists in institutional agglomeration.

Within the realm of politics, Weber defines a state as "a human community that (successfully) claims the *monopoly of the legitimate use of physical force* within a given territory".[50] The state is considered the sole source of the 'right' to use violence. Other institutions or individuals are allowed to use it only to the extent permitted by the state. Politics therefore means an attempt to share power or an endeavor to influence the distribution of power.[51]

Weber further deals with the distribution of power as part of his discussion of bureaucracy. The bureaucratic organization is technically the most highly developed means of power in the hands of a man who controls it.[52] Although Weber gives most weight, in terms of the use of power, to the head of the bureaucratic apparatus, he equally acknowledges that within that apparatus, 'the staff' disposes of a certain degree of power. His role consists of a responsibility to the superior and his command or judgment as a participant in the power process.[53] Power is therefore dispersed within the power structure. In the era of mass consumption the bureaucracy has gained enormous influence that may be called *bureaucratic sovereignty.*[54]

It should be noted that Weber's definition of power also brings into play the concept of 'resistance' or counterpower, which the power has to suppress. The crucial point here is not that resistance is necessary for the existence of all power relations, but that the subjugation of resistance, if present, is an essential feature of these relations.

Arendt represents yet another step in the diffusion of power. Intrinsic to her philosophical lexicon are 'plurality', 'natality' and 'publicity'. For Arendt, politics begins with a plurality of agents, who exist in relation to one another. Plurality then transforms itself into a source of uniquely human power.[55] Plurality "is specifically *the* condition … of all

---

47 Weber, *Basic Concepts in Sociology*, p. 117.

48 *Cf.* Walliman *et al.*, 'On Many Weber's Definition of Power', p. 237.

49 Id.

50 M. Weber, 'Politics as a Vocation', *in* H.H. Gerth & C. Wright Mills, *From Max Weber: Essays in Sociology*, Routledge, London, 1991, p. 78.

51 Id.

52 M. Weber, Max, 'Bureaucracy', *in* Gerth & Wright Mills, *From Max Weber: Essays in Sociology*, p. 232.

53 *Cf.* E. Shils, 'Charisma, Order and Status', *in* P. Hamilton (Ed.), *MAX WEBER: Critical Assessments 1*, Routledge, London-New York, vol. III, p. 276.

54 *See* W. Mommsen, *Max Weber et la politique allemande : 1890-1920*, PUF, Paris, 1985, trans. J. Amsler *et al.*, pp. 218-219.

55 L.J. Disch, *Hannah Arendt and the Limits of Philosophy*, Cornell University Press, Ithaca-London, 1996, p. 31.

political life".[56] Most simply, plurality means human multiplicity. Natality, on the other hand, is the capacity to begin something anew and an enabling condition of power to exist only when people speak and act together in public.[57] Publicity in terms of political action means openness and arises whenever a question, problem or event is submitted to the process of argumentation.[58] The activity of interpretive contestation sustains the integrity of the public realm and as such represents a contestation for power.[59]

Power resides in the interspaces where human beings are, on one hand, joined together *and*, on the other hand, distinguished from one another by their participation in speech and action.[60] It is not surprising, therefore, that other theorists have named this communicative power.[61] Arendt explained power in the following terms:

> Power corresponds to the human ability not just to act but to act in concert. Power is never the property of an individual; it belongs to a group and remains in existence only so long as the group keeps together.[62]

Arendt's understanding of power thus comprises two distinctive currents: the urge towards integration of individuals in the public realm and their diversification through the originality of their action therein. Power "springs up whenever people get together and act in concert";[63] however, all materializations of power – including political institutions – decay as soon as the living power of the people ceases to uphold.[64]

Therefore, Arendt does not recognize an institutional setup as an achieved finality of power, something that is qualitatively different from the process of the concerted action in a group. The institutionalized or focalized power immediately disperses as soon as the group itself falls apart.

Power is therefore dependant on the existence of the group and it dissolves if the group dissolves. The original perspective of the communicative power thus goes from an individual to a focalized center. However, if we turn this perspective around, we find the durability of the concept challenged by its fluidity, instability and inherent tendency towards dissolution. As such, the concept of communicative power follows the trend of the dissolution of power in society as previously identified in Weber's thought. Arendt's

---

56 H. Arendt, *The Human Condition*, The University of Chicago Press, Chicago, 1958, p. 7.

57 Ibid., p. 9 and Disch, *Hannah Arendt and the Limits of Philosophy*, p. 56.

58 Disch, *Hannah Arendt and the Limits of Philosophy*, p. 34.

59 *Cf.* ibid., p. 104.

60 Ibid., p. 50.

61 Steven Lukes characterized it as 'communicative power' (*see* Lukes, *Power*, pp. 59-74) while Jürgen Habermas named it 'communications concept of power' (*see* J. Habermas, 'Hannah Arendt's Communications Concept of Power', *in* ibid., pp. 75-93).

62 H. Arendt, *On Violence*, Allen Lane-The Penguin Press, New York-London, 1970, p. 44.

63 Ibid., p. 52.

64 Ibid., p. 41.

concept of communicative power thus represents a further step in the disaggregation of power.

An exploration of French philosopher Michel Foucault represents the last stage in the conceptual dispersion of power. For Foucault, power relations are rooted deep in the social nexus and are not a supplementary structure over and above 'society'. A society without power relations can only be an abstraction.[65] Foucault departs from the understanding of aggregated power, particularly through the invention of the notion of 'biopower'.[66]

Biopower evolved in two basic forms; the first comprising the disciplines of the body and the second including the regulation of life. The first pole centered on the body as a machine; in the forms of achieving discipline over it, the optimization of its capabilities, the extortion of its force, and its integration into systems of efficient and economic controls (anatomo-politics of the human body). The second pole formed later and focused on the species body. By this term Foucault understood that the body is permeated with the mechanics of life and serves as the basis of biological progress in the forms of reproduction, birth and death, the level of health, life expectancy and longevity (biopolitics of the population).[67] While the two currents were still far apart in the eighteenth century, they merged in the nineteenth century in the form of concrete arrangements in which the use of sexuality becomes the most important.[68]

Foucault studies power through details of individuals' behavior and the conduct of their bodies and gestures. These dynamics he called *microphysics* or *micropowers*. Foucault's intention is to show that power 'comes from below'. In other words, he sought to show that global hierarchical structures of domination within society depended on and operated through low-level 'capillary' circuits of power relationships.[69] In this context, Foucault focuses on several modes of behavior linked to the concept of political sovereignty, such as *lettres de cachet*, governmentality and panopticism.[70] They all share a common dynamic of a continuous circulation of power from the bottom (individuals) to the top (government) or *vice versa*.

65 M. Foucault, 'The Subject and Power', *in* M. Foucault, *Power, Essential Works of Foucault 1954-1984*, Penguin Books, London-New York, 2000, J.D. Faubion (Ed.), trans. R. Hurley *et al.*, vol. 3, p. 343.

66 *See* M. Foucault, 'Right of Death and Power Over Life', *in* P. Rabinow (Ed.), *The Foucault Reader*, Penguin Books, London-New York, 1984, pp. 261-263.

67 Ibid., pp. 262-263.

68 For the treatment of sexuality, *see* M. Foucault, *Ethics: Subjectivity and Truth, Essential Works of Foucault 1954-1984*, The New Press, New York, 1997, vol. 2, P. Rabinow (Ed.), trans. R. Hurley *et al.*, pp. 121 *et seq.*

69 C. Gordon, 'Introduction', *in* Foucault, *Power*, pp. xxiv-xv and M. Foucault, 'The Body of the Condemned', *in* Rabinow, *The Foucault Reader*, pp. 173-174. *See also* F. Gros, *Michel Foucault*, PUF, 1998, Paris, pp. 66-67 and B. Allen, 'Foucault and Modern Political Philosophy', *in* J. Moss (Ed.), *The Later Foucault: Politics and Philosophy*, Sage Publications, London-Thousand Oaks-New Delhi, 1998, p. 165.

70 *See* M. Foucault, 'Lives of Infamous Men', p. 167, M. Foucault, 'Governmentality', pp. 219-220, M. Foucault, 'Truth and Juridical Forms', p. 70, all *in* Foucault, *Power*, and M. Haralambos & M. Holborn, *Sociology: Themes and Perspectives*, Harper Collins, London, 2013, pp. 618-620.

'Domination' and 'resistance' are also relevant in Foucault's consideration of power. Foucault understands domination as a situation in which power relations, instead of being mobile and thereby allowing various actors to modify them, remain blocked or frozen.[71] Resistance, on the other hand, is more than just a power that comes out of the initial power struggle as a dominated component. In a way, it is superior to the forces of the process because the existence of resistance obliges power relations to change with it. In this post-struggle situation, resistance is a key element of power dynamics.[72]

Overall, Foucault considers power to be a positive phenomenon. Power relations are not bad in and of themselves, although they always entail certain risks: for example, in terms of security.[73] What makes power remain good and accepted is that it traverses and produces things, induces pleasure, creates knowledge and produces discourse.[74] Power is an essential component of a society and circulates all around through a particular social fabric.[75] Power is therefore dispersed throughout the social body.

This section followed the movement of power from the buildup within the body politic to the sphere of an individual body, turning the focus from the realm of the political to the individual. Weber's explorations represent a combination of agglomerated power and skilful individuals. Although Weber takes agglomerated power as a model, he proceeds to the dispersion of power in organizational structures, such as the bureaucratic apparatus. Arendt adds an additional contribution to the process of dissolution. According to her, the agglomerated conception of power is impossible. Power can exist only on the basis of communication among individuals when they come together. However, as soon as the group disperses, power itself likewise dissolves. Finally, Foucault represents the last step in the dissolution of power. For him, power resides everywhere in the society. It circulates and therefore does not reside in any particular locus. Power expresses itself through individuals and parts of their bodies. Because it is inherently attached to living persons, Foucault called this kind of power *biopower*.

1.4 Systematic Approaches to Power

The preceding three sections on power as an omnipresent, agglomerated and dispersed phenomenon follow the historical evolution of doctrines in philosophical and political thought. Power typically represents only one element in those doctrines. This section deals with theories devoted solely to the phenomenon of power. Such a development is

71 M. Foucault, 'The Ethics of the Concern for Self as a Practice of Freedom', *in* Foucault, *Ethics*, p. 283.

72 *Cf.* M. Foucault, 'Sex, Power, and the Politics of Identity', *in* ibid., p. 167. On the notions of domination and resistance *see also* P. Patton, 'Foucault's Subject of Power', *in* Moss, *The Later Foucault: Politics and Philosophy*, pp. 67-73.

73 M. Foucault, 'The Risks of Security', *in* Foucault, *Power*, p. 372.

74 M. Foucault, 'Truth and Power', *in* ibid., p. 120.

75 Gros, *Michel Foucault*, p. 78.

mainly a consequence of the blossoming of social sciences in the twentieth century and interdisciplinary considerations of power, which allowed for the comprehensive consideration of this phenomenon.

Bertrand Russell was one of the first contemporary scholars to assess the phenomenon of power systematically. He starts with Hobbes's premise that man's primary desires are power and glory. The desire for glory, however, prompts the same actions as the desire for power and the two motives may in practical terms be regarded as one.[76] Russell speaks of the desire for power in the form of love of power. This desire is an essential part of human nature, particularly in energetic men. "Love of power, in the widest sense, is the desire to be able to produce intended effects upon the outer world, whether human or non-human."[77] For Russell, therefore, power is the "production of intended effects".[78] Love of power is the cause of important activities in social affairs and it is only on that basis that history can be rightly interpreted.[79]

Russell distinguished between 'traditional power', 'naked power' and 'revolutionary power'. Traditional power relies on historically observed practices and has on its side force and habit. It does not have to justify itself in every moment or prove that opposition cannot overthrow it. In addition, it is associated with religious or quasi-religious beliefs denoting resistance as depraved.[80] Naked power is usually equated with military power and may take the form of internal tyranny or foreign conquest.[81] Power is naked when it results merely from the power-loving impulses of individuals or groups and wins support by submission through fear, rather than by active cooperation.[82] When a traditional form of power ceases to exist, it may give way to naked power or, more commonly, to revolutionary power.[83] Power is revolutionary when it depends upon a large group united by a new creed, program or sentiment.[84] The success of 'revolutionary power' in replacing 'traditional power' depends on the willing assent of a large majority of the population, which has to lend it much more vigorous and active popular support that is needed by a traditional authority.[85]

Important characteristics of power which follow from Russell's work are its fluidity, density and expansion. Russell compared power to energy in physics. Its fluid nature comes from the fact that it is continually passing from any one of its forms into any other.[86] Additionally, its density represents the tendency to concentrate power, partic-

76 B. Russell, *Power: A new Social Analysis*, George Allen & Unwin Ltd, London, 1938, p. 9.
77 Ibid., p. 274.
78 Ibid., p. 35.
79 Ibid., p. 10.
80 Ibid., p. 38.
81 Ibid., p. 39.
82 Ibid., p. 41.
83 *Cf.* ibid., p. 84.
84 Ibid., p. 41.
85 Ibid., p. 40.
86 Ibid., pp. 11-12.

ularly in the political sphere. Since men love power, and those who achieve power love it the most, they can be expected to desire an increase in its internal activities.[87] Finally, there is the tendency of power to expand further. When two entities with different but not incompatible objects coalesce, the result is something more powerful than either previous one or even both together. A logical outcome is that the most powerful organization (usually the state) absorbs the others.[88]

Another holistic scholar of power was Bertrand de Jouvenel. For him, the most noteworthy feature of power is that it commands and thereby provokes obedience. This is a necessary and a sufficient condition for its existence.[89] Power has its *raison d'être* solely as a social phenomenon. He classifies articulations of power in two groups, each one with two additional subgroups.

The first group comprises theories that explain and justify power through the existence of a sovereign. The theory of divine sovereignty posits a sovereign whose power is of divine origin and therefore absolute. Sovereign power that originates in the people, on the other hand, manifests itself in parliamentary sovereignty or plebiscitary absolutism. What is common to both theories is that, within a multitudinous environment, power appears as a governing center.[90] The second of de Jouvenel's groups views power from the perspective of organic theories explaining and justifying power through its function and its ends, which are to guarantee material and moral coherence to a society. The first organic theory sees power as a hub of crystallization or as a shining zone from which light propagates. The second theory sees power as an organ within an organism.

In each of the theories, power's tendency to command is either absolute or is ever-growing.[91] In a given society, de Jouvenel also envisaged the existence of a plurality of powers. However, he underlined that there is only one major power, the public power, which defeats its rivals and integrates all others.[92] Therefore, the logical conclusion arising from this dynamic is that power tends towards construction of its 'absolute empire'.[93]

Harold Lasswell and Abraham Kaplan wrote another seminal study on power. In contradistinction to both Russell and de Jouvenel, who consider power from the historical-sociological perspective, Lasswell and Kaplan place the issue of power at the heart of political science studies. For them the "concept of power is perhaps the most fundamental in the whole of political science".[94] They take a note of Russell's definition of power, but argue that power in political science cannot aim at producing general effects. It can only

87 *Cf.* ibid., pp. 168 and 173-174.
88 Ibid., p. 179.
89 B. De Jouvenel, *Du pouvoir : histoire naturelle de sa croissance*, Les éditions du cheval ailé, Genève, 1945, p. 150.
90 Ibid., pp. 47, 94-95.
91 Ibid., pp. 94-95.
92 Ibid., pp. 183, 197-198, 237.
93 Ibid., p. 94.
94 H.D. Lasswell & A. Kaplan, *Power and Society: A Framework for Political Inquiry*, Yale University Press, New Haven (CT)-London, 1969, p. 75.

produce effects that directly involve other persons. In this vein, Lasswell and Kaplan define power as "participation in the making of decisions: G has power over H with respect to the values K if G participates in the making of decisions affecting the K-policies of H."[95] Since it presupposes a relationship between subjects, this definition is relational and reminiscent of Weber's definition of power.

Similar to Russell and de Jouvenel, Lasswell and Kaplan highlight the expansive nature of power, which they argue tends to increase until it is restrained by other power-holders. However, they underline that it is not only one expression of power that limits the other expression of power. Other factors, such as technical factors and the social order, may also set limits to power.[96] In addition, Lasswell and Kaplan situate power within the structural setting of a society. As 'structures' they understood the continuing arrangements by which power is shaped and shared within the community.[97] Two specific structures of power they name are 'hierarchy' and 'co-archy'. Hierarchy is a structure of power relationships based on a vertical echelon of superiors over subordinates. Co-archy, on the other hand, is a structure of equal and horizontal power relationships; the power exerted in one direction is the same as that exerted in the opposite direction.[98] Both structures rely on power as a constituent element, which brings us to the fundamental conclusion that the structural arrangements in a given society elementarily rely on the power relationships.

The importance of the considered theories of power lies in their systemic approach that leads to the identification of a number of power's characteristics. Power is essentially a relational phenomenon; however, it also shapes the structural contours of society. Owing to its fluctuating nature, power takes many forms. It is fluid and tends towards concentration and further expansion. It usurps compatible sources of power and tries to break down competing centers, and then to possibly assimilate them. Competition between sources of power may result in a balance between them, which can be a consequence of equilibrium, of the limits of the social order, or simply of the technical factors. Power's expansive drive is therefore not infinite and can reach a point of saturation, finality and subsequent decline.

1.5 Concluding Remarks on Power

The analysis of power involved an examination of certain doctrines in the social sciences. Although these doctrines vary and sometimes oppose each other, they contain a common thread; the phenomenon of power, which represents an essential building block in those

95 Id.
96 Ibid., pp. 94-95.
97 Ibid., p. 200.
98 Ibid., p. 204.

doctrines. On the basis of a continuous analysis of the phenomenon of power, the following essential characteristics of power can be summarized.

One of the essential characteristics of power is that it is a *relational* and thus a *reciprocal* occurrence. At the most basic level, it denotes a capacity or a change. Both these forms suggest the *dynamic* characteristic of power. However, this dynamism is not an end in itself: power always strives to certain *finality*. That is, the process functions in anticipation of an end. Due to its intangible origin, power is *fluid*. It easily propagates from one locus to another. It is *immaterial* since it cannot be localized and isolated. Furthermore, it is also *spontaneous* because its occurrences are unpredictable.

As a result of its dynamic nature, power tends towards concentration or *agglomeration* in order to augment its weight and it is *expansive* because it always attempts to win exterior forces and invade outer spaces. The drive towards multiplication is not eternal. Once a specific power achieves its high, it is subject to the process of dissolution or *dispersion*. Although the majority of writers emphasize public power, power is essentially a *plural* occurrence, which arises as a consequence of power's residing in numerous human beings. Different drives of power contest with each other. Apart from the possibilities of assimilating compatible powers, and of neutralizing competing powers, there is also a model of equilibrium with a *coexistence* of plural powers. Power also has a tendency to express itself in the form of institutional constructions. This is an *institutional* or *superstructural* dimension of power in the social domain.

After the detailed consideration of the phenomenon of power, the relevant question is how power assumes the form of more tangible phenomena. Emmanuel-Joseph Sieyès provides a useful model of the transformation of power from *pouvoir constituant* (constituent power) to *pouvoir constitué* (constituted power).[99] This concept marks the process of the crystallization of power into a more institutionalized shape. While the constituent power has the quality of the creative spontaneity and fluidity, the constituted power is a derivative power that assumes a form of a finalized structure. For Sieyès, the constituent power is the power of the people, which is institutionalized as the body politic according to a constitution in a given society.

The model of passage from constituent to constitute power can be used to describe a transition from the concept of power to institutionalised phenomena of hegemony and constitutionalism. While power by itself is fluid, spontaneous, immaterial and expansive, it also strives towards finality and institutionalization. In this sense power creates hegemony and constitutionalism as two phenomena that are central to this book.

99 *See, generally,* P. Bastid, *Sieyès et sa pensée*, Slatkine Reprints, Genève, 1978, M. Forsyth, *Reason and Revolution: The Political Thought of the Abbé Sieyes*, Holmes & Meier Publishers Inc., New York, 1987 and R. Zapperi (Ed.), *Emmanuel-Joseph SIEYÈS: Ecrits politiques*, Editions des archives contemporaines, Paris-Montreux, 1985.

2 The Meaning of Hegemony

The term *hegemony* does not have a unified meaning. Its interpretations are multifaceted and come close either to the understanding of other similar phenomena, which are imperialism and empire. They may even stand for these phenomena. The illustration of their interrelatedness is evident, for example, in a reference to the ancient Assyrian Empire where words imperial, hegemony and empire are used interchangeably.[1] Conceptually, these phenomena reflect the same logic – the dominance of the powerful center over the surrounding and heterogeneous periphery.

In general, hegemony means a loose control of the center over the periphery. This control mostly relies on the center's predominant power and also very often on its leadership. Imperialism or imperial rule usually represents a more intense and formalized form of that control. An empire most frequently represents the institutionalization of the imperial rule. However, in many cases these terms have different connotations, which lead to their substantive rapprochement. For example, empire may utilize a loose form of control, and thus more closely resemble hegemony, as it did during the Victorian-era British Empire. On the other hand, as the example of the United States demonstrates, a hegemon can be more powerful than an empire. Finally, imperialism may also exert influence in the space outside the imperial ambit, which makes its control informal and indirect.[2]

Hegemony provides the most generic framework to depict relations of dependence between the powerful center and the subordinate periphery.[3] Therefore, hegemony will be used as a common term that encompasses, as subcategories, hegemony in a narrower sense, imperialism and empire. Nevertheless, the differences between these three phenomena will sometimes be significant and will be distinguished where relevant.

---

1 *Cf.*: "Nous parlons conventionnellement de domination « *impériale* » pour caractériser une *hégémonie* politique et parfois même spirituelle, exercée sur une fraction notable du monde connu, à un moment donné. Nous faisons donc intervenir des critères d'étendue spatiale et de multiplicité ethnique, linguistique et religieuse. De ce point de vue, on peut opposer l' « *empire* » assyrien aux « royaumes » antérieures, qui n'englobaient que des espaces et des peuples restreints." (P. Garelli, 'L'Etat et la légitimité royale sous l'empire assyrien', *in* M.T. Larsen (Ed.), *Power and Propaganda: A Symposium on Ancient Empires*, Mesopotamia, Copenhagen Studies in Assyriology, vol. 7, Akademisk Forlag, Copenhagen, 1979, p. 319.)

2 For the description and examples *see* N. Ferguson, *Colossus: The Rise and Fall of the American Empire*, Penguin Books, London-New York, 2005, pp. 7-13.

3 For a contemporary study of the phenomenon at the international level from early nineteenth century until today, *see* I. Clark, *Hegemony in International Society*, OUP, Oxford, 2011.

2.1 Hegemony in a Narrower Sense

The word *hegemony* is of classical Greek origin. Dictionaries usually translate hegemony as: leading; leading the way, going first; lead in war; rule command; to take or have command; to have authority; to have the primacy; political supremacy, capable of command, authoritative; guiding; imperial; presidency; and mastery. To the notion of a hegemon they give the meaning of: a guide; one who does things first, shows the way to others; one who leads; leader, commander, chief.[4] Diderot-D'Alembert's *Encyclopédie* gives an interesting etymological insight. According to ancient mythology, the word *hegemon* was attributed to the goddess Artemis in Greece (or her equivalent Diana in Rome). In the sense of a hegemon (*Hégémoné*), Artemis represented a leader (*conductrice*) carrying light in order to show the path forward.[5]

This notion of the hegemon as an enlightened leader has a further reflection in the Greek political sphere where hegemony meant the leadership or predominance of one particular state over others in a group of federated or loosely united states. It was mainly Athens and Sparta, which at different times enjoyed a position of predominance among other equal and autonomous states. In particular, hegemony signified the conduct of military operations, usually against the external, non-Greek enemy.[6] Sparta had a hegemonic position in the Peloponnesian confederation, while Athens enjoyed this position in the League of Delos. After wars against Persians, the hegemony became a subject of the rivalry between Sparta and Athens which led to the durable and draining Peloponnesian Wars[7] on the course of which there is a detailed recount of Thucydides.[8]

This classical account of the phenomenon hegemony offers contemporary perspectives as the model of hegemony identified in Ancient Greece can be applied to nineteenth century Europe. One example is the quest of Prussia to unify Germany.[9] This process commenced first in the international economic field with the creation of the customs

4 *See* H.G. Liddel & R. Scott, *A Greek-English Lexicon*, Clarendon Press, Oxford, 1968, *s.v. hgemon-eia* and *hgemon*, J.J. Courtand-Divernesse, *Dictionnaire Français-Grec*, vol. I, L'auteur-éditeur, Delagrave et Cie, J. Lecoffre et Cie, 1874, Paris, *s.v. hégémon* and *hégémonios*, P. Chantraine, *Dictionnaire étymologique de la langue grecque: histoire des mots*, vol. I, Editions Klincksieck, Paris, 1968, *s.v. hgeomai*, and P. Chassang, *Nouveau Dictionnaire Grec-Français*, vol. I, Garnier Frères, Paris, 1872, *s.v. hgemoneus* and *hgemonia*.

5 *See* Diderot & D'Alembert, *Encyclopédie ou dictionnaire raisonné des sciences des arts et des métiers*, Nouvelle impression en facsimilé de la première édition de 1751-1780, vol. 8, Stuttgart-Bad Cannstatt, 1967, Friedrich Frommann Verlag (Günther Holzboog), *s.v. HEGEMONE* and *HEGEMONIES*.

6 For a survey of hegemony in ancient Greece, *see* J. Wickersham, *Hegemony and Greek Historians*, Rowman and Littlefield Publishers, London, 1994.

7 *See Encyclopaedia Britannica*, vol. 11, Encyclopaedia Britannica Ltd., Chicago-London-Toronto, 1960, *s.v. hegemony* and Berthelot & Laurent (Eds.), *La grande encyclopédie*, vol. 19, H. Lamirault et cie., Paris, 1885, *s.v. hégémonie*.

8 *See* Thucydides, *History of the Peleponnesian War*, Penguin Books, London, 1972.

9 P.K. O'Brien, 'The Pax Britannica and American Hegemony: Precedent, Antecedent or Just Another History', *in* P.K. O'Brien & A. Clesse (Eds.), *Two Hegemonies: Britain 1846-1914 and the United States 1941-2001*, Ashgate, Aldershot-Burlington (VT), 2002, p. 3.

union, the *Zollverein*. The nucleus of the *Zollverein* was the customs union between Prussia and Hesse-Darmstadt (in 1828), which gradually increased to consist of eighteen states at the time of its end (in 1866). A similar economic hegemonic example in that time period was the United Kingdom. Britain served as an initiator and leader of the international trade liberalization and of the monetary gold standard to which the majority of other European states adhered in the second half of the nineteenth century.[10] In both cases, the dominant state initiated the process, which other states joined because they benefited from the arrangement.

Therefore, still following the classical model, the contemporary exercise of hegemony can take shape of

> the persistent and consistent actions taken by a single dominant state, in pursuit of its own national self-interest, that also provides public goods or externalities for the international system as a whole.[11]

In this sense, a hegemonic power becomes an alternative and second-best substitute for a benign universal empire or an efficient system of world governance. In a hegemonic system, one paramount state maintains a semblance of order and uses power and persuasion to impose flexibly enforced rules in what could otherwise be a potentially anarchic system of international relations. Such a situation is therefore of benefit to all nations. Among the 'public goods' a hegemon can guarantee are peace, access to international waterways and air spaces, the legal framework for property rights, the enforcement of transnational contractual agreements, a stable regime for foreign trade, an international monetary system, environmental protection, and so on.[12] In short, the contemporary understanding of hegemony

> refers to the deployment of power and persuasion by a dominant state to defend the planet, avoid warfare and to promote economic stability, commerce and cultural exchanges on a global scale.[13]

The world-systems theory of Immanuel Wallerstein provides another interesting perspective on the phenomenon of hegemony.[14] He situates the beginnings of the modern world-system in the sixteenth century and extends its functioning to the present era.

---

10 *See* V.K. Aggarwal & C. Dupont, 'A Leader in Institutional Design? Europe and the Governance of Trade and Monetary Relations', *in* H. Kierzkowski (Ed.), *Europe and Globalization*, Palgrave Macmillan, Houndmills-New York, 2002, pp. 122-123, 125, 131, 139 (n. 12).

11 O'Brien, 'The Pax Britannica and American Hegemony', pp. 3-4.

12 Ibid., p. 4.

13 Id.

14 For a short overview of the work of Wallerstein, *see* A. Papisca & M. Mascia, *Le relazioni internazionali nell'era dell'interdipendenza e dei diritti umani*, CEDAM, Padova, 1991, pp. 55-57.

Wallerstein understands the world-system not as the system of the world, but a system that is a world and that can be, and most often has been, located in an area less than the entire globe.[15] The world-systems analysis envisages two varieties of world-systems: world-empires and world-economies.[16]

A world-empire consists of a single political system over most of an area however attenuated the degree of its effective control.[17] There have been three attempts to create a world-empire in the last 500 years, all unsuccessful. The first was by Charles V in the sixteenth century, the second by Napoleon at the beginning of the nineteenth century, and the third by Hitler in the mid-twentieth century.[18] While the world-economy is consonant with the needs of a capitalist system, a world-empire would stifle capitalism. If a world-empire were to exist, it would necessarily entail a political structure capable of overriding the grasp for the endless accumulation of capital. For that reason, serious attempts to forge world-empires have been met with hostility from capitalist elites.[19]

In the world-economy, in contrast, there is no single political system. The defining element of the contemporary world-economy is capitalism as the form of economic organization, which has been able to flourish precisely because the world-economy had within its bounds a multiplicity of political systems. Capitalism as an economic model is based on the fact that the economic factors operate within an arena that is larger than any political entity can control, which gives capitalists freedom to maneuver. This dynamic made possible the constant economic expansion of the world-system.[20]

In the world-economy the political structure tends to link culture with a physical location. According to Wallerstein, there is a distinction between core, hegemonic states and weaker, peripheral areas. In between there are also buffer zones in the shape of semi-peripheral areas.[21] For him, hegemony took place in three instances. The first was hegemony of the United Provinces (contemporary Netherlands) in the mid-seventeenth century; the second was the United Kingdom in the mid-nineteenth century and the third was the United States in the mid-twentieth century.[22]

---

15 *Cf.*: "[Modern World System] refers to an institutional structure that shapes the *interplay* between the political variables associated with the world-wide capitalist exchange network." (D. Garst, 'Wallerstein and His Critics', 14 *Theory and Society* 1985, p. 470.) On the importance of the notion of class in the work of Wallerstein *see also* A.Y. So & M. Hikam, '"Class" in the Writings of Wallerstein and Thompson: toward a Class Struggle Analysis', 32 *Sociological Perspectives* 1989, pp. 453-457, 463.

16 I. Wallerstein, *World-Systems Analysis: An Introduction*, Duke University Press, Durham-London, 2004, pp. 98-99.

17 I. Wallerstein, *The Modern World-system I: Capitalist Agriculture and the Origins of the European World-Economy in the Sixteenth Century*, Academic Press, Inc., San Diego-London, 1974, p. 348.

18 Wallerstein, *World-Systems Analysis: An Introduction*, p. 57.

19 Ibid., p. 58.

20 Wallerstein, *The Modern World-system I*, p. 348. *See also* R.S. DuPlessis, 'Wallerstein, World Systems Analysis, and Early Modern European History', 21 *The History Teacher* 1988, p. 223.

21 *See* Wallerstein, *The Modern World-system I*, pp. 349-350, 353 and Garst, 'Wallerstein and His Critics', pp. 475-476.

22 Wallerstein, *World-Systems Analysis: An Introduction*, p. 57.

The hegemon thus exerts its power in political, military, economic and cultural domains. In this way, it is able to impose a set of rules on the inter-state system and thereby temporarily create a new political order.[23] For example, among the three existing hegemonies in the world-system analysis, the Dutch offered religious tolerance, the British offered the vision of the liberal state, constitutionalism, the gold standard and the end of slavery, and the Unites States offered multiparty elections, human rights, moderate decolonization and free movement of the capital. These visions were the basis on which the hegemonic power claimed legitimacy for its dominant position and contributed to each state's ability to maintain world order.[24]

Antonio Gramsci provided another valuable perspective on hegemony, which is a central phenomenon in his political thought. For Gramsci, the state is divided between civil society and political society.[25] Hegemony is the unity of the functions of domination, education and leadership of one social class, which is dominant in a given historical period, over the other social class (and even over all classes in a society), through the intermediate of civil society. This leading group is the proletariat.[26] He distinguishes hegemony according to the prerevolutionary and revolutionary phase.

In the prerevolutionary phase, hegemony first signified criticism. On the basis of being critical, the proletariat was able to become aware of itself as a 'class for itself', and to become hegemonic after elaborating its proper philosophy (i.e., Marxism). The aim of the proletariat's hegemony at this stage is to obtain 'active consent' of the masses, who identify themselves with the new vision of the world and the interests of the hegemonic class, and mobilize them to participate in the formation of a 'collective national-popular will'.[27] The proletariat takes hold of the civil society in order to affirm itself as an initiator and a carrier of a new order and vision of the universal value ('historical bloc')[28] and, subsequently, to assume cultural and moral leadership of the society.[29] In this conception, we have hegemony opposed to political society.

In the second, revolutionary phase of hegemony, the proletariat first takes hold of political society and asserts and preserves its position through domination. Gramsci's innovative contribution here lies in bringing the concept of hegemony into the sphere of the political society. Gramsci was not satisfied with Lenin's logic of the dictatorship of proletariat based on domination. Having gained moral and cultural leadership in the

23 *See* I. Wallerstein, 'Three Hegemonies', *in* O'Brien & Clesse, *Two Hegemonies*, pp. 357, 360-361 and Wallerstein, *World-Systems Analysis: An Introduction*, pp. 57-58, 94.

24 Wallerstein, 'Three Hegemonies', p. 359.

25 The term *state* in Gramsci's thought includes both, the civil and the political society, and the dialectic between the two. *See* D. Grisoni & R. Maggiori, *Lire Gramsci*, Editions Universitaires, 1973, *s.v. ETAT*, pp. 177-178, and *s.v. SOCIETE POLITIQUE*, pp. 257-258.

26 Ibid., *s.v. HEGEMONIE*, pp. 179-180.

27 Ibid., p. 181.

28 On the historical bloc *see more* ibid., *s.v. BLOC HISTORIQUE*, pp. 159-160 and H. Portelli, *Gramsci et le bloc historique*, PUF, Paris, 1972, in particular pp. 68-96.

29 Grisoni & Maggiori, *Lire Gramsci, s.v. HEGEMONIE*, p. 182.

prerevolutionary phase, the class of proletariat should continue to exercise its ideological leadership when in power. In fact, the historical mission of the proletariat is to exercise permanent persuasion and spread its influence throughout society, using civil and political society alike. Once the revolution is completed, hegemony enables the creation of a 'new type of the state' through dialectic articulation of leadership and dominance.[30]

The originality of Gramsci's contribution to the study of the phenomenon of hegemony lies in the effort to demonstrate that in the most desirable, 'Gramscian' vision of the society – of the union between the civil and the political society – hegemony conceptually consists of leadership and domination, consent and coercion, persuasion and power.[31] In this way, the interplay of the two elements encountered in the classical definition of hegemony (the Ancient Greek and Prussian) and in the world-systems theory gets a much-needed conceptual clarification.

2.2 IMPERIALISM

British scholar Keith Hancock is credited with a saying, "Imperialism is not a word for scholars".[32] There is a grain of truth in this thought as due to various expressions of imperialism this phenomenon is hard to define. However, the problem is not that there is no definition of imperialism, but that there are as many definitions as there are authors who wrote about it.[33] Nonetheless, in spite of all diverging views scholars can agree on some common denominators.[34] This section shall follow the most widely accepted clas-

30 *Cf.* ibid., pp. 182-183. *See also* P. Anderson, *The Antinomies of Antonio Gramsci*, Verson, London-New York, 2017.

31 A. Gramsci, 'Cahier 13 (XXX), 1932-1934, Petites notes sur la politique de Machiavel', *in Cahiers de prison : Cahiers 10, 11, 12, 13*, Gallimard, Paris, 1978, R. Paris (Ed.), trans. P. Fulchignoni & N. Negri, p. 434. *See also* G. Arrighi, *The Long Twentieth Century: Money, Power and the Origins of Our Times*, Verso, London-New York, 1994, pp. 28-29 and S. Reich & R.N. Lebow, *Good-bye Hegemony! Power and Influence in the Global System*, Princeton University Press, Princeton-Oxford, 2014, pp. 17, 23. The dichotomy between consent and coercion is also a recurrent theme in P. Anderson, *The H-Word: The Peripeteia of Hegemony*, Verso, London-New York, 2017.

32 H.L. Wesseling, 'Imperialism and Empire: An Introduction', *in* W. Mommsen & J. Osterhammel (Eds.), *Imperialism and After: Continuities and Discontinuities*, Allen & Unwin, London-Boston-Sydney, 1986, p. 1 and B.J. Cohen, *The Question of Imperialism – The Political Economy of Dominance and Dependence*, Basic Books, Inc., Publishers, New York, p. 9.

33 H.L. Wesseling, 'Imperialism, History of', *in* N.J. Smelser & P.B. Baltes (Eds.), *International Encyclopedia of the Social & Behavioral Sciences*, Elsevier Science Ltd., Oxford, vol. 11, 2001, p. 7226. *See also* P. Braillard & P. de Senarclens, *L'impérialisme*, PUF, Paris, 1980, p. 10.

34 Recently, there has been an upsurge of studies in imperialism at the intersection of history and international law. *See* L. Benton, *A Search for Sovereignty: Law and Geography in European Empires, 1490-1900*, CUP, Cambridge, 2010, M. Koskenniemi *et al.* (Eds.), *International Law and Empire: Historical Explorations*, OUP, Oxford, 2011, L. Benton & L. Ford, *Rage for Order: The British Empire and the Origins of International Law, 1800-1850*, Harvard University Press, Cambridge (MA)-London, 2016, J. Pitts, *Boundaries of the International: Law and Empire*, Harvard University Press, Cambridge (MA)-London, 2018 and G. Gozzi, *Rights and Civilization: A History and Philosophy of International Law*, CUP, Cambridge, 2019 (Italian original published in 2010).

sifications on imperialism. At the same time the conventional views will be supplemented with atypical ones to add different shades of gray into a black-and-white picture of imperialism.

Another problem with imperialism is that its use is polemical given its appropriation for political ends.[35] Early critics of imperialism, such as Hobson and Lenin, articulated the 'devil theory' of imperialism, arguing that imperialism is essentially a metropolitan disposition of ruthless investment bankers to satisfy their lust for profit.[36] However, history does not support this view as imperialism has proven to be a consequence of a variety of complex factors, such as economic pressures, human aggressiveness and greed, the search for security, the drive for power and prestige, nationalist emotions, humanitarianism, and so on.[37] Bernard Porter emphasizes that imperialism and empire are the rule in human history, not exceptions.[38] For these reasons, it is appropriate to consider imperialism as an objective phenomenon, whose history is as old as the history of man himself,[39] and which conceptually represents a particular phenomenon in the domain of the history of ideas.[40]

Etymologically, imperialism derives from the Roman word *imperium*[41] which, in turn, was of Etruscan origin. *Imperium* was the public power conferred upon the highest magistrates in the Roman Republic, such as dictators, consuls and praetors. *Imperium* consisted of civilian and military acts. Under *imperium*, the magistrate had a right to force any citizen to execute his orders and, in the event of failure, to impose a prescribed penalty upon him. Augustus assumed a proconsular *imperium*, which assured him the absolute power over all military, administrative and judicial organizations of the Roman state. All emperors after him enjoyed the same privilege for the course of their lifetimes.[42] Thus, *imperium* denotes a relationship of a complete dominance of a public officer over his subordinates.

The word *imperialism* as we know it appeared in the first half of the nineteenth century in France and signified the expansionist governing style of Napoleon Bonaparte and his successor Louis Napoleon. In the second half of the century, English liberals took it up

35 Braillard & de Senarclens, *L'impérialisme*, p. 9.

36 M.W. Doyle, *Empires*, Cornel University Press, Ithaca-London, 1986, p. 20.

37 *Encyclopaedia Britannica*, vol. 11, *s.v. imperialism*, pp. 121, 122, 123.

38 B. Porter, *The Lion's Share: A History of British Imperialism 1850 to the Present*, Pearson, Harlow, 2012, pp. 2-3. Similarly, Y.N. Harari, *Sapiens: A Brief History of Humankind*, Vintage, London, 2015, p. 214.

39 Cohen, *The Question of Imperialism*, p. 20.

40 Similar is the approach of Philip D. Curtin in his book *Imperialism*, wherein he assembled and commented on a variety of texts with 'imperialistic' undertones. *See* P.D. Curtin, 'Introduction: Imperialism as Intellectual History', *in* P.D. Curtin (Ed.), *Imperialism*, MacMillan, London-Basingstoke, 1972, pp. ix-x. *See also* Porter, *The Lion's Share*, pp. 2-3.

41 D. Lieven, *Empire: The Russian Empire and Its Rivals*, John Murray, London, 2000, p. 7. Encyclopaedia Britannica also makes a link between Empire and *imperium*. (*Encyclopaedia Britannica*, vol. 8, *s.v. empire*, p. 402).

42 *See* M. Mourre, *Dictionnaire encyclopédique d'histoire*, Bordas, Paris, 1987, vol. 4, *s.v. imperium*, p. 2273 and M. Humbert, *Institutions politiques et socials de l'Antiquité*, Dalloz, Paris, 1999, p. 230.

to describe the expansionist policies of the British government. After that it acquired universal significance.[43]

In broader terms, contemporary dictionaries define imperialism as "the extension or imposition of power, authority, or influence"[44] or a natural tendency toward expansion.[45] This broader meaning of the phenomenon demonstrates its close link with power and actually posits it, at its very basics, as an expression of power.

Contemporary definitions of imperialism point to another problem, which is whether imperialism is a process, an institutionalized phenomenon or both? It seems that all three answers are possible. David Lake defines imperialism as "a form of international hierarchy in which one political unit, or polity, effectively governs or controls another polity."[46] Here, imperialism stands for an institutionalized hierarchy and a process within that hierarchy. Johan Galtung offers a more elaborate definition of imperialism. First he defines imperialism as

> a system that splits up collectivities and relates some of the parts to each other in relations of *harmony of interests*, and other parts in relations of *disharmony of interests*, or *conflict of interests*.[47]

He goes on to explain these relations in more detail. Imperialism is the relationship between the center and the periphery such that:

1. there is a harmony of interest between the center in the Center nation and the center in the Periphery nation,
2. there is more disharmony of interest within the Periphery nation than within the center nations,
3. there is disharmony of interest between the periphery in the Center nation and the periphery in the Periphery nation.[48]

---

43 Mourre, *Dictionnaire encyclopédique d'histoire, s.v. impérialisme*, p. 2263, W.J. Mommsen, *Theories of Imperialism*, The University of Chicago Press, Chicago, trans. P.S. Falla, 1982, pp. 3-4, Cohen, *The Question of Imperialism*, p. 10, and Braillard & de Senarclens, *L'impérialisme*, pp. 3-5.

44 Merriam-Webster On-line Dictionary, *s.v. imperialism*, www.merriam-webster.com.

45 Mourre, *Dictionnaire encyclopédique d'histoire, s.v. impérialisme*, p. 2263 and Porter, *The Lion's Share*, p. 4.

46 D.A. Lake, 'Imperialism: Political Aspects', *in* Smelser & Baltes, *Encyclopedia of the Social & Behavioural Sciences*, p. 7232. *See also* S. Howe, *Empire: A Very Short Introduction*, OUP, Oxford, 2002, p. 30, Porter, *The Lion's Share*, p. 3 and B. Porter, *British Imperial: What the Empire Wasn't*, I.B. Tauris, London-New York, 2016, pp. 22, 177.

47 J. Galtung, 'A Structural Theory of Imperialism', 8 *Journal of Peace Research* 1971, p. 81.

48 Ibid., p. 83.

Since Galtung's view is structuralist,[49] his definition of imperialism has an institutional character.[50] Benjamin Cohen depicts imperialism as "any relationship of effective domination or control, political or economic, direct or indirect, of one nation over another."[51] It seems that Cohen's definition implies a dynamic component[52] and therefore looks upon imperialism as a process. Finally, Doyle clearly sees imperialism as a process, which he distinguishes from an institution – an empire. To put it simply: "[i]mperialism is the process of establishing and maintaining an empire."[53] The central element of imperialism is the imperial control. According to Doyle, imperial control is one form of the exercise of asymmetrical influence and power.[54] Its scope involves the political processes and the political outcomes controlled by the metropole.[55] Imperial control is effective either formally or informally through influence over the environment of periphery, political articulation, aggregation, decision-making, adjudication and implementation. Usually, it is local peripheral elites who help effectuating this control.[56]

Scholars framed three main theories of imperialism: metrocentric, pericentric and systemic theories.[57] Metrocentric theories focus on the internal characteristics of imperial states. Imperialism stands for the metropolitan society to expand its rule. The major proponents of the metrocentric views were John Hobson, Vladimir I. Lenin and Joseph Schumpeter. Hobson, who was the first to produce a scientific account of imperialism, focused on the analysis of British imperialism.[58] He portrays the British need for the overseas territorial expansion as the result of the special interests of financiers who encouraged an expansionist foreign policy in order to export their surplus capital.[59] Hob-

49 For a short overview of Galtung's work *see* Papisca & Mascia, *Le relazioni internazionali nell'era dell'interdipendenza e dei diritti umani*, pp. 59-61.

50 Alexander Motyl, *e.g.*, understands the above definition as that of an empire, not of imperialism. (A.J. Motyl, *Imperial Ends: The Decay, Collapse, and Revival of Empires*, Columbia University Press, New York, 2001, pp. 12-13.)

51 Cohen, *The Question of Imperialism*, p. 16 (italics omitted).

52 *See*, in particular his explanation on the taproot of imperialism, which he finds in the anarchic nature of an international system. The anarchic circumstances prompt states to strive for the maximization of their power in order to achieve dominant positions. (Ibid., p. 245.)

53 Doyle, *Empires*, p. 19. In fact, Doyle derives imperialism from the definition of an empire that will be refered to in the subsequent section on empire.

54 Ibid., p. 34.

55 Ibid., p. 36.

56 Ibid., p. 40 and Howe, *Empire*, 18.

57 This classification comes from Doyle. *See also* Lake, 'Imperialism: Political Aspects', pp. 7232-7233, B. Parrot, 'Analyzing the Transformation of the Soviet Union in Comparative Perspective', *in* K. Dawisha & P. Parrot (Eds.), *The End of Empire? The Transformation of the USSR in a Comparative Perspective*, M. E. Sharpe, Armonk (NY)-London, 1997, p. 8, D.A. Lake, 'The Rise, Fall, and Future of the Russian Empire: A Theoretical Interpretation', *in* Dawisha & Parrot, *The End of Empire?*, pp. 31-32 and W.J. Mommsen, 'The End of Empire and the Continuity of Imperialism', *in* Mommsen & Osterhammel, *Imperialism and After*, p. 337.

58 For more on Hobson's treatment of imperialism *see* P. Cain, 'Free Trade, Social Reform and Imperialism: J. A. Hobson and the Dilemmas of Liberalism, 1890-1914', *in* A. Marrison (Ed.), *Free Trade and Its Reception 1815-1960, Freedom and Trade*, vol. 1, Routledge, London, 1998, pp. 207-223.

59 *See* J.A. Hobson, *Imperialism: A Study*, James Pott & Company, New York, 1902, p. 377.

son's analysis prompted Lenin to depict imperialism as the highest stage of capitalism. However, for Lenin, imperialism is not the product of the special interests of high finance, as Hobson argues, but of capitalism itself, which transformed from the stage of competition to the stage of monopolies. This, the highest stage of capitalism is driven to search for overseas profits, raw materials and markets overseas and to participate in the partition and exploitation of the world. Lenin thus considers imperialism as a derivation of capitalism.[60] Schumpeter, on the other hand, follows a different line of argument. For him pure capitalism and imperialism are unrelated and antithetical to each other. He defines imperialism as the objectless disposition of a state to unlimited forcible expansion.[61] This process originated in the aggressive instincts of ancient and modern 'war machines'.[62]

The pericentric theories suggest that imperialism does not originate in the metropoles but in the peripheries, particularly from the forces that pull imperialists into hierarchical relationships. The pioneering analysis of John Gallagher and Ronald Robinson crucially interpreted imperialism as the interaction between international economy and the social structure of (non)collaboration.[63] They define imperialism as

> a sufficient political function of this process of integrating new regions into the expanding economy; its character is largely decided by the various and changing relationships between the political and economic elements of expansion in any particular region and time.[64]

They add that imperialism may be only indirectly connected to economic integration. It may extend beyond areas of economic development but nevertheless supports their strategic protection.[65] Another asset of the Gallagher-Robinson's findings lies in the importance of local elites for the change in intensity of imperialism from an informal to a formal one. If peripheral polities possessed stable regimes and effective collaborators, imperialists could govern these polities indirectly through informal empires. Only if the peripheral society were politically unstable or if they lacked efficient elites would metropoles intervene to create formal empires and govern them directly.[66]

Finally, there are systemic theories of imperialism, which make part of the wider realist theories of international relations and focus on international power politics. The

60 Doyle, *Empires*, p. 23 and V.I. Lenin, 'Imperialism, the Highest Stage of Capitalism: A Popular Outline', *in* V.I. Lenin, *Selected Works in Three Volumes*, Progress Publishers, Moscow, 1970, vol. 1, p. 736.

61 *See* J. Schumpeter, *Impérialisme et classes sociales*, Flammarion, Paris, 1972, trans. S. de Segonzac & P. Bresson, pp. 43, 44.

62 Ibid., pp. 65-66 and Doyle, *Empires*, pp. 23-24.

63 Doyle, *Empires*, p. 25 and Lake, 'Imperialism: Political Aspects', p. 7233.

64 J. Gallagher, & R. Robinson, 'The Imperialism of Free Trade', 6 *The Economic History Review, New Series* 1953, pp. 5-6.

65 Ibid., p. 6. *See also* Porter, *The Lion's Share*, p. 104.

66 Lake, 'Imperialism: Political Aspects', p. 7233 and Robinson & Gallagher, 'The Imperialism of Free Trade', p. 13.

struggle for survival and influence between great powers creates the condition of competition that influences metropoles to seize territories in order to augment their resources. This race also allows great powers to compensate one another using peripheral territories to maintain the balance of power. Disparities in power thus provide both opportunities and motives for imperialist drive. The case of imperialism driven by the systemic competition was the so-called race for Africa in the late nineteenth century.[67]

From the above considerations it follows that the two essential attributes of the relation between the metropole (or center) and the periphery are – asymmetry and dominance. However, it is not entirely correct to equate imperialism with forceful dominance, because the imperialistic relations are not always a consequence of a simple impulse for dominance. The degree of inequality between the metropole and the periphery may not come as a consequence of asserted imperialism, but of the initial unequal position in the world-system. Robinson, for example, presents an 'eccentric idea of imperialism', which sees imperialism as a system of collaboration between the metropole and peripheral elites. Naturally, the imperialist form of collaboration is an unequal one, because the dominant partner is more powerful.[68] However, even so, there is always a price to be paid to the collaborators, and imperialism is therefore a question of bargaining.[69]

This insight is also supported by Galtung's structural perspective on imperialism and a harmony of interests between the center of the metropole and the center of the periphery. Because there is the harmony of interests, such a situation supports finding the consent between the imperialist authorities and subordinated elites. This relationship at the same time represents grounds for a move from inequality towards equality. In this way, we depart from the initial and conventional perception of imperialism, which understands its inner relations simply as dominance of the center over the periphery. The contents of imperialism are multifaceted and its components in many instances include, beside coercion, also consent, and, apart from inequality, also degrees of equality.

---

67 Lake, 'Imperialism: Political Aspects', p. 7233, Doyle, *Empires*, p. 26 and Cohen, *The Question of Imperialism*, p. 245.

68 However, this is so because the enormous imbalance in economic, intellectual, military and political power potential existed between the two entities from the start. (Mommsen, 'The End of Empire and the Continuity of Imperialism', p. 335.)

69 Wesseling, 'Imperialism and Empire', p. 3. For a detailed analysis, *see* R. Robinson, 'The Excentric Idea of Imperialism, with or without Empire', *in* Mommsen & Osterhammel, *Imperialism and After*, pp. 267-289. For a comprehensive overview of the relation between British and Indian elites *see* D. Judd, *The Lion and the Tiger: The Rise and Fall of the British Raj*, OUP, Oxford, 2003 and J. Darwin, *Unfinished Empire: The Global Expansion of Britain*, Penguin Books, London, 2013, pp. 75, 207-214, 265.

2.3 Empire

Doyle, who defined imperialism as the process of establishing empire, defines empire as

> a relationship, formal or informal, in which one state controls the effective political sovereignty of another political society. It can be achieved by force, by political collaboration, by economic, social, or cultural dependence.[70]

Focusing on the institutional character of empire, it is a state of a large size and usually of composite character, which is often ruled by an emperor. The state may take the shape of a federation (*e.g.*, the German empire 1870-1918), a unitary state (*e.g.*, the Russian empire), or a loose commonwealth of free states united with a number of subordinate dependencies (*e.g.*, the British Empire).[71]

Relying on Foucault's notion of biopower, Michael Hardt and Antonio Negri introduced a post-modern understanding of the empire. For them empire is

> a *decentered* and *deterritorializing* apparatus of rule that progressively incorporates the entire global realm within its open, expanding frontiers. Empire manages hybrid identities, flexible hierarchies, and plural exchanges through modulating networks of command.[72]

They underline that their perception of empire is something altogether different from imperialism and conceive empire without territorial limits or boundaries. In addition, Hardt and Negri understand empire not as a historical regime originating in conquest but as an order that suspends history and fixes the existing state of affairs for eternity.[73] They detach the attribute of territoriality from the concept of empire and substitute it with fluid networks. However, the concept still retains, as its major element, the domination of the powerful center over the periphery.

Another valuable perspective on the term *empire* comes from a study of the ancient empires. Although many authors point out the differences between empires in time, it is

70 Doyle, *Empires*, p. 45. For similar definitions *see* Parrot, 'Analyzing the Transformation of the Soviet Union in Comparative Perspective', p. 7, Howe, *Empire*, pp. 14, 30 and Porter, *The Lion's Share*, p. 11.

71 *Encylopaedia Britannica*, vol. 8, *s.v. empire*, p. 402. Naturally, these are not the only instances of empire. Empires were regular occurrences in non-European regions, as well as ideas to revive them together with their lost grandeur. (*See, e.g.*, N. Ferguson, *Civilization*, Penguin Books, London, 2012, T. Ballantyne & A. Burton, *Empires and the Reach of the Global: 1870-1945*, The Belknap Press of Harvard University Press, Cambridge (MA)-London, 2012 and P. Mishra, *From the Ruins of Empire*, Penguin Books, London, 2013.)

72 M. Hardt, & A. Negri, *Empire*, Harvard University Press, Cambridge (MA)-London, 2000, p. xii.

73 Ibid., pp. xii-xiii, xiv.

interesting to note similarities that unite all forms of empire in a single concept.[74] On the basis of the study of empires in Mesopotamia, Mogens Trolle Larsen comes to the following definition:

> [E]mpire is a relationship between a ruling and controlling power and one or more subjugated and dominated peoples. I would suggest that an empire be defined as a supernational system of political control, and such a system may have either a city-state or a territorial state as its center.[75]

This definition is almost identical to the previously mentioned definitions of empire and, disregarding the element of territoriality, also to Hardt & Negri's definition.

Apart from being an institutional or systemic phenomenon, empire is arguably a process as political conquest and consolidation is accompanied by institutional and symbolic restructuring.[76] The concept of the empire is not a single unitary structure or idea but encompasses a recurrent and irregular process of growth and decay.[77] The growing complexity of empires goes hand in hand with a move towards larger units and stronger centralization so that more extensive areas come under direct rule.[78] This, imperial phase has a tendency to integrate more peripheral space into the center or, reciprocally, incites an increasing expansion of the center into the periphery.[79]

Again consideration must be paid to the issue of equality. A deeper analysis of the concept of empire unveils, similar to hegemony and imperialism, instances that enable the appearance of equality in an otherwise prevailing relation of dominance. Lake uses the systemic approach to show the degree of residual rights in the structure of the empire in which one partner cedes substantial rights of residual control directly to the other one. In this way, the two entities take part in a political relationship in which one party controls the other. However, the complete dominance of one party over the other seldom exists. In the structure of the empire, local officials often enjoy some independence in implementing local residual rights.[80] Lake's analysis is similar to that of Galtung with regard to imperialism. Finally, there is also a general and interdependent influence between the center and the periphery. As a rule, the center usually attempts to exploit,

74 For comprehensive studies on empires, ancient and/or modern, *see* Doyle, *Empires*; *Encyclopaedia Britannica, s.v. empire*; Larsen, *Power and Propaganda*; M. Duverger (Ed.), *Le concept d'empire*, PUF, Paris, 1980; and S.E. Finer, *The History of Government from the Earliest Times*, OUP, Oxford, 1999, 3 volumes.

75 M.T. Larsen, 'The Tradition of Empire in Mesopotamia', *in* Larsen, *Power and Propaganda*, p. 91.

76 R. McC. Adams, 'Common Concerns but Different Standpoints: A Commentary', *in* Larsen, *Power and Propaganda*, p. 393 and S.N. Eisenstadt, 'Observations and Queries about Sociological Aspects of Imperialism in the Ancient World', *in* Larsen, *Power and Propaganda*, p. 21.

77 McC. Adams, 'Common Concerns but Different Standpoints', p. 393.

78 Larsen, 'The Tradition of Empire in Mesopotamia', p. 93.

79 P. Garelli, 'Les empires mésopotamiens', *in* Duverger, *Le concept d'empire*, p. 25. Although the above findings come from the treatment of empires in Mesopotamia they are applicable to all forms of empires.

80 Lake, 'The Rise, Fall, and Future of the Russian Empire', pp. 33-35.

permeate and reconstruct the periphery economically. However, in many empires the peripheries developed potential tendencies toward at least partial impingement on the center.[81] All these examples render the issue of the absolute domination within the empire relative. Periphery gains increasing weight and puts some equilibrium in relation towards the center. In some instances the relationship between the center and the periphery can result in equality.

2.4 Concluding Remarks on Hegemony

Consecutive treatment of hegemony, imperialism and empire aimed at showing that these phenomena essentially stand for the same concept. For that reason they can be put under a 'generic umbrella' of hegemony. They all represent the relation of dominance of the center over multiple peripheries. Usually the element of dominance is less evident in the case of hegemony and more so in imperialism and empire. However, even hegemony in most extreme cases such as in the ancient Greece turns into imperialist control. On the other hand, imperialism and empire often stand for a less formal and intense degree of control as, for example, the British Empire in the eighteenth century. Another element in favor of conceptual unification comes from the fact that all three phenomena imply the condition of dominance as an institution or as a process. The distinction between institution and process is thus not the decisive factor.

What perhaps comes as the most important outcome of the previous analysis is the importance of a simultaneous existence of consent and coercion (or leadership and domination; persuasion and power) in all three concepts. While initially hegemony would be leadership, implying consent or persuasion, it is now clear that hegemony presupposes consent and coercion (or power).[82] Conversely, although the defining element of imperialism seemed to be premised on dominance, it follows from the preceding analysis that the relation between the center and the periphery is much more complex and commonly includes the consent from the peripheral (and, of course, metropolitan) side.[83] Thus, in this context hegemony is premised upon both elements: consent *and* coercion. The degrees of both elements may vary in different circumstances. Sometimes there may be less consent and more coercion and *vice versa*. What is exluded from the understanding of

81 Eisenstadt, 'Observations and Queries about Sociological Aspects of Imperialism in the Ancient World', p. 25 and Judd, *The Lion and the Tiger*, p. 200.

82 *See* M. Delević Đilas, 'The Power of Ideas or How Political Conditionality Differs from Other Forms of Economic Statecraft?', *in* M. Delević Đilas & V. Đerić (Eds.), *O međunarodnom i narodnom – eseji u čast Vojina Dimitrijevića / The International and the National – Essays in Honour of Vojin Dimitrijević*, Beogradski centar za ljudska prava, Belgrade, 2003, pp. 72-73.

83 *See* Howe, *Empire*, pp. 126-127.

hegemony in this book are situations of pure consent (consensual agreement) or of exclusive coercion (forceful domination).[84]

This has significant consequences for our understanding of hegemony. The importance of consent makes the framework of dominance relative. Coexistence between coercion and consent may lead to the emergence of relative equality between the center and entities in the periphery or between elites in the center and in the periphery. In this sense, there is coexistence between the concepts of hierarchy and egalitarianism.[85] Alexander the Great conceived the imperial idea of fusing all peoples, Greek and barbaric, under his authority of a sovereign of the universe (*cosmocrator*) in which all of the empire's citizens would live harmoniously in equality. He assigned high administrative and military posts to the defeated opponents and encouraged mixed marriages.[86] The British Empire in Victorian times represented a complex model of racial and social hierarchy, which nevertheless instituted a general, although not unqualified, principle of equality before the law.[87] Relativization of dominance also leads to the lessening of suppression and to the appearance of liberty within the hegemonic framework.[88] In particular, the ancient empires excelled in allowing liberty to flourish. In a general definition of the empire, Maurice Duverger underlined the issue of autonomy for governed peoples.[89] Roman Emperor Caracala extended Roman citizenship in 212 to all free individuals in the territory of the Roman Empire (*constitutio Antoniana*), through which they acquired a plethora of civic rights.[90] With regard to the British Empire, Niall Ferguson listed nine positive influences in which the idea of liberty occupies the ninth place. He explains his choice with an argument that the British society was always alert to judge Britain's imperial conduct by the yardstick of liberty. Once the peripheries adopted institutions the British brought

84 Examples of forceful domination include processes that began as hegemony, imperialism or empire but later turned into an oppressive rule and led to massive atrocities by colonial administrators, such as the Belgian oppression in Congo during the rule of King Leopold II, German violence in Namibia against Herera and Namaqua peoples, and the practice of systematic torture by the British during the Mau Mau rebellion in Kenya. These instances of oppression were morally and legally reprehensible already at the time of commission. They are unacceptable from the contemporary perspective and would, according to the current international criminal law, classify as atrocity crimes. (*See* A. Hochschild, *King Leopold's Ghost: A Story of Greed, Terror, and Heroism in Colonial Africa*, Marine Books, Boston, 1999, J. Burke & P. Olterman, 'Germany Moves to Atone for "Forgotten Genocide" in Namibia', 25 December 2016, *The Guardian*, www.theguardian.com/world/2016/dec/25/germany-moves-to-atone-for-forgotten-genocide-in-namibia and M. Parry, 'Uncovering the Brutal Truth about the British Empire', 18 August 2016, *The Guardian*, www.theguardian.com/news/2016/aug/18/uncovering-truth-british-empire-caroline-elkins-mau-mau.)

85 In terms of anthropological studies, *see* L. Poyer, 'Egalitarianism in the Face of Hierarchy', 49 *Journal of Anthropological Research* 1993, pp. 111-131.

86 Mourre, *Dictionnaire encyclopédique d'histoire, s.v. impérialisme*, p. 2265 and *Encyclopaedia Britannica, s.v. imperialism*, p. 121.

87 Ferguson, *Colossus*, p. 12 and Howe, *Empire*, 127.

88 For the propagation of various aspects and degrees of liberty within the British Empire, *see* J.P. Greene (Ed.), *Exclusionary Empire: English Liberty Overseas, 1600-1900*, CUP, Cambridge, 2010.

89 M. Duverger, 'Le concept d'empire', *in* Duverger, *Le concept d'empire*, p. 11.

90 *See* V. Korošec, *Rimsko pravo: I. del [Roman Law: Ist Part]*, ČZ Uradni list SRS, Ljubljana, 1987, pp. 94-96. For a tendency towards universality in the Roman Empire *see* Lieven, *Empire*, pp. 8-10.

with them, it was hard for them to prohibit political liberty.[91] In the context of an expansion of the American state across the continent of the Northern America, Thomas Jefferson labelled the United States as the 'empire of liberty'.[92]

Besides equality and liberty, there is another important asset of the hegemonic influence which came to the fore in the late stage of imperialism, namely, the rule of law.[93] Ferguson puts the common law on the fourth place of the list mentioned earlier.[94] In the nineteenth and early twentieth centuries, there was no organization apart from the British Empire which did more to impose Western norms of law, order and governance around the world.[95] In addition, one of the driving forces of the American imperialism, comparable perhaps to an earlier European religious drive to spread Christianity, was to propagate the rule of law.[96] American proliferation of the rule of law occurred, for example, in the form of legal competences of the American military commanders in the occupied Germany and Japan after World War II.[97]

This brings us to the conclusion of the chapter on hegemony and to the following definition of hegemony, to be used for further explorations in this book:

> Hegemony in a generic sense is the expansion of power, which stabilizes a given structure of interactions through the relation of dominance of the commanding center over the asymmetric periphery. The relationship of dominance is not absolute and is checked by the relational power of the periphery. Therefore, hegemony implies coercion and consent, leadership and domination, and persuasion and power. As a consequence, hegemony in many instances leads to the introduction of equality, liberty and the rule of law in the overarching framework of relative dominance.

---

91 N. Ferguson, *Empire: The Rise and Demise of the British World Order and the Lessons for Global Power*, Basic Books, London-New York, 2002, p. xxv. *See also* Howe, *Empire*, p. 66.

92 Ferguson, *Colossus*, p. 2. On the role of Jefferson in the construction of the American empire *see* J.G. Wilson, *The Imperial Republic: A Structural History of American Constitutionalism from the Colonial Era to the Beginning of the Twentieth Century*, Ashgate, Aldershot, 2002, in particular pp. 21-26. *See also* R. Aron, *République impériale : Les États-Unis dans le monde 1945-1972*, Calmann-Lévy, Paris, 1973.

93 On this issue, *see* S. Humphreys, *The Theatre of the Rule of Law: Transnational Legal Intervention in Theory and Practice*, CUP, Cambridge, 2010, pp. 109-121.

94 Ferguson, *Empire*, p. xxv.

95 Ibid., pp. 359, xxiv. For details regarding India, *see* Judd, *The Lion and the Tiger*, in particular pp. 87-89, 91, 94-96, Porter, *The Lion's Share*, p. 37 and Harari, *Sapiens*, pp. 228-229.

96 Wilson, *The Imperial Republic*, p. 254.

97 *See* Ferguson, *Colossus*, pp. 69-76. For Japan, *see, e.g.*, Y. Hasebe, 'Constitutional Borrowing and Political Theory', 2 *International Journal of Constitutional Law* 2003, pp. 224-226. For Germany *see, e.g.*, L. Loewenstein, 'Reconstruction of the Administration of Justice in American-Occupied Germany', 62 *Harvard Law Review* 1948, pp. 419-467.

3 The Meaning of Constitutionalism

This chapter aims to demonstrate, on the basis of an assessment of the development of constitutionalism, that conceptually there is a common understanding of constitutionalism. Naturally, sets of its components vary from one author to the other, and differ from one political entity to another, which is a consequence of the development of constitutionalism in time (through history) and space (in different socio-political *milieus*).[1] Consequently, this chapter will present relations between the common meaning of constitutionalism and its ensuing components that evolved through time and space. It is important to bear in mind that constitutionalism resides at the intersection of law and politics.[2]

Sieyès's model on the crystallization of power serves as a starting point for the exploration of constitutionalism. Constitutionalism consists of two components. The first is the agglomeration of power in the form of government. The second element is an imposition of controls on the government to limit the exercise of its power.

Maurice Vile follows this approach when he opts for "the frank acknowledgment of the role of government in society, linked with the determination to bring that government under control and to place limits on the exercise of its power".[3] Charles McIlwain pleads for the creation of a strong government and for putting legal limitations on it:[4]

> A constituted authority is one that is defined, and there can be no definition which does not of necessity imply a limitation. Constitutional government is and must be 'limited government' if it is constitutional at all.[5]

True constitutionalism, therefore, has never signified government enfeebled by divisions within itself but rather government limited by law.[6] Similarly, Graham Maddox under-

---

1 *Cf.* P. Zumbansen, 'Carving Out Typologies and Accounting for Differences Across Systems: Towards a Methodology of Transnational Constitutionalism', *in* M. Rosenfeld & A. Sajó (Eds.), *Oxford Handbook of Comparative Constitutional Law*, OUP, Oxford, 2012, p. 79.

2 A.F. Lang & A. Wiener, 'A Constitutionalising Global Order: An Introduction', *in* A.F. Lang & A. Wiener (Eds.), *Handbook on Global Constitutionalism*, Edward Elgar Publishing, Cheltenham-Northampton (MA), 2017, pp. 2, 17.

3 M.J.C. Vile, *Constitutionalism and the Separation of Powers*, Liberty Fund, Indianapolis, 1998, p. 2.

4 C.H. McIlwain, *Constitutionalism and the Changing World*, CUP, Cambridge, 1939, pp. 258, 263-264.

5 Ibid., p. 244.

6 Ibid., p. 282. *See also* C.H. McIlwan, *Constitutionalism: Ancient and Modern*, Great Seal Books, Ithaca (NY), 1958, pp. 21-22.

stands constitutionalism as a balance between a strong government, which creates a secure and stable order, and a firm control of governmental power.[7] Giovanni Sartori agrees that constitutionalism seeks to balance the efficient exercise of power within its control and furthermore, a constitution in which the controls "outpower power" leads to an impotent government.[8] In the British national context, Michael Foley understands constitutionalism as a distinctive and substantive code of political life, which not only organizes and rationalizes government but at the same time restricts the exercise of power to agreed limits.[9] Donald Kommers and W.J. Thompson describe constitutionalism as a two-edged concept, with a positive and a negative aspect, "A constitution both empowers and delimits power, both grants authority and specifies its scope and purpose."[10] Ulrich Preuss, likewise, follows this definition and describes the role of a constitution as contradictory "in erecting a strong political power and at the same time limiting and domesticating that power."[11]

All these authors understand constitutionalism to consist of two elements: the accumulation of power, which then assumes a juridical expression, and a formal imposition of limits upon that concentration of power. Boštjan M. Zupančič explains the two-stage evolution in more detail:

> [T]here are two figurative stages in the establishment of a state. In the *first stage* the greater power (of the future state) establishes its absolute prevalence in society, stops the war of everybody against everybody and introduces peace. ... [I]n the *second stage* the state must offer an alternative mode of conflict resolution on all different levels from private controversies, to the conflict between the individual and the state (as in criminal law) to the political conflicts between the different structured interests in the state. The legal order, in the end constitutional, does just that.[12]

---

7 G. Maddox, 'A Note on the Meaning of "Constitution"', 76 *The American Political Science Review* 1982, pp. 805, 809.

8 G. Sartori, 'Comment on Maddox', 78 *The American Political Science Review* 1984, p. 497.

9 M. Foley, *The Politics of the British Constitution*, Manchester University Press, Manchester-New York, 1999, p. 13.

10 D.P. Kommers & W.J. Thompson, 'Fundamentals in the Liberal Constitutional Tradition', *in* J.J. Hesse & N. Johnson (Eds.), *Constitutional Policy and Change in Europe*, OUP, Oxford, 1995, p. 24. *See also* M. Loughlin, *Sword and Scales: An Examination of the Relationship between Law and Politics*, Hart, Oxford-Portland (OR), 2000, pp. 190, 193 and R. Hirschl, *Comparative Matters: The Renaissance of Comparative Constitutional Law*, OUP, Oxford, 2016, p. 152.

11 U.K. Preuss, 'Patterns of Constitutional Evolution and Change in Eastern Europe', *in* Hesse & Johnson, *Constitutional Policy and Change in Europe*, pp. 95, 100.

12 B.M. Zupančič, 'From Combat to Contract: "What Does the Constitution Constitute?"', 1 *European Journal of Law Reform* 1998/1999, p. 70 (footnote omitted, emphasis by A.Z.).

In the broadest sense, constitutionalism stands for the 'minimization of the maximization of power'. It is important to add that the construction of the body politic through agglomeration and limitation of power has a function of the pursuit of the common good in a given community. The pursuit of the common good is a central element of constitutionalism.[13] The common good is the opposite of the concern for self-interest, power and whim,[14] which is logical if one sees the process of agglomeration of power as transcendence of these particularized tendencies. Various thinkers conceived of the common good differently; they viewed it in terms of justice, preservation, material welfare, or maximized utility.[15] One of the most relevant definitions describes the common good as "a value that represents the fundamental goals of a collectivity and is in many ways at the core of its raison d'être."[16] This perspective aligns the common good with collective interests of the members of a given community.[17]

Although the term *constitutionalism* is semantically a recent one, the idea it embodies dates back to classical antiquity.[18] It is not certain when the term as such came into use. Some authors claim it was coined during the American Revolution, while others set its origins in the 1830s. It is closely linked to the words 'constitutional' and 'constitution'.

The term *constitutional* came in to regular use in the second half of the eighteenth century, whereas the use of the term *constitution* dates back to the period between twelfth and thirteenth centuries where it signified an institution. It acquired a modern meaning during the debates that led to the outbreak of English Civil War in 1642. Constitutionalism, through the term *constitution*, derives from the Latin term *constitutio*.[19] A widely accepted contemporary definition of the constitution understands it as

> [t]he organic and fundamental law of a nation or state, which may be written or unwritten, establishing the character and conception of its government, laying the basic principles to which its internal life is to be conformed, organizing the government, and regulating, distributing, and limiting the functions of its different departments, and prescribing the extent and manner of the exercise of sovereign powers.[20]

---

13 M.N.S. Sellers, 'Niccolò Machiavelli: Father of Modern Constitutionalism', 28 *Ratio Juris* 2015, p. 224.

14 R.J. Lipkin, 'The Quest for the Common Good: Neutrality and Deliberative Democracy in Sunstein's Conception of American Constitutionalism', 26 *Connecticut Law Review* 1994, p. 1045.

15 M. Jaede, 'The Concept of the Common Good', Working Paper, University of Edinburgh, p. 1, www.thebritishacademy.ac.uk/sites/default/files/Jaede.pdf and B. Cronin, *Institutions for the Common Good: International Protection Regimes in International Society*, CUP, Cambridge, 2003, pp. 4, 12.

16 Cronin, *Institutions for the Common Good*, p. 12.

17 *See* ibid., pp. 12-13.

18 S. Gordon, *Controlling the State: Constitutionalism from Ancient Athens to Today*, Harvard University Press, Cambridge (MA)-London, 1999, p. 5.

19 Ibid., p. 5, n. 3 and P. Goyard, 'Constitution', *in* Jacob & Auroux, *Encyclopédie philosophique universelle : les notions*, p. 446.

20 H.C. Black, *Black's Law Dictionary*, West Publishing Co., St. Paul (MN), 1990, *s.v. constitution.*

However, the need to control the exercise of the state power goes all the way back to the classical antiquity. The idea of a 'constitutional' political order is as old as Western political thought.[21] Therefore, it is correct to say that the "tradition of constitutionalism begins in ancient Athens and has had a long, interrupted, and irregular history to the present day."[22] This highly interesting development through history demands a brief consideration of its most interesting episodes.

3.1 THEORY OF THE MIXED GOVERNMENT

The most influential contribution of the Greeks to the evolution of constitutionalism was the doctrine of mixed government. The doctrine derives from the idea that there are three basic or pure forms of the state – monarchy, aristocracy and democracy, or government by the one, the few, or the many. Aristotle advocated a slightly different classification where the pure forms of state are monarchy, aristocracy and constitution, or 'constitutional government' (*politeia* in Greek).[23] In contrast, he considered tyranny, oligarchy and democracy as deviations of the form of government.[24]

Aristotle made another interesting observation with regard to the separation of the elements of government. If a particular constitution encapsulates three well-ordered elements, it enjoys supremacy over other forms of constitution:

> Of these three factors one is, what is to be the body that deliberates about the common interests, second the one connected with the magistracies, that is, what there are to be and what matters they are to control, and what is to be the method of their election, and a third is, what is to be the judiciary.[25]

In this explanation, some authors saw the roots of what would later become the doctrine of the 'separation of powers'. However, what Aristotle had in mind was that every orderly government consists of law-making, law-administration and law-adjudication. He did not propose that these functions reside in distinct institutions, nor did he suggest that these functions serve as a limitation of government through their interaction and interdependence.[26] The doctrine of the separation of powers arose several centuries later with

---

21 Gordon, *Controlling the State*, p. 2.

22 F.D. Wormuth, *The Origins of Modern Constitutionalism*, Harper & Brothers Publishers, New York, 1949, p. 3.

23 Aristotle, *Politics*, p. 207, 1279a.

24 Ibid., p. 207, 1279b.

25 Ibid., p. 345, 1297b-1298a.

26 Gordon, *Controlling the State*, p. 83 and M.I. Finley, *Politics in the Ancient World*, CUP, Cambridge, 1994, p. 58. *See also* L. Pitamic, *A Treatise on the State*, Ministry of Justice, Ljubljana, 2008 (repr.), pp. 43-44, 64.

Montesquieu. Before advancing to that stage, the theory of the mixed government first had to evolve into an arrangement that provided mutual checks on the exercise of power.

This conceptual adjustment occurred with Polybius who applied the initially Greek idea to the governmental design of the Roman Republic. According to his doctrine, the Senate embodied the aristocratic element in the Roman Republic, the popular assemblies the democratic element, and the elected consuls the monarchical one.[27] Each of these institutions of the Roman government used its power to curtail the other institutions as well as to cooperate with them. The aim of this dynamic was that the constitution remained in a condition of equilibrium through a long period of time. This version of mixed government differed significantly from that of Plato and of Aristotle. Although the two Greek philosophers envisaged the idea of balance in their political analysis, they did not go so far as to vest distinct powers into different organs as a means of checks and balances.[28] Thus, Polybius set the stage for the transformation of the theory of the mixed government into a theory of checks and balances in which the agencies of government did not principally represent a class, but provided an institutional check within a governmental structure.[29]

The theory of the mixed government thus represents a particular component of the general theory of limited government. It aims to prevent the concentration of power in one organ of the state. Its original contribution lay in the premise that in order to prevent arbitrary rule separate governmental branches are needed. A suitable name for such a distribution of competencies is the 'separation of agencies'. Namely, the various branches were expected to play a part in exercising all functions of government, but their representative character enabled them to prevent the use of power in ways prejudicial to the interests they represented.[30]

3.2 MAGNA CARTA AND CHECKS AND BALANCES IN THE VENETIAN REPUBLIC

Another phase in the history of the limitation of government comes with *Magna Carta Libertatum* in 1215. From the contemporary perspective, the rebellion of the barons against King John may look like a fight for their liberties but at its base, it was an act of imposing limits on the arbitrary monarchic power. As in antiquity, there was no trace of the doctrine of civil liberties in feudal England. These began to emerge as a corollary of the advancement of liberalism only in the seventeenth century. The *Magna Carta* became

27 Gordon criticized the monarchical element arguing that consuls could not represent it since a popular Assembly had elected them for a period of one year. He also invoked arguments defending Polybius's choice. (*See* Gordon, *Controlling the State*, p. 108, including n. 33.)

28 Ibid., pp. 108-109, Wormuth, *The Origins of Modern Constitutionalism*, pp. 22-23 and Finer, *The History of Government from the Earliest Times*, vol. 1, p. 396.

29 Vile, *Constitutionalism and the Separation of Powers*, p. 40.

30 Ibid., pp. 38, 40.

the symbol of the principle that the authority of the monarch was subordinate to what came to be called the *ancient constitution* of England.[31]

The events leading to the creation of *Magna Carta* attest to the fact that the rebels organized a quasi-'constitutional' opposition to John in order to do away with abuses. The main issue was the King's practice of attacking the barons, seizing them as well as their families and property, and ill-treating them without first convicting them in a court. This is the most important element of *Magna Carta* (embodied in Chapter 39),[32] which had long-term repercussions for the advancement of constitutionalism.[33] Chapter 39 led to the creation of Courts of 'Common Pleas', replacing a system whereby courts were part of the king's administrative bureaucracy that accompanied him on his travels to adjudicate pending cases. Although, at the time, the establishment of a system of local courts probably seemed more a matter of convenience, this achievement contributed greatly to the progressive emancipation of judiciary from the Crown in the seventeenth century and, finally, to its complete independence at the end of the eighteenth century.[34]

Zupančič argued that the constitutional significance of the *Magna Carta* lay in the fact that:

> For the first time in history the power had to be exercised in *reference to a legal document* governing its sharing. The future sharing of power seems to be at the core of this paradigmatic situation, the constitution being nothing else but a contract (a *compromissum*) projected into the general rules of the political, legal and power games played between parties.[35]

The checks and balances at that stage were a factual alternative to civil war and a prerequisite for the establishment of the state, constituted as a contract between the protagonists of power in the society. Therefore, it is important to understand that the constitution is essentially a contract.[36]

The theory of the mixed government further evolved after its articulation in the antiquity and had an important role for constitutionalism of the Middle Ages. One of the polities in which the theory played an important part was the Republic of Venice. That Venice achieved a gracious appellation *Serenissima* is not only a consequence of its

---

31 Gordon, *Controlling the State*, p. 230. For recent historical studies on Magna Carta *see* D. Carpenter, *Magna Carta*, Penguin Classics, London, 2015, D. Starkey, *Magna Carta: The True Story behind the Charter*, Hodder & Stoughton, London, 2015 and N. Vincent, *Magna Carta: A Very Short Introduction*, OUP, Oxford, 2012.

32 For all the historical documents in English language in the section on constitutionalism *see* the Internet site of the Avalon Project at the Yale School of Law, http://avalon.law.yale.edu and the Constitution Society, www.constitution.org.

33 McIlwain, *Constitutionalism and the Changing World*, p. 103.

34 Gordon, *Controlling the State*, p. 231 and Pitamic, *A Treatise on the State*, pp. 116-117.

35 Zupančič, 'From Combat to Contract', p. 66.

36 Id.

wealthy status, but also of its equilibrated and nonturbulent way of governance, in contradistinction to other Italian city-states of that period. Florence, for example, repeatedly attempted to set up a constitutional political order, but Venice was the only city that succeeded in elevating a durable one. Even Machiavelli, no admirer of the Venetian system of government (because it did not serve his model of an expansive state), had to admit its constitutional preeminence.[37]

To preserve the notion of liberty, the Venetians constructed constitutional machinery. They made sure that the exercise of power belonged to many incumbents and that no one was able to monopolize power.[38] At the head of the Venetian administration was the Doge who had very restrained competences. Other important institutions were the Great Council, the Senate and the Council of Ten.[39] The Venetian constitution reflected the theory of the mixed government as developed by Polybius. The relationship between institutions was of government offices rather than social classes.[40] Different institutions represented various centers of power and also acted as controlling agencies of other institutions. The constitutional system in Venice consisted of political authorities that were interdependent due to the overlapping membership in various bodies, intersection of their spheres of competence, and accountability of each and every governmental official. In this way, the Venetian political system embodied the principle of 'checks and balances' in its pure form.[41] Venetians were practical men of quotidian politics, who constructed their constitution through solving the concrete and actual problems.[42] Thus, the constitutional machinery with a task to curtail the lust for power was their main contribution to the political history of the West.[43] However, while the Venetian example had some political impact in Europe, it did not bear any influence on American political thought.[44]

3.3 The Doctrine of the Separation of Powers and the Mechanism of Checks and Balances

Under the influence of English writers, particularly John Locke, Montesquieu developed the doctrine of the separation of powers in his masterpiece *De l'Esprit des Lois*. His premise was an effective control of the coercive authority of the state for the prevention of

37 Gordon, *Controlling the State*, pp. 137, 158.
38 Ibid., p. 145.
39 *See* ibid., pp. 137-143. *See also* Finer, *The History of Government from the Earliest Times*, vol. 2, pp. 987-991 and T.F. Madden, *Venice: A New History*, Viking, New York, 2012, pp. 169-172, 174-179, 226-227.
40 Gordon, *Controlling the State*, p. 145.
41 *Cf.* ibid., pp. 145-146.
42 Ibid., p. 137.
43 Ibid., p. 145.
44 *See* ibid., pp. 155-165, 324. This is due to the fact that in the decaying epoch of the Venetian Republic the growing *anomie* led to corruption and decadence.

liberty of an individual.[45] Montesquieu drew from Locke's division between the legislative and the executive powers; however, he emphasized certain elements that were overlooked before, particularly in relation to the judiciary.[46] Within the framework of the protection of liberty, Montesquieu formulated the doctrine of the separation of powers, arguing that there could be no liberty if the judicial powers are not separated from the legislative and executive powers.[47] He explained that if the judicial power were fused with the legislative power, a judge could be a legislator with arbitrary control over the life and liberty of citizens. Furthermore, if judicial powers were fused with executive powers, judges would have the might of an oppressor.[48] Montesquieu went on to underline that everything would be lost if the same person, or the same body of noblemen or people, could exercise all three powers: enact laws, execute the public resolutions, and adjudicate the crimes and disputes of individuals.[49]

Although Montesquieu was the first to put judicial power on a par with executive and legislative powers, he was not a proponent of the strong judiciary. He dispensed with the role of judges, treating them as a mere mouthpiece of the law.[50] While Montesquieu conceived the judiciary as an independent branch of government, in his design, the courts did not possess any power over the other two branches. There were still steps to be made before the courts gained the power of the judicial review.[51]

After America proclaimed independence from the British Empire, they devised a new formulation of the doctrine of constitutionalism, which drew from theories of seventeenth and eighteenth century England and their experience of English and colonial government. Although American constitutionalism relied on the same basic purposes and dangers of political power as in England, it was a new formulation with a very different emphasis, which served to the Americans as a launching pad into the new world of independence.[52]

The constitution of Virginia of 1776, the first of the American state constitutions, ordained that the "legislative, executive and judiciary departments shall be separate and distinct, so that neither exercise the powers properly belonging to the other".[53] This declaration was one of the most precise statements of the doctrine of separation of powers at the time[54] and was replicated in many subsequent state constitutions. The meaning of

45 *Cf.* ibid., p. 282 and Vile, *Constitutionalism and the Separation of Powers*, p. 99.
46 *See* Montesquieu, *De l'Esprit des Lois I*, Garnier-Flammarion, Paris, 1979, livre XI, ch. 6, p. 294. Vile, *Constitutionalism and the Separation of Powers*, p. 95 and Wormuth, *The Origins of Modern Constitutionalism*, p. 195.
47 *See* Loughlin, *Sword and Scales*, pp. 181-182.
48 Montesquieu, *De l'Esprit des Lois I*, p. 294.
49 Ibid., p. 295.
50 Montesquieu, *De l'Esprit des Lois I*, p. 301.
51 Vile, *Constitutionalism and the Separation of Powers*, p. 102.
52 Ibid., p. 175.
53 www.consource.org/document/final-draft-of-the-virginia-constitution-of-1776/.
54 Ibid., p. 131 and Pitamic, *A Treatise on the State*, p. 66.

these provisions on the institutional separation was to protect the liberties of people from the power of the state.[55] The national constitution of the United States of America, which was proposed in 1787 and entered into force in 1789, did not explicitly articulate the doctrine of the separation of powers. This gave rise to serious concerns at the Philadelphia preparatory meetings and in the ratification debates in the several states. The concern was that the state is inherently a dangerous social institution: it must dispose with great power to serve to the benefit of the people, but the liberty of citizens is threatened if its power is not controlled and limited. These preoccupations are reflected in the detailed structure of the federal constitution.[56]

An ex-post facto explanation and authoritative interpretation of the fundamental principles behind the American federal constitution came from a group of strong believers in the constitution – the Federalists – Alexander Hamilton, James Madison and John Jay. In the *Federalist Papers*, written as a series of newspaper articles to facilitate the ratification process in the state of New York, they presented the design of the federal constitution and wrote commentary in its favor. In paper No. 47 Madison pleaded in favor of the principle of the separation of powers.[57] He highlighted that the accumulation of all powers – legislative, executive and judiciary – in the same hands would be the very definition of tyranny.[58] In paper No. 51, Madison went on to link the doctrine of the separation of powers with the mechanism of checks and balances. He emphasized that power should reside in separate and distinct governmental departments and that each of these departments should have constitutional means and personal motives to exercise checks on other departments.[59] Thus, despite any explicit provisions in the American federal constitution, the Federalists pointed to the establishment of the executive, the judiciary and the legislative as separate institutions, each with its own constitutional status and none subservient to another. To this framework, the mechanism of checks and balances comes as a device to constrain the power of the state by enabling each institution to negate the acts of the others.[60]

3.4 Judicial Review and the Rule of Law

The doctrine of the separation of powers and the mechanism of checks and balances represents a necessary prerequisite for the development of another guarantee against

55 Gordon, *Controlling the State*, pp. 296-297.

56 Ibid., p. 300.

57 *See* J. Madison, 'Number XLVII: The Meaning of the Maxim, which Requires a Separation of the Departments of Power, Examined and Ascertained', *in* J. Madison, A. Hamilton & J. Jay, *The Federalist Papers*, Penguin Books, Harmondsworth, 1987, pp. 303-308.

58 Ibid., pp. 302-303.

59 J. Madison, 'Number LI: The Same Subject Continued with the Same View and Concluded', *in* Madison, Hamilton & Jay, *The Federalist Papers*, pp. 319-320.

60 Gordon, *Controlling the State*, p. 310.

tyranny – judicial review.[61] Judicial review is, in turn, a necessary prerequisite for the advancement of the rule of law. Again it was one of the Federalists, Hamilton, who expounded the rationale for judicial review of actions of the other branches of government. In paper No. 78, Hamilton stated that among the separated governmental powers, the judiciary was the least dangerous to constitutional rights. For that reason it could never successfully attack either of the other two branches. However, all possible care is necessary to enable it to defend itself against attacks of the two more powerful branches.[62]

The strength of the judiciary comes from its complete independence in the system of a constitutional government, which presupposes limitations upon the arbitrary exercise of power of the legislative branch.[63] For Hamilton, limitations of this kind can be, in practice, preserved solely through the courts of justice, which possess a duty to declare void all acts contrary to the constitution.[64] There is no doubt that the judiciary has a final say in the interpretation of the constitution:

> The interpretation of the laws is the proper and peculiar province of the courts. A constitution is, in fact, and must be regarded by the judges as, a fundamental law. It therefore belongs to them to ascertain its meaning as well as the meaning of any particular proceeding from the legislative body.[65]

It took several years before the Supreme Court of the United States put the doctrine of the judicial review into practice in the celebrated *Marbury v. Madison* case in 1803. Chief Justice John Marshall, who wrote the opinion for the Court, found that the Section 13 of the Judiciary Act of 1789 conflicted with Article III of the Constitution and was therefore unconstitutional. He considered it the essence of judicial duty to interpret the law and, in case of a conflict between acts of Congress and the Constitution, to uphold the Constitution.[66] He concluded that, following a judicial review, any law that is incompatible with the Constitution must be considered void and that all governmental organs must respect the decision of the court:

> The particular phraseology of the Constitution of the United States confirms and strengthens the principle, supposed to be essential to all written constitutions, that a law repugnant to the constitution is void, and that courts, as well as other departments, are bound by that instrument.[67]

61 Vile, *Constitutionalism and the Separation of Powers*, p. 173.
62 A. Hamilton, 'Number LXXVII: A View of the Constitution of the Judicial Department in Relation to the Tenure of Good Behaviour', *in* Madison, Hamilton & Jay, *The Federalist Papers*, p. 437.
63 *Cf.* ibid., p. 438.
64 Id.
65 Ibid., p. 439.
66 *Marbury v. Madison*, U. S. Supreme Court, February 1803, 5 U.S. 137 (Cranch), pp. 177-178.
67 Ibid., p. 180.

Subsequently, the judgment in *Marbury v. Madison* became a defining document in American constitutional law and the mechanism of the judicial review a fundamental component of American constitutionalism.[68] Henceforth, the doctrine of the judicial review spread worldwide to become an essential feature of any form of modern constitutionalism.[69]

Another fundamental feature of modern constitutionalism is the rule of law. The concept of the rule of law has its origins in Aristotle's political philosophy. According to Aristotle, "the law is wisdom without desire".[70] The law is therefore firmly grounded in the rules of logic and rationality that apply to legal reasoning. In this sense, the rule of law signifies that the authority of a government is embedded in the rule of law rather than of men.[71] Jeffrey Jowell understands the rule of law as "a principle that requires feasible limits on official power so as to constrain abuses on the part of even the most well-intentioned and compassionate of governments."[72] Tom Bingham imbued this principle with more elements and according to his definition the rule of law means

> that all persons and authorities within the state ... should be entitled to the benefit of laws publicly made, taking effect (generally) in the future and publicly administered in the courts.[73]

Modern constitutionalism, therefore, implements the rule of law in that it introduces predictability and security in the relations between individuals and their governments through defining, in advance, the powers and limits of that government.[74] At the same time, the prescriptive force of the rule of law compels organs of all three branches of

---

68 Gordon, *Controlling the State*, p. 321. For the description of the case *see* Wormuth, *The Origins of Modern Constitutionalism*, pp. 200-201, H.A. Johnson, 'Marbury v. Madison', *in* K.L. Hall (Ed.), *The Oxford Companion to the Supreme Court of the United States*, OUP, New York-Oxford, 1992, p. 521 and A.M. Bickel, *The Least Dangerous Branch: The Supreme Court at the Bar of Politics*, Yale University Press, New Haven (MA)-London, 1986, pp. 1-14.

69 *Cf.* M. Cappelletti, 'Judicial Review in Comparative Perspective', 5 *California Law Review* 1970, p. 1052.

70 Aristotle, *Politics*, p. 265, 1287a.

71 Preuss, 'Patterns of Constitutional Evolution and Change in Eastern Europe', p. 96.

72 J. Jowell, 'The Rule of Law and Its Underlying Values', *in* J. Jowell & D. Oliver (Eds.), *The Changing Constitution*, OUP, Oxford, 2011, p. 34.

73 T. Bingham, *The Rule of* Law, Penguin Books, London, 2011, p. 37. Bingham lists the following components of the rule of law: (1) the law must be accessible and so far as possible intelligible, clear and predictable; (2) questions of legal right and liability should be resolved by application of the law and not the exercise of discretion; (3) the laws should apply equally to all (except with regard to objective and justified differences); (4) public officials must exercise the power in good faith, fairly, purposely and reasonably; (5) the law must afford adequate protection of human rights; (6) there must be means for the resolution of disputes without undue cost or delay; (7) adjudicative procedures must be fair; and (8) compliance by the state with its obligations in international and national law. (Id.)

74 L. Alexander, 'Introduction', *in* L. Alexander (Ed.), *Constitutionalism: Philosophical Foundations*, CUP, Cambridge, 1999, p. 4.

government to abide by them in their own spheres of functioning.[75] As the judiciary is entrusted with interpreting the law, it infuses the content of these rules with interpretations that the other two branches of government must respect. The judiciary therefore functions as the generator, promoter and defender of the rule of law.

In comparative terms, the idea of the rule of law corresponds to the German doctrine of *Rechtsstaat* and French *Etat de droit* (or *préëminence du droit).* Although these two concepts are similar in content, their historical origins are different.[76] The major difference seems to be that the rule of law is primarily a dynamic and procedural phenomenon, while *Rechtsstaat* and *Etat de droit* are static and substantive phenomena,[77] although it can be said that nowadays both phenomena comprise dynamic and static elements. In one of the most comprehensive studies on the rule of law, the Venice Commission of the Council of Europe succeeded in synthesizing the rule of law and concepts of *Rechtsstaat* and *Etat de droit.* According to the Venice Commission, the necessary elements of the rule of law are: (i) legality, including a transparent, accountable and democratic process for enacting law; (ii) legal certainty; (iii) prohibition of arbitrariness; (iv) access to justice before independent and impartial courts, including judicial review of administrative acts; (v) respect for human rights; and (vi) nondiscrimination and equality before the law.[78]

3.5 The Doctrine of Human Rights; Liberty and Equality

After the American and French Revolutions at the end of the eighteenth century, a new period in the development of constitutionalism began which can be called *modern constitutionalism.* There are two main differences when compared to the 'ancient' constitutionalism. After the end of the eighteenth century, one can speak of the doctrine of human rights and of the tendency to adopt written constitutions to limit the exercise of governmental power.[79] This is rather surprising from the modern perspective, which takes the doctrine of human rights and written constitutions for granted.

---

75 R.S. Kay, 'American Constitutionalism', *in* Alexander, *Constitutionalism*, p. 48.

76 *See, e.g.*, Zupančič, 'From Combat to Contract', p. 68, n.18, K. Milewicz, 'Emerging Patterns of Global Constitutionalization: Toward a Conceptual Framework', 16 *Indiana Journal of Global Legal Studies* 2009, p. 418, R. Grote, 'Rule of Law, Rechtsstaat and "Etat de droit"', *in* C. Starck (Ed.), *Constitutionalism, Universalism and Democracy*, Nomos Verlagsgesellschaft, Baden-Baden, 1999, pp. 269-306, L. Favoreu *et al.*, *Droit constitutionnel*, Dalloz, Paris, 2003, pp. 23-24, 80-81 and M. Zamboni, '"Rechtsstaat": Just What is Being Exported by Swedish Development Organisations?' *Law, Social Justice & Global Development (LGD) 2001(2)*, www2.warwick.ac.uk/fac/soc/law/elj/lgd/2001_2/zamboni.

77 B.M. Zupančič, *Prvine (pravne) kulture [The Cultural Elements of the Rule of Law]*, FDV, Ljubljana, 1995, p. 51, n. 12.

78 European Commission for Democracy through Law (Venice Commission), 'Report on the Rule of Law', 4 April 2011, CDL-AD(2011)003rev, p. 10. The Venice Commission further elaborated (sub)components of the rule of law in the report on the rule of law checklist. *See* Venice Commission, 'Rule of Law Checklist', 18 March 2016, CDL-AD(2016)007.

79 *See* A. Clapham, *Human Rights: A Very Short Introduction*, OUP, Oxford, 2007, pp. 6-10 and E. Bates, 'History', *in* D. Moeckli *et al.* (Eds.), *International Human Rights Law*, OUP, Oxford, 2014, p. 19.

The French *Declaration of the Rights of Man and of the Citizen* of 1789 is one of the first texts to fuse individual liberties[80] and the basic tenets of constitutionalism, namely, the creation of a body politic and limitation of its power.[81] As follows from the Preamble to the Declaration, the Constituent Assembly primarily understood the proclamation of human rights as a limit on the arbitrary use of governmental power.[82] Similar conclusions apply to the *Virginia Declaration of Rights* of 1776, an integral part of the constitution of Virginia, which antedated and strongly influenced the French Declaration.[83]

However, the design of the *United States Bill of Rights* is different. Originally, the US Constitution of 1789 did not include the Bill of Rights but dealt solely with the question of organization and limitation of the governmental power. The Bill of Rights became part of the US Constitution only some years later (in 1791) through a set of amendments to the Constitution. However, these amendments have a different narration than the previously mentioned texts. They represent provisions in the form of individual rights with which the government must not interfere. The doctrine of human rights *per se* became a constituent part of constitutionalism only after the American and French Revolutions.[84] The doctrine of human rights and its specific articulation in the Bills of Rights thus originated in the general constitutional exigency of the limitation of the governmental power.[85] The doctrine of human rights acquired its important conceptual standing within the notion of constitutionalism following the development of liberalism and individualism.[86]

80 *See*, in particular, Art. 2 (second part) and Arts. 6-11. (For the text of the Declaration in French, *see* www.legifrance.gouv.fr/Droit-francais/Constitution/Declaration-des-Droits-de-l-Homme-et-du-Citoyen-de-1789.)

81 *See* notably Arts. 2 (first part), 12 and 16.

82 *Cf.*: "Les représentants du peuple français, constitués en Assemblée nationale, *considérant que l'ignorance, l'oubli ou le mépris des droits de l'homme sont les seules causes des malheurs publics et de la corruption des gouvernements…*" (Emphasis by A.Z.) *See also* Pitamic, *A Treatise on the State*, p. 122.

83 Bates, 'History', p. 19.

84 Ibid., pp. 21-22.

85 Revealing in this regard is the nature of the English *Bill of Rights* of 1689. In contradistinction to the bills and declaration of rights that appeared one hundred years later, the English Bill does not confer rights to individuals, but to the English parliament and to members of the parliament. Therefore, the English *Bill of Rights* represents a limitation of the royal power by the English parliament.

86 The contemporary doctrine even speaks of the 'human rights constitutionalism'. (*See* L. Henkin, 'A New Birth of Constitutionalism: Genetic Influences and Genetic Defects', *in* M. Rosenfeld (Ed.), *Constitutionalism, Identity, Difference and Legitimacy: Theoretical Perspectives*, Duke University Press, Durham-London, 1994, pp. 39-53 and L.W. Beer, 'Introduction', *in* L.W. Beer (Ed.), *Constitutional Systems in Late Twentieth Century Asia*, University of Washington Press, Seattle (WA)-London, 1992, pp. 9-10 and N. Johnson, 'Constitutionalism: Procedural Limits and Political Ends', *in* Hesse & Johnson, *Constitutional Policy and Change in Europe*, p. 47.)

Two essential postulates of the doctrine of human rights are liberty and equality.[87] Logically, their importance increases with the development of the general doctrine of human rights. Liberty did not gain a significant political value until the years of the Civil War in the mid-seventeenth century England. The *Magna Carta* spoke of liberties more in terms of privileges than in terms of rights. Liberty had emerged as a prime political concept following the rivalry between the Levellers and the English Parliament during the Civil War. In the course of the eighteenth century, liberty acquired the status of a prime political value.[88] The idea of equality is linked to the modern constitutionalism through an opposition to the privileges of status and birth that were characteristic of the feudal order. Historically, equality as a legal value first emerged in the form of procedural framework as a surrogate to the use of power for the conflict resolution, as happened with *Magna Carta.* This procedural framework of legal equality then served as a factual precondition for any legal adjudication.[89] The modern perspective requires a levelling of status-based hierarchies in favor of an order that provides that all human beings are equal, with an inherent capacity for moral choice, self-respect and dignity.[90] An historical example of the political equality of citizens was the Florentine Republic.[91] Jean-Jacques Rousseau envisaged both liberty and equality as fundamental characteristics of the political constitution of the body politic.[92]

3.6 Contemporary Contributions to Constitutionalism: Coordination and Autopoiesis

Contemporary perspectives on constitutionalism, such as coordinative and self-referential (*autopoietic*) approaches, add innovative contributions to its further development. Both approaches accept the logic of constitutionalism of minimization of the maximization of power for the pursuit of the common good.[93]

87 *See* Loughlin, *Sword and Scales*, p. 184, Pitamic, *A Treatise on the State*, pp. 134-144 and Clapham, *A Very Short Introduction*, p. 13. There are also other fundamental components of human rights, such as dignity and solidarity. All four values (dignity, freedom or liberty, equality and solidarity), *e.g.*, constitute the axiological core of the *Charter of Fundamental Rights* of the European Union. Samantha Besson refers to some of those categories – equality, dignity and autonomy – as (moral) justifications for human rights. (S. Besson, 'Justifications', *in* Moeckli *et al.*, *International Human Rights Law*, p. 35.)

88 *See* Wormuth, *The Origins of Modern Constitutionalism*, pp. 163-168.

89 Zupančič, 'From Combat to Contract', pp. 66-67, 71 and 73 (including n. 27).

90 M. Rosenfeld, 'Modern Constitutionalism as Interplay between Identity and Diversity', *in* Rosenfeld, *Constitutionalism, Identity, Difference and Legitimacy*, p. 8.

91 Finer, *The History of Government from the Earliest Times*, vol. II, p. 984.

92 J.-J. Rousseau, *Du contrat social*, GF Flammarion, Paris, 2001, p. 9 and G. Lafrance, 'Montesquieu and Rousseau on Constitutional Theory', *in* A.S. Rosenbaum (Ed.), *Constitutionalism: The Philosophical Dimension*, Greenwood Press, New York-Westport (CT)-London, 1988, p. 63.

93 *Cf.* R. Hardin, *Liberalism, Constitutionalism, and Democracy*, OUP, Oxford, 2008, pp. 18, 82-83 and M. King & C. Thornhill, *Niklas Luhmann's Theory of Politics and Law*, Palgrave Macmillan, Houndmills, 2003, p. 111.

In the contemporary era the governmental coordination has become an essential function for attaining the ends of modern society and one of the indispensable attributes of contemporary constitutionalism.[94] Taking as example the drafting of the US Constitution, Russell Hardin distinguished between the coordination on the Constitution and the coordination under the Constitution. The coordination on the Constitution is the form of negotiations between various political actors. It is a prerequisite for the Constitution to be adopted in the first place. Coordination under the Constitution, on the other hand, refers to its quotidian operation by successfully coordinating actions under its purview.[95] The most successful cooperation occurs if there is a broad consensus among subjects, which leads to the spontaneous coordination and self-enforcement of the Constitution.[96] Instead of Constitution as a contract in the sense of a normative grounding, the coordinative approach favors the Constitution as a workable arrangement leading to the enforcement of common interests.[97]

Gillian Hadfield and Barry Weingast upgraded this perspective with an insight that the coordination function nonetheless necessitates additional legal principles.[98] Inspired by Lon Fuller's work,[99] they composed the following list of legal attributes of coordinative constitutionalism: generality, stability, clarity, publicity and consistency. These principles reflect the components of the rule of law.[100] In addition, coordinative constitutionalism presupposes a process of public reasoning as it is applied over time and in new circumstances. Finally, successful constitutional coordination supports a social equilibrium in which actors with divergent views and interests are willing to coordinate to uphold the constitution.[101] Coordinative constitutionalism is thus a "decentralized enforcement activity that supports interactions rather than coordination of underlying interactions themselves."[102] In this way the coordination process functions as a guarantee for social stability.[103]

Another contemporary view, developed by Niklas Luhmann, sees constitutionalism as an autopoietic or self-referential system. Autopoiesis represents the most complex case of circular causality, in which causal chains constitute a complex array of various feedback loops in a closed system characterized by self-organization. Such a system not only orga-

94 *Cf.* Vile, *Constitutionalism and the Separation of Powers*, p. 367.

95 Ibid., pp. 90, 103-107.

96 Ibid., p. 139.

97 Ibid., p. 87.

98 G.K. Hadfield & B.R. Weingast, 'Constitutions as Coordinating Devices', *in* S. Galiani & I. Sened (Eds.), *Institutions, Property Rights, and Economic Growth: The Legacy of Douglas North*, CUP, Cambridge, 2014, p. 124 and G.K. Hadfield & B.R. Weingast, 'What is Law? A Coordination Model of the Characteristics of Legal Order', 4 *Journal of Legal Analysis* 2012, p. 505.

99 *See* L.L. Fuller, *The Morality of Law*, Yale University Press, New Haven (CT), 1969.

100 *See* Hadfield & Weingast, 'Constitutions as Coordinating Devices', pp. 148, 131-133.

101 Ibid. pp. 135-136, 148.

102 Ibid., p. 126.

103 Hardin, *Liberalism, Constitutionalism, and Democracy*, p. 98 and Hadfield & Weingast, 'Constitutions as Coordinating Devices', pp. 135-136.

nizes itself but reproduces the very components of which it consists.[104] Correspondingly, legal autopoiesis means that the legal system presupposes and reproduces itself. In this conceptual framework, law is a special communications system that reproduces itself through self-referential processes, such as legal norms, legal decisions or legal doctrines. To determine whether a communication is part of the system, the legal system operates pursuant to the binary code: law/nonlaw or legal/illegal.[105] The autopoietic legal system develops an epistemology according to its own criteria, which orchestrate its internal operation and influence legal developments.[106]

Luhmann links the development of constitutionalism to the formation of the modern state at the end of the eighteenth century.[107] The democratic system emerges with the constitutional formalization of the separation of powers in the modern state, and with the separation of politics and administration into two distinct subsystems. These early legal-state constitutions continue the tendency towards internal differentiation in which the separation of powers assumes a more expansive form. Democracy develops a variety of resources and points of reference, making it a formula for self-reference of the differentiated system of modern society.[108] The self-referential dynamic is premised on the argument that the political system itself produces all the characteristic attributes of modern democracies in order to serve and meet its own functional necessity.[109]

The constitution acts as structural coupling (or structural coalescence) between the legal and political systems. When constitutions emerged in the eighteenth century, their role was to assist in recombining functionally differentiated political and legal systems. From the autopoietic perspective, they were adopted to bridge problems of self-reference, paradoxes and asymmetries that existed between the legal and political systems.[110] Thus, "the constitution provides political solutions for the problem of the self-reference of the legal system and legal solutions for the problem of self-reference of the political system."[111] The constitution generates a constitutional synthesis for the continuation of the functional differentiation and operative closure of the political and legal systems.[112] Once a democracy as a political system begins to function, it regenerates itself *ad infini-*

104 B.R. Hornung, 'The Theoretical Context and Foundations of Luhmann's Legal and Political Sociology', *in* M. King & C. Thornhill (Eds.), *Luhmann on Law and Politics: Critical Appraisals and Applications*, Hart Publishing, Oxford-Portland (OR), 2006, p. 203.

105 R. Rogowski, 'Law, Autopoiesis in', *in* J.D. Wright (Ed.), *International Encyclopedia of the Social and Behavioral Sciences*, Second Edition, vol. 13, Elsevier, Amsterdam, 2015, p. 554.

106 Ibid. p. 555.

107 N. Luhmann, *Law as a Social System*, OUP, Oxford, 2004, trans. K.A. Ziegert, p. 404.

108 King & Thornhill, *Niklas Luhmann's Theory of Politics and Law*, p. 111.

109 Ibid., p. 127.

110 Rogowski, 'Law, Autopoiesis in', p. 555.

111 Luhmann, *Law as a Social System*, p. 410.

112 A. Philippopoulos-Mihalopoulos, *Niklas Luhmann: Law, Justice, Society*, Routledge, Abingdon, 2010, p. 153 and Luhmann, *Law as a Social System*, p. 410.

tum. Constitutionalism in this respect acts as an enabling force for the continuation and regeneration of self-referential processes in a given society.

3.7 Concluding Remarks on Constitutionalism

Constitutionalism is a complex phenomenon, which stretches over a time span of over 2,500 years. The historical development of constitutionalism covers a number of doctrines, theories and achievements. Different as they are, they all have one common denominator – the limitation of agglomerated power. Constitutionalism is therefore intrinsically linked with the notion of power. It relates to it in two, somewhat contradictory, ways: constitutionalism first presupposes the aggregation of power in the form of the governmental design and then imposes limits upon the so constituted framework of power. It is a work of art to bring these two components together, which explains why constitutionalism took the shape of so many concrete expressions. The concrete expression of constitutionalism depends on the time period and the characteristics of a given political system. The theory of the mixed government, checks and balances, the doctrine of the separation of powers, judicial review, rule of law, the doctrine of human rights, the constitution (in written or unwritten form), all reflect the axiom of 'minimization of the maximization of power'. Therefore, it is not so important that one provides an enumeration of all possible expressions of the limitation of power. What is more important is to acknowledge that all these expressions stand for the aim of constitutionalism – the function of putting limits on the exercise of the constituted power.[113] Constitutionalism is therefore a legal method of the limitation of government, to which people had often resorted to in the last 2,500 years.[114] There is no doubt that they will have to continue using this method provided they wish to continue to live in the constitutional order.

There are other attributes of constitutionalism also. Constitutionalism comprises both dynamic and static attributes. The dynamic characteristic of constitutionalism comes from the fact that it is a continuous process aimed at the limitation of the constituted power. The static element resides in a strong institutional character through which this process goes on. In the preceding analysis, it is possible to identify five functional components of constitutionalism: institutional, normative, judicial, coordinative and self-referential functions.

The institutional component sees constitutionalism as advocating certain types of institutional arrangements on the grounds that certain ends will be achieved.[115] The historical survey of constitutionalism demonstrates that the institutional component is

113 McIlwain, *Constitutionalism and the Changing World*, pp. 244-245 and Lang & Wiener, 'A Constitutionalising Global Order: An Introduction', p. 2.

114 McIlwain, *Constitutionalism and the Changing World*, p. 240 and Wormuth, *The Origins of Modern Constitutionalism*, p. 215. *Similarly* Vile, *Constitutionalism and the Separation of Powers*, p. 408.

115 Vile, *Constitutionalism and the Separation of Powers*, pp. 8-9.

the essential component of constitutionalism; institutions are essential to shape the governmental power if it is to govern a given social structure.[116] Furthermore, institutions are essential to limit the exercise of power and prevent its arbitrariness. The Federalists formulated the best account of the institutional component in the doctrine of the separation of powers, linked to the mechanism of checks and balances, and to judicial review. Nevertheless, the institutional component alone does not suffice to perform all the tasks of constitutionalism. Institutions are inextricably linked with the normative component.

The importance of the normative component is most obvious through the existence of the constitution, the doctrine of human rights and the rule of law. The constitution is, first and foremost, a fundamental law, which through general and abstract norms defines basic governmental institutions and relations between them. For Hans Kelsen, the constitution represents the highest level of the positive law and its essential function consists in governing the organs and the process of general law creation.[117] In addition, the normative component includes the doctrine of human rights and its connection to the mechanism of judicial review. Individuals can claim their rights on the basis of the normative formulation of those rights, invoking them before the courts. Apart from the protection of rights of individuals, judicial review also contributes to the respect and development of the rule of law in the form of general and prospective rules, which apply to the functioning of the governmental sphere as a whole.

The judicial function of constitutionalism is the most recent of the three traditional constitutional functions. However, nowadays it is extremely important and one cannot envisage constitutionalism without the functioning of the adjudicatory organs. Adjudication of conflicts is the essence of the organized society and at the center of advancement from unrestrained natural aggression to 'law and order' and in turn to 'the rule of law'. In most basic terms adjudication is a surrogate to the use of force between people.[118] In this sense, the power of logic replaces the logic of power. In the context of the legal argumentation, this power of logic is called *justice*.[119] The central role in the process of adjudication falls to the judge, who has to remain impartial and uncommitted throughout this process if the dispute is to be resolved successfully.[120]

In addition to the three traditional constitutional functions, novel constitutional perspectives evolved reflecting challenges of the contemporary area. The fourth constitutional function is constitutionalism as a coordinative phenomenon. As governments are increasingly confronted with the need to pursue new aims, the coordination became an essential function for attaining the ends of modern society. The function of coordination

116 For a comprehensive overview of institutional theories, *see* G.B. Peters, *Institutional Theory in Political Science: The 'New Institutionalism'*, Continuum, London-New York, 2005.

117 H. Kelsen, *Introduction of the Problems of Legal Theory*, Clarendon Press, Oxford, 1992, trans. B. Litschewski Paulson & S.L. Paulson, p. 64.

118 Zupančič, *The Owl of Minerva*, pp. 23-25.

119 Ibid., p. 33.

120 Ibid., pp. 50, 76.

is primarily a function of workability that contributes to a social stability. With relation to the constitution there are two different phases of coordination. Firstly, the content of the constitution has to be agreed on as a matter of coordination and, secondly, the constitution thereafter works as a platform that allows for a successful coordination between subjects under its purview for the pursuit of common ends. Rather than being ordained from the top to the bottom, coordination is a decentralized process that allows for actions of various social agents in the constitutional framework.

The fifth constitutional function understands constitutionalism as a self-referential system. This system is centered on a system of communication loops that provide feedback information while enabling reproduction of self-referential processes. The legal system follows the same self-referential logic through the operation of legal categories and procedures. The rise of the modern state went hand in hand with the evolution of constitutions. They function as structural coupling in the sense of bridging the gap between the political and legal systems by making a synthesis between the two of them. Democracy as a contemporary political system emerges from various political processes and enables the propagation of the separation of powers across the political system. Overall, autopoietic constitutionalism is an enabling tool for the infinite reproduction of self-referential processes intrinsic to a given social system.

The functional components of contemporary constitutionalism, therefore, include the following ones: institutional, normative, judicial, coordinative and self-referential. With a view of using the term *constitutionalism* in the international perspective, and on the basis of the preceding analysis, constitutionalism can be defined as follows:

> Constitutionalism in the broadest sense denotes agglomeration of power in the form of a structural framework for the pursuit of the common good, accompanied by the exigency of putting limitations on the so constituted power. Concrete expressions of the limitation of power include the doctrine of the separation of powers, the mechanism of checks and balances, the judicial review, the rule of law, the doctrine of human rights (including its essential components liberty and equality) and the constitution (written or non-written). Functional components of contemporary constitutionalism are: institutional, normative, judicial, coordinative and self-referential functions.

4 Antinomy between Hegemony and Constitutionalism

After the respective treatment of hegemony and of constitutionalism, the next step is to juxtapose the two phenomena. The intuitive approach would be to consider hegemony and constitutionalism as opposites. At the most basic level, hegemony stands for the expansion of power, which gains the attribute of dominance, while constitutionalism stands for the limitation of the aggregated power. The premises from which the two phenomena derive are therefore contrasting at the general level: expansion versus limitation. However, as previously analyzed, the contents of both phenomena can get extremely complex when applied to specific situations and therefore encompass more than these generalized features. In spite of being expansionist, hegemony can promote liberty, equality and the rule of law, which are all expressions of constitutionalism. On the other hand, while constitutionalism encapsulates values of egalitarianism, liberty and common interest (solidarity), its dynamic is conditioned by the flow of power mimicking hegemonic processes.

Therefore, in concrete circumstances the expression of one phenomenon may not differ significantly from the expression of the other phenomenon. A practical articulation of hegemony and constitutionalism may reveal a certain 'likeness' that stands at the intersection of the two phenomena. Applied back to the general level this similarity indicates that hegemony and constitutionalism cannot exist without each other. Hegemony needs the stability that is inherent in the legitimacy of constitutionalism,[1] while constitutionalism is premised upon the dynamism of hegemonic processes.[2] This reveals a continuous and circular movement from hegemony to constitutionalism and *vice versa*. In short, the two phenomena represent the relationship of antinomy.

Antinomy is a philosophical category. According to Hegel, the world

---

1 *See* I. Clark, *Legitimacy in International Society*, OUP, Oxford, 2007, pp. 63, 166, 167, 220, 248, 252, 256.

2 Two relevant examples are transitions from hegemonic to constitutional regimes ('polyarchies') and the existence of political hegemonic processes within the democratic form of government. *See* R. Dahl, *Polyarchy: Participation and Opposition*, Yale University Press, New Haven (CT)-London, 1971, pp. 7, 10, 14, 23-24, 26, 44-45, 152-162, 208-209, 218, A. Lijphart, *Patterns of Democracy: Government Forms and Performance in Thirty-Six Countries*, Yale University Press, New Haven (CT)-London, 1999, pp. 116-142 and S. Bose, 'Fading Echoes: Legacy of Empire and Democracy in India', *in* K. Nicolaïdis *et al.* (Eds.), *Echoes of Empire: Memory, Identity and Colonial Legacies*, I.B. Taurus, London-New York, 2015, pp. 47-62.

> gets involved in *antinomies*, i.e., in the assertion of two *opposed* propositions about *the same* ob-ject; and it finds, moreover, that each of the propositions must be affirmed with equal necessity.[3]

Antinomy is a dialectical relationship between the two notions that simultaneously reaffirm and oppose each other.[4] In earlier philosophical treatments of the topic, Kant dealt with antinomy in the perspective of the world defined as an entirety of phenomena (cosmology).[5] Hegel, on the other hand, went further in saying that "antinomy is found not only in the four particular ob-jects taken from cosmology, but rather in *all* objects of all kinds, in *all* representations, concepts, and ideas."[6] Contemporary legal philosopher Roberto Unger outlines the antinomy of theory and fact, the antinomy of reason and desire, and the antinomy of rules and values within liberal thought.[7] In international law, Martti Koskenniemi analyzed the antinomy between apology (realism) and utopia (idealism).[8] From the Hegelian perspective, the dynamic of antinomy is important because it represents a force of historical progress.[9]

However, consideration of hegemony and constitutionalism in the international community must go deeper in exploring the dynamic and contents of this antinomic relationship. Antinomy operates at the abstract level,[10] which means that its pace in the concrete world cannot follow. However, the dynamic of antinomy can be traced and analyzed through the process of its deconstruction. There are two approaches to the deconstruction: the *general approach* focusing on abstract premises and the *empirical approach* through the pragmatic reality.

3 G.W.F. Hegel, *The Encyclopaedia Logic (with Zusätze)*, Hackett Publishing Company, Indianapolis, 1991, trans. T. F. Gerates *et al.*, p. 91 (§48).

4 Zupančič, *The Owl of Minerva*, pp. 6, 34.

5 *See* E. Kant, *Critique de la raison pure*, PUF, Paris, 2004, trans. A. Tremesaygues & B. Pacaud, p. 327 *et seq.*, E. Kant, *Critique de la raison pratique*, PUF, Paris, 2003, trans. F. Picavet, p. 122 *et seq.* and Jacob & Auroux, *Encyclopédie philosophique : les notions, s.v. Antinomie*, pp. 112-115.

6 Hegel, *The Encyclopaedia Logic*, p. 92.

7 R.M. Unger, *Knowledge and Politics*, Free Press, New York, 1984, pp. 31-36, 51-55, 88-100, 138.

8 *See* M. Koskenniemi, *From Apology to Utopia: The Structure of International Legal Argument – Reissue with New Epilogue*, CUP, Cambridge, 2005.

9 Zupančič, *The Owl of Minerva*, pp. 6, 34 and G.W.F. Hegel, *Hegel's Philosophy of Right*, Clarendon Press, Oxford, 1942, trans. T. M. Knox, pp. 34-35. For implications of Hegel's philosophy on the legal thought *see* W.E. Conklin, *Hegel's Laws: The Legitimacy of a Modern Legal Order*, Stanford University Press, Stanford, 2008.

10 *Cf.*: "This antinomy rests, like all others, on the abstract thinking which asserts both the moments of an Idea in separation from one another and clings to each of them in its independence and so in its inadequacy to the Idea and in its falsity." (Hegel, *Hegel's Philosophy of Right*, p. 48.)

The first, *general approach* to deconstruction looks at the conceptual foundations of the two phenomena in antinomy, that is, at the common premises that the antinomic pair shares. This approach follows the deductive method of reasoning which starts with the general premise and through inference deduces consequences from it.[11] A deductive inference is one that draws a conclusion that is latent but implicit in the information given in the general premise.[12] A deductively correct argument is one in which the conclusion is true in any state of affairs in which premises are true.[13] The conclusion in this sense is a logical extension of the premise in a particular context. However, as such deductions are inevitably provisional,[14] their meaning is much stronger if it benefits from a confirmation in practice.

Unger understands antinomy as "a contradiction among conclusions derived from the same or from equally plausible premises."[15] The general approach to deconstruction therefore disregards a contradiction between the two antinomic notions. Instead it looks at the origin of the notions that are common to both of them. The contradiction is substituted with the category of totality that accommodates both antinomic notions.[16] Given that the two opposing perspectives represent definite concepts, this approach is workable only after putting aside the contradiction and focusing instead on the category of totality that both phenomena derive from.[17] In the context of the antinomy between hegemony and constitutionalism power is such a general and abstract premise. From previous sections it follows that both phenomena can be defined on the basis of power: hegemony is an extension of power, while constitutionalism is an agglomeration and limitation of power. Power is therefore the key factor for the understanding of the antinomy between hegemony and constitutionalism.

The second, *empirical approach* to deconstruction focuses on the empirical encounters of the two phenomena in reality. In doing so it likewise ignores the contradiction between the two concepts. But instead of looking at the common premise, this approach looks at how the two phenomena factually interact. Essentially, it follows the inductive

---

11 *See* J.St.B.T. Evans, S.E. Newstead & R.M.J. Byrne, *Human Reasoning: The Psychology of Deduction*, Lawrence Erlbaum Associates, Hove-Hillsdale, 1993, pp. 2-4, W.T. Worster, 'The Inductive and Deductive Methods in Customary Law Analysis: Traditional and Modern Approaches', 45 *Georgetown Journal of International Law* 2014, pp. 447-448, 455-456 and S. Talmon, 'Determining Customary International Law: The ICJ's Methodology between Induction, Deduction and Assertion', 26 *EJIL* 2015, p. 420.

12 Evans, Newstead & Byrne, *Human Reasoning*, p. 2.

13 L.J. Rips, *The Psychology of Reasoning: Deductive Reasoning in Human Thinking*, MIT Press, Cambridge (MA)-London, 1994, p. 3.

14 G. Schwarzenberger, 'The Inductive Approach to International Law', 60 *Harvard Law Review* 1947, p. 566.

15 Unger, *Knowledge and Politics*, p. 13.

16 Jacob & Auroux, *Encyclopédie philosophique: les notions*, p. 113.

17 Ibid., p. 114. *See* Kant, *Critique de la raison pure*, pp. 338-357. Kant envisages totality in the concept of transcendence. (*See* ibid., pp. 381, 411-412.)

reasoning which implies inferences from concrete and specific instances to general statements.[18] Different from the process of deduction, these inferences cannot be absolutely true but are only provisionally correct to a certain degree of confidence. The degree to which the conclusion is probably true depends on the quality of evidence used to support it.[19] The aim of the inductive method is to correlate seemingly unrelated specific instances and generate conceptual knowledge from the available quantity of cases.[20]

A survey of possible interactions between the two antinomic concepts in practice reveals that reality is full of empiric, concrete and pragmatic solutions in which manifestations of the two concepts coexist side by side.[21] Thus, brushing away the contradictory concepts reveals instances of their coexistence as empirical manifestations. These occurrences share a close conceptual proximity, which justifies situating them in a category of the intersection between hegemony and constitutionalism that can be named a *hegemo-constitutional* space. The space is a hybrid category,[22] as it comprises elements belonging to both antinomic notions. The empirical approach to deconstruction goes through three phases and graphically looks as follows:

18 N. Chater *et al.*, 'Inductive Logic and Empirical Psychology', *in* D.M. Gabbay, S. Hartmann & J. Woods (Eds.), *Handbook of the History of Logic: Inductive Logic*, vol. 10, North-Holland, Oxford-Amsteram, 2011, p. 572.

19 Worster, 'The Inductive and Deductive Methods in Customary International Law Analysis', p. 456 and Talmon, 'Determining Customary International Law', p. 420.

20 *Cf.* J.H. Holland, *et al.*, *Process of Inference, Learning and Discovery*, MIT Press, Cambridge (MA)-London, 1986, p. 1.

21 *See* Kant, *Critique de la raison pure*, pp. 358, 366-369, 371-372, 411-413. *See also Encyclopédie philosophique : les notions*, pp. 114-115 and F. Ost & M. van de Kèrchove, *De la pyramide au réseau: pour une théorie dialectique du droit*, Publications des Facultés universitaires Saint-Louis, Bruxelles, 2002, p. 181.

22 For the notion of hybridity *see* B. Latour, *Nous n'avons jamais été modernes: Essai d'anthropologie symétrique*, La Découverte, Paris, 1997, in particular pp. 21, 22, 47, 105, Ost & van den Kèrchove, *De la pyramide au réseau*, pp. 15, 27, 31, 127, F. Ost, & M. van de Kèrchove, 'De la « bipolarité des erreurs » ou de quelques paradigmes de la science du droit', 33 *Archives de philosophie du droit* 1988, pp. 180, 206, N. Walker, *Intimations of Global Law*, CUP, Cambridge, 2015, p. 126; and B. de Carvalho, 'The Modern Roots of Feudal Empire', p. 145, R.D. Lipschutz, 'The Assemblage of American Imperium', pp. 226-227, 235-236 and S. Halperin & R. Palan, 'Conclusions', pp. 245-246, all *in* S. Halperin & R. Palan (Eds.), *Legacies of Empire: Imperial Roots of the Contemporary Global Order*, CUP, Cambridge, 2015.

Phase A: Hegemony and constitutionalism look as two opposite phenomena.

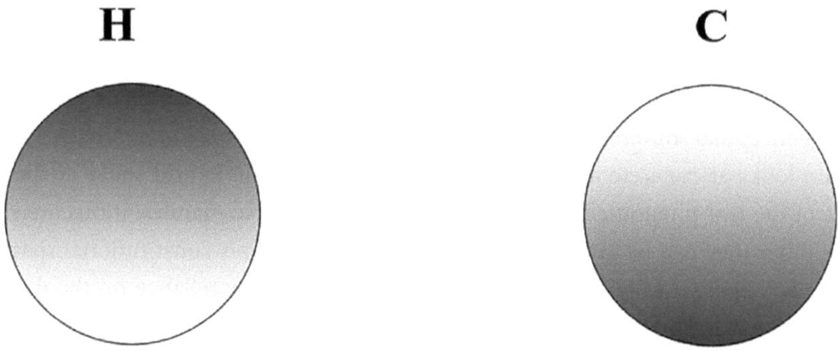

Phase B: In reality, the two phenomena have a number of concrete elements in common.

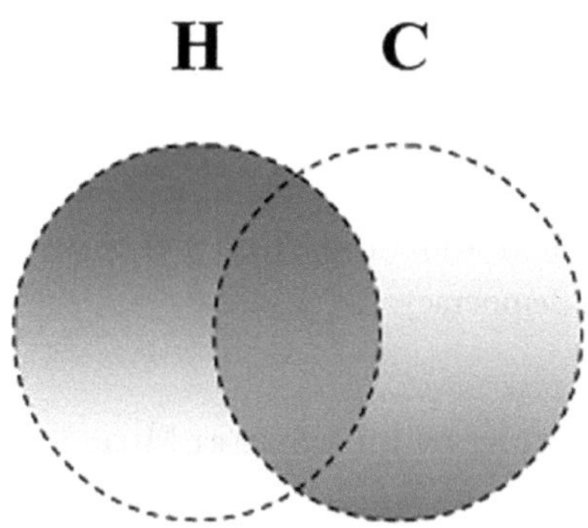

Phase C: Abandonment of general contours of the two contradictory phenomena leads to the identification of a group of concretized but similar elements at the intersection of the two (abandoned) phenomena that can be called the *hegemo-constitutional space.*

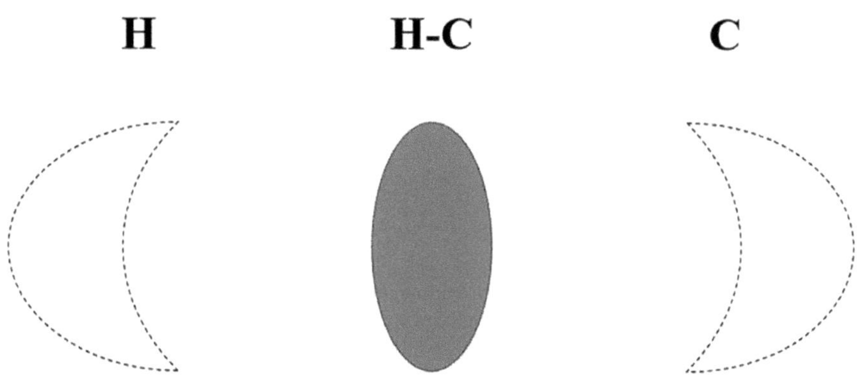

The two approaches to deconstruction relate to the interplay between hegemony and constitutionalism in the following way. The *general approach* to deconstruction seeks to elucidate the antinomy in reverting to the common premise, which leads to the discovery that both phenomena stand for the expression of power. The factor of power is the original conceptual source behind the two phenomena. The *empirical approach* to deconstruction looks at concrete and specific manifestations in the hybrid space at the intersection of the two phenomena in practical reality. Since these manifestations are similar to each other they can be grouped and branded as the hegemo-constitutional space.

The two approaches of deconstruction, together with their reliance on the deductive and inductive reasoning, are mutually reinforcing in paving the way towards new knowledge about the antinomy between hegemony and constitutionalism and their accommodation. The general approach demonstrates that the element of power is crucial for any future consideration. The empirical approach, on the other hand, is useful in bringing together a great amount of similar manifestations that form a new conceptual space.

The empirical approach to deconstruction, in particular, provides a resourceful tool for a further study and analysis of the antinomy between hegemony and constitutionalism in reality. The following sections are going to apply it to the following cases: (i) the political thought of John Stuart Mill; (ii) the theory of postwar international orders; and (iii) the concept of radical democracy.

4.1 The Political Thought of John Stuart Mill

John Stuart Mill has a reputation as one of the most fervent champions of liberalism, in part, because of the acclaim he received for his book *On Liberty*. What is less known is that he spent his whole career as an administrator at the East India Company – an agent of British imperialism in India at the time.[23] According to some writers, he was one of the most important intellectual figures to fabricate a theory of an expanding British Empire.[24] Clearly, being a major proponent of liberalism and a leading theorist of the British Em-

23 D.M. Peers, 'Mill's Defence of the East India Company', *in* M.I. Moir *et al.* (Eds.), *J.S. Mill's Encounter with India*, University of Toronto Press, Toronto-Buffalo-London, 1999, p. 203 and L. Zastoupil, *John Stuart Mill and India*, Stanford (CA), Stanford University Press, 1994, pp. 170-171.

24 E.P. Sullivan, 'Liberalism and Imperialism: J. S. Mill's Defense of the British Empire', 44 *Journal of the History of Ideas* 1983, p. 617 and U.S. Mehta, *Liberalism and Empire: A Study in Nineteenth-Century British Liberal Thought*, The University of Chicago Press, Chicago-London, 1999, p. 76.

pire is a contradiction and therefore warrants a closer examination of Mill's intellectual work.[25]

In his essay *On Liberty*, Mill defines liberty as "the nature and limits of the power which can be legitimately exercised by society over the individual."[26] Liberty was meant as protection against the tyranny of the political rulers.[27] To prevent the arbitrary use of power the aim of patriots was to set limits on the exercise of power over the community.[28] Mill's understanding of liberty therefore corresponds to the definition of constitutionalism; practically, liberty is constitutionalism. But Mill understood liberty more widely, in the sense that "the individual is not accountable to society for his actions in so far as these concern the interests of no person but himself."[29] No society, whatever its form of government, is free unless liberty is respected and none is completely free unless liberty exists in absolute and unqualified terms.[30] Mill therefore gave liberty the status of a nearly absolute category.[31]

But subsequent passages in *On Liberty* make the categorical statement relative. Mill adds a reservation that the doctrine of liberty applies only to mature human beings and extends this logic to states: liberty does not apply to backward states in which the race is considered to be in its nonage.[32] For a proponent of the absolute liberty, he adds the following, rather unexpected remarks:

> Despotism is a legitimate mode of government in dealing with barbarians, provided the end be their improvement and the means justified by actually effecting that end. Liberty, as a principle, has no application to any state of things anterior to the time when mankind have become capable of being improved by free and equal discussion. Until then, there is nothing for them but implicit obedience to an Akbar or a Charlemagne, if they are so fortunate to find one.[33]

However, Mill explains that as soon as mankind attains the capacity to be guided to their own improvement by conviction or persuasion, coercion becomes no longer admissible as a means to their own good.[34]

---

25 Two other prominent British intellectuals, who were simultaneously proponents of the British Empire and constitutionalism, are lawyers Albert Venn Dicey and Henry Sumner Maine. (*See* D. Lino, 'Albert Venn Dicey and the Constitutional Theory of Empire', 36 *Oxford Journal of Legal Studies* 2016, pp. 751-780 and K. Mantena, *Alibis of Empire: Henry Maine and the Ends of Liberal Imperialism*, Princeton University Press, Princeton (NJ), 2010.)

26 J.S. Mill, *On Liberty*, Penguin Books, London, 1985, p. 59.

27 Id.

28 Ibid., p. 60.

29 Ibid., p. 163.

30 Ibid., pp. 71-72.

31 G. Himmelfarb, 'Editor's Introduction', *in* Mill, *On Liberty*, p. 7.

32 Mill, *On Liberty*, p. 69.

33 Id.

34 Id.

Reasons for this 'authoritarian' stand in Mill's thought can be attributed to the utilitarian influences of his father, James Mill and Jeremy Bentham.[35] Nonetheless, Mill developed his own original blend of a theory of moral rights and utilitarian philosophy.[36] Some authors named Mill's synthesis a *system of liberal gradualism*[37] or a *ladder of civilization*, which reflects the perspective of a hierarchical classification of all societies.[38] The main point of this synthesis resides in the proposal that indigenous representatives should participate in imperial administration.[39] It is true to say that liberty in this case lost its absolute meaning, but it is equally correct to say that despotism lost its absolute reach, too.

Mill classifies dependent territories in two groups. The first category includes countries composed of a people similar to the ruling countries and thus ripe for representative government, such as the British possessions in America and Australia. The second category consists of countries that are still at a great distance from the state of self-governance, such as India.[40] He envisages the following two possibilities to bring progression to backward nations, both of which have a character of the 'enlightened despotism'. One way was that the nation would be led by an enlightened ruler (hence a reference to Akbar and Charlemagne in an earlier paragraph).[41] The other, much more preferable and realistic way of development is to subject backward nations to superior, more civilized foreigners who would lead them rapidly through several stages of progress to a more advanced state of society.[42] However, Mill was mindful of the danger that colonial administrators might fall to the danger of despising the natives and of situations of the abuse of force against the local population.[43] Therefore, he underlined that foreign des-

35 *See* E. Halévy, *La formation du Radicalisme Philosophique III : Le Radicalisme Philosophique*, PUF, Paris, 1995, p. 80, E. Stokes, *The English Utilitarians and India*, OUP, Delhi, 1989, p. 309, J. Pitts, *A Turn to Empire: The Rise of Imperial Liberalism in Britain and France*, Princeton University Press, Princeton (NJ)-Oxford, 2005, pp. 103-162, Mehta, *Liberalism and Empire*, pp. 2, 111-112, Zastoupil, *John Stuart Mill and India*, pp. 11-13, 24-25, 75-76, 129, Himmelfarb, 'Editor's Introduction', pp. 11-17 and S. Kurtz, 'Democratic Imperialism: A Blueprint', 118 *Policy Review* April-May 2003, www.hoover.org/research/democratic-imperialism-blueprint.

36 *See* D. Habibi, 'The Moral Dimensions of J. S. Mill's Colonialism', 30 *Journal of Social Philosophy* 1999, pp. 132-133.

37 Kurtz, 'Democratic Imperialism: A Blueprint', sec. 'Competing administrative schools', para. 9.

38 T.R. Metcalf, *Ideologies of the Raj*, The New Cambridge History of India, III.4, CUP, Cambridge, 1994, p. 31.

39 Kurtz, 'Democratic Imperialism: A Blueprint', sec. 'Competing administrative schools', para. 9.

40 J.S. Mill, 'Considerations on Representative Government', *in* J.M. Robson (Ed.), *Essays on Politics and Society*, The Collected Works of John Stuart Mill, vol. 19, University of Toronto Press-Routledge & Kegan Paul, Toronto-London, 1963-1991, p. 562.

41 *See* Mill, 'Considerations on Representative Government', pp. 415-417, 419.

42 Ibid., pp. 418, 419.

43 *See* ibid., p. 569 and J.S. Mill, 'A Few Words on Non-Intervention', *in* J.M. Robson (Ed.), *Essays on Equality, Law and Education*, The Collected Works of John Stuart Mill, vol. 21, University of Toronto Press-Routledge & Kegan Paul, Toronto-London, 1963-1991, p. 120.

pots who rule in the name of a foreign master, should be under the control of the constitutional rule at home.[44] In this sense, Mill emphasized the importance of the liberal tradition and upheld the tenets of constitutionalism during the imperial enterprise.[45]

As the most appropriate solution to the British rule in India, he envisaged the institution of self-government for the Indian people.[46] Mill argued that the way to bring democracy to relatively uncivilized colonies was to create local democratic assemblies. These assemblies would not compete with the central power but would be auxiliary to it.[47] Mill observed that in the Asiatic villages, people had considerable practice in managing their village or town interests; however, they were incapable of transcending to the higher level, which would make them all feel as a people. He envisaged that such a process would happen on the basis of deference of people to a central authority. Through participation and learning through governance processes led by the central authority, local representatives would be able to capture the conception of large interests in the frame of a wider geographic extent.[48] The synthesis of these seemingly contradictory views comes in Mill's notion of the 'representative institutions without representative government', which comprises the centralized foreign governance, on the one hand, and political education and participation of the local people in this process of governance, on the other.[49]

Because of the mix between liberalism and imperialism, the views of Mill on local democracy gave inspiration for the construction of the term *liberal imperialism* or *democratic imperialism*.[50] From our perspective, the relevant hegemo-constitutional components in the political thought of John Stuart Mill concerning the British Empire are the following: the submission of the hegemonic rule to the constitutional control at home; the support of the hegemonic administration to the locally grown constitutionalism; the check (or better, the limit) by the locally grown constitutionalism on the hegemonic rule; and the cooperation between the hegemonic rule and institutions of local constitutionalism.

4.2 The Theory of Post-War International Order(s)

The contemporary political scientist, John Ikenberry, elaborated on the shape of an international design that emerges after great wars. According to him, the postwar international system has to find a new equilibrium, which may go in the way of hegemony,

44 Mill, 'Considerations on Representative Government', p. 568. *E.g.*, Mill was one of the most outspoken critics of a violent suppression of a small-scale unarmed rebellion in Jamaica by the Governor of Jamaica, Eyre. (Metcalf, *Ideologies of the Raj*, p. 52.)
45 Metcalf, *Ideologies of the Raj*, p. 52.
46 Ibid., p. 33.
47 Kurtz, 'Democratic Imperialism: A Blueprint', sec. 'Liberal imperialism?', para. 10.
48 Mill, 'Considerations on Representative Government', p. 417.
49 Ibid., pp. 417-418.
50 *See* Kurtz, 'Democratic Imperialism: A Blueprint'.

constitutionalism, or a set-up between the two of them. Ikenberry envisages the last possibility through the transformation from one order to the other and *vice versa*.

A starting premise for the theory of postwar international orders is Robert Gilpin's claim that wars serve as a principal mechanism of change throughout history. The basic form of control in every international system resides in the distribution of power among states.[51] Therefore, a political change arises from a disjuncture between the existing international system and those actors that would benefit from the change of that system.[52] As a consequence, the international system moves from a condition of equilibrium to the situation of disequilibrium.[53] This disjuncture leads to a crisis in the international system. Historically, the principal mechanism of change has been through hegemonic wars that also determine the new dominant state in the international system.[54] The most important consequence of the hegemonic war, however, is that it changes the system in accordance with the new distribution of power. It leads to a reordering of the international system. The conclusion of one hegemonic war, according to Gilpin, marks the beginning of another cycle of growth, expansion and eventual decline.[55] Uneven growth of states continues to redistribute power in the system, which undermines the *status quo* that arose out of the prior hegemonic war. Disequilibrium again replaces equilibrium, and the international system comes to a new round of a hegemonic struggle.[56]

Ikenberry builds upon Gilpin's assumption that hegemonic wars were traditionally the most common cause for the change in the international system. But he goes one step further in that he identifies an additional model, apart from the hegemonic one, of a postwar international hierarchical system – the constitutional order.[57] In general, Ikenberry understands the political order as a governing arrangement among a group of states that includes fundamental rules, principles and institutions.[58] The two ideal types of such an order at the international level are the hegemonic order and the constitutional order.[59]

51 R. Gilpin, *War and Change in World Politics*, CUP, Cambridge, 1986, p. 29.

52 Ibid., p. 9.

53 Ibid., p. 14.

54 Ibid., p. 15. From the contemporary perspective this assertion seems too categorical. For a recent reevaluation of Gilpin's work, *see* G.J. Ikenberry (Ed.), *Power, Order and Change in World Politics*, CUP, Cambridge, 2014.

55 Gilpin, *War and Change in World Politics*, p. 198.

56 Ibid., p. 210.

57 In fact, Ikenberry distinguishes between three international orders: the hegemonic order, the constitutional order and the balance of power order. However, he puts them in two groups. One group, where the defining character is the distribution of power, consists of the hegemonic order and balance of power order. The other group, where institutions put a check on the exercise of power, comprises the constitutional model. For these reasons, the relevant distinction for this work is between a hegemonic and constitutional order. (*See* G.J. Ikenberry, *After Victory: Institutions, Strategic Restraint, and the Rebuilding of Order after Major Wars*, Princeton University Press, Princeton (NJ)-Oxford, 2001, pp. 23-26, 28-29, 36.)

58 Ibid., p. 23.

59 Ibid., p. 24. As stated above, the balance of power order is excluded from the analysis, although Ikenberry characterizes it as an ideal type.

However, these two ideal types are based on the strong form. In concrete circumstances, any one of the two orders can assume many different expressions.[60]

The strong version of the hegemonic order presupposes direct and coercive dominance of the hegemon over weaker and secondary states. However, the hegemonic order can also assume a more benevolent and less coercive shape when it is organized in the form of reciprocal, consensual and institutionalized elements. In these circumstances, the hegemonic order still relies on the asymmetrical power relations, but the most significant attribute of the order, the dominance, loses its significance. This, 'weak' version of the hegemonic order assimilates the presence of rules and institutional processes that diminish the pure operation of hegemonic coercion.[61] Therefore, we can describe such a system as 'benign hegemony'. However, in such a situation a metamorphosis of the hegemonic order can occur: "In these circumstances of benign hegemony, the order takes on characteristics of what might be called 'weak' constitutionalism."[62] The leading state agrees to limits upon its power for the exchange of acquiescence and participation of secondary powers and the order moves towards the constitutional settlement.[63]

On the other hand, a strong constitutional order denotes a political order with a high level of acceptance, observance and institutionalization of the rules, rights and protections. In practice, constitutional characteristics of an international order crystallize in the degree to which international institutions bind powerful and weaker states together. This institutional cohesion also imposes limits on the arbitrary exercise of state power.[64] The constitutional order can likewise vary in terms of the strength of the rules and institutions that bind states together and so limit the exercise of the state power. As is the case with hegemonic orders, constitutional orders can likewise run on the scale from strong to weak.[65] However, if binding institutions and credible commitments vanish away, the constitutional order loses its essential capacity to reassure threatened and insecure states. When the order loses its constitutional attributes it moves towards the shape of the hegemonic order.[66]

Thus, Ikenberry's design of a postwar order anticipates situations at the intersection of hegemonic and constitutional orders. If the compelling power of the dominant state fades away, the order can move to the structure comprising institutions and rules that impose constitutional rules on the exercise of state power. On the other hand, if the constitutional order loses its institutional and normative guarantees with regard to the common restraints of the state power, states may recede back to the logic of power, which puts the

60 Ibid., pp. 36, n. 42, p. 49.
61 Ibid., pp. 28, 49.
62 Ibid., p. 28.
63 G.J. Ikenberry, *Liberal Order and Imperial Ambition: Essays on American Power and World Politics*, Polity Press, Cambridge, 2006, p. 112.
64 Ikenberry, *After Victory*, p. 36.
65 Ibid., p. 49.
66 Ibid., p. 48.

most potent state to the forefront of the international order. According to Ikenberry, therefore, 'weak' hegemonic orders may display characteristics that are identical to the characteristics of the 'weak' constitutional orders and *vice versa*. The practical reality of postwar international orders therefore anticipates the occurrence of hegemo-constitutional spaces.

4.3 The Concept of Radical Democracy

Contemporary intellectuals of the Left, Ernesto Laclau and Chantal Mouffé, built upon the theory of Antonio Gramsci to develop the concept of radical democracy in terms of the socialist political thought. As an overarching framework, Laclau and Mouffé use the grounds of the discourse theory.[67] The notion of discourse has its roots in the type of analysis addressed not to facts but to their conditions and possibility.[68]

Laclau and Mouffé understand Gramsci's notion of the historical bloc as a cohesive factor, which brings together different elements to form regularity in dispersion. This corresponds to the concept of a discursive formation, which takes a shape of the hegemonic formation in the field of the antagonistic terrain.[69] The hegemonic formation also embraces what opposes it, insofar as the opposing force accepts the basic articulations of the formation.[70] Laclau and Mouffé extend Gramsci's perspective of hegemony from a single hegemonic center to a plural landscape:

> Hegemony is, quite simply, a political *type of relation, a form,* if one so wishes, of politics; but not a determinable location within the topography of the social. In a given social formation, there can be a variety of hegemonic nodal points.[71]

Laclau explains the process of transformation of hegemony from the center to the plurality through the lens of a dichotomy between universal and particular. Here, again, he takes Gramsci as a starting point and describes that the only universality a society can achieve is a hegemonic universality, that is, universality contaminated by *particularity*.[72] Laclau claims that hegemony exists only if the dichotomy universality/particularity is

---

67 For a comprehensive presentation of the discourse theories, *see* J. Torfing, *New Theories of Discourse: Laclau, Mouffé and Žižek*, Blackwell Publishers, Oxford-Malden (MA), 1999.

68 E. Laclau, 'Discourse', *in* R.E. Goodin & P. Pettit (Eds.), *A Companion to Contemporary Political Philosophy*, Blackwell Reference, Oxford-Cambridge (MA), 1993, p. 431.

69 E. Laclau & C. Mouffé, *Hegemony & Socialist Strategy: Towards a Radical Democratic Principles*, Verso, London-New York, 1985, p. 136.

70 Ibid., p. 139.

71 Id.

72 E. Laclau, 'Identity and Hegemony: The Role of Universality in the Constitution of Political Logics', *in* J. Butler, E. Laclau & S. Žižek, *Contingency, Hegemony, Universality: Contemporary Dialogues on the Left*, Verso, London-New York, 2000, p. 51.

surpassed. Universality can subsist solely if it is incarnated in some particularity. However, no particularity can become political without becoming the locus of universalizing effects.[73] The hegemonic relation therefore, encapsulates a typical antinomic situation where the universal and particular reject but nevertheless require each other.[74]

Laclau and Mouffé conceived their socialist strategy as a response to what they see as the antidemocratic neoconservative offensive (of the 1980s). As a solution for the Left, they applied their model of hegemony to the system of liberal democracy. The task of the Left is therefore to deepen and expand liberal-democratic ideology in the direction of a radical and plural democracy. In this respect, they argue that the meaning of the liberal discourse on individual rights is not definitely fixed. Just as this 'unfixity' permits articulation with elements of conservative discourse, it also allows for articulation and redefinition, which accentuate the democratic moment. Since the elements, which make up the liberal discourse never appear as totally crystallized, the liberal discourse may be a field of hegemonic struggle. The possibility of the hegemonic strategy of the Left resides not in the abandonment of the democratic terrain but, on the contrary, in the extension of the field of democratic struggles to the whole of civil society and the state.[75] A democratic struggle has an ability to inundate a certain space in which it develops and produces effects of equivalence with other struggles in different political spaces.[76]

This process leads to the principle of democratic equivalence, which represents the process of the construction of a new 'common sense' changing the identity of different groups in such a way that the demands of each group are articulated equivalently with those of the others.[77] This equivalence (or equality) has a hegemonic character because it not only establishes an alliance between relevant interests, but it also modifies the very identity of the forces engaging in that alliance. For example, the defense of the interests of the workers should not occur at the expense of the rights of women, immigrants or consumers if the aim is to establish equivalence between these different struggles. Struggles against power become truly democratic only in the context of respect for the rights to equality of all other subordinated groups.

However, the principle of democratic equivalence also has its necessary limits. Total equivalence never exists because each equivalence is penetrated by a constitutive precariousness, which is derived from the unevenness of the social. Therefore, the precariousness of each equivalence demands that it is complemented and limited by the logic of autonomy:[78]

---

73 Ibid., p. 56.

74 Id.

75 Laclau & Mouffé, *Hegemony & Socialist Strategy*, p. 176.

76 Ibid., p. 181.

77 Ibid., p. 183.

78 Ibid., pp. 183-184.

> It is for this reason that the demand for *equality* is not sufficient, but needs to be balanced by the demand for *liberty*, which leads us to speak of a radical and *plural* democracy.[79]

Radical democrats do not reject liberal democratic values, such as liberty and equality, but argue that they should be deepened and radicalized.[80] Equality and liberty are thus constitutive phenomena of the radical democracy.

It is necessary to emphasize that no hegemonic project can rely solely on a democratic logic, but must also consist of a set of proposals for the positive organization of the social. A situation of the real hegemony is one in which the management of the positivity of the social and the articulation of the diverse democratic demands achieves a maximum of integration. The opposite situation, in which social negativity leads to the disintegration of every stable system of differences, corresponds to an organic crisis.[81] The radical democracy, therefore

> must base itself upon the search for a point of equilibrium between a maximum advance for the democratic revolution in a broad range of spheres, and the capacity for the hegemonic direction and positive reconstruction of these spheres on the part of subordinated groups.[82]

A brief summary of Laclau-Mouffé's theory of a radical democracy leads to the following insights. Although they base themselves on the Gramscian theory of hegemony, they depart from it in many significant ways. The notion of a single hegemony is dissolved into a number of hegemonies, radiating from different nodal points. Such dynamic comes from the reinterpretation of Gramsci's notion of the hegemonic bloc, which abandons the domain of the class and builds alliances around equivalent subordinated groups. Laclau describes this process in terms of a relation between the universal and the particular(s). While the original notion of hegemony has universal meanings, all subsequent particularistic instances of hegemony reflect this universality in their own way. However, although particularities can never achieve the original universality, they can come closer to it, when each of the particularistic centers assumes the universal identity which unifies them in the form of a representation.

Radical democracy is such a representation in the context of the liberal democracy. It is predicated upon hegemony that evolves from the one-dimensional hegemony to a

79 Ibid., p. 184.

80 L. Tønder & L. Thomassen, 'Introduction', C. Mouffé, 'For an Agonistic Public Sphere', T.B. Dyrberg, 'Radical and Plural Democracy: In Defence of Right/Left and Public Reason', E. Laclau, 'The Future of Radical Democracy', *all in* L. Tønder & L. Thomassen (Eds.), *Radical Democracy: Politics between Abundance and Lack*, Manchester University Press, Manchester, 2014, pp. 4, 126, 168, 259.

81 Laclau & Mouffé, *Hegemony & Socialist Strategy*, p. 189.

82 Id.

plurality of hegemonies. At the same time, radical democracy also contains elements of constitutionalism, as its two essential components are equality and liberty, which inscribe themselves in the context of the 'democratic rights'.[83] In the framework of the liberal democracy, these components connect with other familiar concepts representing a check on the exercise of power, such as the doctrine of separation of powers, representative democracy, doctrine of human rights and rule of law (*Rechtsstaat*). In other words, equality and liberty in radical democracy epitomize the concept of constitutionalism.[84] The representation of the radical democracy therefore results from the process of hybridization between hegemony and constitutionalism and, as such, provides another example of the hegemo-constitutional space.

4.4 Concluding Remarks on the Antinomy between Hegemony and Constitutionalism

This chapter analyzed the relationship between hegemony and constitutionalism as the notion of antinomy, a relationship of two phenomena that simultaneously exclude and confirm each other. Although the antinomy cannot be resolved, it can be accommodated for further explorations and insights. There are two relevant approaches. The first, *general approach* is to retract both phenomena to the original premise, in this case to the notion of power. Such an insight brings a deeper understanding of the context in which the antinomy between hegemony and constitutionalism operates. It is an environment in which the power dynamic has an important place.

The second, *empirical approach* to accommodating the tension between the two phenomena leads to the empirical entity, which contains elements of both and can, due to being porous and fluid, move from one concept to the other. The empirical category does not represent a dialectical synthesis or a new construction in qualitative terms. Rather, it represents an independent category as a result of the process of hybridization at the intersection of the two phenomena. The interaction between these elements leads to the process of shared identification, which amalgamates them in a new concept and elevates it above the irrelevance of unrelated atomic dispersions. At the same time, the process of amalgamation emancipates the empirical category from the confrontation of the two phenomena at the abstract level. This empirical category is thus emancipated from both the abstract and the specific levels alike.

In the framework of the antinomy between hegemony and constitutionalism the category at the intersection of the two phenomena can be labelled as the hegemo-constitutional space. The above survey of the political thought of John Stuart Mill, the theory of

83 *See* ibid., pp. 184-185.
84 *Cf.* Torfing, *New Theories of Discourse*, p. 249, A. Ryan, 'Liberalism', and A. Gutman, 'Democracy', *in* Goodin & Pettit, *A Companion to Contemporary Political Philosophy*, pp. 298, 307, 413-415.

postwar international orders and the concept of the radical democracy provided three relevant examples. As such the hegemo-constitutional space is a useful analytical tool that can be applied to the discipline of international law. However, before coming to that consideration in Part Three of the book, further connections between power, hegemony, constitutionalism and international law have to be established, which is the topic of Part Two.

Part II
Power, Hegemony and Constitutionalism in International Law

5 Power and International Law

The relationship between power and law is complex. As previously demonstrated, power encapsulates different meanings and all of these meanings influence the shape of law. Many scholars see power as an instigator of normative developments.[1] The relationship between power and law has three dimensions: power may be a creator of a normative system; it may be an instigator of the inner structure of the normative system; and it may be a prescriptive and coercive element of a legal norm. These three dimensions can be labelled as power on the law, power in the law, and power by the law. *Power on the law* signifies the external power that shapes the law; *power in the law* relates to the power within the legal system; and *power by the law* stands for power manifested by the law with an aim to influence the reality, including social power.[2]

Although power at first appears as a formative phenomenon with law as its derivative, this is the case only while power is creating the legal system. After establishing the legal system, law assumes an autonomous expression, and power becomes an important, but not a preeminent, element within the legal system. Additionally, the social power of the community is limited by the legal system. Thus, power creates law, penetrates the legal system, converts into legal power and ultimately limits social power. The social power therefore, creates law and, in doing this, also limits itself. Although consideration of the dynamic between power and law usually takes place within the ambit of the general theory of law, this dynamic applies equally to international law.[3] In graphic terms, the described relationship between power and (international) law is illustrated in the following way:

1 *See, e.g.*, R. von Ihering, *Law as a Means to an End*, The Lawbook Exchange, Union (NJ), 1999, trans. I. Husik, G. Burdeau, *Traité de science politique, Présentation de l'univers politique : Le pouvoir politique*, Tome 1, vol. 2, LGDJ, Paris, 1980, Reale, 'Law and Power and Their Correlation', pp. 238-270 and M.S. McDougal, W.M. Reisman & A.R. Willard, 'The World Process of Effective Power, The Global War System', *in* M.S. McDougal & W.M. Reisman, *Power and Policy in Quest of Law: Essays in Honor of Eugene Victor Rostow*, Martinus Nijhoff Publishers, Dordrecht-Boston-Lancaster, 1985, pp. 353-414.

2 *Cf.* K. Tuori, 'Law, Power and Critique', *in* K. Tuori, Z. Bankowski & J. Uusitalo (Eds.), *Law and Power: Critical and Social-Legal Essays*, Deborah Charles Publications, Liverpool, 1997, p. 10. However, my account of correlations between power and law differs from Tuori's analysis.

3 *See* R.H. Steinberg & J.M. Zasloff, 'Power and International Law' 100 *AJIL* 2006, p. 64, M. Klamberg, *Power and Law in International Society: International Relations as the Sociology of International Law*, Routledge, London & New York, 2015, pp. 96-99.

Power and (International) Law

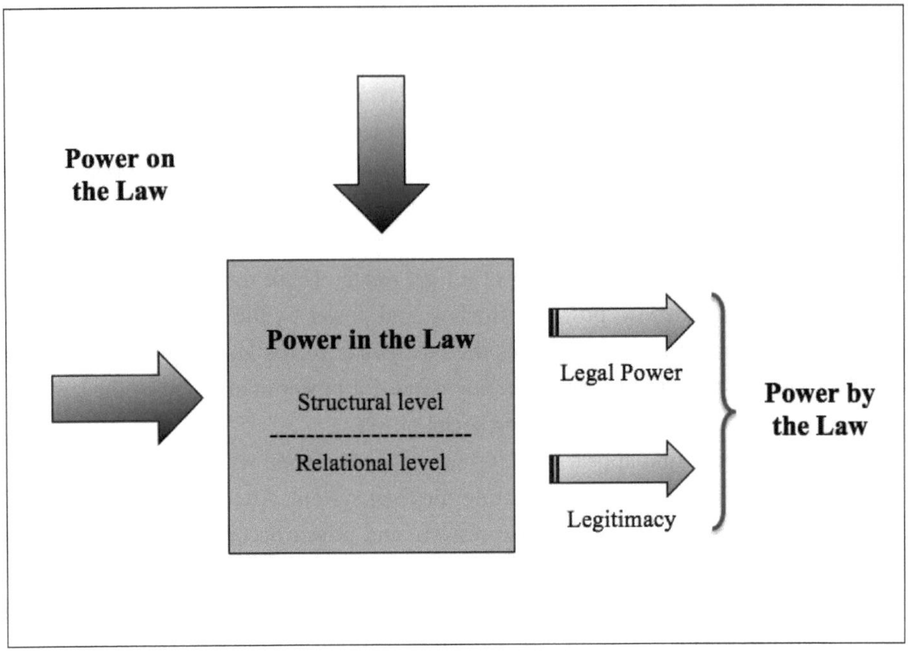

5.1 POWER ON THE LAW

Power on the law deals with the tension between power and law. Since power belongs to the domain of politics, we can equally speak of a relationship between politics and law. As such, the terms power and politics shall be used interchangeably.

According to Hobbes, the natural condition of mankind consists of a 'war of everybody against everybody'. This hostile 'state of nature' endangers the survival of mankind. As war between two approximately equal parties would lead to fruitless and mutual injury, warring parties resort to negotiation and compromise. Therefore, the origin of justice lies in the bargaining process, the conclusion of which results in each party getting something that is worth more than their approximately equal positions of strength.[4] All individual bearers of power are obliged to enter the social contract and transfer their power to the commonwealth – Leviathan.[5] Nevertheless, in the commonwealth all men

4 *See* F. Nietzsche, *Human, All-Too-Human*, 1909-1913, trans. H. Zimmern, para. 92, http://nietzsche.holtof.com/Nietzsche_human_all_too_human/index.htm and von Ihering, *Law as a Means to an End*, pp. 183-184.

5 Hobbes, *Leviathan*, pp. 40-41, 226-227.

remain, as they were in the state of nature, equals.[6] The body politic exercises a monopoly on the use of force. In return, it must provide an alternative mode for the resolution of conflicts that substitutes the brutal power game (war) for a language game (justice) in the context of the peaceful resolution of disputes.[7]

From an abstract perspective, the shift from warfare to adjudication reflects the realization that in order to secure its existence, power must succumb to normative control:

> Force thus sets a limit to itself, which it desires to respect; it recognizes a norm to which it intends to subordinate itself, and this norm approved by itself is law.[8]

Rudolf Ihering refers to this as the *proto-legal* moment in which power transforms itself into law. However, this moment does not lead to the annihilation of power. Rather, power retains its social importance by adding law as a constitutive element and becoming legal power.[9] From this point, power assumes competing characteristics. It is contained both in the 'law and order' of the body politic, which enforces the rule of law, and in the 'rule of law', which places normative limits on the 'law and order'. As Zupančič underlines, these two components represent a dialectical relationship because they simultaneously necessitate and exclude each other:

> In simplest possible terms, 'law and order' necessitates the 'rule of law' because lacking the latter, conflicts would remain unresolved and would continue to destabilize the matrix of human relationships. Thus without 'law and order,' the 'rule of law' would not be enforceable whereas without the 'rule of law,' i.e. adjudication, the 'law and order' would not achieve its main purpose of social stability.[10]

However, the community sponsored legal system as a nonviolent system of resolution of disputes can be binding only if the 'law and order' enforces the 'rule of law' decisions by means of constant threat of violent implementation. Violence continues as a sponsor of nonviolence.[11]

This dynamic relationship between power and law is ingrained also in theories of other scholars. Walter Benjamin portrayed it as a dialectical relationship between 'law-

6 B. de Spinoza, *A Theologico-Political Treatise, and A Political Treatise*, Cosimo Classics, New York, 2005, trans. R.H.M. Elwes, p. 207. *See also* R.H.M. Elwes, 'Introduction', ibid., p. xxxii.
7 *See* Zupančič, *The Owl of Minerva*, pp. 21-25.
8 Ihering, *Law as a Means to an End*, p. 184.
9 *Cf.* ibid., p. 187.
10 Zupančič, *The Owl of Minerva*, p. 33. *See also ibidem* pp. 31-35 and Ihering, *Law as a Means to an End*, pp. 187, 233.
11 Zupančič, *The Owl of Minerva*, pp. 34-35. *See also* Ihering, *Law as Means to an End*, pp. 178 and 231.

making violence' and 'law-preserving violence'[12] whereas Herman Heller pictured it as a dynamic between 'law formative character of power' and 'power formative aspect of law'.[13] Hans Kelsen eloquently summarizes the relationship between power and law:

> Law and force must not be understood as absolutely at variance with one another. Law is an organization of force. For the law attaches certain conditions to the use of force in relations among men, authorizing the employment of force only by certain individuals and only under certain conditions.[14]

This dialectics between power and law applies also to international law. Pashukanis based his approach to law on the logic of equivalence. As a Marxist thinker, he sees the essence of everything legal in the relationship of commodity exchange – the logic of the legal form reverberates with the logic of the commodity form.[15] This relationship can apply to individuals, organized communities or institutions of international law.[16] The economic relationship of exchange is reflected in the legal relationship of the 'purchase and sale' contract.[17] On the basis of aggregation of legal disputes before the courts, a superstructure in the form of a legal system emerges.[18] However, since at the international level the organizational force with coercive powers is present to a lesser extent, the relationships of equivalence between states only exists under the conditions of the real balance of forces, which represents the basis of international law.[19] The international legal form thus juxtaposes juridical equality with the unequal distribution of power between sovereign states,[20] which points to the inherent paradox of international law: "force is determining, but determining between relations which cannot be understood except as equal in fundamentally constitutive and constituting ways."[21]

---

12 *See* W. Benjamin, 'Critique of Violence', *in* W. Benjamin, *Reflections: Essays, Aphorisms, Autobiographical Writings*, Schocken Books, New York, 1978, P. Demetz (Ed.), trans. E. Jephcott, pp. 284-288, 295, 300.

13 *See* H. Heller, 'The Nature and Structure of the State', 18 *Cardozo Law Review* 1996, trans. D. Dyzenhaus, pp. 1139-1216 and D. Dyzenhaus, *Legality and Legitimacy: Carl Schmitt, Hans Kelsen and Hermann Heller*, OUP, Oxford, 1999, pp. 202, 214.

14 H. Kelsen, *General Theory of Law and State*, Lawbook Exchange, Union (NJ), 1999, trans. A. Wedberg, p. 21.

15 A. Bianchi, *International Law Theories: An Inquiry into Different Ways of Thinking*, OUP, Oxford, 2016, p. 78.

16 E. Pashukanis, *The General Theory of Law and Marxism*, *in* P. Bierne & R. Sharlet (Eds.), *Pashukanis: Selected Writings on Marxism and Law*, Academic Press, London-New York, 1980, trans. P.B. Maggs, p. 175 and C. Miéville, *Between Equal Rights: A Marxist Theory of International Law*, 2005, Pluto Press, London, 2005, p. 131.

17 Pashukanis draws inspiration from Ihering. *See* Ihering, *Law as a Means to an End*, pp. 101-102.

18 Pashukanis, *The General Theory of Law and Marxism*, p. 67.

19 E. Pashukanis, 'International Law', *in* Bierne & Sharlet, *Pashukanis: Selected Writings on Marxism and Law*, pp. 108, 179.

20 *Cf.* Mièville, *Between Equal Rights*, p. 293.

21 Ibid., p. 8.

At the international level, power likewise pursues human ends.[22] International law exerts important influence and constraints on power.[23] Often power and international law are indistinguishable and the fields of international relations and international law coincide. This is particularly true if international law is understood as a decision-making process by authorized decision-makers. As Rosalyn Higgins emphasizes:

> [I]t is *not* the case, as is frequently supposed, that international law is concerned with authority *alone*, and that 'power' stands somehow counterpoised to authority, and is nothing to do with it, and is indeed inimical to it. This view - which banishes power to the outer darkness (that is to say, to the province of international relations) - assumes that authority can exist in the total absence of supporting control, or power. But this is fantasy. The authority which characterizes law exists not in a vacuum, but exactly where it intersects with authority. Law, far from being authority battling against power, is the interlocking of authority with power.[24]

Seen from a dynamic perspective, this intersection between power and international law is an antinomy in which one phenomenon turns into the other and *vice versa*. For example, formal equality can be seen as a device established by the powerful actors in order to substantiate and prolong their power.[25] At the same time, the fundamental concepts and principles of international law, such as international community and sovereign equality, places limits on exceptional treatment of great powers. These foundational aspects of the international system enhance the power and influence of those actors who operate within the rules of international law.[26] Miguel Reale points out that while power affects rules, rules similarly exert influence over power:

> [L]aw divested of power is impotent; it becomes a mere *desideration* or logical affirmation without the possibility of *accomplishments* [...]; on the other hand,

22 *See* C. de Visscher, *Theory and Reality in Public International Law*, Princeton University Press, Princeton (NJ), 1957, trans. P.E. Corbett, pp. 92-93, 120-129. *Cf. also* G. Niemeyer, *Law without a Force: The Function of Politics in International Law*, Transaction Publishers, New Brunswick (NJ)-London, 2001, pp. 396, 401.

23 De Visscher, *Theory and Reality in Public International Law*, pp. 133, 139-140, O. Schachter, 'The Nature and Process of Legal Development in International Society', *in* R.St.J. Macdonald & D.M. Johnston (Eds.), *The Structure and Process of International Law: Essays in Legal Philosophy Doctrine and Theory*, Martinus Nijhoff Publishers, The Hague-Boston-Lancaster, 1983, pp. 753-754 and O. Schachter, 'The Role of Power in International Law', 93 *ASILP* 1999, p. 205.

24 R. Higgins, *Problems and Process: International Law and How We Use It*, Clarendon Press, Oxford, 1994, p. 4. For a similar approach which sees the interaction between power and international law as a process, *see* J. Fawcett, *Law and Power in International Relations*, Faber and Faber, London, 1982, in particular pp. 9-47.

25 J. Crawford, 'Foreword', *in* G. Simpson, *Great Powers and Outlaw States: Unequal Sovereigns in the International Legal Order*, CUP, Cambridge, 2005, p. vii.

26 M. Byers, 'Introduction: The Complexities of Foundational Change', *in* M. Byers & G. Nolte (Eds.), *United States Hegemony and the Foundations of International Law*, CUP, Cambridge, 2003, p. 22.

> power deprived of juridical or law reference or not confined to objective limits becomes pure strength or arbitrariness. Power and law hence make reciprocal demands and so reciprocally do they light each other.[27]

In the international community, power conceptually belongs to the sphere of international relations, while legal rules are part of the realm of international law. What follows is a constant metamorphosis of power into rules – or politics into law – and *vice versa*. In order to demonstrate this relationship Koskenniemi uses the metaphor of the perception of a landscape:

> In the morning we see the colors of the trees and the reflection of the leaves on the water; in the evening, we notice the outline of the cliffs against the grey sky, and the shadow of the forest stretches far into the sea. The landscape is the same, the messages it conveys are different. The images are equally self-contained and full. We can reproduce both separately, but we cannot mix them. Likewise, law and politics seemed coherent and separate, yet related to one single reality.
> And yet reality has a temporal dimension: morning turns into day and the evening begins sooner than we had noticed.[28]

Therefore, the reality of international politics is such that power and international law are two phenomena that continuously morph into each other.[29] International politics, power included, and international law represent two sides of the same social reality.[30]

5.2 Power in the Law

At their very base, legal systems mirror the legal power structure. This presupposes a power structure in the shape of a social institution.[31] Every political community has a constitution in the form of a power structure, which is characteristic of that community,

---

27 Reale, 'Law and Power and Their Correlation', p. 251.

28 M. Koskenniemi, 'The Place of Law in Collective Security', 17 *Michigan Journal of International Law* 2006, p. 475.

29 *See* ibid., p. 484, Klamberg, *Power and Law in International Society*, p. 261, G. Shaffer, 'The New Legal Realist Approach to International Law', 28 *LJIL* 2015, p. 206 and A. Carty, 'Sociological Approaches to International Law', *in* R. Wolfrum (Ed.), *Max Planck Encyclopedia of Public International Law*, vol. 9, OUP, Oxford, 2012, p. 263.

30 *Cf.* R. Maspetiol, 'Le droit et la politque : deux visions partielles et fragmentaires d'une meme réalité sociale', 16 *Archives de philosophie de droit* 1971, p. 37.

31 *See* N. Timasheff, *An Introduction to the Sociology of Law*, Harvard University Committee on Research in the Social Sciences, Cambridge (MA), 1939, pp. 171-187, 203-210, 223-226.

as well as a minimal number of legal norms concerning the power structure.[32] A similar logic applies to the international community and international law. Max Huber emphasizes that international law must remain close to its sociopolitical substrate and the realities of political life.[33] In this vein, Bart Landheer identifies three fundamental components of international law:

> [I]nternational law is partially an expression of power politics, partially aimed at greater real equality by postulating legal equality between unequal partners, and partially a structural law which regulates certain matters in a functional manner.[34]

The process by which power arrives at a norm corresponds to the construction of the legal system. In essence, the legal system is constructed once the political system in the form of social institutions takes shape. In contradistinction to the 'power on the law', the norm comes first and (legal) power comes later.[35] Along with this process, there is a shift from particular interests to the common interest of the social fabric or, in the international arena, from bilateralism to community interests.[36] Thus, power builds an institution, which asserts itself through time and creates a legal system in the name of that institution.[37] Historically, this has been a drastic process in that it represents a move away from naked power. Law (including international law) always reflects the existing constellations of social forces.[38] In this sense international law is not an end in itself but a tool to further certain social values and ends.[39] At the same time, however, law limits the arbitrariness of these constellations. Once a political ideal assumes the form of a positive

32 Heller, 'The Nature and Structure of the State', pp. 1195, 1206.

33 J. Delbrück, 'Max Huber's Sociological Approach to International Law', 18 *EJIL* 2007, pp. 104-105, 111-112 and J. Klabbers, 'The Sociological Jurisprudence of Max Huber: An Introduction', 43 *Austrian Journal of Public International Law* 1992, pp. 200-201.

34 B. Landheer, 'Contemporary Sociological Theories in International Law', *in RCADI*, vol. 91, 1957-I, A.W. Sijthoff, Leyde, 1958, p. 35.

35 *Cf.* Ihering, *Law as a Means to an End*, pp. 186-187.

36 Ibid., pp. 220-221. Bruno Simma transposed this logic to international law. (*See* B. Simma, 'From Bilateralism to Community Interest in International Law', *in RCADI*, vol. 250, VI, Martinus Nijhoff Publishers, The Haugue-Boston-London, 1994.)

37 *See* M. Hauriou, *Aux sources de droit : le pouvoir, l'ordre et la liberté*, Librairie Bloud & Gay, Paris, 1933, pp. 96-97, 94, 128, Burdeau, *Traité de science politique*, pp. 10, 24-26, 118-119, 149, S. Romano, *L'ordre juridique*, Dalloz, Paris, trans. F. Lucien & P. Gothot, 1975, pp. 16-19, 37-38.

38 M. Hirsch, *Invitation to the Sociology of International Law*, OUP, Oxford, 2015, p. 1.

39 R. Pound, 'Philosophical Theory and International Law', 1 *Bibliotheca Visseriana* 1923, p. 89, R. Pound, 'The Call for a Realist Jurisprudence', 44 *Harvard Law Review* 1930-1931, pp. 709-711 and A. Pellet, 'Values and Power Relations – The "Disillusionment" of International Law', KFG Working Paper Series, No. 34, Berlin Potsdam Research Group "The International Rule of Law – Rise or Decline?", Berlin, May 2019, pp. 7, 13.

legal system, power inscribes itself into the domain of law and every norm of the legal system imposes limits on the exercise of power.[40]

Therefore, international law reflects the actual power structure of the international community and remains closely associated with international politics.[41] At the structural level, the international community consists of states and international organizations as main building blocks. Given that states remain principal international actors, the existing system of international law needs "powerful states to enforce international rules and principles."[42] However, the degree of influence of power that states exert upon international law varies.[43] Georg Schwarzenberger devises a stratified concept of the international legal system that expands through concentric circles from the sphere of the law of power, through the sphere of the law of reciprocity, to the sphere of the law of coordination. Power is most concentrated in the sphere of the law of power and its influence diminishes gradually through each concentric circle.

In the sphere of the *law of power*, which typically encompasses laws on the use of force, peace treaties and hegemonic expansion, power exerts a prevailing influence on the shape of international law. In this area, international law is instrumental and serves the interests of power. The sphere of the *law of reciprocity* is more detached from power. Reciprocal cooperation between states in the international community leads to the establishment of the law of reciprocity in the form of diplomatic law, extradition law and economic, social and cultural law. Finally, in the area of activities distant from power politics, international law shows traces of community law or *law of coordination*. In this sphere, international law promotes the common interests of humankind and exerts the greatest influence on social reality. These common interests lead to the development of human rights law, the law of humanitarian assistance and environmental law.[44]

With regard to international organizations the dynamic between power and law is mediated through a set of institutional features. According to René-Jean Dupuy, the institutional model deals with the process of creation of superior legal norms and with organs designed to implement norms.[45] This model has the following attributes: concentration of power, conditioning of power and repression of power. Concentration of power occurs when states become members of international organizations. In this way they enter into a position of concentration within organs of that organization. The next attribute, the conditioning of power, consists of different layers. The first check upon the state

40 Reale, 'Law and Power and Their Correlation', pp. 257, 265.

41 *Cf.* Klamberg, *Power and Law in International Society*, pp. 93-95.

42 A. Paulus, 'The War against Iraq and the Future of International Law: Hegemony or Pluralism?', 25 *Michigan Journal of International Law* 2004, p. 732.

43 Klamberg, *Power and Law in International Society*, p. 256.

44 *See* G. Schwarzenberger, *Power Politics: A Study of World Society*, Steven & Sons Limited, London, 1964, pp. 199-209.

45 R.-J. Dupuy, *La communauté internationale entre le mythe et l'histoire*, Economica-UNESCO, Paris, 1986, pp. 40, 41.

power occurs when the organization admits the state as a member. Then, the conditioning on the part of the international organization continues through the autonomous functioning of the organization. Institutions also presuppose a certain normative hierarchy. This enables the organization to bring a group of states together and to further common ends. Finally, the repression of power occurs through the rules proscribing the use of force and through the institutionalization of the peaceful settlement of disputes.[46]

At the relational level, social power permeates the content of legal rules through different processes. Concepts such as the 'open texture of rules',[47] 'juridical nomogenesis'[48] or 'decisionism'[49] describe a phase in the lawmaking process where the indeterminate nature of legal rules interacts with the corresponding factual situation. In the process of the formation of rules, decision-makers (such as judges, politicians, public officials and legal advisers) take into account facts and nonlegal factors from their social reality – in short, the social context – which influences their final decision on the normative output.[50] As power is one of the main factors in the social field, these avenues of juridical permeability allow for the penetration of social power into the legal structure and for the influencing of legal norms. It has to be added that international law is formally premised upon relations of juridical equality among relevant international actors, as is encapsulated in the principle of sovereign equality of states (Article 2(1) of the UN Charter). However, the sub-component of 'sovereignty' in that principle suggests that formal equality is in practice often pondered with extra-legal features such as power.[51] At the same time, the juridical acknowledgment of equality limits the influence of such features.

Being a system of law, international law distinguishes itself from other disciplines of law, principally with regard to its sources. The two main formal sources of international law are, pursuant to the Article 38(1) of the Statute of the International Court of Justice (ICJ), treaty law and customary international law.

In the international legal system, custom still occupies an important role as a form of lawmaking due to the decentralized structure of the international community. Customary

46 *See* ibid., pp. 48-57.

47 H.L.A. Hart, *The Concept of Law*, OUP, Oxford, 1997, pp. 127-128, 135.

48 Reale, 'Law and Power and Their Correlation', p. 244. This statement reflects what Reale conceived as a 'three-dimensional theory of law', in which law is a dialectical process of implication and polarity between facts, values and norms. *See* M. Reale, *Filosofia del diritto*, G. Giappichellli editore, Torino, 1956, trans. L. Bagolini & G. Ricci, pp. 319-380.

49 C. Schmitt, *Les trois types de pensée juridique*, PUF, Paris, 1995, trans. M. Köller & D. Séglard, pp. 81, 83 and G. Marramao, 'Pouvoir et puissance : Àpropos de Carl Shmitt', *in* C.-M. Herrera (Ed.), *Le droit, le politique : autour de Max Weber, Hans Kelsen and Carl Schmitt*, Ed. L'Harmattan, Paris, 1994, p. 70.

50 G. Shaffer, 'The New Legal Realist Approach to International Law', pp. 193, 194.

51 *See* Chapter 6 of this book.

international law consists of two essential elements: state practice and *opinio juris.*[52] Power has an important influence on both elements.[53]

With regard to the element of the state practice, Charles de Visscher provides useful insight in saying that there are always some actors

> who mark the soil more deeply with their footprints than others, either because of their weight, which is to say their power in this world, or because their interests bring them more frequently this way.[54]

In this vein, the elements of the state strength and national interests are important in the formation of state practice. Although allusions to powerful states initially bring to mind naked or military force, state power can also comprise economic and cultural force.[55] The notion of power may be derived from almost any of the forces that exist in the international community at a given time.[56] In this sense, custom "concerns the implicit creation of norms through the behaviour of a few politically relevant factors."[57] In addition, national interests are also determinative of state practice in that they prompt states to action. In the *North Sea Continental Shelf* cases, the ICJ emphasized that the formation of customary international law requires widespread and representative participation, including participation by states whose interests are specially affected by a proposed new rule of customary international law.[58]

The notion of 'specially affected' states is multifaceted. On one hand, it may serve as a guise for important, powerful states that would necessarily be 'specially affected' by nearly all political and legal developments in the international community.[59] This understanding is premised on the responsibility of powerful states for the shape of the international community and their subsequent involvement in global affairs. On the other hand, the phrase *specially affected* suggests that the process of customary formation of international

---

52 The literature on customary international law is extensive. *See, e.g.,* M. Shaw, *International Law*, CUP, Cambridge, 2014, pp. 51-66, I. Brownlie, *Principles of Public International Law*, OUP, Oxford, 2008, pp. 6-12, G. Abi-Saab, *Cours général de droit international public, in RCADI*, vol. 207, Martinus Nijhoff Publishers, The Hague-Boston-London, 1996, pp. 169-184 and P. Haggenmacher, 'La doctrine de deux elements du droit coutumier dans la pratique de la Cour internationale', 90 *RGDIP* 1986, pp. 5-126.

53 *See* Schwarzenberger, *Power Politics*, p. 199 and de Visscher, *Theory and Reality of International Law*, p. 149.

54 De Visscher, *Theory and Reality of International Law*, p. 149.

55 *Cf.* Kelsen, 'Théorie du droit international coutumier', *in* C. Leben (Ed.), *Hans Kelsen. Écrits français de droit international*, PUF Paris, 2001, p. 79.

56 M. Byers, *Custom, Power and the Power of Rules: International Relations and Customary International Law*, CUP, Cambridge, 1999, p. 220.

57 M.W. Reisman, 'The Cult of Custom in the Late 20th Century', 17 *California Western International Law Journal* 1987, p. 133.

58 *North Sea Continental Shelf Cases*, Judgment, 20 February 1969 (ICJ Reports 1969, p. 3), para. 73.

59 G.M. Danilenko, *Law-making in the International Community*, Martinus Nijhoff Publishers, Dordrecht, 1993, pp. 96, 236.

rules considers the interests of affected states, regardless of their power.[60] Some states may be, on the basis of geographical, cultural, political or historical factors, more active in certain areas of international law, such as the law of the sea, environmental law and human rights law. Their continuous activity makes them leading players in those areas, which increases their international influence. In this sense, legitimate interests may be the inspiration or motive behind certain practices of states that lead to the evolution of customary law.[61]

The influence of the powerful states is not absolute. The consistent behavior of the leading powers alone cannot create norms of customary international law against the resistance of other, less powerful states.[62] Nevertheless, the process of the creation of customary norms relies on the power dynamic in the international community and the influence of states that make unilateral determinations on the basis of their interests, still remains paramount in this process.[63]

Power is also present in relation to *opinio juris*. For Brigitte Stern, the content of *opinio juris* of each state depends on its position of power in the international order.[64] The customary process is essentially the relation between the more powerful and less powerful states in which the element of power transpires through the will of the stronger:

> The will of a state, even if it is not a will power, implies an element of power. Thus certain states will feel bound because they wanted to be, because they freely consented to be, and other states, on the contrary, will feel bound because they cannot not want to be, because the rule is imposed upon them.[65]

Such a realist approach advocates that states with coercive power determine the existence of rules of customary international law.[66] A similar perspective emphasizes the role of power in the process of the spontaneous necessity-driven creation of customary rules. The important element in this process is the formation of the collective legal awareness in the existence of social necessity. This process often mirrors constellations of power at the international level; the 'silent majority' often bows to the analysis of the most powerful states as to what constitutes the social necessity.[67] Power therefore has a major role in the creation of *opinio juris*. It is possible to go even further and say that *opinio juris*

60 Byers, *Custom, Power and the Power of Rules*, p. 38.
61 G. Fitzmaurice, 'The Law and Procedure of the International Court', 30 *BYIL* 1953, pp. 69-70. As an example of legitimate interests Fitzmaurice mentions economic interests.
62 J. Kunz, 'The Nature of Customary International Law', 47 *AJIL* 1953, p. 666.
63 Reisman, 'The Cult of Custom in the Late 20th Century', p. 144.
64 B. Stern, 'Custom at the Heart of International Law', 11 *Duke Journal of Comparative and International Law* 2001, trans. M. Byers & A. Denise, p. 108.
65 Id.
66 Id.
67 P. Daillier & A. Pellet, *Droit international public*, L.G.D.J, Paris, 1999, p. 320.

reflects the prevalence of the will of the most powerful states over weaker states.[68] However, one has to add a more relative nuance to this view. From the perspective of autolimitation of powerful states, *opinio juris* has traditionally served two closely related functions. The first function is to distinguish legally relevant from legally irrelevant state practice. The second function is to serve as a means of self-control of powerful states against their tendency to abuse power in the process of formation of customary law.[69]

This leads to the conclusion that power is intrinsic to both elements of customary international law, state practice and *opinio juris*, as well as to the branch of customary international law itself.[70] The traditional view that powerful states have a greater say in the development of international law is correct. Their role in the customary process is predominant because they have the means of power, ranging from the effective diplomatic service to the threat with economic measures or military weapons (for example, in the form of the 'gunboat diplomacy').[71] By implication, their predominant position presupposes an interest in the regulation of the international community, often in accordance with their national interests. In this way, the principle of the balance of power has a prevailing role in the customary process. However, as previously discussed, the power of leading states is not absolute. With regard to both state practice and *opinio juris*, less important states, likewise, have a role to play. Without the support of the smaller states, the powerful states cannot create general customary law. Therefore, the relationship between powerful and less powerful states is not one of simple domination but one of power and counterpower.[72]

The dynamic of power politics likewise exists in the domain of the law of treaties. An essential characteristic of treaty lawmaking is free will or free consent, which implies that states subscribe only to those international conventions to which they have agreed.[73] Although the process of treaty-making unfolds on the basis of formal equality, extralegal factors can perform an important role in the conclusion of treaties.[74] These factors take the shape of power or its more tempered expressions, such as influence or pressure. At the same time, power – in the form of the predominance of the great powers or the power equilibrium – represents guarantees of the binding nature of concluded treaties and a decisive factor in upholding the international legal order.[75]

---

68 *See* Stern, 'Custom at the Heart of International Law', p. 108.

69 Byers, *Custom, Power and the Power of Rules*, p. 212.

70 M. Byers, 'Introduction: Power, Obligation, and Customary International Law', 11 *Duke Journal of Comparative and International Law* 2001, p 87.

71 *See* Byers, *Custom, Power and Power of Rules*, p. 205.

72 Hirsch, *Invitation to the Sociology of International Law*, p. 2.

73 Schwarzenberger, *Power Politics*, p. 203 and N. Krisch, 'More Equal than the Rest? Hierarchy, Equality and US predominance in International Law', *in* Byers & Nolte, *United States Hegemony and Foundations of International Law*, p. 142.

74 *See* Krisch, 'More Equal than the Rest?', p. 137 *et seq.* and L. Oppenheim, *International Law: A Treatise*, Longmans, Green and Co., London, vol. I, 1920, pp. 196-200.

75 Delbrück, 'Max Huber's Sociological Approach to International Law', pp. 109-111.

In the case of a disparity in obligations of state parties to the treaty – such as imbalanced or nonreciprocal rights and duties – the doctrine speaks of 'unequal treaties'.[76] These treaties have a long historical tradition.[77] In the era of imperialism, great powers imposed such treaties on countries in Africa and Asia under the pretext that they still needed to reach the stage of civilization that would qualify them as equal international actors.[78] During the Cold War, socialist doctrine classified all treaties concluded between capitalist states and developing states concerning military bases in the foreign territory, economic and technical assistance and credits and loans as unequal.[79] Nowadays, disparities in treaty obligations exist primarily between developed and less developed states in the field of investment treaties.[80]

Treaties can be unequal in terms of both substance and procedure.[81] Inequality with regard to substance relates to the imbalance between rights and duties of two contracting parties. The position and influence of great powers, pursuant to factors such as the actual size, strength and economic influence, make smaller states agree to the arrangements of the great powers.[82] A treaty represents a legal transaction between two parties and the substantive reciprocity resulting from actual advantages deriving from treaty performance.[83] The condition of reciprocity allows that the transaction occurs between unequals to the benefit of both. There is nothing wrong if parties to the legal transaction are unequal and if the content of the treaty was influenced by factors of power. In fact, reciprocity acknowledges and accepts heterogeneity.[84] The concept of reciprocity blurs the distinction between legal and political considerations in the law of treaties.[85] What is at stake concerning unequal treaties is an imbalance of obligations in a given treaty,

76 *See* A. Peters, 'Treaties, Unequal', *in* Wolfrum, *The Max Planck Encyclopedia of Public International Law*, vol. X, pp. 38 and 44-46.

77 For a critical account *see* M. Craven, 'What Happened to Unequal Treaties? The Continuities of Informal Empire', 74 *Nordic Journal of International Law* 2005, pp. 335-383.

78 *See* M. Koskenniemi, *The Gentle Civilizer of Nations: The Rise and Fall of International Law 1870-1960*, CUP, Cambridge, 2001, C.H. Alexandrowicz, *An Introduction to the History of the Law of Nations in the East Indies (16th, 17th and 18th Centuries)*, Clarendon Press, Oxford, 1967, pp. 149-184 and 224-239, C.H. Alexandrowicz, *The European-African Confrontation: A Study in Treaty Making*, A.W. Sijthof, Leiden, 1973, pp. 29-55, 117-128, G.W. Gong, *The Standard of 'Civilization' in International Society*, Clarendon Press, Oxford, 1984, pp. 239-248 and M.J. van Ittersum, 'Global Constitutionalism in the Early Modern Period: The Role of Empires, Treaties and Natural Law', in Lang & Wiener, *Handbook on Global Constitutionalism*, pp. 47-59.

79 Peters, 'Treaties, Unequal', pp. 43-44.

80 A.T. Guzman, 'Why LDCs Sign Treaties that Hurt Them: Explaining the Popularity of Bilateral Investment Treaties', 38 *Virginia Journal of International Law* 1998, pp. 639-688.

81 Peters, 'Treaties, Unequal', pp. 39, 43-44.

82 Oppenheim, *International Law*, p. 199.

83 B. Simma, 'Reciprocity', *in* Wolfrum, *The Max Planck Encyclopedia of Public International Law*, vol. VIII, p. 652.

84 E. Wyler & A. Papaux, 'The Search for Universal Justice', *in* R.St.J. Macdonald & D. Johnston (Eds.), *Towards World Constitutionalism: Issues in the Legal Ordering of the World Community*, Martinus Nijhoff, Leiden, 2005, p. 302. *See also* Schwarzenberger, *Power Politics*, p. 208 and Simma, 'Reciprocity', p. 652.

85 *Cf.* Simma, 'Reciprocity', pp. 652-653 and Oppenheim, *International Law*, pp. 198-199.

which must be assessed in the overall context of treaty relations between the concerned states. In this wider context, 'inequality' in one treaty may be compensated by reverse 'inequality' in another.[86]

A flagrant imbalance of obligation in the context of a relationship of domination or subordination would not by itself suffice to make an unequal treaty null and void,[87] especially in a case where there is a balance in this relationship on the basis of a wider framework, which – apart from legal – includes political, economic and other elements. It is worth noting that an imbalance of duties and obligations may also go in the other direction. Some multilateral treaties (*e.g.*, the *General Agreement on Tariffs and Trade*) allow for positive discrimination in order to rectify economic weaknesses of some states or institute special arrangements, such as the regime of differentiated responsibilities for developing countries, in the post-Rio environmental treaties. These treaties aim to realize substantial equality.[88]

Therefore, inequality in treaty of obligations may not be the consequence of the exercise of power, nor is every inequality in treaty relations unacceptable.[89] However, a manifest imbalance through an extended period of time would point to the problematic relationship of subordination of one contracting party to the other one.

Procedural inequality, on the other hand, pertains to a set of arguments related to the conclusion of treaties.[90] In the course of this process, a stronger state may use power to exert pressure on a weaker party. Article 52 of *Vienna Convention on the Law of Treaties* (VCLT) stipulates:

> A treaty is void if its conclusion has been procured by the threat or use of force in violation of the principles of international law embodied in the Charter of the United Nations.[91]

The ICJ confirmed this rule in the *Fisheries Jurisdiction* case.[92]

While the VCLT prohibits the threat or use of force by one contracting party over another,[93] it does not address the issues of other forms of coercion, such as economic or

86 L. Caflisch, 'Unequal Treaties', 35 *GYIL* 1992, p. 69.
87 Ibid., p. 68.
88 Peters, 'Treaties, Unequal', p. 48.
89 *Cf.* Simma, 'Reciprocity', p. 652.
90 Peters, 'Treaties, Unequal', p. 45.
91 Vienna Convention on the Law of Treaties, 23 May 1969, entered into force on 27 January 1980, UNTS, vol. 1155, p. 18. The Vienna Convention on the Law of Treaties between States and International Organizations or between International Organizations (1986) contains the same provision.
92 *Fisheries Jurisdiction Case (United Kingdom v. Iceland)*, Jurisdiction of the Court, ICJ, 2 February 1973 (ICJ Reports 1973), para. 24.
93 *Cf.* M. Fitzmaurice, 'The Practical Working of the Law of Treaties', *in* M. Evans (Ed.), *International Law*, OUP, Oxford, 2006, pp. 194-195.

political pressure.[94] Nevertheless, such kind of pressure would constitute an illegal threat if it represented conduct comparable to physical violence in the economic field, such as economic blockades, causing unlawful damage to states.[95] The level of pressure must therefore reach the violent intensity of an illegal threat or use of armed force to be deemed unacceptable by the international community.[96]

The real reason for imbalance of treaties in substantive and procedural terms is that the use of economic and political pressure exploiting the extreme power disparities is a common feature in inter-state relations. By upholding imbalanced treaties, international law accepts differences of social and political power in international relations and thus allows for the intervention of power in the domain of international law.[97] Since international law remains – for the greater part – a horizontal legal system, it relies upon the logic of reciprocity that takes into account a broader plethora of nuances in inter-state relations.[98]

In the case of a problematic unequal treaty characterized by "a major and striking imbalance,"[99] such a treaty could be made invalid or voidable, or the unequal character of the treaty could be a ground for its unilateral termination, suspension or a claim for revision, in accordance with the VCLT regime.[100] However, as there is currently no comprehensive and compulsory dispute settlement mechanism with regard to treaties, the identification of unfairness or inequity in treaty obligations falls to the contracting parties themselves. They usually have divergent views on these issues.[101] Nonetheless, on the basis of its advisory jurisdiction the ICJ recently stated in the advisory opinion on *the Chagos Archipelago* that the consent between contracting parties must be based on the free and genuine expression of the will.[102]

---

94 For more on this issue *see* Caflisch, 'Unequal Treaties', pp. 71-75, P. Reuter, *Introduction au droit des traités*, PUF, Paris, 1995, pp. 159-161 and Daillier & Pellet, *Droit international public*, pp. 197-199.

95 Caflisch, 'Unequal Treaties', pp. 75. *See also* M. Schröder, 'Treaties, Validity', *in* Wolfrum, *The Max Planck Encyclopedia of Public International Law*, vol. X, p. 54.

96 Caflisch, 'Unequal Treaties', p. 75.

97 Peters, 'Treaties, Unequal', pp. 48, 50.

98 Simma, 'Reciprocity', p. 655.

99 Caflisch, 'Unequal Treaties', p. 66.

100 Peters, 'Treaties, Unequal', p. 47. *See* Schröder, 'Treaties, Validity', pp. 51-56.

101 Peters, 'Treaties, Unequal', p. 50.

102 The advisory opinion dealt with the issue of the right of self-determination of the people of Mauritius during the decolonization process, with a special focus on the status of the Chagos Islands. The ICJ concluded that the agreement on the Chagos Archipelago between the United Kingdom and Mauritius, in which the latter agreed to the detachment of the Chagos Islands from the colony of Mauritius, cannot constitute an international agreement given that Mauritius at that time was under the authority of the United Kingdom. Therefore, the supposed consent "was not based on the free and genuine expression of the will of the people concerned." Consequently, the process of decolonization of Mauritius was not lawfully completed when the country became independent in 1968. The continued administration of the Chagos Islands by the United Kingdom constitutes an internationally wrongful act and should be, according to the ICJ, brought to an end as rapidly as possible. (*Legal Consequences of the Separation of the Chagos Archipelago from Mauritius in 1965*, Advisory Opinion, 25 February 2019 (General List No. 169), in particular paras. 160, 171-174, 177-178.)

Power in the law represents the penetration of power into and its flow within the international legal system. Power inevitably shapes the contours of international law in structural terms, be it through states or international organizations. The extent to which power shapes the international legal systems is multifaceted. The influence of power has the greatest impact in areas that are closest to the exercise of power in international relations. On the other hand, in areas that are remote from power dynamics, power exercises minimal imprints on international law. International organizations have a role in directing and limiting power within the purview of their functional competences. While the importance of international courts and tribunals is growing, their ambit in limiting the exercise of power is still rather limited.[103] In relational terms, power can shape the formation of international law through the formation of customary international law and treaty law. It is worth emphasizing that the influence of powerful states in both spheres of international lawmaking can be countered by smaller states. Such use of lawmaking rules and mechanisms can be considered as counterpower.

5.3 Power by the Law

The expression *power by the law* embraces two components: the issue of the coercive character of law (legal power) and the issue of the legitimacy of law.

In the design of a body politic as a social organization of coercion, the state is the bearer of the regulated and disciplined coercive force. Law, on the other hand, is the total sum of principles on the basis of which the body politic exercises its coercive function. In the social design of the state, it is power (or force) that comes at law, as described above.[104] The correlation between power and law goes beyond mere mutual dependence. Force is an inherent element of law if law is to have any effect at all. The issue of legal power is also referred to as the efficacy of the legal system.[105]

If law is understood as the organization of power,[106] efficacy becomes extremely important. While efficacy is not to provide validity for a norm, it is a condition of its validity. The norm is valid only if it belongs to the legal order which, on the whole, is efficacious. Efficacy, in essence, means that a legal order relates to the social reality. It means that the power of law successfully regulates human behavior and thus shapes the social domain.[107] The existence of a legal system therefore depends on the executive force, which is inherent in the legal order and originates in the social power.[108]

103 *See* Chapters 6, 7, 10 of this book.

104 Ihering, *Law as a Means to an End*, pp. 178, 231, 233.

105 *Cf.*: "The efficacy of law belongs to the realm of reality and is often called the power of law." (Kelsen, *General Theory of Law and State*, p. 121.)

106 Id.

107 *See* ibid., pp. 121, 190, Kelsen, *Introduction to the Problems of Legal Theory*, pp. 29, 60-61, 104-105 and N. Bobbio, *Diritto e potere : Saggi su Kelsen*, Edizioni Scientifiche Italiane, Napoli-Roma, 1992, p. 148.

108 Romano, *L'ordre juridique*, pp. 37-38 and Abi-Saab, *Cours général de droit international public*, p. 112.

These essential characteristics correspond to the constitutive process of the New Haven School policy-oriented approach to international law. The constitutive process of international law is a phenomenon whereby "a variety of groups and individuals on the basis of effective power and its authority seek to create, sustain or change the fundamental institutions of decision-making in a community."[109] The constitutive process does not represent an organic process but stands for an aggregate of decisions in which the power element can exercise a strong role.[110] A central part of the constitutive process in any community is the prescribing function of law. Its focus is not on the content of particular norms but on the process by which such norms are made.[111] The importance of the prescriptive process is that its outcomes - prescribed norms - are effective, rational and inclusive.[112]

Therefore, rather than a system of fixed legal rules, the New Haven School sees law as a process of authoritative decisions based on power.[113] As power is an essential element in the constitutive process, it also plays a fundamental role in the prescriptive process. Power is such an integral part of law that law is itself a type of power, that is, a manifestation of power.[114] The international institutional framework, in particular, absorbs, and to a degree, transcends power and its logic. It furthers legal standards of the international community and, through institutional mechanisms, contributes to the implementation of legal rules.[115]

International law is a coercive legal order, consisting of a set of normative prescriptions that regulate human behaviour by attaching certain coercive acts, or sanctions, as consequences to certain behaviours.[116] As we have seen before, coercion is an essential precondition for the efficacy of law. It epitomizes the transformation of power in the law to the legal power encapsulated in the legal rule as a prescription to influence and change social reality. Legal power retains attributes of being law and power at the same time. The legal power is legal because it is intrinsically linked to the normative prescription. It is also power because through coercion it makes the social reality conform to these legal prescriptions.

---

109 M.W. Reisman, 'Law from the Policy Perspective', *in* M. McDougal & M.W. Reisman, *International Law Essays: A Supplement to International Law in Contemporary Perspective*, The Foundation Press, Mineola (NY), 1981, p. 11.

110 Ibid., pp. 11-12 and M.S. McDougal, 'The Law School of the Future: From Legal Realism to Policy Science in the World Community', 56 *Yale Law Journal* 1947, p. 1348.

111 M.S. McDougal & M.W. Reisman, 'The Prescribing Function in World Constitutive Process: How International Law Is Made', 6 *Yale Studies in World Public Order* 1980, p. 272.

112 Ibid., p. 273.

113 *Cf.* Koskenniemi, *The Gentle Civilizer of Nations*, p. 478.

114 B. Rosenthal, *Etude de l'oeuvre de Myres Smith McDougal en matière de droit international public*, L.G.D.J., Paris, 1970, p. 131.

115 Schachter 'The Nature and Process of Legal Development in International Society', pp. 753-754 and Schachter, 'The Role of Power in International Law', p. 205. *See also* R.-J. Dupuy, *La communauté internationale entre le mythe et l'histoire*, pp. 48-57.

116 Kelsen, H., *Pure Theory of Law*, Lawbook Exchange, Union (NJ), 2002, trans. Max Knight, p. 320.

Another essential component of the power by law is legitimacy. The question of legitimacy goes to the heart of the legal system. If legal rules are not generally accepted by the governed, the legal system amounts to an authoritarian regime and power by the law degrades to arbitrary power. A number of scholars emphasize the axiological aspect of rules as a condition for people to accept law as legitimate.[117] The legitimacy of rules requires the psychological acquiescence of the people in order to elevate the repetitive practice to a legal form. Again, people, states and other subjects consent to rules not solely because of the coercive power behind them but because they accept that legal rules are consistent with their interests, values and principles.

In the realm of international law, Thomas Franck understands legitimacy as

> that quality of a rule which derives from a perception on the part of those to whom it is addressed that it has come into being in accordance with right process.[118]

Indicators of legitimate rules include: determinacy, symbolic validation, coherence, and adherence to a normative hierarchy.[119] In this context, "legitimacy is the capacity of a rule to pull those to whom it is addressed toward consensual compliance."[120] The challenge here is to understand how this 'pull to compliance' happens and why. Explanation can be found in the theory of normative integration. Zupančič describes normative integration as "a process in which social norms get accepted, that is, integrated through the process of punishment and other adjudicative methods."[121]

The process of normative integration presupposes, firstly, successful identification of the progressive values that would 'pull' the community forward. Secondly, this process necessitates consistent implementation of the socially progressive norms by coercion where necessary. Finally, the addressees should perceive these norms as truly progressive and worthy of acceptance and internalization. However, this process is demanding because society is not homogenous. While society is stratified according to inequalities,

---

117 *See* Hart, *The Concept of Law*, pp. 56-57, 88-89, 112, G. Jellinek, *L'état moderne et son droit: Théorie générale de l'Etat*, vol. I, V. Giard & E. Brière, Paris, 1911, trans. G. Fardis, pp. 504-505, 519-536, R. Dworkin, *Law's Empire*, Hart Publishing, Oxford-Portland (OR), 1998, pp. 191-192 and Fuller, *The Morality of Law*, pp. 42, 96-97.

118 T.M. Franck, 'Legitimacy in the International System', 82 *AJIL* 1988, p. 706. *See also* T.M. Franck, 'Why a Quest for Legitimacy?', 21 *UC Davis Law Review* 1988, pp. 535-547 and T.M. Franck, 'The Power of Legitimacy and the Legitimacy of Power: International Law in an Age of Power Disequilibrium', 100 *AJIL* 2006, pp. 88-106.

119 Franck, 'Legitimacy in the International System', p. 712.

120 Franck, 'The Power of Legitimacy and the Legitimacy of Power', p. 93 and Franck, 'Legitimacy in the International System', p. 708.

121 Zupančič, *The Owl of Minerva*, p. 232. *See also* Hirsch, *Invitation to the Sociology of International Law*, pp. 6-7.

which implies that social consciousness is different for different interest groups,[122] successful identification with social values is possible.

One of the catalysts of normative integration in the international community is the work of international courts such as the European Court of Human Rights. It would be inaccurate to perceive any process of interpretation, including judicial interpretation, as a value neutral operation.[123] After all, the role of the prominent courts is precisely to provide 'moral leadership'. This may happen through the introduction of uncharacteristic and even entirely new legal criteria based on 'ethical adequacy' with regard to important social issues.[124] Normative integration through international courts proceeds on the basis of the institutionalization of new legal standards in concrete cases. Through consistent application by lower instances of adjudication, these new values, if adequate, take root and become assimilated.[125] Values are integrated into the law because they have become socially indispensable. Their integration therefore brings about social appeasement and reconciliation.[126] Given that such values meet the needs of pressing social reality, they fall on fertile ground and are readily accepted. This is the essence of the legitimacy of legal rules and of the 'pull to compliance'.

Power by the law therefore consists of two components: coercion or legal power and legitimacy of the law. Legal power carries power as an indispensable coercive component of the norm. Without coercion there is no efficacy of law that would lead to changes in behavior and to the transformation of social reality. However, in order for these norms to be implemented, they have to be perceived as legitimate by subjects who are agents of prescribed changes. The process of social transformation unfolds when there is a match between the axiological substance of norms and perception of these norms as socially progressive by subjects in that society. Consequently, power by the law warrants the process of internalization of prescribed norms.

5.4 Concluding Remarks on Power and International Law

The transformations of power with regard to international law can be portrayed in the following dynamic terms. On the basis of the need for self-preservation, social power is compelled to create the normative system (power on the law). But the normative system makes only a part of the larger international reality and social power still remains the main acting force in the larger context of international affairs. Social power consists of a

122 *Cf.* Zupančič, *The Owl of Minerva*, p. 224.

123 A. Bianchi, 'Enforcing International Law Norms against Terrorism: Achievements and Prospects', *in* A. Bianchi (Ed.), *Enforcing International Law Norms against Terrorism*, Hart Publishing, Oxford-Portland (OR), 2004. pp. 499-500.

124 Zupančič, *The Owl of Minerva*, p. 238.

125 Ibid., p. 239.

126 Id.

power structure of the most important states and partly, in terms of their functional importance, also of international organizations. However, together with the creation of the international legal system, a portion of social power metamorphoses into the power within that legal system (power in the law). The main traits of power in international law are that it influences the distribution of competences within the international legal system and provides limits on the exercise of legal power. In particular, power in the law may exercise influence on the formation of norms through the emergence of customary international law and the conclusion of treaties. Through the functioning of the international legal system, power emerges with an aim to influence the reality of international relations. This is power by the law, which includes legal power and legitimacy of law. Legal power represents coercion, whereas legitimacy of legal rules implies their acceptance by actors due to the 'inner morality of law'.[127] In the end, power by the law puts constraints on the movement of social power in international affairs.[128] This scheme portrays the circular flow of power in the international community – from the power on the law, to the power in the law and, finally, to the power by the law. In the end, we see that power imposes prescriptive limits upon itself. Generally, the function of law is to evolve as a superstructure and to restrain social power for the preservation of a community and its social ends. This ambivalent logic likewise applies to the relationship between international law and power in international relations. On the one side, international law has been formed to express, in legal terms, the preferences of the most powerful countries. On the other, it has been formed to put limits on the international behavior of those same countries.[129] International law thus acts as a tool and a constraint on the social power in the international reality.

127 *See* Fuller, *The Morality of Law*. For more on legitimacy in the international system *see* Clark, *Legitimacy in International Society*.

128 *Cf.* Tuori, 'Law, Power and Critique', p. 18.

129 J.M. Pureza, 'Defensive and Oppositional Counter-Hegemonic Uses of International Law: From the International Criminal Court to the Common Heritage of Humankind', *in* B. de Sousa Santos & C.A. Rodríguez-Garavito (Eds.), *Law and Globalization from Below: Towards a Cosmopolitan Legality*, CUP, Cambridge, 2005, p. 279.

6 Hegemony and International Law

The expression hegemonic international law links the phenomenon of hegemony with international law. It points to the influence of hegemony on the shaping of international law. As demonstrated previously, hegemony is a particular expression of the constellation of power. Defined in a generic sense, hegemony is an expansion of power, which stabilizes a given structure of interactions through the relation of dominance of the commanding center over the asymmetric periphery. However, the relation of dominance is not absolute; it implies coercion and consent. As a consequence, hegemony in some instances leads to the introduction of equality, liberty and the rule of law in the overarching framework of relative dominance (see Chapter 4).

On the basis of the interplay between power and law, it is possible to observe how hegemony molds international law according to its inner dynamic. Hegemony, as an expression of power, tends to create hegemonic law. Hegemonic international law in this sense denotes those contents of international law under the preponderant influence of hegemony. But the reverse is also true. As shown before, law always re-acts and puts limits on any kind of power. Even though hegemony shapes international law, law restrains the drive of hegemonic power. Therefore, in the case of an encounter between hegemony and international law it is reasonable to speak of international law which bears the distinctive mark of hegemony.[1] Hegemonic international law may find expressions across many areas in international law. The aim of this chapter is to explore the various expressions and contents of hegemonic international law.

6.1 Hegemonic International Law

The expression *hegemonic international law (HIL)* comes from the American scholar Detlev Vagts.[2] Following the publicist Charles Krauthammer, Vagts understands HIL as

---

1 *See* N. Krisch, 'International Law in Times of Hegemony: Unequal Power and the Shaping of the International Legal Order', 16 *EJIL* 2005, pp. 369-408.

2 *See* Vagts's ground-breaking article: D.F. Vagts, 'Hegemonic International Law', 95 *AJIL* 2001, pp. 843-848. The expression hegemonic international law was consequently retaken by others. *See, e.g.,* J.E. Alvarez, 'Hegemonic International Law Revisited', 97 *AJIL* 2003, pp. 873-888 and A. Ramiro Brotóns, 'New Imperial Order or (Hegemonic) International Law?', 8 *Austrian Review of International and Comparative Law* 2003, pp. 25-34. For insightful contemporary analyses of the relationship between hegemony and international law from the Marxist and New Haven School perspectives, respectively, *see* R. Knox, 'Hegemony', *in* J. D'Aspremont, S. Sing & G.C. McBain (Eds.), *Concepts for International Law: Contributions to Disciplinary Thought,* Edward Elgar Publishing, Cheltenham-Northampton (MA), 2019, pp. 328-360 and C.J. Borgen, 'Whose Public, whose Order? Imperium, Religion and Normative Friction', 32 *Yale Journal of International Law* 2007, pp. 331-362.

a capacity to reshape norms, alter expectations and create new realities. He applies this pattern to the fields of the use of force (intervention), treaty law and customary international law.[3] According to Vagts, "the historical records shows that it can be convenient for the hegemon to have a body of [international] law to work with, provided it is suitably adapted."[4] Another contemporary scholar, Nico Krisch, enlightens encounters between hegemony and international law with insights from the discipline of international relations.[5] As an outcome of these encounters, he frames four strategies of hegemonic countries with regard to international law: (i) instrumentalization of international law; (ii) withdrawal from the international legal system; (iii) reshaping of international rules; and (iv) replacement with domestic law. Of the four strategies, the reshaping of international rules is the most frequent.[6] For Krisch, international law needs to adapt to demands of hegemonic powers so as not to be completely sidelined. At the same time, it must not bow to them completely because only in this way it can provide them with the legitimacy they seek.[7]

The idea of HIL has roots in the works of two German international lawyers, Heinrich Triepel and Wilhelm Grewe. Triepel wrote a book on hegemony which, after many decades, still remains one of the leading monographs on hegemony in international law.[8] Grewe, on the other hand, produced a historical survey of international law in which he demonstrated the prevailing influence of the hegemonic powers on the development of

3 *Cf.* Vagts, 'Hegemonic International Law', pp. 843, 845-848.
4 Ibid., p. 845.
5 Krisch, 'International Law in Times of Hegemony', pp. 369-408. *See also* N. Krisch, *Imperial International Law*, Global Working Paper 01/04, New York University School of Law and N. Krisch, 'More Equal than the Rest? Hierarchy, Equality and US Predominance in International Law', *in* M. Byres & G. Nolte (Eds.), *United States Hegemony and the Foundations of International Law*, CUP, Cambridge, 2003, pp. 135-175.
6 *See* Krisch, 'International Law in Times of Hegemony', pp. 381-407.
7 Ibid., p. 408.
8 *See* H. Triepel, *Hegemonie: Ein Buch von führenden Staaten*, Stuttgart, 1938. Hereinafter the reference is to the Italian version of this book: *L'egemonia*, Casa editrice Sansoni, Firenze, 1949, trans. G. Battino. For overviews of the book in English *see* Vagts, 'Hegemonic International Law', p. 844, C. Kruszewski, 'Hegemony and International Law', 35 *American Political Science Review* 1941, pp. 1127-1144, J.H. Herz, 'Review', 55 *Political Science Quarterly* 1940, pp. 600-602 and O. Jászi, 'Review', 34 *American Political Science Review* 1940, pp. 345-347. For biographical details on Triepel *see* M. Schmöckel, 'Ulrich Gassner and Heinrich Triepel', 11 *EJIL* 2000, pp. 744-745 and B. Fassbender, 'Stories of War and Peace: On Writing the History of International Law in the "Third Reich" and After', 13 *EJIL* 2002, pp. 496-498, 501-503. Triepel's book on hegemony is not free from controversy. In particular Schmöckel points to Triepel's alleged link with Nazism. Other authors, however, underscore Triepel's intellectual honesty and objectivity given the fact that the book was published during the Nazi era. A thorough reading of the book confirms these views.

international law.[9] Although both books deal primarily with historical dimensions of hegemony, their findings are important because they provide insights into the concept of hegemony and its impact on international law.

The studies of both, Triepel and Grewe are in the context of the relation between power and international law.[10] Triepel considers hegemony as an expression of power; every hegemony derives from the aspiration of power of an actor which already possesses some power and has the will to aggrandize that power.[11] Grewe maintains even more directly that every epoch of international law is an expression of power of the hegemonic state of that period.[12] Hegemony therefore develops on the basis of activities of the leading actor. According to Triepel the leading actor may comprehend either individuals or social groups (including states). Such an actor pulls forward the others and performs leadership or predominance.[13] Triepel establishes a distinction between the factual hegemony and the legal hegemony. Legal hegemony is an extrapolation of the factual hegemony and its confirmation in the legal field. It is, of course, not necessary for the factual hegemony to seek its legal confirmation. But in general it is true that the more hegemonic the status of a particular state, the more hegemonic is the nature of legal rules that deal with that state.[14] In this sense, legal hegemony represents legal confirmation of the hegemonic position and of hegemonic aims.[15] This is also in line with the contemporary views, which see hegemony as the striving for leadership or the institutionalized supremacy of some states over the others. This constellation of power then shapes international political order and international law in a given period of time.[16]

On the basis of the predominant powers, Grewe conceives the following epochs in the history of international law: the Spanish period, in which international law bore religious

9 *See* W.C. Grewe, *The Epochs of International Law*, Walter de Gruyter, Berlin-New York, 2000, trans. & rev. M. Byers. For the relevant book reviews and summaries, *see* Vagts, 'Hegemonic International Law', p. 844, C. Landauer, 'Book Review: Wilhelm Grewe, *The Epochs of International Law*', 16 *LJIL* 2003, pp. 191-201, M. Koskenniemi, 'Review', 51 *ICLQ* 2002, pp. 746-775 and Fassbender, 'Stories of War and Peace', pp. 479-512. As in the case of Triepel, reviewers point to the issue of Grewe's intellectual involvement with the Nazi regime and alleged influences of the work of Schmitt on Grewe's book. However, as Fassbender points out, Schmitt's influences are negligible. In addition, after the war Grewe had a prominent career in the diplomatic service of the democratic Germany.

10 More precisely, the approach of Triepel is interdisciplinary. In his study, he uses insights from sociology, psychology, history, public law and international law.

11 Triepel, *L'egemonia*, pp. 143, 186.

12 Grewe, *The Epochs of International Law*, p. 6.

13 *See* Triepel, *L'egemonia*, pp. 3-76 (leadership of an individual), 79-126 (leadership of a group) and 129 *et seq.* (leadership of a state).

14 *See* Triepel, *L'egemonia*, pp. XII-XIII, 218-219.

15 Ibid., pp. 216-217.

16 K. Ginther, 'Hegemony', *in* R. Bernhardt (Ed.), *Encyclopedia of Public International Law*, vol. 2, North Holland-Elsevier, London-Amsterdam, 1995, p. 685.

elements, the French period, with the preponderant influence of *raison d'Etat* in the form of absolute power, and the British period, marked by ideology of the 'universal' international law in the community of 'civilized' nations.[17] Thus, the intellectual and political style of the leading power of a particular historical period shapes international law of that time.[18] Similar are some contemporary approaches to international law. According to Phillip Bobbitt, history of international law develops in sequences following epochal wars. Each of these epochal or transformative wars leads to the establishment of a new constitutional order at the international level. But Bobbitt adds a military factor to the historical categorization. Winners of such epochal wars are those great powers that adopt innovative military strategies. In this sense, military strategies of the winning powers determine the contents of international law of their time.[19]

One of the most fundamental issues of HIL concerns the relationship between hegemony and the principle of equality of states. The standard answer to this issue is a blend of realism and idealism in the sense: "Of course states are unequal but, at least, they are legally equal."[20] However, from the standpoint of history of international law, in particular during the 'age of empire',[21] there were numerous scholars who braced the legal gradation of countries in the international community according to their factual weight and cultural influence.[22] The Scottish legal scholar James Lorimer even claimed that the equality of states is a baseless theory repudiated by history.[23] The scale was usually threefold, in the range from civilized states to barbaric communities. For example, Lorimer classified nations as civilized, barbaric and savage;[24] Franz von Liszt made a distinction between civilized, semi-civilized and uncivilized peoples or states;[25] Stelios Seferiades

17 From the contemporary perspective, it is possible to make a slighlty different historical periodization of international law. (*See* I. de la Rasilla, 'The Problem of Periodization in the History of International Law', 37 *Law and History Review* 2019, pp. 1-34.) However, the one made by Grewe remains most intellectually compelling for this study.

18 Grewe, *The Epochs of International Law*, pp. 23-24, 167 and Landauer, 'Book Review: Wilhelm Grewe, *The Epochs of International Law*', pp. 198-199.

19 *See* P. Bobbitt, *The Shield of Achilles: War, Peace and the Course of History*, Penguin Books, London, 2002, in particular pp. 23, 34, 67, 206-208, 335-336, 362, 813.

20 G. Simpson, *Great Powers and Outlaw States: Unequal Sovereigns in the International Legal Order*, CUP, Cambridge, 2003, pp. 38-39.

21 *See* E. Hobsbawm, *The Age of Empire: 1875-1914*, Vintage Books, New York, 1989.

22 *See* Simpson, *Great Powers and Outlaw States*, p. 122 *et seq.* and Koskenniemi, *The Gentle Civilizer of Nations*, p. 98 *et seq.*

23 J. Lorimer, *The Institutes of the Law of Nations*, William Blackwood and Sons, Edinburgh-London, 1883, vol. 1, pp. 44, 170-171. *See also* Simpson, *Great Powers and Outlaw States*, p. 124 and M. Koskenniemi, 'Race, Hierarchy and International Law: Lorimer's Legal Science', 27 *EJIL* 2016, pp. 421-424.

24 Lorimer, *The Institutes of the Law of Nations*, pp. 102, 156-160 and Abi-Saab, *Cours général de droit international public*, p. 56. For more on Lorimer *see* A. de La Pradelle, *Maîtres et doctrines du droit des gens*, Les éditions internationales, Paris, 1950, pp. 219-229 and the symposium "The European Tradition in International Law: James Lorimer", *in* 27 *EJIL* 2016, pp. 409-492.

25 Abi-Saab, *Cours général de droit international public*, p. 56.

wrote about civilized, semi-barbaric and savage states;[26] while Vladimir Hrabar used a more traditional division between great powers and smaller states.[27] The main repercussion of this gradation is that according to these scholars (with the exception of Hrabar) international law does not apply to 'uncivilized communities'; they enjoy only a partial recognition by international law or are left completely to the discretion (or mercy) of the members of the international community and their sense of (in)justice. Similarly, 'semi-civilized' communities are only partially recognized as subjects and only to the extent that they are linked to 'civilized countries' with treaties.[28] Hrabar, on the other hand, emphasized that solely great powers possess the capacity to solve big political issues and administer world affairs.[29] He saw a solution in the official proclamation of legal inequality in a newly established international organization in which the great powers would have the dominant, hegemonic role.[30] The work of these authors, marked by the era of imperialism, testifies that in historical terms international law can function as a tool to serve or endorse the imperialistic aims of great powers.[31]

However, smaller states did not agree with doctrines of domination of greater powers and continued to claim the position of equality at the international level. A conceptual breakthrough occurred at the Hague conference in 1907 where Latin American states, headed by the Brazilian delegate and politician Rui de Barbosa, proposed a solution in the form of the sovereign equality which was until then known and applied only in the American practice of international law.[32] In the Americas, the doctrine of sovereign equality was acceptable to the small, middle and the greater states alike. For small and middle states, it represented recognition of their equal status. For the greater state (the US) it stood for the recognition of its powerful position and a device to legitimize the

26 *See* T. Skouteris, *The Notion of Progress in International Law Discourse*, T.M.C. Asser Press, The Hague, 2010, p. 74 *et seq.*

27 *See* V.Z. Grabar (Hrabar), *Nachalo ravensta gosudarstv' v' sovremennom' mezhdunarodnom' prave* [The Principle of the Equality of States in Contemporary International Law], Izvestiya Ministerstva Inostrannyh del' [Bulletin of the Ministry of Foreign Affairs], St. Petersburg, 1912, vol. 1 and L. Mälksoo, 'The Science of International Law and the Concept of Politics: The Arguments and Lives of the International Law Professors at the University of Dorpat/Iur'ev/Tartu 1855-1985', 76 *BYIL* 2005, p. 453.

28 Abi-Saab, *Cours général de droit international public*, p. 56.

29 Grabar, *Nachalo ravensta gosudarstv' v' sovremennom' mezhdunarodnom' prave*, p. 4.

30 *See* ibid., pp. 20-22, 29, 36-37.

31 On the historical use of international law for imperialistic and colonial ends, *see* A. Anghie, *Imperialism, Sovereignty and the Making of International Law*, CUP, Cambridge, 2005, in particular pp. 13-195, P. Fitzpatrick, *Modernism and the Grounds of Law*, CUP, Cambridge, 2001, pp. 146-182, E. Jouannet, 'Universalism and Imperialism: The True-False Paradox of International Law', 18 *EJIL* 2007, pp. 379-407 and N. Berman, 'Les ambivalences impériales' and M. Xifaras, 'Commentaire', both *in* E. Jouannet & H. Ruiz Fabri (Eds.), *Impérialisme et droit international en Europe et aux Etats-unis*, Société de législation comparé, Paris, 2007, pp. 131-181, 183-209.

32 Simpson, *Great Powers and Outlaw States*, pp. 129, 133 *et seq.*

Monroe Doctrine.[33] In the end, the Hague conference signified introduction of this principle in the diplomatic discussions but not yet its formal acceptance.[34]

The principle of the sovereign equality came to the forefront towards the end of World War II, when the allied powers were preparing the plan for the new postwar order. In the Moscow Declaration of 1943, they recognized "the necessity of establishing at the earliest practicable date a general international organization, based on the principle of the sovereign equality of all peace-loving nations".[35] The preparatory proceedings on the Charter of the United Nations (UN) posited sovereign equality as one of the leading principles of the Charter and Organization.[36] In doing so the drafters succeeded in synthesizing two distinctly different notions of sovereignty and equality and hence the dual notion of this fundamental concept.[37] While the component of sovereignty embodies the notion of power,[38] together with its tendency for further growth, the notion of equality epitomizes the need for the equivalent position of states in legal terms (in terms of equality before the law).[39] The concept of sovereign equality embodies the inherent contradiction of international law according to which states exist side by side, while their individual weight differs according to their power. Despite this contradiction, the UN Charter posits the sovereign equality as one of its most fundamental principles, essential for the effective pursuit of purposes and aims of the Organization.[40] In this vein, Ian Brownlie considers the principle of sovereign equality as the basic constitutional doctrine of international law.[41]

Sovereign equality therefore oscillates between two poles: the accent on sovereignty and the accent on equality. The emphasis on the sovereign power is most visible in the dominant position of the permanent members in the Security Council (the power of veto) and in international financial institutions, such as the International Monetary Fund

33 Ibid., pp. 130-131.

34 *See* F.C. Hicks, 'Equality of States and the Hague Conferences', 2 *AJIL* 1908, pp. 530-561.

35 Joint Four-Nation Declaration, October 1943, Moscow, para. 4, http://avalon.law.yale.edu/wwii/moscow.asp.

36 K. Mbaye, 'Article 2, paragraphe 1', *in* J.-P. Cot & A. Pellet (Eds.), *La Charte des Nations unies : Commentaire article par article*, Economica, 1991 pp. 84-85 and Simpson, *Great Powers and Outlaw States*, p. 192.

37 *See* A. van Wynen Thomas & A.J. Thomas Jr., 'Equality of States in International Law: Fact or Fiction?', 37 *Virginia Law Review* 1951, p. 817 and Krisch, 'More Equal than the Rest?', pp. 138-140, 141, 149.

38 H. Kelsen, 'The Principle of Sovereign Equality of States as a Basis for International Organization', 53 *Yale Law Review* 1944, p. 208.

39 *See* H. Steinberger, 'Sovereignty', vol. 10, p. 412, J.M. Castro Rial, 'States, Sovereign Equality', vol. 10, pp. 477-480 and G. Arangio-Ruiz, 'Friendly Relations Resolution', vol. 9, p. 139, all *in* Bernhardt, *Encyclopedia of Public International Law*.

40 *Cf.*: "The Organization and its Members, in pursuit of the Purposes stated in Article 1, shall act in accordance with the following Principles: [/] 1. The Organization is based on the principle of sovereign equality of all its Members. ..." (Art. 2 of the UN Charter.). The most authoritative interpretation of the principle of sovereign equality is the so-called Friendly Relations Declaration, adopted in a resolution of the General Assembly No. 2625 (XXV) on 24 October 1970. *See also* Daillier & Pellet, *Droit international public*, pp. 425-426 and C. Warbrick, 'States and Recognition in International Law', *in* M. Evans (Ed.), *International Law*, OUP, Oxford, 2006, pp. 222-224.

41 Brownlie, *Principles of Public International Law*, p. 289.

(IMF) and the World Bank (voting rights). Some authors consider this to be an example of dominance or hegemony of the great powers.[42] On the other hand, the focus on the principled equality is most visible through its legal-formal character. In this sense, it denotes juridical capability of states to hold all rights and obligations in international law, notwithstanding any political, military, cultural, socioeconomic or other differences.[43] The principle of sovereign equality aptly resonates with hegemonic international law: the component of power allows for the growing influence of hegemonic countries, whereas the element of equality curbs the domination of greater powers over smaller states.

In 1979, the UN General Assembly adopted the resolution with an interesting title *Inadmissibility of the policy of hegemonism in international relations.*[44] This is the only official UN document addressing the issue of hegemony and international law. The resolution affirms the fundamental principles of the UN Charter: sovereignty; sovereign equality; national independence of States; nonintervention; and the prohibition of the use of force.[45] The General Assembly understood hegemony as

> a manifestation of the policy of a State, or a group of States, to control, dominate and subjugate, politically, economically, ideologically or militarily, other States, peoples or regions of the world[46].

The resolution reconfirms the condemnation of the coercive measures as manifestations of hegemony, however, it extends the scope of prohibition also to the policy of the block divisions; all forms of domination, subjugation, interference or intervention; all forms of pressure, including political, cultural and ideological; and the creation of spheres of influence.[47]

---

42 *See* Simpson, *Great Powers and Outlaw States*, pp. 147, 185-186, Krisch, 'More Equal than the Rest?', pp. 156-158, van Wynen Thomas & Thomas, 'Equality of States in International Law', p. 818, Castro Rial, 'States, Sovereign Equality', p. 480, Anghie, *Imperialism, Sovereignty and the Making of International Law*, pp. 258-272 and B.S. Chimni, 'International Institutions Today: An Imperial Global State in the Making', 15 *EJIL* 2004, pp. 1-37, in particular 2, 20.

43 Steinberger, 'Sovereignty', p. 412 and Castro Rial, 'States, Sovereign Equality', p. 477.

44 UN GA Res. A/34/103, 14 December 1979. Hereinafter, the term hegemony will be used instead of hegemonism, because it is grammatically more correct.

45 Ibid., preambular paras. 1, 2, 5.

46 Ibid., preambular para. 3.

47 Ibid., operative paras. 1-6.

Such a general condemnation of all forms of hegemony makes the resolution problematic.[48] There is no doubt that hegemony, if conducted through military means or coercive measures, is contrary to international law, notably to the purposes and principles of the UN Charter (Articles 1 and 2).[49] However, a sweeping condemnation of hegemony on the basis of the domination, political, economic, cultural or ideological pressure, and the spheres of influence – whenever these forms do not amount to coercion – is questionable.[50] This is not to say that such expressions of hegemony are free from controversy, but they are not necessarily contrary to international law.[51] One should judge the (in)admissibility of hegemony only on the basis of a thorough analysis of all relevant factors. Most often the conclusion would come on the basis of a case-by-case consideration.

This overview demonstrates that hegemonic powers have an important influence on the formation of international law that can vary in degree, ranging from empire to first among equals.[52] As hegemony resides amid the two poles, implying some coercion and some consent, such a blend usually applies also to international law.[53] Consistently with its power the hegemon tries to 'lay down the law', which means "that a hegemonic authority has the ability to influence the content of international law, especially in those areas that matter most for the exercise of such authority."[54] The hegemon's tendency to mold international law has a long-standing historical record.[55]

---

48 To evaluate the normative relevance of the resolution one must take into account other, nonlegal considerations. Although at first sight it seems that the resolution was initiated by the nonaligned movement (NAM), its true author was the Soviet Union. The resolution was directed against the hegemony of the United States and China, and their rapprochement at the time. (*See* A.V. Kozyrev, 'Politika gegemonizma – ugroza miru i mezhdunarodnomu pravoporyadku' [The Policy of Hegemony – A Threat to Peace and International Legal Order], 1982 *Sovetskoe gosudarstvo i pravo* [*Soviet State and Law*], pp. 85-86, 88-91.) However, not long after the adoption of the resolution, the Soviet Union launched a military intervention in Afghanistan. At a special session, the UN General Assembly strongly condemned the Soviet military campaign in Afghanistan. (*See* UN GA Res. A/ES-6/2, 14 January 1980.)

49 *See* Ginther, 'Hegemony', p. 688.

50 A similar assessment applies to the right of self-determination in the context of neocolonialism. *See* M. Hébié, 'Was There Something Missing in the Decolonization Process in Africa? The Territorial Dimension', 28 *LJIL* 2015, p. 535.

51 *See* A. Randelzhofer, 'Great Powers', p. 146, Steinberger, 'Sovereignty', p. 411 and H. Neuhold, 'Spheres of Influence', pp. 357-359, all *in* Bernhardt, *Encyclopedia of Public International Law*, vol. 9.

52 *Cf.* Vagts, 'Hegemonic International Law', p. 848.

53 *See* C. Tomuschat, 'Multilateralism in the Age of US Hegemony', *in* Macdonald & Johnston, *Towards World Constitutionalism*, pp. 33-34 and M. Mastanduno, 'Hegemony in International Law', 30 August 2016, *Oxford Bibliographies*, www.oxfordbibliographies.com/view/document/obo-9780199796953/obo-9780199796953-0141.xml.

54 R. Müllerson, 'International Law between Anarchy and Hegemony', *in* J. Petman & J. Klabbers (Eds.), *Nordic Cosmopolitanism: Essays in International Law for Martti Koskenniemi*, Martinus Nijhoff Publishers, Leiden-Boston, 2003, p. 226.

55 For comprehensive presentations, *see* Krisch, 'International Law in Times of Hegemony', Triepel, *L'egemonia* and Grewe, *The Epochs of International Law*.

Nonetheless, it has to be emphasized that even if international law falls under the influence of hegemony, it does not necessarily play a subservient role to it.[56] Legal rules can exert a role of restraining the growth of hegemony and there are many examples in which international treaties prohibited or impeded the occurrence of hegemony,[57] which points to the dialectical relation between hegemony and law. This is a refined restatement of the dynamics between power and law encountered previously. In this sense, the international law part in hegemonic international law may act as a restraint on hegemony. Consequently, hegemony and international law may be compatible.

Hegemony can be contrary to international law when dominance passes a certain threshold. That threshold is the threat of the use of force, the actual use of force, infringements of sovereignty, political independence and territorial integrity when these would violate the fundamental principles of international law. In this case we cannot speak of HIL, but of infringements of international law in general. However, if dominance does not surpass this threshold, even if it takes the form of ideological, economic or political pressure, hegemony does not need to be contrary to international law.

The hegemon may eventually have a temptation to completely disregard international law. Such an action would provoke the legitimacy crisis. One of the fundamental attributes of law is to provide legitimacy to those in power. If legitimacy is gone the rule of power comes to the forefront. But his state of play works only in the short term. In the long term, such an attitude leads to the collapse of the hegemon. No hegemon can rule by sheer force only.[58]

Apart from respecting the law and disregarding the law, the hegemon may also resort to the third option. Superficially, it may consent to the validity of international law, but in reality it uses it as an instrument for unilateral ends. However, in such a situation, international law loses its integrity and autonomy, leading to the abuse of international law. This is a phenomenon of the 'imperial legal overstretch'[59] whereby the hegemon distorts legal rules in the sense that its interpretation goes far beyond the normative meaning of the rule. The end result in such a situation is again a loss of legitimacy, which deprives hegemony of its consensual character and announces a turn to the rule by brute power.

56 *Cf.* D. Thürer, 'Hegemony', *in* R. Wolfrum (Ed.), *Max Planck Encyclopedia of Public International Law*, OUP, Oxford, 2012, vol. IV, pp. 777, 781.

57 Triepel, *L'egemonia*, pp. 221-222.

58 For an interplay between legitimacy and power, *see* Paulus, 'The War against Iraq and the Future of International Law', pp. 729-733.

59 This expression is inspired by Paul Kennedy's term 'imperial overstretch' in the context of his seminal study on the rise and fall of the great powers. Imperial overstretch denotes a situation in which the total sum of the hegemon's interests and obligations exceeds the country's power to defend them all at the same time. Imperial overstretch usually marks the end of hegemony of one power. (*See* P. Kennedy, *The Rise and Fall of the Great Powers: Economic Change and Military Conflict from 1500 to 2000*, Vintage Books, New York, 1989, p. 517.) In the context of this book, 'imperial legal overstretch' means an erroneous interpretation.

The only proper way that hegemony may use international law is through HIL. Hegemonic international law functions as a legal tool of hegemony, but at the same time it also works, paradoxically, as a counter-hegemonic device.[60] HIL is therefore a synthesis of the two phenomena.

6.2 Three Contemporary Models of Hegemonic International Law

The hegemonic pair of center and periphery in the international community assumes three different forms of appearance. Each of them is relevant in the context of contemporary international law and has a slightly different constellation. The classification of different international hegemonic models is based on the innovative work of Alejandro Lorite.[61] For the analysis of American doctrine on international law, Lorite devised a set of categories: the 'inner realm', the 'outer realm' and the 'sovereign border'.[62] The inner realm denotes the hegemonic center, the outer realm stands for the international periphery, whereas the sovereign border is a dividing line between the center and the periphery. The permeability of that border depends on the importance of sovereignty for the center. Different constellations of these components lead to the following three hegemonic models of international law: (i) nationalist model, (ii) rational choice model, and (iii) interventionist model.

In nationalist hegemonic international law model, there is a strong center (the inner realm), which is anchored in the strict understanding of sovereignty. In general, the center does not show much interest in the periphery and is mostly focused on itself. For that matter, the division between the inner realm and the outer realm is strong. The strong center is able to project its national law to the outer realm of international law. The center therefore understands international law according to its national perceptions. Therefore, the strong center is able to expand its contents into the outer realm, while the outer realm is not able to substantially influence the inner realm. In graphic terms this model looks as follows:

60 *Cf.* Krisch, 'International Law in Times of Hegemony', p. 408 and Krisch, *Imperial International Law*, p. 61.

61 *See* A. Lorite Escorihuela, 'Cultural Relativism the American Way: The Nationalist School of International Law in the United States', 5 *Global Jurist* 2005, Frontiers 5, Article 2, pp. 1-166 and A. Lorite Escorihuela, 'L'impérialisme comme produit dérivé : la doctrine internationaliste contemporaine aux Etats-Unis', *in* Jouannet & Ruiz Fabri, *Impérialisme et droit international en Europe et aux Etats-unis*, pp. 223-285.

62 Lorite, 'Cultural Relativism the American Way', pp. 24-25. Lorite understands the sovereign border as a hybrid concept between the inner and the outer realm, which has its own substance. (*See* ibid., pp. 38-41.) My understanding of the sovereign border is more instrumental in terms of a border between the two realms.

Nationalist Model

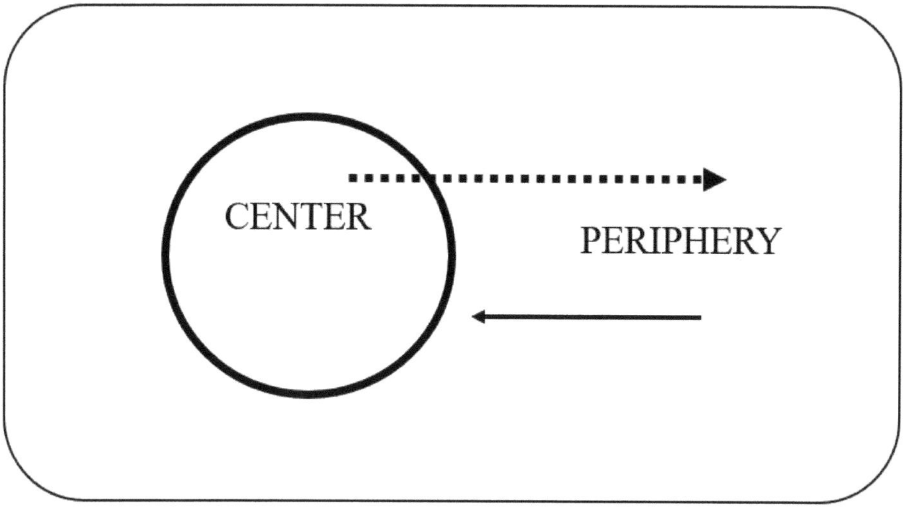

The next model is the rational choice theory model. Here the sovereign center remains strong. However, the sovereign border is more permeable. Again, there is a strong urge for dominance from the center that is tempered by the influence from the periphery of the center. The interaction occurs on the basis of the cost-benefit analysis of the hegemon. This means that the hegemon engages in cooperation with the periphery when it is in the interest of the hegemon and defects from the cooperation when it is not. Usually, this model applies when the hegemon participates in international regimes (treaties or organizations). Although interaction between the center and periphery is reciprocal, the influence of the center is much greater than that of the periphery. The scheme of this model is the following:

Rational Choice Model

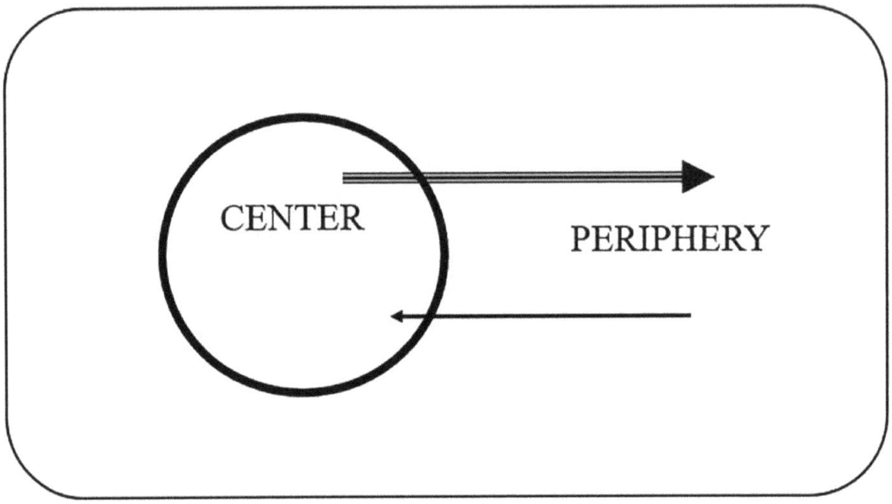

The final model is the interventionist model. In this constellation, the center does not confine itself to the national perspective, but instead focuses on the international perspective. The aim of the center is to intervene in the international realm. Three variants of the model can be distinguished: liberal, conservative and realist interventionism. As the name indicates, the three variants originate from a particular conceptual viewpoint: liberalism, conservatism or realism. All three viewpoints have an internationalist orientation through which they attempt to shape international periphery. Consequently, the sovereign border between the center and periphery is more flexible than in the two previous models. However, the influence travels in one direction only – from the center to the periphery. The influence of the periphery stops at the sovereign border. This border is therefore flexible only from the point of view of the center.

Interventionist Model

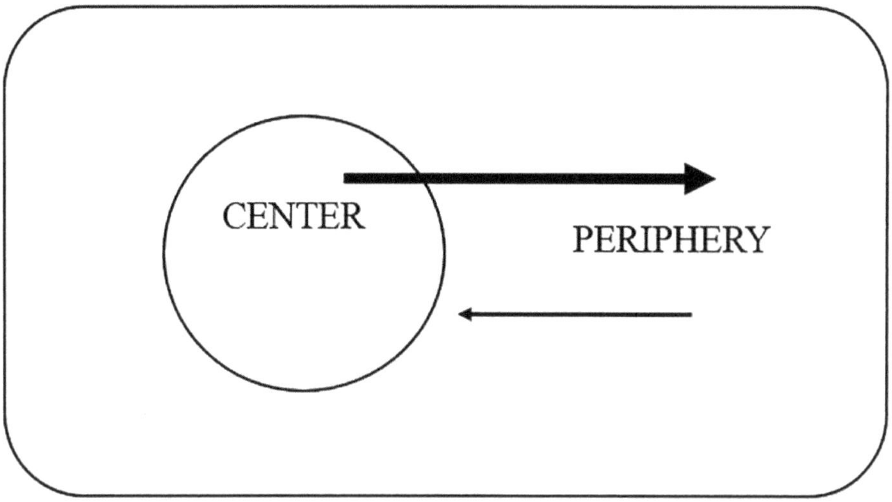

These are the three models of hegemony that occur in the contemporary international community. Due to their significant impact on international law they shall be examined in more detail below. Given their weight in international relations, the actions of the following international actors will feature in these hegemonic models: the United States of America, China, Russia and the European Union.

6.2.1 *Nationalist Model*

In conceptual terms, the nationalist model comes very close to what some authors termed as national perspectives of international law. The main idea behind national perspectives of international law is that states use law in order to promote their own interests.[63] One of the first scholars who devoted more attention to the consideration of this topic, Charles Rousseau, pointed out that national perceptions of international law tend to reflect aspirations and demands of a particular country in order to make international law suit that country's preferences.[64] The key issue for national perspectives on international law is the issue of sovereignty. Precepts of domestic sovereignty serve as a projection of national

63 J.-P. Cot, 'Tableau de la pensée juridique américaine', 110 *RGDIP* 2006, p. 593.

64 C. Rousseau, 'Les conceptions nationals du droit des gens', *in Mélanges offerts à Paul Reuter – Le droit international : unité et diversité*, Editions A. Pedone, Paris, 1981, pp. 441, 446.

political preferences at the international level. There can be various perspectives on national international law: French, Italian, Swiss, British, American and so on.[65] There can be as many national perspectives of international law as there are states. In essence, national perspectives of international law stand for the promotion of national interests in the framework of international law.

The nationalist model represents a step further from national perspectives of international law. The nationalist model subordinates international law to domestic law and interprets it through domestic, mainly constitutional law.[66] The main feature of the nationalist perspectives on international law is a strong dualism between the domestic and international legal system, which serves as a gatekeeper between the inner and the outer realm. Dualism is a tool that assures the impermeability of the sovereign border. Essentially, it ensures that international law does not enter the sovereign realm, or, when it does enter it, the 'intrusion' remains under the control of the center.[67] Often the hegemon would go even further in claiming that there is no law at international level and that the international dynamic is a subject not of law, but of politics.[68] In legal terms, two concepts have been developed that reflect the structure of the nationalist model of HIL. The first concept is that the sovereign center is exclusively or predominantly entitled to interpret international law in line with domestic law. Consequently, in case of conflict domestic law prevails over international law. The second concept is extraterritorial application or projection of hegemon's domestic law abroad. The law of the center is thus extended to regulate behavior outside the territory of the hegemon.

In the contemporary international community, we can identify three hegemonic countries that impose their nationalist perceptions of international law at the universal level: the United States, China and Russia.

---

65 *See* ibid., pp. 441-443. A similar development, albeit with a harmonizing tendency, in the contemporary doctrine goes in the direction of 'comparative international law'. *See* M. Koskenniemi, 'The Case for Comparative International Law', 20 *Finnish Yearbook of International Law* 2009, pp. 1-8 and A. Roberts, 'Comparative International Law? The Role of National Courts in International Law', 60 *ICLQ* 2011, pp. 57-92.

66 *Cf.* A. Bianchi, 'International Law and US Courts: The Myth of Lohengrin Revisited', 15 *EJIL* 2004, p. 774, D. Vagts, 'Treaty Interpretation and the New American Ways of Law Reading', 4 *EJIL* 1993, pp. 491-494 and R.F. Turner, 'American Unilateralism and the Rule of Law', *in* Macdonald & Johnston, *Towards World Constitutionalism*, pp. 99-101.

67 *See* Lorite, 'Cultural Relativism the American Way', pp. 34-35, C.A. Bradley, 'Breard, Our Dualist Constitution, and the Internationalist Conception', 51 *Stanford Law Review* 1999, pp. 529-566 and J. Rabkin, *Law without Nations? Why Constitutional Government Requires Sovereign States*, Princeton University Press, Princeton-Oxford, 2005, p. 258.

68 *See* Lorite, 'Cultural Relativism the American Way', pp. 38-39, 72.

6.2.1.1 United States

In the United States, it was initially the so-called neoconservative thinkers (also called the *neocons*)[69] during the George W. Bush administration that pursued the above arguments. The neoconservative thinkers derive their views from the preponderant power of the United States in international relations. Two most outspoken neoconservative lawyers are John Bolton and Jeremy Rabkin. Due to their preoccupation with the concept of sovereignty, they also gained the label of 'new sovereignists'.[70] Discussing the relationship between international law and the American constitution, they both give precedence to the US Constitution. Bolton says: "We should be unapologetic, uncompromising American constitutional hegemonists. International law is *not* superior to, and does not trump, the Constitution."[71] In a similar display of constitutional isolationism,[72] Rabkin contends that the power of making laws can never migrate from the constitutional framework to international authorities.[73] Both authors therefore favor American constitutionalist hegemony over international law. This approach assumes that the US national and cultural values are superior, which leads to extending the American way of doing things to other countries and cultures.[74]

In the context of the nationalist or sovereignist conception of international law a doctrine of the 'last-in-time-rule' needs to be mentioned.[75] The last-in-time-rule doctrine considers as valid a piece of law that was enacted at a later date.[76] In this sense this doctrine operates on the basis of a classical legal postulate *lex posteriori derogat legi priori*. However, as Andrea Bianchi points out,

---

69 On neoconservatism generally *see* J.F. Drolet, *American Neoconservatism: The Politics and Culture of A Reactionary Idealism*, Hurst & Company, London, 2011 and E. Drew, 'The Neocons in Power', 50 *The New York Review of Books* 2003, www.nybooks.com/articles/2003/06/12/the-neocons-in-power/.

70 *See* Lorite, 'Cultural Relativism the American Way', pp. 15, 21-22 and P. Spiro, 'The New Sovereignists: American Exceptionalism and its False Prophets', 79 *Foreign Affairs* 2000, pp. 9-15.

71 J. Bolton, 'Is There Really "Law" in International Affairs?', 10 *Transnational Law & Contemporary Problems* 2000, p. 48.

72 I. de la Rasilla y del Moral, 'Review Essay – Remarks on Post-Sovereignty and International Legal Neoconservatism: Reading Jeremy Rabkin', 8 *German Law Journal* 2007, p. 811.

73 Rabkin, *Law without Nations?*, pp. 266, 267.

74 R.B. Persaud, 'Shades of American Hegemony: The Primitive, the Enlightened, and the Benevolent', 19 *Connecticut Journal of International Law* 2004, p. 266.

75 Vagts, 'Hegemonic International Law', pp. 846-847 and Bianchi, 'International Law and US Courts', pp. 761-763.

76 Origins of this doctrine go back to the *Chinese Exclusion Case*, US Supreme Court, 13 May 1889, 130 US 581, p. 600. It was later reaffirmed in contemporary cases such as *Breard v. Greene, Warden*, US Supreme Court, 14 April 1998, 523 U.S. 371 (1998) and *Medellín v. Texas*, 25 March 2008, US Supreme Court, No. 06-984, 552 US 491 (2008).

> a closer look at the operation of the principle in practice … casts some doubts on the alleged equality of treaties and federal statutes as well as on the alleged neutrality of the last-in-time principle.[77]

As the US Supreme Court stated in the *Chinese Exclusion Case*: in the final end it is the expression of the American sovereign will that controls the validity of a legal provision, whether it is an international treaty or an Act of Congress.[78] Such a legal operation may result (and it often does) in a violation of an international treaty.[79]

In terms of legal outcomes, the sovereignist mind-set paved the way to the so-called 'torture memos'. The memos by government lawyers in the Bush Jr. administration John Yoo, Robert Delahunty and Jay Bybee are an exercise in the misinterpretation of international human rights standards that led to the worldwide ill-treatment of prisoners in the American 'war on terror'.[80] These memos venerate the constitutional sovereignty and unlimited powers of the US President in military operations, including the interrogation and treatment of prisoners. Under the US Constitution, the argument goes, presidential powers cannot be restricted by the Congress and hence the US legislation prohibiting torture does not apply.[81] Similarly, international law does not bind the US President. If he ever decides to apply international legal norms, their contents are up to his interpretation.[82] Legal advisers ended in dismantling essentials of the international protection against torture, as stipulated by the *UN Convention against Torture* (CAT) to which the

77 Bianchi, 'International Law and US Courts', p. 761. *See also* D. Vagts, 'The United States and Its Treaties: Observance and Breach', 95 *AJIL* 2001, pp. 313-321.

78 *Chinese Exclusion Case*, p. 600. For the defense of the last-in-time rule, *see* J. Ku, 'Treaties as Laws: A Defense of the Last-in-Time Rule for Treaties and Federal Statutes', 80 *Indiana Law Journal* 2005, pp. 319-390; for a criticism of the doctrine *see* E.S. Bremer, 'The Dynamic Last-in-Time Rule', 20 *Indiana International & Comparative Law Review* 2012, pp. 27-69.

79 Bianchi, 'International Law and US Courts', p. 763.

80 *See* A. Lewis, 'Introduction', *in* K.J. Greenberg & J.L. Dratel, (Eds.), *The Torture Papers: The Road to Abu Ghraib*, CUP, Cambridge, 2005, pp. xiii-xvi and D. Luban, *Legal Ethics and Human Dignity*, CUP, Cambridge, 2007, pp. 162-205. The US Senate report released in 2014 officially condemned the CIA's use of torture in the 'war on terror'; however, no legal sanctions followed so far. *See* Senate Select Committee on Intelligence, *Committee Study of the Central Intelligence Agency's Detention and Interrogation Program*, 13 December 2012.

81 *See* J. Yoo & R.J. Delahunty, 'Application of Treaties and Laws to al Qaeda and Taliban Detainees', 9 January 2002, p. 47, J.S. Bybee, 'Standards of Conduct for Interrogation under 18 U.S.C. §§ 2340-2340A', 1 August 2002, p. 200 and 'Working Group Report on Detainee Interrogations in the Global War on Terrorism: Assessment of Legal, Historical, Policy, and Operational Considerations', pp. 256-257, all *in* Greenberg & Dratel, *The Torture Papers*.

82 *See* Yoo & Delahunty, 'Application of Treaties and Laws to al Qaeda and Taliban Detainees', pp. 39, 52, 72-73, 77, 79 and J.S. Bybee, 'Application of Treaties and Laws to al Qaeda and Taliban Detainees', 22 January 2002, pp. 112-113, *in* Greenberg & Dratel, *The Torture Papers*.

United States is a state party. The sovereignist argument dispensed with the absolute prohibition of torture in any circumstances,[83] and drastically narrowed the understanding of torture to physical pain equivalent to that of serious physical injury (such as organ failure, impairment of bodily function, or death) and mental pain of significant psychological harm and duration (lasting for months or years).[84] The case of 'torture memos' demonstrates that the constitutional hegemonic logic, when pushed to the extreme, can lead to dramatic violations of international law.[85]

Another legal tool that exemplifies the nationalist international law model is extraterritorial legislation. This kind of legislation can produce effects outside a sovereign jurisdiction of one state in fields as distinct as antitrust matters, export controls, protection of environment, corporate governance and others.[86] These measures consequently override the power of the foreign territorial sovereign to regulate the same course of conduct.[87] Examples of extraterritorial legislation that stand out as hegemonic legislation are the *Helms-Burton Act* and the *Kennedy-D'Amato Act*, both adopted in 1996 by the US Congress.

The rationale of the Helms-Burton Act[88] has been to put additional political pressure on Cuba. The legislative history reveals that the US lawmakers openly understood this act

83 Bybee, 'Standards of Conduct for Interrogation', p. 209, n. 23. *But see* Art. 2, para. 2 of the UN Convention against Torture and Other Cruel, Inhuman or Degrading Treatment or Punishment, adopted by the General Assembly resolution 39/46 of 10 December 1984, entered into force on 26 June 1987. It seems that the Trump administration adheres to a similar interpretation regarding torture. (*See* H.H. Koh, *The Trump Administration and International Law*, OUP, Oxford, 2019, p. 34 *et seq.*)

84 Bybee, 'Standards of Conduct for Interrogation', p. 172. *But see* Art. 1 of CAT.

85 *See* critical examination of the US obligations under CAT by the Committee against Torture: *Conclusions and Recommendations of the Committee against Torture – United States of America*, 25 July 2006, CAT/C/USA/CO/2.

86 *See, e.g.*, R.P. Alford, 'Extraterritorial Application of Antitrust Laws: The United States and the European Community Approaches', 33 *Virginia Journal of International Law* 1992, pp. 1-50, A. Bianchi, 'Extraterritoriality and Export Controls: Some Remarks on the Alleged Antinomy between European and U.S. Approaches', 35 *GYIL* 1992, pp. 366-434, B.C. Lewis, 'It's a Small World after All: Making the Case for the Extraterritorial Application of the National Environmental Policy Act', 25 *Cardozo Law Review* 2004, pp. 2143-2187, D.F. Vagts, 'Extraterritoriality and the Corporate Governance Law', 97 *AJIL* 2003, pp. 289-294 and C.A. Bradley, *International Law in the U.S. Legal System*, OUP, Oxford, 2015, pp. 169-199.

87 Bianchi, 'Extraterritoriality and Export Controls', p. 373. In doctrinal terms, the extraterritorial legislation rests on the US jurisdiction to prescribe and its 'substantial effect' concept, as phrased in the *Restatement (Third) of the Foreign Relations Law of the US. The United States*, American Law Institute, Washington (DC), 1990, Sec. 402 (1) (c) (available through Westlaw).

88 Officially known as Cuban Liberty and Democratic (LIBERTAD) Act, adopted on 12 March 1996. However, application of the act has been waived by every US administration since it was passed. Interestingly, the Trump administration refrained from its suspension and for the first time made it fully effective in April 2019, which triggered lawsuits against companies dealing with assets nationalized or seized in Cuba. (*See* BBC, 'Helms-Burton Act: US Firms Face Lawsuits over Seized Cuban Land', 3 May 2019, www.bbc.com/news/world-us-canada-48113549.)

as an instrument of the political, social and economic transformation of Cuba.[89] It has a hegemonic feature in Section III, which institutes extraterritorial jurisdiction with regard to 'trafficking' in property confiscated by Cuba.[90] Consequently, any person in the world that engages in commercial activity touching upon confiscated property in Cuba that once belonged to American citizens, may be subject to a civil suit before the US court.[91] Thus, the primary aim of the act was to control the conduct of the foreign nationals and to impose a secondary economic boycott against Cuba.[92]

A similar law, the D'Amato-Kennedy Act, regulates behavior of persons who engage in economic relations with Iran.[93] The main purpose of this Act is to prevent foreign investments into the petrol and gas sector of the country that, according to the US, has been the sponsor terrorism and has a tendency to acquire weapons of mass destruction.[94] The D'Amato-Kennedy Act attempts at regulating foreign conduct under the threat of denial of American financial resources and trade possibilities on the US market. It also extends sanctions to the behavior of wholly foreign corporations with no ties to American business or property.[95] Similar to the Helms-Burton Act, the aim of the D'Amato-Kennedy Act is to impose a secondary boycott on foreign persons.[96] It is not surprising, therefore, that a number of scholars depicted both acts as imperialistic measures[97] or

89 *See* R.L. Muse, 'A Public International Law Critique of the Extraterritorial Jurisdiction of the Helms-Burton Act (Cuban Liberty and Democratic Solidarity (LIBERTAD) Act of 1996)', 30 *George Washington Journal of International Law and Economics* 1996-1997, pp. 208-209 and A.F. Lowenfeld, 'Congress and Cuba: The Helms-Burton Act', 90 *AJIL* 1996, pp. 422-425.

90 The use of the word 'trafficking' was problematic as its usual use was limited to trafficking in narcotics, its scope was very broad and there was no link between the value of property and the transaction. (*See* Lowenfeld, 'Congress and Cuba', pp. 425-426.)

91 Lowenfeld, 'Congress and Cuba', p. 426 and A. Reinisch, 'Widening the US Embargo against Cuba Extraterritorially: A Few Public International Law Comments on the 'Cuban Liberty and Democratic Solidarity (LIBERTAD) Act of 1996', 7 *EJIL* 1996, p. 550.

92 *See* Lowenfeld, 'Congress and Cuba', pp. 428-429 and B. Stern, 'Vers la mondialisation juridique ? Les lois Helms-Burton et D'Amato-Kennedy', 100 *RGDIP* 1996, p. 992.

93 The official name of this act is *Iran and Libya Sanctions Act*, signed on 5 August 1996. Subsequently Libya accepted some American demands and the Congress excluded it from the Act. (*See* K. Katzman, 'The Iran Sanctions Act', CRS Report for Congress, 12 October 2007, p. 3.)

94 *See* C.T. Graves, 'Extraterritoriality and its Limits: The Iran and Libya Sanctions Act of 1996', 21 *Hastings International and Comparative Law Review* 1998, pp. 717-719 and Stern, 'Vers la mondialisation juridique ?', pp. 980, 981.

95 *See* Stern, 'Vers la mondialisation juridique ?', pp. 984-985 and T.S. Dunning, 'D'Amato in a China Shop: Problems of Extraterritoriality with the Iran and Libya Sanctions Act of 1996', 19 *University of Pennsylvania Journal of Economic Law* 1998, pp. 186-187.

96 Dunning, 'D'Amato in a China Shop', pp. 186-187.

97 *See* M. Gibney & D.R. Emerick, 'The Extraterritorial Application of United States Law and the Protection of Human Rights: Holding Multinational Corporations to Domestic and International Standards', 10 *Temple International and Comparative Journal* 1996, p. 145, A. Gattini, 'Two Faces of Hegemony', 8 *Austrian Review of International and European Law* 2003, p. 54, and Stern, 'Vers la mondialisation juridique ?', p. 986.

made a conclusion that with these two pieces of legislation the US is trying to act as a world government.[98]

The practice of targeted killings, in particular with the remotely piloted aircrafts ('drones'), was a reflection of the hegemonic mentality of the Obama administration.[99] Recent data show that the number of targeted killings during the Obama administration increased dramatically in comparison with the Bush Jr. administration.[100] The number of drone strikes further increased during the Trump presidency.[101] In March 2019, Trump revoked the Executive Order adopted by his predecessor, which required intelligence officials to publish the number of civilians killed in drone attacks outside of war zones.[102]

The line of argument for the use of drones rests on the following elements: (i) the US is engaged in an non-international armed conflict with Al-Qaeda and associated terrorist groups; (ii) the United States is justified to use force against those members of the terrorist groups that represent a 'continuous' and 'imminent' threat to the interests of the United States; (iii) the United States has a right to use force against imminent threat under constitutional and international law; and (iv) the United States is under an obligation to comply with the laws of war when conducting such operations.[103] The domestic

---

98 Krisch. 'More Equal than the Rest?', pp. 136, 173.

99 *See* R. Singh, *Barack Obama's Post-American Foreign Policy: The Limits of Engagement*, Bloomsbury Academic, London, 2012, pp. xii, 18, 71.

100 C. Savage & S. Shane, 'U.S. Reveals Death Toll From Airstrikes Outside War Zones', *The New York Times*, 1 July 2016. According to official data as of July 2016, the US killed around 2.500 terrorists and 64-112 civilian bystanders in areas other than conventional war zones.

101 J. Haltiwanger, 'Trump Inherited Obama's Drone War and He's Significantly Expanded It in Countries where the US Is Not Technically at War', *Business Insider*, 27 November 2018, https://www.businessinsider.com/trump-has-expanded-obamas-drone-war-to-shadow-war-zones-2018-11.

102 BBC, 'Trump Revokes Obama Rule on Reporting Drone Strike Deaths', 7 March 2019, https://www.bbc.com/news/world-us-canada-47480207.

103 *See* Koh, 'The Obama Administration and International Law', Annual Meeting of the American Society of International Law, Washington (DC), 25 March 2010, https://2009-2017.state.gov/s/l/releases/remarks/139119.htm, E. Holder, 'Attorney General Eric Holder Speaks at Northwestern University School of Law', Chicago, 5 March 2012, www.justice.gov/opa/speech/attorney-general-eric-holder-speaks-northwestern-university-school-law, B.J. Egan, 'International Law, Legal Diplomacy, and the Counter-ISIL Campaign', American Society of International Law, Washington (DC), 1 April 2016, https://digital-commons.usnwc.edu/ils/vol92/iss1/7/, D.J. Barron, 'Re: Applicability of Federal Criminal Laws and the Constitution to Contemplated Lethal Operations Against Shaykh Anwar al-Aulaqi', US Department of Justice, Office of Legal Counsel, 16 July 2010, pp. 21, 25, 30, 39, www.aclu.org/files/assets/2014-06-23_barron-memorandum.pdf, 'Department of Justice White Paper: Lawfulness of a Lethal Operation Directed Against a U.S. Citizen Who Is a Senior Operational Leader of Al-Qa'ida or an Associated Force', pp. 1-3, 5, 7, 9, 15-16, www.justice.gov/sites/default/files/oip/legacy/2014/07/23/dept-white-paper.pdf and 'Presidential Policy Guidance: Procedures for Approving Direct Action Against Terrorist Targets Located Outside the United States and Areas of Active Hostilities', 22 May 2013, https://fas.org/irp/offdocs/ppd/ppg-procedures.pdf. *See also* Bradley, *International Law in the U.S. Legal System*, pp. 330-331.

legal basis for the practice of targeted killings is the Congress resolution *Authorization for Use of Military Force*[104] and the US Constitution.[105]

However, as many critics note, the above advocacy contains elements that challenge the established precepts under international law: (i) the protracted theater of the armed conflict is territorially unlimited; (ii) consequently, the application of the use of force is extraterritorial; (iii) extraterritoriality is problematic if in violation with the principle of sovereignty of other countries; (iv) the interpretation of the 'imminent threat' is very broad and left to the discretion of US officials in which domestic concerns prevail.[106] Although competent international bodies highlighted the need for the restrictive interpretation of international law that touches upon targeted killings, they nevertheless acknowledged that further consultations are needed to establish consensus about the applicable legal principles.[107] In this sense, the US official position is a blend of constitutional and international legal rules – with an anchor in the US domestic law – in which the national legal perspective dominates over the international one.[108]

The Trump administration is the most eloquent proponent of the nationalist or sovereignist model encapsulated in the slogan 'America First'. This approach is further extended to the rational choice model with an emphasis on national interests, as will be shown later. The US *National Security Strategy* (NSS) of 2017 describes the approach of the Trump administration as 'principled realism', which is "based upon the view that peace, security and prosperity depend on strong, sovereign nations that respect their citizens at home and cooperate to advance peace abroad."[109] Perhaps a more apt description of this approach would be 'pragmatic realism' as it recognizes the central role of power in international politics and reaffirms sovereignty of states and the pursuit of national interests.[110] Rather than taking principles and values as inspiration, pragmatic

---

104 S.J.Res. 23 – 107th Congress, adopted on 14 September 2001, Pub. L. No. 107-40.

105 *See* The White House, 'Remarks by the President at the National Defense University', 23 May 2013, www.whitehouse.gov/the-press-office/2013/05/23/remarks-president-national-defense-university, 'Department of Justice White Paper', pp. 2, 15, Barron, 'Re: Applicability of Federal Criminal Laws and the Constitution to Contemplated Lethal Operations Against Shaykh Anwar al-Aulaqi', p. 21, 'Presidential Policy Guidance', pp. 13, 17 and Holder, 'Attorney General Eric Holder Speaks at Northwestern University School of Law'.

106 *See, e.g.*, M.E. O'Connell, 'Unlawful Killing with Combat Drones: A Case Study of Pakistan, 2004-2009', *in* S. Bronitt *et al.* (Eds.), *Shooting to Kill: Socio-Legal Perspectives on the Use of Lethal Force*, Hart, Oxford & Portland (OR), 2012, pp. 263-291, Falk, *Power Shift*, pp. 44-71, 225-232, Bradley, *International Law in the U.S. Legal System*, pp. 330-331, R. Brooks, 'Drones and the International Rule of Law', 28 *Ethics & International Affairs* 2014, pp. 83-103 and ICRC, 'The Use of Armed Drones Must Comply with Laws', 10 May 2013, https://www.icrc.org/eng/resources/documents/interview/2013/05-10-drone-weapons-ihl.htm.

107 *See* UN GA, *Report of the Special Rapporteur on the Promotion and Protection of Human Rights and Fundamental Freedoms While Countering Terrorism, Ben Emmerson*, 11 March 2014, A/HRC/25/59 and UN GA, *Report of the Special Rapporteur on Extrajudicial, Summary or Arbitrary Executions, Christof Heyns*, 1 April 2014, A/HRC/26/36, pp. 20-22.

108 *Cf.* Bradley, *International Law in the U.S. Legal System*, p. 330.

109 The White House, *National Security Strategy of the United States of America*, Washington (DC), December 2017, p. 1 (hereinafter *NSS 2017*).

110 Ibid., pp. 4, 25, 55,

realism is driven by the pursuit of power in various international contexts.[111] In this dynamic, the US sovereignty and national interests are of primary importance.

A number of actions of the Trump administration are anchored in the sovereignist legal framework and projected on the international arenas. In April 2017 and in April 2018 the administration reacted to the use of chemical weapons against civilians by the Assad regime in Syria with a limited missile attack on the Assad forces (2017) and on manufacturing facilities in Syria (2018). However, the US abstained from providing any meaningful legal argumentation in support of these military actions.[112] With regard to the April 2018 intervention, the then Secretary of Defense James Mattis referred to the authority of the US President as military commander in chief under Article II of the US Constitution to defend national interests abroad.[113] For some scholars, this is not a valid legal authority for the strikes.[114] Other scholarly opinions range from manifest illegality to the exemption of unlawfulness due to humanitarian considerations (inspired by the law of state responsibility), as an emerging norm of customary international law.[115] Trump himself explained that the purpose of missile attacks was to establish a strong deterrent against the production, spread, and use of chemical weapons, which is a vital national security interest of the United States.[116] However, relying solely on national security interests to support missile strikes in Syria is not a valid legal justification for these actions.

In the economic field, the Trump administration imposed tariffs on steel (25%) and aluminum (10%) against a range of countries (Canada, China, Japan, Mexico, the EU and others).[117] As a basis, Trump invoked Section 232 of the Trade Expansion Act of 1962.[118] The relevant norm allows for the introduction of tariffs if an item is imported in the

111 *See* The White House, 'Remarks by President Trump to the 73rd Session of the United Nations General Assembly', New York, 25 September 2018, https://www.whitehouse.gov/briefings-statements/remarks-president-trump-73rd-session-united-nations-general-assembly-new-york-ny/.

112 Koh, *The Trump Administration and International Law*, pp. 128, 135.

113 US Department of Defense, 'Statement by Secretary James N. Mattis on Syria', 13 April 2018, https://dod.defense.gov/News/News-Releases/News-Release-View/Article/1493610/statement-by-secretary-james-n-mattis-on-syria/.

114 J. Goldsmith & O. Hathaway, 'Bad Legal Arguments for the Syria Airstrikes', *Lawfare*, 14 April 2018, www.lawfareblog.com/bad-legal-arguments-syria-airstrikes.

115 *See* blog posts by M. Milanović on EJIL: *Talk!*, www.ejiltalk.org, M. Schmitt & C. Ford, M. Lederman, A. Deeks, H.H. Koh, A. Henriksen and R. Goodman on *Just Security*, www.justsecurity.org and *Lawfare*, www.lawfareblog.com. For a more elaborate version of these arguments, *see* Koh, *The Trump Administration and International Law*, pp. 127-140 and M.N. Schmitt & C.M Ford, 'Assessing U.S. Justifications for Using Force in Response to Syria's Chemical Attacks: An International Law Perspective', 9 *National Security Law and Policy* 2017, pp. 283-303.

116 J. Kirby, 'Read Trump's Statement on Syria Strike: "They Are Crimes of a Monster"', *Vox*, 13 April 2018, https://www.vox.com/2018/4/13/17236862/syria-strike-donald-trump-chemical-attack-statement.

117 D.A. Irwin, 'Trade under Trump: What He's Done So Far – and What He'll Do Next', *Foreign Affairs*, 6 November 2018, sec. 'I Want Tariffs', https://www.foreignaffairs.com/articles/2018-11-06/trade-under-trump.

118 *See* S.T. Mercer & M. Khan, 'America Trades Down: The Legal Consequences of President Trump's Tariffs', 13 March 2018, www.lawfareblog.com/america-trades-down-legal-consequences-president-trumps-tariffs.

United States "in such quantities or under such circumstances as to threaten to impair the national security."[119] The administration specifically targeted China for unfair trade practices. Using Section 301 of the Trade Act of Act 1974,[120] Trump imposed tariffs of $50 billion worth on imports from China.[121] This move led to a series of counter tariffs from China totaling $110 billion and from the United States in the total amount of $250 billion.[122] Several rounds of trade talks were held between the United States and China and consequences of this 'tariffs war' are still to be seen.[123] It seems that the rationale behind tariffs against China is not merely short-term protection of the American economy but also an attempt at a longer-term restructuring and containment of the Chinese economy.[124]

The Trump administration exerts the sovereignist reflex with regard to the International Criminal Court (ICC) to which the United States is not a state party. As the Obama administration tried to reengage with the legal regime under the ICC, the reaction of the Trump administration is to block any activities of the ICC that would infringe upon US interests. In 2017, the ICC Prosecutor Fatou Bensouda opened an investigation in Afghanistan that could have included crimes committed by American soldiers during the American intervention after 2001.[125] John Bolton, the National Security Adviser in the Trump administration and an outspoken opponent of the ICC, heavily criticized the Court in a speech at the Federalist Society stating that it "unacceptably threatens American sovereignty and US national security interests."[126] Soon afterwards the Secretary of State Mike Pompeo announced that the United States shall withdraw or deny visas to the ICC personnel investigating possible crimes by US forces in Afghanistan with a further possibility to introduce economic sanctions them.[127] The ICC responded that it is an

119 *See* the amended and currently valid version: 19 U.S. Code §1862, Safeguarding national security, https://www.law.cornell.edu/uscode/text/19/1862. For Trump, economic security equals national security. (*NSS 2017*, p. 17.)

120 This provision may be used if foreign acts, practices and policies violate or are inconsistent with an international agreement or are unjustifiable and burden or restrict US commerce. (*See* W.M Morrison, 'Enforcing U.S. Trade Laws: Section 301 and China', 13 March 2019, *Congressional Research Service*, p. 1.)

121 Irwin, 'Trade under Trump', sec. 'Fighting China'.

122 Morrison, 'Enforcing U.S. Trade Laws', p. 1.

123 G. Davies, "China's New Trade Offer is Better than a Tariff War', 17 February 2019, *The Financial Times*, https://www.ft.com/content/b64a5c44-3034-11e9-8744-e7016697f225.

124 Irwin, 'Trade under Trump', sec. 'Fighting China'.

125 S. Tisdall, 'Trump Attack on ICC is the Unacceptable Face of US Exceptionalism', *The Guardian*, 10 September 2018, www.theguardian.com/us-news/2018/sep/10/trump-attack-on-icc-is-the-unacceptable-face-of-us-exceptionalism.

126 Al Jazeera, 'Full Text of John Bolton's Speech to the Federalist Society', 10 September 2018, www.aljazeera.com/news/2018/09/full-text-john-bolton-speech-federalist-society-180910172828633.html.

127 In April 2019, the United States revoked the entry visa of the prosecutor of the ICC Fatou Bensouda. Consequently, she cannot attend UN meetings in New York. (Reuters, 'U.S. Revokes ICC Prosecutor's Entry Visa over Afghanistan Investigation', 4 April 2019, www.reuters.com/article/us-usa-icc-prosecutor/u-s-revokes-icc-prosecutors-entry-visa-over-afghanistan-investigation-idUSKCN1RG2NP.)

independent and impartial institution and will continue its work 'undeterred' by US actions.[128]

6.2.1.2 China

As a growing major power and the anticipated hegemonic contender to the United States,[129] China is another country that falls in the nationalist model of HIL. The official foreign policy doctrine of China articulated these aspirations through concepts of leader states and, even more patently, the Chinese Dream.[130] Concrete expressions of Chinese hegemonic aspirations are most visible with regard to the maritime dimension and relevant territories: Taiwan, Senkaku (Diaoyu) Islands in the East China Sea, and Paracel (Xinsha) and Spratly (Nansha) Islands in the South China Sea. These territories belong to the so-called *First Ring* perimeter of the Chinese national security and represent core national interests of China.[131] In addition, China believes that territories of the East China and South China seas are rich in oil and gas reserves.[132] Arguments surrounding these issues are a classical example of the sovereign projection to the outer realm.

The legal picture of China is a complex one, given its distinct historical and civilizational development. Nonetheless, for contemporary China the principle of sovereignty is the fundamental postulate in international relations.[133] Reasons for insistence on nearly absolute sovereignty[134] derive from the longstanding Chinese imperial past that was abruptly put to end by numerically modest but militarily superior Western forces in the

---

128 Reuters, 'U.S. Imposes Visa Bans on International Criminal Court Investigators – Pompeo', 15 March 2019, www.reuters.com/article/uk-usa-icc/u-s-imposes-visa-bans-on-international-criminal-court-investigators-pompeo-idUSKCN1QW1ZH and ICC, 'Statement by the President of the Assembly, O-Gon Kwon, Reiterating Strong Support for the ICC', 15 March 2019, www.icc-cpi.int/Pages/item.aspx?name=pr1442.

129 *See* J.S. Nye Jr., *Is the American Century Over?* Polity, London, 2015, pp. 46-70 and J. Fenby, *Will China Dominate the 21st Century?*, Polity, London, 2014, pp. 101-126.

130 Xinhua, 'Xi Pledges "Great Renewal of Chinese Nation"', 29 November 2012, http://news.xinhuanet.com/english/china/2012-11/29/c_132008231.htm and Editorial, 'Xi Jinping and the Chinese Dream', *The Economist*, 4 May 2013, www.economist.com/news/leaders/21577070-vision-chinas-new-president-should-serve-his-people-not-nationalist-state-xi-jinping.

131 A.J. Nathan & A. Scobell, *China's Search for Security*, Columbia University Press, New York, 2014, pp. 3-4.

132 Ibid., p. 173.

133 *See* H. Xue, *Chinese Contemporary Perspectives on International Law: History, Culture and International* Law, AIL-Pocket, The Hague, 2012, pp. 32-33, 95-96, 256, S. Ogden, 'China and International Law: Implications for Foreign Policy', 49 *Pacific Affairs* 1976, pp. 31-36, 38, 47-48, H. Xue, 'Chinese Observations on International Law', 6 *Chinese Journal of International Law* 2007, pp. 84-86 and J. Wen, 'Carrying Forward the Five Principles of Peaceful Coexistence in the Promotion of Peace and Development', 3 *Chinese Journal of International Law* 2004, p. 365.

134 *See* Ogden, 'China and International Law', p. 48 and J. deLisle, 'China's Approach to International Law: A Historical Perspective', 94 *ASILP* 2000, p. 273.

nineteenth century. Until then, China had perceived itself as the 'central country' (*zhongguo*) of the Far Easter region and projected its power to other countries through concentric zones of influence (Sinocentrism).[135] The contemporary Chinese establishment sees this interruption as an anomaly in a longer perspective and is willing to resume its position in the world as a great power.[136]

The first turn to a more active role in the world occurred with the concept of 'harmonious world' proclaimed by Hu Jintao in 2005. According to Hu, the harmonious world leads to lasting peace and common prosperity.[137] However, important for the realization of the harmonious world order are leader states that help to formulate or refine a proper vision of the international system. China is seen to be such a state.[138] In 2012, Hu's successor Xi Jinping went further with the announcement of the 'Chinese Dream'. This concept is supposed to lead to "the great renewal of the Chinese nation, make the Chinese nation stand rock-firm in the family of nations, and make even greater contribution to mankind".[139] Hand in hand with the real power is also the intention of Chinese officials and scholars to exert more influence in international law.[140] These are signs of China aspiring to become "the bearer and driver of a new world, with which it will enjoy an increasingly hegemonic relationship."[141] An important expression of this attitude is the colossal Chinese initiative named *Belt and Road Initiative* (*BRI*).[142] While positioning China as the center of the world community, the purpose of the BRI is to establish unimpeded connections between China and the rest of the world to stimulate trade and economic relations. The tool for achieving such interconnectedness are massive infrastructure and investment projects (construction of highways, railways, ports and bridges) in numerous countries with generous Chinese financial support, which is usually forma-

135 *See* Z. Li, 'Traditional Chinese World Order', 1 *Chinese Journal of International Law* 2002, p. 25, M. Jacques, *When China Rules the World: The End of the Western World and the Birth of a New Global Order*, Penguin Books, London, 2012, pp. 82-116, 294-341 and T. Ruskola, 'China in the Age of the World Picture', *in* A. Orford, F. Hoffmann & M. Clark (Eds.), *The Oxford Handbook of the Theory of International Law*, OUP, Oxford, 2016, pp. 145-146.

136 Xue, *Chinese Contemporary Perspectives on International Law*, pp. 256-257, Jacques, *When China Rules the World*, pp. 526-535 and Fenby, *Will China Dominate the 21st Century?*, pp. 46-52.

137 J. Hu, 'Build towards a Harmonious World of Lasting Peace and Common Prosperity', Statement at the UN Summit, New York, 15 September 2005, pp. 4 *et seq.*, www.un.org/webcast/summit2005/statements15/china050915eng.pdf.

138 S. Yee, 'Towards a Harmonious World: The Roles of the International Law of Co-progressiveness and Leader States',7 *Chinese Journal of International Law* 2008, pp. 104-105 and S. Yee, 'Sovereign Equality of States and the Legitimacy of "Leader States"', *in* Macdonald & Johnson, *Towards World Constitutionalism*, pp. 763-772.

139 'Xi Jinping's Remarks to the Press', 18th CPC Congress, 15 November 2012, www.china.org.cn/china/18th_cpc_congress/2012-11/16/content_27130032.htm.

140 Chatham House, 'Exploring Public International Law and the Rights of Individuals with Chinese Scholars – Part 2', International Law Programme, 14-15 November 2014, London, pp. 2-3.

141 Jacques, *When China Rules the World*, p. 16. *See also* ibid., p. 583 and E.C. Economy, 'China's Imperial President: Xi Jinping Tightens His Grip', 93 *Foreign Affairs* 2014, pp. 87-91.

142 *See* 'Belt and Road Portal', https://eng.yidaiyilu.gov.cn/.

lized through legally nonbinding Memoranda of Understanding (MOU).[143] Although the updated strategy of the BRI refers to building 'a harmonious international community' and 'a global community of shared future',[144] the hegemonic push of China behind this initiative is patent.[145]

Concrete hegemonic tendencies have already materialized in China's dealings with the territories of Taiwan, Senkaku Islands, Paracel Islands and Spratly Islands. With regard to Taiwan, China persistently reasserts the 'One China Policy' according to which Taiwan would 'reunite' with the mainland China.[146] Taiwan, however, enjoys some attributes of an international entity.[147] The Taiwanese prefer a status quo between reunification with China and proclamation of independence of Taiwan, which was also an option for some political actors.[148] Annoyed by the growth of the pro-independence movement, China in 2005 resorted to the adoption of the *Anti-Secession Law* with extraterritorial effects.[149] The law uses the constitutional framework in that it refers to the Chinese Constitution, which in the Preamble stipulates that Taiwan is part of China and calls for the reunification of Taiwan with China.[150] The law unequivocally proclaims the 'Taiwan question' as China's internal affair, which allows for no interference from the 'outside'.[151] It goes on to

143 *See* A. Chatzky & J. McBride, 'China's Massive Belt and Road Initiative', 21 February 2019, *Council on Foreign Relations*, www.cfr.org/backgrounder/chinas-massive-belt-and-road-initiative, N. Rolland, 'Reports of Belt and Road's Deat Are Greatly Exaggerated: Don't Underestimate China's Resilience', 29 January 2019, *Foreign Affairs*, www.foreignaffairs.com/articles/china/2019-01-29/reports-belt-and-roads-death-are-greatly-exaggerated and A. Giuffrida, 'Italy and China in Plan for New Silk Road-style Trade Network', 23 March 2019, *The Guardian*, www.theguardian.com/world/2019/mar/23/italy-china-new-silk-road-belt-and-road-g7.

144 *See* Office of the Leading Group for Promoting the Belt and Road Initiative, 'The Belt and Road Initiative Progress, Contributions and Prospects', Foreign Languages Press, Beijing, 2019, sec. II, 2, 4, www.beltandroad.news/report_19832742. Lorenzo Zucca identifies certain constitutional elements in the BRI. (*See* L. Zucca, 'Two Conceptions of Global Constitutional Order', 19 September 2018, King's College London Law School Research Paper No. 2018-22, pp. 2, 6-10, https://papers.ssrn.com/sol3/papers.cfm?abstract_id=3188161.)

145 *See* DW, '"New Silk Road" and China's Hegemonic Ambitions', 15 May 2017, https://www.dw.com/en/new-silk-road-and-chinas-hegemonic-ambitions/a-38843212.

146 *See* 'Taiwan and the Question of Reunification of China', 2 *Chinese Journal of International Law* 2003, pp. 717-731, 'The One China Principle and the Taiwan Issue', 2 *Chinese Journal of International Law* 2003, pp. 732-746 and F.Y. Chiang, 'One-China Policy and Taiwan', 28 *Fordham International Law Journal* 2004, pp. 1-87.

147 For a balanced consideration of this issue, *see* A.H. Hsiao, 'Is China's Policy to Use Force against Taiwan a Violation of the Principle of Non-Use of Force under International Law?', 32 *New England Law Review* 1998, pp. 732-742 and L. Chen, 'Taiwan's Current International Legal Status', 32 *New England Law Review* 1998, pp. 675-683.

148 *See* K.M. Campbell & D.J. Mitchell, 'Crisis in the Taiwan Strait?', 80 *Foreign Affairs* 2001, pp. 14-39, M.D. Swaine, 'Trouble in Taiwan', 83 *Foreign Affairs* 2004, pp. 39-49 and R.S. Ross, 'Taiwan's Fading Independence Movement', 85 *Foreign Affairs* 2006, pp. 141-148.

149 The law was adopted by the National People's Congress on 14 March 2005. For the text, *see* 'Anti-Secession Law', 4 *Chinese Journal of International Law* 2005, pp. 461-463.

150 K. Zou, 'Governing the Taiwan Issue in Accordance with Law: An Essay on China's Anti-Secession Law', 4 *Chinese Journal of International Law* 2005, p. 456.

151 Art. 3, para. 2.

enumerate a number of confidence-building measures and elements for the achievement of peaceful reunification through consultations and negotiations.[152] Finally, Article 8 prescribes the use of non-peaceful measures if the Taiwanese leadership would opt for secession from China or if possibilities for a peaceful reunification would be completely exhausted.[153] The key effect of this law is that it extends Chinese constitutional sovereignty, with the threat of the use of military means, to Taiwan and formally subsumes it to the Chinese legal order. Such a military option can be seen as contrary to international law[154] and it is understandable that Taiwan objected to this hegemonic measure.[155]

On the basis of historical factors China projected its sovereignty over remote islands in East China and South China Seas using domestic maritime and air space legal measures. In 1992 China adopted the *Law Concerning the Territorial Sea and the Contiguous Zone*, which listed the Senkaku, Paracel and Spratly Islands as sovereign territory of China.[156] The characteristics of the three respective island groups are different, although they are all subject to competing claims of several adjacent countries. Japan exercises effective control over the Senkaku islands and a number of elements speak in favor of Japanese sovereignty over this group of islands.[157] However, in 2013 China declared an air defense identification zone (ADIZ) in East China Sea.[158] While ADIZ is a permissible instrument under international law,[159] the Chinese proclamation is problematic for two reasons. Firstly, the East China Sea ADIZ included the Senkaku islands in its ambit,[160] which means that China again resorted to the extraterritorial legal regulation. In explaining the announcement of the ADIZ, the Chinese government said that the zone "aims at

152 *See* Arts. 6 and 7.

153 *See* Art. 8, para. 1. *See also* Art. 2.

154 Hsiao, 'Is China's Policy to Use Force against Taiwan a Violation of the Principle of Non-Use of Force under International Law?', p. 742 and D.L. Dupree, 'The Potential Costs of Capitalism: Why China's Market Economy is at the Root of its Anti-secession Law', 6 *Washington University Global Studies Law Review* 2007, pp. 405, 412, 419.

155 Zou, 'Governing the Taiwan Issue in Accordance with Law', p. 459.

156 *See* Art. 2, para. 2, www.un.org/depts/los/LEGISLATIONANDTREATIES/PDFFILES/CHN_1992_Law.pdf.

157 *See, e.g.*, M. Asada, 'Diaoyu/Senkaku Islands', *in* Wolfrum, *Max Planck Encyclopedia of Public International Law*, vol. III, pp. 90 *et seq.*, C. Ramos-Mrosovsky, 'International Law's Unhelpful Role in the Senkaku Islands', 29 *University of Pennsylvania Journal of International Law* 2008, pp. 903-946 and M.H. Loja, 'Status Quo Post Bellum and the Legal Resolution of the Territorial Dispute between China and Japan over the Senkaku/Diaoyu Islands', 27 *EJIL* 2016, pp. 979-1004.

158 The legal basis for the proclamation is Chinese domestic legislation: the *Law on National Defense*, the *Law on Civil Aviation* and the *Basic Rules on Flight*. (*See* Xinhua, 'China Exclusive: Defense Ministry Spokesman Responds to Air Defense Identification Zone Questions', 23 November 2015, http://news.xinhuanet.com/english/china/2013-11/23/c_132912145.htm.) *See also* M. Green *at al.*, 'Counter-coercion Series: East China Sea Air Defense Identification Zone', 13 June 2017, *Asia Maritime Transparency Initiative* <https://amti.csis.org/counter-co-east-china-sea-adiz/>.

159 *See, e.g.*, P.A. Dutton, 'Caelum Liberam: Air Defense Identification Zone Outside Sovereign Airspace', 103 *AJIL* 2009, pp. 1-19 and R. Almond, 'Clearing the Air Above the East China Sea: The Primary Elements of Aircraft Defense Identification Zones,' 7 *Harvard National Security Journal* 2016, pp. 126-198.

160 BBC News, 'China Establishes "Air-Defence Zone" over East China Sea', 23 November 2013, www.bbc.com/news/world-asia-25062525.

protecting its state sovereignty and territorial and airspace security, and maintaining flying orders."[161] Secondly, rules that regulate the East China Sea ADIZ envisage, apart from information gathering, the use of military measures also if an aircraft in the zone does not comply with instructions of Chinese authorities (Ministry of Defense).[162] This is in stark contrast with ADIZ rulebooks of other countries which focus on information gathering measures, not military ones.[163] Chinese measure on ADIZ is thus another example of hegemonic legal regulation most likely to bring insecurity in the skies above East China Sea, rather than security and order.

As mentioned in the preceding text, China considers Paracel and Spratly Islands in the South China Sea as the sovereign territory of China. However, territorial claims of China conflict with other coastal states in that region: Vietnam, Philippines, Brunei and Malaysia.[164] China's claims in this region are based on an ambiguous concept of 'nine-dash line', inspired by the map drawn in 1948, which China started referring to in international affairs only in 2009.[165] The nine-dash line projects Chinese maritime interests well into the South China Sea and it interferes with maritime zones of other coastal states. The official interpretation is that the line represents a historic title of China to maritime resources in the South China Sea.[166] However, its legal value under the contemporary law of the sea is highly questionable.[167] Chinese reliance on the nine-dash line as a legal argument seems to be in correlation with its ambition to become a great maritime nation and exercise regional hegemony in the South China Sea.[168]

---

161 'China Exclusive: Defense Ministry Spokesman Responds to Air Defense Identification Zone Questions'.

162 *Cf.*: "China's armed forces will adopt defensive emergency measures to respond to aircraft that do not cooperate in the identification or refuse to follow the instructions." (Xinhua, 'Announcement of the Aircraft Identification Zone of the P.R.C.', 23 November 2013, http://news.xinhuanet.com/english/china/2013-11/23/c_132911634.htm.)

163 J. Lee, 'China's Declaration of an Air Defense Identification Zone in the East China Sea: Implications for Public International Law', 17 *ASIL Insights* 2014, www.asil.org/insights/volume/18/issue/17/china's-declaration-air-defense-identification-zone-east-china-sea.

164 *See* C.R. Symmons, 'Maritime Zones from Islands and Rocks', *in* S. Jayakumar *et al.* (Eds.), *The South China Sea Disputes and Law of the Sea*, Edward Elgar, Cheltenham-Northampton (MA), 2014, pp. 60-61, S. Talmon & B.B. Jia (Eds.), *The South China Sea Arbitration: A Chinese Perspective*, Hart Publishing, Oxford-Portland (OR), 2014, p. 2 and P. Strupp, 'Spratly Islands', *in* Wolfrum, *Max Planck Encyclopedia of Public International Law*, vol. IX, p. 448 *et seq.*

165 *See* T.L. McDorman, 'Rights and Jurisdiction over Resources in the South China Sea: UNCLOS and the "nine-dash line"', *in* Jayakmar *et al.*, *The South China Sea Disputes and Law of the Sea*, pp. 145-149 and Z. Gao & B.B. Jia, 'The Nine-Dash Line in the South China Sea: History, Status and Implications', 107 *AJIL* 2013, pp. 100-108.

166 *See* Gao & Jia, 'The Nine-Dash Line in the South China Sea', pp. 108-124.

167 *See* F. Dupuy & P.-M. Dupuy, 'A Legal Analysis of China's Historic Rights Claim in the South China Sea', 107 *AJIL* 2013, pp. 124-141.

168 K. Morton, 'China's Ambition in the South China Sea: Is a Legitimate Maritime Order Possible?', 92 *International Affairs* 2016, pp. 910-911, 932 and H.W. French, 'What's Behind Beijing's Drive to Control the South China Sea?' *The Guardian*, 28 July 2015, www.theguardian.com/world/2015/jul/28/whats-behind-beijings-drive-control-south-china-sea-hainan.

Already in 2002 countries of the Association of South East Asian Nations (ASEAN) and China signed a *Declaration on the Conduct of Parties in the South China Sea*, stipulating that the "Parties undertake to exercise self-restraint in the conduct of activities that would complicate or escalate disputes and affect peace and stability" in the South China Sea.[169] Nonetheless, tensions kept growing in particular after China started fortifying maritime features (rocks and reefs) in the Spratly Islands that fall within the alleged Exclusive Economic Zone (EEZ) of the Philippines.[170] In 2013, the Philippines decided to launch an arbitration procedure against China before the Permanent Court of Arbitration (PCA), in line with the *UN Convention on the Law of the Sea* (UNCLOS).[171] Although China, as a State Party to the UNCLOS, was obliged to participate in the arbitration, it declined to take part in it.[172] The arbitral tribunal continued with the proceedings and issued an award that significantly curtailed China's claims in the South China Sea. The tribunal stripped the 'nine dash line' of any legal meaning under the contemporary law of the sea.[173] In addition, it classified several maritime features under China's control either as rocks or low-tide elevations, which effectively cancels out Chinese claims to extensive maritime zones (EEZ and Continental Shelf) in the South China Sea.[174] The tribunal also condemned China's construction works on these maritime features on ecological grounds.[175] The judgment of the tribunal is valid *inter partes* and applies only to the Spratly islands. However, the argumentation adopted therein will have repercussions in the whole South China Sea (including the Paracel islands).[176] The straightforward judgment of the arbitral tribunal serves as a prime example of how international law can limit excessive and speculative aspirations of a hegemonic country. Nonetheless, given that China refused the arbitral award and continues with a military build-up in the

169 Art. 5, http://asean.org/?static_post=declaration-on-the-conduct-of-parties-in-the-south-china-sea-2. *See also* Xue, *Chinese Contemporary Perspectives on International Law*, pp. 241-243.

170 *See, e.g.*, J. Borger & T. Phillips, 'How China's Artificial Islands Led to Tension in the South China Sea', *The Guardian*, 27 October 2015, www.theguardian.com/world/2015/oct/27/tensions-and-territorial-claims-in-the-south-china-sea-the-guardian-briefing. Another conflict worth mentioning is the intrusive drilling by the Chinese oil rig Haiyang Shiyou 981 in the EEZ and Continental Shelf of Vietnam in May 2014. *See* V. Hai Dang, 'Disputes between Vietnam and China in the South China Sea: A Legal Analysis', *in* M. Hiebert *et al.* (Eds.), *Perspectives on the South China Sea: Diplomatic, Legal and Security Dimensions of the Dispute*, CSIS, Rowman & Littlefield, Lanham, 2014, pp. 35-43,

171 For a summary of legal issues of the case, *see* R.C. Beckman, 'The *Philippines v. China* Case and the South China Sea Disputes', *in* J. Huang & A. Billo (Eds.), *Territorial Disputes in the South China Sea: Navigating Rough Waters*, Palgrave MacMillan, Houndmills, 2015, pp. 54-65.

172 For the Chinese position, *see* 'Position Paper of the Government of the People's Republic of China on the Matter of Jurisdiction in the South China Sea Arbitration Initiated by the Republic of the Philippines', 7 December 2014, www.fmprc.gov.cn/mfa_eng/zxxx_662805/t1217147.shtml.

173 *South China Sea Arbitration: Philippines v. China*, Award, PCA Case No. 2013-19, 12 July 2016, para. 278.

174 *See South China See Arbitration Award*, paras. 305-648.

175 *See* ibid., paras. 976-992, 1181 and T. Davenport, 'Island Building in the South China Sea: Legality and Limits', 8 *Asia Journal of International Law* 2018, pp. 89-90.

176 H.D. Phan & L.N. Nguyen, 'The South China Sea Arbitration: Bindingness, and Compliance with UNCLOS Dispute Settlement Decisions', 8 *Asia Journal of International Law* 2018, p. 49.

South China Sea,[177] a more stable solution among coastal and other countries will have to be found, probably with the use of diplomatic means.[178]

6.2.1.3 Russia

As the principal successor state of the former Soviet Union and the world's biggest country, Russia has become more assertive in international affairs in the past decade. Many scholars describe Russia's international assertiveness after the Cold War as postimperial or newly imperial.[179] Traditionally, Russia – whether in the form of the Tzarist Russia, the leading part in the Soviet Union or the Russian Federation – has been oscillating between two civilizational traditions: the European and the Eurasian one. Although at the end of the Cold War it seemed that Russia would get closer to the European tradition, recent developments attest that Putin's Russia is leaning towards Eurasia.[180] In geopolitical terms, the Eurasian perspective presupposes a strong Russia, anchored in the Eurasian continental plateau, with a strong influence in its zones of influence, for example, neighboring states that used to be part of the former Soviet Union.[181] This perspective "reflects Russia's overarching concerns over security, defense of its borders, and the desire for international prestige."[182]

In this respect, one of the most important tools is the concept of the 'Russian World' (*Russkiy mir*). Initially, the Russian World Foundation was created by President Putin's decree to promote the Russian language as "a significant aspect of Russia and world culture".[183] Gradually, the role of the Russian World extended from the linguistic to the spatial dimension. According to Putin, the

177 Reuters, '"Give Them a Bloody Nose": Xi Pressed for Harder South China Sea Response', 31 July 2016, www.reuters.com/article/us-southchinasea-ruling-china-insight-idUSKCN10B10G.

178 *See* Phan & Nguyen, 'The South China Sea Arbitration', p. 50 and M. Rapp-Hooper, 'Parting the South China Sea: How to Uphold the Rule of Law', 95 *Foreign Affairs* 2016, www.foreignaffairs.com/articles/china/2016-07-22/parting-south-china-sea.

179 *See* A. Grigas, *Beyond Crimea: The New Russian Empire*, Yale University Press, New Haven-London, 2016, M. Kalb, *Imperial Gamble: Putin, Ukraine and the New Cold War*, The Brookings Institution, Washington (DC), 2015 and D. Trenin, *Post-imperium: A Eurasian Story*, Carnegie Endowment for International Peace, Washington (DC), 2011. Trenin's analysis is somewhat contradictory. While he labels Russia's behavior as past imperial, his findings portray Russia as a great power, which falls in the discourse of imperialism (*see* Trenin, *Post-imperium*, pp. 13, 37, 86, 231).

180 *See* Trenin, *Post-imperium*, pp. 13-38, 73, A. Lukin, 'What the Kremlin Is Thinking: Putin's Vision for Eurasia', 93 *Foreign Affairs* 2014, pp. 85-93 and L. Mälksoo, *Russian Approaches to International Law*, OUP, Oxford, 2015, pp. 161-167.

181 *See* Trenin, *Post-imperium*, pp. 33, 36-37, 86-87, 209.

182 Borgen, 'Whose Public, whose Order?', p. 347.

183 Decree by the President of the Russian Federation on the Establishment of the Ruskiy mir Foundation', No. 796, 21 June 2007, https://russkiymir.ru/en/fund/decree.php.

> Russian language not only preserves an entire layer of truly global achievements but is also the living space for the many millions of people in the Russian-speaking world, a community that goes far beyond Russia itself.[184]

This civilizational reorientation of Russia also influenced the Russian legal tradition. With the role of the universalist-globalist school diminishing, the traditional sovereignist school now exercises a predominant influence on the Russian thinking about international law.[185]

The most eloquent exposition of the sovereignist stance appeared in the 2015 judgment of the Russian Constitutional Court on the enforceability of judgments of the European Court of Human Rights (ECtHR).[186] As Russia is a contracting party of the European Convention for Human Rights (ECHR), these judgments are binding upon it by virtue of Article 46 of the ECHR. The Russian Constitutional Court characterized principles of sovereign equality and noninterference in internal affairs of states as *jus cogens* norms.[187] This is a questionable interpretation, given that the mentioned categories are structural principles of the international community, whereas *jus cogens* rules have the quality of norms (rules).[188] The Russian Constitutional Court went on to explore the possibility of a conflict between the judgment of the ECtHR and the Russian Constitution. Should such a normative conflict occur, the Constitutional Court held the constitutional norms would have supremacy over the ECtHR judgment. It would be up to the Constitutional Court to examine the alleged conflict and rule on the (non)enforceability of the ECtHR judgment.[189] This line of argument was later translated into amendments to the Federal Constitutional Law on the Constitutional Court, adopted by the Russian Duma on 15 December 2015. In the case of an apparent collision between the ECtHR judgment and the Russian Constitution, the law stipulates that competent state organs must turn to the Constitutional Court for a final decision.[190] Dilemmas described in the preceding text fall within the so-called 'dialogue of judges', a practice that evolved be-

---

184 https://russkiymir.ru/en/fund/index.php.

185 R. Tkatova, 'Russian Spirit, Soviet Heritage and Western Temptation: "Un-'Peaceful Coexistence'" in Russia's International Doctrine and Practice', 12 *BaYIL* 2012, pp. 11-16, Mälksoo, *Russian Approaches to International Law*, pp. 121-127, 137-138, 143 and Trenin, *Post-imperium*, p. 34.

186 Judgment of the Russian Constitutional Court on the case concerning the review of constitutionality of Art. 1 of the Convention for the Protection of Human Rights and Fundamental Freedoms and Protocols thereto, 14 July 2015, No. 21-P/2015, available in Russian at: http://doc.ksrf.ru/decision/KSRFDecision201896.pdf.

187 Ibid., pp. 13-14. *See also* L. Mälksoo, 'Russia's Constitutional Court Defies the European Court of Human Rights', 12 *European Constitutional Law Review* 2016, p. 381.

188 *See* Charter of the United Nations, Art. 2(1)(7) (1 UNTS XVI) and VCLT, Art. 53.

189 *See* Judgment of the Russian Constitutional Court, 14 July 2015, in particular pp. 15, 24-25, 27-28 and M. Smirnova, 'Russian Constitutional Court Affirms Russian Constitution's Supremacy over ECtHR Decisions', EJIL: *Talk!*, 15 July 2015, www.ejiltalk.org/russian-constitutional-court-affirms-russian-constitutions-supremacy-over-ecthr-decisions/.

190 Amendments to the Federal Constitutional Law on the Constitutional Court of the Russian Federation, 14 December 2015, www.venice.coe.int/webforms/documents/default.aspx?pdffile=CDL-REF(2016)006-e.

tween international and highest national courts. The end result of such an argumentative process is usually a solution that is acceptable to all principal judicial authorities.[191]

However, the solution embedded in the Russian Constitutional Law is more robust in the sense that it puts down an institutionalized mechanism and procedure, according to which judgments of the ECtHR could be declared unenforceable in Russia.[192] The Venice Commission criticized such a solution, in particular the power to declare the whole ECtHR judgment unenforceable, as potentially contrary to international law and called upon the Russian Duma to amend it accordingly.[193] Nevertheless, as the Russian Constitutional Court already passed a judgment on the unenforceability of a specific ECtHR judgment,[194] it seems that the sovereignist mentality put a strong imprint on the Russian legal system.

The most visible expression of the Russian hegemony comes out of its activities connected to the territorial issues in the Arctic Sea, Georgia and Ukraine. The melting of Arctic ice is opening up the transport possibilities through the Northern Passage, which in 2007 prompted the Russian exploratory submarine to plant the Russian titanium flag on the seabed beneath the North Pole.[195] This move, which many portrayed as a reminiscence of the fifteenth century land-grab imperialism, is based on the Russian claims to the Continental Shelf adjacent to the Russian EEZ in the Arctic Ocean.[196] Russia filed several claims with the UN Commission on the Limits of Continental Shelf, which functions on the basis of UNCLOS as the authoritative body on the delimitation of the Continental Shelf.[197] There is no doubt that Russia is entitled to the Continental Shelf in the

191 Probably the best known example of such a dialogue is between the German Constitutional Court and the European Court of Justice in so-called *Solange* cases. For an overview of a judicial dialogue in the context of the ECHR *see* Venice Commission, 'Interim Opinion on the amendments to the Federal Constitutional Law on the Constitutional Court of the Russian Federation', 13 June 2016, CDL-AD(2016)005, pp. 17-19.

192 *Cf.* Mälksoo, 'Russia's Constitutional Court Defies the European Court of Human Rights', p. 394,

193 Venice Commission, 'Russian Federation – Final Opinion on the Amendments to the Federal Constitutional Law on the Constitutional Court', 13 June 2016, CDL-AD(2016)016, pp. 11-12.

194 *See* Judgment of the Russian Constitutional Court on the case concerning the resolution of the question of possibility to execute the judgment of the European Court of Human Rights of 4 July 2013 in the case of *Anchugov and Gladkov v. Russia*, 14 April 2016, No. 12-P/2016, www.ksrf.ru/en/Decision/Judgments/Documents/2016_April_19_12-P.pdf. For a comprehensive analysis of the topic, *see* R.M. Fleig-Goldstein, 'The Russian Constitutional Court versus the European Court of Human Rights: How the Strasbourg Court Should Respond to Russia's Refusal to Execute ECtHR Judgments,' 56 *Columbia Journal of Transnational Law* 2017, pp. 172-218.

195 Trenin, *Post-imperium*, pp. 43-44, 140-141 and BBC News, 'Russia Plants Flag under N Pole',2 August 2007, http://news.bbc.co.uk/2/hi/europe/6927395.stm.

196 T. Parfitt, 'Russia Plants Flag on North Pole Seabed', *The Guardian*, 2 August 2007, https://www.theguardian.com/world/2007/aug/02/russia.arctic and V. Isachenkov, 'Russia Submits Revised Claim for Vast Arctic Seabed Territories at United Nations', *The Associated Press*, 4 August 2015, www.usnews.com/news/business/articles/2015/08/04/russia-bids-for-vast-arctic-territories-at-un.

197 *See* RT News, 'Russia Submits Revised Claims for Extending Arctic Shelf to UN', 10 February 2016, https://www.rt.com/news/332089-russia-arctic-claim-un/ and Annex II of the UNCLOS, www.un.org/depts/los/convention_agreements/texts/unclos/annex2.htm.

Arctic Ocean.[198] However, Russia's claims, including to the seabed under the North Pole, are anchored in the absolute understanding of state sovereignty and are greatly excessive. It can be said that Russian claims amount to imperialistic territorial expansion.[199] While the decision of the UN Commission is pending, it will be interesting how Russia will react to the decision of the Commission, should it significantly curtail its claims in the Arctic Ocean.

The legal framework for exercising Russian hegemonic influence in the neighboring countries is centered on the argument of defending interests of Russian citizens in the 'Near Abroad'.[200] This is a fluid expression that usually implies the republics of the former Soviet Union, with the possible exception of Baltic States.[201] Agnia Grigas uses a broader term *compatriots*, which includes ethnic Russians and Russian speakers (*i.e.*, Russian diaspora) in countries in the Russian zone of influence, of which formal Russian citizens form a subgroup. The protection of compatriots has become part and parcel of the concept of the 'Russian World' as a tool to project Russian geopolitical interests and power beyond Russia's borders.[202]

A closer look at the Russian official policy in the recent years reveals a move from the broader category of compatriots to a more formalized status of citizens.[203] As Grigas demonstrates, the projection of Russian influence abroad advances through seven stages of the 'reimperialization policy trajectory': (i) soft power; (ii) humanitarian policies; (iii) compatriot policies; (iv) passportization; (v) information warfare; (vi) protection; and (vii) informal control or formal annexation of territories.[204] The so-called passportization represents the process of extending Russian citizenship to compatriots, usually on the basis of a generous, massive dissemination of Russian passports. The Russian Constitu-

198 For the detailed analysis of Russia's claims, *see, e.g.*, J. Trent Warner, 'One Small Step for a Submersible, One Giant Land Grab for Russian-kind: An Evaluation of Russia's Claims to the North Pole under International Law', 57 *Naval Law Review* 2009, pp. 49-103 and I. Nossova, *Russia's International Legal Claims in Its Adjacent Seas: The Realm of Sea as Extension of Sovereignty*, Tartu University Press, Tartu, 2013, http://dspace.ut.ee/bitstream/handle/10062/31198/nossova_irina.pdf.

199 Nossova, *Russia's International Legal Claims in Its Adjacent Seas*, pp. 162,163.

200 Grigas, *Beyond Crimea*, pp. 2-3, 93.

201 I. Bērziņa *et al.*, *Russia's Footprint in the Nordic-Baltic Information Environment*, NATO Strategic Communications Centre of Excellence, Riga, 2018, p. 9.

202 *See* M. Suslov, '"Russian World": Russia's Policy towards its Diaspora', *Notes de l'Ifri, Russie.Nei.Visions* 103, July 2017, https://www.ifri.org/sites/default/files/atoms/files/suslov_russian_world_2017.pdf, O. Lutsevytch, *Agents of the Russian World: Proxy Groups in the Contested Neighbourhood*, Chatham House, April 2016, https://www.chathamhouse.org/sites/default/files/publications/research/2016-04-14-agents-russian-world-lutsevych.pdf and R. Allison, 'Russian "Deniable" Intervention in Ukraine: How and why Russia Broke the Rules', 6 *International Affairs* 2014, pp. 1282-1289.

203 For a detailed survey, *see* Grigas, *Beyond Crimea*, pp. 57-93.

204 Ibid., p. 26.

tion is evoked as a legal basis for this measure.[205] Its aim is to instrumentalize the status of citizenship to justify territorial claims, which can be characterized as a new form of imperialism by civic means.[206] In realistic terms, passportization serves as a tool to enlarge the pool of Russian citizens abroad, open the way for claims of protection and build a pretext for an eventual military intervention. The military scenario occurred with regard to Georgia in 2008 and Ukraine in 2014, after their steps towards Western integration processes (NATO and EU) endangered Russia's geopolitical interests.[207]

When Russian forces intervened Georgia in August 2008 to defend Russian citizens in South Ossetia and Abkhazia (as a response to a hasty military action by Georgian forces), the legal argument was put together on the basis of constitutional provisions. Valeriy Zorkin, the Chairman of the Russian Constitutional Court, emphasized the need for the protection of Russian citizens under the Russian Constitution and linked it to the (unfounded) claims that genocide was taking place in Georgia.[208] After the intervention in Georgia, Russia amended its Law on Defense in 2009 with several permissible grounds for the use of military force abroad; one of them is "to protect Russian Federation Citizens beyond the territorial boundaries of the Russian Federation from armed attack".[209] A similar provision was included in the Russian Military Doctrine of 2010.[210] However, the Venice Commission found this legislative change to be potentially in conflict with international law, in particular if the domestic authorization of the use of force would not

205 Ibid., pp. 41-43 and F. Mühlfried, 'Citizenship at War: Passports and Nationality in the 2008 Russian-Georgian Conflict', 26 *Anthropology Today* 2010, pp. 8-13. *See* Arts. 61 and 62 of the Constitution of the Russian Federation, www.constitution.ru/en/10003000-03.htm. The latest use of this tool is with regard to Russian speaking inhabitants in the eastern Ukraine. *See* S. Greene, 'Putin's "Passportization" Move Aimed At Keeping the Donbass Conflict on Moscow's Terms', 26 April 2019, *The Moscow Times*, www.themoscowtimes.com/2019/04/26/putins-passportization-move-aimed-at-keeping-the-donbass-conflict-on-moscows-terms-a65405 and A. Peters, 'Passportisation: Risks for International Law and Stability', Parts I-II, 9-10 May 2019, as well as E. Fripp, 'Passportisation: Risks for International Law and Stability – Response to Anne Peters', 30 May 2019, all on EJIL: *Talk!*, available at: www.ejiltalk.org.

206 Mühlfried, 'Citizenship at War', pp. 9, 13.

207 For a critical assessment of the Western support of these processes, *see* J.J. Mearsheimer, 'Why the Ukraine Crisis Is the West's Fault: The Liberal Delusions That Provoked Putin', 93 *Foreign Affairs* 2014, pp. 77-89.

208 *See* V. Zorkin, 'Proyti po lezviyu britvi: prinuzhdenie k miru i prava cheloveka' ['Pass Over the Razor's Edge: Peace Enforcement and Human Rights'], *Rossiyskaya Gazeta* [*Russian Gazette*], 13 August 2008, https://rg.ru/2008/08/13/zorkin.html. Zorkin referred to Art. 61 of the Russian Constitution, which stipulates: "2. The Russian Federation shall guarantee to its citizens protection and patronage abroad."

209 Federal Law No. 252-FZ of 9 November 2009 "Amending the Federal Law 'On Defence'", published on 13 November 2009, entered into Force on 24 November 2009, amending Art. 10(2) of the Federal Law "On Defence", www.venice.coe.int/webforms/documents/?pdf=CDL(2010)056rev-e.

210 The Military Doctrine of the Russian Federation, approved by Russian Federation presidential edict on 5 February 2010, paras. 20, 26, 27(j), http://carnegieendowment.org/files/2010russia_military_doctrine.pdf.

comply with international norms on the use of force.[211] The Venice Commission somehow predicted the turn of events.

In 2014, Russia reacted to the political turmoil in Ukraine with the military intervention. In February, Russian forces occupied Crimea and the Russian leadership was quick to annex it to the Russian Federation. The annexation was later approved by the Russian Constitutional Court.[212] In the meantime troops, officially non-affiliated but factually linked to Russian armed forces, intervened in the Eastern Ukraine and mounted an armed rebellion against the Ukranian government.[213] Russia justified intervention in Ukraine on three legal grounds: (i) the claim to be protecting Russian citizens from danger; (ii) the claim to be intervening by invitation, premised on the consent by the deposed president Yanukovich who fled the country; and (iii) the need to rectify human rights violations against the Russian speaking minority through the use of the 'remedial secession'. However, all three arguments are based on weak legal argumentation and unfounded assertions of facts.[214] Although international law allows for rescue operations of one's state nationals abroad, they cannot be a pretext for military interventions on the scale of the use of force within Article 2(4) of the UN Charter.[215]

Both Russian interventions (in Georgia and Ukraine) have been conducted in obvious violation of fundamental norms of international law, such as sovereign equality, prohibition of the use of force and respect of territorial integrity. From a historical perspective, it seems that the ground for military intervention on the basis of the socialist international

211 Venice Commission, 'Opinion on the Federal Law on the Amendments to the Federal Law on Defence of the Russian Federation', 21 December 2010, CDL-AD(2010)052, pp. 4, 58. For a Russian view on the use of force *see* B. Tuzmukhamedov, 'Legislative Regulation of Trans-boundary Use of Armed Force: Russian Case Study', 12 *BaYIL* 2012, pp. 57-74; for the Georgian view on the Russian use of force in Georgia *see* L. Alexidze, 'Kosovo and South Ossetia: Similar or Different? Consequences for International Law', 12 *BaYIL* 2012, pp. 75-101.

212 *See* I. Nuzov, 'National Ratification of an Internationally Wrongful Act: The Decision Validating Russia's Incorporation of Crimea: Constitutional Court of the Russian Federation Decision of 19 March 2014, No. 6-P', 12 *European Constitutional Law Review* 2016, pp. 353-376.

213 *See* Office of the Prosecutor, 'Report on Preliminary Examination Activities 2016', International Criminal Court, 14 November 2016, pp. 35-38.

214 *See* Allison, 'Russian "Deniable" Intervention in Ukraine', pp. 1259-1268. For legal controversy surrounding the Russian intervention in Ukraine, *see* S. Sayapin & E. Tsybulenko (Eds.), *The Use of Force against Ukraine and International Law: Jus Ad Bellum, Jus In Bello, Jus Post Bellum*, T.M.C. Asser Press, The Hague 2018, H.J. Yue, 'Crimea's Independence from Ukraine and Incorporation into Russia: The Unlawfulness of Russia's Use of Force', 6 *Beijing Law Review* 2016, pp. 181-191, W.W. Burke-White, 'Crimea and the International Legal Order', 56 *Survival* 2014, pp. 65-80, TASS, 'Putin's Letter on Use of Russian Army in Ukraine Goes to Upper House', 1 March 2014, http://tass.com/russia/721586 and 'Address by President of the Russian Federation', 18 March 2014, http://en.kremlin.ru/events/president/news/20603.

215 Venice Commission, 'Opinion on the Federal Law on the Amendments to the Federal Law on Defence of the Russian Federation', p. 12, C. Marxsen, 'The Crimea Crisis: An International Law Perspective', 2014 *Zeitschrift für ausländisches öffentliches Recht und Völkerrecht* 74, pp. 373-374 and Allison, 'Russian "Deniable" Intervention in Ukraine', pp. 1262, 1284, 1285. Art. 2(4) of the UN Charter says: "All Members shall refrain in their international relations from the threat or use of force against the territorial integrity or political independence of any state, or in any other manner inconsistent with the Purposes of the United Nations."

solidarity (the Brezhnev doctrine) has been replaced by a paternalistic ideology of providing help to Russian citizens and compatriots in need (the Putin doctrine).[216] The examples in Georgia and Ukraine demonstrate how international law was twisted to suit the expansive and sovereignist mentality of the Russian leadership. They also show how a hegemonic power can break fundamental rules and principles of international law when these are not in line with its national interests.

6.2.1.4 Conclusion on the Nationalist Model

The main elements of the nationalist model are sovereignty at the center and a projection of this inner realm to the periphery. The most typical legal form of projecting sovereignty to the outer realm is through extraterritorial legislation. Likewise, legal doctrine in hegemonic countries – United States, China and Russia – understands the concept of sovereignty in nearly absolute terms. In this sense hegemonic countries lean on domestic constitutional and public law, rather than on international law, in pursuit of their interests at the international level. Interpretation of legal rules with a strong sovereignist twist can be compatible with international law. Such interpretive conciliations add new elements to the body of HIL. However, as demonstrated before, sovereignist interpretation and actions can be in obvious violation of international law, in particular when rules deal with geopolitical categories, such as territorial sovereignty, the use of force and foreign intervention. Another important result also comes from the considerations discussed in the preceding text. A projection of hegemony under the nationalist model of HIL in most cases occurs on the basis of the constitutional order and leads to a curious blend of constitutionalism and hegemony.

6.2.2 Rational Choice Model

This model derives from the rational choice theory that first emerged in economics and later set foot in political science and in law. The rational choice model is similar to the nationalist model in that they both have a strong center. The main difference is that in the rational choice model the center engages in communication with the periphery more willingly. However, this does not signify that the sovereign border between the inner realm and the outer realm is less firm. The center still relies on the strong concept of sovereignty. Therefore, the exchange that occurs between the center and periphery works to the profit of the center. The channel of communication from the inner realm to the periphery is stronger than in the opposite way. The biggest difference with regard to the nationalist model is that here the influence of the outer realm reaches and influences the inner realm. Nevertheless, the impact of this influence is modest. The reason for a more open interaction between the two realms is that the hegemon finds cooperation at the

216 Mühlfried, 'Citizenship at War', p. 13 and Kalb, *Imperial Gamble*, p. xviii.

international level beneficial to its interests. It operates on the basis of the rational choice theory (*e.g.*, the cost-benefit analysis). So long as international cooperation corresponds to hegemon's interests, it will participate in the framework of an international regime. When international cooperation goes against interests of the hegemon – when the calculus would be negative – then the hegemon withdraws from the regime. But the hegemon opts for isolation only as long as the rational choice calculus favors withdrawal. When the result speaks in favor of the international cooperation, the hegemon will decide to rejoin the international realm. Everything therefore depends on the cost-benefit analysis.[217]

In international relations, Joseph Nye and Robert Keohane framed the theory of hegemonic stability that operates on the basis of the cost-benefit logic.[218] This theory presupposes that the hegemon strives to create an international system that provides for the exercise of hegemony and at the same time enables multilateral cooperation. Therefore, hegemony and cooperation are not alternatives, but often perform a symbiotic relationship with one another and form what we can call hegemonic cooperation.[219] Within this realm, the hegemon's behavior can assume various forms: leadership, consent, compliance and internalization.[220]

The relationship in the condition of hegemonic cooperation builds on interests of states. The hegemon seeks to persuade other actors to accept its vision of the world order, and its leadership.[221] Benefits of the hegemonic cooperation for both sides are the following. The hegemon is more willing to enter into agreements in which it makes initial sacrifices for future gains because it expects to have considerable control over its partners in the future. Smaller states, on the other hand, expect that the hegemon will enforce a general pattern of rules that will bind all actors, the hegemon included.[222] With regard to the influence on international law, the hegemonic stability theory presupposes that

> one state is powerful enough to maintain the essential rules governing interstate relations, and willing to do so. In addition to its role in maintaining a regime, such a state can abrogate existing rules, prevent the adoption of rules that it opposes, or play the dominant role in constructing new rules.[223]

---

217 See Krisch, 'International Law in Times of Hegemony', p. 373 and Krisch, *Imperial International Law*, pp. 4-6.

218 *See* R.O. Keohane & J.S. Nye Jr., *Power and Interdependence: World Politics in Transition*, Little, Brown and Company, Boston (MA)-Toronto, 1977. Keohane later adapted the hegemonic stability theory to the field of international political economy. *See* his work *After Hegemony: Cooperation and Discord in the World Political Economy*, Princeton University Press, Princeton (NJ), 1984.

219 Keohane & Nye, *Power and Interdependence*, pp. 46, 55.

220 *See* M.A. Pollack, 'Who Supports International Law, and Why? The United States, the European Union and the International Legal Order', 13 *EJIL* 2016, pp. 874-884.

221 Keohane & Nye, *Power and Interdependence*, p. 137.

222 Ibid., p. 180.

223 Ibid., p. 44.

The hegemonic cooperation in the normative field therefore depends on the cost-benefit calculations of the hegemon, based on its particular interests, rather than solely on factors of power and persuasion. But the cooperation also depends on preferences of other actors interested in the stability of the international system.

Rational choice explanations in international legal thinking draw upon the factor of power and on other nonlegal influences,[224] which makes it a close relative of political realism. In the legal field, the most visible representatives of the rational choice model are Jack Goldsmith and Eric Posner.[225] They summarize their approach as follows:

> our theory is that international law emerges from states acting rationally to maximize their interests, given their perceptions of the interests of other states and the distribution of state power.[226]

This leads them to adopt an instrumentalist approach, according to which international law is a product of state self-interest.[227] International law can never compel states to comply if this goes against their interests. The reach of international law is confined to the configuration of state interests and the distribution of state power.[228] Their perspective, however, fails to distinguish between long-term and short-term state interests. It is much easier for the hegemon to defect from an arrangement contrary to its short-term interests. If an international regime, on the other hand, coincides with its long-term interests, then the hegemon is less likely to abandon such a regime.

Nevertheless, Goldsmith and Posner acknowledge some features of autonomy to international law. International law, notably in the form of treaties, serves as a means to articulate what counts as cooperation or coordination in inter-state interactions. This helps states to achieve mutually beneficial outcomes.[229] States comply with international norms because they fear that their defection therefrom would provoke either retaliation from other countries or would harm their reputation.[230] Both responses to noncooperation could worsen the position of a defecting state.[231] In the context of the rational choice model, this implies that states commit to the international system predominantly due to the rational calculus. Among greater powers, the United States and China frequently use the rational choice model of hegemony.

---

224 J.L. Goldsmith & E.A. Posner, 'Introduction', 31 *Journal of Legal Studies* 2002, p. S3.

225 *See* a symposium with critical contributions assessing their approach: 'The Limits of International Law', *in* 2 *Georgia Journal of International and Comparative Law* 2006.

226 J.L. Goldsmith & E.A. Posner, *The Limits of International Law*, OUP, Oxford, 2005, p. 1.

227 Ibid., p. 13.

228 Id.

229 Id.

230 Goldsmith and Posner do not see the issue of reputation as relevant. *But see* G.W. Downs & M.A. Jones, 'Reputation, Compliance, and International Law', 31 *Journal of Legal Studies* 2002, pp. S95-S114.

231 *See* Goldsmith & Posner, *The Limits of International Law*, pp. 100-104 and Krisch, 'International Law in Times of Hegemony', p. 374.

6.2.2.1 United States

The United States has a particular attitude with regard to international treaties and to regimes. One can best describe it as the United States agreeing to international law as long as it is in tune with the US law and suits its national interests.[232] In literature, such an attitude is known as the *American exceptionalism*.[233] Consequently, the US attitude towards international legal regimes is not uniform; the US involvement depends on the degree of compatibility of international interests with national interests.[234] The US attitude toward international regimes can be categorized in three ways: (i) nonadherence to an international regime, (ii) adherence to an international regime subject to certain conditions from the United States, and (iii) adherence to an international regime followed by the subsequent withdrawal from it. The first category of nonadherence to an international regime includes examples of the US refusal of the Kyoto Protocol and the Anti-Personnel Landmines Treaty.[235] The second category of adhering to an international regime under certain conditions is most visible with regard to international human rights treaties. There, the United States developed a practice of submitting reservations, understandings and declarations to international treaties.[236] Finally, in the third category the United States entered into an international regime, but then left it when it was not consonant with its national interests. The relevant examples here are withdrawals from the Anti-Ballistic Missile Treaty (ABMT) and the Statute of the ICC.[237]

The Bush administration was not in favor of the rational choice model and rather preferred the sovereignist and interventionist hegemonic models. However, with regard to the ICC Statute, the attitude of the Bush administration evolved from the hostility to

232 A. Paulus, 'The Influence of the US on the Concept of International Community', p. 81, A. Pellet, 'Comments on Chapters 13 and 14', pp. 418, 421 and J. Delbrück, 'Comment on Chapters 13 and 14', p. 416, all *in* Byers & Nolte, *United States Hegemony and the Foundations of International Law*.

233 *See* E.C. Luck, 'American Exceptionalism and International Organization: Lessons from the 1990s', *in* R. Foot *et al.* (Eds.), *US Hegemony and International Organizations*, OUP, Oxford, 2003, pp. 25-48 and H.H. Koh, 'On American Exceptionalism', 55 *Stanford Law Review* 2003, pp. 1479-1527.

234 *See* P. Klein, 'Law of Treaties', pp. 363-391 and C. Redgwell, 'US Reservations to Human Rights Treaties: All for One and None for All?', pp. 392-415, both *in* Byers & Nolte, *United States Hegemony and the Foundations of International Law*.

235 *See* S. Hopgood, 'Looking Beyond the "K-Word": Embedded Multilateralism in American Foreign Environmental Policy', *in* Foot *et al., US Hegemony and International Organizations*, pp. 139-164 and J. Brunnée, 'The United States and International Environmental Law: Living with an Elephant', 15 *EJIL* 2004, pp. 617-649 and K. Anderson, 'The Ottawa Convention Banning Landmines, the Role of International Non-governmental Organizations and the Idea of International Civil Society', 11 *EJIL* 2000, pp. 91-120.

236 *See* L. Henkin, 'U.S. Ratification of Human Rights Conventions: The Ghost of Senator Bricker', 89 *AJIL* 1995, pp. 341-350 and K. Roth, 'The Charade of US Ratification of International Human Rights Treaties', 1 *Chicago Journal of International Law* 2000, pp. 347-353.

237 *See* C.C. Sabis, 'Congress and the Treaty Power: An Originalist Argument against Unilateral Presidential Termination of the ABM Treaty', 21 *Denver Journal of International Law and Policy* 2002, pp. 223-263 and L.R. Helfer, 'Exiting Treaties', 91 *Virginia Law Review* 2005, pp. 1579-1648.

hegemonic cooperation. In 2002, President Bush 'unsigned' the Statute to liberate the United States from any restrictions imposed by the ICC regime.[238] This was followed with a campaign to secure immunity for peacekeepers from states that were not parties to the ICC Statute.[239] Eventually, however, the Bush administration with an abstention vote in the Security Council de facto supported the referral of Darfur to the ICC regime.[240] Later the Obama administration voted in favor of the referral of Libya to the ICC.[241]

The Obama administration used the cost-benefit model more frequently. The main components of the Obama foreign policy doctrine – known also as *leading from behind* – were commitment to principled engagement and strategic multilateralism, which presuppose the support of international regimes with the leading role of the United States in them.[242] This doctrine relentlessly followed a cost-benefit logic and sought a pragmatic balance in the US foreign policy.[243] Harold Koh, former Legal Adviser of the State Department during the Obama administration, calls this approach 'engage-translate-leverage' as a way of exerting smart power over other international actors.[244] As a general rule the United States engaged with the international system on ad hoc basis.[245] Practical application of the Obama doctrine in the legal diplomacy has had various expressions: engaging with states parties of the ICC Statute and supporting ICC's prosecutions, participation in the global health system against infectious diseases, membership of the United States in human rights bodies, application of treaty regimes as customary international law (*e.g.*, UNCLOS, VCLT) and the increasing use of nonconventional and nonbinding arrangements (*e.g*,. MOUs on enhancing the cooperation with the Arab League, the Arctic Council mechanism).[246]

As the approach of the Trump administration is to put US interests at the forefront ('America First'), there has recently been a fallback from the engagement with interna-

---

238 *See* D.C Scott, 'Presidential Power to "Un-sign" Treaties', 6 *The University of Chicago Law Review* 2002, pp. 1447-1477 and C.A. Bradley, 'U.S. Announces Intent Not to Ratify International Criminal Court Treaty', *ASIL Insights*, May 2002.

239 *See* C. Stahn, 'The Ambiguities of Security Council Resolution 1422 (2002)', 14 *EJIL* 2003, pp. 85-104.

240 C. Heyder, 'The U.N. Security Council's Referral of the Crimes in Darfur to the International Criminal Court in Light of U.S. Opposition to the Court: Implications for the International Criminal Court's Functions and Status', 24 *Berkeley Journal of International Law* 2006, p. 652. *See* UN SC, Resolution S/RES/1564 (2004), 18 September 2004, para. 12.

241 Human Rights Watch, 'UN: Security Council Refers Libya to ICC', 27 February 2011, www.hrw.org/news/2011/02/27/un-security-council-refers-libya-icc.

242 The White House, *National Security Strategy of the United States of America*, May 2010, Washington (DC), pp. 1, 3 (hereinafter cited as *NSS 2010*) and Koh, 'The Obama Administration and International Law'.

243 Singh, *Barack Obama's Post-American Foreign Policy*, pp. 41, 13.

244 Koh, *The Trump Administration and International Law*, pp. 9, 12-13.

245 *NSS 2010*, 13.

246 *See* ibid., p. 48-49, 49-50 and Koh, 'The Obama Administration and International Law' and H.H. Koh, 'Twenty-First Century International Lawmaking', Georgetown University Law Center, Washington (DC), 17 October 2012, https://digitalcommons.law.yale.edu/cgi/viewcontent.cgi?article=5696&context=fss_papers.

tional regimes practiced under the Obama doctrine.[247] The NSS of 2017 supports American participation in multilateral forums; however, with an important condition that American interests and principles must be protected.[248] The NSS 2017 acknowledges the need that the United States must lead and engage in the multilateral arrangements and shape many rules that affect US interests and values. However, while participating in them, the United States must protect American sovereignty, advance American interests and values and oppose any claims to authority over American citizens that are in conflict with the US constitutional framework.[249] In multilateral regimes, the Trump administration pursues the maximalist cost-benefit outcome; if that is not acceptable to other participants, the subsequent step is to withdraw from the regime. This US stance comes very close to the sovereignist model to the point that both models become interconnected and morph into each other when applied in daily practice.

From the outset, Trump made it clear that he disagreed with the 2015 Paris Agreement on Climate Change and stated his intent to withdraw from it. However, Article 28 of the Paris Agreement stipulates that a party cannot give notice of withdrawal until three years from the date it entered into force. The notification then takes one year before the withdrawal becomes valid.[250] The Paris Agreement entered into force on 4 November 2016, so the earliest date that such legal notice would take effect would be 4 November 2019.[251] Thus, the United States will stay a party to the Paris Agreement at least until 4 November 2020.[252]

Trump was also a critic of the North American Free Trade Agreement (NAFTA), which he saw as damaging to US economic interests. Therefore, the Trump administration requested renegotiation of the NAFTA agreement with Canada and Mexico. The renegotiation resulted in a restructured agreement (*United States Mexico Canada Agreement*). The new arrangement, however, is only a little different from the original NAFTA agreement.[253] Linked to the unilateral increase of tariffs to some extent is the request of the Trump Administration to 'reform' the WTO dispute settlement mechanism, which could be a great obstacle in pursuing the US unilateral economic policy.[254] The Trump

247 Koh, *The Trump Administration and International Law*, pp. 9, 13-14.
248 *NSS 2017*, pp. 4, 25.
249 Ibid., p. 40.
250 *See* https://unfccc.int/sites/default/files/english_paris_agreement.pdf.
251 Koh, *The Trump Administration and International Law*, p. 41.
252 Ibid., pp. 39, 41-42 and K. Birmingham Bontekoe, 'What Will a Trump Administration Mean for International Agreements with the United States?' *EJIL: Talk!*, 13 December 2016, www.ejiltalk.org/what-will-a-trump-administration-mean-for-international-agreements-with-the-united-states/.
253 Ibid., pp. 55-56 and Irwin, 'Trade under Trump'.
254 Koh, *The Trump Administration and International Law*, pp. 59-60.

administration blocked the nomination of new members to the WTO Appellate Body that decimated its membership and slowed down its functioning.[255] Currently, talks are underway on how to modernize the WTO system that would have a weaker dispute settlement (judicial) component.[256]

In the area of disarmament, the Trump administration withdrew from two international regimes. The first was the 2015 Joint Comprehensive Plan of Action (the Iran Nuclear Deal) concluded among P5+1 (US, UK, France, China, Russia and Germany) and Iran. After protracted negotiations, Iran agreed to specified limits on its nuclear development program in exchange for the relaxation of sanctions imposed through the UN.[257] However, in 2018, after describing it as a bad deal, Trump announced the US withdrawal from the Iran Nuclear Deal and the imposition of US economic sanctions.[258] Intentions of the United States to negotiate a new, harsher nuclear deal with Iran have yielded no result so far.[259] In 2019, after accusing Russia of developing intermediate nuclear missiles prohibited under the Intermediate-Range Nuclear Forces (INF) Treaty, Trump announced his decision to suspend the treaty for six months; should Russia not destroy the missiles during this period, the United States would formally withdraw from the INF Treaty.[260] However, soon afterwards Russia reciprocated with the same formula: suspension and withdrawal from the INF Treaty in six months. While Russia's swift reaction dispelled any legal uncertainty about this issue, it mounted fears of the renewed nuclear arms race.[261] The tendency for withdrawal from international regimes continued

255 J. Brinkley, 'Trump Is Close to Shutting Down the WTO's Appeals Court', *The Forbes*, 27 September 2018, www.forbes.com/sites/johnbrinkley/2018/09/27/trump-is-close-to-shutting-down-the-wtos-appeals-court/#3d8a6a167ab6 and T. Miles, 'U.S. Blocks WTO Judge Reappointment as Dispute Settlement Crisis Looms', *Reuters*, 27 August 2018, www.reuters.com/article/us-usa-trade-wto/u-s-blocks-wto-judge-reappointment-as-dispute-settlement-crisis-looms-idUSKCN1LC19O. *See also* Chapter 7 of this book.

256 E. Moyle, '2019 Forecast: WTO Reform and Appellate Body', *Foreign Brief*, 1 January 2019, www.foreignbrief.com/forecast/2019-forecast-wto-reform-and-the-appellate-body/.

257 Koh, *The Trump Administration and International Law*, p. 61 and K. Daverport, 'The Joint Comprehensive Plan of Action (JCPOA) at a Glance', *Arms Control Association*, May 2018, www.armscontrol.org/factsheets/JCPOA-at-a-glance.

258 S.K. Dehghan, 'What is the Iran Deal and why Does Trump Want to Scrap It?' *The Guardian*, 9 May 2018, www.theguardian.com/world/2018/may/08/iran-nuclear-deal-what-is-it-why-does-trump-want-to-scrap-it.

259 J. Kruzel, 'Donald Trump's Vow to Renegotiate a Deal with Iran is at a Standstill', *Politifact*, 4 January 2019, www.politifact.com/truth-o-meter/promises/trumpometer/promise/1368/renegotiate-iran-deal/. In response Iran, in May 2019, announced a partial withdrawal from the Nuclear Deal. (J. Griffiths, J. Berlinger & S. McKenzie, 'Iranian Leader Announces Partial Withdrawal from Nuclear Deal', *CNN*, 8 May 2019, https://edition.cnn.com/2019/05/08/middleeast/iran-nuclear-deal-intl/index.html.)

260 The White House, 'President Donald J. Trump to Withdraw the United States from the Intermediate-Range Nuclear Forces (INF) Treaty', 1 February 2019, www.whitehouse.gov/briefings-statements/president-donald-j-trump-withdraw-united-states-intermediate-range-nuclear-forces-inf-treaty/.

261 J. Borger, 'Donald Trump Confirms US Withdrawal from INF Nuclear Treaty', *The Guardian*, 1 February 2019, www.theguardian.com/world/2019/feb/01/inf-donald-trump-confirms-us-withdrawal-nuclear-treaty, N. Hodge & S. McKenzie, 'Russia Will Exit the INF Nuclear Missile Treaty in Six Months', *CNN*, 6 February 2019, https://edition.cnn.com/2019/02/06/europe/russia-exit-inf-treaty-intl/index.html and T. Nichols, 'Mourning the INF Treaty: The United States Is Not Better for Withdrawing', *Foreign Affairs*, 4 March 2019, www.foreignaffairs.com/articles/2019-03-04/mourning-inf-treaty.

with the announcement of Trump to revoke the status of the United States as a signatory of the UN Arms Trade Treaty, which Obama signed in 2013 but has not yet been ratified by the US Senate.[262]

A similar confrontational approach was used also with regard to the UN Human Rights Council. The Trump administration claimed that the Human Rights Council was working against national interests of the United States and its allies as well as infringing upon US sovereignty. A major flaw of the human rights regime, according to the United States, was that country membership of the Human Rights Council included many abusers misusing their position to work against human rights. The Trump administration required the Human Rights Council to undergo necessary reforms. After the plan for a radical reform was clearly rejected by other states, the United States withdrew from its membership.[263]

The overview of the actions of the Trump administration reveals a pattern of a transactional approach in the sense of a maximalist *quid* for a minimal *quo*.[264] In some international regimes, such imbalance of interests was acceptable to other members but to many it was not. In the latter cases, the confrontation resulted in the withdrawal of the United States from respective regimes. A logical follow-up to the withdrawal from the regime would be a move of the Trump administration to the framework of the nationalist hegemonic model.

6.2.2.2 China

China persistently uses the rational choice model in the context of its *Fourth Ring*, which covers outer dimensions of security in regions of Europe, Middle East, Africa, North and South America. China has made a visible entrance in this farthest circle since the late 1990s, mainly to secure energy resources, pursue its interests in international economy and seek diplomatic support on bilateral and multilateral issues.[265] In order to be part of international regimes, China subjected itself to international rules. However, China abides by the rules in different degrees, depending on how a particular regime suits its needs and interests; in some cases compliance is substantive, in others it is formal.[266]

262 J. Colvin & L.M. Paine, 'President Trump Announces Decision to Withdraw U.S. from Arms Trade Treaty in NRA Speech', *The Time*, 26 April 2019, http://time.com/5578872/trump-nra-speech-arms-trade-treaty/.

263 US Department of State, 'Remarks on the UN Human Rights Council', 19 June 2018, www.state.gov/secretary/remarks/2018/06/283341.htm, BBC, 'US Quits "Biased" UN Human Rights Council', 20 June 2018, www.bbc.com/news/44537372 and The Graduate Institute Geneva, 'Nikki Haley: US May Leave Human Rights Council', 8 June 2017, http://graduateinstitute.ch/home/relations-publiques/news-at-the-institute/news-archives.html/_/news/corporate/2017/nikki-haley-us-may-leave-human-r.

264 *Cf.* T. Wright, 'Trump's Foreign Policy is No Longer Unpredictable', *Foreign Affairs*, 18 January 2019, sec. 'A Unified Foreign Policy', www.foreignaffairs.com/articles/world/2019-01-18/trumps-foreign-policy-no-longer-unpredictable and V. Perthes, 'President Trump and International Relations', *EurActiv.com*, 23 November 2016, www.euractiv.com/section/global-europe/opinion/president-trump-and-international-relations/.

265 Nathan & Scobell, *China's Search for Security*, pp. 6-7, 347.

266 Ibid., p. 13.

These regimes are, in particular, international criminal justice, international peacekeeping and international human rights system.

Although China is not a party to the ICC Statute, it continues to engage in international criminal justice as a permanent member of the UN Security Council. China voted in favor of the Security Council resolution creating the International Criminal Tribunal for the former Yugoslavia and supported its functioning in nominating a number of Chinese judges to the tribunal. China abstained on (and thus did not veto) the resolution establishing the International Criminal Tribunal for Rwanda. Similar to the United States, China also abstained (thus de facto approving) the resolution referring the situation in Darfur to the ICC and supported a resolution on the referral of Libya. China continues to attend the ICC State Parties Assembly as an observer state.[267] While it remains reluctant to the use of force by the Security Council under Chapter VII of the UN Charter, it has made a significant contribution to peacekeeping operations (also called Chapter VI and a half) since the 1990s. Usually, China's contribution had been restricted to the deployment of engineers, medical aid, police and other noncombat personnel. A major shift occurred with regard to the peacekeeping operation in Mali in 2013, where China for the first time participated with combat troops. The important role of China in peacekeeping missions is likely to continue in the future.[268] Finally, China has a particular attitude with regard to the international human rights system. In the 1990s, a number of Western countries led a campaign, unsuccessfully, to single out China as a human rights violator at the UN Commission for Human Rights. But this prompted China to support the transformation of the Commission into the Human Rights Council.[269] The main novelty of the Human Rights Council is the Universal Periodic Review process, which reduces the political pressure as all countries are evaluated for their compliance with human rights standards (the principle of nonselectivity). During its membership in the Human Rights Council (2006-2012), China kept a low profile, mainly keeping an eye on the protection of its interests and supporting solidarity with the developing world. However, there are signs that China's role is becoming more assertive.[270]

---

267 Chatham House, 'Exploring Public International Law and the Rights of Individuals with Chinese Scholars', International Law Programme, 14-17 April 2014, London, p. 8 and B.B. Jia, 'China and the International Criminal Court: Current Situation', 10 *Singapore Year Book of International Law* 2006, pp. 1-2, 6, 11.

268 Chatham House, 'Exploring Public International Law and the Rights of Individuals with Chinese Scholars', p. 9, Xue, *Chinese Contemporary Perspectives on International Law*, pp. 227-229, Nathan & Scobell, *China's Search for Security*, pp. 185-186 and F.P van der Putten, 'China's Evolving Role in Peacekeeping and African Security: The Deployment of Chinese Troops for UN Force Protection in Mali', Clingendael Report, September 2015. For a comprehensive analysis of China's role in peacekeeping *see* a special issue: 18 *International Peacekeeping* 2011, Issue 3, entitled 'China's Evolving Approach to Peacekeeping'.

269 Xue, *Chinese Contemporary Perspectives on International Law*, pp. 158-160.

270 Chatham House, 'Exploring Public International Law and the Rights of Individuals with Chinese Scholars – Part 2', pp. 4-5, Nathan & Scobell, *China's Search for Security*, pp. 190, 336, S. Sceats & S. Breslin, *China and the International Human Rights System*, Chatham House, October 2012, pp. 10-32 and N. Jiang, 'China's Human Rights Cooperation with the International Community', 2015 *Intellectual Properties Rights* 3, pp. 1-4.

China has joined the international human rights framework by signing or becoming a state party to a wide range of human rights treaties. It tends to see them as aspirational rather than legally binding, which reduces the level of its compliance with the human rights regime.[271] In general, China seems to be engaged with the international human rights system but a closer look reveals that it primarily acts from within to defend its interests.[272]

6.2.2.3 Conclusion on the Rational Choice Model

At the heart of the rational choice model is a calculus about the long- and short-term interests of the hegemon. If its outcome is positive for the hegemon, it is very likely that the hegemon will participate in the relevant international regime. The greatest benefit for the hegemon in the international regime is that it can forge a normative and institutional pattern which imposes obligations on other states (as well as on the hegemon). However, often it is not easy to distinguish between long- and short-term state interests. This has important repercussions, as the reliance on long-term interests keeps the leading state in the regime, while the observance of short-term interests leads to a less stable commitment of the leading state to the regime. The modalities of the hegemon's participation in international regimes are various: from a leading role, through a more reserved one to a passive role. In all these modalities there is some exchange between the hegemon and members of the regime. However, transactions from the hegemon to the regime are much stronger than the other way round. The role of international law in this context is that it functions as a social catalyst in allowing the hegemon to pursue its interests. On the other hand, through its normative and institutional framework international law acts as a check on the hegemon's exercise of power.

6.2.3 Interventionist Model

The last expression of hegemonic international law is the interventionist model. As the name implies, this model is more open to the international realm. The center is inclined to interact with the outer realm and exercise its influence there. For that reason, the sovereign border is not that strong as with two previous models. The main difference with regard to the two models is precisely this 'openness' to influence the outer realm more willingly. On the other hand, the main similarity between the interventionist model and the nationalist model is that the outer realm is not able to exercise any substantial influence on the inner realm of the center. It seems somehow paradoxical that the interventionist model is less prone to the outer influence; however, this is precisely its main hegemonic attribute. The model is more willing to communicate with the outer realm

---

271 Sceats & Breslin, *China and the International Human Rights System*, Summary Points, p. 35.
272 Ibid., p. 55.

because of the center's intention to shape periphery according to its interests. This is also the main difference compared to the rational choice model, which allows for a feedback influence, albeit a very limited one, from the outer realm on to the inner realm. Motivations behind actions in the outer realm come from a conservative, liberal or realist conceptual background. Somewhat paradoxically, the interventionist model brings together all these approaches.

Analyzing the prospects for an American Empire, Philip Bobbitt refers to a group of thinkers that overtly favor the creation of a worldwide 'Pax Americana'. Bobbitt points out that this group unites a curious blend of neoconservative and liberal thinkers who are all in favor of projecting American power worldwide.[273] There is, however, a difference between neoconservatives and liberals. Neoconservatives openly support the need for a dominant position of the United States in the world. Liberals, on the other hand, subscribe to the same views in a more indirect way.[274] Additionally, the liberal strand of the interventionist model comprises not only thinkers who favour the American domination, but also liberals who depict other international actors as global hegemons, such as the EU. Thus, there is a distinction between American and European imperial liberals. All differences apart, what in the very end unites neoconservative and liberal interventionists is their desire to shape the world according to their own design.[275] In addition, the intervention abroad may be prompted by typical realist considerations, such as the projection of power abroad and protection of geostrategic interests, as was the case with Russia's intervention in Syria. This section will survey the development of the interventionist approach in the United States, the EU and Russia.

6.2.3.1 United States

The most important generator of neoconservative views was a conservative think tank *The Project for the New American Century* (PNAC).[276] Its membership included Paul Wolfowitz, Dick Cheney, Donald Rumsfeld, William Kristol, Donald Kagan, Robert Kagan and other neoconservative figures. In July 1997, a group of PNAC protagonists had supported the case for American global leadership. According to the PNAC's statement of principles, the requirements for the revitalization of the American leadership are:

---

273 P. Bobbitt, 'Better than Empire', *The Financial Times*, 13-14 March 2004, p. W8.

274 *See* B. Mabee, 'Discourses of Empire: The US "Empire", Globalisation and International Relations', 25 *Third World Quarterly* 2004, pp. 1361-1362.

275 *See* D.K. Simes, 'America's Imperial Dilemma', 82 *Foreign Affairs* 2003, p. 102, J. Vaïsse, *Neoconservatism: The Biography of a Movement*, The Belknap Press of Harvard University Press, Cambridge (MA)-London, 2010, trans. A. Goldhammer, pp. 251-252 and I. Parmar, 'Foreign Policy Fusion: Liberal Interventionists, Conservative Nationalists and Neoconservatives: The New Alliance Dominating the US Foreign Policy Establishment', 46 *International Politics* 2009, pp. 177-209.

276 *See* relevant websites: http://rightweb.irc-online.org/profile/Project_for_the_New_American_Century/ and http://web.archive.org/web/20070810114230/www.newamericancentury.org/. The PNAC had its own web page over many years. However, since July 2008 the web page of the PNAC is inaccessible and PNAC materials are available at previously mentioned websites.

i. to increase defense spending significantly so as to carry out global responsibilities and modernize the US armed forces;
ii. to strengthen ties to democratic allies and to challenge regimes hostile to US interests and values;
iii. to promote the cause of political and economic freedom abroad;
iv. to accept responsibility for America's unique role in preserving and extending an international order friendly to the US security, prosperity and principles.[277]

In an important report entitled *Rebuilding America's Defenses* PNAC mainly deals with the issue of how to transform the American military force to become an even more powerful tool to propagate American interests across the globe.[278] Introduction to the report identifies the United States "as the world's only superpower, combining pre-eminent military power, global technological leadership, and the world's largest economy."[279] In addition, the report positions the United States as a leader of the world's leading democratic powers with a mission to preserve and enhance the existing *Pax Americana* in the coming century.[280] This is to happen on the basis of the US military operations abroad with an aim to safeguard American security.[281] One of the common options for the achievement of the American security in particular regions of the world is a regime change.[282]

As numerous PNAC protagonists assumed high-ranking positions in the Bush Jr. administration, it is not surprising that many contents of the PNAC framework were transplanted to the US *National Security Strategy* (NSS) of 2002.[283] In the NSS of 2002, President Bush stated that the US national security strategy is based "on a distinctly American internationalism that reflects the union of our values and our national interests."[284] In the introduction, Bush identifies contemporary time period as a unique opportunity for the United States to extend the benefits of freedom, democracy, develop-

---

277 'Statement of Principles', *The Project for the New American Century*, 3 June 1997. *See also* Drolet, *American Neoconservatism*, pp. 146-147 and G. Dorrien, *Neoconservatism and the New Pax Americana*, Routledge, New York-Milton Park, 2004, pp. 114-164.

278 *See Rebuilding America's Defenses: Strategy, Forces and Resources for a New Century*, A Report of The Project for the New American Century, September 2000, https://archive.org/details/RebuildingAmericasDefenses.

279 Ibid., p. i.

280 Ibid., pp. i, iv, 75-76.

281 Ibid., pp. 74, 75.

282 *See* ibid., pp. 10, 25, 61.

283 For links between the neoconservatives (including the PNAC) and NSS of 2002 *see also* S. Soederberg, 'American Empire and "Excluded States": The Millennium Challenge Account and the Shift to Pre-Emptive Development', 25 *Third World Quarterly* 2004, pp. 280-289, 297-298.

284 The White House, *National Security Strategy of the United States of America*, Washington (DC), September 2002, p. 1 (hereinafter *NSS 2002*).

ment and free trade to every corner of the world.[285] This means that the American administration sees American interests as international interests.[286] At its core, such a viewpoint is typically Schmittean: the Sovereign has the power to decide on the ultimate interpretation of what is legitimate in a certain situation.[287] The interventionist model is different from the nationalist model in that rulers at the center posit themselves in the international context and feel under an obligation to shape the international realm. Essentially, their viewpoint is international, whereas in the nationalist model the perspective is domestic.

The NSS of 2002 is a typical example of the outer realm which assumes the top position in the world hierarchy with an aim to dominate and regulate international periphery. The most obvious tools of such hegemonic governance are the following. The first tool is the doctrine of preemptive action allowing the US military forces to take action against an imminent danger of attack.[288] In literature this doctrine earned the label the 'Bush doctrine' of preemptive self-defense.[289] However, the Bush doctrine is very broad and expressed in political, rather than legal terms. This raises the question of what are its exact contents.[290] Does it mean anticipatory self-defense, preemptive self-defense or even preventive war?[291] While it is difficult to give precise answers, it is important to note that the term *preemptive action* or *preventive action* signals an intention to 'act alone', that is, unilaterally. Therefore, the main feature of the Bush doctrine, whatever its concrete ex-

---

285 Ibid., p. iv.

286 I.I. Lukashuk & D.S. Boklan, 'The Concept of the US National Security and International Law: A View from Moscow', 2 *Chinese Journal of International Law* 2003, pp. 590, 592.

287 P. Owens, 'The Return of Realism? War and Changing Concepts of the Political', *in* H. Strachan & S. Schelpers (Eds.), *The Changing Character of War*, OUP, Oxford, 2011, pp. 484-485.

288 *See NSS 2002*, pp. 6, 15.

289 *See* C. Gray, 'The Use of Force and the International Legal Order', *in* Evans, *International Law*, pp. 603-604.

290 *Cf.* M.W. Reisman & A. Armstrong, 'The Past and Future of the Claim of Preemptive Self-Defense', 100 *AJIL* 2006, pp. 525, 547. On the Bush doctrine, *see* also contributions in D.J. Ceraley (Ed.), *American Hegemony: Preventive War, Iraq, and Imposing Democracy*, The Academy of Political Science, New York, 2004.

291 Anticipatory self-defense derives from the Caroline dispute of 1837. The Caroline case served as a catalyst for a transformation of the doctrine of self-defense from a political excuse to a legal doctrine. Conditions for the anticipatory self-defense, according to the US Secretary of State Daniel Webster, are the following. Anticipatory self-defense must be instant, overwhelming, leaving no choice of means, and no moment of deliberation. Further, such an action must be limited by necessity. Anticipatory self-defense therefore covers the cases of an attack that is about to come. The attack is imminent, but not yet underway. In contrast, preemptive self-defense occurs when the danger of the attack is there, but the attack itself is still not imminent. The danger of the attack is contingent on the mere possibility of an attack at some future time. Under contemporary international law preemptive self-defense is not permissible. Finally, preventive war means a war launched in order to prevent the rise of a competing sate to the leading position. While preventive war was a regular occurrence in history, it is not legal under current international law. It has to be added that scholarship is not unanimous on the content of the three categories and their legality under international law. For definitions *see, e.g.*, Reisman & Armstrong, 'The Past and Future of the Claim of Preemptive Self-Defense'. pp. 525-550, R.Y. Jennings, 'The *Caroline* and McLeod Cases', 32 *AJIL* 1938, pp. 82-99, C. Gray, 'The US *National Security Strategy* and the New "Bush Doctrine" on Preemptive Self-defense', 1 *Chinese Journal of International Law* 2002, pp. 437-447 and A.D. Soafer, 'On the Necessity of Pre-emption', 14 *EJIL* 2003, pp. 209-226.

pression, was to withdraw the decision on the use of force from the international framework and confer it to the US administration.

The second tool is to propagate the spread of democracy worldwide.[292] The United States sees the economic development closely connected with the advancement of democracy.[293] In this respect the NSS 2002 represents a convenient combination of power and principles and some authors even consider it to be thoroughly Wilsonian.[294] Nonetheless, the conceptual accent of the NSS 2002 is on the use of force and preemptive action and the spread of democracy is contingent upon the security concerns. But this quality changed in the subsequent NSS adopted in 2006, which restricted the scope of preemptive action and devoted more attention to the universal growth of democracy.

The most explicit application of the Bush doctrine was the US military attack on Iraq in 2003. The controversial nature of this military action sparked a lively scholarly debate and generated a vast amount of literature on the war in Iraq.[295] It seems that the majority of international legal scholarship finds the Iraqi war to be unlawful, with notable exceptions in the US and partly in the UK legal community. Nonetheless, the real issue goes beyond the issue of lawfulness and is more about methodology than substance.[296] The stand on this question depends on whether one ascribes to the so-called extensive or

292 J.L. Gaddis, 'A Grand Strategy of Transformation', No. 133 *Foreign Policy* 2002, p. 53.

293 *See NSS 2002*, pp. 2, 4, 21-25.

294 Gaddis, 'A Grand Strategy of Transformation', p. 54.

295 *See, e.g.,* Paulus, 'The War against Iraq and the Future of International Law', pp. 691-733, Soafer, 'On the Necessity of Pre-emption', pp. 220-226, G. Simpson, 'The War in Iraq and International Law', 6 *Melbourne Journal of International Law* 2005, pp. 167-188, K. Bannelier *et al.* (Ed.), *L'intervention en Irak et le droit international*, CEDIN, Paris, 2004, I. Johnstone, 'US-UN Relations after Iraq: The End of the World (Order) as We Know It?' 15 *EJIL* 2004, pp. 830-836, BBC, 'Iraq War Illegal, Says Annan', 16 September 2004, http://news.bbc.co.uk/2/hi/middle_east/3661134.stm and a series of articles in the agora of the *AJIL* on the Iraq war, vol. 97 (2003): W.H. Taft IV and T.F. Buchwald, 'Preemption, Iraq and International Law', pp. 557-563; R. Wedgewood, 'The Fall of Saddam Hussein: Security Council Mandates and Preemptive Self-Defense', pp. 576-585; R.N. Gardner, 'Neither Bush nor the Jurisprudes', pp. 585-590; M. Sapiro, 'The Shifting Sands of Preemptive Self-Defense', pp. 599-607; T.S. Franck, 'What Happens Now – The United Nations after Iraq', pp. 607-620 and T.J. Farer, 'The Prospect for International Law and Order in the Wake of Iraq', pp. 621-628. *See also* Sir John Chilcot's *Report of the Iraq Inquiry*, 6 July 2016, www.iraqinquiry.org.uk. From the UK perspective the Chilcot report found the intervention against Iraq to be unjustified. However, it did not make any judgments as to its legality. (*See* K. Sengupta, 'Chilcot Report: Intelligence on WMDs Exaggerated to Justify Going to War, Inquiry Finds', *The Independent*, 6 July 2016, www.independent.co.uk/news/uk/politics/chilcot-report-intelligence-was-exaggerated-and-omitted-to-justify-iraq-war-inquiry-finds-a7122481.html.)

296 *See* O. Corten, 'The Controversies over the Customary Prohibition on the Use of Force', 16 *EJIL* 2006, pp. 805-822 and A. Bianchi, 'The International Regulation of the Use of Force: The Politics of Interpretive Method', 22 *LJIL* 2009, pp. 651-675.

restrictive interpretation of the use of force. The first perspective favors extra-legal considerations (such as interests of great powers, perceived security concerns and values of the international community), while the second follows a narrower black-letter approach anchored in legal categories.[297]

The US led 'Coalition of the Willing' (including the UK, Australia and Poland) intervened in Iraq on the basis of the Security Council resolution 1441 (2002).[298] This resolution, adopted under Chapter VII, recognized that Iraq's noncompliance with previous disarmament obligations constitutes a threat peace and security.[299] The resolution established what some authors named a 'golden thread' of legal argumentation justifying an attack on Iraq:[300] finding a material breach of the disarmament obligations deriving from the cease-fire resolution 687 (1990)[301] and, consequently, reviving the authority of the resolution 678 (1990) to use all necessary means against Iraq to secure international peace and security.[302] In this way, the intervening countries situated arguments for the military action against Iraq within the 'Bush doctrine'.[303] Overall, skeletal legal arguments, weak evidentiary basis and magnified extra-legal considerations (such as a threat of weapons of mass destruction and authoritarian nature of the Iraqi regime) prevailed as a basis for action and brought this issue on the brink of the requirement of lawfulness.[304]

In legal terms, the most apt description of the military actions described above is the unilateral enforcement of the collective will or community objectives.[305] On the basis of common interests expressed in the Security Council resolutions, the mentioned states opted to proceed to unilateral action. Consequently, the end result of this hegemonic

---

297 On the two approaches, *see* a symposium in *LJIL*, vol. 29 (2016): J. Kammerhofer, 'Introduction: The Future of Restrictivist Scholarship on the Use of Force', pp. 13-18; R. van Steenberghe, 'The Law of Self-Defence and the New Argumentative Landscape on the Expansionists' Side', pp. 43-65; W.C. Banks & E.J. Criddle, 'Customary Constraints on the Use of Force: Article 51 with an American Accent', pp. 67-93; and A.-C. Martineau, 'Concerning Violence: A Post-Colonial Reading of the Debate on the Use of Force', pp. 95-112.

298 *See* SC Res. 1441 (2002), 8 November 2002.

299 Ibid., preambular para. 3.

300 Simpson, 'The War in Iraq and International Law', pp. 181-182.

301 *See* SC Res. 1441, paras. 1, 4 and SC Res. 687 (1991), 3 April 1991.

302 *See* SC Res. 1441, preambular paras. 10, 11 and SC Res. 678 (1990), 29 November 1990. This line of argument is extensively developed in the legal opinon by the UK Attorney General Lord Goldmisth of 7 March 2003. (*See* 'Full Text: Iraq Legal Advice', *The Guardian*, 28 April 2005, www.theguardian.com/politics/2005/apr/28/election2005.uk.)

303 Taft & Buchwald, 'Preemption, Iraq and International Law', pp. 557-563 and J. Allain, 'The True Challenge to the United System of the Use of Force: The Failures of Kosovo and Iraq and the Emergence of the African Union', 8 *Max Planck Yearbook of United Nations Law* 2004, p. 257.

304 For a useful presentation of the weakness of US rhetorical arguments *see* D. Zarefsky, 'Making the Case for War: Colin Powell at the United Nations', 10 *Rhetoric & Public Affairs* 2007, pp. 275-302.

305 *Cf.* N. Krisch, 'Unilateral Enforcement of the Collective Will: Kosovo, Iraq, and the Security Council', 3 *Max Planck Yearbook of United Nations Law* 1999, p. 60 and V. Gowlland Debbas, 'The Limits of Unilateral Enforcement of Community Objectives in the Framework of UN Peace Maintenance', 11 *EJIL* 2000, pp. 362-363.

use of force shook the foundations of the UN system of collective security and opened the way for subsequent unilateral actions of great powers.

The NSS of 2006 is a follow-up document to the NSS of 2002, in particular with regard to the proliferation of democracy.[306] Although the NSS of 2006 confirmed the doctrine of preventive action, it nevertheless significantly limited its reach.[307] It seems that the lesson from Iraq tamed the will for power that pervaded the contents of NSS of 2002. Instead, the NSS of 2006 demonstrates more willingness to resort to the multilateral framework and diplomacy.[308] The single most important tool of the NSS of 2006 was the concept of 'transformational diplomacy'. According to the NSS of 2006 the transformational diplomacy

> means working with our many international partners to build and sustain democratic, well-governed states that will respond to the needs of their citizens and conduct themselves responsibly in the international system. Long-term development must include encouraging governments to make wise choices and assisting them in implementing those choices.[309]

The origins of this concept came from the State Department.[310] Transformational diplomacy represents a move from the traditional diplomacy to encompass public diplomacy, military security concerns, peace-building aims and promotion of democracy. Transformational diplomacy puts an emphasis on the local presence of 'transformational diplomats' who exercise their functions in a post-conflict environment as: political advisors to the military forces; police officers; judges; electricians; engineers; bankers; economists; legal experts; and election monitors.[311] If one understands transformational diplomacy in these terms one can surely speak of transformational aspirations, but hardly of diplomacy. The concept of transformational diplomacy resembles a unilateral substitution for the UN peace-building missions in which the US 'colonial administration' replaces the

306 *See* The White House, *National Security Strategy of the United States of America*, Washington (DC), March 2006, pp. ii, 1, 2-7, 11, 31-34, 46 (hereinafter *NSS* 2006) and Gray, 'The Bush Doctrine Revisited', pp. 555, 558-559.

307 *See* C. Gray, 'The Bush Doctrine Revisited: The 2006 National Security Strategy of the USA', 5 *Chinese Journal of International Law* 2006, pp. 555, 559, 561-563, Reisman & Armstrong, 'The Past and Future of the Claim of Preemptive Self-Defense', pp. 531-532, and J.R. Crook, 'Contemporary Practice of the United States relating to International Law', 100 *AJIL* 2006, pp. 690-691.

308 *NSS 2006*, p. 23.

309 Ibid., p. 33.

310 *See* C. Rice, 'Transformational Diplomacy', U.S. Department of State, 18 January 2006, https://2001-2009.state.gov/secretary/rm/2006/59306.htm and C. Oleszycki, 'Update on Department of State and Department of Defense Coordination of Reconstruction and Stabilization Assistance', 24 *The Army Lawyer* 2006, p. 22.

311 *See* Rice, 'Transformational Diplomacy', Department of State, 'Transformational Diplomacy', Office of the Spokesman, 18 January 2006, https://2001-2009.state.gov/r/pa/prs/ps/2006/59339.htm and Oleszycki, 'Update on Department of State and Department of Defense Coordination of Reconstruction and Stabilization Assistance', pp. 22-23.

UN field staff. In this sense, it is an upgrade of the Bush doctrine and the strategy for the global proliferation of democracy. After demolition of autocratic regimes, there is a need to build democratic regimes with the assistance of the US administrators. As such, transformational diplomacy works as an instrument of interventionist hegemony.[312]

Like neoconservatives, the liberals had an influential think-tank the Princeton Project on National Security (PPNS) led by liberal academics Anne-Marie Slaughter and John Ikenberry, with a wide cross-party membership.[313] The final report of PPNS made an intellectual case in support of liberal interventionism across the world.[314] After the election of Barack Obama as the US President some vocal proponents of liberal interventionism took office in the State Department:[315] Hillary Clinton as State Secretary,[316] Samantha Power as US Ambassador to the United Nations[317] and Anne-Marie Slaughter as Director of Policy Planning.[318]

President Obama articulated his views on the use of force in the Nobel Peace Prize acceptance speech. Somewhat surprisingly – given the occasion – Obama did not take a stand against a war. He said that at times the use of force is not only necessary but also morally justified. Obama referred to the concept of 'just war', according to which war is permissible under justified conditions, such as that it is waged as a last resort or in self-defense; the use of force is proportionate; and that civilians are spared from violence whenever possible. He went on to support the use of force on humanitarian grounds in situations of massive human rights violations by oppressive governments.[319] These 'open textured' views were conceptually articulated in the NSS of 2010. The NSS explicitly

312 This resonates with ideas expressed in literature. *See, e.g.*, S. Mallaby, 'The Reluctant Imperialist', 81 *Foreign Affairs* 2002, pp. 2-7, G.J. Ikenberry, 'America's Imperial Ambition', 81 *Foreign Affairs* 2002, pp. 44-60, N. Fergusson, 'Hegemony or Empire?', 82 *Foreign Affairs* 2003, pp. 154-161 and E.A. Cohen, 'History and the Hyperpower', 83 *Foreign Affairs* 2004, pp. 49-63.

313 *See* wws.princeton.edu/news-and-events/news/item/princeton-project-national-security-releases-working-group-reports.

314 G.J. Ikenberry & A.-M. Slaughter (Co-Directors), *Forging a World of Liberty Under Law: U.S. National Security In The 21st Century*, 27 September 2006, Princeton University, www2.world-governance.org/IMG/pdf_0080_Forging_a_World_of_Liberty_Under_Law.pdf.

315 Mazower, *Governing the World*, pp. 393-394.

316 *See* J.A. Stacey, 'The Hillary Clinton Doctrine', *Foreign Affairs*, 17 May 2016, www.foreignaffairs.com/articles/2016-05-17/hillary-clinton-doctrine. Clinton's concept of 'civilian power' comes very close to Rice's transformational diplomacy. (*See* H.R. Clinton, 'Leading Through Civilian Power: Redefining American Diplomacy and Development', 89 *Foreign Affairs* 2010, pp. 13-24.)

317 *See* S. Power, *"A Problem from Hell": America and the Age of Genocide*, Basic Books, New York, 2013 and E. Osnos, 'In the Land of the Possible', *The New Yorker*, 22 & 29 December 2014, www.newyorker.com/magazine/2014/12/22/land-possible.

318 *See* A.-M. Slaughter, 'How the World Could—and Maybe Should—Intervene in Syria', *The Atlantic*, 23 January 2012, www.theatlantic.com/international/archive/2012/01/how-the-world-could-and-maybe-should-intervene-in-syria/251776/ and L. Feinstein & A.-M. Slaughter, 'A Duty to Prevent', 83 *Foreign Affairs* 2004, pp. 135-150.

319 *See* The White House, 'Remarks by the President at the Acceptance of the Nobel Peace Prize', Oslo City Hall, 10 December 2009, https://obamawhitehouse.archives.gov/the-press-office/remarks-president-acceptance-nobel-peace-prize.

envisaged participation of the United States in the framework of the Responsibility to Protect (R2P), which presupposes the collective use of military force against those states that commit genocide and mass atrocities against their own population.[320]

Intellectual underpinnings of liberal interventionism had a limited practical influence on President Obama. During his mandate, only two areal military interventions took place: in Libya and in Syria.[321] Rather than expressions of hegemonic interventionism, the two cases of the use of force were undertaken on the basis of common community interests in the conceptual framework of R2P. In Libya this doctrine was activated successfully, while in Syria the initial action inspired by the R2P vocabulary dissolved into a myriad of unilateral applications of the use of military force.[322]

6.2.3.2 European Union

Similar to American interventionists, there are Europeans who portray the European Union (EU) as a hegemonic power with the capacity to project its values, principles and interests abroad. For a long time the EU had perceived itself as a civilian and a normative power.[323] Some scholars refer to the so-called 'European exceptionalism'.[324] Additionally, there are tendencies to see the EU as a potent global player with a capacity to project its power beyond its territory.[325] According to Federica Mogherini, EU's High Representative for Foreign Affairs and Security Policy, the EU has the strength to contribute to peace and security in the European region and in the world by combining soft and hard power.[326]

The *Laeken Declaration* of the EU Council, adopted in 2001, stated that in the post-Cold War world, the EU is supposed to be "a power resolutely doing battle against all

---

320 *NSS 2010*, pp. 48, 22.

321 *Cf.* Stacey, 'The Hillary Clinton Doctrine', Singh, *Barack Obama's Post-American Foreign Policy*, p. 183 and CNN, 'Transcript: President Obama's Speech on Combating ISIS and Terrorism', 11 September 2014, available at: https://edition.cnn.com.

322 *See* Chapter 9 of this book.

323 *See* T. Diez (Ed.), *A Different Kind of Power? The EU's Role in International Politics*, IDEBATE Press, New York, London & Amsterdam, 2014, in particular contributions by F. Duchêne, 'The European Community and the Uncertainties of Interdependence', pp. 21-36 and T. Diez & I. Manners, 'Reflecting on Normative Power Europe', pp. 55-73. *See also* Z. Laïdi, *La norme sans la force : l'énigme de la puissance européenne*, Presses de la fondation nationale des sciences politiques, Paris, 2005.

324 *See* M. Ličková, 'European Exceptionalism in International Law', 19 *EJIL* 2008, pp. 463-490 and G. Nolte & H.P. Aust, 'European Exceptionalism?', 2 *Global Constitutionalism* 2013, pp. 407-436.

325 B. Delcourt, 'La séduction du concept d'impérialisme liberal auprès des elites européennes : vers une redéfinition de la politique étrangère de l'Union européenne ?', *in* Jouannet & Ruiz Fabri, *Impérialisme et droit international en Europe et aux Etats-unis*, p. 101, R. Prodi, 'A Wider Europe – A Proximity Policy as the Key to Stability', Brussels, 5-6 December 2002, President of the European Commission, SPEECH/02/619, Peace, Security and Stability – International Dialogue and the Role of the EU, Sixt ECSA-World Conference, Jean Monnet Project, p. 2, Borgen, 'Whose Public, whose Order?', p. 344 and J. Rabkin, 'Is the EU Policy Eroding the Sovereignty of the Non-Member States?', 1 *Chicago Journal of International Law* 2000, p. 290.

326 F. Mogherini, 'Foreword', *in* EU, *Shared Vision, Common Action: A Stronger Europe, A Global Strategy for the European Union's Foreign And Security Policy*, June 2016, pp. 4, 5 (hereinafter *EU Global Strategy*).

violence, all terror and fanaticism, but which also does not turn a blind eye to the world's heartrending injustices."[327] The subsequent *European Security Strategy* of 2003 elaborated these views in more detail.[328] Similarly, the *EU Global Strategy* of 2016 underscores a nexus between EU's interests and values: peace, democracy, prosperity and a rules-based global order are vital interests that underpin EU's external action.[329] At the same time, a link exists between internal and external security. EU's home security presupposes peace in neighboring and surrounding countries, which implies a broader interest in preventing conflict, promoting human security, addressing the root causes of instability and working towards a safer world.[330] As a guiding maxim, the *EU Global Strategy* posits 'principled pragmatism' to steer the EU between the Scylla of isolationism and the Charybdis of rash interventionism.[331] According to the strategy, the EU will engage in peace building and support human security through all stages of the conflict. The EU will be focusing on prevention, responding responsibly and decisively to crises, investing in stabilization, and avoiding premature disengagement from conflicts.[332] The thoughts described in the preceding paragraphs reflect an inherent contradiction between liberalism and realism in the EU documents on foreign and security policy:

> At a first glance, they appear to endorse a traditional liberal view by legitimising the use of force on humanitarian grounds. On the other hand, modes of action and reasons for action are still justified in realistic terms, mainly through references to the specific interests of the Union and its Member states.[333]

In essence, the EU is an expression of liberal ideology and as such "universalist or at least open in aspiration."[334] But it is equally true that, in the world of global governance, the EU increasingly operates as a projection of its model and power on the rest of the world.[335] Some years ago, the then President of the EU Commission, Jose Manuel Barro-

327 *See* EU, 'Laeken Declaration on the Future of the European Union', *in* Presidency Conclusions, European Council Meeting in Laeken, 14-15 December 2001, The EU Council, No. SN 300/1/01 REV 1, p. 20.

328 *See* EU, 'A Secure Europe in a Better World: European Security Strategy', Brussels, 12 December 2003 www.cvce.eu/content/publication/2004/10/11/1df262f2-260c-486f-b414-dbf8dc112b6b/publishable_en.pdf.

329 *EU Global Strategy*, p. 13. For more on the EU Global Strategy, *see* J. Larik, 'The EU's Global Strategy, Brexit and "America First" ', 23 *European Foreign Affairs Review* 2018, pp. 343-364.

330 *EU Global Strategy*, p. 14.

331 Ibid., p. 16.

332 Ibid., pp. 9-10.

333 B. Delcourt, 'The Normative Underpinnings of the Use of Force. Doctrinal Foundations and Ambiguities in the CFSP/ESDP Discourse', 6 *BaYIL* 2006, pp. 158-159. *See also* B. Delcourt, 'Les paradoxes de l'Europe puissance normative, civile … et tranquille?', *in* B. Adam *et al., Europe puissance tranquille ? Rôle et identité sur la scène mondiale*, Coédition GRIP-Éditions Complexe, Bruxelles, 2006, pp. 92-93, 96-97 and G. Frankenberg, 'Commentaire', *in* Jouannet & Ruiz Fabri, *Impérialisme et droit international en Europe et aux Etats-unis*, pp. 116-120.

334 K. Nicolaïdis & R. Howse,'"This is my EUtopia …": Narrative as Power', 40 *Journal of Common Market Studies* 2002, p. 789.

335 Ibid., pp. 767 and 782.

so, said that the EU is an anti-imperial empire, which enables the EU to administer globalization in accordance with its values.[336] The EU is therefore a proponent of liberal imperialism.[337] As such it plays an important role in the context of the interventionist model of hegemony.

There are notably three authors who portray the EU as an example of liberal imperialism: Robert Cooper, Jan Zielonka and József Böröcz. All of them underline the permeable character of the contemporary notion of sovereignty, which intensifies interaction between the powerful center and the receptive periphery, but they also see this neo-imperial constellation as the source of stability and order.[338] Cooper divides the world into three categories: premodern world, modern world, and postmodern world. The EU is an example of a postmodern system and as such a model for the future.[339] While the EU can coexist with the modern world of nation states, the turbulent premodern world of failed states represents the greatest danger.[340] As a solution for orderly world governance, Cooper proposes to resort to a liberal imperialism inspired by human rights and cosmopolitan values.[341] Zielonka sees the EU in the shape of a neo-medieval empire.[342] He emphasizes that the EU's ways of organizing governance and projecting power abroad are not unique, but originate in history. Although the neo-medieval model presupposes a lax border between the center and periphery, the EU represents a strong center with an ability to influence diluted peripheries. Böröcz, likewise, construes the idea of the EU as an empire on the basis of the European colonial history and sees it as a predictable and inescapable actuality of the EU. He applies the imperial order based on domination of the center over the periphery, notably to the Eastern European enlargement process.[343]

The EU influences the periphery mainly through the propagation of norms, values and principles by dint of its capacity as a normative power. The concept of normative

---

336 Le Monde, 'M. Barroso, président de la Commission européenne: « Nous avons le devoir de ne pas nous attaquer aux institutions européennes »', 7 October 2005.

337 *See* Delcourt, 'La séduction du concept d'impérialisme liberal auprès des elites européennes', pp. 73-114 and B. Hettne & F. Söderbaum, 'Civilian Power or Soft Imperialism? The EU as a Global Actor and the Role of Interregionalism', 10 *European Foreign Affairs Review* 2005, pp. 535-552.

338 *Cf.* R. Cooper, 'The New Liberal Imperialism', *The Observer*, 7 April 2002, www.theguardian.com/world/2002/apr/07/1, J. Zielonka, *Europe as Empire: The Nature of the Enlarged European Union*, OUP, Oxford, 2006, pp. 18, 143 and J. Böröcz, 'Introduction: Empire and Coloniality in the "Eastern Enlargement" of the European Union', *in* J. Böröcz & M. Kovács (Eds.), *Empire's New Clothes: Unveiling EU Enlargement*, Central Europe Review Ltd., Shropshire, 2001, pp. 12-19.

339 *See* R. Cooper, *The-Post Modern State and the World Order*, Demos-The Foreign Policy Centre, London, 2000 pp. 17-33. *See also* Rabkin, 'Is the EU Policy Eroding the Sovereignty of Non-Member States?', pp. 275, 277.

340 Cooper, 'The New Imperialism'.

341 Ibid.

342 *See* Zielonka, *Europe as Empire*, pp. 9-11, 13, 143-144, 170 (*see also* tables at pp. 12, 153) and J. Zielonka, *Is the EU Doomed?*, Polity, Cambridge, 2014, p. xi.

343 *See* Böröcz, 'Introduction', pp. 4-19.

power is a blend between EU's core values and EU's procedural and institutional machinery, which projects these norms to the international realm.[344] EU's core values are human dignity, freedom, democracy, equality, the rule of law and human rights.[345] While these values are constitutive for EU member states, they are also instrumental for EU's external action to which one must also add values such as support for international law, including the UN Charter.[346] In this vein, Article 3(5) of the Lisbon Treaty states that in "relations with the wider world, the Union shall uphold and promote its values and interests." To achieve the stated purpose, these values have to find their practical expression in legal norms.[347] The EU is using its foreign policy primarily for the promotion of values, for building values and for protection of values.

With regard to the promotion of values, the EU is proliferating them in the context of neighborhood, enlargement and conditionality policies as well as in a wider framework.[348] The main purpose of these practices is to align foreign legal orders with the EU's normative structure. Nonetheless, a coercive element is an inherent part of the promotion of values process.[349] Should partner states choose not to follow EU's imperatives, the EU would retract its political, expert, economic or diplomatic support. The modalities of the promotion of EU values include: (i) exporting values via forms of unilateral action (*e.g.*, trade policy); (ii) exporting values via technical assistance; (iii) exporting values via bilateral 'soft' instruments, such as human rights dialogues or the European Neighbourhood Policy (ENP);[350] (iv) shared values as a basis for developing a relationship (bilateral or multilateral), such as the Stabilization and Association Process and the ENP; and (v) shared values as an essential element of a contractual relationship.[351]

---

344 *See* I. Manners, 'Normative Power Europe: A Contradiction in Terms?', 40 *Journal of Common Market Studies* 2002, pp. 242-245.

345 TEU Art. 2 (Consolidated Version of the Treaty on European Union, Official Journal of the European Union, No. C 326, 26 October 2012).

346 M. Cremona, 'Values in EU Foreign Policy', *in* M. Evans & P. Koutrakos (Eds.), *Beyond the Established Legal Orders*, Hart Publishing, Oxford-Portland (OR), 2011, pp. 276, 313. *See also* Art. 21 of the Lisbon Treaty.

347 Cremona, 'Values in EU Foreign Policy', p. 275.

348 Ibid., pp. 292-293. *See also* Zielonka, *Europe as Empire*, pp. 13-14, 55, 149, 162, Hettne & Söderbaum, 'Civilian Power or Soft Imperialism?', pp. 540-543, 549-550, Cooper, 'The New Liberal Imperialism' and contributions in Böröcz & Kovács, *Empire's New Clothes*. For more on neighborhood, enlargement and conditionality policies, *see EU Global Strategy*, pp. 9, 24-25, F. Casolari, 'The Janus-Faced New European Neighbourhood Policy: Normative (Hard) Power vs. the Pragmatic (Soft) Approach', Istituto Affari Internazionali, Documenti IAI 13/08, November 2013, S. Koch, 'A Typology of Political Conditionality Beyond Aid: Conceptual Horizons Based on Lessons from the European Union', 75 *World Development* 2015, pp. 97-108 and S. Blockmans, 'La Nouvelle Vague: The Introduction of a More Significant Ost-politik in the EU's Security Policies', *in* A. Łazowski (Ed.), *The Application of EU Law in the New Member States: Brave New World*, T.M.C. Asser Press, The Hague, 2010, pp. 31-64.

349 *Cf.* Zielonka, *Europe as Empire*, p. 170 and A. Hyde-Price '"Normative Power" Europe: A Realist Critique', 13 *Journal of European Public Policy* 2006, p. 227.

350 *See* https://eeas.europa.eu/diplomatic-network/european-neighbourhood-policy-enp_en?page=1.

351 Cremona, 'Values in EU Foreign Policy', p. 278. For a detailed analysis, *see* ibid., pp. 292-307.

The process of building values has a more diplomatic character and includes advocacy for and creation of new norms as well as their interpretation and enforcement. This activity is part of a wider commitment by the EU to solve common problems through multilateral forums.[352] The process of building values involves: (i) diplomatic consensus-building among member, candidate (formal and potential) and neighbor states, the elaboration of EU strategies and Common Positions; and (ii) negotiation, decision-making and treaty-making, including within international organizations.[353]

The activity of protecting values is connected to peace and state building efforts on the European continent, in particular in post-conflict countries such as Bosnia and Herzegovina (BiH) and Kosovo. EU's involvement in these countries presupposes its presence in international field institutions and participation with civilian personnel.[354] The EU presence is necessary to pacify these still instable areas and to protect EU's core values.[355] The High Representative for BiH, who has always been a national of the EU, is in charge of the civilian implementation of the Dayton Agreement and ensuring that Bosnia and Herzegovina evolves into a peaceful and viable democracy on course for integration into Euro-Atlantic institutions.[356] In addition, the EU has a Special Representative of the EU in BiH with a task to pursue EU policy objectives of continuous progress with the aim of a stable, viable, peaceful and multiethnic and united BiH; peaceful cooperation with its neighbors; and irreversibility on track towards membership in the EU.[357] In Kosovo, the institutional arrangement is similar. There, the EU Special Representative's mandate is to offer the EU's advice and support in the political process and promote overall EU political coordination in Kosovo.[358] In the field of the administration of justice, the EU established a civilian field mission called *EULEX* with the task of assisting the Kosovo authorities in areas concerned with the development of the rule of law and administration of justice.[359]

While there is no doubt that the EU is a dynamic actor in international relations,[360] there is also no doubt that on the basis of projecting its values abroad the EU is acting as an interventionist hegemon.

---

352 Mogherini, 'Foreword', p. 4 and *EU Global Strategy*, pp. 10, 15-16, 39, 42-44.

353 Cremona, 'Values in EU Foreign Policy', p. 278. For a detailed analysis, *see* ibid., pp. 307-313.

354 Cooper, 'The New Liberal Imperialism'.

355 *Cf.* Zielonka, *Europe as Empire*, p. 162.

356 *See* www.ohr.int/?lang=en.

357 *See* EEAS, 'EU Special Representatives', 14 June 2016, sec. 'EUSR in Bosnia and Herzegovina', https://eeas.europa.eu/headquarters/headquarters-homepage/3606/eu-special-representatives_en.

358 *See* ibid, sec. 'EUSR for Kosovo'.

359 *See* www.eulex-kosovo.eu/.

360 F. Amtenbrink & D. Kochenov, 'Conclusion: Messianism, Mission, or *Realpolitik*? Some Concluding Observations on the EU's Role in Shaping the International Legal Order', *in* D. Kochenov & F. Amtenbrink (Eds.), *The European Union's Shaping of the International Legal Order*, CUP, Cambridge, 2014, pp. 349, 352.

6.2.3.3 Russia

In recent years, Russia has started to project its power globally, in accordance with its geopolitical interests, to assume the role of the global power that once belonged to the Soviet Union.[361] As part of its strategy to expand influence abroad Russia established a set of military bases in Vietnam, Cuba, Venezuela, Nicaragua, Seychelles, Singapore and Belarus. The list would be incomplete without a naval base in the Syrian town of Tartus that once belonged to the Soviet Union and was subsequently taken over by Russia. As soon as the crisis in Syria erupted in 2011, Russia showed interest in being one of the international players involved in solving it. Unsurprisingly, when the situation in Syria deteriorated, Russia decided to intervene militarily in the Syrian crisis.[362] The reasons for the military intervention by Russia in Syria reflect traditional realist concerns of power expansion and the pursuit of national interests.[363]

The impetus for greater involvement by Russia came from the Syrian President Assad Al-Bashir who invited Russia to intervene in the Syrian crisis in order to fight international terrorism.[364] Although in this case the prevailing belligerent context is a civil war rather than an international conflict, such intervention by invitation is in accordance with international law.[365] The Russian Law on Defense allows for sending Russian troops abroad in order "to repel or prevent an armed attack on another State which makes a corresponding request to the Russian Federation".[366] The purpose of the intervention abroad is to protect the "interests of the Russian Federation and its citizens and supporting international peace and security", under condition that the deployment of troops is in accordance with international law and international treaties concluded by Russia.[367] Under the Russian Constitution and the Law of Defense, the President of Russia is empowered to make a decision on the operational deployment of troops abroad on the basis of the authorization by the Council of the Federation (upper house of the Russian parlia-

---

361 A. Stent, 'Putin's Power Play in Syria', 95 *Foreign Affairs* 2016, p. 106. For more details, *see* 'Russian National Security Strategy', 31 December 2015, www.ieee.es/Galerias/fichero/OtrasPublicaciones/Internacional/2016/Russian-National-Security-Strategy-31Dec2015.pdf and 'The Foreign Policy Concept of the Russian Federation', 30 November 2016, www.rusemb.org.uk/rp_insight/.

362 S. Al-Saadi, 'Russia Long-term Aims in Syria', *Carnegie Endowment for International Peace*, 6 October 2015, https://carnegieendowment.org/sada/61521.

363 *See* Stent, 'Putin's Power Play in Syria', pp. 108-109.

364 B. Chappell, 'Russia Begins Airstrikes in Syria After Assad's Request', *NPR*, 30 September 2015, www.npr.org/sections/thetwo-way/2015/09/30/444679327/russia-begins-conducting-airstrikes-in-syria-at-assads-request and Reuters, 'Syria's Assad wrote to Putin over military support: statement', 30 September 2015, www.reuters.com/article/us-mideast-crisis-syria-putin-idUSKCN0RU17Y20150930.

365 L. Visser, 'Russia's Intervention in Syria', *EJIL: Talk!*, 25 November 2015, www.ejiltalk.org/russias-intervention-in-syria/.

366 Art. 10, para. 2.2 of the Federal Law No. 252-FZ of 9 November 2009 'Amending the Federal Law "On Defence"'.

367 Ibid., Art. 10, para 2.

ment).[368] In addition, the Russian Law on the Counteraction of Terrorism allows for the deployment of Russia troops abroad to fight international terrorism.[369]

This legal framework was followed by Putin to order air strikes by Russian forces in Syria in the fight against international terrorism,[370] under which Syria and Russia understood not solely the forces of the 'Islamic State' but also anti-regime armed groups.[371] Russian political leaders justified the decision to intervene militarily in Syria with a need to defend Russian national security interests, to uphold Russia's growing role in global affairs and to stabilize the legal authority in Syria in order to find a political compromise to the crisis.[372] When explaining the decision to intervene in Syria, Putin stated that the Russian military action solely implies the use of the airforce activities without the use of ground troops.[373] Nonetheless, in the following years the presence of Russian ground troops in Syria increased. Russian military presence grew notably through the deployment of private military companies.[374] This was facilitated on the basis of the amendment to the Law on military conscription, which came into force in January 2017. According to it every person who completed military service or is a member of the reserve force can be considered as a member of the Russian military if he participates in activities against international terrorism outside the Russian territory. Russian mercenaries in Syria thus have a status of being members of the Russian military forces.[375]

Russia further cemented its military presence in Syria with international agreements. The first international agreement signed in August 2015 and ratified by the Russian parliament in October 2016 allowed for the deployment of Russian air forces to the

368 *See* ibid., Art. 10, para. 1.1 and Art. 102, para. 1.d of the Constitution of the Russian Federation, www.constitution.ru/en/10003000-06.htm.

369 Art. 5, para. 1.3 and Art. 10, www.legislationline.org/en/topics/country/7/topic/5.

370 *See* Ria novosti [Ria News], 'Zakonodatel'stvo o vozmozhnosti primeneniya VS Rossii za ee predelami' ['Legislation on the Possibility of Using the Armed Forces of Russia beyond its Borders], 30 September 2015, https://ria.ru/20150930/1293155963.html.

371 J. Daher, 'Three Years Later: The Evolution of Russia's Military Intervention in Syria', *The Atlantic Council*, 27 September 2018, www.atlanticcouncil.org/blogs/syriasource/three-years-later-the-evolution-of-russia-s-military-intervention-in-syria.

372 AP, 'Russian Parliament Approves Military Intervention in Syria', 30 September 2015, https://mashable.com/2015/09/30/russia-approves-military-intervention-syria/?europe=true and Interfax, 'Putin nazval osnovnuyu zadachu rossiyskih voennyh v Sirii' ['Putin Identified the Main Task of the Russian Military in Syria], 11 October 2015, www.interfax.ru/russia/472593.

373 The Moscow Times, 'Putin Wins Parliamentary Support for Russian Airstrikes in Syria', 30 September 2015, www.themoscowtimes.com/2015/09/30/putin-wins-parliamentary-support-for-russian-air-strikes-in-syria-a49935.

374 Daher, 'Three Years Later'.

375 W. Neumann & S. Dobbert, 'Putin's Mercenaries', 6 February 2017, *Zeit Online*, https://www.zeit.de/politik/ausland/2017-02/russia-vladimir-putin-military-mercenary-soldiers-syria.

Syrian territory and for the permanent establishment of the Russian air base at the airport Hmeymim in the province of Latakia.[376] The second agreement, on the use of the port of Tartus by Russia, was signed in January 2017 and ratified by the Russian parliament in December 2017. Russia and Syria agreed on the prolongation of the cost-free use of the Tartus naval base for 49 years and on the enlargement of the base for the activities of the Russian naval forces.[377]

It is therefore not surprising that the potent and whole-scale involvement of Russia in the Syrian conflict was the tipping point in consolidating the Assad regime and aided in bringing the Syrian conflict to an end.[378] The Russian intervention in Syria and its military build-up there were in accordance with international law. However, several operations by Syrian forces under the sponsorship of Russia are dubious from the point of view of international humanitarian norms, in particular due to the high rate of civilian casualties and attacks on civilian objects. This may trigger responsibility by Russia for these military actions.[379]

The end result of the Russian military intervention in Syria is the strengthening of the position of Russia in the Middle East as a peacemaker and guarantor of global security and establishing a durable alliance with Syria on the fight against international terrorism.[380] The Russian intervention in Syria is a typical example of the hegemonic interventionist model following the realist logic: the use of the internationally oriented domestic legal framework and international agreements to project Russian power abroad to augment its global position and protect national interests in the international arena.

---

376 Sputnik News, 'Russian Military Bases Abroad: Facts and Details', 8 October 2016, https://sputniknews.com/military/201610081046123220-russian-abroad-military-bases/ and Sovet Federacii [Council of the Federation], 'Sovet Federacii odobril Soglashenie o razmeshchenii aviacionnoy gruppy Vooruzhennyh Sil Rossii v Sirii' ['The Federation Council Approved the Agreement on the Deployment of the Aviation Group of the Armed Forces of Russia in Syria'] 12 October 2016, http://council.gov.ru/events/news/72364/.

377 RFE/RL, 'Russia Establishing Permanent Presence at Bases in Syria', 26 December 2017, https://www.rferl.org/a/russia-syria-bases-permanent-presence-shoigu/28939539.html and TASS, 'Russia's State Duma Ratifies Agreement with Syria on Expanding Tartus Naval Base', 21 December 2017, http://tass.com/politics/982210.

378 E. Burrows & J. Masters, 'Putin Orders Withdrawal of Russian Troops in Visit to Syrian Base', *CNN*, 11 December 2017, https://edition.cnn.com/2017/12/11/middleeast/putin-russia-syria-withdrawal/index.html, DW, 'New Russia-Syria Accord Allows Up to 11 Warships in Tartus Port Simultaneously', 20 January 2017, www.dw.com/en/new-russia-syria-accord-allows-up-to-11-warships-in-tartus-port-simultaneously/a-37212976 and P. Isa, A. Rosa & M. Alleruzzo, 'US-allied Syrian Force Declares Victory over Islamic State', *AP News*, 23 March 2019, https://apnews.com/ced0b1d5bd9b4447a3d36039213c8b3b. For a comprehensive overview of the Russian involvement in Syria, *see* Wikipedia, 'Russian Military Intervention in the Syrian Civil War', https://en.wikipedia.org/wiki/Russian_military_intervention_in_the_Syrian_Civil_War.

379 *See* R. Lawless, 'A State of Complicity: How Russia's Persistent and Public Denial of Syrian Battlefield Atrocities Violates International Law', 9 *Harvard National Security Journal* 2018, pp. 180-226.

380 RFE/RL, 'Russia Defense Minister Meets With Syria's Assad, Hands Him Message From Putin', 19 March 2019, www.rferl.org/a/russia-defense-minister-meets-with-syria-s-assad-hands-message-from-putin/29830752.html and S. Rosenberg, 'Syria War: Putin's Russian Mission Accomplished', 13 December 2017, *BBC News*, www.bbc.com/news/world-europe-42330551.

6.2.3.4 Conclusion on the Interventionist Model

The interventionist model brings together a curious alignment of neoconservative, liberal and realist strands of thoughts, be it American, European or Russian. This might be surprising; however, the basic tenets of all these concepts have roots in the factor of power. In this model, the center is eager on projecting its principles, values, norms and interests abroad in order to shape the periphery according to its preconceptions. In this sense, the interventionist model is the most ambitious of the three hegemonic models in its desire to mold the periphery according to hegemonic designs. In terms of international law, the intervention can take the form of the use of force (unilateral, collective or intervention by invitation), establishment of military bases abroad, peace and state building efforts, and the creation of international norms to subsume the periphery under the hegemon's legal order.

6.2.4 Concluding Remarks on Hegemonic International Law

Hegemonic international law revolves around the legal interaction between the dominant center and the subordinate international periphery. Depending on the nature of this interaction there are three different models: the nationalist model, the rational choice model and the interventionist model. In the nationalist model, the hegemonic center shapes the international periphery on the basis of its domestic constitutional and public law framework. The rational choice model presupposes participation of the hegemon in the international regime, depending on benefits it receives through international cooperation. The interventionist model implies the projection of the hegemon's preferences to the international periphery in order to transform its environment. Dominance is the essential element that characterizes the shape of HIL generally and is constitutive of all three models. Because of the prevalence of one major power over other international actors, the logical question arises as to the autonomous nature of HIL.

As stated earlier, the main function of law is to tame the free flow of power. Another main function of law is to shape its rules according to the interests of power. Therefore, when law confronts the dominant power, it does not necessarily bow to the display of force. Similarly, in the case of HIL, the factor of dominance does not automatically prevail over law. In general, HIL functions as any kind of law. Although there may be tension between HIL and fundamental principles of international law,[381] such as sovereign equality, noninterference in domestic affairs, and the prohibition of the use of force, HIL is in accordance with international law. Characteristically, the major part of the previous sur-

381 *See* A. Tanzi, 'Remarks on Sovereignty in the Evolving Constitutional Features of the International Community', *in* M.H. Arsanjani *et al.* (Eds.), *Looking to the Future: Essays on International Law in Honor of W. Michael Reisman*, Martinus Nijhoff, Leiden-Boston, 2011, pp. 307-310, 321-322.

vey between hegemony and international law dealt with the body of law that constitutes HIL as a specific branch of international law.

There is, however, a realistic possibility that hegemonic power may eventually prevail over law. The preceding survey expounded several examples of misinterpretation of international law due to interests of hegemonic powers. These examples are: erroneous understanding of torture in the 'war on terror' by the Bush administration; substitution of the law of the sea rules with historical considerations by China concerning the South China Sea; appropriation of the rules on the use of force by Russia regarding the occupation of Crimea and intervention in Ukraine; to this many would add misinterpretation of international law by the United States with regard to the military intervention in Iraq in 2003.

It has to be emphasized that the cases mentioned in the preceding text do not represent examples of HIL for one simple reason – they are contrary to international law and thus fall out of the legal framework. Although hegemonic countries tried to use international law in accordance with their interests and preferences, their actions ultimately ended in violations of international law. Modalities of the misuse of international law are many: false or wrong factual account as a basis for the use of international rules; injection of extra-legal (historical, political, security, practical) features that eventually overwhelm the meaning of legal concepts; imposition of domestic legal canons and perceptions on the interpretation of international rules; and a misinterpretation or misunderstanding of international legal rules in line with hegemon's interests and preferences. The use of one modality or a combination of them leads to what can be called the *imperial legal overstretch*.[382] Instead of relying on the substance within the law, the hegemonic interpreter adds something to the law that is not contained in it.[383] This corresponds to the situation where the hegemon ignores an underlying juridical idea of the international rule and, consequently, the fabricated interpretive construction abandons the realm of law.[384] Imperial legal overstretch therefore traverses limits of an acceptable teleological interpretation of international rules.

However, the main problem in the contemporary international community is an absent international judicial authority with a power to deliver final and authoritative judgments on controversial legal issues, including the ones involving hegemonic powers.[385] As there are a number of competing but judicially unchecked interpretations, it is most apt to describe this arrangement as a system of 'decentralized interpretation'.[386] Therefore, paraphrasing a recent account of the Marxist legal thinker one can say: between

382 *See* above note 59.

383 *Cf.* L. Pitamic, 'Some Aspects of the Problem of Interpretation', 19 *American Bar Association Journal* 1933, p. 584.

384 Id.

385 *See also* Chapter 10 of this book.

386 B.-O. Bryde, 'International Democratic Constitutionalism', *in* Macdonald & Johnson, *Towards World Constitutionalism*, p. 110.

plural interpretations, the interpretation of the most powerful prevails.[387] If quantity of such hegemonic interpretations would increase drastically, then international law would change its aggregate condition. International law, universal by design, could be supplanted by HIL, together with its specific appearances in nationalist, rational choice and interventionist models. This can be one consequence of monopolized hegemonic interpretations. The other is more dangerous. In case of a number of competing hegemonic interpretations, law may fall back on interests of particular powers and, subsequently, on the formations of sheer power. This may lead to the situation of *anomie*, triggering a disintegration of the international legal system as we know it.[388]

However, for most of the time, HIL operates as international law with a task of facilitating the performance of hegemons in the international legal system. As presented previously, in such a system hegemons have a decisive say. Generally, this logic implies that the hegemon pursues its own interests. Nevertheless, it also has to take into account the preferences of smaller countries. If an international system is to persist it must be legitimate for all participants. Legitimacy in the international hegemonic system implies that the hegemon uses its dominant position for the benefit of a system as a whole and pursues the common good or collective interests. As long as smaller states feel that the hegemon takes into account their interests, they are willing to accept the leading role of the hegemon and the shape of HIL. In this sense, we speak of shared values and solidarity between the hegemon and smaller states.[389] This is also the reason why international hegemony on various occasions, surprisingly, takes the shape of constitutionalism, as will be shown later.

---

387 *See* Miéville, *Between Equal Rights.*

388 *See* Zupančič, *The Owl of Minerva*, pp. 209-210 and B.M. Zupančič, 'Criminal Law and Its Influence upon Normative Integration', 7 *Acta Criminologica* 1974, pp. 56-58, 63-64. For the concept of anomie, *see also* R.K. Merton, *Social Theory and Social Structure*, The Free Press, Glencoe, 1962, 131-194.

389 *See* Clark, *Legitimacy in International Society*, pp. 156-157.

7 Constitutionalism and International Law

Until recently it was not commonplace to visualize international law (essentially a horizontal phenomenon) through the lens of constitutionalism (preponderantly based on the vertical dynamic). During the interwar period, several authors started applying a constitutionalist approach to international law.[1] Among them, Georges Scelle merits a special mentioning for his pioneering contribution to international constitutional law. From the old adage of *ubi societas, ibi jus* Scelle extrapolated the conclusion that if there is an international community, there has to be an international constitution.[2]

Part One defined constitutionalism as the agglomeration of power in the form of a structural framework for the pursuit of common goals, followed by the exigency of putting limitations on the so constituted power in the form of the doctrine of the separation of powers, the mechanism of checks and balances, the judicial review, the rule of law, the doctrine of human rights and the constitution. This dynamic can be summarized as the minimization of the maximization of power. It transpires through functional components of constitutionalism, which are normative, institutional, judicial, coordinative and self-referential.

In line with the previous appraisal of power and law, the application of constitutionalism to international law leads to the agglomeration of power in the international community and to the development of corresponding limitations upon it. As this dynamic is reflected in constitutional functions, constitutionalism as a process also shapes the development of constitutional functions at the international level. This mode of legal thinking, which is at the same time constitutionalist and internationalist, gives rise to the new discipline of international law – international constitutional law (ICL). ICL therefore deals with the agglomeration of international power and restraints upon it and, in more detail, with a survey of international constitutional functions.

1 *See* G. Scelle, 'Le droit constitutionnel international', *in Mélanges Raymond Carré de Malberg*, Recueil Sirey, Paris, 1933, pp. 501-516, B. Mirkine-Guetzévitch, *Droit constitutionnel international*, Sirey, Paris, 1933, O. Hoijer, *La pacte de la Société des nations : Commentaire théorique et pratique*, Editions Spes, Paris, 1926, p. 7, A. Zimmern, *The League of Nations and the Rule of Law 1918-1935*, MacMillan and Co., London, 1939, p. 304 and A. Verdross, *Die Verfassung der Völkerrechtsgemeinschaft*, J. Springer, Vienna, 1926.

2 Scelle, 'Le droit constitutionnel international', pp. 505-506.

7.1 International Constitutional Law

Looking from the organic perspective, ICL encapsulates a process of increased cross-fertilization between the disciplines of constitutional law and international law. Bianchi underlines that while international law is undergoing a process of constitutionalization, the main problem remains that these changes materialize in ad-hoc solutions rather than in a conceptual move to a higher evolutionary level of legal development.[3] Scholarly discussions deal with a question of whether it is constitutionalization of international law that is underway or is it rather internationalization of constitutional law. The process of internationalization of constitutional law puts an accent on the hierarchical constitutional order and impregnates it with some international elements.[4] The process of constitutionalization of international law, on the other hand, essentially attempts at transgressing the horizontal realm of international law. In this sense, constitutionalization of international law supplements international law with constitutional doctrines and logic.[5]

This interaction between international and constitutional law leads to the growing influence of constitutional legal thinking in international fora. Zupančič emphasizes that "at bottom the universal and large scale international process is, in the mode of autonomous legal reasoning, indistinguishable from internal, national constitutionalization of law."[6] This is especially patent with regard to human rights treaties whose methodology is clearly constitutionalist.[7] The structure of international legal system is therefore up-grading from its initial contract-law logic,[8] to a hierarchical global structure. At the core of this process is a transformation from the horizontal constellation of power(s) to a vertical alignment of power. Responding to the demand for an imaginative constitutional thinking in international law, constitutional law is progressively enriching the contents of international law with constitutional logic. As the constitutional reasoning is at the center of any legal system, it makes it rather easy to permeate all other branches of law.[9]

---

3 Bianchi, 'Ad-hocism and the Rule of Law', pp. 267, 269-270.

4 For a comprehensive study of globalization of constitutional law, *see* A. Peters, 'The Globalization of State Constitutions', *in* J. Nijman & A. Nollkaemper (Ed.), *New Perspectives on the Divide between National and International Law*, OUP, Oxford, 2007, pp. 251-308.

5 *See* Zupančič, *The Owl of Minerva*, pp. 355, 364-365, 391, 392, G. Malinverni, 'Propos introductifs', *in* J.-F. Flauss (Ed.), *L'enseignement du droit constitutionnel*, Bruylant, Bruxelles, 2000, pp. 7-8, 10, Bryde, 'International Democratic Constitutionalism', pp. 120-121 and T. Cottier & M. Hertig, 'The Prospects of 21st Century Constitutionalism', *in* T. Cottier, *The Challenge of WTO Law: Collected Essays*, Cameron May, London, 2007, pp. 418-424.

6 Zupančič, *The Owl of Minerva*, p. 392 (footnote omitted).

7 Bryde, 'International Democratic Constitutionalism', p. 112.

8 Ibid., p. 109, A. Peters, 'Global Constitutionalism in a Nutshell', *in* K. Dicke (Ed.), *Weltinnenrecht: Liber amicorum Jost Delbrück*, Duncker & Humblot, Berlin, 2005 and Zupančič, *The Owl of Minerva*, p. 362, n. 22.

9 Malinverni, 'Propos introductifs', p. 8 and J.-F. Flauss, 'Conclusions générales – Deux siècles d'enseignement de droit constitutionnel : esquisse d'un bilan', *in* Flauss, *L'enseignement du droit constitutionnel*, p. 214.

There is no doubt that an intense cross-fertilization between constitutional and international law is elevating ICL to a novel and autonomous branch of international law.[10] The dichotomy between 'the international' and 'the constitutional' therefore seems to be overcome.[11] Since pragmatism is a short-term strategy that does not pay off in the long run,[12] it is important to abandon the patchy approach and start considering ICL as a discipline in its own right.[13]

International constitutionalism inscribes in the general definition of constitutionalism in that the migration of power to the international sphere leads to the agglomeration of international power and forming limitations that restrain it.[14] This is the process of internationalization of the constitutive power (*pouvoir constituant*).[15] Constitutionalism in this sense denotes establishment of an international political authority, which is followed by imposing limitations on that political power.[16] Constitutional principles that limit international power are, for example, the rule of law, checks and balances, human rights protection and democracy.[17]

The main difference to the domestic realm is that the process of the agglomeration of power is dispersed and materializes through various international regimes. Regimes can be defined as arrangements for subject areas that embody implicit rules and norms that guide behaviour of important actors in a particular issue area.[18] They are relatively efficient and cohesive power structures, since their principles, rules, and institutions prompt actors to identify common issues and reach mutually beneficial agreements.[19] In the

---

10 *Cf.* B. Fassbender, 'The United Nations Charter as Constitution of the International Community', 36 *Columbia Journal of Transnational Law* 1998, p. 617 and E. de Wet, 'The Constitutionalization of Public International Law', *in* M. Rosenfeld & A. Sajó (Eds.), *The Oxford Handbook of Comparative Constitutional Law*, OUP, Oxford, 2012, p. 1213.

11 Fassbender, 'The United Nations Charter as Constitution of the International Community', p. 561.

12 Bianchi, 'Ad-hocism and the Rule of Law', p. 272.

13 B. Fassbender, 'The Meaning of International Constitutional Law', *in* N. Tsagourias (Ed.), *Transnational Constitutionalism: International and European Models*, CUP, Cambridge, 2007, p. 308. It seems that this approach is increasingly gaining influence. *See, e.g.*, contributions in Macdonald & Johnston, *World Constitutionalism*, Tsagourias, *Transnational Constitutionalism*, and C. Joerges, I.-J. Sand & G. Teubner (Eds.), *Transnational Governance and Constitutionalism*, Hart Publishing, Oxford, 2004.

14 *Cf.* I. Pernice & F.C. Mayer, 'De la constitution composée de l'Europe', 36 *Revue trimestrielle de droit européen* 2000, p. 627.

15 *Cf.* Peters, 'Global Constitutionalism in a Nutshell', p. 539, C. Möllers, '*Pouvoir Constituant—Constitution —Constitutionalisation*', *in* A. von Bogdandy & J. Bast (Eds.), *Principles of European Constitutional Law*, Hart Publishing, Oxford-Portland (OR), 2006, p. 186 *et seq.*, and A. von Bogdandy, 'Constitutional Principles for Europe', *in* E. Riedel & R. Wolfrum (Eds.), *Recent Trends in German and European Constitutional Law*, Springer, Berlin-Heidelberg-New York, 2006, p. 4.

16 Peters, 'Global Constitutionalism in a Nutshell', p. 540, W. Werner, 'The Never-ending Closure: Constitutionalism and International Law', *in* Tsagourias, *Transnational Constitutionalism*, pp. 349, 356, 366-367, and A. Verhoeven, *The European Union in Search of a Democratic and Constitutional Theory*, Kluwer Law International, The Hague-London-New York, 2002, p. 16.

17 A. Peters, 'Compensatory Constitutionalism: The Function and Potential of Fundamental International Norms and Structures', 19 *LJIL* 2006, p. 583.

18 Keohane, *The Theory of Hegemonic Stability*, p. 133.

19 *Cf.* ibid., p. 97.

context of this book, the term regime is understood widely to include states, international organizations, non-governmental organizations and other relevant entities.

Most frequently international constitutionalism stands for the creation of an international institution on the basis of the constituent treaty.[20] P.-M. Dupuy labels the advancement of constitutionalism *within* the framework of international organizations as micro-constitutionalism. Additionally, there is also the growth of constitutionalism at the global level, with regard to the legal order *as a whole* and can be understood as macro-constitutionalism.[21] Some authors try to overcome the dichotomy between micro- and macro-constitutionalism with a structure of multi-layered constitutionalism. Thomas Cottier and Maya Hertig propose a five-layer structure of constitutionalism spanning from a local to a global level.[22] The first three layers consist of entities from the domestic law: communes, the cantons or sub-federal entities, and federal units. At the international level, they envisage the fourth layer, consisting of regional organizations and, as the fifth layer, emerging structures of global integration such as the WTO, the Bretton Woods institutions and the United Nations.[23] Ingolf Pernice also proposed the model of multi-level constitutionalism. Here, the future structure of a global constitution relies on a number of supranational organizations, organized according to the logic of cascade. At one level there would be different regional organizations, which would all come under an umbrella of one unified system.[24] Nonetheless, the current global structure does not function on the basis of the logic of hierarchy and regional institutions often do not see themselves as being subordinate to universal institutions. Therefore, the most appropriate way to describe the current state of international constitutionalism is that it represents a transnational network of diverse and partial expressions of constitutionalism at the international level.[25] However, multiple processes of international constitutionalism "do not cancel each other out, but are apt to co-exist, to reinforce each other and even mutually to

---

20 *See* R. Monaco, 'Le caractère constitutionnel des actes institutifs d'organisations internationales', *in Mélanges offerts à Charles Rousseau – La communauté internationale*, Editions A. Pedone, Paris, 1974, pp. 153-172 and Peters, 'Compensatory Constitutionalism', pp. 593-594.

21 P.-M. Dupuy, *L'unité de l'ordre juridique international : Cours général de droit international public (2000), in RCADI*, vol. 297, Martinus Nijhoff Publishers, Leiden-Boston, 2003, pp. 227-228. P.-M. Dupuy uses the term *macro-constitutionalism* with regard to the Charter of the UN. *See also* J. Klabbers, A. Peters & G. Ulfstein, *The Constitutionalization of International Law*, OUP, Oxford, 2009, p. 20.

22 Cottier & Hertig, 'The Prospects of 21st Century Constitutionalism', pp. 414-415.

23 Ibid., p. 444.

24 I. Pernice, 'The Global Dimension of Multilevel Constitutionalism: A Legal Response to the Challenges of Globalisation', *in* P.-M. Dupuy (Ed.), *Völkerrecht als Wertordnung: Festschrift für Christian Tomuschat*, N.P. Engel, Kehl, 2006, p. 1005. *See also* Pernice & Mayer, 'De la constitution composée de l'Europe', pp. 623-647.

25 *Cf.* A. Peters, 'There is Nothing more Practical than a Good Theory: An Overview of Contemporary Approaches to International Law', 44 *GYIL* 2001, p. 36, C. Walter, 'International Law in a Process of Constitutionalization', *in* Nijman & Nollkaemper, *New Perspectives on the Divide between National and International Law*, p. 194 and N. Walker, 'Reframing EU Constitutionalism', *in* J.L. Dunoff & J.P. Trachtman (Eds.), *Ruling the World? Constitutionalism, International Law, and Global Governance*, CUP, Cambridge, 2009, p. 151.

compensate each others' deficiencies."[26] In graphic terms, this state of play would correspond to a raised-relief map in which elevations such as hills and mountains would represent various instances and degrees of international constitutionalism.

Given that human agency has a vital influence on the shape and functioning of regimes,[27] it is reasonable to portray these centers of international constitutionalism as epistemic communities in charge of exercising relevant constitutional functions.[28] An epistemic community is "a network of professionals with recognized expertise and competence in a particular domain and an authoritative claim to policy-relevant knowledge within that domain or issue-area."[29] These professionals share their belief or faith in particular forms of knowledge or specific professional truths.[30] In the international legal system, such communities emerge from discursive interaction between participants in a particular field or enterprise and are vital in defining international rules and norms.[31] Members of a given epistemic community may exert a strong influence at the international level. An epistemic community that consolidates its power within a specific international forum has a tendency to propagate its views to other fora in the international community.[32] If epistemic communities operate on the basis of a constitutional mindset, this leads to the "extension of constitutionalist thinking to world order".[33]

Importantly, epistemic communities perform social functions. Generally, the functionalist approach is understood "in the sense that every social pattern is analysed as performing some function in order to preserve the existing society."[34] The essential attribute of functionalism is a practice of interpreting data and implying their consequences for larger structures in which they are implicated.[35] In this sense, social functionalism

---

26 A. Peters, 'Fragmentation and Constitutionalization', *in* Orford, Hoffmann & Clark, *The Oxford Handbook of the Theory of International Law*, p. 1022.

27 Peters, *Institutional Theory*, pp. 162-163.

28 *Cf.* A.L. Paulus, 'From Territoriality to Functionality? Towards a Legal Methodology of Globalization', *in* I.F. Dekker & W.G. Werner (Ed.), *Governance and International Legal Theory*, Martinus Nijhoff Publishers, Leiden-Boston, 2004, pp. 59-60, 93.

29 P.M. Haas, 'Introduction: Epistemic Communities and International Policy Coordination', 46 *International Organization* 1992, p. 3. In the context of the EU Neil Walker developed a comparable phenomenon of 'epistemic pluralism'. (*See* N. Walker, 'The Idea of Constitutional Pluralism', 65 *The Modern Law Review* 2002, p. 338 *et seq.*)

30 Haas, 'Introduction', p. 4.

31 I. Johnstone, 'The Power of Interpretive Communities', *in* M. Barnett and R. Duvall (Eds.), *Power in Global Governance,* CUP, Cambridge, 2004, p. 186.

32 *Cf.* Haas, 'Introduction', p. 4.

33 R.A. Falk, 'The Pathways to Global Constitutionalism', *in* R.A. Falk, R.C. Johansen & S.S. Kim (Eds.), *The Constitutional Foundations of World Peace*, State University of New York Press, Albany, 1993, p. 14. *See also* M. Koskenniemi, 'Constitutionalism as Mindset: Reflections on Kantian Themes about International Law and Globalization', 8 *Theoretical Inquiries in Law* 2007, pp. 9-36.

34 M. Hirsch & A. Lang, 'Introduction', *in* M. Hirsch & A. Lang (Eds.), *Research Handbook on the Sociology of International Law*, Edward Elgar, Cheltenham, 2018, p. 2.

35 Merton, *Social Theory and Social Structure*, pp. 19-84, in particular pp. 46-47. For application of functionalism to international law *see* J.L. Dunoff & J.P. Trachtman, 'A Functional Approach to International Constitutionalization', *in* Dunoff & Trachtman, *Ruling the World?*, pp. 9-18.

presupposes professional interaction with an aim to advance comprehension, knowledge and expertise about broader social processes. A legal perception of social functionalism sees law as a social concept and proposes a way forward in a social reality on the basis of the normative prescription.[36] In line with this perspective international constitutionalism – through the work of epistemic communities – instils and reinforces constitutional features in the international community.[37] These features, as illustrated in Part One, amalgamate into the following constitutional functions: normative, institutional, judicial, coordinative and self-referential.

Each of these constitutional functions operates on the basis of a certain epistemic logic. The task of the normative function is to provide the international community with necessary and adequate legal rules. However, norms can lead to desired effects only on the basis of a solid and working institutional framework, which is also the best guarantee for the efficient implementation of norms. In addition, there is a need for the judicial function to keep resolving conflicts in a highly differentiated international community and mediate between different norms and between different institutions. The coordinative function serves the purpose of aligning international regulatory aggregations into an ordered and concerted whole. Finally, the self-referential function deals with spontaneous phenomena, which leads to new developments in the international community and raises fresh dilemmas about their regulation. Each of these constitutional functions is essential for the proper social functioning of the international community. Each of them also works as a check on the other constitutional functions. The relationship between them is therefore one of interdependence and correlation: one does not exist without the other whereas they all reinforce and limit each other. Below is a graphic design symbolizing their interaction.

36 *Cf.* Koskenniemi, *From Apology to Utopia*, pp. 573-574, R. Prandini, 'The Morphogenesis of Constitutionalism', *in* P. Dobner & M. Loughlin (Eds.), *The Twilight of Constitutionalism?*, OUP, Oxford, 2010, p. 313 and J.L. Cohen, *Globalization and Sovereignty: Rethinking Legality, Legitimacy and Constitutionalism*, CUP, Cambridge, 2012, p. 53.

37 *See* Dunoff & Trachtman, 'A Functional Approach to International Constitutionalization', pp. 4-5, 9-10, A. Peters, 'Global Constitutionalism', *in* M. Gibbons (Ed.), *The Encyclopedia of Political Thought*, Wiley & Sons, London, 2015, p. 1485 and A. Peters, 'Fragmentation and Constitutionalization', *in* Orford, Hoffmann & Clark, *The Oxford Handbook of the Theory of International Law*, p. 1016.

Repartition of Constitutional Functions in the International Community

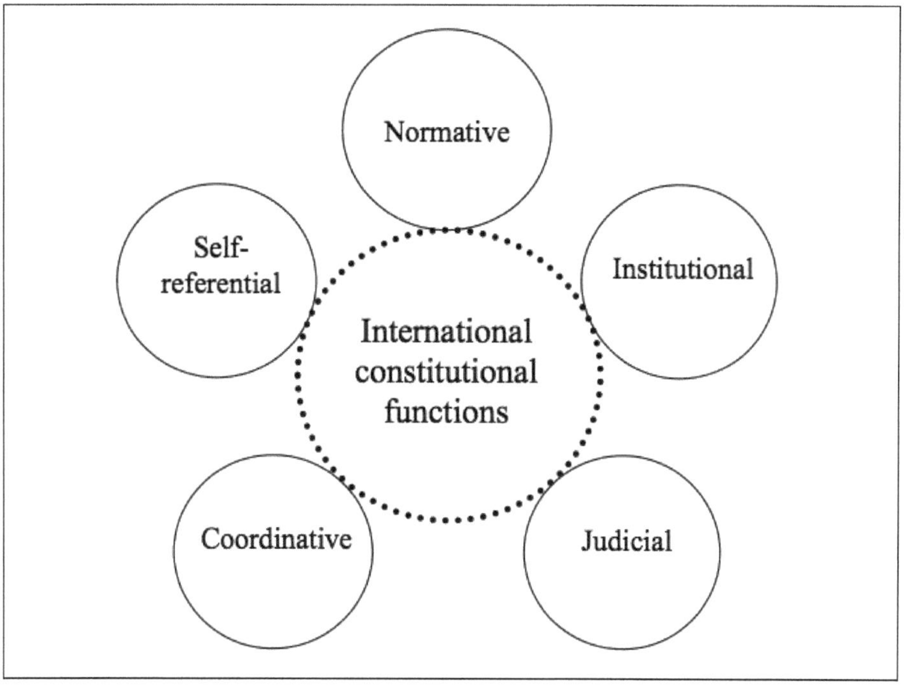

ICL deals with international constitutionalism in line with its characteristic dynamic. It is presupposed on the inherent tension in international constitutionalism between the process of agglomeration of international powers(s) and limitations that are imposed on these power structures. Regimes that spring from these power centers are the home of epistemic communities radiating constitutional features into the international community. In the international realm, these features amalgamate into distinct international constitutional functions: normative, institutional, judicial, coordinative and self-referential.[38] Most appropriately this concept can be labelled as integrative international consti-

38 International lawyers usually refer to general constitutional analogies of normative, institutional and judicial functions, to which sometimes coordinative and/or self-referential functions are added in a less systematic fashion. (*See* Klabbers, Peters & Ulfstein, *The Constitutionalization of International Law*, pp. 28, 46-47, 80, D. Grimm, 'The Achievement of Constitutionalism and its Prospects in a Changed World', *in* Dobner & Loughlin, *The Twilight of Constitutionalism?*, p. 46 and A. Clapham, *Brierly's Law of Nations: An Introduction to the Role of International Law in International Relations*, OUP, Oxford, 2012, pp. 102-103.)

tutionalism.[39] These functions are going to be subject of a more detailed appraisal in the following pages.

7.2 Normative Function of International Constitutionalism

The normative function of international constitutionalism primarily focuses on norms as bearers of fundamental values. In the context of the definition of a constitution scholars refer to this component as a material element of the constitution. In this sense, a material component of a constitution stands for a set of legal principles of paramount importance to all the subjects belonging to a particular social community.[40] Juxtaposed to the material component is also the organic element of the constitution. But since that component deals with institutional issues,[41] it shall be considered in the section on the institutional function of international constitutionalism. The normative function of international constitutionalism deals with norms with a strong ethical underpinning. These norms have acquired a special hierarchical standard. Consequently, they form an international value system superior to other norms of international law.[42] In the context of the general international law, the focus will be on norms *jus cogens*, obligations *erga omnes* and international human rights law (non-derogable rights). Furthermore, with regard to the development of international norms within international organizations, this section will take into consideration the universal level (the UN and the World Trade Organization, WTO) and the regional level (the European Union and the Council of Europe). Norms of ICL are therefore a subset of international rules and principles of such importance that they deserve the label *constitutional*.[43]

---

39 The word integrative implies integration of various strands into a common concept. For similar approaches, *see* J. Tully *et al.*, 'Editorial: Introducing Global Integral Constitutionalism', 5 *Global Constitutionalism* 2016, pp. 1-15 and C.E.J. Schwöbel, *Global Constitutionalism in International Legal Perspective*, Martinus Nijhoff Publishers, Leiden, 2011, pp. 2-3, 17 *et seq.*

40 P.-M., Dupuy, 'The Constitutional Dimension of the Charter of the United Nations Revisited', 1 *Max Planck Yearbook of United Nations Law* 1997, p. 3.

41 Id.

42 *Cf.* Bianchi, 'Ad-hocism and the Rule of Law', p. 268 and E. De Wet, 'The Emergence of International and Regional Value Systems as a Manifestation of the Emerging International Constitutional Order', 19 *LJIL* 2006, pp. 612-613. *See also* T. Rensmann, 'The Constitution as a Normative Order of Values: The Influence of International Human Rights Law on the Evolution of Modern Constitutionalism', *in* Dupuy, *Völkerrecht als Wertordnung*, pp. 260-278 and P. Tavernier, 'L'identification des reglès fondamentales, un problème résolu ?', *in* C. Tomuschat & M. Thouvenin, (Eds.), *The Fundamental Rules of the International Legal Order: Jus Cogens* and *Obligations Erga Omnes*, Martinus Nijhoff Publishers, Leiden-Boston, 2006, p. 18.

43 *Cf.* A. Peters & K. Armingeon, 'Introduction – Global Constitutionalism from an Interdisciplinary Perspective', 16 *Indiana Journal of Global Legal Studies* 2009, p. 387.

7.2.1 *Fundamental Norms of the International Community*

An early example of the normative understanding of international constitutionalism emerged within the concept of the international community as a legal community. The bearers of this approach are predominantly lawyers coming from the German-speaking tradition of international law, notably Alfred Verdross, Hermann Mosler and Christian Tomuschat.[44] The concept of the international legal community sees the constitution of this community as the conglomerate of the most important international norms. While this perspective is paramount for the development of international constitutionalism, it is sometimes reductionist to the point that it situates the concept of the international constitution exclusively within the axiological framework.

The process of constitutionalization of the normative function evolved particularly through the development of normative categories of the higher value throughout the twentieth century.[45] In this contest, it is adequate to speak of gradation in the normativity of international law.[46] Doctrine and jurisprudence developed various concepts of dichotomy between higher and lower norms. These concepts can be classified as follows: norms of *jus cogens v. jus dispositivum*, obligations *erga omnes v.* obligations *inter partes*, and non-derogable human rights *v.* derogable human rights. A pioneer of the critique on the hierarchy of international norms, Prosper Weil, called this phenomenon 'relative normativity'.[47]

The idea of *jus cogens* derives from the concept of natural law,[48] which attempted to command human behaviour on the basis of religious or rational discovery of higher

44 *See* Fassbender, 'The United Nations Charter as Constitution of the International Community', pp. 541-544, 546-551, B. Simma, 'The Contribution of Alfred Verdross to the Theory of International Law', 6 *EJIL* 1995, pp. 33-54, H. Mosler, *The International Society as a Legal Community, in RCADI,* 1974, IV, vol. 140, A.W. Sijthoff, Leyde, 1976, pp. 32-36, C. Tomuschat, 'Obligations Arising for States without or against their Will', *in RCADI,* 1993, IV, vol. 241, Martinus Nijhoff Publishers, Dordrecht-Boston-London, 1994, pp. 216-240 and C. Tomuschat, 'International Law as the Constitution of Mankind', *in International Law on the Eve of the Twenty-first Century: Views from the International Law Commission,* United Nations, New York, 1997, pp. 37-50.

45 *Cf.* Bianchi, 'Ad-hocism and the Rule of Law', p. 268.

46 *See* U. Fastenrath, 'Relative Normativity in International Law', 4 *EJIL* 1993, p. 338 and D. Shelton, 'International Law and "Relative Normativity"', *in* Evans, *International Law,* pp. 159-160 and Daillier & Pellet, *Droit international public,* p. 201.

47 P. Weil, 'Towards Relative Normativity in International Law?', 77 *AJIL* 1983, pp. 413-442.

48 A. Verdross, 'Jus Dispositivum and Jus Cogens in International Law', 60 *AJIL* 1966, p. 56, Koskenniemi, *From Apology to Utopia,* p. 323, n. 54, C. Dominicé, 'Le grand retour du droit naturel en droit des gens', *in* C. Dominicé, *L'ordre juridique international entre tradition et innovation: Recueil d'études,* PUF, 1997, Paris, p. 41 and G.M. Danilenko, 'International *Jus Cogens*: Issues of Law-Making', 2 *EJIL* 1991, p. 44.

ethical values.[49] The work of the International Law Commission (ILC), in particular, transformed the concept of *jus cogens* from the realm of natural law to become a positive legal rule in the VCLT.[50] Article 53 defines *jus cogens* in the following terms:

> [A] peremptory norm of general international law is a norm accepted and recognized by the international community of States as a whole as a norm from which no derogation is permitted and which can be modified only by a subsequent norm of general international law having the same character.

In case of a conflict between a treaty provision and a norm of *jus cogens* a "treaty is void if, at the time of its conclusion, it conflicts with a peremptory norm of general international law."[51] The concept of *jus cogens* devises norms of international law that cannot be downscaled by other norms not having the same character. The concept of *jus cogens* therefore establishes a distinction between higher peremptory norms and lower, 'ordinary' norms or the *jus dispositivum* of international law. The difference between two layers of norms comes from the fact that *jus cogens* norms are not discretionary in nature. As such, they stand above the will of states and the voluntarist conception of international law.[52] Although the VCLT originates from the treaty law, this normative differentiation is applicable to the entire international legal system.[53]

However, the concept of *jus cogens* is not free from controversy.[54] While the VCLT in its Article 53 implies that peremptory norms are of a higher rank,[55] it does not define

49 *Cf.* S.C. Neff, 'A Short History of International Law', *in* Evans, *International Law*, p. 32, A. Pellet, 'The Normative Dilemma: Will and Consent in International Law-making', *in* 12 *Australian Yearbook of International Law* 1988-1989, pp. 22-23, A. Verdross, 'Forbidden Treaties in International Law: Comments on Professor Garner's Report on "The Law of Treaties"', 31 *AJIL* 1937, p. 572, Dominicé, 'Le grand retour du droit naturel', p. 33 and A. Bianchi, 'Human Rights and the Magic of *Jus Cogens*', 19 *EJIL* 2008, pp. 493-494, 495.

50 *Cf.* Bianchi, 'Human Rights and the Magic of *Jus Cogens*', pp. 492-493, M. Virally, 'Réflexions sur le « jus cogens »', *in* M. Virally, *Le droit international en devenir : essais écrits au fil des ans*, PUF, Paris, 1990, p. 156 and K. Zemanek, 'How to Identify Peremptory Norms of International Law', *in* Dupuy, *Völkerrecht als Wertordnung*, p. 1110.

51 Art. 53 of the VCLT. Art. 64 of the VCLT applies to the conflict between an earlier treaty and a new peremptory norm: "If a new peremptory norm of general international law emerges, any existing treaty which is in conflict with that norm becomes void and terminates."

52 J.A. Carillo Salcedo, 'Reflections on the Existence of a Hierarchy of Norms in International Law', 8 *EJIL* 1997, pp. 583-595 and J.A. Frowein, 'Jus Cogens', *in* Bernhardt, *Encyclopedia of Public International Law*, vol. 3, pp. 65-66.

53 *Cf.* M. Akehurst, 'The Hierarchy of the Sources of International Law', 47 *BYIL* 1974-1975, pp. 281-282.

54 For a realistic assessment of *jus cogens*, *see* A. D'Amato, 'It's a Bird, It's a Plane, It's Jus Cogens!' 6 *Connecticut Journal of International Law* 1990, pp. 1-6 and Bianchi, 'Human Rights and the Magic of *Jus Cogens*', pp. 491-508.

55 Reuter even says that they enjoy an absolute character. (Reuter, *Introduction au droit des traités*, p. 127.)

their contents.[56] The concept of *jus cogens* is therefore essentially self-referential.[57] Who is then to decide on the precise meaning of *jus cogens* and how?[58] The only viable solution would be that there is a judicial body to control the contents of peremptory norms and its violations.[59] Up until now international courts and tribunals were not very eager to employ the concept of *jus cogens.* The explicit mention of *jus cogens* features in a few judgments of international judicial bodies,[60] for example, in *Congo v. Uganda* of the ICJ,[61] the *Furundžija* case of the ICTY[62] and the *Al-Adsani* case of the ECtHR.[63] Such reserved attitude points to the possible haphazard impact of *jus cogens* and to the danger of its abuse. It is possible to imagine that the imperative character of *jus cogens* could instil hegemonic dominance over other spheres of international law.[64] In addition, determination of what constitutes the contents of the peremptory norms may amount to cultural imperialism.[65]

Obligations *erga omnes* derive from the logic that there are certain obligations in the international community, which pertain to that community as a whole. While the ICJ is not so open to the concept of *jus cogens*, it invented the concept of obligations towards the international community as a whole. In the *Barcelona Traction* case, the ICJ said:

56 Virally, 'Réflexions sur le « jus cogens »', p. 164 and Tavernier, 'L'identification des reglès fondamentales', p. 1. However, scholars in general agree that the following norms represent *jus cogens*: prohibition of aggression, genocide, crimes against humanity, war crimes, the principle of self-determination and the fundamental rights of the human person. (Reuter, *Introduction au droit des traités*, p. 127, A. Paulus, '*Jus cogens* in a Time of Hegemony and Fragmentation – An Attempt at a Re-appraisal', 74 *Nordic Journal of International Law* 2005, p. 306 and H. Ruiz-Fabri, 'L'ordre public en droit international', *in* M.-J. Redor (Ed.), *L'ordre public : Ordre public ou ordres publics, Ordre public et droits fondamentaux*, Nemesis-Bruylant, Bruxelles, 2001, p. 92.) Currently, the work is underway in the ILC to identify peremptory norms of international law. Special Rapporteur on the topic, Dire Tladi, proposed the following list of *jus cogens* norms: the prohibition of aggression, the prohibition of torture, the prohibition of genocide, the prohibition of crimes against humanity, the prohibition of apartheid and racial discrimination, the prohibition of slavery, the right to self-determination, the basic rules of international humanitarian law and other possible *jus cogens* norms. As this list is illustrative, the work of the ILC on the topic will continue. (*See* ILC, 'Fourth Report on Peremptory Norms of General International Law (Jus Cogens) by Dire Tladi, Special Rapporteur', 31 January 2019, A/CN.4/727.)

57 Daillier & Pellet, *Droit international public*, p. 202, Abi-Saab, *Cours général de droit international public*, p. 427, Zemanek, 'How to Identify Peremptory Norms of International Law', p. 1113, Dupuy, *L'unité de l'ordre juridique international*, p. 283 and Shelton, 'International Law and "Relative Normativity"', p. 165.

58 *Cf.* Dominicé, 'Le grand retour du droit naturel', p. 41 and Bianchi, 'Human Rights and the Magic of *Jus Cogens*', pp. 493-494, 507-508.

59 *Cf.* Zemanek, 'How to Identify Peremptory Norms of International Law', p. 1117.

60 *See* Shelton, 'International Law and "Relative Normativity"', pp. 167-170, Bianchi, 'Human Rights and the Magic of *Jus Cogens*', pp. 501-502 and Tavernier, 'L'identification des reglès fondamentales', pp. 8-10.

61 *See Case concerning Armed Activities on the Territory of the Congo (New Application: 2002) (Democratic Republic of the Congo v. Rwanda)*, Jurisdiction of the Court and Admissibility of the Application, 3 February 2006 (General List No. 126), paras. 15, 64, 69, 78, 125.

62 *See Prosecutor v. Anto Furundžija*, Judgement, 10 December 1998, paras. 153-155.

63 *See* case *Al-Adsani v. the United Kingdom*, 21 November 2001, para. 60.

64 R. Kolb, *Théorie du ius cogens international : Essai de relecture du concept*, PUF, Paris, 2001, p. 48.

65 Zemanek, 'How to Identify Peremptory Norms of International Law', p. 1114 and M.J. Glennon, 'De l'absurdité du droit impertif (*jus cogens*)', 110 *RGDIP* 2006, p. 534.

> [A]n essential distinction should be drawn between the obligations of a State towards the international community as a whole, and those arising vis-à-vis another State in the field of diplomatic protection. By the very nature the former are the concern of all States. In view of the importance of the rights involved, all States can be held to have a legal interest in their protection; they are obligations erga omnes.[66]

A state invokes such an obligation in the context of the international community as a whole. Or, looking from the opposite perspective, all states of the world community have an interest in the protection of such obligations.[67] The ICJ transformed the protection from narrow bilateralism to the universal protection of certain fundamental norms.[68] The reason for a distinction derives from an extraordinary nature of such an obligation.[69] Obligations *erga omnes* consist of a substantive and procedural component. The above argumentation of the ICJ suggests that obligations *erga omnes* have specific as well as broad procedural consequences because of the substantive importance of norms they put forward.[70] In this way, essential community interests enjoy protection even with no effective organs in the international community.[71]

However, the concept of obligations *erga omnes* can pose a danger to national sovereignty if there are no criteria for a determination by the majority of states that a certain conventional regime is contrary to obligations *erga omnes*.[72] The formula of obligations *erga omnes* presupposes that a wide group of states can refer to the general interest of the international community and determine the universal content of international rules.[73] But in a poorly organised community dominated by the great powers, such a phenomenon could turn into a factual international government of the oligarchic type. In a contemporary system of international law-making, the end result of the content of the norms usually reflects a quasi-universal consensus. However, the process can also go proceed to reflect the will of the great powers.[74]

---

66 *Barcelona Traction* case, para. 33.

67 *Cf.* Dupuy, *L'unité de l'ordre juridique international*, p. 290, Shelton, 'International Law and "Relative Normativity"', p. 163 and Villalpando, *L'émergence de la communauté internationale dans la responsabilité des Etats*, pp. 97, 104, 281.

68 Weil, 'Towards Relative Normativity in International Law?', p. 432.

69 Among obligations of *erga omnes* are the prohibition of genocide, respect of the fundamental human rights, in particular prohibition of slavery and racial discrimination. (Barcelona Traction *case*, para. 34, Dupuy, *L'unité de l'ordre juridique international*, p. 290 and Shelton, 'International Law and "Relative Normativity"', p. 163.)

70 Shelton, 'International Law and "Relative Normativity"', p. 163.

71 Fassbender, 'The Meaning of International Constitutional Law', p. 319.

72 Daillier & Pellet, *Droit international public*, p. 247. On the difficulty of the determination of the community interests in the context of *erga omnes* obligations, *see also* Villalpando, *L'émergence de la communauté internationale dans la responsabilité des Etats*, p. 98.

73 Daillier & Pellet, *Droit international public*, p. 246.

74 Ibid., p. 247.

With regard to international norms some scholars invoke another distinction – that of non-derogable and derogable human rights. Dinah Shelton underlines that this hierarchy applies to human rights within a particular human rights treaty.[75] According to Article 4 of the ICCPR, Article 15 of the ECHR, and Article 27 of the IACHR states parties can take measures to suspend certain rights to the extent strictly required by the exigencies of the situation, provided that such obligations are not inconsistent with other obligations under international law and that they do not represent any discrimination in the most basic form.[76] The lists of non-derogable rights in these documents are not completely identical.[77] But if we take the three instruments as a whole, we can identify the five core non-derogable rights: right to life, freedom from torture, prohibition of slavery, inadmissibility of *ex post facto* criminal laws, and the right to be free from discriminatory treatment in respect of derogations.[78] However, that does not mean that these are the sole rights to enjoy the status of non-derogability. All three human rights charters proclaim that states should not adopt measures that would be inconsistent with their obligations under international law. The Human Rights Committee (HRC), for example, supplements the above list to include prohibitions of taking hostages, imposing collective punishments, practicing arbitrary deprivations of liberty, or deviating from fundamental principles of fair trial (including the presumption of innocence).[79] All these rights constitute, according to the HRC, *jus cogens*, which is why they are protected as non-derogable rights although the ICCPR does not enumerate them as such.[80]

All these essential categories – *jus cogens*, obligations *erga omnes*, and non-derogable rights – overlap at the higher level of the normative structure of the international community.[81] These norms therefore represent the constitutional normative dimension of

75 Shelton, 'International Law and "Relative Normativity"', p. 174.

76 For a basic assessment of these provisions, *see* the following contributions: M. Nowak, 'The International Covenant on Civil and Political Rights', pp. 89-90, J.G. Merrills, 'The Council of Europe (I): The European Convention on Human Rights', pp. 231-233 and H. van der Wilt, 'The OAS System for the Protection of Human Rights', p. 307, all *in* R. Hanski & M. Suksi (Eds.), *An Introduction to the International Protection of Human Rights: A Textbook*, Institute for Human Rights, Åbo Akademi University, Turku-Åbo, 1998.

77 *See* Marks & Clapham, *International Human Rights Lexicon, s.v. terrorism*, p. 353.

78 Shelton, 'International Law and "Relative Normativity"', p. 174. There are other non-derogable rights in the context of each human rights instrument. The ICCPR and the IACHR recognize as non-derogable rights to recognition as a person before the law, and the right to the freedom of thought, conscience, and religion. The ICCPR considers as non-derogable the right to be free from imprisonment for a failure to perform a contractual obligation. The ECHR, together with Protocols, considers the freedom from double jeopardy and abolition of death penalty as non-derogable. Finally, the IACHR declares as non-derogable also protection of the family, rights of the child, the right to a nationality, the right to participate in government, as well as fundamental rights of due process. (Id.)

79 Ibid., p. 170 and HRC, 'General Comment No. 29, States of Emergency (article 4)', U.N. Doc. CCPR/C/21/Rev.1/Add.11 (2001), para. 13.

80 'General Comment No. 29', para. 11.

81 *Cf.* A. Bianchi, 'Immunity versus Human Rights: The *Pinochet* Case', 10 *EJIL* 1999, p. 271 and W.E. Conklin, 'The Peremptory Norms of the International Community', 23 *EJIL* 2012, pp. 861-862.

international law.[82] It seems that the main difference is not in the nature of norms, but in focus of the category to which they belong. *Jus cogens* norms, with their value orientation and natural law origins, tend to appeal to the conscience of the power-holders.[83] Obligations *erga omnes*, on the other hand, focus on collective interests of the world community.[84] Finally, non-derogable human rights emphasize a concern for survival and integrity of a human person.

7.2.2 Norms in International Organizations

Further components of the normative function of international constitutionalism can be found in constituent treaties or fundamental charters of different international organizations: the UN, the WTO, the EU and the Council of Europe (in the context of the ECHR). All these legal orders comprise norms in the sense of values of the international community.

7.2.2.1 United Nations

In the framework of the UN the constitutional provisions are part of the Charter of the UN.[85] These provisions comprise notably the preamble of the UN Charter[86] and the first chapter which proclaims purposes and principles of the UN.[87] In this sense, the normative constitutional principles of the UN are the maintenance of peace and security;[88] the prohibition of the use of force;[89] the peaceful settlement of disputes;[90] the principle of equal rights and self-determination of peoples;[91] the principle of cooperation in solving international problems of an economic, cultural or humanitarian character;[92] promotion of respect for human rights and fundamental freedoms for all;[93] and the respect of the

82 S. Kirchner, 'Relative Normativity and the Constitutional Dimension of International Law: A Place for Values in the International Legal System?', 5 *German Law Journal* 2004, p. 57 and Bianchi, *International Law Theories*, pp. 49-50.

83 Pellet, 'The Normative Dilemma', pp. 22-23.

84 ILC, *Draft Articles on Responsibility of States for Internationally Wrongful Acts, with commentaries, in Report of the International Law Commission, Fifty-third session (23 April-1 June and 2 July-10 August 2001)*, General Assembly, Official Records, Fifty-sixth session, Supplement No. 10 (A/56/10), United Nations, New York, 2001, p. 281.

85 Bianchi, *International Law Theories*, p. 47.

86 S. Schmahl, 'An Example of *Jus Cogens*: The Status of Prisoners of War', *in* Tomuschat & Thouvenin, *The Fundamental Rules of the International Legal Order*, pp. 47-48.

87 M. Virally, 'L'O.N.U. devant le droit', *in* Virally, *Le droit international en devenir*, p. 260.

88 *Charter of the United Nations*, United Nations, New York, 1995, Art. 1, para. 1. The UN Charter was signed on 26 June 1945, entered into force on 24 October 1945.

89 Art. 2, para. 4.

90 Art. 1(2), Art. 2(3) and Art. 33.

91 Art. 1(2).

92 Art. 1(3).

93 Id.

sovereign equality of all members of the UN.[94] In addition to the UN Charter, there are a number of other legal instruments that comprise normative provisions of a constitutional nature. The leading document is the *Universal Declaration of Human Rights* (UDHR), which introduced a comprehensive catalogue of human rights.[95] These fundamental normative provisions were elaborated in more detail in the nine universal core human rights instruments, the Genocide convention and the Statute of the International Criminal Court.[96] All these legal instruments originate from the UN framework. Therefore, it is adequate to name them 'constitutional by-laws'[97] because they are supplementary in the sense of adding to and implementing objectives of the law of the Charter.[98]

7.2.2.2 World Trade Organization

Due to its wide-ranging importance, fundamental norms constitutive of the WTO can be labeled as an economic constitution.[99] In the framework of the WTO the leading norms (basic principles and objectives) make part of the preamble of the WTO constituent *Agreement.*[100] In addition, the Agreement assumes substantive normative provisions by asserting legal supremacy of more than twenty worldwide trade agreements, which are listed in the WTO Annexes.[101] Moreover, the WTO legal system also incorporates the 50

---

94 Art. 2(1) and Dupuy, 'The Constitutional Dimension of the UN Charter', pp. 5-6.

95 See *Universal Declaration of Human Rights, in Human Rights: A Compilation of International Instruments*, vol. I (First Part), United Nations, New York-Geneva, 1994, pp. 1-7. The UDHR was adopted and proclaimed by the resolution of the General Assembly No. 217 A (III) on 10 December 1948. For more on the UDHR, *see* Clapham, *Human Rights: A Very Short Introduction*, pp. 42-48.

96 *Cf.* Fassbender, 'The United Nations Charter as Constitution of the International Community', p. 588. The nine core human rights charters are: the ICCPR, the International Covenant on Economic, Social and Cultural Rights, the International Convention on the Elimination of All Forms of Racial Discrimination, the Convention against Torture, the Convention on the Rights of the Child, the Convention on the Elimination of All Forms of Discrimination against Women, the International Convention on the Protection of the Rights of All Migrant Workers and their Families, the International Convention for the Protection of All Persons from Enforced Disappearance and the Convention on the Rights of Persons with Disabilities. For more, *see* Clapham, *Human Rights: A Very Short Introduction*, pp. 48-51.

97 Bylaw is an expression of English juridical terminology. It denotes a legal rule which derives from a higher legal rule (*e.g.*, law) and must stay within the limits of the higher legal rule. Bylaws are classed as 'subordinate' or 'delegated' legislation. (*See* Pitamic, *A Treatise on the State*, p. 168.)

98 Fassbender, 'The United Nations Charter as Constitution of the International Community', p. 588 and E. de Wet, 'The International Constitutional Order', 55 *ICLQ* 2006, pp. 57-58.

99 J.H. Jackson, *The World Trade Organization: Constitution and Jurisprudence*, The Royal Institute of International Affairs, London, 1998, pp. 1, 101-104 and J.P. Trachtman, 'Global Commercial Constitutionalization: The World Trade Organization', *in* Lang & Wiener, *Handbook on Global Constitutionalism*, pp. 396-397.

100 *Cf.* WTO, Agreement Establishing the World Trade Organization, preambular para. 5 (adopted on 15 April 1994 and entered into force 1 January 1995). *See* E.-U. Petersmann, 'Human Rights, Constitutionalism and the World Trade Organization: Challenges for World Trade Organization Jurisprudence and Civil Society', 19 *LJIL* 2006, pp. 635, 642-643 and D.Z. Cass, *The Constitutionalization of the World Trade Organization: Legitimacy, Democracy, and Community in the International Trading System*, OUP, Oxford-New York, 2005, pp. 146-162, 176.

101 E.-U. Petersmann, 'The WTO Constitution and Human Rights', 3 *Journal of International Economic Law* 2000, p. 20.

years of the previous GATT practice and decisions (known as the 'GATT *acquis*').[102] In these annexes and in the GATT *acquis* we find the most important normative provisions of the WTO legal system. The following normative components of the WTO constitutionalism are worth emphasizing: (i) the *WTO Agreement* and the *Dispute Settlement Understanding* (DSU) aims to ensure the rule of international (trade) law; (ii) the WTO protects freedom and nondiscrimination in international trade and is committed to sustainable development; (iii) compulsory WTO dispute settlement system protects horizontal and vertical separation of powers; and (iv) the WTO objectives or raising standards of living, promoting sustainable development and ensuring that developing countries have an adequate share in the growth of international trade, reflect a concern for social justice.[103] To these norms one must also add a requirement to protect and preserve the environment.[104] Looking from a comparative perspective, the most important of the above-enumerated normative commitments is the principle of nondiscrimination or the principle of equality. The WTO guarantees of nondiscrimination go beyond national constitutional guarantees in most countries which tend to discriminate against foreign goods, foreign services and foreign economic operators. By extending equal freedoms across the frontiers, the WTO exercises constitutional functions in rendering human rights and the corresponding governmental obligations more effective in the area of trade policy.[105]

7.2.2.3 Council of Europe

After the horrors of World War II, the European governments in 1949 decided to establish an international organization, the Council of Europe (COE), committed to the rule of law and common spiritual and moral traditions.[106] In this spirit, Article 1 of the COE Statute calls for the achievement of a greater unity between its members in various fields and also in the maintenance and further realization of human rights and fundamental

---

102 P. Lamy, 'The Place of the WTO and its Law in the International Legal Order', 5 *EJIL* 2007, pp. 971-972. On the process of the development of norms in the WTO *see* A. von Bogdandy, 'Law and Politics in the WTO – Strategies to Cope with a Deficient Relationship', 5 *Max Planck Yearbook of United Nations Law* 2001, pp. 625-644.

103 Petersmann, 'Human Rights, Constitutionalism and the World Trade Organization', p. 645 and J.L. Dunoff, 'Constitutional Conceits: The WTO's 'Constitution' and the Discipline of International Law', 17 *EJIL* 2006, pp. 653-654.

104 *Cf.* Agreement Establishing the WTO, preambular para. 1 and Lamy, 'The Place of the WTO and its Law in the International Legal Order', p. 978.

105 E.-U. Petersmann, 'Time for a United Nations "Global Compact" for Integrating Human Rights into the Law of Worldwide Organizations: Lessons from European Integration', 13 *EJIL* 2002, pp. 643-644 and Lamy, 'The Place of the WTO and its Law in the International Legal Order', p. 973.

106 J.G. Merrills, 'Promotion and Protection of Human Rights within the European Arrangements', *in* Hanski & Suksi, *An Introduction to the International Protection of Human Rights*, p. 209.

freedoms.[107] The first fruit of this commitment was the *European Convention on Human Rights* (ECHR), adopted in 1950.[108] In the Preamble, the ECHR first refers to the UDHR as a source of inspiration for the protection of human rights in the regional framework.[109] The ECtHR labeled the ECHR as a constitutional instrument of European public order (*ordre public*).[110] Other most important instruments within the COE framework are the *European Social Charter*, the *European Convention for the Prevention of Torture* and the *Framework Convention for the Protection of National Minorities*.[111] Therefore, the European public order contributes to the reinforcement of the international value system as a whole.[112]

7.2.2.4 European Union

In the last two decades, there has been a noticeable turn to a normative component of constitutionalism in the EU. The founding treaties of the European Community did not refer to the protection of fundamental rights.[113] The credit for the introduction of human rights into the European legal order goes to the European Court of Justice (ECJ). The ECJ started infusing the European communitarian order with the fundamental legal rights for which it found inspiration in the ECHR and constitutional tradition of the member states.[114] The real breakthrough with regard to human rights occurred with the elabora-

---

107 Merrills, 'Promotion and Protection of Human Rights within the European Arrangements', p. 209 and D. Gomien, *Short Guide to the European Convention on Human Rights*, Council of Europe Publishing, Strasbourg, 1998, p. 5.

108 Merrills, 'Promotion and Protection of Human Rights within the European Arrangements', pp. 209-210 and Gomien, *Short Guide to the European Convention on Human Rights*, pp. 5-6. *See also* R.C.A. White & C. Ovey, *The European Convention on Human Rights*, OUP, Oxford, 2010 and D. Harris *et al., Law of the European Convention on Human Rights*, OUP, Oxford, 2009.

109 European Convention on Human Rights as Amended by Protocol No. 11, Council of Europe, Strasbourg, 1998, preambular paras. 1, 2.

110 *See* case *Loizidou v. Turkey (Preliminary Objections)*, 23 March 1995, para. 75. For the treatment of the topic in doctrine, *see* F. Sudre, 'L'ordre public européen', *in* M.-J. Redor (Ed.), *L'ordre public : Ordre public ou ordres publics, Ordre public et droits fondamentaux*, Nemesis-Bruylant, Bruxelles, 2001, pp. 109-131, J.-F. Renucci, *Droit européen des droits de l'homme*, L.G.D.J., Paris, 1999, pp. 350-351 and J. Frowein, 'The European Convention on Human Rights as the Public Order of Europe', *in Collected Courses of the Academy of European Law*, 1990, Martinus Nijhoff Publishers, Dordrecht-Boston-London, 1992, vol. 1, Book 2, pp. 267-358.

111 *See* Merrills, 'Promotion and Protection of Human Rights within the European Arrangements', pp. 213-216 and D. Harris, 'The Council of Europe (II): The European Social Charter', *in* Hanski & Suksi, *An Introduction to the International Protection of Human Rights*, pp. 243-263.

112 De Wet, 'The Emergence of International and Regional Value Systems as a Manifestation of the Emerging International Constitutional Order', p. 629.

113 S. Besson, 'The European Union and Human Rights: Towards a Post-national Human Rights Institution?', 6 *Human Rights Law Review* 2006, p. 343.

114 Ibid., pp. 343-344, J. Dutheil de la Rochère, 'The EU and the Individual: Fundamental Rights in the Draft Constitutional Treaty', 41 *Common Market Law Review* 2004, p. 345 and M. Dougan, 'The Treaty of Lisbon: Winning Minds, not Hearts', 45 *Common Market Law Review* 2008, p. 661.

tion of the *Charter of Fundamental Rights*.[115] The Charter consists of several chapters, which group a number of rights under the following categories: human dignity, freedoms, equality, solidarity, citizen's rights and justice was also its accent on the principle of equality, which encompassed the equality of citizens and the equality of the EU member states.[116] The Lisbon Treaty contains references to the Charter without incorporating it as a whole.[117] However, when the Treaty of Lisbon entered into force on 1 December 2009, the Charter acquired, by virtue of Article 6(1) TEU, the same legal value as the Treaties, thereby becoming a binding source of primary law.[118] The Charter thus represents an authoritative source of protection of fundamental rights in the EU and is an instrument of a constitutional nature.[119] In the years after the Lisbon Treaty, the Charter improved the centrality of human rights in the reasoning of the ECJ and made them a parameter of constitutionality in the EU legal system.[120]

7.2.3 *Conclusion on the Normative Constitutional Function*

The normative development in recent decades (in particular after World War II) instituted a normative hierarchy in the international community in that two layers of norms can be discerned. The upper layer consists of the fundamental norms of the international community (norms *jus cogens*, obligations *erga omnes*, non-derogable human rights) anchored in essential human values, whereas the lower level comprises subordinated norms. This distinction is reminiscent of a constitutional classification from domestic jurisdictions which makes a difference between higher, constitutional and lower, legislative norms and values. In addition, regimes of international organizations are premised upon a set of norms of a constitutional character that define and further articulate func-

115 Charter of Fundamental Rights of the European Union, No. 2000/C 364/01, Official Journal of the European Communities, 18 December 2000. For a substantive analysis of the Charter *see* F. Pocar, 'A New Catalogue of Human Rights: the Charter of Fundamental Rights of the European Union", in Delević Đilas & Đerić, *O međunarodnom I narodnom – eseji u čast Vojina Dimitrijevića / The International and the National – Essays in Honour of Vojin Dimitrijević*, pp. 165-172.

116 *See* J. Zemanek, 'The Principle of Equality', *in* C. Kaddous & A. Auer (Eds.), *Les principes fondamentaux de la Constitution européenne*, Helbing & Lichtenhahn-Bruylant-L.G.D.J., Genève-Bâle-Munich-Bruxelles-Paris, 2006, pp. 237-243.

117 Dougan, 'The Treaty of Lisbon', pp. 619-662.

118 *See* European Parliament, 'The Protection of Fundamental Rights in the EU', www.europarl.europa.eu/factsheets/en/sheet/146/the-protection-of-fundamental-rights-in-the-eu.

119 *Cf.* Dougan, 'The Treaty of Lisbon', p. 665, Dutheil de la Rochère, 'The EU and the Individual: Fundamental Rights in the Draft Constitutional Treaty', p. 349, 'Editorial Comments: A Constitution for Europe', 41 *Common Market Law Review* 2004, pp. 903-903, G. de Búrca, *The EU Constitution: in Search of Europe's Identity*, Europa Law Publishing, Groningen, 2005, p. 7 and A.J. Menéndez, 'Three Conceptions of the European Constitution', *in* E.O. Eriksen *et al.* (Eds.), *Developing a Constitution for Europe*, Routledge, London-New York, 2004, p. 120 (footnote omitted).

120 S. Iglesias Sánchez, 'The Court and the Charter: The Impact of the Entry of the Lisbon Treaty on the ECJ's Approach to Fundamental Rights', 49 *Common Market Law Review* 2012, pp. 1565, 1576.

tions of these organizations and are as such pivotal for the proper functioning of the international community. Altogether, the network of these sets of fundamental norms constitutes the normative function of international constitutionalism.

7.3 INSTITUTIONAL FUNCTION OF INTERNATIONAL CONSTITUTIONALISM

A precondition for an efficient legal system is that the level of normative density corresponds to the level of institutional density.[121] The normative function of international constitutionalism is inextricably linked to the institutional function in that it guarantees the effective implementation of norms in practice. The most important feature of an institution is that it is a structural feature of the community.[122] The institutional dimension deals with organs and mechanisms whose task is to implement the normative contents.[123] The term *institution* also comprises *legal institution*. Legal institution is a regime of legal norms perpetuating a legal practice which originates from a belief that the regime is an existent unity.[124]

Looking from a realist perspective the constitution is essentially a living institution built around a particular document.[125] An institution is in the first instance a set of ways of doing things and not a matter of words or rules.[126] In the broadest sense, the constitution as an institution embraces the interlocking ways and attitudes of different actors and groups in a community by blending them in a well-organized whole.[127] This depiction chimes with an institutional constitutional function that amalgamates different centers and epistemic communities into a functional whole at the international level.

It is a particular characteristic of international organizations that their constituent acts imply normative as well as an institutional component. This also opens the way for the development of the judicial component.[128] Since the constituent treaties of international organizations represent constitutions of these organizations,[129] it is apt to speak of international organizations as promoters of international constitutionalism.[130] In comparison

---

121 Abi-Saab, *Cours général de droit international public*, pp. 95-96.
122 Peters, *Institutional Theory in Political Science*, p. 18.
123 *See* Dupuy, The Constitutional Dimension of the UN Charter, pp. 3-4, 19.
124 *See* I.F. Dekker & R.A. Wessel, 'Governance by International Organizations: Rethinking the Normative Force of International Decisions', *in* Dekker & Werner, *Governance and International Legal Theory*, pp. 220-221.
125 K.N. Llewellyn, 'The Constitution as an Institution', 34 *Columbia Law Review* 1934, p. 3.
126 Ibid., p. 17.
127 Ibid., p. 18.
128 *See* Monaco, 'Le caractère constitutionnel des actes institutifs d'organisations internationales', p. 155 *et seq.* and C. Chevallier-Govers, 'Actes constitutifs des organisations internationales et constitutions nationales', 105 *RGDIP* 2001, pp. 374-375.
129 *Cf.* Monaco, 'Le caractère constitutionnel des actes institutifs d'organisations internationales', p. 155.
130 On this process, in general terms, *see* J. Klabbers, 'Constitutionalism Lite', 1 *International Organizations Law Review* 2004, pp. 31-58.

to national constitutionalism, the main difference of international constitutionalism is in the dynamic between actors. Essentially, it falls to the states to create international organizations.[131] Therefore, the relationship between states and international organizations resonates in a constant dialectic between development of communitarian interests and the respect of state sovereignty.[132]

The institutional component is essential for the development of constitutionalism at the international level. Norms are ineffective if there is no institution to materialize them. On the other hand, institutions are not an end in themselves. Without norms, institutions remain empty mechanisms. Therefore, it is not surprising that the normative component and the institutional component sometimes intertwine to the point that it is sometimes difficult to distinguish between the two of them. This is notably the case with regard to the legislative function of international organizations. In the framework of the institutional function, the following organizations shall be analyzed in more detail: the UN; the WTO; the Council of Europe; and the EU.

7.3.1 United Nations

With reference to the UN system, it is important to note that the UN Charter establishes an institutional union of states.[133] Although the UN pursues many important goals, its main goal is to safeguard and restore peace.[134] The UN Charter emerged as a response to the experiences of the WWII with an aim not only to prohibit the unilateral use of force by states, but also to centralize control of the use of force in the Security Council (within the ambit of Chapter VII).[135] The purpose of the enforcement action under Chapter VII is not to "maintain and restore the law, but to maintain, or restore peace, which is not necessarily identical with the law."[136] After the fall of the Berlin Wall, many scholars advocated a perspective that the UN Charter must represent a constitution of the international community.[137] However, important developments outside the scope of the UN

131 This pertains solely to international governmental organizations, but there may be other forms of international organizations, which are less important for this consideration. *See generally*, Klabbers, J., *An Introduction to International Institutional Law*, CUP, Cambridge, 2007.

132 *See* ibid., pp. 5-6, 81. Klabbers labels the relationship between member states and international organizations as 'schizophrenic'. *See* J. Klabbers, 'The Changing Image of International Organizations', *in* J.-M. Coicaud & V. Heiskanen (Eds.), *The Legitimacy of International Organizations*, United Nations University Press, Tokyo-New York-Paris, 2001, pp. 224-227.

133 G. Arangio-Ruiz, 'The "Federal Analogy" and UN Charter Interpretation: A Critical Issue', 8 *EJIL* 1997, pp. 3, 10.

134 J.M. Hanhimäki, *The United Nations: A Very Short Introduction*, OUP, Oxford, 2015, p. 15.

135 Gray, 'The Use of Force and the International Legal Order', p. 590.

136 H. Kelsen, *The Law of the United Nations: A Critical Analysis of Its Fundamental Problems*, Stevens & Sons Limited, London, 1950, p. 294. *Cf. also* M. Koskenniemi, 'The Police in the Temple – Order, Justice and the UN: A Dialectical View', 6 *EJIL* 1995, p. 341.

137 Fassbender, 'The Meaning of International Constitutional Law', pp. 321, 327-328 and Paulus, 'From Territoriality to Functionality?', p. 64 *et seq.*

Charter make the idea of the Charter as a world constitution irrelevant. Nonetheless, the UN system may still provide important contribution and inspiration to the development of international constitutionalism, within and outside the UN.

Under Article 24 of the Charter, the Security Council enjoys a primary responsibility for the maintenance of international peace and security,[138] which makes it a central organ under the architecture of the UN system.[139] The end of the Cold War brought significant imbalances in the relationship between the Security Council and the General Assembly. As the tensions between the permanent powers within the Security Council eased, the Council began to rediscover its powers under the UN Charter and to expand them. Some authors speak of the revival of the role of the Security Council during the post-Cold War era.[140] This growth can best be assessed through the framework of various articles of the UN Charter that relate to the functioning of the Security Council.

First, Article 25 stipulates that the members of the UN are under obligation to accept and carry out decisions of the Security Council, which gives these decisions an obligatory character. Next, the Security Council greatly expanded understanding of what constitutes a threat to peace under Article 39 (Chapter VII) and made a shift from a 'hard' understanding to a 'soft' concept of peace.[141] This change signifies that the Security Council expanded a threat from particular and specific situations of the armed hostilities to threats of a general and hypothetical nature, such as the danger of international terrorism and proliferation of WMDs (weapons of mass destruction).[142] Still further, within the powers of Chapter VII, the Security Council settled the border dispute between Iraq and Kuwait,[143] established the Compensatory Commission to provide reparation for war damage stemming from the first Iraqi war,[144] and created two ad-hoc international tribunals (for the former Yugoslavia and Rwanda, respectively).[145] This points to the fact that the Security Council exercises the judicial function, or, that it established judicial

138 Art. 24(1) of the UN Charter.

139 *Cf.* Daillier & Pellet, *Droit international public*, p. 807 and L. Fasulo, *An Insider's Guide to the UN*, Yale University Press, New Haven, 2015, p. 55-56. On the Security Council, *see* Higgins *et al.*, *Oppenheim's International Law - United Nations*, vol. I, OUP, Oxford, 2017, pp. 13-61.

140 Id. For a similar assessment, *see* V. Gowlland-Debbas, 'Security Council Enforcement Action and Issues of States Responsibility', 43 *ICLQ* 1994, p. 56 and Dupuy, *L'unité de l'ordre juridique international*, p. 335.

141 Dupuy, *L'unité de l'ordre juridique international*, pp. 336, 353 and Koskenniemi, 'The Police in the Temple', p. 341.

142 For a detailed overview of these developments, *see, e.g.*, M. Selkirk, 'Judge, Jury and Executioner? Analysing the Nature of the Security Council's Authority under Article 39 of the UN Charter', 9 *Auckland University Law Review* 2003, pp. 1101-1139.

143 *See* SC Res. 687 and SC Res. 773 (1992) 26 August 1992.

144 *See* SC Res. 687, SC Res. 705 (1991) 15 August 1991 and SC Res. 706 (1991) 15 August 1991.

145 *See* SC Res. 827 (1993), 25 May 1993 and SC Res. 955 (1994), 8 November 1994. *See* S. Talmon, 'The Security Council as World Legislature', 99 *AJIL* 2005, p. 175.

organs (the two ad hoc tribunals) within the sphere of its competence.[146] In addition, the Security Council prescribed general and abstract measures (financing of terrorism, non-proliferation of WMDs and foreign terrorist fighters) akin to legal rules.[147] With reference to Article 25, member states of the UN are under obligation to implement these legal rules. This shows that the Security Council possesses a law-making or legislative function.[148] Finally, on the basis of Article 103 of the Charter, in the event of a conflict between the obligations of members of the UN under the Charter and their obligations under any other agreement, it is the Charter obligations that prevail. This means that legal acts of the Security Council prevail over international agreements.[149] Considering these developments in a cumulative fashion leads to the conclusion that the Security Council has assumed a new and prominent institutional capacity of a global legislator.[150] This stands as a major contribution of the UN system to the growth of international constitutionalism.

This is not to underestimate the role of the General Assembly.[151] Together with the Security Council, the General Assembly is one of the six principal organs of the UN.[152] The General Assembly enjoys important prerogatives within the UN system, such as administrative, constitutional, financial and other powers.[153] There is a distinction between general competences and special competences of the General Assembly. General competences pertain to those relating to the functioning of the UN itself and to those

146 *Cf.* P. Hulsroj, 'The Legal Function of the Security Council', 1 *Chinese Journal of International Law* 2002, pp. 71-74, Koskenniemi, 'The Police in the Temple', p. 326 (including note 8), J.E. Alvarez, *International Organizations as Law-Makers*, OUP, Oxford, 2005, pp. 421-428 and *Prosecutor v. Duško Tadić a/k/a "Dule"*, Decision on the Defence Motion for Interlocutory Appeal on Jurisdiction, ICTY, 2 October 1995, para. 38.

147 *See* SC Res. 1373 (2001), 28 September 2001, SC Res. 1540 (2004), 28 April 2004 and SC Res. 2178 (2014), 24 September 2014. *See also* Chapter 8 of this book.

148 In general terms *see* Hulsroj, 'The Legal Function of the Security Council', pp. 60-65, 93 and Alvarez, *International Organizations as Law-Makers*, pp. 184-198.

149 *See* R. Bernhardt, 'Article 103', *in* B. Simma (Ed.), *The Charter of the United Nations: A Commentary*, OUP, Oxford-New York, 2002, pp. 1292-1302, T. Flory, 'Article 103', *in* Cot & Pellet, *La Charte des Nations unies*, pp. 1381-1396, A. Toublanc, 'L'article 103 et la valeur juridique de la Charte des Nations Unies', 108 *RGDIP* 2004, pp. 439-460, J.-M. Thouvenin, 'Article 103', *in* J.-P. Cot, A. Pellet & M. Forteau (Eds.), *La Charte des Nations Unies*, Economica, Paris, 2005, vol. II, pp. 2133-2147, Kelsen, *The Law of the United Nations*, 111-121.

150 *See* P.C. Szasz, 'The Security Council Starts Legislating', 96 *AJIL* 2002, pp. 901-904, Talmon, 'The Security Council as World Legislature', pp. 175-193 and E. Rosand, 'The Security Council as "Global Legislator": Ultra Vires or Ultra Innovative?', 28 *Fordham International Law Journal* 2005, pp. 542-591.

151 On the General Assembly, *see* Higgins *et al.*, *Oppenheim's International Law – United Nations*, vol. I, pp. 62-99.

152 Other principal organs are: an Economic and Social Council, a Trusteeship Council, an International Court of Justice, and a Secretariat. (Art. 7(1) of the UN Charter.)

153 M. Bennani, 'Article 10 : Fonctions et pouvoirs', *in* Cot & Pellet, *La Charte des Nations unies*, p. 247. For the functions and powers of the General Assembly, *see notably* Arts. 10-18 of the UN Charter.

entrusted for the realization of aims and objectives of the UN.[154] Special competences, on the other hand, carry a particular character, such as the contribution of the General Assembly to international peace and security.[155] In this area, the General Assembly shares competences with the Security Council, under condition, that the competence of the Security Council is primary.[156] However, the competence of the Security Council is not exclusive. The utmost expression of the rivalry with the Security Council was General Assembly's resolution 377 (V) of 1950, better known as the *Uniting for Peace Resolution*. This resolution authorized the General Assembly to consider issues of international peace and security whenever the Security Council would become inoperative.[157] In practice, that would mean that the General Assembly would take over whenever one of the permanent members would paralyze the work of the Security Council with the use of veto.[158] Such practice was common during the decades of the Cold War. Although in the end UN member states activated the *Uniting for Peace Resolution* relatively rarely, this resolution stands out as a symbol of an era in which the factual powers of the Security Council and of the General Assembly stood at an equal footing.

7.3.2 World Trade Organization

Another important contribution to the institutional function of international constitutionalism at the universal level occurred in the WTO. A major move in this framework was a transformation of the GATT system, which functioned on the basis of the 'club model' trade regime,[159] to a fully fledged international trade institution in 1995.[160]

---

154 Bennani, 'Article 10', pp. 247-253. On the competences and activities of the General Assembly, *see also* D. Akande, 'The International Court of Justice and the Security Council: Is there Room for Judicial Control of Decisions of the Political Organs of the United Nations?', 46 *ICLQ* 1997, pp. 300-301, Alvarez, *International Organizations as Law-Makers*, pp. 122-129, Daillier & Pellet, *Droit international public*, pp. 814-816, E. Suy, 'The Role of the United Nations General Assembly', *in* H. Fox (Ed.), *The Changing Constitution of the United Nations*, BIICL, London, 1997, pp. 55-69 and G. Abi-Saab, '"Unused Charter Capacity" for Global Governance?', *in Issues in Global Governance: Papers Written for the Commission on Global Governance*, Kluwer Law International, London-The Hague-Boston, 1995, pp. 154-156.

155 Bennani, 'Article 10', p. 247.

156 Id. and Daillier & Pellet, *Droit international public*, pp. 810-811, 814, 952.

157 For the GA resolution 377 *see* Bennani, 'Article 10', pp. 259, 261-262, H. Cassan, 'Article 11 : Paragraphes 2 et 3', pp. 274, 277-278, M.-C. Smouts, 'Article 12 : Paragraphe 1', pp. 298, R. Degni-Segui, 'Article 24 : Paragraphes 1 et 2', pp. 451-458, all *in* Cot & Pellet, *La Charte des Nations unies*, and J. Andrassy, 'Uniting for Peace', 50 *AJIL* 1956, pp. 563-582.

158 *Cf.* Suy, 'The Role of the United Nations General Assembly', p. 55 and Virally, 'L'O.N.U. devant le droit', p. 254.

159 D. Esty, 'The World Trade Organization's Legitimacy Crisis', 1 *World Trade Review* 2002, p. 11.

160 Lamy, 'The Place of the WTO and its Law in the International Legal Order', pp. 971, 984 and Klabbers, *An Introduction to International Institutional Law*, p. 320.

Although the WTO is a successor of the GATT system in terms of the normative substance,[161] this transformation represents a new quality in many respects.

First, it marks a movement from the logic of diplomatic bargaining towards greater 'juridification' of international trade.[162] Second, it represents a move in international trade from ad hoc multilateral brokering in the pursuit of the community interests within the WTO. In the contemporary system of international trade, trade markets unavoidably need effective international institutions to provide the framework that protects the market function.[163] In this sense, institution enhances the international trade system with unity and coherence.[164] Finally, as international institutions include elements of efficiency and the capacity to carry out institutional goals, they tend to develop techniques for overcoming 'treaty rigidity' so that they can keep pace with the changing world. A necessary part of this framework is a juridical institutional structure with a task to constrain the use of power impinging on local societies.[165] Therefore, the evolution and centrality of an institutional component in the world trading system invests that system with a much needed constitutional structure.[166] The word constitution in the world trading system can be understood as an institutional structure, which includes informal mechanism and practice.[167]

The WTO institutional-constitutional framework comprises an internal and an external dimension. The external dimension includes relationships of power-sharing between the WTO bodies, and between the WTO and states. The internal dimension, on the other hand, consists of the internal structures of the WTO and it is this dimension which initiated the constitutionalization of the WTO and overcame the defects of the previous GATT system.[168] Distinctive characteristics of institutional constitutionalism in the

161 The WTO functions on the basis of the following main pillars: the General Agreement on Tariffs and Trade (GATT), the General Agreement on Trade in Services (GATS), the Agreement on Trade-Related Aspect of Intellectual Property Rights (TRIPS) and the Dispute Settlement Understanding (DSU). (*See* G. Loibl, 'International Economic Law', *in* Evans, *International Law*, pp. 699-706, Daillier & Pellet, *Droit international public*, pp. 1063-1066 and P. Malanczuk, *Akehurst's Modern Introduction to International Law*, Routledge, London-New York, 1998, pp. 231-233.)

162 *See* J.H.H. Weiler, *The Rule of Lawyers and the Ethos of Diplomats: Reflections on the Internal and External Legitimacy of WTO Dispute Settlement*, Harvard Jean Monnet Working Paper 9/00, Cambridge (MA), 2000 and P.B. Stephan, 'Sheriff or Prisoner? The United States and the World Trade Organization', 48 *Chicago Journal of International Law* 2000, pp. 51-52.

163 J.H. Jackson, 'Sovereignty-Modern: A New Approach to an Outdated Concept', 97 *AJIL* 2003, p. 799 and J.H. Jackson, 'The WTO "Constitution" and Proposed Reforms: Seven "Mantras" Revisited', 4 *Journal of International Economic Law* 2001, p. 70.

164 *Cf.* Cass, *The Constitutionalization of the World Trade Organization*, p. 100.

165 Jackson, 'Sovereignty-Modern', p. 802.

166 Cass, *The Constitutionalization of the World Trade Organization*, p. 101 and Jackson, *The World Trade Organization*, p. 57.

167 Jackson, 'The WTO "Constitution" and Proposed Reforms', pp. 70-71 and T. Cottier, 'John H. Jackson, Sovereigny-Modern and the Constitutional Approach to International Law', 19 *Journal of International Economic Law* 2016, p. 327.

168 Cass, *The Constitutionalization of the World Trade Organization*, p. 105.

WTO are openness to pragmatic and empirical analysis and eagerness for practical solutions. Therefore, the institutional component of WTO constitutionalism can be labeled 'managerial institutionalism'.[169]

The basic institutional structure under the WTO Agreement is the following. Article II of the Agreement states that the "WTO shall provide the common institutional framework for the conduct of trade relations among its Members."[170] The main lawmaking organ is the Ministerial Conference composed of representatives of all WTO members, which meets every two years.[171] In the intervals between the meetings of the Ministerial Conference, the Agreement designates the General Council as the main decision-making organ of the WTO that likewise consists of all member states.[172] The General Council establishes a range of permanently functioning bodies.[173] In general, the WTO serves as the forum for negotiations for its members concerning their multilateral trade agreements.[174] One of the most important constitutional rules in this sense is that the WTO continues the practice under GATT of conducting the decision-making on the basis of consensus. An exception is that if consensus cannot be achieved, a decision is reached on the basis of voting.[175] The Agreement also sets up the Secretariat of the WTO headed by a Director General.[176] The Agreement requires that the Director General and the staff should not accept instructions from any government. On the other hand, the WTO members should not influence the Director General and staff in the discharge of their duties.[177]

All these institutional developments represent a great step forward with regard to the pre-1995 GATT system in the sense that they constructed the WTO as a specific constitutional framework for the international trading system.

7.3.3 *Council of Europe*

The mission of the Council of Europe (COE) is to contribute to the promotion of the rule of law and the maintenance and further realization of human rights and fundamental

169 *See* ibid., pp. 67-144, in particular 133-134, 137.

170 Art. II(1).

171 Art. IV(1), Loibl, 'International Economic Law', p. 700 and Alvarez, *International Organizations as Law-Makers*, p. 115.

172 Art. IV(2) of the Agreement and Malanczuk, *Akehurst's Modern Introduction to International Law*, p. 23.

173 The General Council operates as the Dispute Settlement Body and the Trade Policy Review Body. Three councils operate under the general guidance of the General Council: a Council for Trade in Goods, a Council for Trade in Services and a Council for Trade-Related Aspects of Intellectual Property. (Loibl, 'International Economic Law', p. 700 and Art. IV(3-5).)

174 Art. III(2).

175 *Cf.* Art. IX(1), Klabbers, *An Introduction to International Institutional Law*, p. 230 and Loibl, 'International Economic Law', p. 700.

176 Art. VI(1).

177 Art. VI(2).

freedoms across the European Continent.[178] This mission is inextricably linked to a vast normative framework of more than 200 treaties, including the European Convention on Human Rights (ECHR) as the prime normative instrument of the COE.[179] Nevertheless, the drafting process and application of the ECHR, other treaties and normative standards would not have been possible without a solid institutional structure. New instruments usually originate from the Parliamentary Assembly and are then transformed into action by the Committee of Ministers, assisted by its committees of governmental experts and, in the final phase, presented to member states for signature and ratification.[180] The European Court of Human Rights (ECtHR) includes norms that give an important role to COE organs in the implementation of the Convention. Thus, the Secretary General of the COE can ask state parties to the ECHR for an explanation of the manner in which their domestic law ensures the effective implementation of ECHR provisions.[181] The Committee of Ministers, on the other hand, has an essential role in supervising the execution of ECtHR's judgments in domestic legal systems by state parties.[182] The supplementary and consultative role in this process has been assumed lately also by the Parliamentary Assembly.[183] Although not an organ mentioned in the ECHR, the High Commissioner for Human Rights has important preventive functions in monitoring compliance with ECHR and other COE human rights standards by member states in their domestic law.[184] Worth mentioning is also the Venice Commission, which was created in 1990 on the basis of a partial and enlarged agreement that includes membership beyond the European Continent. The Venice Commission is an independent body of experts specialized in constitutional issues. Although its powers are advisory, the Venice Commission conducts a very rigorous screening of member states' legislation for compliance with established constitutional, international and human rights standards.[185]

---

178 F. Benoît-Rohmer & H. Klebes, *Council of Europe Law: Towards a Pan-European Legal Area*, Council of Europe Publishers, Strasbourg, 2005, p. 20.

179 Merrills, 'Promotion and Protection of Human Rights within the European Arrangements', pp. 209-210 and White & Ovey, *The European Convention on Human Rights*, p. 17.

180 Merrills, 'Promotion and Protection of Human Rights within the European Arrangements', p. 210.

181 Art. 52 of the ECHR. *See* White & Ovey, *The European Convention on Human Rights*, pp. 14-16.

182 Art. 46(2) of the ECHR. *See* White & Ovey, *The European Convention on Human Rights*, pp. 52-55, 61-62, Harris *et al., Law of the European Convention on Human Rights*, pp. 871-880, pp. 885-886 and Benoît-Rohmer & Klebes, *Council of Europe Law*, pp. 53-54.

183 White & Ovey, *The European Convention on Human Rights*, pp. 60-61.

184 Ibid., pp. 16-17 and Benoît-Rohmer & Klebes, *Council of Europe Law*, p. 76.

185 *See* J. Jowell, 'The Venice Commission: Disseminating Democracy through Law', 24 *Public Law* 2001, pp. 675-683 and W. Hoffmann-Riem, 'The Venice Commission of the Council of Europe – Standards and Impact', 25 *EJIL* 2014, pp. 579-597.

7.3.4 European Union

In the framework of the European Union an institutional component is particularly strong.[186] Ever since the beginning of the European integration in the 1950s, institutions of the EU (and its predecessors) were main promoters of community interests, which pushed forward the integration process. In this sense, constitutionalism of the EU consists in the continuous contributions of the European institutions to further integration. The EU constitutionalism[187] therefore corresponds to an understanding according to which "constitutions institutionalize the political community as a whole, yet they consist of an aggregation of institutions themselves."[188] The main institutions that contribute to the evolution of constitutionalism are the ECJ,[189] the Council, the Commission and the European Parliament.[190]

Nonetheless, the leading motion within the EU constitutional framework is a tension between supranationalism and intergovernmentalism (also called the *institutional balance*).[191] Member states of the EU still retain the upper hand with regard to the formal decision-making in the EU. The intergovernmental conference (IGC) of member states, which usually meets every four to five years, is the most important body to fix the institutional structure of the EU.[192] Nonetheless, normally it is the main organ of the EU that opens the pertinent issues and only after this will these issues become part of the

186 *Generally, see* D.M. Curtin & I.F. Dekker, 'The EU as a "Layered" International Organization: Institutional Unity in Disguise', *in* P. Craig & G. de Búrca (Eds.), *The Evolution of EU Law*, OUP, Oxford, 1999, pp. 83-132.

187 Drawing upon rich literature on European constitutionalism, Matej Avbelj identifies six forms of 'EU constitutionalisms': classical constitutionalism, socio-teleological constitutionalism, epistemic meta-constitutionalism, best fit universal constitutionalism, harmonious discursive constitutionalism and multilevel classical constitutionalism. (*See* M. Avbelj, 'Questioning EU Constitutionalisms', 9 *German Law Journal* 2007, pp. 1-26.)

188 A. Wiener, *Towards a Transnational Nomos: The Role of Institutions in the Process of Constitutionalization*, Jean Monnet Working Paper 9/03, Heidelberg, 2003, p. 4. *Cf. also* Avbelj, 'Questioning EU Constitutionalisms', p. 1.

189 The role of the ECJ in this process is pivotal. *E.g.*, since the mid-80s onwards, the ECJ described the Community treaties as the constitutional charter of the Community. (G. De Búrca, 'The Institutional Development of the EU: A Constitutional Analysis', *in* Craig & de Búrca, *The Evolution of EU Law*, pp. 55-57.) For a theoretical presentation of this dynamic, *see* A. Stone Sweet, *Governing with Judges: Constitutional Politics in Europe*, OUP, Oxford, 2000, pp. 194-204. The contribution of the ECJ is analyzed in more detail below in the section on the judicial function of international constitutionalism.

190 *See* De Búrca, 'The Institutional Development of the EU: A Constitutional Analysis', pp. 55-60. For a classification of different phases of constitutionalism in the EU, *see* Wiener, *Towards a Transnational Nomos*, pp. 12-33.

191 De Búrca, 'The Institutional Development of the EU', p. 65 and Y. Devuyst, 'The European Union's Constitutional Order? Between Community Method and *Ad-hoc* Compromise', 18 *Berkeley Journal of International Law* 2000, pp. 8-9, 51-52.

192 N. Nugent, *The Government and Politics of the European Union*, Duke University Press, Durham, 2003, p. 93 and D. Phinnemore, 'Towards European Union', *in* M. Cini (Ed.), *European Union Politics*, OUP, Oxford, 2007, p. 33.

agenda of IGCs.[193] Every IGC represents a European 'constitutional moment' of its own. This makes European constitutionalism an open-ended and flexible phenomenon. The most important recent steps in this process were Maastricht (1991), Amsterdam (1996), Nice (2000) and Lisbon (2007).[194]

An important albeit not finalized constitutional moment emerged after the Nice conference, when the European leaders decided to frame the constitution of the European Union. For this purpose, the EU entrusted a special ad hoc constitutional convention with the task of producing a draft of the Constitutional Treaty. Member states adopted, with minor changes and adjustments, the constitutional treaty at the meeting of the European Council in Brussels in 2004. However, subsequent referenda in France and in the Netherlands in 2005 put the Constitutional Treaty to rest.[195] But the constitutional idea survived in a more traditional form of EU law-making. After a period of reflection, the member states decided to actualize the constitutional contents through the process of a traditional treaty-amending procedure.[196] This resulted in the adoption of the Lisbon Treaty in 2007 (that entered into force in 2009). The Lisbon Treaty differs little from the Constitutional Treaty with regard to substantive issues.[197] The major contribution of both – the Constitutional Treaty and the Lisbon Treaty – to the constitutional framework was to design the institutions of the EU in the field of foreign (or external) affairs.[198] If the EU is to become a potent and efficacious player in the interdependent and globalizing world, it will necessarily have to adopt an institutional structure which will centralize and streamline its structure – at least when it comes to relations with the rest of the world.[199]

---

193 Wiener, *Towards a Transnational Nomos*, pp. 22-23.

194 For more on these conferences and adopted treaties, *see* Nugent, *The Government and Politics of the European Union*, pp. 60-108, D. Dinan, *Ever Closer Union: An Introduction to European Integration*, Palgrave-MacMillan, Houndmills, 2005, pp. 118-128, 163-173 and EU, 'Intergovernmental Conferences', www.consilium.europa.eu/en/documents-publications/intergovernmental-conferences/.

195 On the Constitutional Treaty, *see* C. Church & D. Phinnemore, 'The Rise and Fall of the Constitutional Treaty', *in* Cini, *European Union Politics*, pp. 47-64, Dinan, *Ever Closer Union*, pp. 174-183, 'Editorial Comments: A Constitution for Europe', pp. 899-907 and I. Pernice, 'Institutional Settlements for an Enlarged European Union', *in* G.A. Bermann & K. Pistor (Eds.), *Law and Governance in an Enlarged European Union*, Hart Publishing, Oxford-Portland (OR), 2004, pp. 3-34.

196 'Editorial Comments: From the Constitution to a New Round of Treaty Amendments: Step-by-step', 44 *Common Market Law Review* 2007, pp. 1230-1231.

197 *See* ibid., pp. 1231-1232 and Dougan, 'The Treaty of Lisbon', p. 620.

198 *See* De Búrca, *The EU Constitution*, pp. 7-9 and 13-14. The Lisbon Treaty added two institutions to the institutional structure of the EU: the European Central Bank and the European Council. At the head of the European Council there is a President with two-and-a-half years of a term in office. The Lisbon Treaty also establishes a post of the High Representative for Foreign Affairs. (*See* Dougan, 'The Treaty of Lisbon', pp. 626-629, 636-637.) Institutional provisions of the Lisbon Treaty draw largely on similar provisions of the Constitutional Treaty. *See* http://eur-lex.europa.eu/legal-content/EN/TXT/?uri=uriserv%3Aai0033.

199 *See* S. Duke, *Europe as a Stronger Global Actor: Challenges and Strategic Responses*, Palgrave Macmillan, London, 2017, pp, 4-8.

7.3.5 *Conclusion on the Institutional Constitutional Function*

The institutional component of international constitutionalism is the backbone of the international community in that it establishes organs, procedures and mechanisms that enable international organizations to exist and function. For the exercise of institutional functions it is extremely important that these institutional frameworks are permanent, dynamic and stable. Institutional developments within international organizations can be instigated by institutional organs or member states. The institutional constitutional function is further strengthened through coordination and cooperation of multiple international institutions in the international community. Given its 'mechanical' character it is therefore not surprising that the institutional constitutional function is inextricably linked with other constitutional functions to the point that sometimes is it hard to properly differentiate between them.

7.4 JUDICIAL COMPONENT OF INTERNATIONAL CONSTITUTIONALISM

As demonstrated in Chapter 3, of all governmental constitutional functions the judiciary was the last to emerge as a completely emancipated branch only in the eighteenth century. It is similar in the international community. The first notable step in this direction was the creation of the Permanent Court of International Justice, which started functioning in 1922. The judicial component of the international community rose to prominence only after the World War II. The main bearers of this process were the ICJ and regional courts, such as the ECJ and the ECtHR.[200] The recent period, especially after the fall of the Berlin Wall, has witnessed an incredible multiplication of international adjudicatory organs.[201] But multiplication also implies that there is a strong diversification within the international judicial function. For that reason, it is not possible to speak of a judicial function that would reside in one, central international judicial organ.[202] Nonetheless, it is possible to speak of international adjudication in terms of a judicial function that connects all international adjudicatory bodies.[203]

The functional crystallization of the role of the judicial epistemic community goes hand in hand with the growth of international constitutionalism in the adjudicative do-

---

200 *Cf.* S. Oeter, 'The International Order and Its Judicial Function', *in* Dupuy, *Völkerrecht als Wertordnung*, p. 589.

201 C.P.M. Romano, 'The Proliferation of International Judicial Bodies: The Pieces of the Puzzle', 31 *N.Y.U. Journal of International Law and Politics* 1999, pp. 709-710, 728 *et seq.*

202 Oeter, 'The International Order and Its Judicial Function', pp. 590-593, 597 and Paulus, 'From Territoriality to Functionality', pp. 68-69.

203 G. Abi-Saab, 'Fragmentation or Unification: Some Concluding Remarks', 31 *N.Y.U. Journal of International Law and Politics* 1999, pp. 926-927 and Oeter, 'The International Order and Its Judicial Function', p. 597.

main. This process goes beyond the horizontal structure of the international community.[204] If a judicial function is to keep pace with constitutional developments at the international level, it has to evolve according to constitutional logic.[205] The real challenge for ICL is a successful cross-fertilization between the disciplines of constitutional and international law. In this sense, it is useful to take a proper look at traditional characteristics of constitutional adjudication: the judicial review; *erga omnes* effects of judgments; and adequate remedies for violations.[206] The subsequent survey will analyze achievements of the most visible and advanced bodies of international adjudication: the ICJ, the WTO Appellate Body, the ECtHR and the ECJ. Not all these judicial bodies extended their constitutional functioning in all categories; however, taken in the aggregate, their contribution is extremely important for the evolution of the judicial function of international constitutionalism.

7.4.1 Judicial Review

The relationship between global constitutionalism and international judicial review is co-constitutive in the sense that judicial review relies on the constitutionalist understanding of international law and is, at the same time, an important force to uphold global constitutionalism.[207] Judicial review is an effective way of constraining power by subjecting its exercise to judicial scrutiny.[208] Many authors tend to portray the ICJ as the world's

204 *See* V. Bore Eveno, 'Le contrôle juridictionnel des resolutions du Conseil de securité : vers un constitutionnalisme international ?', 110 *RGDIP* 2006, pp. 828-832.

205 *Cf.* Klabbers, Peters & Ulfstein, *The Constitutionalization of International Law*, pp. 150, 217.

206 *See* Bickel, *The Least Dangerous Branch*, pp. 202-203, V.C. Jackson & M. Tushnet (Eds.), *Comparative Constitutional Law*, Foundation Press, New York, 2006, H. Steinberger, *Models of Constitutional Jurisdiction*, European Commission for Democracy through Law, Council of Europe Press, Strasbourg, 1994, H. Steinberger, 'Decisions of the Constitutional Court and their Effects', *in The Role of the Constitutional Court in the Consolidation of the Rule of Law*, Proceedings of the UniDem Seminar Organised in Bucharest on 8-10 June 1994, Council of Europe Press, Strasbourg, 1994, pp. 72-101, K.L. Hall, (Ed.), *The Oxford Companion to the Supreme Court of the United States*, OUP, New York-Oxford, 1992, p. 464 *et seq.*, 663, M. Cappelletti, 'Judicial Review in Comparative Perspective', 58 *California Law Review* 1970, pp. 1033-1053, Zupančič, *The Owl of Minerva*, pp. 351-355, 368-376, 391, D. Shelton, 'Human Rights, Remedies', *in Max Planck Encyclopedia of Public International Law*, 2006 (available at: http://opil.ouplaw.com/home/EPIL), J. Crawford, '*Marbury v. Madison* at the International Level', 36 *George Washington International Law Review* 2004, pp. 505-514.

207 B. Çali, 'International Judicial Review', *in* A.F. Lang & A. Wiener (Eds.), *Handbook on Global Constitutionalism*, p. 301.

208 Bianchi, *International Law Theories*, p. 57.

constitutional court.[209] However, in order for the ICJ to assume the role of the constitutional court, it would need to dispose of the mechanism of judicial review. Authors usually understand the power of judicial review as "a process by which a court of law determines whether a legal person has acted substantively within the scope of its powers and procedurally in a correct manner."[210] In the context of the UN, the ICJ could exercise judicial review in a horizontal and a vertical way. At the vertical level, the ICJ would review acts of national organs of states that are parties to the case. At the horizontal level, the ICJ would review acts of political organs of the UN. The Charter of the UN designates the ICJ as the "principal judicial organ of the United Nations,"[211] which may also imply a power of judicial review.[212] However, a question whether the ICJ has a power of judicial review is very ambiguous,[213] especially at the horizontal level. The issue of judicial review arose in several cases and advisory opinions: in the *Certain Expenses* advisory opinion,[214] in the *Namibia* advisory opinion,[215] in the case of the application of the *Genocide Convention*[216] and in the *Lockerbie* case.[217] In all these cases, the ICJ, presumably for political reasons,[218] brushed aside the issue of judicial review and left it at the stage of potential-

209 *See* E. McWhinney, 'Judicial Wisdom, and the World Court as Special Constitutional Court', *in* U. Beyerlin *et al.* (Eds.), *Recht zwischen Umbruch und Bewahrung: Völkerrecht, Europarecht, Staatsrecht: Festschrift für Rudolf Bernhardt*, Springer Verlag, Berlin, 1995, pp. 705-712, R. Abraham, 'La Cour internationale de justice, juge constitutionnel ?', *in* R. Chemain & A. Pellet (Eds.), *La Charte des Nations Unies, constitution mondiale ?*, Editions Pedone, Paris, 2006, pp. 105-108, Klabbers, Peters & Ulfstein, *The Constitutionalization of International Law*, pp. 64-67 and F. Orrego Vicuña, *International Dispute Settlement in an Evolving Society: Constitutionalization, Accessibility, Privatization*, CUP, Cambridge, 2004, pp. 18-28.

210 E. Lauterpacht, 'Judicial Review of Acts of International Organizations', *in* L. Boisson de Chazournes & P. Sands (Eds.), *International Law, the International Court of Justice and Nuclear Weapons*, CUP, Cambridge, 1999, p. 92.

211 Art. 92 of the Charter. For a scholarly assessment of this qualification, *see* 'Rapport présenté par le Professeur Alain Pellet' and 'Commentary by Professor Vera Gowlland-Debbas', in C. Peck & R.S. Lee (Eds.), *Increasing the Effectiveness of the International Court of Justice: Proceedings of the ICJ/UNITAR Colloquium to Celebrate the 50th Anniversary of the Court*, Martinus Nijhoff Publishers, The Hague-Boston-London, 1997, pp. 234-266.

212 G.R. Watson, 'Constitutionalism, Judicial Review, and the World Court', 34 *Harvard International Law Journal* 1993, p. 5.

213 For a conservative view, *see* A. Aust, *Handbook of International Law*, CUP, Cambridge, 2010, p. 424 and M.J. Matheson, 'ICJ Review of Security Council Decisions', 36 *George Washington International Law Review* 2004, pp. 615-622.

214 *See Certain Expenses of the United Nations*, Advisory Opinion, 20 July 1962 (ICJ Reports 1962, p. 151).

215 *See Legal Consequences for States of the Continued Presence of South Africa in Namibia (South West Africa) notwithstanding Security Council Resolution 276 (1970)*, Advisory Opinion, 21 June 1971 (ICJ Reports 1971, p. 16).

216 *See Application of the Convention on the Prevention and Punishment of the Crime of Genocide (Preliminary Objections)*, 11 July 1996 (ICJ Reports 1996, p. 595).

217 *See Questions of Interpretation and Application of the 1971 Montreal Convention arising from the Aerial Incident at Lockerbie (Libyan Arab Jamahiriya v. United Kingdom)*, Provisional Measures, Order of 14 April 1992 (ICJ Reports 1992, p. 9.)

218 These political reasons imply noninterference with the permanent members of the Security Council. (*See* Watson, 'Constitutionalism, Judicial Review, and the World Court', pp. 43-44.)

ity.[219] The ICJ based itself on the presumption of validity of resolutions of the Security Council and the General Assembly.[220] On the other hand, a court in the framework of the UN did review a resolution of the Security Council. In the *Tadić* case, the ICTY reviewed the Security Council resolution in order to decide upon the legality of its creation.[221] The ICJ, therefore, is yet to construe its own *Marbury v. Madison* case.[222] However, there are increasing calls that the ICJ should undertake judicial review if the UN organs would violate rules of *jus cogens* or other fundamental human rights.[223] In the context of measures against individuals in the fight against terrorism, this danger of abuse of authority is becoming more tangible.[224] For example, the European Court of First Instance did not hesitate to assume, of its own motion, an indirect judicial review of the Security Council measures against individuals presumably involved in financing of terrorism.[225] In the appeals procedure to this case, the stand of the ECJ was even stronger. The ECJ asserted that the Community judicature must ensure full judicial review of Community acts which give effect to the resolutions of the Security Council in the light of the fundamental rights secured in the Community legal order.[226] Therefore, if the ICJ is to retain its position of the central adjudicatory organ in the world community, it will have to follow contemporary developments and actualize its power of judicial review.[227]

The next possibility for judicial review is within the competences of the WTO's Appellate Body. The creation of the Appellate Body signifies an important paradigm shift in

219 On the above-mentioned cases, *see* ibid. pp. 14-28, Bore Eveno, 'Le contrôle juridictionnel des resolutions du Conseil de securité', pp. 830, 839-840, 852, 858, Crawford, '*Marbury v. Madison* at the International Level', p. 512 and Akande, 'The International Court of Justice and the Security Council', pp. 309-343.

220 Watson, 'Constitutionalism, Judicial Review, and the World Court', pp. 17-18, 25.

221 *See Tadić* case, paras. 32-40.

222 Crawford, '*Marbury v. Madison* at the International Level', p. 508 and J. Alvarez, 'Theoretical Perspectives on Judicial Review by the World Court', 85 *ASILP* 1995, p. 89.

223 *See* E. Lauterpacht, 'Judicial Review of Acts of International Organizations', 95-97, I. Brownlie, 'The Decisions of Political Organs of the United Nations and the Rule of Law', *in* R.St.J. Macdonald (Ed.), *Essays in Honour of Wang Tieya*, Martinus Nijhoff Publishers, Dordrecht-Boston-London, 1994, pp. 93-102 and A. Tzanakopoulos, *Disobeying the Security Council: Countermeasures against Wrongful Sanctions*, OUP, Oxford, 2011.

224 *See* A. Bianchi, 'Assessing the Effectiveness of the UN Security Council's Anti-terrorism Measures: The Quest for Legitimacy and Cohesion', 17 *EJIL* 2007, pp. 903-910.

225 In doctrinal terms, the two most relevant in a set of cases regarding Kadi are *Case T-306/0, Yusuf and Al Barakaat International Foundation v. Council and Commission*, 21 September 2005, paras. 281-282 and *Case T-315/01, Kadi v. Council and Commission*, 21 September 2005, paras. 230-231. For analysis of these two cases, *see* Bore Eveno, 'Le contrôle juridictionnel des resolutions du Conseil de securité', p. 831 *et seq.*, C. Tomuschat, 'Case Law', 43 *Common Market Law Review* 2006, pp. 537-551 and M. Nettesheim, 'U.N. Sanctions against Individuals – A Challenge to the Architecture of European Union Governance', 44 *Common Market Law Review* 2007, pp. 567-600.

226 *See* Joined Cases C-402/05 P and C-415/05 P, *Kadi, Al Barakaat International Foundation v. Council, Commission, and UK*, 3 September 2008, para. 256.

227 Watson, 'Constitutionalism, Judicial Review, and the World Court', p. 45, Orrego Vicuña, *International Dispute Settlement in an Evolving Society*, p. 19 and Crawford, '*Marbury v. Madison* at the International Level', p. 514.

that it brought a strong adjudicatory character to the WTO.[228] The Appellate Body serves as a review body on points of law with regard to decisions made by ad hoc panels under the WTO dispute settlement mechanism (DSM).[229] While panels function as a blend of diplomatic and juridical approaches to dispute settlement, the Appellate Body works as a real international court.[230] As the WTO is a 'member-driven' organization, this characteristic weakens a possibility for a judicial review in the horizontal sphere, which is nearly nonexistent.[231] Therefore, judicial review in the WTO exists in the form of the vertical review.[232] In the course of the adjudicatory process, the Appellate Body adopted a position "that national authorities can no longer make decisions without these decisions being subject to international judicial oversight by WTO Panels."[233] Judicial review in the WTO thus consists of the administration of superior norms by the Appellate Body against the entities subject to those norms, that is, member states.[234] In doing so the role of the Appellate Body is truly constitutional.[235]

However, in 2018 the functioning of the Appellate Body suffered a major backlash when the United States blocked the nomination process of its members under the pretext that they have become too activistic and that it should be reformed.[236] At present it is

---

228 *See* Klabbers, Peters & Ulfstein, *The Constitutionalization of International Law*, pp. 215-216, E.-U. Petersmann, 'Between "Member-Driven" WTO Governance and "Constitutional Justice": Judicial Dilemmas in GATT/WTO Dispute Settlement', 21 *Journal of International Economic Law* 2018, pp. 103-122, R. Howse, 'The World Trade Organization 20 Years On: Global Governance by Judiciary', 27 *EJIL* 2016, pp. 7-99 and a series of articles under the heading 'Afterword: Robert Howse and His Critics', *in* 27 *EJIL* 2016, pp. 1075-1129. Geraldo Vidigal goes a step further and lables the aggregation of judicial powers by the Appellate Body as 'hegemonic' (*see* G. Vidigal, 'Living without the Appellate Body: Hegemonic, Fragmented and Network Authority in International Trade', 4 March 2019, pp. 12-17, https://papers.ssrn.com/sol3/papers.cfm?abstract_id=3343327.)

229 S. Picciotto, 'The WTO's Appellate Body: Legal Formalism as a Legitimation of Global Governance', 18 *Governance* 2005, pp. 477-478. For more on the WTO DSM, *see* T. Bernauer, M. Elsig & J. Pauwelyn, 'Dispute Settlement Mechanism – Analysis and Problems', pp. 485-506 and M. Matsushita, 'The Dispute Settlement Mechanism at the WTO: The Appellate Body – Assessment and Problems', pp. 507-534, both *in* A. Narlikar, M. Daunton & R.M. Stern (Eds.), *The Oxford Handbook on the World Trade Organization*, OUP, Oxford, 2014 and Jackson, *The World Trade Organization*, p. 59 *et seq.*

230 *See* Weiler, *The Rule of Lawyers and the Ethos of Diplomats*, pp. 7-16 and C.D. Ehlermann, 'Reflections on the Appellate Body of the WTO', 6 *Journal of International Economic Law* 2003, p. 697.

231 *Cf.* C.M. Vázques, 'Judicial Review in the United States and in the WTO: Some Similarities and Differences', 36 *George Washington International Law Review* 2004, p. 596.

232 Ibid., pp. 596, 601.

233 Cass, *The Constitutionalization of the World Trade Organization*, p. 188.

234 Vázques, 'Judicial Review in the United States and in the WTO', p. 596.

235 D.Z. Cass, 'The "Constitutionalization" of International Trade Law: Judicial Norm-Generation as the Engine of Constitutional Development in International Trade', 12 *EJIL* 2001, p. 42 and von Bogdandy, 'Law and Politics in the WTO', p. 625.

236 T. Miles, 'U.S. Blocks WTO Judge Reappointment as Dispute Settlement Crisis Looms', *Reuters*, 27 August 2018, www.reuters.com/article/us-usa-trade-wto/u-s-blocks-wto-judge-reappointment-as-dispute-settlement-crisis-looms-idUSKCN1LC19O and USTR, 'Statement of the United States by Ambassador Dennis Shea at the 14th WTO Trade Policy Review of the United States of America', 17 December 2018, Geneva, https://ustr.gov/about-us/policy-offices/press-office/press-releases/2018/december/statement-united-states-ambassador.

difficult to foresee how the reform would look like.[237] Nonetheless, empirical evidence suggests that the DSM system under the WTO, including the judicial role of the Appellate Body, visibly contributes to the growth of the world trade.[238] While the move by the United States may hamper the further work of the Appellate Body, the development of the judicial component in world trade shall possibly seek other avenues, such as the use of binding arbitration proceedings under Article 25 of the DSU or through regional trade agreements.[239] It is therefore unlikely that such a hegemonic move by the United States would result in blocking the judicial function in world trade whose operation is prompted by demands of the increasingly interconnected world.

The ECtHR likewise performs judicial review in pursuing its mission of protecting human rights in Europe. Judicial review of the ECtHR is analogous to constitutional complaint procedure in national legal systems.[240] The basic similarity between a complaint to the ECtHR and a constitutional complaint is the task of reviewing whether a challenged governmental act represents a violation of fundamental rights.[241] Although the mechanism of a constitutional complaint focuses on an act of public authority, which violates an individual right, this act may have its source in a piece of legislation.[242] The ECtHR is formally not a constitutional court; however, it gradually assumed the role of the European constitutional court of human rights.[243] The main turning point in this evolution was Protocol No. 11, which posited the ECtHR as a permanent court and

---

237 For an overview of the pertinent issues and possible solutions *see* Petersmann, 'Between "Member-Driven" WTO Governance and "Constitutional Justice"', pp. 109-122, A. Bahri, '"Appellate Body Held Hostage": Is Judicial Activism at Fair Trial?', 53 *Journal of World Trade* 2019, pp. 293-315 and P.J. Kuijper, 'The US Attack on the WTO Appellate Body', 45 *Legal Issues of Economic Integration* 2018, pp. 1-11.

238 *See* W. Shin & D. Ahn, 'Trade Gains from Legal Rulings in the WTO Dispute Settlement System', 18 *World Trade Review* 2019, pp. 1-31.

239 *See* B.H. Malkawi, 'Can Article 25 Arbitration Serve as a Temporary Alternative to WTO Dispute Settlement Process?', *Kluwer Arbitration Blog*, 5 January 2019 and Vidigal, 'Living without the Appellate Body', pp. 17-30, http://arbitrationblog.kluwerarbitration.com/2019/01/05/can-article-25-arbitration-serve-as-a-temporary-alternative-to-wto-dispute-settlement-process/?doing_wp_cron=1551681355.8135259151458740234375.

240 Zupančič, *The Owl of Minerva*, p. 351.

241 *See* Steinberger, *Models of Constitutional Jurisdiction*, pp. 29-30.

242 Id.

243 *See* B.M. Zupančič, *Sur la Cour européenne des droits de l'homme : Rétrospective d'un initié (1998-2016)*, Harmattan, Paris, 2019, pp. 21-22, J.-F. Flauss, 'La Cour européenne des droits de l'homme est-elle une Cour constitutionnelle ?', 36 *Revue française de Droit constitutionnel* 1998, p. 728, W. Wildhaber, 'A Constitutional Future for the European Court of Human Rights', 23 *Human Rights Law Journal* 2002, pp. 161-165 and J.L. Jackson, '*Broniowski v. Poland*: A Recipe for Increased Legitimacy of the European Court of Human Rights as a Supranational Constitutional Court', 39 *Connecticut Law Review* 2006, pp. 759-806, in particular pp. 777-781.

enabled individuals to address complaints directly to the Court.[244] This arrangement *de facto* transformed complaints under the ECHR into a constitutional complaint. The constitutional quality is particularly present with regard to the so-called 'pilot judgments',[245] which concern structural causes for violations of human rights in domestic legal systems.[246] The ECtHR, as well as domestic constitutional courts, adjudicate on the basis of constitutional argumentation. This epistemic compatibility lends synthetical effects, which leads to harmonization between the Strasbourg legal order and domestic legal systems.[247] Protocol No. 14 further strengthened the power of the judicial review by reinforcing the Court's filtering capacity, new admissibility criteria which rule out trivial cases, and measures for dealing with repetitive cases.[248] Furthermore, Protocol No. 16 vested the Court with a power to issue advisory opinions, upon the request of the highest national courts, on questions of principle relating to the interpretation or application of rights under the ECHR.[249] An important feature of the constitutional character of the ECtHR is a growing two-way dialogue with the highest national courts.[250]

Judicial review in the European Union exists at the horizontal level, as well at the vertical level. Therefore, the ECJ serves as the supreme guardian of the Community law.[251] The horizontal review vests the ECJ with authority to review the legality of acts

244 For more on Protocol No. 11, *see* A. Drzemczewski, 'The European Human Rights Convention: A New Court of Human Rights in Strasbourg as of November 1, 1998', 55 *Washington and Lee Law Review* 1998, pp. 697-717, F. Sudre, 'La réforme du mécanisme de contrôle de la Convention européenne des droits de l'homme : le Protocole 11 additionnel à la Convention', 69 *La Semaine Juridique* 1995, pp. 234-240 and *Protocol No. 11 to the European Convention on Human Rights and Explanatory Report*, May 1994, Council of Europe, Strasbourg, No. H (94) 5.

245 *See* cases *Broniowski v. Poland*, 22 June 2004, *Lukenda v. Slovenia*, 6 October 2005 and *Sejdović v. Italy*, 1 March 2006. *See also Broniowski v. Poland (friendly settlement)*, 28 September 2005, para. 35.

246 On a pilot procedure and the problem of structural violations, *see* L. Wildhaber, 'The European Court of Human Rights in Action', 21 *Ritsumeikan Law Review* 2004, pp. 90-91, L.R. Helfer, 'Redesigning the European Court of Human Rights: Embeddedness as a Deep Structural Principle of the European Human Rights Regime', 19 *EJIL* 2008, pp. 146-149, 154 and V. Colandrea, 'On the Power of the European Court of Human Rights to Order Specific Non-Monetary Measures: Some Remarks in Light of the *Assanidze, Broniowski* and *Sejdovic* Cases', 7 *Human Rights Law Review* 2007, pp. 403-408.

247 *See* Zupančič, *The Owl of Minerva*, pp. 366-368.

248 *See* Protocol No. 14, adopted on 12 May 2004 and L. Caflisch, 'The Reform of the European Court of Human Rights: Protocol No. 14 and Beyond', 6 *Human Rights Law Review* 2006, pp. 403-415.

249 *See* Protocol No. 16 on the Convention on the Protection of Human Rights and Fundamental Freedoms, Council of Europe Treaty Series – No. 214, signed on 2 October 2013, entered into force 1 August 2018, www.echr.coe.int/Documents/Protocol_16_ENG.pdf. *See also Advisory Opinion concerning the recognition in domestic law of a legal parent-child relationship between a child born through a gestational surrogacy arrangement abroad and the intended mother, Requested by the French Court of Cassation*, Grand Chamber, 10 April 2019.

250 G. Ulfstein, 'The European Court of Human Rights as a Constitutional Court?', PluriCourts Research Paper No. 14-08, 2014, p. 7.

251 M.G. Puder, 'Supremacy of the Law and Judicial Review in the European Union: Celebrating *Marbury v. Madison* with *Costa v. Enel*', 36 *George Washington International Law Review* 2004, pp. 581-582.

of EU institutions.[252] Under horizontal review, the ECJ has a competence to review acts of the Council, the Commission, the European Parliament and the European Central Bank. In conducting the horizontal review, the ECJ based itself on practices from administrative and constitutional jurisprudence of member states highest courts.[253] Interestingly, the horizontal review may turn into a vertical review, as happened in the *Tobacco Advertising* case.[254] In this case, the ECJ invalidated a particular EU directive. But since the EU directive imposed obligations on member states, its invalidation preserved constitutional authority of member states at the vertical level.[255]

Vertical judicial review is much more important for the construction of the Community legal order and operates on the basis of preliminary ruling procedure for preliminary questions.[256] Under this procedure, national courts of member states may request the ECJ to give an interpretation on the compatibility of domestic legal rules with the Community law.[257] The preliminary ruling procedure closely resembles concrete review as one of the most typical mechanisms in constitutional legal theory.[258] The ECJ used this procedure to adopt a series of far-reaching judgments that permeated a classical international architecture with the pillars of a constitutional order.[259] The first landmark judgment introduced the doctrine of direct effect of the Community law in the member states.[260] Subsequently, the ECJ supplemented the doctrine of direct effect with a doctrine

252 A legal basis for horizontal review is Art. 263(1) of the Consolidated version of the Treaty on the Functioning of the European Union, Official Journal C 326, 26 October 2012 (TFEU). *See* P. Craig, 'Legal Control of Regulatory Bodies: Principle, Policy, and Teleology', *in* P. Birkinshaw & M. Varney (Eds.), *The European Union Legal Order after Lisbon*, Kluwer Law International, Alphen aan der Rijn, 2010, p. 95 and G.A. Bermann, '*Marbury v. Madison* and European Union "Constitutional" Review', 36 *George Washington International Law Review* 2004, p. 561. For an overall assessment of the horizontal judicial review, *see* P. Craig & G. de Búrca, *EU Law: Text, Cases, and Materials*, OUP, Oxford, 1998, pp. 453-514.

253 Bermann, '*Marbury v. Madison* and European Union "Constitutional" Review', p. 563. Bermann explicitly mentions the German Constitutional Court and the French Conseil d'Etat.

254 *See* Case C-376/98, *Germany v. Parliament and Council, Directive 98/43/EC – Advertising and sponsorship of tobacco products*, 5 October 2000.

255 Bermann, '*Marbury v. Madison* and European Union "Constitutional" Review', pp. 564-565.

256 TFEU Art. 267.

257 *See* Bermann, '*Marbury v. Madison* and European Union "Constitutional" Review', p. 560 and J.H.H. Weiler, *The Constitution of Europe: "Do the New Clothes have an Emperor" and Other Essays on European Integration*, CUP, Cambridge, 1999, pp. 27-28. For more on the preliminary reference procedure, *see* M. Broberg & N. Fender, *Preliminary References to the European Court of Justice*, OUP. Oxford, 2014, T. de la Mare, 'Article 177 in Social and Political Context', *in* Craig & de Búrca, *The Evolution of EU Law*, pp. 215-250 and Craig & de Búrca, *EU Law*, pp. 406-450.

258 Stone Sweet, *Governing with Judges*, pp. 156, 160, Puder, 'Supremacy of the Law and Judicial Review in the European Union', p. 583 and Steinberger, 'Decisions of the Constitutional Court and their Effects', p. 90.

259 R. Dehousse, *La Cour de justice des Communautés européennes*, Montchrestien, Paris, 1994, p. 42.

260 *See* Case 26-62, *NV Algemene Transport-en Expeditie Onderneming van Gend & Loos v. Netherlands Inland Revenue Administration*, 5 February 1963, Sect. II/B.

of supremacy in the sense that Community law can have full impact only if the Community norms enjoy supremacy over national norms.[261] It is interesting to note that national judges readily embraced participation in the preliminary ruling procedure which makes them agents of the Community order whenever they resolve disputes of the Community law.[262] In this respect, national judges form a central part of a Community-wide judicial hierarchy, with the ECJ sitting at the top.[263] Eventually, judicial review on the basis of preliminary ruling procedure led to a greater constitutionalization of the Community law and to enhanced European integration.[264] It also enabled the ECJ to position itself as a constitutional court.[265]

7.4.2 *Erga Omnes Effects of Judgments*

The next category in the constitutional classification is the *erga omnes* effects of decision of adjudicatory bodies. *Erga omnes* effects can be considered as synonymous with doctrines of precedents and of *stare decisis*. Such effects are based on a premise that any "system of law requires a minimum of certainty, and any dispute settlement system a minimum of foreseeability."[266] Constitutional theory defines *erga omnes* effects as those consequences of a particular judgment that go beyond the subject matter and rights and obligations of specific parties of that case. *Erga omnes* effects extend to the abstract object of the procedure that becomes a standard of reference for all similar cases in the future. Importantly, not only the tenor of the decision but also the argumentation (*rationes decidendi*) forms part of the *erga omnes* effect.[267] In other words, the *erga omnes* effect implies that the interpretation proper of a particular judgment extends to parallel cases or cases successive to the first case by other parties. This judicial interpretation may comprise a decision on the merits, as well as a decision on a prejudicial question.[268] It is also typical of constitutional adjudication that constitutional courts themselves are not bound

---

261 *See* Case 6/64, *Flaminio Costa v. E.N.E.L.*, 15 July 1964 and Weiler, *The Constitution of Europe*, pp. 20-22, Dehousse, *La Cour de justice des Communautés européennes*, p. 47, E. Stein, 'Lawyers, Judges and the Making of a Transnational Constitution', 75 *AJIL* 1981, p. 10 and Stone Sweet, *Governing with Judges*, pp. 161-162, 178.

262 Stone Sweet, *Governing with Judges*, pp. 163-164, 178.

263 Craig & de Búrca, *EU Law*, p. 408.

264 Stone Sweet, *Governing with Judges*, p. 165, Stein, 'Lawyers, Judges and the Making of a Transnational Constitution', p. 1, B. Ackerman, 'The Rise of World Constitutionalism', 83 *Virginia Law Review* 1997, p. 793, de la Mare, 'Article 177 in Social and Political Context', p. 249 and Craig & de Búrca, *EU Law*, p. 407.

265 De la Mare, 'Article 177 in Social and Political Context', p. 216.

266 G. Guillaume, 'The Use of Precedent by International Judges and Arbitrators', 2 *Journal of International Dispute Settlement* 2011, p. 6.

267 Steinberger, 'Decisions of the Constitutional Court and their Effects', p. 76.

268 Id.

by these *erga omnes* effects. In order to keep constitutional law open for further development the constitutional courts may overrule prior cases and their doctrines.[269]

From the perspective of the constitutional reasoning described in the preceding paragraphs, all bodies under consideration faced a significant setback in this regard at the time of their creation. International treaties upon which they operate restrict effects of their decisions only to parties to a dispute[270] or underline advisory or interpretative nature of adjudication.[271] However, if international tribunals are to exercise a role of a pivotal adjudicatory organ within their particular international legal regime, such an arrangement is untenable. It is not surprising that all international adjudicatory bodies under consideration went on to construe their own jurisprudential *acquis* upon which they rely in prospective adjudication and which all entities within their sphere of jurisdiction are obliged to respect. Technical solutions on this issue vary from one system to another, but the end result is the same – decisions of international adjudicatory organs have *erga omnes* effects. The ICJ in both procedures at its disposal, contentious proceedings and advisory jurisdiction, exercises a function of constitutional interpretation[272] and in doing so managed to establish the doctrine of precedent.[273] An important part of WTO's Appellate Body quasi judicial role is that its decisions constitute a *de facto* system of precedent.[274] In the Strasbourg system for the protection of human rights, the ECtHR instituted the practice of *de facto erga omnes* effect of its judgments.[275] Some authors speak also of the doctrine of *l'autorité de la chose interprétée* (*res interpretata*) according to which the Court's interpretation of the ECHR has a binding effect on all (*erga*

269 Ibid., pp. 76-77.

270 *See* Art. 59 of the Statute of the ICJ, Art. 46, para. 1 of the ECHR, and Art. 17, para. 14 of the DSU (however, a possibility of member states expressing their views in the course of the adoption of the Appellate Body reports indicates that effects of these reports transgress a strict *inter partes* effect).

271 *See* Art. 65 of the Statute of the ICJ, Art. 47 of the ECHR, and Art. 267 of the TFEU on the preliminary ruling procedure. *See also* Protocol No. 16 to the ECHR.

272 Abraham, 'La Cour internationale de justice, juge constitutionnel ?', p. 107.

273 Watson, 'Constitutionalism, Judicial Review, and the World Court', p. 40, Alvarez, 'Theoretical Perspectives on Judicial Review by the World Court', p. 87 and R.Y. Jennings, 'The Judiciary, International and National, and the Development of International Law', 45 *ICLQ* 1996, p. 11.

274 P.J. Kelly, 'Judicial Activism at the World Trade Organization: Developing Principles of Self-Restraint", 22 *Northwestern Journal of International Law & Business* 2002, p. 354 and R. Bhala, 'The Precedent Setters: De Facto Stare Decisis in WTO Adjudication', 9 *Transnational Law & Policy* 1999, p. 4 and R.H. Steinberg, 'Judicial Lawmaking at the WTO: Discursive, Constitutional, and Political Questions', 98 *AJIL* 2004, p. 254. For an overall treatment of precedential effect of the Appellate Body decisions, *see* A. Chua, 'The Precedential Effect of WTO Panel and Appellate Body Reports', 11 *LJIL* 1998, pp. 45-61.

275 Zupančič, *Sur la Cour européenne des droits de l'homme*, pp. 30-31, 35, Zupančič, *The Owl of Minerva*, pp. 354, 351-383, Flauss, 'La Cour européenne des droits de l'homme est-elle une Cour constitutionnelle?', p. 724 and Wildhaber, 'A Constitutional Future for the European Court of Human Rights', p. 164.

omnes).[276] The effects in the Community legal system are similar. Judicial review at the horizontal level (under Article 263 of the TFEU) brings about the *erga omnes* effect, if the ECJ declares the Community act as void.[277] With regard to preliminary ruling procedure (vertical level) the situation was not so clear at the outset. However, in the consequent jurisprudence, the ECJ introduced *erga omnes* effects also in judicial review at the vertical level.[278] This summary overview shows that all international adjudicatory bodies developed *erga omnes* effect of their judgments which situates them solidly in the ambit of constitutional adjudication.[279]

7.4.3 Remedies

The last element of the constitutional model of international adjudication is the notion of remedies. Words that are usually used as synonyms for remedies in international law are reparation, redress, compensation and just satisfaction.[280] Remedies are essentially interrelated to rights: without remedies there are no rights.[281] However, the notion of remedies goes beyond the substantive scope of violated rights and of their reconstitution.[282] The notion of remedies comprises ways and means in which rights can be claimed. In other words, remedies comprise procedural and institutional elements. One essential expression of these elements is the power of judicial organs that adjudicate upon violation of rights and afford redress. In the context of constitutional adjudication, remedies in the first place presuppose powers of constitutional courts to order measures that subordinate organs must respect and execute.[283] This necessarily implies an interaction between international adjudicatory bodies and organs in national legal systems.

---

276 *See* O.M. Arnardóttir, '*Res Interpretata, Erga Omnes* Effect and the Role of the Margin of Appreciation in Giving Domestic Effect to the Judgments of the European Court of Human Rights', 28 *EJIL* 2017, pp. 819-843 and A. Drzemczewski & P. Tavernier, 'L'exécution des "decisions" des instances internationales de contrôle dans le domaine des droits de l'homme', *in La protection des droits de l'homme et l'évolution du droit international, Colloque de Strasbourg*, Société Française pour le Droit International, Editions A. Pédone, Paris, 1998, p. 251 *et seq*. The expression comes from *l'autorité de la chose jugée (res judicata).*

277 *See* Craig & de Búrca, *EU Law*, pp. 510-511.

278 Ibid., pp. 512, 407-408 and 414-418. In this context, Paul Craig and Gráinne de Búrca speak also of the system of precedents.

279 For a general overview, *see* N. Gal-Or, 'The Concept of Appeal in International Dispute Settlement', 19 *EJIL* 2008, pp. 43-65.

280 For comprehensive studies on the issue of remedies, *see* C. Gray, *Judicial Remedies in International Law*, OUP, Oxford, 1990, D. Shelton, *Remedies in International Human Rights Law*, Oxford, 2001 and ILC, *Draft Articles on Responsibility of States for Internationally Wrongful Acts, with commentaries*, pp. 91-94.

281 Zupančič, *The Owl of Minerva*, p. 50.

282 Shelton describes the essence of remedies as follows: "Remedies thus are designed to place an aggrieved party in the same position as he or she would have been had no injury occurred." (Shelton, *Remedies in International Human Rights Law*, p. 38.)

283 This is the very essence of constitutional jurisdiction. *See* Steinberger, *Models of Constitutional Jurisdiction*, pp. 3-4.

The topic of remedies before the ICJ is a complex one.[284] Although the ICJ essentially works in the domain of international law, it is possible to consider its attitude towards judicial remedies from a constitutional perspective. Until recently, the ICJ rarely used the word 'remedies'.[285] The issue of remedies came to the fore in particular with regard to the application of the *Vienna Convention on Consular Relations* after a number of foreign citizens in the United States were sentenced to capital punishment in disregard of rights enumerated in Article 36 (right to communication with consular officers) of the Vienna Convention on Consular Relations (VCCR).[286] In cases *Breard, LaGrand* and *Avena*, the ICJ issued provisional measures ordering the stay of an execution of capital punishment.[287] In a judgment on the merits of the *LaGrand* case, the ICJ decided, as the United States disregarded the previous order, that the order was binding and created a legal obligation on the United States.[288] This was the first time that the ICJ prescribed provisional measures as binding.[289] Furthermore, the ICJ further found a violation of Article 36 of the VCCR and ordered, as an appropriate remedy, the "review and reconsideration of the conviction and sentence by taking account of the violation of the rights set forth in that Convention."[290] In the *Avena* case, the ICJ further clarified that "the process of review and reconsideration should occur within the overall judicial proceedings relating to the individual defendant concerned."[291] On this basis, the ICJ again ordered judicial re-

284 Christine Gray, *e.g.*, considers the following components in the context of remedies before the ICJ: jurisdiction, interim measures, damages, other remedies, and advisory opinions (in terms of their declaratory nature). (*See* Gray, *Judicial Remedies in International Law*, pp. 59-119.) This viewpoint still considers remedies largely from the horizontal perspective.

285 Crawford, '*Marbury v. Madison* at the International Level', p. 513. The legal basis for the ICJ to order remedies is Art. 36, para. 2(d) of the ICJ Statute according to which the jurisdiction of the Court comprises "the nature or extent of the reparation to be made for the breach of an international obligation." In terms of case law, the leading case is the *Chorzów Factory* case of ICJ's predecessor, the Permanent Court of International Justice. *See Case concerning the Factory at Chorzów (Claim for Indemnity)*, Merits, 13 September 1928, Permanent Court of International Justice, Series A, No. 17, p. 47.

286 Vienna Convention on Consular Relations, Done at Vienna on 24 April 1963, entered into force on 19 March 1967, UNTS vol. 596, p. 261.

287 *See Case concerning the Vienna Convention on Consular Relations (Paraguay v. United States of America)*, Provisional Measures, Order of 9 April 1998 (ICJ Reports 1998, p. 248), para. 41(I), *LaGrand (Germany v. United States of America)*, Provisional Measures, Order of 3 March 1999 (ICJ Reports 1999, p. 9), paras. 28-29 and *Avena and Other Mexican Nationals (Mexico v. United States of America)*, Provisional Measures, Order of 5 February 2003 (ICJ Reports 2003, p. 77), para. 59(I, a).

288 *See LaGrand (Germany v. United States of America)*, Judgement, 27 June 2001, (ICJ Reports 2001, p. 466), paras. 110-115.

289 A.P. Llamzon, 'Jurisdiction and Compliance in Recent Decisions of the International Court of Justice', 18 *EJIL* 2007, pp. 820-821, 841 and C. Tomuschat, *Human Rights: Between Idealism and Realism*, OUP, Oxford, 2008, pp. 238-239.

290 Case *Avena*, Provisional Measures, para. 128(7). For a consideration as to what would constitute appropriate review and reconsideration, *see* M. Sheik, 'From *Breard* to *Medellin*: Supreme Court Inaction or ICJ Activism in the Field of International Law?', 94 *California Law Review* 2006, pp. 555-556, 568-570 and D. Cassell, 'International Remedies in National Criminal Cases: ICJ Judgment in *Germany* v. *United States*', 15 *LJIL* 2002, pp. 69-86.

291 Case *Avena and Other Mexican Nationals (Mexico v. United States of America)*, Judgment, 31 March 2004 (ICJ Reports 2004, p. 12), para. 141.

view and reconsideration in the *Avena* case.[292] Although initially the United States showed signs towards compliance of the ICJ judgment in the *Avena* case,[293] the US Supreme Court in the *Medellin* case held that the ICJ judgment was not directly enforceable.[294] Mexico asked the ICJ for the interpretation of the judgment and the ICJ again called for judicial review and reconsideration of relevant cases.[295] Thus, the behavior of the ICJ in recent years reveals a shift to bolder understanding of its remedial powers.[296]

The legal basis for remedial powers of the WTO panels and the Appellate Body is Article 19(1) of the DSU.[297] That provision stipulates that when a panel or the Appellate Body finds a violation of the WTO agreement, it recommends the member concerned to bring measure in conformity with that agreement. This expression is a standard formula for remedies.[298] Under the DSU, the Appellate Body is competent to decide solely the matters of law,[299] which makes it function as a court of cassation.[300] Theoretically, this legal design provides a solid basis for remedial framework. The traditional understanding of the word *recommendation* in GATT/WTO jurisprudence has been that it constitutes a legally binding order.[301] In addition to recommendations, the panel or the Appellate Body may suggest ways in which the member can implement the recommendations. Suggestion, which is not binding, implies that the Appellate Body indicates which of

292 Ibid., para. 153(I, 9). *See also* D. Shelton, 'Case concerning Avena and Other Mexican Nationals', 98 *AJIL* 2004, pp. 564-566.

293 Llamzon, 'Jurisdiction and Compliance in Recent Decisions of the International Court of Justice', pp. 841-842.

294 *See* case *Medellin v. Texas*, pp. 8-37. For an analysis of this case in relation to the ICJ cases on the Vienna Convention, *see* A.M. Tranel, 'The Ruling of the International Court of Justice in *Avena and Other Mexican Nationals*: Enforcing the Right to Consular Assistance in U.S. Jurisprudence', 20 *American University International Law Review* 2005, pp. 943-974 and Sheik, 'From *Breard* to *Medellin*', pp. 531-573.

295 *See Request for Interpretation of the Judgment of 31 March 2004 in the Case concerning Avena and Other Mexican Nationals (Mexico v. United States of America)*, Judgment, 19 January 2009, paras. 55, 60 and 61(3).

296 M. Schnetter, 'Remedies at the International Court of Justice: A New Analytical Approach', No. 1 *Bucerius Law Journal* 2017, p. 89.

297 This section does not deal with an overall issue of remedies in the WTO (notably remedies available if there is noncompliance with the Appellate Body Reports, such as economic retaliation). For a general consideration of WTO remedies *see* R.E. Hudec, 'Broadening the Scope of Remedies in WTO Dispute Settlement', *in* F. Weiss & J. Wiers (Eds.), *Improving WTO Settlement Procedures*, Cameron May Publishers, London, 2000, pp. 345-376, P. Grané, 'Remedies under WTO Law', 4 *Journal of International Economic Law* 2001, pp. 755-772, M. Bronckers & N. van den Broek, 'Financial Compensation in the WTO: Improving the Remedies of the WTO Dispute Settlement', 8 *Journal of International Economic Law* 2005, pp. 101-126 and P.C. Mavroidis, 'Remedies in the WTO Legal System: Between a Rock and a Hard Place', 11 *EJIL* 2000, pp. 763-813.

298 'The WTO Appellate Body: The First Four Years', 2 *The Journal of World Intellectual Property* 2005, p. 437 (remark of Edwin Vermulst).

299 *See* Art. 17(6) of the DSU.

300 Lamy, 'The Place of the WTO and its Law in the International Legal Order', p. 976 and Gal-Or, 'The Concept of Appeal in International Dispute Settlement', p. 43 *et seq.*

301 Hudec, 'Broadening the Scope of Remedies in WTO Dispute Settlement', p. 10 and Mavroidis, 'Remedies in the WTO Legal System', pp. 783, 788.

the available options is preferable for successful implementation of the general recommendation.[302]

Recommendations have a wide scope. If a violation of international trade obligations originates from domestic legislation, recommendations of the Appellate Body may indicate revision of domestic laws. An example of this legislative review is the *Gasoline* case where the Appellate Body reviewed the US Gasoline Rule.[303] On the other hand, if non-compliance results from the system, guidelines and procedure, as it happened in the *Shrimp-Turtle* case,[304] the Appellate Body may recommend the noncomplying state to bring its measures in conformity with trade obligations.[305] However, recommendation as a rule consist of one paragraph at the end of the report in which the Appellate Body recommends the Dispute Settlement Body to request a member state to bring its measure into conformity with international trade obligations.[306] Therefore, it seems that the tool of binding recommendation of the Appellate Body could be developed in a stronger remedy.[307]

In the Strasbourg legal system, we find a legal basis for remedial powers of the ECtHR in Articles 41 and 46 of the ECHR. Article 41 says that in the case of a violation, the Court may, if necessary, afford just satisfaction to the injured party.[308] Additionally, Article 46 stipulates that state parties have to abide by the final judgment of the ECtHR and that the Committee of Ministers of the COE supervises its execution. The text of Article 41 is essentially modeled on the inter-state logic of bilateral and multilateral arbitrage treaties.[309] Until the reform of Protocol No. 11, the Court accepted just satisfaction primarily in the form of monetary compensation.[310]

But the provision on just satisfaction, as it formally stands, is inadequate with the central position of the ECtHR under the ECHR (especially after Protocol No. 11) and

302 Hudec, 'Broadening the Scope of Remedies in WTO Dispute Settlement', pp. 10-11 and Mavroidis, 'Remedies in the WTO Legal System', p. 784, 788.

303 *See* case *United States – Standards for Reformulated and Conventional Gasoline*, WT/DS2/AB/R, 29 April 1996.

304 *See* case *United States – Import Prohibition of Certain Shrimp and Shrimp Products*, WT/DS58/AB/R, 12 October 1998.

305 'The WTO Appellate Body: The First Four Years', p. 437 (Vermulst).

306 *See* case *Shrimp and Shrimp Products*, p. 188 and the *Gasoline* case, *in fine*.

307 Lamy has more optimistic views with regard to implementation of the Appellate Body' reports: "[T]heir implementation is subject to continuous multilateral monitoring until full satisfaction of the complainant where a violation has been found." (Lamy, 'The Concept of Appeal in International Dispute Settlement', p. 976.) *See also* R. Rajesh Babu, *Remedies under the WTO Legal System*, Brill-Nijhoff, Leiden, 2012, pp. 217-218.

308 Art. 46 stipulates: "If the Court finds that there has been a violation of the Convention or the Protocols thereto, and if the internal law of the High Contracting Party concerned allows only partial reparation to be made, the Court shall, if necessary, afford just satisfaction to the injured party."

309 *See* H. Golsong, 'Quelqeus reflections à propos du pouvoir de la Cour européenne des droits de l'homme d'accorder une satisfaction equitable (article 50 de la Convention européenne des Droits de l'Homme),' *in René Cassin amicorum discipulorumque liber*, vol. 1, Paris, 1969, pp. 92.

310 H.C. Krüger, 'Reflections on Some Aspects of Just Satisfaction under the European Convention for Human Rights', *in Liber Amicorum Marc-André Eissen*, Bruylant-L.G.D.J., Bruxelles-Paris, 1995, p. 256.

in marked contrast to similar provisions of other comparable human rights instruments.[311] Gradually, through case law the ECtHR significantly expanded the scope of Article 41 and brought it closer to the proper remedial design.[312] As the first landmark judgment, *Scozzari and Giunta* introduced a possibility for the ECtHR to prescribe general and individual measures to the state party.[313] General measures pertain to changes of domestic legislation. This option is particularly potent with regard to the mechanism of pilot judgments (case *Broniowski*). On the other hand, the Court directs individual measures to a violating state party so that it can remedy the situation of a particular individual. In this vein, in the cases *Assanidze v. Georgia* and *Ilaşcu and Others v. Moldova and Russia*, the Court ordered release of arbitrarily detained applicants.[314] This development represents a true revolution in the ECtHR's functioning given that only a decade ago the Court refused to order such measures.[315] What is extremely important is that prescribed general and individual measures are directed (specific) in nature, which gives instructions to the state party on how to implement them.[316]

Although after Protocol No. 11 the ECtHR has managed to restore remedial powers in line with remedial prerogatives of constitutional courts, in recent years the Court encountered a certain backlash from several constitutional courts. In a show of defiance, termed also as *principled resistance*, they reserved the right to have the final say as to whether measures ordered by the ECtHR are compatible with relevant domestic legislation.[317] While normally such normative conflicts are solved through a dialogue of judges,[318] the case of Russia is a cause for concern. It was mentioned before that the

311 *Cf.* Art. 63(1) of the Inter-American Convention of Human Rights. For an overview of preparatory works on remedial powers of the ECtHR *see* A. Zidar, 'The European Court of Human Rights and the Question of Remedies', *in* A. Creta *et al.*, *European Master's Degree in Human Rights and Democratization Awarded Theses of the Academic Year 1998/1999*, Marsilio, Venice, 2001, pp. 343-352.

312 Colandrea, 'On the Power of the European Court of Human Rights to Order Specific Non-Monetary Measures', p. 410.

313 *See* case *Scozzari and Giunta v. Italy*, 13 July 2000, para. 249.

314 *See* case *Assanidze v. Georgia*, 8 April 2004, paras. 202-203, and 14 (a) of the holding and case *Ilaşcu and Others v. Moldova and Russia*, 8 July 2004, para. 490 and 22 of the holding.

315 The origins of this development can be identified in separate opinions of Judge Zupančič who from the very beginning of the creation of the 'new Court' (post-Protocol 11) insisted that Protocol No. 11 endowed the Court with adequate remedial powers. In the context of violation of essential fair trial and due process rights Judge Zupančič claimed that the only legally and morally justified remedy in such cases was a retrial before the court of law. (*See* Partly Dissenting Opinion of Judge Zupančič, case *Cable and Others v. United Kingdom*, 18 February 1999, pp. 11-12 and Partly Concurring Opinion of Judge Zupančič, case *Lucà v. Italy*, pp. 12-17.)

316 Jackson, '*Broniowski v. Poland*', pp. 763, 783-784, 800. For a thorough analysis of the ECtHR's remedial practice, *see* A. Donald & A.-K. Speck, 'The European Court of Human Rights' Remedial Practice and its Impact on the Execution of Judgments', 19 *Human Rights Law Review* 2019, pp. 83-117.

317 *See* Venice Commission, 'Interim Opinion on the amendments to the Federal Constitutional Law on the Constitutional Court of the Russian Federation', pp. 17-24 and the conference entitled 'Principled Resistance against ECtHR Judgments – a New Paradigm?', https://recht.uni-konstanz.de/echr-conference/.

318 *See* F.G. Jacobs, 'Judicial Dialogue and the Cross-Fertilization of Legal Systems: The European Court of Justice', 38 *Texas International Law Journal* 2002, pp. 547-556.

Russian Duma passed legislative changes in 2015 that give a mandate to the Russian Constitutional Court to declare a certain judgment of the ECtHR unenforceable in the Russian legal system. The Russian Constitutional Court ignored the opinion of the Venice Commission that such an arrangement may be contrary to international law and went on to block execution of several ECtHR judgments.[319]

It is widely acknowledged that the ECJ has been the generator of the European integration. The ECJ has been an activist court in particular in the field of judicial remedies.[320] If the Community (EU) law was to have direct effect in member states there had to be adequate remedies available before national courts.[321] Since neither the European treaties nor the Community law lay down a general scheme or procedures and remedies for enforcement of the Community law,[322] the ECJ necessarily needs national courts to implement the Community law through national remedies.[323] Remedial powers of the ECJ evolved through four phases.[324] In the early phase, the ECJ emphasized autonomy of domestic courts in providing remedies for breaches of the Community law.[325] In the second phase, the ECJ abandoned the assumption that the legal systems of member states are sufficiently developed to enable individuals to protect their Community rights and moved to intensify its supervision of domestic legal rules. In the case *Factortame I* the ECJ instructed courts of the United Kingdom to disregard, in a Community-related case, domestic rules precluding the award of interim relief against the Crown.[326] In the *Francovich* case, the ECJ stated that it was a principle of the Community law that a member state has to pay compensation for harm caused to individuals through violation of the

---

319 Venice Commission, 'Russian Federation – Final Opinion on the Amendments to the Federal Constitutional Law on the Constitutional Court', pp. 35-36, P. Pustorino, 'Russian Constitutional Court and the Execution "à la carte" of ECtHR Judgments', 1 *Questions of International Law* 2014, pp. 5-18 and M. Timofeyev, 'Money Makes the Court Go Round: The Russian Constitutional Court's Yukos Judgment', *Verfassungsblog*, 26 January 2017, http://verfassungsblog.de/money-makes-the-court-go-round-the-russian-constitutional-courts-yukos-judgment/.

320 R. Craufurd Smith, 'Remedies for Breaches of EU Law in National Courts: Legal Variation and Selection', *in* Craig & de Búrca, *The Evolution of EU Law*, p. 287 (referring to W. van Gerven).

321 Craig & de Búrca, *EU Law*, p. 213 and M. Ruffert, 'Rights and Remedies in European Community Law: A Comparative View', 34 *Common Market Law Review* 1997, p. 316.

322 Id.

323 *Cf.* Craufurd Smith, 'Remedies for Breaches of EU Law in National Courts', p. 289.

324 There is naturally no sharp division between these four phases. Sometimes different phases may overlap.

325 Ruffert, 'Rights and Remedies in European Community Law', p. 329. *See* case 33/76, *Rewe-Zentrafinanz and Rewe-Zentral AG v. Landwirtschaftskammer für das Saarland*, 16 December 1976, para. 5 and case 45/76, *Comet BV v Produktschap voor Siergewassen*, 16 December 1976, para. 13. *See also* Craig & de Búrca, *EU Law*, pp. 214-215.

326 Ibid., pp. 300-301. Case C-213, *The Queen v. Secretary of State for Transport, ex parte: Factortame Ltd and Others*, 19 June 1990, para. 20.

Community law for which it was responsible.[327] In the third phase, the ECJ adopted a more interventionist approach of effective protection.[328] The majority of cases in this phase involved restrictions on remedies available for sex discrimination in areas of employment and social security. The ECJ established that individuals must have access to a judicial process in order to attain efficacious realization of their Community rights in these fields.[329] In the final stage, the ECJ touched upon the question of domestic rules and confirmed that an evaluation of the rationale behind procedural rules was an essential component of the test whether remedies are effective.[330] The attitude of the ECJ towards remedies therefore evolved over time from initial reserved approach to a purposive evaluation of procedural rules.[331]

7.4.4 *Conclusion on the Judicial Constitutional Function*

The incredible multiplication of international adjudicatory organs after the fall of the Berlin Wall likewise implies that there is a strong diversification within the international judicial function. For that reason, it is reasonable to speak of a judicial function that connects all international adjudicatory bodies. The judicial component is a branch of international constitutionalism that most closely resembles the judicial power in the traditional constitutional understanding of the separation of powers. Recent development demonstrates that the international judicial function gradually, but inevitably transcended the logic of inter-state dispute resolution. Major developments with regard to judicial review, effects of judgments and remedies brought international judicial function closer to the typology of constitutional adjudication. However, the reliance on the principle of sovereignty by some highest domestic courts puts practical limitations on the evolving power of international courts.

---

327 Ruffert, 'Rights and Remedies in European Community Law', p. 319. Joined cases C-6/90 and C-9/90, *Andrea Francovich and Danila Bonifaci and Others v. Italian Republic*, 19 November 1991 (ECR 1991, p. I-5357), para. 37. For impact of the *Francovich* case on the Community law, *see, e.g.*, W. van Gerven, 'Bridging the Unbridgeable: Community and National Tort Laws after Francovich and Brasserie', 45 *ICLQ* 1996, pp. 507-544.

328 *Cf.* Ruffert, 'Rights and Remedies in European Community Law', p. 330.

329 Craufurd Smith, 'Remedies for Breaches of EU Law in National Courts', pp. 307-308. *See* case 14/83, *Sabine von Colson and Elisabeth Kamann v. Land Nordrhein-Westfalen*, 10 April 1984 (ECR 1984, p. 1891), para. 23, Case 222/84, *Marguerite Johnston v. Chief Constable of the Royal Ulster Constabulary*, 15 May 1986 (ECR 1986, p. 1651), paras. 18, 21, and case C-271/92, *M. Hellen Marshall v. Southampton and South West Hampshire Area Health Authority*, 2 August 1993 (ECR 1993, p. I-04357), paras. 22, 24.

330 Craufurd Smith, 'Rights and Remedies in European Community Law', pp. 314-315. *See* case C-312/93, *Peterbtroeck, Van Campenhout & Cie SCS v Belgian State*, 14 December 1995 (ECR 1995, p. I-4599), para. 14 and C-430/93, *Jeroen van Schijndel and Johannes Nicolaas Cornelis van Veen v Stichting Pensioenfonds voor Fysiotherapeuten*, 14 December 1995 (ECR 1995, p. I-4705), paras. 17, 19-22. On this issue *see more* C.N. Kakouris, 'Do the Member States Possess Judicial Procedural "Autonomy"?', 34 *Common Market Law Review* 1997, pp. 1389-1412.

331 Craufurd Smith, 'Rights and Remedies in European Community Law', p. 317.

7.5 COORDINATIVE COMPONENT OF INTERNATIONAL CONSTITUTIONALISM

The fourth function of international constitutionalism is coordination. The idea here is not to envisage a global, centralized government, but to constitutionalize global governance.[332] It is based on the presupposition that the sovereignty of the states is disaggregating. Consequently, the interaction between the domestic and the international levels is flexible.[333] Domestic centers of public power reach the global arena and liaise with other holders of power in order to exercise functions that are necessary for the maintenance of a global system.[334] The coordinative function is based on the respect of mutually agreed constitutional essentials between these actors, which leads them to defer to one another's decisions. Coordination works through mutual monitoring, adjustment, informal negotiation and peer review.[335] This process is called *global governance.*[336]

7.5.1 *Transgovernmental Networks*

There are several important differences between government and governance. The governmental domain suggests activities that originate in formal authority. Implementation of governmental policies relies on coercive powers. Governance, on the other hand, performs functions on the basis of shared goals that are necessary for the persistence of a system. These activities do not necessarily rely on formally prescribed responsibilities, or on coercive powers to attain compliance. The important feature of governance is that it is a system of rules dependent on intersubjective meanings or formal documents that work only if accepted by the majority.[337]

On this basis Anne-Marie Slaughter developed a concept of transgovernmentalism that is premised upon the existence of transgovernmental networks.[338] It builds directly on the fact that the state power is in the process of disaggregation.[339] This enables governmental power holders to interact with their counterparts at the international level and

332 Peters, 'Compensatory Constitutionalism', p. 610.

333 A.-M. Slaughter, 'Government Networks: The Heart of the Liberal Democratic Order', *in* G.H. Fox & B.R. Roth (Ed.), *Democratic Governance and International Law*, CUP, Cambridge, 2000, pp. 200-201. *See also* A.-M. Slaughter, 'International Law in a World of Liberal States', 6 *EJIL* 1995, pp. 534-537.

334 J.N. Rosenau, 'Governance, Order, and Change in World Politics', *in* J.N. Rosenau & E.-O. Czempiel (Eds.), *Governance without Government: Order and Change in World Politics*, CUP, Cambridge, 1992, p. 3.

335 C.F. Sabel & O. Gerstenberg, 'Constitutionalising an Overlapping Consensus: The ECJ and the Emergence of a Coordinate Constitutional Order', 16 *European Law Journal* 2010, p. 512 and T.A. Börzel, 'European Governance: Governing with or without the State?', *in* Dobner & Loughlin, *The Twilight of Constitutionalism?*, p. 77.

336 *See* Slaughter, 'Government Networks', p. 200.

337 Rosenau, 'Governance, Order, and Change in World Politics', pp. 4-5.

338 Slaughter, 'Government Networks', p. 203.

339 A.-M. Slaughter, 'Governing the Global Economy trough Government Networks', *in* Byers, M. (Ed.), *The Role of Law in International Politics – Essays in International Relations and International Law*, OUP, Oxford-New York, 2000, p. 178.

to form adequate regulatory networks.[340] Transgovernmentalism in this sense is "a distinctive mode of global governance: horizontal rather then vertical, composed of national governmental officials rather than international bureaucrats, decentralized and informal rather than organized and rigid."[341]

There are various classifications of transgovernmental networks. According to the different regulatory contexts in which they arise and operate, Slaughter distinguishes between: (i) a network of national regulators in the context of international organizations; (ii) a network of national regulators under the umbrella of an agreement negotiated by heads of state; and (iii) networks of national regulators that develop outside of any formal network.[342] Following traditional repartition of constitutional functions another important classification situates regulators' activities in the framework of transnational judicial, legislative and executive networks.[343] At the international level, these functional expressions of constitutionalism materialize on the basis of interaction among bearers of each respective constitutional function.[344] This scheme led Slaughter to announce "the possibility of a genuinely new conception of world order in which networked institutions perform the functions of a world government – legislation, execution, administration, and adjudication – without the form."[345] In addition, it is possible to imagine the exercise of regulatory functions in other fields at the international level, as will be shown in the next section on the self-referential function.

7.5.2 Conclusion on the Coordinative Constitutional Function

The coordinative function of international constitutionalism builds upon the process of disaggregation of states and the need to establish a governing regime at the global level. Members of governmental structures from disaggregated states reach to the global level to form transgovernmental regulatory networks. The creation of these networks is premised upon the constitutional division of powers from domestic governmental frameworks, although their further development may transgress that classification. The essential fea-

340 A.-M. Slaughter, 'Global Government Networks, Global Information Agencies, and Disaggregated Democracy', *in* K.-H. Ladeur (Ed.), *Public Governance in the Age of Globalization*, Ashgate, 2004, p. 122 and Slaughter, *A New World Order*, pp. 217-218.

341 Slaughter, 'Governing the Global Economy through Government Networks', p. 178.

342 Slaughter, 'Global Government Networks, Global Information Agencies, and Disaggregated Democracy', p. 129. For a further explanation of these networks, *see* ibid., pp. 129-133.

343 *See* Slaughter, 'International Law in a World of Liberal States', pp. 522-528.

344 Slaughter applies the principle of the separation of powers to transgovernmental networks in her book entitled *A New World Order*. For the executive transnational network, *see* pp. 36-64 ('new' diplomats), for the judicial transnational network, *see* pp. 65-103 and for the legislative transnational network, *see* pp. 104-130. She notes that of all three transnational networks, the legislative network is least developed. (*See* ibid., pp. 104-107.) For a comparable approach with regard to the judicial transnational network, *see* J. Allard & A. Garapon, *Les juges dans la mondialisation: la nouvelle révolution de droit*, Seuil, Paris, 2004.

345 Slaughter, 'Government Networks', p. 235 and Slaughter, *A New World Order*, p. 1.

ture of the international constitutional coordinative process is that networks interact pursuant to mutually agreed premises as a basis for their continuous cooperation, while also exercising constraint upon each other.

7.6 SELF-REFERENTIAL COMPONENT OF INTERNATIONAL CONSTITUTIONALISM

The fifth function of international constitutionalism is self-referential (*autopoietic*) in the sense that global processes generate a set of problems intrinsic to law, which lead to the self-deconstruction of the dominant lawmaking processes related to the inter-state logic and, consequently, to the processes of a novel law construction.[346] However, these developments are not a derivation of the usual understanding of the process of globalization. Rather, they represent an accelerated differentiation of society into autonomous social systems which crosses territorial confines and constitutes itself globally. Globalization so understood is not economy-led globalization but 'polycentric globalization'.[347] From these fragmented sectors emerge autonomous legal orders that are closely connected with socioeconomic processes and are, as such, global in its design.[348] Consequently, fragmented processes lead to the creation of autonomous sources of power producing autonomous systems of law.[349]

7.6.1 *Societal Constitutionalism*

As these processes pursue the dynamic between the growth and limitation of power, they are an expression of the phenomenon of constitutionalism.[350] The main proponent of this approach, Gunther Teubner, labels them societal constitutionalism.[351] The logic of autonomous or autopoietic sources of law is non-statal. In this vein societal constitutionalism is constitutionalism without a state.[352] At the transnational level this kind of constitutionalism is prompted by constitutional developments in various autonomous sub-

346 G. Teubner, 'Global Private Regimes: Neo-Spontaneous Law and Dual Constitution of Autonomous Sectors?', *in* Ladeur, *Public Governance in the Age of Globalization*, pp. 72-73.

347 G. Teubner & A. Fischer-Lescano, 'Regime Collisions: the Vain Search for Legal Unity in the Fragmentation of Global Law', 25 *Michigan Journal of International Law* 2004, pp. 1005-1006. For a criticism of this premise, *see* J. Friedrichs, 'The Neomedieval Renaissance: Global Governance and International Law in the New Middle Ages', *in* Dekker & Werner, *Governance and International Legal Theory*, pp. 32, 35, 36.

348 G. Teubner, '"Global Bukowina": Legal Pluralism in the World Society', in G. Teubner (Ed.), *Global Law without a State*, Dartmouth, Aldershot-Brookfield-Singapore-Sidney, 1997, pp. 4, 5.

349 Teubner, 'Global Private Regimes', pp. 74-75.

350 G. Teubner, *Constitutional Fragments: Societal Constitutionalism and Globalization*, OUP, Oxford, 2012, trans. G. Norbury, p. 18 and Schwöbel, *Global Constitutionalism in International Legal Perspective*, p. 18.

351 *See* G. Teubner, 'Fragmented Foundations: Societal Constitutionalism beyond the Nation State', *in* Dobner & Loughlin, *The Twilight of Constitutionalism?*, pp. 327-341.

352 *See* G. Teubner, 'Constitutionnalisme sociétal et globalisation : alternatives à la théorie constitutionnelle centre sur l'État', 3 *Revue Juridique Themis* 2005, pp. 445-447.

systems of the world community (auto-constitutional regimes).[353] Each of these functional processes can be depicted as "a self-reproducing, worldwide legal discourse which closes its meaning boundaries by the use of the legal/illegal binary code and reproduces itself by processing a symbol of global (not national) validity."[354] Characteristically, societal constitutionalism amalgamates developments by international, non-statal, public and private actors and thus transcends the divide between international law and domestic law, as well as between public and private law.[355] Its plural nature situates societal constitutionalism within the theoretical framework of legal pluralism.[356]

The norms of the autopoietic transnational regime must fulfil the following four criteria to count as constitutional norms:

a. constitutional functions: transnational regimes must produce legal norms that perform not merely regulatory or conflict-solving functions, but act as constitutive rules or limitative rules;
b. constitutional arenas: transnational arenas of constitutionalization must be comparable to arenas of organized political processes and the spontaneous process of public opinion as regulated in state constitutions;
c. constitutional processes: transnational regime norms must develop a close connection to their social and functional contexts;
d. constitutional structures: transnational regimes must form typical constitutional structures as they are known in nation states, such as supremacy of norms and judicial review.[357]

Fields of autopoietic law at the transnational level are constantly growing and currently it is possible to list the following emerging areas: *lex mercatoria* (private economic law), Internet law, transport law, sports law, health law, tourist law and others.[358] Due to its autonomous drive, it is not surprising that the shape of autopoietic constitutionalism differs from the traditional notion of constitutionalism. Instead of the separation of law-making, law-application and law-enforcement functions there is a nuclear fusion of these three elements.[359] These regimes have the capacity not just to juridify but also to constitutionalize themselves, which leads to the existence of an array of smaller constitutions.[360]

---

353 Teubner, 'Fragmented Foundations', pp. 329, 333.

354 *Cf.* Teubner, 'Global Bukowina', p. 12 (changed to normal script). *See also* Teubner, 'Constitutionnalisme societal et globalisation', p. 442.

355 *See* Teubner, *Constitutional Fragments*, p. 73.

356 *Cf.* Teubner, 'Global Bukowina', p. 11.

357 Teubner, *Constitutional Fragments*, pp. 74-75.

358 *See* ibid., pp. 17-22, G. Teubner, 'Societal Constitutionalism: Alternatives to State-Centred Constitutional Theory', *in* Joerges, Sand & Teubner, *Transnational Governance and Constitutionalism*, pp. 21-22 and Teubner, 'Fragmented Foundations', p. 330.

359 *Cf.* Teubner, 'Societal Constitutionalism', p. 26.

360 Bianchi, *International Law Theories*, p. 67.

In Teubner's autopoietic design, there are actually two concepts of societal constitutionalism: the weak and the strong conception.[361] The weak conception implies the factual process of institutionalizing constitutional elements in global sectors.[362] The strong conception, on the other hand, dispenses with all public law expressions and situates constitutionalism exclusively in the private law domain.[363] Global constitutionalism in this sense represents a network of autonomous private constitutions.[364] This division basically means that there are two parallel forms of constitutionalism: the first based on the nation state and the second rooted in global civil society. Teubner calls this formation a dual constitution of a global society.[365] Both conceptions, however, rely on the original premise that the law is self-producing and is paradoxically founded in itself.[366] Both classifications question the viability of interconnecting partial autopoietic constitutions and it seems that these cannot unite in a bigger whole.[367] The only way of aligning multiple autopoietic systems is through communication and cooperation between different sectorial systems,[368] which over time leads to the establishment of some sort of transnational public policy (*ordre public transnational*).[369]

7.6.2 *Conclusion on the Self-Referential Constitutional Function*

Self-referential function of international constitutionalism follows the basic dynamic between agglomeration and limitation of power. But in contradistinction to the growth of public power in traditional constitutionalism, it is premised upon the generative movement within self-contained regimes in the global society. The prime mover for such a development is an intrinsic need of the regime itself, which corresponds to the autonomous source of sectoral power that springs up in global society. A single most important contribution of the self-referential conception to international constitutionalism is the ability to generate self-sustained constitutional regimes premised on the constitutional logic and incited by global social processes. According to the self-referential constitu-

---

361 *See* T. Vesting, 'Constitutionalism or Legal Theory: Comments on Gunther Teubner', *in* Joerges, Sand & Teubner, *Transnational Governance and Constitutionalism*, pp. 30-31.

362 Ibid., p. 30.

363 For an extreme position on this point, which calls for the erasure of duality between public/private and for its reconstruction by the multiplicity of social perspectives within the law, *see* G. Teubner, 'State Policies in Private Law? A Comment on Hanoch Dagan', 56 *American Journal of Comparative Law* 2008, pp. 842-843.

364 *Cf.* Vesting, 'Constitutionalism or Legal Theory', pp. 30, 31, 39, and Peters, 'Compensatory Constitutionalism', p. 593.

365 *See* Teubner, 'Global Private Regimes', pp. 82-87 and Teubner, 'Constitutionnalisme societal et globalisation', p. 457.

366 Vesting, 'Constitutionalism or Legal Theory', p. 29.

367 *See* ibid., pp. 37-39.

368 *See* Teubner & Fischer-Lescano, 'Regime Collisions', pp. 1017-1019 and Teubner, 'Constitutionnalisme societal et globalisation', pp. 457-458.

369 Bianchi, *International Law Theories*, p. 240.

tional function legal regimes in the international community can spring of their own motion. These legal regimes lead to the creation of an array of smaller constitutions that are interconnected through cooperation and coordination between regimes.

7.7 Concluding Remarks on International Constitutional Law

The first conclusion after the survey of ICL is that it has achieved an independent standing as a discipline uniting international law and constitutional law.[370] ICL combines the horizontal logic of international law with vertical reasoning of constitutional law. The trend goes clearly in the direction of verticalization of international law.[371] This means that international law will have to open up more to constitutional reasoning. Verticalization of international law is a logical consequence of disaggregation of state power and its migration to the international level. In this sense, there is a patchwork of constituent powers – in the form of a cross between regimes and epistemic communities – at the international level. However, there is no central agglomeration of power. For that reason international constitutionalism cannot be streamlined along the ideal typology of constitutional doctrines such as the separation of powers, checks and balances, judicial review and others, although these doctrines serve as an inspiration for further developments. Rather, international constitutionalism evolves through various functions. The purpose of the normative constitutional function is to generate higher norms of the international community. These comprise fundamental norms as well as constitutional norms developed by international organizations. The institutional constitutional function serves as the backbone of ICL in that it creates organs, procedures and mechanisms necessary for the growth of constitutionalism. One of the most dynamic constitutional functions is the judicial one as evidenced by the proliferation of international adjudicatory bodies and their increasing reliance on constitutional judicial tools, such as judicial review, *erga omnes* effects of judgments and remedies. The coordinative constitutional function is important for synchronizing workings of transgovermental regulatory networks that arise at the international level as a result of disaggregaton of states. Finally, the self-referential constitutional function emphasizes the generative processes that create autonomous, self-contained global legal regimes as a consequence of the differentiation of the world community. These regimes likewise operate pursuant to the constitutional logic. All listed constitutional functions are interdependent and interrelated.

International constitutionalism follows the basic logic of the phenomenon of constitutionalism. First, it presupposes existence of power through a network aggregation of

---

370 *Cf.* M. Rosenfeld, 'Is Global Constitutionalism Meaningful or Desirable?', 25 *EJIL* 2014, p. 199 and A. O'Donoghue, 'International Constitutionalism and the State', 11 *International Journal of Constitutional Law* 2013, p. 1045.

371 *See* Ziccardi Campaldo, *The Pillars of Global Law*, pp. xv-xvi.

various centers of power. Second, international constitutionalism puts limits on the flow of power through diverse constitutional functions. The preceding analysis shows a tendency of all constitutional functions for their further evolution: the development of higher and other fundamental international norms; the strengthening of the institutional structure of international organizations; the tendency of international adjudicatory organs to posit themselves as judicial organs in a vertical sense; the continuous build-up of transgovernmental coordinative networks; and the multiplication of self-generative functional regimes at the global level. If these trends going beyond the inter-state architecture are to continue, international law will be compelled to reach for legal instruments that exist in the domain of constitutional law. In the long term, this trend may lead towards a more centralized constellation of power in the world community, together with a tendency for more elaborate limitations of that power.

Part III
Hegemo-Constitutional Instances in the World Community

8 International Organizations

The third part the book focuses on is the antinomy between hegemony and constitutionalism and its deconstruction in the sense of the 'in-betweenness' devised in Chapter 4 that leads to the occurrence of a hegemo-constitutional space in the international legal reality. The hegemo-constitutional space is an autonomous category consisting of concrete and empiric residual elements of hegemony and constitutionalism in a particular setting. For this category to crystallize, there first needs to be a confrontation (antinomy) between the two phenomena, which leads – through the abandonment of their premises – to a factual coexistence of similar elements belonging to both antinomic notions. Part Three analyzes instances of the hegemo-constitutional space in the following domains of international law: (i) international organizations; (ii) the intervention on humanitarian grounds; and (iii) international adjudication.

An important interaction between hegemony and constitutionalism occurs in the domain of international organizations. Within the constitutional setting of the organization hegemony takes the shape of a power structure that allows for dominance of some actors. Constitutionalism, on the other hand, develops in the sense of allocation of powers and putting limitations on their exercise, which channels and constrains various displays of hegemony within that particular international forum.

A useful category expressing the interplay between the two phenomena in the international community is the category of legalized hegemony.[1] Gerry Simpson defines it as

> the existence within an international society of a powerful elite of states whose superior status is recognized by minor powers as a political fact giving rise to the existence of certain constitutional privileges, rights and duties and whose relations with each other are defined by adherence to a rough principle of sovereign equality.[2]

In simplified terms legalized hegemony stands for an institutional constitutional order that brings hegemony of some states and the egalitarian principle into a precarious systemic balance.[3]

Simpson confers the superior status to an elite group of states on the basis of their power. A typical example is the UN Security Council, which enjoys a privileged position and wide powers in the UN, in particular in the area of international peace and security.

1 *See* Triepel, *Egemonia*, pp. xiii, 217, 219.
2 Simpson, *Great Powers and Outlaw States*, p. 68 (changed to normal script).
3 Ibid., p. 195.

Within the Security Council still, a group of world's most powerful states has a special standing as permanent members of the organ (P5) with a right to veto. The Security Council and P5 are good examples of legalized hegemony. In addition to the factor of power, states may become members of various elite clubs on the basis of other considerations, such as being progressive in a certain area of international activities.

An important element of legalized hegemony is the convergence of interests between the 'elite group' of states and common interests of a particular institutional setting. While enjoying a superior status, a club of states takes into account also the pursuit of interests of the international organization. The focus on the harmony of interests allows for the extension of legalized hegemony from power relations to the more flexible concept of leadership premised on functionality. The particular club of progressive states may assume a certain function within the international setting with an aim to pursue, enhance or enforce common interests of that institution. In doing so, the elite or core countries intertwine their particular interest with common institutional interests.

Such a functional hegemony developed in the UN after the Security Council started exercising the role of a global legislator. In the EU, the leadership of a core group of states is possible under the aegis of enhanced cooperation. Similarly, a possibility to adopt plurilateral agreements in the WTO may enable the reshaping of the organization into a polycentric 'club-of-clubs'. All these examples represent legalized hegemony and embody a mix of constitutional and hegemonic elements in a particular international organization. They are considered in more detail in the following sections.

8.1 The UN Security Council as a Global Legislator

As noted in Chapter 7, the growth of the Security Council into a global legislator represents one of the most remarkable developments of international constitutionalism in the United Nations.[4] On the other hand, the Security Council also stands as an example of legalized hegemony in the sense that it is a forum of 15 countries that enjoy wide powers to decide on issues of international peace and security. Ten of those countries are non-permanent members and rotate every two years according to equitable geographic distribution, while five are permanent members (P5) with a right to veto (China, France, Russia,[5] UK and US). This arrangement defines the Security Council as a leading organ in

4 *See* Szasz, 'The Security Council Starts Legislating', pp. 901-904, Talmon, 'The Security Council as World Legislature', pp. 175-193, Rosand, 'The Security Council as "Global Legislator"', pp. 542-591 and V. Popovski & T. Fraser (Eds.), *The Security Council as Global Legislator*, Routledge, London-New York, 2014.

5 As a successor to the Union of Soviet Socialist Republics, Russia took over its seat without any formal amendment of the Charter. (D. Schweigman, *The Authority of the Security Council under Chapter VII of the UN Charter: Legal Limits and the Role of the International Court of Justice*, Kluwer Law International, The Hague-London-Boston, 2001, p. 45, n. 186 and F.L. Kirigs, 'The Security Council's First Fifty Years', 89 *AJIL* 1995, p. 537.)

the international community. In addition, it enables P5 countries to exert influence over other members of the Security Council.[6] The growth of constitutionalism coupled with the display of hegemony represents a unique dynamic between these two phenomena in the United Nations.

Until recently the mainstream doctrine claimed that the present system of international law does not have an international legislative organ[7] and that the Security Council cannot perform such a task.[8] On the other hand, the work of Edward Yemin on legislative powers in the UN system led to a conclusion that the Security Council had a potential to become an international legislator.[9] This qualitative change in the functioning of the Security Council has become particularly visible after 9/11. On the basis of the general theory of law, Yemin put forward a set of conditions for legislation at the international level. He defined legislation as the "creation of general legal norms for the community by an organ thereof".[10] This process is also called the *legislative act*, which has three essential characteristics: (i) it is unilateral in form; (ii) it creates or modifies some element of a legal norm; and (iii) the norm is generic and abstract (hypothetical) in nature.[11]

The international legislator is a collegiate international organ with the competence to adopt obligatory international legal norms. The norms are adopted in a unilateral form, which means that a decision derives from that organ as a whole. The norms are generic in nature and address an indeterminate number of subjects. International norms primarily address states as the traditional subjects of international law. However, since the role of other actors (*e.g.*, non-state actors and individuals) at the international level is growing, international norms may pertain to them as well.[12] It is possible, therefore, to consider

6 *See* D.M. Malone, 'US-UN Relations in the UN Security Council in the Post-Cold War Era', *in* Foot *et al.*, *US Hegemony and International Organizations*, pp. 73-91 and Alvarez, 'Hegemonic International Law Revisited', pp. 873-888.

7 *See, e.g.*, Hart, *The Concept of Law*, p. 214, M. Virally, 'Sur la prétendue «primitivité» du droit international', *in* Virally, *Le droit international en devenir*, p. 91 and F. Sudre, *Droit international et européen des droits de l'homme*, PUF, Paris, 1995, p. 21. *See also Tadić* case, para. 43.

8 *Cf.* G. Abi-Saab, 'A "New World Order"? Some Preliminary Reflections', 7 *Hague Yearbook of International Law* 1994, p. 90 and D.W. Bowett, 'Judicial and Political Functions of the Security Council and the International Court of Justice', *in* Fox, *The Changing Constitution of the United Nations*, pp. 79-80.

9 *Cf.* E. Yemin, *Legislative Powers within the United Nations and Specialised Agencies*, A.W. Sijthoff, Leyden, 1969, p. 2.

10 Ibid., p. 23.

11 Ibid., p. 6 and Talmon, 'The Security Council as World Legislature', pp. 176, 181. In his definition, Yemin does not consider that a norm should be abstract. However, since he invokes an argument that legal norms are hypothetical in character when he deals with the second element of legislative process (creation of law) it seems that the abstract element is implied therein. Legislators commonly produce generic and abstract norms. (*Cf.* Favoreu *et al.*, *Droit constitutionnel*, p. 589.)

12 *E.g.*, the SC Resolution 1540 (2004) has references directed towards non-state actors and SC Resolution 2178 (2014) to individuals. For the latter resolution, *see* A. Peters, 'Security Council Resolution 2178 (2014): The "Foreign Terrorist Fighter" as an International Legal Person, Part I', *EJIL: Talk!*, 20 November 2014, www.ejiltalk.org/security-council-resolution-2178-2014-the-foreign-terrorist-fighter-as-an-international-legal-person-part-i/.

the Security Council as the global legislator.[13] In addition, the generic and hypothetical nature of norms implies that they cover an undetermined array of acts susceptible to repeated application in the course of time.

The Security Council assumed the role of the global legislator on the basis of accumulation of powers under different Articles of the UN Charter that deal with the Council's prerogatives. Article 25, which stipulates that member states accept and carry out decisions of the Security Council, is one of the key provisions of the Charter.[14] It was drafted to be one of the pillars of a system of international security, with the predominant role of the Security Council. Since Article 24 confers the primary responsibility for the maintenance of peace and security to the Security Council, it is logical that its decisions have a compulsory character, which binds all members of the UN.[15]

Article 103 addresses the problem of relations between the Charter of the UN and the order of international treaties. It establishes a hierarchy of international treaty norms, based on the primacy of the Charter. This quality originates from the foundational San Francisco conference where the delegates opted for superior and constitutional characteristics of the Charter in relation to other international treaties.[16] Article 103 therefore gives to the UN Charter primacy in the legal order of international treaties.[17] According to the authoritative interpretation of the ICJ in the *Lockerbie* case, the decisions of the Security Council represent obligations under the Charter and as such prevail over obligations in other international agreements.[18]

The next step in the growth of legislative powers of the Security Council pertains to Article 39. This article triggers action under Chapter VII with respect to threats to the peace, breaches of the peace and acts of aggression.[19] In the context of legislative measures, the expression 'threat to peace' is the most important. Given that the determination of the threat to peace falls within discretion of the Security Council,[20] the scope for

13 This is a standard expression of contributors in the book Popovski & Fraser, *The Security Council as Global Legislator.*

14 E. Suy, 'Article 25', *in* Cot & Pellet, *La Charte des Nations unies*, p. 471.

15 Id. and L.M. Goodrich, E. Hambro & A.P. Simons, *Charter of the United Nations: Commentary and Documents*, Columbia University Press, New York-London, 1969, pp. 207-208.

16 Flory, 'Article 103', p. 1381 and Bernhardt, 'Article 103', p. 1294.

17 Flory, 'Article 103', p. 1388 and Thouvenin, 'Article 103', pp. 2133-2134.

18 *Lockerbie* case, para. 39, p. 15.

19 J.A. Frowein, 'Article 39', *in* B. Simma (Ed.), *The Charter of the United Nations: A Commentary*, C.G. Beck, München 1995, p. 608.

20 Kelsen, *The Law of the United Nations*, p. 727, G. Cohen Jonathan, 'Article 39', *in* Cot & Pellet, *La Charte des Nations unies*, p. 646, M. Hilaire, *United Nations Law and the Security Council*, Ashgate, Aldershot, 2005, p. 297 and T.D. Gill, 'Legal and Some Political Limitations on the Power of the UN Security Council to Exercise its Enforcement Powers under Chapter VII of the Charter', 26 *Netherlands Yearbook of International Law* 1995, p. 42.

interpretation is very wide and may include generic and hypothetical assumptions as to what could constitute a threat to peace.[21]

After the determination of the existence of a threat to peace under Article 39, the Security Council may call upon members to apply nonmilitary enforcement measures under Article 41. The second sentence of Article 41 enumerates measures such as breaking off economic and diplomatic relations and communication links. Although these were the measures that the Security Council applied most commonly, they are not the exclusive ones. The second sentence, which begins with the words "These [measures] may include," points to their inexhaustive nature.[22] The open-ended nature of this formulation allows for the adoption of such measures that habitually fall within the purview of legislative organs.

The Security Council adopted generic and hypothetical norms in the context of the fight against international terrorism, under Chapter VII of UN Charter.[23] The first measure was resolution 1373 (2001) that the Security Council adopted in the aftermath of the terrorist attacks of 11 September.[24] This resolution mainly (but not exclusively) focused on the problem of financing of terrorism. The second measure was resolution 1540 (2004), which addressed the danger of proliferation of WMDs.[25] One of the major concerns of the Security Council in this regard was that WMDs could fall into the hands of terrorists.[26] The third legislative instrument was resolution 2178 (2014) on the sanction-

21 *Cf.* Selkirk, 'Judge, Jury and Executioner?', pp. 1114-1116, Talmon, 'The Security Council as World Legislature', pp. 181-182 and Bianchi, 'Assessing the Effectiveness of the UN Security Council's Anti-terrorism Measures', pp. 889-990.

22 J.A. Frowein, 'Article 41', *in* Simma, *The Charter of the United* Nations, 1995, p. 625 and P.M. Eisemann, 'Article 41', *in* Cot & Pellet, *La Charte des Nations unies*, p. 695.

23 V. Popovski, 'The Legislative Role of the Security Council's Thematic Resolutions', pp. 1, 2 and M. Heupel, 'Security Council Legislation in Counter-terrorism', pp. 125, 129, both *in* Popovski & Fraser, *The Security Council as Global Legislator.*

24 SC Res. 1373 (2001), 28 September 2001.

25 SC Res. 1540 (2004), 28 April 2004. Another set of resolutions, which could fall under the scope of international legislation, are resolutions on international peacekeeping in relation to the ICC Statute (1422 (2002) and 1487 (2003)) and on piracy (1816 (2008), 1851 (2008), 2015 (2011) and others.) However, as these resolutions were adopted for a limited period of time (international peacekeeping) or did not articulate comprehensive legislative obligations (piracy), they are less important for our consideration. For more on these issues *see* Talmon, 'The Security Council as World Legislature', pp. 177-178, 186-187, Y. Gottlieb, 'The Security Council's Maritime Piracy Resolutions: A Critical Assessment', 24 *Minnesota Journal of International Law* 2015, pp. 1-72 and P. Lehr, 'Security Council Resolutions on Somali Piracy', *in* Popovski & Fraser, *The Security Council as Global Legislator*, pp. 145-158.

26 *See* J.R. Bolton, 'The Bush Administration's Forward Strategy for Nonproliferation', 5 *Chicago Journal of International Law* 2005, pp. 395-404, in particular p. 399.

ing of foreign terrorist fighters. Although adopted in the framework of the fight against terrorism, it encountered criticism that it expands the criminalization of terrorist offenses beyond established international law norms.[27]

Resolution 1373 adopted generic and abstract norms in its first paragraph obliging the states to prevent and suppress the financing of terrorist acts.[28] The first paragraph requires the states to prevent and suppress the financing of terrorist acts, to freeze financial assets of terrorists, and to prohibit their nationals to provide financial assets to terrorists.[29] The Security Council modeled these provisions on the *International Convention for the Suppression of the Financing of Terrorism* of 9 December 1999, which was not yet in force at the time.[30] In addition, in the second paragraph of resolution 1373, the Security Council imposed a number of normative obligations upon states in the fight against terrorism, such as to refrain from providing any support to entities or persons involved in terrorist acts, to deny safe haven to terrorists and to bring them to justice, to enact criminal legislation for terrorist offences and others.[31] These provisions address all states, which means that they have a generic character, and pertain to an array of non-concretized acts, which makes them abstract in nature. Resolution 1373 norms directly create new obligations for member states and, on the assumption of the action of the governments, indirectly for persons under their jurisdiction. Thus, with resolution 1373 the Security Council imposed new obligations on the member states in the field of suppression of the financing of terrorism. In order to secure implementation of these norms, the resolution established a special subsidiary organ, the Counter-Terrorism Committee, to monitor implementation of that resolution.[32]

---

27 S. Krähenmann, 'Foreign Fighters under International and National Law', 20 *Recueils de la Société Internationale de Droit Pénal Militaire et de Droit de la Guerre* 2015, p. 256, Human Rights Watch, *"Foreign Terrorist Fighter" Laws: Human Rights Rollbacks under UN Security Council Resolution 2178*, December 2016 and K. Ambos, 'Our Terrorists, Your Terrorists? The United Nations Security Council Urges States to Combat "Foreign Terrorist Fighters," but Does Not Define "Terrorism,"' *EJIL: Talk!*, 2 October 2014, www.ejiltalk.org/our-terrorists-your-terrorists-the-united-nations-security-council-urges-states-to-combat-foreign-terrorist-fighters-but-does-not-define-terrorism/.

28 *Cf.* Bianchi, 'Assessing the Effectiveness of the UN Security Council's Anti-terrorism Measures', pp. 882-883.

29 SC Res. 1373, para. 1.

30 Szasz, 'The Security Council Starts Legislating', p. 903, Alvarez, 'Hegemonic International Law Revisited', p. 196 and Talmon, 'The Security Council as World Legislature', pp. 177,184. The Convention entered into force on 10 April 2002.

31 SC Res. 1373, para. 2.

32 Ibid., para. 6. For the implementation of the resolution 1373 *see* A. Bianchi, 'Security Council's Anti-terror Resolutions and their Implementation by Member States', 4 *Journal of International Criminal Justice* 2006, pp. 1048-1059, Bianchi, 'Assessing the Effectiveness of the UN Security Council's Anti-terrorism Measures', pp. 892-897, Alvarez, *International Organizations as Law-Makers*, p. 196 and E. Rosand, 'Security Council Resolution 1373, the Counter-Terrorism Committee, and the Fight against Terrorism', 97 *AJIL* 2003, pp. 333-341.

The substance of resolution 1540 is very similar to resolution 1373.[33] The first two paragraphs of this resolution impose generic and abstract obligations on the member states of the UN.[34] The first paragraph demands all states to refrain from providing any form of support to non-state actors that attempt to produce or deal with weapons of mass destruction (WMD).[35] Obligation in the second paragraph is even more prescriptive.[36] The Security Council requires all states to adopt and enforce appropriate effective laws, which would prohibit any non-state actor to develop or traffic with weapons of mass destruction, in particular for terrorist purposes.[37] Finally, in paragraph three the Council requires all states to establish domestic controls to prevent proliferation of WMDs. Following the example of resolution 1373, resolution 1540 establishes a special committee with a task to monitor implementation of resolution 1540.[38]

Finally, resolution 2178 in paragraph 6 requires all states to adopt relevant laws and regulations to criminalize offenses with regard to foreign terrorist fighters. The resolution makes a reference to resolution 1373 and recalls its obligation that persons who are in any way engaged in terrorist acts should be brought to justice. The proscribed offenses related to foreign terrorist fighters cover the following components: (i) the travelling (or attempted travelling) of individuals to countries abroad "for the purpose of the perpetration, planning, or preparation of, or participation in, terrorist acts, or the providing or receiving of terrorist training"; (ii) the wilful provision or collection of funds for the purpose of financing activities under (i); and (iii) the wilful organization or other facilitation, including acts of recruitment, of activities under (i).[39] Monitoring of the implementation of resolution 2178, including the aspect of criminalization of foreign terrorist fighters, is entrusted to the UN Counter-Terrorism Committee Executive Directorate.[40]

The above analysis of resolutions 1373, 1540 and 2178 demonstrate that the Security Council, by adopting generic and abstract norms, ventured into a novel activity of global legislation. This change was not instantaneous but rather reflects a gradual process of

---

33 B.N. Patel, 'Security Council Resolution 1540 and Non-proliferation of Weapons of Mass Destruction', 11 *African Yearbook of International Law* 2003, p. 302.

34 *Cf.* S. Sur, 'La resolution 1540 du Conseil de Securité (28 avril 2004) : entre la proliferation des armes de destruction massive, le terrorisme et les acteurs non étatiques', 108 *RGDIP* 2004, p. 857.

35 SC Res. 1540, para. 1.

36 Serge Sur speaks of the 'contexte normatif' of the resolution 1540. (Sur, 'La resolution 1540 du Conseil de Securité (28 avril 2004)', p. 857.)

37 SC Res. 1540, para. 2. *See also* Sur, 'La resolution 1540 du Conseil de Securité (28 avril 2004)', p. 867.

38 Alvarez, *International Organizations as Law-Makers*, p. 197. On the implementation of the resolution 1540 and the role of the committee, *see* Sur, 'La resolution 1540 du Conseil de Securité (28 avril 2004)', pp. 867-868 and M. Heupel, *Implementing UN Security Council Resolution 1540: A Division of Labor Strategy*, Carnegie Papers, Carnegie Endowment for International Peace, Washington (DC), 2007, pp. 6-11, 14-16.

39 SC Res. 2178 (2014), 24 September 2014, para. 6.

40 *See* ibid., paras. 24-26, UN SC CTC, *Special Meeting of the Counter-Terrorism Committee on Stemming the Flow of Foreign Terrorist Fighters and Related Documents*, S/2015/939, 23 December 2015 and UN SC CTCED, *Implementation of Security Council Resolution 2178 (2014) by States Affected by Foreign Terrorist Fighters: A Compilation of Three Reports (S/2015/338; S/2015/683; S/2015/975).*

accumulating powers under Chapter VII. Under Article 39 of the Charter the Security Council widened the scope of the determination of a 'threat to peace', which was until then mainly restricted to armed conflicts, to general phenomena such as prevention of terrorism and nonproliferation of WMDs. Through Article 41, the Council extended the nature of nonmilitary measures to the legal field, to include legal norms on the suppression of the acts of financing of terrorism, the prohibition of acquiring WMDs and the criminalization of activities of foreign terrorist fighters. The interpretation of Articles 25 and 103 of the Charter by the ICJ elevated binding decisions of Chapter VII above any other international agreements. The aggregation of all the enumerated steps transformed the Security Council into a new quality of the global legislator.[41] As this quality is a typical illustration of the normative and institutional functions, it represents a significant step in the development of international constitutionalism.

It is likely that the Security Council will continue to act as the global legislator. The question arises whether its activities at the same time represent an occurrence of legal hegemony. Several issues come to mind with regard to the legitimacy of the Security Council in this role.

As mentioned before, the Security Council is a club of states with a privileged position of big powers under the UN Charter. One cannot ignore the factual reality that in many cases the initiatives in the Security Council are led by P1 (US),[42] which gives the impression that the Security Council's activities are instrumentalized by one hegemon for the protection of its own interests.[43] Nonetheless, the Security Council acts as a collegiate organ. Although a powerful country can influence other members, the responsibility for accepted decisions rests on the Security Council as a collective organ. From this perspective the growth of the Security Council stands as the example of a collective hegemony, which has important repercussions for other members of the international community.

A metamorphosis of the Security Council into the global legislator represents a major shift in the functioning of the international community. Until recently, the rule of consent of states was undisputed as a major principle of international lawmaking. By assuming the role of the global legislator, the resolutions of the Security Council can override

41 Bianchi, 'Assessing the Effectiveness of the UN Security Council's Anti-terrorism Measures', p. 883, Alvarez, *International Organizations as Law-Makers*, pp. 197 and Rosand, 'The Security Council as "Global Legislator"', p. 567.

42 Tono Eitel describes the decision-making process of the Security Council as follows: "According to my experience a Council decision (Resolution or Presidential Statement) is, in most cases, prepared through the following steps, the sequence of which may change:

a. Kick off by the U.S. or in many other cases with the support of the U.S.;
b. Preparation by the Secretary-General in a report (often in consultation with one or all of the P 5 and, of course, principally interested other members);
c. Harmonising among the P 5;
d. Lobbying with reluctant Council members by the proponents and the U.S. (or the U.S. alone);
e. Taking of the decision of the Council." (T. Eitel, 'The UN Security Council and Its Future Contribution in the Field of International Law', 4 *Max Planck Yearbook of United Nations Law* 2000, pp. 58-59.)

43 Alvarez, 'Hegemonic International Law Revisited', p. 887.

the will of the states.[44] It is important that at the time of the adoption the legislative resolutions did not raise significant objections from the member states. In all probability this was so because all three resolutions pursued legitimate community interests within the Security Council's mandate to maintain international peace and security, that is, to fight international terrorism and to prevent the proliferation of WMD. There are, however, important differences with regard to three legislative resolutions when it comes to the process of their adoption.

In the aftermath of the terrorist attack on 9/11, the need for a speedy adoption of resolution 1373 was self-evident. The legislative provisions were modeled on the existing international agreement on the suppression of the terrorist financing. In subsequent discussions before the Security Council, states supported the resolution. Although nonproliferation of WMD is likewise in the common interest of the international community, the approach with regard to resolution 1540 was slightly different. The resolution not only summarized the existing international obligations on the nonproliferation of WMD but also extended them to non-state actors.[45] In addition, preparatory negotiations lasted for several months and included two open discussions before the Security Council.[46] Finally, the process leading to resolution 2178 was less transparent. In this case, the Security Council prescribed an entirely new set of provisions criminalizing activities of foreign terrorist fighters. The discussions about the content of these norms were practically nonexistent. After the adoption, some scholars criticized this resolution for the nontransparency of the process and for its vagueness allowing member states to arbitrarily expand the field of criminalization in their domestic legislation.[47]

The evolution of the Security Council into the role of the global legislator necessarily opens a question about the limits of its legislative activities, as well as a general question about legitimacy to act in this role.[48] Already in the process of expanding its powers under Chapter VII – but also after passing the first legislative resolution 1373 – several commentators criticized the Security Council for its excessive activity leading to a hege-

---

44 *See* Rosand, 'The Security Council as "Global Legislator"', pp. 573-578, Heupel, 'Security Council Legislation in Counter-terrorism', pp. 131, 132 and M. Fremuth & J. Griebel, 'On the Security Council as a Legislator: A Blessing or a Curse for the International Community?', 76 *Nordic Journal of International Law* 2007, pp. 354-355.

45 Patel, 'Security Council Resolution 1540 and Non-proliferation of Weapons of Mass Destruction', p. 306.

46 Popovski, 'The Legislative Role of the Security Council's Thematic Resolutions', p. 5 and O. Bosch, 'A Legislative Evolution: Security Council Resolution 1540 Revisited', *in* Popovski & Fraser, *The Security Council as Global Legislator*, pp. 102, 112.

47 M. Scheinin, 'Back to Post-9/11 Panic? Security Council Resolution on Foreign Terrorist Fighters', *Just Security*, 23 September 2014, www.justsecurity.org/15407/post-911-panic-security-council-resolution-foreign-terrorist-fighters-scheinin/ and Ambos, 'Our Terrorists, Your Terrorists?'. However, the subsequent monitoring of the implementation of resolution 2178 by CTC, also from the perspective of the rule of law and human rights, significantly reduced these concerns. (*See Implementation of Security Council Resolution 2178 (2014) by States Affected by Foreign Terrorist Fighters: A Compilation of Three Reports.*)

48 For the problem of legitimacy, *see* Chimni, 'International Institutions Today', pp. 20-21 and Bianchi, 'Assessing the Effectiveness of the UN Security Council's Anti-terrorism Measures', p. 918.

monic position in the international community.[49] The exercise of the legislative role through the adoption of binding normative obligations, overlooking consent of states, cemented the Security Council as a global hegemon in this regard.[50] The Security Council draws legitimacy from fulfilling the function of protecting wider community interests within its mandate for the maintenance of peace and security under the UN Charter.[51] As long as it continues to act within that purview, which depends on a set of concrete assessments in each particular case, its actions shall be seen as legitimate.[52] However, given that other components of international constitutionalism – such as the judicial function – are likewise on a continuous rise, it is viable that legality and legitimacy of the Security Council's legislative actions will be soon assessed by the evolving checks and balances mechanism.

As the process of globalization is accelerating, its negative consequences in the form of international terrorism appear as novel threats to international peace and security. The UN Charter clearly identifies the protection of international peace and security as a common end of the international community. The Security Council responded to these threats with a conceptual expansion of the threat to peace and a continual aggregation of its powers. Eventually, the Security Council assumed the position of the global legislator. This agglomeration of powers represents the first stage of constitutionalism,[53] as defined in Chapter 3. However, the constitutional metamorphosis of the Security Council goes hand in hand with its positioning as a global hegemonic actor in the international community.[54] The Security Council of today therefore represents a simultaneous expression of constitutionalism and hegemony. Nonetheless, in order to correspond fully to the requirements of constitutionalism, the hegemonic powers of the Security Council need to

49 Abi-Saab, 'A New World Order?', pp. 89, 91, Koskenniemi, 'The Police in the Temple', p. 339 and M. Koskenniemi, 'International Law and Hegemony: A Reconfiguration', 17 *Cambridge Review f International Affairs* 2004, p. 209. *See also* H. Breaky, 'Parsing Security Council Resolutions: A Five-dimensional Taxonomy of Normative Properties', p. 55 and J. Wouters & J. Odermatt, '*Quis Custodiet Consilium Securitatis*: Reflections on the Law-making Powers of the Security Council', p. 74, both *in* Popovski & Fraser, *The Security Council as Global Legislator*.

50 *See* Alvarez, *International Organizations as Law-Makers*, pp. 199-217, 644-645, A. Anghie, 'Europe and International Law's Colonial Present', 6 *BaYIL* 2006, p. 83 and C. Forcese, 'Hegemonic Federalism: The Democratic Implications of the UN Security Council's "Legislative" Phase', 38 *Victoria University Wellington Law Review* 2007, pp. 185, 195-196.

51 Bosch, 'A Legislative Evolution', p. 112.

52 *See* T. Fraser, 'Conclusion: The Security Council as Global Legislator', *in* Popovski & Fraser, *The Security Council as Global Legislator*, p. 301, Bianchi, 'Assessing the Effectiveness of the UN Security Council's Anti-terrorism Measures', pp. 917-919, Bianchi, 'Security Council's Anti-terror Resolutions and their Implementation by Member States', p. 1072 and Rosand, 'The Security Council as "Global Legislator"', pp. 588-590.

53 Heupel, 'Security Council Legislation in Counter-terrorism', pp. 125, 138.

54 *Cf.* J.E. Alvarez, 'Foreword', *in* Popovski & Fraser, *The Security Council as Global Legislator*, pp. xiv-xv.

be subjected to an efficacious mechanism of checks and balances by other members of the international community. The greatest potential for the operation of this mechanism resides in the judicial function of the international community.[55]

8.2 Enhanced Cooperation in the European Union

The word hegemony is nearly absent in discussions on the European affairs. This is partly understandable. The European integration started precisely to avoid hegemony of one or a few member countries on the European continent and, thus, to prevent a return of power politics of an interwar period. In this vein, a decision-making framework under the original Treaty of Rome attempted to construct a suitable climate for Franco-German reconciliation and ensure the participation of the smaller Benelux countries.[56] This, however, does not rule out the leadership of some EU countries, as in the form of the well-known Franco-German 'privileged friendship'. The Franco-German axis has been the real engine behind much of the European integration project and it looks that this cooperation is going to intensify in the future.[57] Some refer to this form of leadership as the *directoire* formula.[58]

On the other hand, leadership of some countries produces opposition from smaller ones. In fact, an institutional tension between larger and smaller countries – which Paul Magnette and Kalypso Nicolaïdis termed the 'Lilliput Syndrome'[59] – has been part of the European framework since the very beginning.[60] In broader terms, this tension represents an opposition between two key principles: equality between member states and democratic (or proportional) representation. In practice, member states resolved this pressure through three constitutional mechanisms: a system of qualified majority voting (QMV) in the Council of Ministers, independence of the Commission as a supranational organ,

55 On the judicial functioning of international constitutionalism, *see* Chapter 7. At this point, it is useful to add that the judicial organs of the EU (the ECJ and the Court of First Instance) started performing indirect judicial scrutiny of the activities of the Security Council in the fight against terrorism (the process of listing of individuals as terrorist suspects), such as in the *Kadi* case.

56 Devuyst, 'The European Union's Constitutional Order?', p. 33 and P. Magnette & K. Nicolaïdis, 'Coping with the Lilliput Syndrome: Large vs. Small Member States in the European Convention', 11 *European Public Law* 2005, p. 86.

57 Devuyst, 'The European Union's Constitutional Order?', p. 34, D.W. Urwin, 'The European Community: From 1945 to 1985', *in* Cini, *European Union Politics*, pp. 19, 28, Dinan, *Ever Closer Union*, pp. 74-75, 79-80 and DW, 'Merkel and Macron Sign Treaty of Aachen to Revive EU', 22 January 2019, www.dw.com/en/merkel-and-macron-sign-treaty-of-aachen-to-revive-eu/a-47172186.

58 Magnette & Nicolaïdis, 'Coping with the Lilliput Syndrome', p. 87 and Devuyst, 'The European Union's Constitutional Order?', pp. 34-35.

59 According to the Lilliput Syndrome, big countries picture themselves as giants, but are potentially held back by a group of smaller countries. In this way, weighted votes of big countries are under-represented according to the relative weight of the factor of population. (Magnette & Nicolaïdis, 'Coping with the Lilliput Syndrome', pp. 89-90.)

60 Ibid., pp. 85-86 and Devuyst, 'The European Union's Constitutional Order?', pp. 33-36.

and rotating presidency of the Council of Ministers.[61] However, the dynamic of enlargement, in particular the last wave with countries from the Central and Eastern Europe and the Mediterranean, heightened institutional tensions in the EU and led to a revision of the mechanisms that were initially designed to cope with such diversity.[62] All these constitutional mechanisms had to attain a completely new institutional equilibrium, which points to a direct link between enlargement and European constitutionalism.[63] One important issue in this respect is QMV in the Council of Ministers. QMV represents a move away from the tradition of consensual decision-making. However, this is necessary if an increasingly heterogeneous EU is to function in the future.[64] Whereas in the Nice Treaty rules on QMV favored larger states, subsequent negotiation on the defunct Constitutional Treaty and on the Lisbon Treaty took into account concerns from smaller states and adjusted rules on QMV accordingly.[65]

Another important measure to alleviate heterogeneity in the enlarged European Union is the mechanism of the differentiated integration and its more specific variation of enhanced cooperation. Differentiated integration has been present since the beginning of this process.[66] However, a growing interdependence in the process of the European integration inevitably gave rise to the greater differentiation within this structure.[67] The best way to accommodate heterogeneous European interests is by introducing more flexibility without risking the gains achieved through previous integration efforts. Essential elements of such 'flexible integration' are (i) a common base, in which all members of the EU must participate and (ii) a possibility to enter into open partnerships that allow

61 Magnette & Nicolaïdis, 'Coping with the Lilliput Syndrome', pp. 87-88, 102-103.

62 Ibid., pp. 86, 103.

63 *See* N. Walker, 'Constitutionalising Enlargement, Enlarging Constitutionalism', 9 *European Law Journal* 2003, pp. 365-385.

64 Nugent, *The Government and Politics of the European Union*, p. 506, Phinnemore, 'Towards European Union', p. 36 and Pernice, 'Institutional Settlements for an Enlarged European Union', pp. 32-33.

65 The Nice Treaty introduced the requirement of 'double majority', according to which a legislative proposal would pass if it received a qualified majority (72%) of votes, representing an absolute majority of member states, and – subject to a specific request by a member state – a qualified majority (62%) of the EU population. The Constitutional Treaty set the new double majority at 55% of the member states and 65% of the population. This arrangement made it relatively easier for countries to form a blocking majority without, however, allowing the biggest three member states to do so themselves. Finally, the Lisbon Treaty adopted a transitional regime. In the first period (until 2014) the arrangement of the Nice Treaty applied. In the second period (2014-2017), the double majority was set to 55% of member states and to 65% of the population. In the third period (after 2017), only the rules of 55% of member states and 65% population apply. (*See* Dinan, *Ever Closer Union*, pp. 171, 171, Dougan, 'The Treaty of Lisbon', p. 631 and Magnette & Nicolaïdis, 'Coping with the Lilliput Syndrome', pp. 90-91, 101-102.)

66 T. Kubin, 'Enhanced Cooperation, EMU Reforms and Their Implications for Differentiation in the European Union', 7 *Baltic Journal of European Studies* 2017, p. 95.

67 F. Schimmelfennig, D. Leuffen & B. Rittberger, 'The European Union as a System of Differentiated Integration: Interdependence, Politicization and Differentiation', *Political Science Series*, Working Paper No. 137, 10 July 2014, p. 23, www.ihs.ac.at/publications/pol/pw_137.pdf.

groups of countries ('clubs') to integrate further.[68] At the heart of this approach is a proper balance between, on one hand, a firm commitment of all EU states to the values of European integration and, on the other one, a freedom of choice for those who wish to pursue deeper and broader integration as well as for those who do not.[69]

Such a dynamic inevitably brings asymmetry into the structure of the EU. The equality between the EU member states is a constitutional principle of EU law.[70] Nonetheless, although the common basis remains the same for all, an option to deepen and widen integration in certain policy areas is bound to introduce a variety of asymmetric arrangements into the EU.[71] In this sense, differentiated integration brings a certain degree of practical inequality between member states,[72] instituting hegemony in the EU under the guise of avant-garde groups of some member states.[73] At the same time, however, asymmetry "leads to the identification of a constitutional core of principles and values whose respect makes asymmetry 'sustainable': this is also the rationale of asymmetry in EU law".[74] Differentiated integration, in particular in the form of enhanced cooperation, thus allows for the formation of a vanguard group of member states exercising the constitutional function of achieving 'an ever closer union' in new policy areas within the EU constitutional order.[75]

---

68 *Flexible Integration: Towards a More Effective and Democratic Europe*, Monitoring European Integration 6, Center for Economic Policy Research, London, 1995, pp. 9-10.

69 Ibid., p. 10.

70 J. Wouters & P. Schmitt, 'Equality Among Member States and Differentiated Integration in the EU', *in* L.S. Rossi & F. Casolari (Eds.), *The Principle of Equality in EU Law*, Springer, Cham, 2017, p. 50.

71 *See* C.M. Cantore, 'We're One, but We're Not the Same: Enhanced Cooperation and the Tension between Unity and Asymmetry in the EU', 3 *Perspectives on Federalism* 2011, pp. 3-4 and G. Martinico, 'A Multi-Speed EU? An Institutional and Legal Assessment', 15 *IAI Working Papers* 2015, Istituto Affari Intenazionali, pp. 2-6.

72 Woutes & Schmitt, 'Equality Among Member States and Differentiated Integration in the EU', p. 75.

73 *Cf.* R. Geiger, 'Title III: Enhanced Cooperation', *in* R. Geiger, D.-E. Khan & M. Kotzur (Eds.), *European Union Treaties: Treaty on European Union, Treaty on the Functioning of the European Union*, C.H. Beck-Hart, 2015, p. 1012, S. Peers, 'Divorce, European Style: The First Authorization of Enhanced Cooperation', 6 *European Constitutional Law Review* 2010, p. 356 and M. Avbelj, 'Differentiated Integration—Farewell to the EU-27?', 14 *German Law Journal* 2013, p. 191.

74 Martinico, 'A Multi-Speed EU?', p. 5.

75 F. Fabbrini, 'Enhanced Cooperation under Scrutiny: Revisiting the Law and Practice of Multi-Speed Integration in Light of the First Involvement of the EU Judiciary', 40 *Legal Issues of Economic Integration* 2013, pp. 206-207. Ran Hirschl turns this logic on its head in the form of the hegemonic preservation thesis. The reason why larger Western states (especially Germany and France), in anticipation of the enlargement, introduced the mechanism of enhanced cooperation was to preserve their hegemony. This would allow them to go ahead with deeper integration and create a core group of Western states. In this sense, political actors create institutions in order to impose limits on their competitors, rather than to limit themselves. Interestingly, all this occurs in the framework of the EU constitutional order. (R. Hirschl, 'Preserving Hegemony? Assessing the Political Origins of the EU Constitution', 3 *International Journal of Constitutional Law* 2005, pp. 278-279, 286-287, 291.) However, what Hirschl somehow overlooks is that rules on enhanced cooperation are general and open to all member states. Enhanced cooperation is a systemic mechanism in the EU constitutional order that allows for the formation of various instances of hegemony in the EU.

Typologically, we can classify the forms of differentiated integration in three categories: multispeed integration, integration *à la carte*, and concentric circles. All three categories share the same goal – further integration of those member states that are ready to deepen their cooperation in the framework of the EU. Although these categories may interfere conceptually, the main distinguishing factors are the following: multispeed Europe focuses on the time aspect, *à la carte* integration on the policy area and concentric circles on the factor of space.[76]

Differentiated integration recently became part of the high-level political agenda, as a tool to transcend the heterogeneous nature of the EU while staying on the path of joint integration. On this issue, there is a convergence of views between the supranational and the intergovernmental level of the EU. In March 2017, the European Commission issued a *White Paper on the Future of Europe* describing five scenarios on how to move forward. Scenario No. 3 with a title 'Those who want more do more' presupposes that groups of states can emerge in order to work together in specific policy areas. These areas may, for example, cover defense, internal security, taxation or social matters.[77] Shortly thereafter, at the Rome conference celebrating the sixtieth anniversary of the creation of the predecessor of EU, leaders of EU member states and institutions adopted a declaration stating that the EU

> will act together, at different paces and intensity where necessary, while moving in the same direction … in line with the Treaties and keeping the door open to those who want to join later.[78]

These explicit statements confirm the view that "differentiated integration has also become an important and – most probably – permanent feature of European integration."[79]

Nonetheless, when discussing differentiated integration, one must make certain clarifications in order to avoid the danger of a conceptual confusion. Differentiated integration in the general sense stands for a plethora of different options, which allow for ex-

76 *See* A. Stubb, 'A Categorization of Differentiated Integration', 34 *Journal of Common Market Studies* 1996, pp. 287-289, *Flexible Integration*, pp. 52-53, 55-58, K. Junge, 'Differentiated European Integration', *in* Cini, *European Union Politics*, pp. 396-398 and M. Wind, 'The European Union as a Polycentric Polity: Returning to a Neo-medieval Europe', *in* J.H.H. Weiler & M. Wind (Eds.), *European Constitutionalism beyond the State*, CUP, Cambridge, 2003, pp. 111-112.

77 European Commission, *White Paper on the Future of Europe: Reflections and Scenarios for the EU27 by 2025*, 1 March 2017, COM(2017)2025, p. 20, https://ec.europa.eu/commission/sites/beta-political/files/white_paper_on_the_future_of_europe_en.pdf.

78 Council of EU, *The Rome Declaration*, 25 March 2017, 149/17, www.consilium.europa.eu/en/press/press-releases/2017/03/25/rome-declaration/pdf.

79 K. Holzinger & F. Schimmelfennig, 'Differentiated Integration in the European Union: Many Concepts, Sparse Theory, Few Data', 19 *Journal of European Public Policy* 2012, p. 293.

ceptions in favor of certain states while the core majority pursues further cooperation and integration within the EU framework.[80] Its manifestations comprise a range of formal and semi-formal legislative, executive and judicial techniques of regulation, whose outcomes fall short of requiring and establishing uniformity. To these one can add more pronounced legal arrangements in the form of exceptions from the agreed arrangements, such as safeguard clauses, various opt-outs with potential opt-ins, and protocol-based derogations in favor of a selected member state.[81] Two distinct features of differentiated integration are that it normally belongs to the area of primary law (treaties) and that it has been traditionally considered as an exception to the otherwise uniform process of the European integration.[82] Typical examples of differentiated integration are the legal framework on the Economic and Monetary Union (Euro cooperation); the European Stability Mechanism; the Fiscal Compact Treaty; the Schengen regime; and the Area of Freedom, Security and Justice cooperation regarding visa, asylum and immigration policies.[83]

Gradually, as a response to the growing heterogeneity in the EU, another mode of differentiated integration started to develop, which has evolved into a potent phenomenon with the Lisbon Treaty – the mechanism of enhanced cooperation. Enhanced cooperation was constitutionalized in the Treaty of Amsterdam (1996) and transposed to the Nice Treaty (2000). As conditions for its activation were rather rigid it was never used in practice. A more flexible legal arrangement under the Lisbon Treaty enabled this mechanism to become an ordinary tool for members of the EU wishing to deepen cooperation in certain areas.[84]

The Lisbon Treaty covers the mechanism of enhanced cooperation in Article 20 of the Treaty on European Union (TEU) and Articles 326-334 of the Treaty on the Functioning of the European Union (TFEU). The aim of enhanced cooperation is "to further the objectives of the Union, protect its interests and reinforce its integration processes."[85] The rationale of enhanced cooperation is to pursue common interests and objectives of

---

80 *See* D. Leuffen, 'European Union as a Blueprint? Nine Hypotheses on Differentiated Integration in a Comparative Perspective', WAI-ZEI Paper, No. 8, 2013, pp. 14-15, www.zei.uni-bonn.de/dateien/wai-zei-paper/08-2013-wai-zei-leuffen.

81 Avbelj, 'Differentiated Integration – Farewell to the EU-27?' pp. 193-194.

82 *Cf.* ibid., pp. 193-195 and J.W. de Zwaan, *Stability and Differentiation in the European Union*, Eleven International Publishing, The Hague, 2017, pp. 15-16.

83 Wouters & Schmitt, 'Equality Among Member States and Differentiated Integration in the EU', pp. 56-67, de Zwaan, *Stability and Differentiation in the European Union*, pp. 15-16 and D. Thym, 'Competing Models for Understanding Differentiated Integration', *in* B. de Witte, A. Ott & E. Vos (Eds.), *Between Flexibility and Disintegration: The Trajectory of Differentiation in EU Law*, Edward Elgar, Cheltenham-Northampton, 2017, pp. 29, 57, 62.

84 *See* Avbelj, Differentiated Integration – Farewell to the EU-27?', pp. 195, 198-199, Junge, 'Differentiated European Integration', pp. 392, 393, Wind, 'The European Union as a Polycentric Polity', pp. 114, 117 and D.A. Kroll & D. Leuffen, 'Enhanced Cooperation in Practice. An Analysis of Differentiated Integration in EU Secondary Law', 22 *Journal of European Public Policy* 2015, p. 354.

85 TEU Art. 20(1). (*See* Consolidated version of the Treaty on European Union, Official Journal C 326, 26 October 2012.)

the EU, albeit in a smaller circle of EU member states.[86] Enhanced cooperation therefore pursues the goal of fostering a multispeed integration in the EU constitutional order, allowing at the same time the political organs of the EU to impose several limitations on this process.[87]

The enhanced cooperation is based on an agreement between at least nine participating EU member states and must rely on the act of the Council of the EU as the secondary Union Law.[88] At the same time, its activation should be the measure of last resort after the Council has established that objectives of such cooperation cannot be attained within a reasonable period by the EU as a whole.[89] The mechanism leaves the door open for those member states that wish to join such cooperation later.[90] Indeed, participating states and the Commission are under obligation to promote participation of as many EU member states as possible.[91] This arrangement sends a clear message that enhanced cooperation is a measure that takes place within the EU constitutional framework and is premised on the fundamental EU values, principles and interests. It authorizes a group of states to upgrade cooperation in a certain EU policy area, allowing others to join in later.

Any instance of enhanced cooperation must take place within the nonexclusive competences of the EU and comply with the Treaties and EU law.[92] It must not undermine the essential postulates of the EU such as the internal market, or economic, social and territorial cohesion; it must not function as a barrier to or discrimination of trade nor distort competition between member states.[93] The initiative for enhanced cooperation must go through a set of gatekeeping checks for its compatibility with the EU objectives. Member states wishing to establish enhanced cooperation must first address a request to the Commission and specify its scope and objectives. If the Commission agrees with the request it submits a proposal to the Council. However, before the Council considers the matter, the proposal for enhanced cooperation must obtain the approval of the European

---

86 *Cf.* R. Stemplowski, 'Hegemony in the European Union?', 4 *Polish Foreign Affairs Digest* 2004, pp. 9-10 and de Zwaan, *Stability and Differentiation in the European Union*, p. 16.

87 Fabbrini, 'Enhanced Cooperation under Scrutiny', p. 199 and Geiger, 'Title IV: Provisions on Enhanced Cooperation', *in* Geiger, Khan & Kotzur, *European Union Treaties*, p. 115.

88 TEU Art. 20(2) and Geiger, 'Title IV: Provisions on Enhanced Cooperation', p. 116.

89 TEU Art. 20(2).

90 *See* TEU Art. 20(1) and TFEU Arts. 328 and 331.

91 Art. TFEU 328(1).

92 Enhanced cooperation is likewise possible in the area of the common foreign and security policy although rules for its functioning differ slightly from the general framework. (*See* TFEU Arts. 329(2) and 331(2)).

93 TEU Art. 20(1) and TFEU Art. 326.

Parliament. In the last instance, authorization to proceed with the enhanced cooperation is granted by a decision of the Council with qualified majority.[94] The request for enhanced cooperation is thus subject to a three-stage scrutiny by the EU political organs.

After the enhanced cooperation is established, acts adopted within its framework bind only the participating states and do not make part of the EU *acquis* to be accepted by candidate countries.[95] While any case of enhanced cooperation must respect the competences, rights and obligations of nonparticipating EU member states, these must not impede implementation by the participating states.[96] Furthermore, all member states may participate in the deliberations of the enhanced cooperation mechanism. However, only those members of the Council that are participating in a particular case of enhanced cooperation are entitled to take part in the vote.[97] The Council and the Commission are obliged to ensure the consistency of activities undertaken in the context of enhanced cooperation, including with the policies of the EU.[98] In introducing the relationship of mutual respect, such an arrangement gives adequate weight both to the mechanism of enhanced cooperation and member states not participating in it. At the same time, it also ensures that discussions and deliberations in the Council as well as activities within enhanced cooperation veer towards the highest possible convergence of interests between participating states, nonparticipating states and EU institutions.

Although the heterogeneous nature of the EU made the mechanism of enhanced cooperation more acceptable politically, some scholars point to the danger that it may turn into a hegemonic device.[99] Undeniably, the group of participants form an avant-garde in the chosen area of enhanced cooperation. Since the EU is premised upon the "process of creating an ever closer union",[100] other member states are expected to join up as soon as possible and ensure a widely spread participation.[101] But as enhanced cooperation brings together only those states that are willing to advance integration in a certain EU policy area, it is realistically possible that it might lead to the creation of a club of states having a profounder convergence of interests in a certain field. Enhanced cooperation therefore

94 TFEU Art. 329, Geiger, 'Title III: Enhanced Cooperation', pp. 1012-1013, de Zwaan, *Stability and Differentiation in the European Union*, p. 16 and F. Fabbrini, 'The Enhanced Cooperation Procedure: A Study in Multispeed Integration', Research Paper, *Centro Studi del Federalismo*, October 2012, pp. 7-8, www.csfederalismo.it/attachments/article/998/CSF-RP_Fabbrini_ENHANCED%20COOPERATION_October2012.pdf. Within the framework of the common foreign and security policy there is no need for a proposal by the Commission, while the decision of the Council must be unanimous (Geiger, 'Title III: Enhanced Cooperation', p. 1013.)

95 TEU Art. 20(4).

96 TFEU Art. 327 and Fabbrini, 'The Enhanced Cooperation Procedure', p. 9.

97 TEU Art. 20(3), TFEU Art. 330(1) and Geiger, 'Title IV: Provisions on Enhanced Cooperation', p. 117.

98 TFEU Art. 334 and Fabbrini, 'The Enhanced Cooperation Procedure', pp. 8, 9.

99 Junge, 'Differentiated European Integration', p. 401.

100 TEU Art. 2(1).

101 Geiger, 'Title III: Enhanced Cooperation', p. 1012, Fabbrini, 'The Enhanced Cooperation Procedure', p. 13 and de Zwaan, *Stability and Differentiation in the European Union*, p. 17.

facilitates the formation of a hegemonic center encompassing a smaller group of states.[102] However, rather than leading to the creation of static hegemony in the EU, it is more viable that the flexible character of enhanced cooperation will lead to the formation of multiple hegemonic structures, depending on the need for further integration in various policy areas in the EU.[103] Nonetheless, as some EU members are more inclined to the process of further integration, a certain group of core countries in the sense of flexible hegemony might take shape in the EU in the future.[104]

Enhanced cooperation has already become a reality in practical terms.[105] So far, four instances of enhanced cooperation are ongoing,[106] while one is still in the process of being authorized. The functioning examples of enhanced cooperation are on:

i. the European unitary patent, establishing a legal regime for the protection of the European patent with a unitary effect and a related specialized patent court (26 member states participating);
ii. the rules on divorce law, enabling international couples to agree which law would apply to their divorce or, failing to reach such an agreement, setting the common formula for deciding the applicable law (17 member states);
iii. the creation of the European Public Prosecutor's Office with a task to investigate and prosecute cases involving suspected fraud against the EU budget (22 member states) and;
iv. the property regime rules, dealing with the property regimes of international couples laying down clear rules in cases of divorce or death and bringing an end to parallel and possibly conflicting cross-border proceedings (17 member states).[107]

---

102 Stemplowski, 'Hegemony in the European Union?', p. 10.

103 *Cf.* ibid., p. 12.

104 Currently, the group of core countries participating in all instances of enhanced cooperation (those authorized and waiting) is made of Austria, Belgium, France, Germany, Greece, Italy, Portugal and Slovenia. (*See* Kubin, 'Enhanced Cooperation, EMU Reforms and their Implications for Differentiation in the European Union', p. 92 and European Commission, 'Enhanced Cooperation: Already a Reality in the EU', https://ec.europa.eu/commission/sites/beta-political/files/enhanced_cooperation_-_already_a_reality_in_the_eu_1.pdf).

105 *See* European Commission, 'Enhanced Cooperation'.

106 In broader terms, enhanced cooperation covers cooperation in defense matters (permanent structured cooperation in the area of defense and security – PESCO), and investing in supercomputing in the form of the joint undertaking (EuroPhC Joint Undertaking). However, as these two initiatives are subject to a different set of rules than the mechanism of enhanced cooperation, they are not included in the above analysis. PESCO is regulated in TEU Arts. 42(6) and 46, while the joint undertaking in TFEU Arts. 187 and 188 (1). *See* EEAS, 'Permanent Structured Cooperation (PESCO) – factsheet', https://eeas.europa.eu/sites/eeas/files/pesco_factsheet_may_2019.pdf and European Commission, 'Proposal for a Council Regulation Establishing the European High Performance Computing Joint Undertaking', 11 January 2018, https://ec.europa.eu/digital-single-market/en/news/proposal-council-regulation-establishing-european-high-performance-computing-joint-undertaking.

107 European Commission, 'Scenario 3 of the White Paper on the Future of Europe: Those Who Want More Do More', 25 September 2018', p. 2, https://ec.europa.eu/commission/sites/beta-political/files/enhanced-cooperation-factsheet-tallinn_en.pdf.

Additionally, in the waiting room is the enhanced cooperation in the area of financial transaction tax, which will strengthen the Single Market by reducing divergent national approaches to financial transaction taxation and ensure that the financial sector makes a fair and substantial contribution to public revenues (10 member states). This initiative is still subject to further discussions in the Council concerning its implementation.[108]

The examples of enhanced cooperation described in the preceding paragraphs brought to light fears of nonparticipating member states that this mode of cooperation would make incursions into their interests and institute a kind of hegemony of participating states. With regard to the legal regime of the European unitary patent, in particular, Spain and Italy lodged an application for annulment of the EU Council decision authorizing enhanced cooperation in this area.[109] However, the ECJ refuted their claim stating that

> the uniform protection given by it and the arrangements attaching to it will be in force, not in the Union in its entirety, but only in the territory of the participating Member States.[110]

In this case, the ECJ thus unequivocally supported the functioning of the mechanism of enhanced cooperation as such.[111]

The mechanism of enhanced cooperation under the Lisbon Treaty stands for the interplay of constitutionalism and hegemony in the EU. Hegemony occurs because the dynamic design of enhanced cooperation allows for flexible functional liaisons between member states. It leads to the formation of an avant-garde club of states in a particular EU policy area with an aim to further integration on the basis of common objectives and interests of the EU. However, every such initiative is part and parcel of the EU constitutional order. In terms of substance, it has to comply with EU law and fundamental principles of the EU. In procedural terms the initiative on enhanced cooperation is scrutinized by the Commission, the Parliament, the Council and possibly by the ECJ for its compatibility with EU constitutional values, objectives and interests. The mechanism of enhanced cooperation thus allows for an interesting convergence of interests. On the one hand, pursued interests and objectives of the club of states in a particular instance of

108 Ibid., p. 3 and European Parliament, 'Legislative Train Schedule: Deeper and Fairer Internal Market with a Strengthened Industrial Base/Taxation', 14 December 2018, www.europarl.europa.eu/legislative-train/theme-deeper-and-fairer-internal-market-with-a-strengthened-industrial-base-taxation/file-financial-transaction-tax.

109 Council decision 2011/167/EU of 10 March 2011 authorizing enhanced cooperation in the area of creation of unitary patent protection.

110 Joined Cases C-274/11 and C-295/11, *Kingdom of Spain and Italian Republic v. Council of the European Union*, Grand Chamber, 16 April 2013, para. 68. *See also* ibid., para. 82.

111 *See* Wouters & Schmitt, 'Equality Among Member States and Differentiated Integration in the EU', pp. 74-75, 79.

enhanced cooperation must be compatible with community interests. On the other hand, the enhanced cooperation process has a potential to reinforce community interests and push forward the integration process of the entire EU. This is another point of convergence between hegemony and constitutionalism in the EU.

8.3 PLURILATERAL AGREEMENTS IN THE WORLD TRADE ORGANIZATION

The main difference between the WTO and its predecessor GATT is that the WTO has a much more developed constitutional framework.[112] Institutionalization of the WTO system represents constitutionalization of the power structure in the world trade system. However, the normative framework regulating political decision-making within the WTO institutional structure is still rather weak and lax, especially when compared to other international organizations. In practice, it turns out that the decision-making procedure of WTO political organs did not transcend the GATT diplomatic functioning. While it is true that the WTO is a 'member driven' organization,[113] the question remains, who is the driver in the seat?

It is not surprising therefore that, along with its institutional growth and the constitutional positioning, the WTO has been under criticism that it functions as a hegemonic device. Authors accused the WTO of imperialism in terms of Robinson-Gallagher's free trade imperialism and that it had worked for the benefit of hegemonic interests of great powers.[114] A closer look gives some credit to these reproaches as practice shows that within the WTO the big powers tend to operate in terms of the Gramscian notion of hegemony. As demonstrated in Chapter 2, this is a dynamic approach, which bases itself on pressure covering all nuances in between consent and coercion.[115] Paradoxically, it turns out that it is precisely the flexible institutional setup of the WTO which has enabled the functioning of hegemony in the WTO.[116]

In this sense, the principle of consensus and the culture of flexibility and pragmatism traditionally have worked against the poorer and smaller countries. In seeking a consensus, great powers (notably the US and the EU) often overlook voices of smaller countries.

---

112 Jackson, *The World Trade Organization*, pp. 6-8, 101-103.

113 Von Bogdandy, 'Law and Politics in the WTO', pp. 614-615 and Jackson, 'The WTO "Constitution"', p. 72.

114 *See* J. Tully, *Public Philosophy in a New Key, Volume II: Imperialism and Civic Freedom*, CUP, Cambridge, 2008, pp. 128 *et seq.*, 195 *et seq.*, Anghie, *Imperialism, Sovereignty and the Making of International Law*, pp. 245-246, 271, Chimni, 'International Institutions Today', p. 1 *et seq.* and J. Fatoumata & A. Kwa, *Behind the Scenes at the WTO: The Real World of International Trade Negotiations*, Zed Books, London, 2003, pp. 269-271. Reproaches about imperialistic or hegemonic tendencies in the WTO are usually voiced within a broader criticism of international economic institutions, together with the World Bank and the International Monetary Fund.

115 For a theoretical explanation of this approach in the framework of international organizations *see* A.A. Fatouros, 'On the Hegemonic Role of International Functional Organization', 23 *GYIL* 1980, pp. 9-36.

116 A. Narlikar, & R. Wilkinson, 'Collapse at the WTO: A Cancun Post-Mortem', 25 *Third World Quarterly* 2004, pp. 447, 458.

If these countries do not have the possibility of expressing their positions, then it is easy to conclude that there is 'a consensus'.[117] Thus, the mechanism of consensus leads to broad deregulation opening the way for the play of power politics.[118] In addition, the culture of flexibility and pragmatism ('managerial institutionalism') leads to the establishment of informal groups of states (clubs), creation of facilitators who coordinate negotiation of these groups, and a number of 'behind-the-scene' meetings. For most part, protagonists in this dynamic have been representatives of the great powers. Therefore, although the WTO is formally a negotiating forum for all members, usually a narrow and powerful minority negotiates and takes all essential decisions.[119]

During the last years, however, the growing power of non-Western countries in the WTO has reversed the negotiating dynamic. Powerful trading partners (China, Brazil and India) and influential coalitions of developing countries (*e.g.*, Least-Developed Countries – LDCs) emerged in the WTO reality. In particular, since the Doha round these actors managed to assert their positions and counter Western influences.[120] In addition, the pro-Western hegemonic rule-making process, premised upon domestic policy concepts of the developed world, is no longer acceptable to other negotiating countries.[121] During the Doha round, the power play in the WTO framework has started to exhibit counter-hegemonic developments, which curbed until then prevailing positions of developed countries. One negative consequence of these power permutations is damage to the efficient functioning, inclusiveness and future relevance of the organization.[122] The Western countries, in particular the United States, reacted to these power challenges with a request for the profound modernization of the WTO.[123]

It is not surprising, therefore, that during the Doha Round the WTO had come to a standstill, failing to deliver tangible results. One of the reasons for the deadlock in the implementation of the Doha Development Agenda (DDA) is that interests of Western countries (the US and the EU) are at loggerheads with interests of emerging powers and

117 *See* A. Kwa, *Power Politics in the WTO*, Focus on the Global South, Bangkok, 2003, pp. 7, 18, 36, 40 and Narlikar & Wilkinson, 'Collapse at the WTO', pp. 448, 450.

118 Narlikar & Wilkinson, 'Collapse at the WTO', p. 452 and Kwa, *Power Politics in the WTO*, pp. 7, 55.

119 *See* Kwa, *Power Politics in the WTO*, pp. 19-20, 25, 37-39, 40, and Narlikar & Wilkinson, 'Collapse at the WTO', pp. 450-452.

120 The Doha Round kicked off at the fourth ministerial conference in Doha (Qatar) in 2001. Its goal is to introduce lower trade barriers and revised trade rules. The work program, which covers around 20 trade areas, strives to improve trade prospects of developing countries. (*See* WTO, 'Doha Round', www.wto.org/english/tratop_e/dda_e/dda_e.htm.)

121 S. Bhandari, *Global Constitutionalism and the Path of International Law: Transformation of Law and State in the Globalized World*, Brill Nijhoff, Leiden-Boston, 2016, p. 115 and A. Narlikar, 'Collective Agency, Systemic Consequences: Bargaining Coalitions in the WTO', *in* Narlikar *et al., The Oxford Handbook on the World Trade Organization*, pp. 184, 187.

122 B. Vickers, 'The Role of the BRICS in the WTO: System-supporters or Change Agents in Multilateral Trade', *in* Narlikar *et al., The Oxford Handbook on the World Trade Organization*, p. 256.

123 *See* 'Statement of the United States by Ambassador Dennis Shea at the 14th WTO Trade Policy Review of the United States of America'.

less developed countries.[124] At the ministerial meeting in Bali in 2013, for example, the WTO members were able to reach an agreement on a very limited scope of WTO activities (the so-called *Bali Package*). As the largest issues of the DDA remain unresolved to date, it seems that the Doha Round of negotiations will not be successful.[125] Additionally, it is also worrying that the credibility of the WTO as a negotiating forum is called into serious question.[126] The main danger is that WTO member states will start concluding bilateral or regional trade agreements outside the ambit of WTO, thus sidelining its relevance for international trade.

In recent years, proposals started to emerge that member states could use the option of plurilateral trade agreements in the WTO framework.[127] This option became part of diplomatic reality in particular after the WTO ministerial meeting in Buenos Aires in 2017, when representatives of several member states and WTO Director General started mentioning plurilateral agreements as a way out of the Doha round impasse.[128] Conceptually, this option is known also as the *club-of-clubs* approach.[129]

Due to its flexible and pragmatic approach, the WTO and its predecessor GATT have been labeled as the world trade club. The club-of-clubs approach introduces the principle of variable geometry in the WTO in the sense that various groups of countries with

124 For a thorough analysis of this complex issue, *see* M. Elsig & C. Dupont, 'Persistent Deadlock in Multilateral Trade Negotiations: The Case of Doha', *in* Narlikar *et al., The Oxford Handbook on the World Trade Organization*, pp. 587-606. *See also* S. Joseph, *Blame it on the WTO? A Human Rights Critique*, OUP, Oxford, 2011, pp. 276-284.

125 The 'Bali Package' includes several vague decisions on issues such as agriculture, cotton, LDCs and regular work. *See* Bhandari, *Global Constitutionalism and the Path of International Law*, pp. 118-124, 149-152.

126 Ibid., p. 124.

127 *See, e.g.*, P. Sutherland *et al., The Future of the WTO: Addressing Institutional Challenges in the New Millennium*, WTO, Geneva, 2004, pp. 65-66. It is useful to delineate plurilateral agreements from other similar agreements in the WTO framework, such as 'critical mass agreements', regional trade agreements (RTAs) and preferential trade agreements (PTAs). Critical mass agreements likewise cover a specific sector or issue, but they presuppose adherence of states representing a sizeable share of world trade, production and consumption in that domain. In addition, critical mass agreements are based on the most favored nation (MFN) clause, which means that the benefits of such an agreement apply to all WTO members. The purpose of RTAs, on the other hand, is to intensify economic integration, usually on the regional scale by affording reciprocal preferential treatment to state parties. They cover a wide array of horizontal trade issues. The goal of PTAs is to promote economic integration by giving unilateral preferential treatment on a range of trade issues to a closed group of states (*e.g.*, by developed countries to LDCs). RTAs and PTAs are thus not based on the MFN clause. (*See* R. Basedow, 'The WTO and the Rise of Plurilatelarism – What Lessons Can We Learn from the European Union's Experience with Differentiated Integration?' 21 *Journal of International Economic Law* 2018, p. 417, B.M. Hoekman & P.C. Mavroidis, 'WTO "à la carte" or "menu du jour"? Assessing the Case for More Plurilateral Agreements', 26 *EJIL* 2015, p. 319 *et seq.* and WTO, 'Regional Trade Agreements and Preferential Trade Agreements', www.wto.org/english/tratop_e/region_e/rta_pta_e.htm.)

128 *See* ICTSD, 'Trade Officials Weigh Impact of New Initiatives in Post-Buenos Aires Era', 22 *Bridges* 2018, 1 March 2018, https://www.ictsd.org/bridges-news/bridges/news/trade-officials-weigh-impact-of-new-initiatives-in-post-buenos-aires-era.

129 *See* R.Z. Lawrence, 'Rulemaking amidst Growing Diversity: A Club-of-Club Approach to WTO Reform and New Issue Selection', 9 *Journal of International Economic Law* 2006, pp. 823-835.

shared interests establish groups in order to upgrade cooperation in specific WTO areas.[130] They cooperate on the basis of pursuing 'club goods', that is, goods from which exclusion is possible, while the competition for them is low or nonexistent.[131] Absence of rivalry for such goods makes it possible that certain member states intensify cooperation and not deprive others of any benefits. In terms of substance, plurilateral agreements are not wide-ranging trade compacts. They cover a specific issue or sector of world trade, not necessarily within the WTO exclusive domain.[132] The aim of such agreements is not to confer general trade benefits to its parties but to deepen international integration within a specific WTO area of activity for those states that have an interest to do so.[133]

Robert Lawrence structured the WTO club-of-clubs concept around three components: (i) that the club must be related to the mission of the WTO: reducing barriers to trade, reducing discrimination in trade and enhancing development through trade; (ii) that the club is enforceable by the means available to the organization and club members; and (iii) that the club is compatible with maintaining and enhancing legitimacy.[134] In other words, the working of the WTO club must be based on common interests of the WTO, it must be situated within the WTO framework and directed towards further developing an agenda related to WTO common interests.[135] It is not surprising that the club-of-clubs approach sounds very similar to the EU mechanism of enhanced cooperation. In fact, designs for the working of WTO plurilateral agreements often draw inspiration from the EU model, taking into account the institutional and practical differences between the WTO and the EU.[136] Similar to the EU, the club-of-clubs leads to the creation of core groups of member states, thus allowing for the occurrence of hegemony in the WTO. A core group in a particular area of WTO-related activity would need to mobilize expertise and political energy for such a project and be determined to reach agreed outcomes.[137]

---

130 Hoekman & Mavroidis, 'WTO "à la carte" or "menu du jour"?', p. 319 and B.M. Hoekman & P.C. Mavroidis, 'Variable Geometry in the WTO', *in* R. Schütze (Ed.), *Globalisation and Governance: International Problems, European Solutions*, CUP, Cambridge, 2018, pp. 148, 168.

131 Basedow, 'The WTO and the Rise of Plurilatelarism', p. 415 and A. Kölliker, 'Bringing Together or Driving Apart the Union? Towards a Theory of Differentiated Integration', Max-Planck-Projektgruppe Recht der Gemeinschaftsgüter, May 2001, p. 10, available at: https://papers.ssrn.com.

132 B.M. Hoekman & P.C. Mavroidis, 'Embracing Diversity: Plurilateral Agreements and the Trading System', 14 *World Trade Review* 2015, p. 105.

133 Lawrence, 'Rulemaking amidst Growing Diversity', p. 832.

134 Ibid., pp. 826-827.

135 *Cf.* Hoekman & Mavroidis, 'WTO "à la carte" or "menu du jour"?', p. 320 and Hoekman & Mavroidis, 'Variable Geometry in the WTO', p. 159.

136 *See* Basedow, 'The WTO and the Rise of Plurilatelarism', pp. 419-431, Cantore, 'We're One, but We're Not the Same', pp. 14-18 and D. Negrescu & G. Truică, 'Can EU's Enhanced Cooperation Mechanism Provide Solutions to the "Single Undertaking" Problems of the WTO?', 6 *Romanian Journal of European Affairs* 2006, pp. 5-23.

137 R. Adlung & H. Mamdouh, 'Plurilateral Trade Agreements: An Escape Route for the WTO?' WTO Working Paper ERSD-2017-03, 25 January 2017, p. 8, www.wto.org/english/res_e/reser_e/ersd201703_e.pdf. *See also* Hoekman & Mavroidis, 'Variable Geometry in the WTO', p. 159.

Plurilateral agreements represent an exception in taking over legal obligations in the WTO. Ever since the creation of the WTO the main principle for assuming legal obligations of member states has been the single undertaking rule, presupposing that all member states must adhere to all agreements.[138] Plurilateral agreements, on the other hand, were commonplace during the Tokyo Round (in the 1970s) and later superseded by the single undertaking rule during the Uruguay Round (1986-1993).[139] With the creation of the WTO in 1995, the single undertaking rule was co-opted as one of the guiding principles of the organization in Article II.2 of the WTO Agreement.[140] Together with the principle of consensus in Article IX.I, the single undertaking rule represents the most faithful expression of the principle of sovereign equality in the WTO.[141] Nevertheless, Annex 4 to the WTO Agreement incorporated several plurilateral agreements in the WTO institutional framework of which two are still valid today. These are the Agreement on Trade in Civil Aircraft and the Agreement on Government Procurement.[142]

Plurilateral agreements have a limited membership. Article II.4 of the WTO Agreement makes plurilateral agreements binding only for members who accepted them; they do not create any obligations or rights for other member states. Nonetheless, plurilateral agreements are 'open' in principle in the sense that the WTO member states can join them later.[143] Previous practice shows that many plurilateral agreements in the GATT system evolved into multilateral agreements.[144]

Plurilateral agreements are formally incorporated in the WTO framework, upon the request of member parties to such an agreement, on the basis of a consensual decision at the ministerial conference.[145] Therefore, it is reasonable that negotiations on these agreements extend beyond the limited circle of interested parties and take place in the format open to all WTO members.[146] Such interactive dynamic works as a melting pot between

138 Lawrence, 'Rulemaking amidst Growing Diversity', p. 824.

139 Adlung & Mamdouh, 'Plurilateral Trade Agreements', pp. 8-9 and J. Wouters & B. De Maaster, *World Trade Organization: A Legal and Institutional Analysis*, Intersentia, Antwerpen-Oxford, 2007, pp. 11-12.

140 W. Guan, 'Consensus Yet Not Consented: A Critique of the WTO Decision-Making by Consensus', 17 *Journal of International Economic Law* 2014, pp. 82-85.

141 *See* ibid., p. 80 *et seq.*

142 Of these two only the Agreement on Government Procurement is fully effective. The United States questioned the functioning of the Civil Aircraft Agreement due to excessive launch aid by the EU to the Airbus A380 project and initiated a formal dispute on the matter. Nonetheless it still remains in force. Other two plurilateral agreements listed in Annex 4, the International Dairy Agreement and the International Bovine Meat Agreement, were terminated in 1997. (B. Hoekman, 'Proposals for WTO Reform: A Synthesis and Assessment', *in* Narlikar *et al.*, *The Oxford Handbook on the World Trade Organization*, p. 759, including n. 57, M. Matsushita, T.J. Schoenbaum & P.C. Mavroidis, *The World Trade Organization: Law, Practice, and Policy*, OUP, Oxford, 2006, pp. 8-9, Wouters & De Maaster, *World Trade Organization*, pp. 123-126.)

143 Hoekman & Mavroidis, 'Embracing Diversity', pp. 105, 110.

144 A. Ansong, 'Single Undertaking, Different Speeds: Pliable Models for Decision-making in the WTO', 21 *Journal of International Economic Law* 2018, p. 407.

145 WTO Agreement Art. X.9. Bernard Hoekman and Petros Mavroidis suggest that the consensus rule should be relaxed so that the option of plurilateral agreements could become more frequent in practice. (Hoekman & Mavroidis, 'Variable Geometry in the WTO', pp. 165-166.)

146 Lawrence, 'Rulemaking amidst Growing Diversity', p. 828.

common WTO interests, interests of WTO members and a particular plurilateral agenda. The high bar of the consensual approval could be reached much easier if plurilateral agreements would be based on the nondiscriminatory approach (the MFN clause) extending benefits of such agreements to all members of the WTO.[147]

In line with the existing practice, plurilateral agreements should result in establishing a committee that would, on one hand, assist members in the implementation of agreements and, on the other hand, regularly report its activities to the WTO General Council and share information with all WTO member states.[148] This would also enhance transparency of a particular plurilateral process. Additionally, the regime of the plurilateral agreement should refer disputes to the WTO dispute settlement system (WTO Panels and the Appellate Body). This would ensure that the case law related to the plurilateral agreement would be developed harmoniously and in coherence with case law pertaining to the WTO multilateral agreements.[149]

The option of plurilateral agreements internalizes elements of both, hegemony and constitutionalism. It enables a group of interested WTO states to deepen integration in a specific sector or on a particular issue. The circle of state parties can expand and the future accession by other states could metamorphose a plurilateral agreement into a multilateral one.[150] Such a group of states would represent a hegemonic club in the WTO. Given that the practice of plurilateral agreements could become more frequent in the future, the ensuing formation of hegemonic clubs could result in a polycentric hegemony within the WTO.

Simultaneous with pursuing the plurilateral agenda such a group of countries would need to pursue activities within the WTO constitutional framework, on the basis of existing principles, rules and practices. This process would primarily entail screening of compatibility of the plurilateral agenda with common interests of the WTO, as well as with interests of nonparticipating WTO members. Parts of this process would be: participation of all member states during the negotiations for the plurilateral agreement, adoption of the plurilateral agreement by consensus, the possibility of WTO member states joining the agreement later, creation of a particular committee under the agreement to report to the General Council on its activities, and a legal possibility to refer a dispute to the WTO dispute settlement mechanism.

The existent two plurilateral agreements are a heritage of the Uruguay Round. However, the stalemate of the Doha Round and the issue of modernization of the WTO have opened a way for the WTO to pursue regulating the world trade also through plurilateral

147 Adlung & Mamdouh, 'Plurilateral Trade Agreements: An Escape Route for the WTO?', pp. 8, 15, 21-23.

148 Hoekman & Mavroidis, 'Embracing Diversity', pp. 106-107. Such practice currently applies to two existing WTO plurilateral agreements (*see* Wouters & De Maaster, *World Trade Organization*, pp. 199-200).

149 Lawrence, 'Rulemaking amidst Growing Diversity', p. 830 and Hoekman & Mavroidis, 'Embracing Diversity', pp. 107, 110.

150 A. Ansong, 'The WTO Decision-Making Process: Problems and Possible Solutions', Working Paper (2012), pp. 37, 38 available at: https://works.bepress.com/alex_ansong/4/.

agreements. While not solving all the controversial issues on the WTO agenda, plurilateral agreements could broker a way out of the current existential crisis of the WTO.[151] Diplomatic statements after the Buenos Aires ministerial conference certainly anticipate the use of plurilateral agreements as a realistic option.[152] Should this happen, the WTO constitutional framework would be a unique platform, exhibiting a passage from hegemony of Western states, through counter-hegemony of developing countries to polycentric hegemony of issue-specific clubs.[153]

8.4 CONCLUDING REMARKS ON THE COEXISTENCE OF HEGEMONY AND CONSTITUTIONALISM IN INTERNATIONAL ORGANIZATIONS

The concept of legalized hegemony embeds the antinomy of hegemony and constitutionalism in international organizations. When extended from power considerations to common interests, legalized hegemony becomes a category that pertains not solely to configurations of power but also to a functional leadership in a given institutional setting. The three considered cases represent examples of coexistence between concrete hegemonic and constitutional elements in a particular international institution.

The evolution of the Security Council into the role of a global legislator on issues of peace and security is a typical example of hegemonic growth through the accumulation of powers within the UN constitutional setting. A conceptual link between Articles 24, 25, 39, 41 and 103 of the UN Charter vested the Security Council with a novel function of the global legislator in the field of maintenance of international peace and security. Faced with security threats of international terrorism, the Security Council made use of its legislative role and issued a set of resolutions to fight it: resolution 1373 on the prevention of international financing of terrorism; resolution 1540 prohibiting proliferation of WMD particularly by non-state actors; and resolution 2178 criminalizing activities of foreign terrorist fighters. In doing so, the Security Council, as a club of privileged states in the UN, assumed responsibility for the protection of common security interests. A unique feature of these resolutions is that they override one of the traditional principles of international lawmaking: the consent of states. While such functional development has been necessary and stood the test of time, it is intriguing that the newly acquired legisla-

151 Hoekman & Mavroidis, 'Embracing Diversity', pp. 114-115 and Hoekman & Mavroidis, 'Variable Geometry in the WTO', p. 169.

152 *See* 'Trade Officials Weigh Impact of New Initiatives in Post-Buenos Aires Era'.

153 Some WTO scholars dealing with plurilateral agreements envisage that they might lead to hegemony of developed countries as these have more capacity to set agendas for such agreements. Others anticipate that plurilateral agreements might be used when bigger powers would not be interested in pursuing certain issues. There is also a possibility that such agreements would rely on the aid-for-trade component. The plurilateral dynamic can therefore unfold in many directions. (*See* Basedow, 'The WTO and the Rise of Plurilatelarism', p. 419, Ansong, 'The WTO Decision-Making Process', p. 38, Hoekman & Mavroidis, 'Embracing Diversity', pp. 113-114 and Lawrence, 'Rulemaking amidst Growing Diversity', pp. 823-834.)

tive competence is unmatched by checks and balances in the international community. Nonetheless, the international working of checks and balances will probably manifest itself in the future through the international judiciary.

In the EU, the mechanism of enhanced cooperation as framed in the Lisbon Treaty (Article 20 of TEU and Articles 326-334 of TFEU), allows for formation of a core group of states in a certain field of EU competences. While pursuing deeper integration in a particular policy area, objectives of enhanced cooperation must be nevertheless based on the EU *acquis* and compatible with common interests of the EU. Every proposal for enhanced cooperation is screened for its compatibility with the EU legal order by the European Commission, the European Parliament, the European Council and eventually by the ECJ. Hegemony of a group of states must be open-ended so that other members may join later and turn enhanced cooperation into a fully fledged EU activity. However, it would be utopian to expect that every example of enhanced cooperation would later become a pan-EU affair. With growing heterogeneity within the EU, enhanced cooperation is a convenient mechanism to allow for the development of 'diversity within unity' along with 'differentiation within stability' in that institutional framework.[154] A growing number of examples of enhanced cooperation (currently four, plus one in the pipeline) confirms that EU member states have embraced this mechanism in practice.

The flexible constitutional system of the WTO has allowed for the occurrence of hegemony on the side of Western states as well as various coalitions of emerging powers and developing countries in the sense of counter-hegemony. Due to a standstill in the Doha Round and requests for the reform of the WTO by some great powers (the United States and partly by the EU), the plurilateral agreements in the WTO stand as a good mechanism for the convergence of particular interests of states clustered in clubs and common interests of the organization. As plurilateral agreements usually concentrate on a specific trade sector or issue, the hegemonic club would probably crystalize on the basis of a particular functional need rather than around the North-South divide. Still, the plurilateral agreement of such a club of states would have to fulfill all necessary conditions required by the WTO institutional framework: negotiations open to all WTO members, adoption of the agreement with consensus, an open nature of the agreement allowing WTO member states to join in later, the creation of a committee that would report to the General Council, and an option to resort to the dispute settlement system in the WTO.

From the preceding paragraphs, it is possible to conclude that all three examples – the Security Council as a global legislator, enhanced cooperation in the EU and WTO plurilateral agreements – represent a comprehensive mix of hegemonic and constitutional elements. They also represent workable answers to the functional challenges brought by

154 De Zwaan, *Stability and Differentiation in the European Union*, pp. 14-15, 40-41.

two leading tendencies in the world community – hegemony and constitutionalism. All three examples are illustrations of the hegemo-constitutional reality of today.

9 Intervention on Humanitarian Grounds

This chapter deals with doctrines of humanitarian intervention and the responsibility to protect (R2P), from the viewpoint of the interaction between constitutionalism and hegemony. Both doctrines presuppose a situation of gross societal instability within a certain country that failed to protect its own population. The instability usually involves a large-scale use of military violence, be it governmental or paramilitary, against the civilian population. As a response to such an unbearable situation, the two doctrines presuppose an action of the international community, if needed with the use of force.

At the core of the military intervention on humanitarian grounds is a clash between two fundamental international principles: state sovereignty and the protection of humanity. Traditionally, state sovereignty has been considered as a supreme postulate and the protection of humanity within a state only as a secondary concern.[1] On the basis of the constitutionalist understanding of international law, a paradigm shift occurred in the sense that state sovereignty is supposed to embrace concerns for humanity, including the responsibility for the well-being of people in a particular country.[2] These represent common concerns of humankind.[3] This new type of sovereignty is called *humanized sovereignty*. Should that humanitarian aspect of state sovereignty go wrong, the international community has a duty to intervene in that country to protect the lives and well-being of its people.[4]

The humanitarian protection is premised on values that are related to human existence, such as the protection of lives, respect for integrity and dignity of a human person and alleviation of human suffering. They have a strong axiological underpinning similar to other international fundamental norms: atrocity crimes, protection of the fundamental human rights, protection of *jus cogens* norms and *erga omnes* obligations. In this sense, they represent fundamental norms of the international community of constitutional quality.

---

1 *See* A. Peters, 'Humanity as the A and Ω of Sovereignty', 20 *EJIL* 2009, pp. 513-522, 543.

2 T. Ramopoulos, 'International Law and the Application of the Third Pillar Approach', *in* D. Fiott & J. Koops (Eds.), *The Responsibility to Protect and the Third Pillar: Legitimacy and Operationalization*, Palgrave Macmillan, Basingstoke, 2015, pp. 7-8 and P.-T. Stoll, 'The Responsibility to Protect: One-time Incentive of Lasting Advancement for International Law?', *in* P. Hilpold (Ed.), *Responsibility to Protect (R2P): A New Paradigm of International Law?*, Brill Nijhoff, Leiden-Boston, 2015, pp. 152-155. *See also* UN SG, *One Humanity: Shared Responsibility*, Report of the Secretary-General for the World Humanitarian Summit, 2 February 2016, A/70/709.

3 *See* K. Nadakavukaren Schefer & T. Cottier, 'Responsibility to Protect (R2P) and the Emerging Principle of Common Concern', *in* Hilpold, *Responsibility to Protect (R2P)*, pp. 122-142.

4 Peters, 'Humanity as the A and Ω of Sovereignty', pp. 527, 533, 543-544.

But the legal framework for the mobilization of the international community and, more specifically, on the activation of the use of force in such situations is vague and permeable.[5] This leaves the door open for the exercise of international hegemony, be it in a unilateral or multilateral form.[6] The humanitarian use of force can have repercussions for other constitutional tenets of the international order, such as the principles of sovereign equality and of nonintervention. If the humanitarian use of force is pursued outside the valid international legal framework, it could have a damaging impact on the international order. Although intervention on humanitarian grounds has become an international imperative, the doctrines underpinning it still need to be perfected so as to leave no doubt about the motives behind it and the ensuing course of action.

9.1 The Military Intervention in Kosovo

The use of force in foreign countries to protect human lives, known also as the doctrine of humanitarian intervention, is among the most controversial doctrines in international law.[7] Historically, it has evolved as a response of Western powers to large-scale violence against the civilian population in the decaying Ottoman Empire.[8] In situations of gross human rights violations against civilians in foreign countries, the Western powers reserved the right to intervene in these countries. After World War II, humanitarian intervention was perceived as forbidden by the UN legal framework and as a practice that belonged to the past. The UN Charter gave primary responsibility for the use of force to the Security Council sharply limiting the extent of states to use military force. Nonetheless, the minority view, especially within the British tradition of international law, has allowed, under restricted conditions, for the use of humanitarian intervention.[9]

The Kosovo crisis, which erupted in 1998, brought this issue to the limelight again. Systematic violence of the Serbian security forces against the Albanian population pro-

---

5 For an analysis on the use of force in the framework of international constitutionalism, *see* M. Weller, 'The Real Utopia: International Constitutionalism and the Use of Force', *in* Schütze, *Globalisation and Governance*, pp. 131-147.

6 *Cf.* Cohen, *Globalization and Sovereignty*, pp. 177-178, 209, Falk, *Power Shift*, pp. 77-78 and A. Orford, 'Jurisdiction without Territory: From the Holy Roman Empire to the Responsibility to Protect', 30 *Michigan Journal of International Law* 2009, p. 1015.

7 For a historical overview, *see* P. Hilpold, 'R2P and Humanitarian Intervention in a Historical Perspective', *in* Hilpold, *Responsibility to Protect (R2P)*, pp. 60-122.

8 *See* D. Rodogno, 'Humanitarian Intervention in the Nineteenth Century', *in* A.J. Bellamy & T. Dunne (Eds.), *The Oxford Handbook of the Responsibility to Protect*, OUP, Oxford, 2016, pp. 19-37.

9 For an overview, *see* M. Shaw, *International Law*, CUP, Cambridge, 2003, pp. 1045-1048 and I. Brownlie, *Principles of Public International Law*, OUP, Oxford, 2008, pp. 742-745. *See also* A. Garwood-Gowers, 'The Responsibility to Protect and the Arab Spring: Libya as the Exception, Syria as the Norm?', 36 *UNSW Law Journal* 2013, p. 618 and Prime Minister's Office, 'Chemical Weapon Use by Syrian Regime, UK Government Legal Position', 29 August 2013, para. 4, www.gov.uk/government/publications/chemical-weapon-use-by-syrian-regime-uk-government-legal-position/chemical-weapon-use-by-syrian-regime-uk-government-legal-position-html-version.

voked massive exodus of civilians from Kosovo, threatening to assume proportions of a regional humanitarian catastrophe. Consequently, in the spring of 1999, NATO initiated a bombing campaign against Serbian military targets, which brought repression against civilians to a halt.[10]

There is a vast amount of literature dealing with various aspects of the Kosovo intervention.[11] One of the most relevant questions is whether, in the situation of a mounting humanitarian crisis in Kosovo, NATO's military intervention satisfied the condition of legality. The prevailing view is that the intervention was illegal, but legitimate.[12] However, this matter goes beyond the question of (il)legality. The pertinent issue is how to assess the conceptual differences on the collective security system and the prohibition on the unilateral use of force.[13]

The international scholarship articulated a difference between a restrictive and an extensive approach to the prohibition of the use of force, in particular in the context of customary rules. On one hand, the extensive approach takes into account moral and other non-legal considerations. It recognizes a number of exceptions to the prohibition on the use of force, in particular through the practice by major states, which are indispensable actors to satisfy the demand of legitimacy and effectiveness of customary law. The restrictive approach, on the other hand, perceives this method as subjective or ideological and tends to delineate law from politics and morality.[14] It acknowledges the evolution of the customary rules on the use of force solely in terms of their acceptance by the whole international community. The restrictive approach therefore rejects exceptions with regard to the prohibition on the use of force.[15] The fact that two approaches on the use of force coexist in the international reality leads to conflicting justifications on

10 *See* A. Roberts, 'NATO's "Humanitarian War" over Kosovo', 41 *Survival* 1999, pp. 102-123.

11 *See, e.g.*, B. Simma, 'NATO, the UN and the Use of Force: Legal Aspects', 10 *EJIL* 1999, pp. 1-22, A. Pellet, 'Brief Remarks on the Unilateral Use of Force', 11 *EJIL* 2000, pp. 385-392, N. Valticos, 'Les droits de l'homme, le droit international et l'intervention militarie en Yougoslavie', 104 *RGDIP* 2000, pp. 5-18, P. Weckel, 'L'emploi de la force contre la Yougoslavie ou la Charte fissurée', 104 *RGDIP* 2000, pp. 18-35 and C. Tomuschat (Ed.), *Kosovo and the International Community*, Kluwer Law International, The Hague-London-New York, 2002.

12 *See* Simma, 'NATO, the UN and the Use of Force', p. 22, A. Cassese, '*Ex iniuria ius oritur*: Are We Moving towards International Legitimation of Forcible Humanitarian Countermeasures in the World Community?', 10 *EJIL* 1999, pp. 23-24, Cohen, *Globalization and Sovereignty*, p. 174, Pellet, 'Brief Remarks on the Unilateral Use of Force', pp. 385-386, Falk, *Power Shift*, p. 80 and 'Executive Summary – Main Findings', *in The Kosovo Report*, The Independent International Commission for Kosovo, 2000.

13 Paulus, 'The War against Iraq and the Future of International Law', p. 701.

14 Corten, 'The Controversies over the Customary Prohibition on the Use of Force', pp. 821-822. *See also* symposium on this topic in 29 *Leiden Journal of International Law* 2016, pp. 13-112 and Bianchi, 'The International Regulation of the Use of Force: The Politics of Interpretive Method', pp. 651-676.

15 Corten, 'The Controversies over the Customary Prohibition on the Use of Force', p. 822. In the context of the Kosovo humanitarian crisis, some authors expressed this dilemma in the opposition between the positivist approach and the constitutional approach. (*See* R. Uerpmann, 'La primauté des droits de l'homme: licéité ou illicéité de l'intervention humanitaire', pp. 67-74 and J.-F. Flauss, 'La primarité des droits de la personne: licéité ou illécité de l'intervention humanitaire?', pp. 92-93, 101-102, both *in* Tomuschat, *Kosovo and the International Community*.)

the use of force. This reflects a structural deficiency in the international community in the sense that there is no ultimate authority to decide on the legality of the use of force.

The difference between these two approaches is clearly visible in the framework of the decision-making of the Security Council. Under Chapter VII of the UN Charter, which covers threats to peace and security, the Security Council typically deliberates in two phases. The Security Council first decides on the existence of a situation that represents a threat to international peace. If such a threat exists, the Security Council consequently proposes measures on how to remove the threat.[16] While ideally the Security Council would smoothly proceed through both phases, the problem arises if the Council is not unanimous on what measures to employ in order to alleviate a threat to peace.

In the case of Kosovo, the Security Council adopted resolutions 1160 (1998),[17] 1199 (1998),[18] and 1203 (1998).[19] The Security Council adopted all three resolutions in the framework of Chapter VII. Resolutions 1199 and 1203 defined the situation in the Federal Republic of Yugoslavia (FRY) as a threat to peace and security in the region. Resolution 1199 contained a phrase that the Security Council shall "consider further action and additional measures to maintain or restore peace and stability in the region".[20] Faced with a threat of a Russian veto on the subsequent use of force in the Security Council, NATO decided to use this basis and employ force unilaterally against the FRY and the regime of Slobodan Milošević, the main architect of the humanitarian crisis in Kosovo.[21] In order to avert the humanitarian catastrophe and protect a legitimate aim of safeguarding human lives, NATO decided to initiate a military action external to the Chapter VII legal framework.[22] In doing so it relied on the extensive approach by the use of force. From this perspective, NATO's action was legitimate, but contrary to the existing international legal framework.[23]

As stated previously, the most adequate legal description of such a military action is the unilateral enforcement of the collective will or community objectives.[24] Pursuant to common concerns in the Security Council resolutions, NATO embarked on the unilateral

16 R. Wolfrum, 'The Attack of September 11, 2001, the Wars against the Taliban and Iraq: Is There a Need to Reconsider International Law on the Recourse to Force and the Rules in Armed Conflict?', 7 *Max Planck Yearbook of United Nations Law* 2003, pp. 13-14.

17 SC Res. 1160 (1998), 31 March 1998.

18 SC Res. 1199 (1998), 23 September 1998.

19 SC Res. 1203 (1998), 24 October 1998.

20 SC Res. 1199, para. 16.

21 *See* Simma, 'NATO, the UN and the Use of Force', pp. 6-7.

22 *See* BBC, 'Text of Solana's Statement', 24 March 1999 http://news.bbc.co.uk/2/hi/europe/302281.stm.

23 Cassese, '*Ex iniuria ius oritur*', pp. 23-30 and D.H. Joyner, 'The Kosovo Intervention: Legal Analysis and A More Persuasive Paradigm', 13 *EJIL* 2002, pp. 597-619.

24 *Cf.* Krisch, 'Unilateral Enforcement of the Collective Will: Kosovo, Iraq, and the Security Council', p. 60 and Gowlland Debbas, 'The Limits of Unilateral Enforcement of Community Objectives in the Framework of UN Peace Maintenance', pp. 361-362. Here the use of force is considered 'unilateral' given that NATO has an autonomous legal personality as an international organization.

military action.[25] However, the repercussions of the unilateral enforcement of common interests proved very damaging to the system of the collective security and to the normative framework of the United Nations.[26] Jules Lobel, for example, expressed a concern that a mechanism of non-UN-sponsored humanitarian interventions would, under the pretext of human rights protection, project geopolitical interests of great powers throughout the globe and function as their hegemonic tool.[27]

In the end, the Kosovo humanitarian intervention is an example of hegemony of the major Western powers associated in NATO that embraced the extensive understanding of the use of force. Although the intervention in the Kosovo crisis went beyond the Security Council framework, the subsequent course of events brought the situation back under the umbrella of the UN Charter. In 1999, the Council adopted the resolution 1244 (1999),[28] which instituted the UN administration in Kosovo. Nonetheless, in order to minimize the extensive approach that would relegate the use of force outside the United Nations and thus severely damage the international legal order, the international community began to develop a novel concept for the international protection of civilians, known as the responsibility to protect (R2P).[29]

9.2 The Emerging R2P Doctrine

In 2001, Canada convened a meeting of the International Commission on Intervention of State Sovereignty (ICISS), consisting of progressive international thinkers, with a task to develop a new paradigm in the context of the humanitarian intervention.[30] Its task was to come up with a mechanism that had an adequate response to atrocities which would be

25 This practice has origins in the unilateral use of force against Iraq through air raids by the United States, the United Kingdom, and, to a limited extent, France against Iraq in the 1990s. For more, *see* Krisch, 'Unilateral Enforcement of the Collective Will', pp. 64-79, Gowlland-Debbas, 'The Limits of Unilateral Enforcement of Community Objectives in the Framework of UN Peace Maintenance', pp. 372-373, R. Wedgewood, 'Unilateral Action in the UN System', 11 *EJIL* 2000, pp. 358-359 and J. Lobel & M. Ratner, 'Bypassing the Security Council: Ambiguous Authorizations to Use Force, Cease-Fires and the Iraqi Inspection Regime', 93 *AJIL* 1999, pp. 124-154.

26 Krisch, 'Unilateral Enforcement of the Collective Will', pp. 60, 100-101 and Allain, 'The True Challenge to the United System of the Use of Force', p. 258.

27 J. Lobel, 'Benign Hegemony? Kosovo and Article 2(4) of the U.N. Charter', 1 *Chicago Journal of International Law* 2000, p. 28.

28 *See* SC Res. 1244 (1999), 10 June 1999.

29 On the link between the Kosovo humanitarian intervention and the responsibility to protect, *see* R. Thakur, 'Rwanda, Kosovo and the International Commission on Intervention and State Sovereignty', *in* Bellamy & Dunne, *The Oxford Handbook of the Responsibility to Protect*, pp. 94-113, B. Reka, 'NATO's Intervention in Kosovo: The Predecessor to the Concept of the Responsibility to Protect', pp. 417-443 and M.V. Vlasic & P. Atlee, 'NATO and the Responsibility to Protect: Inconsistent but Indispensable', pp. 455 *et seq.*, both *in* V. Sancin & M. Kovič Dine (Eds.), *Responsibility to Protect in Theory and Practice*, GV Založba, Ljubljana, 2013.

30 *See The Responsibility to Protect*, Report of the International Commission on Intervention and State Sovereignty, International Development Research Centre, Ottawa, 2001.

part of the international legal architecture. The ICISS reconceptualized the theme into the notion of the responsibility to protect. It proceeded along two premises: the first was Francis Deng's insight that sovereignty implies responsibility to ensure the safety, welfare and human rights of citizens; the second guiding thought was Kofi Annan's extension of sovereignty to individual sovereignty in the sense of the fundamental freedom of individuals and the need for their protection.[31]

The ICISS redefined sovereignty as a responsibility of a state to protect its own citizens against repression and insecurity, which is a typical constitutionalist concern.[32] Furthermore, if a state would fail to protect its own citizens, the international community would assume that responsibility and intervene in the state to protect the civilians.[33] Intervention is understood as a broad concept of responding to humanitarian crises of which military intervention would be the measure of last resort.[34]

The ICISS defined R2P around three components: (i) the responsibility to prevent (to address root causes and direct causes of internal conflict and human insecurity); (ii) the responsibility to react (to respond to situations of compelling human need with appropriate measures, including coercive measures and military intervention); and (iii) the responsibility to rebuild (to provide in post-conflict situations full assistance with recovery, reconstruction and reconciliation).[35]

Although R2P is not focused merely on the unhindered use of military intervention, the conditions for its use are put down in more detail compared to other components of R2P. It is undeniable that the mechanism of military intervention is one of the most potent parts of R2P. The logical reason is that the use of military force may have a significant impact on human lives and infrastructure. However, as mentioned before, the use of military intervention would be exceptional and subject to strict conditions. Firstly, the humanitarian use of force would be permissible solely in situations of large-scale loss of life or large-scale ethnic cleansing. Secondly, a set of conditions should be satisfied when resorting to military intervention:

---

31 *See* F. Deng, *Protecting the Dispossessed: A Challenge for the International Community*, The Brookings Institution, Washington (DC), 1993 and K. Annan, 'Two Concepts of Sovereignty', *The Economist*, 16 September 1999, www.economist.com/node/324795. *See also* M. Dembinski & T. Reinold, *Libya and the Future of the Responsibility to Protect – African and European Perspectives*, PRIF-Report No. 107, Peace Research Institute, Frankfurt, 2011, p. 3, G. Evans, *The Responsibility to Protect: Ending Mass Atrocity Crimes Once and For All*, Brookings Institution Press, Washington (DC), 2008, pp. 35-38, R. Cohen & F.M. Deng, 'Sovereignty as Responsibility: Building Block for R2P', pp. 74-93 and C. Cater & D.M. Malone, 'The Genesis of R2P: Kofi Annan's Intervention Dilemma', pp. 117-119, both *in* Bellamy & Dunne, *The Oxford Handbook of the Responsibility to Protect*.

32 Klabbers, Peters & Ulfstein, *The Constitutionalization of International Law*, p. 185.

33 G. Evans & M. Sahnoun, 'Foreword', *in The Responsibility to Protect*, p. VIII and Evans, *The Responsibility to Protect*, pp. 38-50.

34 Evans, *The Responsibility to Protect*, p. 4.

35 *The Responsibility to Protect*, p. XI.

a. its purpose should be to halt or avert human suffering (right intention);
b. it should be used as a last resort, after all possible peaceful measures have been explored;
c. the scale, duration and intensity of the use of force should be proportionate to the pursued aim; and
d. there should be a reasonable prospect of halting or averting human suffering.[36]

In addition, the military intervention would have to be approved beforehand by the UN Security Council, in line with the existing legal architecture on the use of force. If the Security Council would reject such a proposal or fail to deal with it in a reasonable period of time, two exceptions could be triggered: (i) the proposal for the military intervention could be considered by the General Assembly under the 'Uniting for Peace' procedure; or (ii) the military intervention could be triggered by regional organizations under the Chapter VIII prerogative, requiring to seek subsequent authorization of the Security Council.[37]

The concept of R2P has important implications on the constitutional principles embodied in the UN Charter. Its emphasis on the protection of human lives and dignity at the level of peremptory norms elevates the protection of human rights above the state centric structure of international law.[38] This axiological awareness infuses a new meaning to other constitutional principles of the international legal order, such as the state sovereignty and nonintervention. State sovereignty, together with its corollary of sovereign equality in Article 2(1) of the UN Charter, embodies an inherent responsibility of the state for the well-being of its citizens.[39] The failure of a state in exercising this humanitarian responsibility would activate the responsibility of the international community. This also casts a new light on the principle of nonintervention enshrined in the UN Charter, prohibiting the threat or use of force by states against territorial integrity or political independence of another state,[40] or the United Nations intervention against any state in matters that essentially fall within the framework of domestic jurisdiction.[41] The R2P doctrine makes clear that international interference, including military inter-

36 Id.
37 Ibid., pp. XII-XIII.
38 A.J. Bellamy & R. Reike, 'The Responsibility to Protect and International Law', 2 *Global Responsibility to Protect* 2010, pp. 276-280, 285-286.
39 *See* N. Tsagourias, 'Whither the Veto: The Responsibility to Protect and the Security Council Veto', *in* Sancin & Dine, *Responsibility to Protect in Theory and Practice*, pp. 164, 173, Klabbers, Peters & Ulfstein, *The Constitutionalization of International Law*, pp. 185-186 and C. Powell, 'Libya: A Multilateral Constitutional Moment', 106 *AJIL* 2012, pp. 298-299. For a somewhat more cautious assessment, *see* B. Tacheva & G. Wallace Brown, 'Global Constitutionalism and the Responsibility to Protect', 4 *Global Constitutionalism* 2015, pp. 428-467.
40 UN Charter Art. 2(4).
41 UN Charter Art. 2(7).

vention, is not merely an option but is necessary to protect human lives and prevent massive human rights violations. This is the main contribution of the R2P doctrine to the constitutionalist 'recalibration' of the international legal order.[42]

At the same time, the purpose of the R2P doctrine is to limit the extensive approach on the use of force and to infuse the restrictive approach with more axiological elements and concerns. However, the rules on the use of force are very broad. The legal framework of Chapter VII has an open-textured character and its procedures and decisions are often underpinned by extra-legal considerations and contexts. The ICISS's concept of military intervention likewise includes a number of conditions and caveats. But its content still remains fluid to a certain degree and may be subject to competing interpretations, which leaves the door open for a hegemonic use of force on humanitarian grounds by a group of states, along with their interests, motives and preferences.[43]

The importance of the ICISS report is that it generated the concept of R2P. Although it was a product of a group of progressive thinkers in an ad hoc setting, with no normative mandate, its reasoning is persuasive and authoritative. It represented a breakthrough in mobilizing international efforts in support of this concept.

The concept was further elaborated in several frameworks related to the UN World Summit in 2005. A preparatory report by a high-level panel of eminent persons included the concept of the 'responsibility to protect'.[44] The report assigns the primary responsibility to protect the civilian population to governments; however, when states are unable or unwilling to protect their own citizens from humanitarian catastrophes, the international community should step in. Responses can span from prevention, reaction to violence, to rebuilding measures. The panel saw military intervention as a measure of last resort, exercisable solely within the competences by the Security Council, in situations of genocide and other large-scale killing, ethnic cleansing or serious violations of international humanitarian law.[45]

UN Secretary-General Kofi Annan reaffirmed such understanding of R2P in his own report 'In Larger Freedom' for the World Summit.[46] A notable contribution of the Secretary-General's report is that it framed a more precise, although still not finalized, under-

---

42 *Cf.* Tsagourias, 'Whither the Veto', p. 164.

43 *See* S. Mohamed, 'Taking Stock of the Responsibility to Protect', 48 *Stanford Journal of International Law* 2012, p. 65, A. Hehir, *The Responsibility to Protect: Rhetoric, Reality, and the Future of the Humanitarian Intervention*, Palgrave Macmillan, Basingstoke-New York, 2012, pp. 13, 189, 206-207, R. Thakur, *The Responsibility to Protect: Norms, Laws and the Use of Force in International Politics*, Routledge, Abingdon-New York, 2011, pp. 139, 159, Evans, *The Responsibility to Protect*, p. 55 *et seq.*, D. Silander, 'NATO (In)actions in Syria?', *in* V. Sancin (Ed.), *Responsibility to Protect: Where Do We Stand Ten Years After?*, University of Ljubljana, Ljubljana, 2015, pp. 230-231 and R. Zongze, 'Responsible Protection: Building a Safer World', 34 *China International Studies* 2012, www.ciis.org.cn/english/2012-06/15/content_5090912.htm.

44 UN GA, *A More Secure World: Our Shared Responsibility*, 2 December 2004, A/59/565, p. 56.

45 Ibid., p. 57.

46 UN SG, *In Larger Freedom: Towards Development, Security and Human Rights for All*, Report of the Secretary-General, 21 March 2005, A/59/2005, p. 35.

standing of humanitarian grounds that trigger collective action, namely, the commission of instances of genocide, ethnic cleansing and crimes against humanity.[47]

Finally, the 'World Summit Outcome' (WSO) document, which was adopted as a consensual resolution of the General Assembly, confirmed the R2P doctrine along almost identical lines as two previous reports. This resolution gives the R2P doctrine a normative confirmation by all UN member states and undoubtedly represents a high mark in the worldwide acceptance of R2P.[48] The contents of R2P are written in paragraphs 138 and 139 of the WSO document and consist of the following main elements:

a. each individual State has the responsibility to protect its citizens from genocide, war crimes, ethnic cleansing and crimes against humanity. Given that all these phenomena stand for atrocities, some scholars refer to them as 'atrocity crimes';[49]
b. prevention is a constituent part of R2P and the international community should encourage and help states to exercise this responsibility and support the UN in establishing an early warning capability;
c. the international community, through the UN, has the responsibility to use appropriate diplomatic, humanitarian and other peaceful means to protect populations from atrocity crimes;
d. should peaceful means be inadequate while national authorities would be manifestly failing to protect their populations from atrocity crime, an important part of R2P is a commitment to take collective action in a timely and decisive manner through the Security Council, including Chapter VII, on a case-by-case basis and in cooperation with relevant regional organizations;
e. the General Assembly should be a forum to continue consideration of R2P in the context of protection from atrocity crimes;
f. the international community is committed to helping states build capacity to protect their populations from atrocity crimes and to assisting those under stress conducive to crises and conflicts.[50]

47 Ibid., p. 59.
48 A. Hehir, *The Responsibility to Protect*, p. 2.
49 *See* the publication R.H. Cooper & J. Voïnov Kohler (Eds.), *Responsibility to Protect: The Global Moral Compact for the 21st Century*, Palgrave Macmillan, Basingstoke-New York, 2009, in particular D. Scheffer, 'Atrocity Crimes Framing the Responsibility to Protect', pp. 77-98.
50 UN GA Res., '60/1. 2005 World Summit Outcome', 24 October 2005, A/RES/60/1.

The adoption of the WSO marks the general acceptance of the R2P doctrine by the international community.[51] Any outstanding dilemmas are henceforth linked to the question of its implementation rather than to the concept itself.[52]

In the WSO document, the concept of R2P is more elaborate than in the two preceding reports and moves closer to the original ICISS concept. However, compared to the original design by ICISS it is also less extensive. This fact prompted some authors to refer to R2P in the WSO document as 'R2P lite'.[53] Three comparisons justify this label. Firstly, the ICISS report referred to large-scale loss of life or large-scale ethnic cleansing as a basis to trigger R2P. This is somewhat broader than atrocity crimes of genocide, war crimes, ethnic cleansing and crimes against humanity.[54] But the WSO list has an advantage of having a more precise meaning in terms of the legal vocabulary, anchored in international criminal law.[55] Second, in terms of military action, ICISS sees the Security Council as the main decision-maker. Nonetheless, in the case of the Security Council paralysis, ICISS allows for alternative options to initiate R2P through regional organizations or the GA 'Uniting for Peace' procedure. The WSO version sees the Security Council as the main decision-making body, and vaguely anticipates cooperation with regional organizations.[56] Finally, ICISS sets down a list of precautionary principles that have to be fulfilled before resorting to military action, whereas the WSO document identifies no such conditions.

It has to be emphasized that although the WSO document gives priority to the Security Council for the military activation of R2P, it allows for military measures through regional organizations (in the sense of Chapter VIII) or on the initiative of the General Assembly ('Uniting for Peace' mechanism). This is in visible contrast with the two reports that mention solely the Security Council's role. It is true that in this respect references in the WSO document are less explicit than in the ICISS report; however, authoritative

51 For the insider's perspective on diplomatic negotiations leading to the adopted text, *see* the account of one of the two facilitators on this issue, the Slovenian Ambassador Roman Kirn. Ambassador Kirn emphasizes that, after initial reluctance, intense negotiations on R2P led to its wide acceptance in the UN fora because the concept underlined the primary responsibility of states to act and included the international responsibility to rebuild post-conflict societies. Furthermore, the eventual use of force is embedded in the UN legal framework. One important feature that made R2P an established and irreversible concept is an appeal in para. 139 of the WSO document that the General Assembly should continue consideration of this topic. It is thus an evolving concept. (R. Kirn, *V službi diplomacije [In Service of Diplomacy]*, Modrijan, Ljubljana, 2017, pp. 241-244.)

52 A. Orford, *International Authority and the Responsibility to Protect*, CUP, Cambridge, 2011, p. 21.

53 T.G. Weiss, *Humanitarian Intervention: Ideas in Action*, Polity Press, Cambridge, 2012, p. 127.

54 Mohamed, 'Taking Stock of the Responsibility to Protect', pp. 71-72.

55 The only exception is ethnic cleansing which can be subsumed under crimes against humanity of persecution. (Scheffer, 'Atrocity Crimes Framing the Responsibility to Protect', p. 89.)

56 *Cf.* Weiss, *Humanitarian Intervention*, p. 127.

interpretation in the subsequent report to the GA confirms the military option through two alternative organs.[57]

Another conceptual contribution to the development of the R2P doctrine is in the 2009 report by the then Secretary-General Ban Ki-moon. In line with the idea of R2P, the report gives preference to responsibility of a state over responsibility of the international community, as well as to prevention over coercive measures. It supports the R2P concept through three pillars. The first pillar focuses on the protection responsibilities of a state, the second pillar deals with the international assistance and capacity-building, whereas the third pillar revolves around timely and decisive response, ranging from prevention, through peaceful measures to coercion.[58] Although this classification is useful for a further application of R2P in various situations, the protracted style of the report as a whole gives a somewhat diluted account of R2P, which evokes many elements of the 1992 'Agenda for Peace', with its focus on preventive diplomacy.[59] Nonetheless, the 2009 report is a confirmation, albeit in a lighter form, of the R2P concept as conceived by ICISS.

There is a certain dissonance in scholarly literature about the legal nature of R2P. Many authors assess its validity in terms of sources of international law, such as customary international law or anticipate its further elaboration in the form of treaty law. Even more frequent is a reference to R2P as an 'emerging norm'.[60] However, analyzing R2P through narrow normative lens is not the adequate approach. R2P is first and foremost a concept (or a doctrine) that has repositioned the constitutional tenets of the international legal order. It confers a constitutional validity to fundamental humanitarian values, and imbues constitutional postulates of state sovereignty, nonintervention and the use of force with this new understanding. If one is to assess the legal character of the WSO resolution, the most appropriate label is that it represents 'soft law'. However, R2P does not introduce a new norm (in the sense of legal obligations) into the international legal system.[61] Rather, it encapsulates a paradigm shift, which serves as authoritative guidance on the application of existing legal norms, infusing them with a humanitarian context. Thus, the WSO document "should be understood as normative in the … sense of provid-

57 UN SG, *Implementing the Responsibility to Protect*, Report of the Secretary-General, 12 January 2009, A/63/677, pp. 9, 23, 25, 27.

58 Ibid., pp. 8-10, Higgins *et al.*, *Oppenheim's International Law - United Nations*, vol. II, pp. 746-747 and V. Sancin, 'Chapter 1: Translating R2P's Theory into Practice', *in* V. Sancin (Ed.), *Responsibility to Protect: Lessons Learned and the Way Forward*, Faculty of Law, University of Ljubljana, Ljubljana, 2019, pp. 27-28.

59 *Cf. Implementing the Responsibility to Protect*, p. 18 *et seq.* Subsequent reports by Secretary General on R2P go in the same direction. *See* www.un.org/en/genocideprevention/key-documents.shtml.

60 *See* Tacheva-Wallace Brown, 'Global Constitutionalism and the Responsibility to Protect', pp. 230-231, C. Stahn, 'Responsibility to Protect: Political Rhetoric or Emerging Legal Norm?', 101 *AJIL* 2007, p. 101, Bellamy & Reike, 'The Responsibility to Protect and International Law', pp. 268-274 and E. Strauss, 'A Bird in the Hand Is Worth Two in the Bush – On the Assumed Legal Nature of the Responsibility to Protect', 1 *Global Responsibility to Protect* 2009, pp. 292-293.

61 *See* J.M. Welsh, 'Norm Contestation and the Responsibility to Protect', 5 *Global Responsibility to Protect* 2013, pp. 365-396.

ing legal authorisation for certain kinds of activities."[62] A common reference to R2P as a 'norm' is meant as a reference to the norm in the widest sense, that is, as the desired way of behavior in the international community.[63] As such, R2P is indeed aimed at changing the behavior of states and other international actors.

9.3 Application of R2P in Practice

In the aftermath of the World Summit the doctrine of R2P received wide diplomatic support and found its way in documents of the Security Council. Until today the concept of R2P has been used in more than 40 Security Council resolutions and numerous presidential statements.[64] This section will consider the Security Council resolutions in the protection of civilians and Sudan, which inaugurated the R2P concept in the work of the Security Council, and the resolutions on Côte d'Ivoire and Libya that represent the most important examples of R2P's practical application, in particular within the third pillar (military intervention).[65]

The Security Council resolution 1674 (2006) on the protection of civilians in armed conflict makes a reference to the WSO document. Its operative paragraph 4 reaffirms those parts of the WSO document that deal with R2P in the sense of protecting populations from atrocity crimes.[66] As there is no explicit reference to Chapter VII, it seems this resolution is nonbinding. Nonetheless, it represents a general endorsement of R2P in the context of the protection of civilians during armed conflicts as a subcomponent of the general international responsibility for civilians.[67]

During the same year, the Security Council adopted resolution 1706 (2006) on Sudan concerning the humanitarian situation in Darfur. In the preamble, the resolution referred to resolution 1674, together with a reaffirmation of R2P in the context of the protection of civilians in armed conflicts.[68] The resolution went a step further. Acting under Chapter VII, it authorized UN Mission in Sudan (UNMIS) to use all necessary means for the implementation of the Darfur Peace Agreement. More specifically, UNMIS was authorized, inter alia, to protect civilians under threat of physical violence and to prevent attacks

---

62 A. Orford, 'From Promise to Practice? The Legal Significance of the Responsibility to Protect Concept', 3 *Global Responsibility to Protect* 2011, p. 421.

63 *See* www.merriam-webster.com.

64 UN SG, *Mobilizing Collective Action: The Next Decade of the Responsibility to Protect*, Report of the Secretary-General, 22 July 2016, A/70/999-S/2016/620, p. 3 and T. Milić, 'Responsibility to Protect and Legal Value of the UN Security Council Presidential Statements', *in* Sancin, *Responsibility to Protect: Where Do We Stand Ten Years After?*, pp. 143-154.

65 *Cf.* P. Hilpold, 'From Humanitarian Intervention to the Responsibility to Protect', *in* Hilpold, *Responsibility to Protect (R2P)*, pp. 2-3.

66 SC Res. 1674 (2006), 28 April 2006, operative para. 4.

67 The Security Council reafirrmed the R2P concept in another resolution on the protection of civilians: SC Res. 1894 (2009), 11 November 2009.

68 SC Res. 1706 (2006), 31 August 2006, preambular para. 2.

and threats against civilians.[69] The link between the endorsement of R2P in the preamble and the authorization of the use of force for the protection of civilians in the operative part makes resolution 1706 the first case of reaffirming R2P in a country specific Security Council resolution.[70] Nonetheless, due to a number of factors in the complex Darfur situation, R2P could not be implemented on the ground.[71]

Another incipient use of R2P concerns the situation in Côte d'Ivoire, a country with a record of prolonged social unrest. In 2010, after presidential elections, the political situation degraded into a vortex of post-electoral violence between support to the incumbent president Laurent Gbagbo, who lost elections, and the winner Alassane Outtara. The fighting spread beyond the capital, Abidjan, and the country descended into a civil war resulting in 3,000 killed, thousands injured and around 1 million displaced persons.[72] In 2011, the Security Council passed resolution 1975 (2011) in which it invoked "the primary responsibility of each State to protect civilians."[73] In addition, the Security Council recalled that the already stationed UN mission there United Nations Operation in Côte d'Ivoire (UNOCI) is authorized

> to use all necessary means to carry out its mandate to protect civilians under imminent threat of physical violence, ... including to prevent the use of heavy weapons against the civilian population.[74]

Eventually, the UNOCI forces, joined with residing French troops, undertook military actions against the Gbagbo forces, which shifted the military power in Outtara's favor and resulted in Gbagbo's deposition.[75] The fact that UN and French forces engaged against one of the warring parties in the internal conflict led to criticism that this military action stood for Western imperialism. It is true that the military force was not used with a direct purpose to protect civilians but rather to end the civil strife in Côte d'Ivoire and oust Gbagbo from presidency. However, there is no doubt that the military action was prop-

69 Ibid., operative para. 12(a).

70 The first reference to R2P in a country specific Security Council resolution was concerning the situation in the Great Lakes Region (SC Res. 1653 (2006)). However, that was a very brief and general reference to the WSO document as such, not to its R2P paragraphs. Alex Bellamy and Tim Dunne emphasize that a reference to R2P in the resolution on Darfur was a hard struck diplomatic deal that stalled the use of the R2P in the context of Sudan and in other situations for several years. (A.J. Bellamy & T. Dunne, 'R2P in Theory and Practice', *in* Bellamy & Dunne, *The Oxford Handbook of the Responsibility to Protect*, p. 9.)

71 *See* A. de Waal, 'Darfur and the Failure of the Responsibility to Protect', 83 *International Affairs* 2007, pp. 1039-1054.

72 C.T. Hunt, 'Côte d'Ivoire', *in* Bellamy & Dunne, *The Oxford Handbook of the Responsibility to Protect*, pp. 693, 695-696, M. Serrano, 'The Responsibility to Protect: Libya and Côte d'Ivoire', 3 *Amsterdam Law Forum* 2011, pp. 94-95 and A.J. Bellamy & P.D. Williams, 'The New Politics of Protection? Côte d'Ivoire, Libya and the Responsibility to Protect', 81 *International Affairs* 2011, p. 829 *et seq.*

73 SC Res. 1975 (2011), 30 March 2011, preambular para. 9.

74 Ibid., para. 6.

75 Hunt, 'Côte d'Ivoire', pp. 700-701.

erly authorized by the UN Security Council and that the general framework for the intervention was the doctrine of R2P, as indicated in resolution 1975.[76] Consistent with the R2P doctrine, the military intervention pursued the humanitarian aim of protection of the civilian population.[77] Although the intervention in Côte d'Ivoire is not an ideal example, it ultimately represents a successful application of R2P in practice.

The situation in Libya in 2011, which preceded the UN action in Côte d'Ivoire for several weeks, stands for the most explicit use of R2P in practical terms. Following the Arab Spring upheaval in Libya and the subsequent repression against civilians and political opponents by the Qaddafi regime, the Security Council decided to take action against Libyan authorities. The preamble of the resolution 1970 (2011) contains several elements of the R2P doctrine. For example, the Security Council condemned violence and the use of force against civilians in Libya; it pointed out that widespread and systematic attacks against the civilian population may amount to crimes against humanity; and recalled that the Libyan authorities have responsibility to protect its population.[78] The resolution was adopted under Chapter VII, which allowed the Security Council to take measures under Article 41 (non-military coercive measures). The Security Council demanded an immediate end to the violence and called for steps to fulfill the legitimate demands of the population.[79] All these features demonstrate that resolution 1970 was adopted in the framework of the R2P concept.

Nonetheless, the deterioration of the situation in Libya led to the diplomatic mobilization at the regional level. The Council of the League of Arab States (LAS) passed a resolution with a call to the Security Council for the imposition of a no-fly zone on Libyan military aviation and for the establishment of safe areas in zones under shelling as a precautionary measure for protection of Libyan people and foreign nationals.[80]

Building upon this regional initiative, the Security Council proceeded to the second, more robust resolution on Libya, 1973 (2011). The Security Council again used the vocabulary belonging to the R2P doctrine. The Security Council reiterated the responsibility of the Libyan authorities to protect its population and pointed out that they failed to comply with the previous resolution.[81] It condemned the gross and systematic violation of human rights and underlined that the widespread and systematic attack against the

76 Ibid., pp. 701-702, 704.

77 *Cf.* Serrano, 'The Responsibility to Protect: Libya and Côte d'Ivoire', pp. 99-100 and Bellamy & Williams, 'The New Politics of Protection?', pp. 836-837.

78 SC Res. 1970 (2011), 26 February 2011, preambular paras. 1, 6, 9. The resolution was adopted by consensus. (T. Dunne & S. Teitt, 'Contested Intervention: China, India, and the Responsibility to Protect', 21 *Global Governance* 2015, p. 379.)

79 SC Res. 1970, para. 1.

80 Arab League Council Res. 7360, 12 March 2011, op. para. 1, http://responsibilitytoprotect.org/Arab%20League%20Ministerial%20level%20statement%2012%20march%202011%20-%20english(1).pdf.

81 SC Res. 1973 (2011), 17 March 2011, preambular paras. 1, 2. Several important members of the Security Council abstained: China and Russia (both permanent members), as well as Germany, Brazil and India. (Dunne & Teitt, 'Contested Intervention', p. 381.)

civilian population may amount to crimes against humanity.[82] Mostly importantly, however, the Security Council stated that the situation in Libya constituted a threat to international peace and security and decided to proceed pursuant to Chapter VII. With regard to the protection of civilians, the Security Council authorized member states

> to take all necessary measures ... to protect civilians and civilian populated areas under threat of attack ... while excluding a foreign occupation force of any form on any part of Libyan territory.[83]

The Security Council also requested members of the LAS to cooperate with other UN member states in the implementation of its decision.[84] Additionally, the Security Council established a ban on all flights in the Libyan airspace (the no-fly zone) in order to help protect civilians and authorized member states to take all necessary measures to enforce compliance with this ban.[85]

Taken together, elements in the two Security Council resolutions on Libya represent an exemplary application of R2P in practice and a multilateral constitutional moment.[86] Resolutions 1970 and 1973 invoked the responsibility of Libya to protect its civilian population, emphasized the danger that atrocity crimes are underway and urged the Libyan authorities to stop repressive actions against the civilian population. Resolution 1970 established no-fly zones and protected areas. Going further, resolution 1973 authorized all necessary measures to protect civilians and instituted a flight ban. In addition, there was an explicit, preceding endorsement of these actions by the regional organization (LAS).[87] All these elements stand for the R2P doctrine as included in the WSO document. They also represent repositioning of constitutional underpinnings of the multilateral system in the sense that (i) the protection of human lives is now part of the new understanding of sovereignty, and (ii) that a failure to observe it gives way to the international intervention.[88]

The international military action pursuant to the Security Council resolution 1973 was led by NATO, together with some associated Arab countries. It consisted mainly of air strikes against Gaddafi's ground forces that were attacking civilians. However, in the course of the international military action cleavages between bigger powers began to emerge. China, Russia and some other actors (India, Brazil, South Africa, the African

---

82 SC Res. 1973, preambular paras. 4, 6.

83 Ibid., para. 4.

84 Id.

85 Ibid., paras. 6, 8. *See also* Higgins *et al., Oppenheim's International Law – United Nations*, vol. II, pp. 1023-1024.

86 *See* Powell, 'Libya: A Multilateral Constitutional Moment?', pp. 298-316.

87 F. Azzam & C. Pison Hindawi, 'The Arab Region', *in* Bellamy & Dunne, *The Oxford Handbook of the Responsibility to Protect*, pp. 456, 462.

88 Powell, 'Libya: A Multilateral Constitutional Moment?', pp. 298-299, 303.

Union) perceived the conduct of the NATO military campaign, upon which they had no influence, as an expression of Western hegemony. This hegemonic reprimand grew even stronger in their claim that the military campaign went beyond the protection of civilians to pursue the goal of the regime change in Libya. They claimed this aim was not covered in resolution 1973.[89] The situation evoked memories of the Kosovo intervention and led to a serious backlash against the use of the R2P doctrine. When the Security Council was soon afterwards confronted with the situation in Syria, despite the pressing humanitarian situation there, China and Russia vetoed all draft resolutions that were tabled and the Security Council became paralyzed.[90] Subsequently, with regard to Syria the collective framework on the use of force disintegrated into a plethora of unilateral but often legally dubious military actions, underpinned by the extensive interpretation of the use of force.[91]

Similar to an overstatement in the case of Libya that R2P achieved its ultimate recognition, the failure of the application of the R2P doctrine in the case of Syria led to pessimistic claims that R2P has met its premature death.[92] While there is no doubt that the most explicit use of R2P was in the case of Libya, it is also appropriate to say that this case demonstrated a realignment of common humanitarian values with geopolitical factors of the biggest international actors.[93] This was not the case in Syria and hence a 'failure' of the application of R2P there.[94] Another criticism of the use of R2P in Libya from the *ex post* perspective may be that Libya is a less safe place after the intervention than it used to be during the Gaddafi era. But one has to take into account that large-scale violence against civilians by the Gaddafi regime was 'a point of no return' and required (military) intervention by the international community. However, a lesson learned is that the military intervention should have been followed by measures in the sense of the responsibility

89 *See* Dunne & Teitt, 'Contested Intervention', pp. 381-382, Garwood-Gowers, 'The Responsibility to Protect and the Arab Spring', pp. 594-595, 606 *et seq.*, Dembinski & Reinold, *Libya and the Future of the Responsibility to Protect*, pp. 12, 25, D. Silander, 'NATO (In)actions in Syria?, *in* Sancin, *Responsibility to Protect: Where Do We Stand Ten Years After?*, p. 231, Falk, *Power Shift*, pp. 117-118 and P. Bolopion, 'After Libya, the Question: To Protect or Depose', *Los Angeles Times*, 25 August 2011, http://articles.latimes.com/2011/aug/25/opinion/la-oe-bolopion-libya-responsibility-t20110825.

90 *See* Dunne & Teitt, 'Contested Intervention', pp. 382-386, Xue, *Chinese Contemporary Perspectives on International Law*, pp. 91-92 and Garwood-Gowers, 'The Responsibility to Protect and the Arab Spring', pp. 610-613.

91 *See, e.g.*, O. Flasch, 'The Legality of the Air Strikes against ISIL in Syria: New Insights on the Extraterritorial Use of Force against Non-state Actors', pp. 37-69, and L. O'Connor, 'Legality of the Use of Force in Syria against Islamic State and the Khorasan Group', pp. 70-96, both *in* 3 *Journal on the Use of Force and International Law* 2016.

92 *See* O. Ribbelink, 'R2P: RIP?', *in* Sancin, *Responsibility to Protect: Where Do We Stand Ten Years After?*, pp. 43-52.

93 Garwood-Gowers, 'The Responsibility to Protect and the Arab Spring', p. 609 and M.W. Doyle, 'The Politics of Global Humanitarianism: R2P before and after Libya', *in* Bellamy & Dunne, *The Oxford Handbook of the Responsibility to Protect*, pp. 685-686.

94 However, R2P was referred to in the Security Council resolutions 1996 on South Sudan (July 2011) and 2014 on Yemen (October 2011). (Bellamy & Dunne, 'R2P in Theory and Practice', p. 10.)

to rebuild. That component was envisaged by the ICISS under the 'responsibility to re-build' but somehow ignored in the WSO document. In the future there should be a closer link between the use of R2P and the post-intervention peace building measures in the sense that peace building becomes a constituent part of the R2P doctrine.[95] Another possible enhancement of the post-conflict international involvement could be a link to the UN Peacebuilding Commission.[96]

9.4 Concluding Remarks on the Coexistence of Hegemony and Constitutionalism Concerning the Intervention on Humanitarian Grounds

The emergence of the concept of R2P is an example of international constitutionalism in which humanitarian concerns permeated other international constitutional categories, such as state sovereignty and the principle of nonintervention. This interaction led to the realignment of constitutional principles of the international legal order. A motive for the development of R2P came after the hegemonic use of humanitarian intervention in the case of Kosovo. The R2P concept was shaped by the ICISS and – in a somewhat lighter version – universally confirmed in the WSO document. In the R2P concept the use of force has an important, although not a primary place. It is considered as a tool of last resort. Nonetheless, the military intervention under R2P, as is typical of rules and practice on the use of force, suffers from an overly discretionary nature of these norms. Thus, the application of R2P in the case of Libya is a simultaneous example of constitutionalism and hegemony in the sense of the hegemo-constitutional reality in the world community. On one hand, the framework for the use of R2P in resolutions 1970 and 1973 stems from the international constitutional structure. On the other hand, the use of military force by the NATO-led coalition pursued goals that some international actors perceived as excessive and hegemonic. Nonetheless, it is undeniable that these goals remained within the humanitarian confines of the R2P concept, as well as within the

95 R. Paris, 'The Blurry Boundary between Peacebuilding and R2P', *in* Bellamy & Dunne, *The Oxford Handbook of the Responsibility to Protect*, pp. 509-523 and Hunt, 'Côte d'Ivoire', pp. 705-707.

96 V. Sancin, 'Odgovornost zaščititi in njeno univerzalno, regionalno in državno uveljavljanje' ['Responsibility to Protect and its Universal, Regional and National Application'], *in* A. Zidar & S. Štiglic (Eds.), *Slovenske misli o mednarodnih odnosih in pravu: prispevki ob 80-letnici dr. Ernesta Petriča* [*Slovenian Reflections on International Relations and Law: Essays in Honour of the 80th Birthday of Professor Ernest Petrič*], FDV-MZZ, Ljubljana, 2017, pp. 380, 382. *See also* C. Stahn, 'Responsibility to Protect', p. 110.

Security Council legal framework, which is a major step forward with regard to the Kosovo intervention.

Despite the success of R2P in the case of Libya, there remain some doubts about the further application of R2P in situations of atrocity crimes.[97] In order to secure a more consistent and frequent application of R2P in the future, a special procedure would have to be instituted.[98] In terms of substance, the ICISS already proposed a set of criteria that should guide the decision-making on the use of force. But a major step should be procedural, such as the establishment of a monitoring mechanism, for example, a panel of international experts, presumably in the form of a subsidiary organ of the Security Council. Such a mechanism would have a mandate to evaluate and endorse all phases of the R2P action, including military intervention, in a particular humanitarian situation. In this way, the mechanism would narrow the discretionary application of the use of force under the R2P concept. It would also strike the adequate balance between the restrictive and extensive approach to the use of force and give a stamp of legality and legitimacy to future R2P actions.

97 There are signs, however, that non-Western powers such as China are again gravitating towards the R2P doctrine. After the NATO intervention in Libya, China developed the 'responsible protection' doctrine that can be seen as a restatement of R2P, albeit in slightly 'softer' terms. (*See* A. Garwood-Gowers, 'China's "Responsible Protection" Concept: Reinterpreting the Responsibility to Protect (R2P) and Military Intervention for Humanitarian Purposes', 6 *Asian Journal of International Law* 2016, pp. 89-118.)

98 *Cf.* Cohen, *Globalization and Sovereignty*, pp. 210-211.

10 International Adjudication

As evidenced in Chapter 7, the development of the international judicial function through a growing number of international adjudicatory bodies is one of the most important features of the contemporary international community. This unprecedented judicial evolution caught some international judges by surprise. At the turn of the century, two consecutive presidents of the International Court of Justice (ICJ), Judge Gilbert Guillaume and Judge Stephen Schwebel, expressed worries that proliferation of international adjudicatory organs might lead to overlapping jurisdictions and consequently, to conflicting judgments. They warned this development could end in overall anarchy.[1]

Another ICJ president, Judge Rosalyn Higgins, was less pessimistic. While foreseeing a possibility of clashing international jurisdictions, she suggested that such judicial conflicts could be readily solved through judicial cooperation.[2] The main reason for the cooperative approach is that international judges belong to the same epistemic community that shares a belief in the aims of international justice and the value of international law.[3] This leads to the practice of borrowing from each other's jurisprudence, inciting a dialogue among judges and cross-fertilization of judicial standards.[4] Unsurprisingly, such close professional cooperation has wider repercussions in the form of an emerging and interconnected judicial system in which seemingly disparate islands of international courts and tribunals are connected in the framework of general international law.[5]

As part of an emerging function of the international community, the international judicial bodies have transcended the traditional role of the peaceful settlement of disputes. While this task remains important, international courts and tribunals as organs of the international public authority started performing other adjudicative tasks. Aside from dispute settlement, international courts perform functions of stabilizing normative

---

1 *See* G. Guillaume, 'The Proliferation of International Judicial Bodies: The Outlook for the International Legal Order', Speech to the Sixth Committee of the General Assembly of the United Nations, 27 October 2000 and S.M. Schwebel, 'Address to the Plenary Session of the General Assembly of the United Nations', 26 October 1999 (*in fine*) (both available at: www.icj-cij.org).

2 *See* R. Higgins, 'A Babel of Judicial Voices? Ruminations from the Bench', 55 *ICLQ* 2006, pp. 791-804.

3 D. Terris, C.P.R. Romano & L. Swigart, *The International Judge: An Introduction to the Men and Women who Decide the World's Cases*, OUP, Oxford, 2007, pp. 63, 65.

4 Ibid., pp. 118-119, J.I. Charney, 'The Impact on the International Legal System of the Growth of International Courts and Tribunals', 31 *N.Y.U. Journal of International Law and Politics* 1999, pp. 706-707 and S. Vasiliev, 'Cross-fertilisation under the Looking Glass: Transjudicial Grammar and Reception of Strasbourg Jurisprudence by International Criminal Tribunals', *in* P. Lobba & T. Mariniello (Eds.), *Judicial Dialogue on Human Rights: The Practice of International Criminal Tribunals*, Brill-Nijhoff, Leiden-Boston, 2017, pp. 16-17.

5 J.S. Martinez, 'Towards an International Judicial System', 56 *Stanford Law Review* 2003, pp. 431, 435 and J. Pauwleyn, 'Bridging Fragmentation and Unity: International Law as a Universe of Inter-connected Islands', 25 *Michigan Journal of International Law* 2004, pp. 904, 915-916.

expectations, judicial lawmaking as well as controlling and legitimating public authority.[6] Armin von Bogdandy and Ingo Venzke labeled this development as a move from a one-dimensional to a multifaceted understanding of international adjudication.[7]

José Alvarez similarly extends functions of international adjudication to the fact-finding function, the law-making function and the governance function.[8] Under the latter function, in particular, international courts exercise constitutional prerogatives, in the sense of adhering to the rule of law, participating in the dynamic of checks and balances, and upholding the respect for human rights. The common purpose of exercising constitutional functions is to uphold the common values of the international community and contribute to its harmonious integration.[9] These developments reflect the general expansion of power of international courts and tribunals as well as internalization of constitutional features, such as judicial review, *erga omnes* effect of judgments, constitutional doctrines and effective remedies.

However, the growth of power of international adjudicatory organs does not stop with judicial constitutionalism. A nearly simultaneous process can be called *judicial hegemony*. Tribunals may regard themselves as separate and different little empires exhibiting a tendency for self-augmentation.[10] In parallel with the growth of constitutional powers there are numerous instances of cross-judicial interference at the international level. One aspect of this interaction is the transplantation of international rules from the original to a different context. This process can have positive implications for comparative jurisprudence in the sense of spreading knowledge about the current judicial practice. Nonetheless, borrowing and adaptation of rules can result in their divergent judicial

---

6 *See* A. von Bogdandy & I. Venzke, 'On the Function of International Courts: An Appraisal in Light of Their Burgeoning Public Authority', 26 *LJIL* 2013, pp. 54-59.

7 Ibid., pp. 49-72.

8 J.E. Alvarez, 'What Are International Judges for? The Main Functions of International Adjudication', *in* C.P.R. Romano, K.J. Alter & Y. Shany (Eds.), *The Oxford Handbook of International Adjudication*, OUP, Oxford, 2014, pp. 166-176.

9 Ibid., pp. 171-172 and von Bogdany & Venzke, 'On the Function of International Courts', pp. 57-58.

10 *See* M. Andenas, 'Reassertion and Transformation: From Fragmentation to Convergence in International Law', 46 *Georgetown Journal of International Law* 2015, pp. 704-706 (referring to Robert Jennings). *See also* J. Pauwelyn, 'Europea, America and the "Unity" of International Law', *in* J. Wouters *et al.* (Eds.), *The Europeanisation of International Law: The Status of International Law in the EU and its Member States*, T.M.C. Asser Press, The Hague, 2008, p. 225.

interpretation in various contexts.[11] These issues are explored in particular in discussions on proliferation of international tribunals and fragmentation of international law.[12]

10.1 Doctrinal Insights on the Interplay between Judicial Hegemony and Constitutionalism

Just like many other areas in international law, the landscape of international adjudication serves as a meeting ground between hegemony and constitutionalism. This hegemo-constitutional scheme is buttressed by insights from the doctrine and practice alike. In doctrinal terms, the most relevant is the hegemonic contestation dynamic by Martti Koskenniemi.[13]

This doctrinal insight is based on the premise that international functional regimes, including international courts and tribunals, tend to create limited or mini-sovereignties out of themselves.[14] The growth of judicial powers at the same time also implies judicial hegemonic contestation. This is hardly surprising as law is a semantic battlefield in which opponents "engage in hegemonic practices, trying to enlist its rules, principles and institutions on their side, making sure they do not support the adversary."[15] By hegemonic contestation, Koskenniemi understands a process in which international actors con-

11 A.-M. Carstens, 'Interpreting Transplanted Treaty Rules', *in* A. Bianchi, D. Peat & M. Windsor (Eds.), *Interpretation in International Law*, OUP, Oxford, 2015, pp. 229, 232 and A. Riccardi, 'The Judicial Dialogue between the ECtHR and the ad hoc Tribunals on the Right to Rehabilitation Offenders', *in* Lobba & Mariniello, *Judicial Dialogue on Human Rights*, pp. 165-183.

12 *Generally see* M. Koskenniemi & P. Leino, 'Fragmentation of International Law? Postmodern Anxieties', 15 *LJIL* 2002, pp. 553-579, M. Koskenniemi, *Fragmentation of International Law: Difficulties Arising from the Diversification and Expansion of International Law*, Report of the Study Group of the International Law Commission, UN Doc. A/CN.4/L.682, 4 April 2006, R. Higgins, 'The ICJ, the ECJ, and the Integrity of International Law', 52 *ICLQ* 2003, pp. 1-20 and contributions in 31 *N.Y.U. Journal of International Law and Politics* 1999, pp. 679-933.

13 The other doctrinal perspectives are Ran Hirschl's hegemonic preservation thesis and Chris Borgen's hegemony as process. The hegemonic preservation thesis sees the reason for the international strengthening of judicial power in a tendency of political elites to preserve their hegemony. By enabling the international judiciary to increase their power through judicial review, the exercise of the rule of law and protection of human rights, the influential groups perpetuate their ideological and political platforms at the international level. The view of hegemony as a process, on the other hand, focuses on the dynamic of the transnational litigation. Such a process is usually portrayed as non-state actors (individuals, groups and companies) versus states. The hegemonic push in this case comes from private litigants exploiting the constitutional expansion of international courts with an aim to perpetuate the desired jurisprudential outcomes. (*See* R. Hirschl, *Towards Juristocracy: The Origins and Consequences of the New Constitutionalism*, Harvard University Press, Cambridge (MA)-London, 2007, pp. 11-12, 16, 214, 216-217, 221-222, R. Hirschl, 'The Struggle for Hegemony: Understanding Judicial Empowerment through Constitutionalisation in Culturally Divided Polities', 36 *Stanford Journal of International Law* 2000, pp. 84-87 and C.J. Borgen, 'Transnational Tribunals and the Transmission of Norms: The Hegemony of Process', 39 *George Washington International Law Review* 2007, pp. 686-688, 749-751, 763-764.)

14 M. Koskenniemi, 'Hegemonic Regimes', *in* M.A. Young (Ed.), *Regime Interaction in International Law: Facing Fragmentation*, CUP, Cambridge, 2015, p. 317.

15 Koskenniemi, 'International Law and Hegemony', p. 200.

stantly challenge each other referring to rules and principles on which they have projected meanings that support their own preferences, while counteracting those of their opponents. 'Battles for meaning' within hegemonic contestation can revolve around interpretation of expressions such as aggression, self-defense, self-determination, *jus cogens*, jurisdiction and many others.[16]

An essential enterprise of hegemonic contestation is to succeed in giving a specific meaning to a universalist characteristic. International actors typically claim to speak in the voice of the universal in that they refer to 'universal values', 'interests of the international community' and, increasingly, 'international constitutionalism'.[17] In this sense, judicial organs are "engaged in a *hegemonic* struggle in which each hopes to have its special interest identified with the general interest."[18] But in invoking the constitutionalist mindset their arguments are no less hegemonic than those of their competitors.[19] In addition to the tendency of setting the universalist meaning, the important question within hegemonic contestation is also who has the power to determine that meaning.[20] One of the eminent questions in recent judicial practice is precisely which international court is authorized to have a final say in a particular matter.[21]

In sum, the hegemonic contestation dynamic focuses on the relationship between various international courts. The growth of international constitutionalism presupposes the growth of judicial powers. As international courts naturally pursue specific functional ends, their extension of power may be hegemonic and clash with activities of other courts. In the exercise of its inherent judicial function, each court feels entitled that its interpretation of the relevant legal vocabulary is universally valid, although it may reflect its own hegemonic preferences. Whenever the issue of contestation over various hegemonic judicial meanings arises, it likewise triggers the question of the ultimate judicial competence for a decision in the particular matter. Such problems are resolved through a continuous communication among international courts. This chapter will address judicial tensions in the areas of (i) state responsibility, (ii) allocation of jurisdiction and (iii) protection of human rights.

10.2 JUDICIAL TENSION ON THE SUBSTANTIVE ISSUE OF STATE RESPONSIBILITY

The field of state responsibility is subject to important developments through the process of articulation of international norms and judicial practice. In 2001, the ILC adopted *Draft Articles on Responsibility of States for Internationally Wrongful Acts*, which encap-

16 Ibid., pp. 198, 199.
17 *See* ibid., pp. 199, 206.
18 Koskenniemi & Leino, 'Fragmentation of International Law?', p. 562.
19 Koskenniemi, 'Hegemonic Regimes', p. 321.
20 Ibid., p. 312.
21 Koskenniemi & Leino, 'Fragmentation of International Law?', pp. 562, 574-579.

sulate fundamental rules on the topic.[22] State responsibility fulfills constitutional functions in two ways. First, its reparatory component is directed towards remedying damage caused to injured states or persons but at the same time also to reconstituting the violated international norm. Secondly, the accountability of states for their internationally wrongful acts is essential for upholding the international rule of law and, by reinforcing the principle of sovereign equality, also for maintaining the international constitutional order. Law of state responsibility is therefore crucial for the protection of the integrity of the international legal system.[23]

At the center of the judicial controversy in the field of state responsibility is hegemonic contestation between the International Tribunal for Former Yugoslavia (ICTY) and the ICJ over rules for the attribution of wrongful conduct to a state, in particular on the understanding of the 'effective control test' as devised by the ICJ.

In the Nicaragua case, the ICJ dealt with the issue of attribution of responsibility for military and paramilitary activities of the contra revolutionaries in Nicaragua to the US government. The Court examined and rejected the direct responsibility of the United States for actions of the *contras* in the sense of their 'complete dependence' on the United States (the so called *agency test*).[24] But it went on to articulate the 'effective control test' as part of customary international law, according to which the responsibility of a foreign government is established if it is engaged in "training, arming, equipping, financing and supplying the *contra* forces or otherwise encouraging, supporting and aiding military and paramilitary activities" in a foreign country.[25] Nonetheless, with regard to the connection between the US government and activities of the *contras*, the Court made an important distinction. It found no evidence that such connection existed in the case of alleged violations of international human rights and humanitarian law perpetrated by the *contras*. It did, however, establish such a connection, on the basis of the effective control test, with regard to the violation of the principle of nonintervention, which triggered state responsibility of the United States for the breach of this international norm.[26]

Reasons for different applications of the effective control test may be that domains of international human rights law and humanitarian law deal primarily with individual responsibility, while the prohibition of intervention in domestic affairs is a typical norm touching upon responsibility of states. Another basis for this distinction is that Nicaragua's pleading before the ICJ failed to identify the US support for individual missions

22 ILC, *Draft articles on Responsibility of States for Internationally Wrongful Acts.*

23 A. Nollkaemper, 'Concurrence between Individual and State Responsibility in International Law', 52 *ICLQ* 2003, p. 622 and A. Nollkaemper, 'Constitutionalization and Unity of the Law of International Responsibility', 16 *Indiana Journal of Global Legal Studies* 2009, pp. 535, 544-545.

24 *Military and Paramilitary Activities in and against Nicaragua (Nicaragua v. United States of America)*, Merits, Judgment, ICJ Rep. 1986, at 14, pp. 62-63.

25 *Nicaragua v. United States of America*, para. 292(3).

26 *See* ibid., paras. 110, 114-116, 247, 292(3).

of the *contras*; rather, they referred to the US involvement with the *contras* in general.[27] The given set of circumstances thus leads to the nexus between the involvement of the United States with the rebel forces in Nicaragua in the sense of its wrongful intervention in the Nicaraguan domestic affairs.

In the process of adjudicating crimes committed during the war in the former Yugoslavia, the ICTY rejected the effective control test and chose instead to develop a new test of an 'overall control'. The ICTY used the issue of state responsibility as a tool to determine the distinction between an international and non-international armed conflict. This distinction was essential for charging Duško Tadić for graver breaches of international humanitarian law in international armed conflicts, rather than for those in non-international armed conflicts.[28] However, in exercising its proper jurisdiction, the ICTY Appeals Chamber ventured into the reinterpretation of the concept of state responsibility, which is a typical issue of general international law. The ICTY Appeals Chamber labelled the effective control test in Nicaragua as "non persuasive" and "unconvincing" from the point of view of the entire system of the law on state responsibility.[29] In going beyond the effective control test, the ICTY reasoned that to attribute the acts of a military or a paramilitary group to a State,

> it must be proved that the State wields overall control over the group, not only by equipping and financing the group, but also by coordinating or helping the general planning of its military activity.[30]

The overall control likewise presupposes organising, coordinating or planning the military actions of the military group.[31] This criterion, according to the ICTY Appeals Chamber, should be essential in determining state responsibility.[32] However, in a separate opinion to the judgment, Judge Mohamed Shahabuddeen explained that the Federal Republic of Yugoslavia (FRY) was using force in Bosnia and Herzegovina through the armed forces of Republika Srpska (VRS). This was sufficient to establish a nexus between FRY and VRS

27 J. Crawford, *State Responsibility: The General Part*, CUP, Cambridge, 2013, p. 148.

28 Ibid., p. 150. *See Prosecutor v. Duško Tadić*, ICTY, Appeals Chamber, Case No. IT-94-1-A, Judgment, 15 July 1999, paras. 88-94, 104, 161.

29 *Prosecutor v. Duško Tadić*, paras. 115, 116.

30 Ibid., para. 131.

31 Ibid, para. 137.

32 For the line of argument, *see* ibid, paras. 141-145. The test became an established standard in the ICTY's case law. *See*, in particular: *Prosecutor v. Aleksovski* (Judgment) IT-95-14/1-A, Appeals Chamber, 24 March 2000; *Prosecutor v. Dedalić and Others (Čelebići case)* (Judgment) IT-96-21-A, Appeals Chamber, 20 February 2001; *Prosecutor v. Kordić and Čerkez* (Judgment) IT-95-14/2-A, Appeals Chamber, 17 December 2004. For a vocal defense of the overall control test, *see* A. Cassese, 'The Nicaragua and Tadić Tests Revisited in Light of the ICJ Judgment on Genocide in Bosnia', 18 *EJIL* 2007, pp. 649-668.

in Bosnia and qualify the conflict as international. An invention of the overall control test and its subsequent application to international humanitarian law was not necessary.[33]

By offering a wholesale criticism of the Nicaragua test for the purposes of state responsibility, the ICTY violated the principle of judicial economy given that the only issue that needed to be decided was whether the armed conflict was international or internal.[34] Furthermore, in venturing into the area not of its primary competence, trying to overwrite the established case law of the ICJ, the ICTY attempted to influence the field beyond its jurisdiction. The ICTY's mandate pertains to the issues of individual criminal responsibility, not state responsibility, and the relevant question was not responsibility but the applicability of relevant rules of international humanitarian law.[35] Given that the ICTY deals with individual criminal responsibility, it overstepped its functional framework. Some authors even referred to this judicial intervention as *ultra vires* action.[36] An excursus of the ICTY into the domain of state responsibility thus represents a vivid example of judicial hegemony.

Through its subsequent case law, the ICJ proffered a fairly balanced response to the above challenge.[37] In the *Armed Activities* case, the ICJ confirmed the effective control test as a tool to evaluate the degree of state responsibility. With regard to Uganda's intervention in DR Congo, the ICJ found Uganda liable for its intervention into Congo's internal affairs. However, concerning the support given by Uganda to the rebel group called *Congo Liberation Movement*, the court decided it did not pass the threshold of the effective control test.[38]

The ICJ dealt with this issue more extensively in the *Bosnian Genocide* case. The issue at stake was similar to in the *Tadić* case: was the Federal Republic of Yugoslavia (Serbia and Montenegro) responsible for acts of genocide committed by Bosnian Serb forces during the war in Bosnia? In reaching the decision, the ICJ applied the rules of the law of state responsibility, including a reference to the Nicaragua case and the effective control test. According to the ICJ, the question of state responsibility was not crucial for the exercise of the ICTY's jurisdiction in the *Tadić* case.[39] Jurisdiction of the ICTY pertains to criminal law issues only and the tribunal is not generally called upon to rule on issues of

33 *See* Separate Opinion of Judge Shahabuddeen, *Prosecutor v. Duško Tadić*, paras. 5, 17-21.

34 R.J. Goldstone & J. Hamilton, '*Bosnia* v. *Serbia*: Lessons from the Encounter of the International Court of Justice with the International Criminal Tribunal for the Former Yugoslavia', 21 *EJIL* 2008, p. 101.

35 *Draft articles on Responsibility of States for Internationally Wrongful Acts, with commentaries*, p. 48.

36 *See* M. Sassòli & L.M. Olsson, 'Prosecutor v. Tadić', 94 *AJIL* 2000, pp. 575, 578 and K. Oellers-Frahm, 'Multiplication of International Courts and Tribunals and Conflicting Jurisdiction: Problems and Possible Solutions', 5 *Max Planck Yearbook of United Nations Law* 2001, pp. 79-80.

37 *Cf.* Goldstone & Hamilton, '*Bosnia* v. *Serbia*', p. 101.

38 *Case concerning Armed Activities on the Territory of Congo (Democratic Republic of the Congo v. Uganda)*, Judgment, ICJ Reports 2005, p. 168, paras. 160, 165, 213.

39 Ibid., para. 403. *See also* P. Webb, *International Judicial Integration and Fragmentation*, OUP, Oxford, 2013, pp. 138-139, 141 and Crawford, *State Responsibility*, pp. 154-155.

general international law, nor on the questions of state responsibility.[40] The ICJ thus rejected ICTY's entitlement to procure authoritative interpretations of general international law that would go beyond ICTY's framework of competence.

With regard to substance, the ICJ diagnosed that the ICTY created the overall control test to determine the question of whether or not an armed conflict was international which triggers different forms of criminal acts. The ICJ estimated that the biggest drawback of the overall control test is that it broadens the scope beyond a fundamental principle that a state is responsible for conduct of persons acting on its behalf.[41] It held that the overall control test is unsuitable because "it stretches too far, almost to the breaking point, the connection which must exist between the conduct of a State's organ and its international responsibility."[42] In this way, the ICJ affirmed relevance of the effective control test, barred the overall control test from the case law of ICJ and put to question the relevance of the overall control test for the law of state responsibility.

In the end, the ICJ came to the conclusion that Serbia did not commit genocide in Bosnia as there was no state responsibility on the part of Serbia for the acts perpetrated by VRS in Bosnia. However, the ICJ found that Serbia violated the obligation to prevent genocide in Bosnia and that it failed to transfer Ratko Mladić, indicted for genocide and complicity in it, to the ICTY for trial.[43]

The 'battle for meaning' between the ICTY and ICJ proceeded as follows: in the course of its process of adjudication, the ICTY developed the overall control test, with which it tried to overwrite the ICJ's effective control test and influence the development of the law of state responsibility and jurisdiction of other courts. But the ICJ reacted in a measured if determined fashion. While holding back on the relevance of the overall test for the ICTY's own jurisdiction, it clearly rejected its validity for the ICJ's work, as well as for general international law. The ICJ's message to ICTY was: we shall not delve upon your work but if it interferes with our competence we shall prevail, as that is our exclusive domain. The solution to accommodate such judicial conflict is that each international court is competent to ensure legal consistency within its own working purview while not projecting its power on other jurisdictions.[44]

---

40 *Application of the Convention on the Prevention and Punishment of the Crime of Genocide (Bosnia and Herzegovina v. Serbia and Montenegro)*, Judgment, 26 February 2007, p. 43, para. 403.

41 In this respect, the ICJ established the framework of state responsibility: (i) for acts carried out by its official organs; (ii) for acts by persons who are in a relationship of complete dependence on the state; or (iii) if a person or a group acted on the instructions or under direction of the state or if the state exercised effective control over the action during which the wrong was committed. (Ibid., paras. 404-406. *See also* Crawford, *State Responsibility*, pp. 155-156.)

42 *Bosnia v. Serbia and Montenegro*, para. 406.

43 Ibid., paras. 413-415, 425-450, 471.

44 *See* Goldstone & Hamilton, '*Bosnia v. Serbia*', pp. 102, 103, 111 and Webb, *International Judicial Integration and Fragmentation*, pp. 139, 141, 151, 144.

10.3 Judicial Tension on the Procedural Issue of Jurisdiction

A series of confrontations about jurisdictional competence arose between the European Court of Justice (ECJ)[45] and international courts and tribunals in the context of two cases: the *MOX Plant case* and the *Achmea case*. Both are important as they deal with a range of constitutional issues at the international level, such as the relationship between international judicial bodies, the autonomy of the EU legal order and the freedom of states to choose international litigation forums.[46] At the same time, the jurisdictional rivalry among international judicial bodies exemplifies traits of judicial hegemony, notably by the ECJ with regard to other international courts and tribunals.

The *MOX Plant case* concerned a dispute between Ireland and the United Kingdom on the potential environmental contamination of the Irish Sea following the production of the so-called *mixed oxide (MOX)* fuel at the British nuclear plant in Sellafield. Ireland considered this dispute of such vital importance that it initiated a series of international judicial proceedings.[47] Various legal aspects of the case crystallized in judicial decisions under three international legal regimes (the *Convention for the Protection of the Marine Environment of the North-East Atlantic* or the OSPAR Convention,[48] the *UN Convention on the Law of the Sea* or the UNCLOS,[49] and the EU legal regime), by four adjudicatory bodies.[50]

Ireland first initiated proceedings under the OSPAR Convention claiming that the UK violated an obligation to provide access to information to Ireland on the protection of the marine environment. Among other grounds, the UK contested the tribunal's jurisdiction with an argument that it touched upon EU law, which implies exclusive jurisdiction of EU institutions.[51] In 2003, the arbitral tribunal rejected the relevance of the EU dimen-

---

45 The Lisbon Treaty renamed the highest EU court as the Court of Justice of the EU (CJEU). Since the survey of jurisprudence in this section partly predates the new name, a more traditional expression of the European Court of Justice (ECJ) is used.

46 *Cf.* N. Lavranos, 'MOX Plant Dispute: Court of Justice of the European Communities', 2 *European Constitutional Law Review* 2006, pp. 463-464 and P.T. Eicher, 'International Forum Shopping: The Mox Plant Case and the ECJ', 30 *Dublin University Law Journal* 2006, pp. 391-392.

47 Eicher, 'International Forum Shopping', pp. 367-368.

48 Convention of the Marine Environment of the North-Atlantic, open for signature on 22 September 1992, entered into force on 25 March 1998.

49 United Nations Convention on the Law of the Sea, opened for signature on 10 December 1982, entered into force on 16 November 1994. Annex VI of the UNCLOS established the permanent International Tribunal for the Law of the Sea (ITLOS).

50 For an incisive analysis of the case law, *see* R. Churchill & J. Scott, 'The MOX Plant Litigation: The First Half-life', 53 *ICLQ* 2004, pp. 643-676, C.P.R. Romano, 'Commission of the European Communities v. Ireland', 101 *AJIL* 2007, pp. 171-178, J. Gao, 'Comments on *Commission of the European Communities v. Ireland*', 7 *Chinese Journal of International Law* 2008, pp. 417-427 and N. Lavranos, 'Protecting the Exclusive Jurisdiction: The *MOX Plant*-Judgment of the ECJ', 5 *The Law and Practice of International Courts and Tribunals* 2006, pp. 479-493.

51 *Dispute concerning Access to Information under Article 9 of the OSPAR Convention (Ireland v. UK)*, Case No. 2001-3, PCA arbitral tribunal, Final Award, 2 July 2003, paras. 110, 143.

sion for the dispute at hand. It stated that the OSPAR Convention and the EU legal order are each "an independent legal source that establishes a distinct legal regime and provides for different legal remedies."[52]

In parallel, Ireland initiated proceedings against the UK before the arbitral tribunal under Annex VII of the UNCLOS asserting violations concerning the protection of the marine environment; the prevention and control of pollution; and cooperation on these issues between the two states.[53] Ireland also lodged a request for provisional measures under the UNCLOS. In the absence of an arbitral tribunal yet to be constituted, the competency to decide on the request for provisional measures was conferred to the ITLOS. The UK again contested jurisdiction under the UNCLOS as the subject matter in their view interfered with the OSPAR Convention and EU law. The latter made it fall within the competence of the EU institutions, notably the jurisdiction of the ECJ.[54] In 2001, the ITLOS held that the dispute under the UNCLOS covers aspects other than in the OSPAR Convention and the EU legal order. Even if these two legal regimes contain rights or obligations similar to those under the UNCLOS, they have a 'separate existence'.[55] Consequently, the ITLOS confirmed that the dispute settlement mechanisms under the UNCLOS were solely relevant to the dispute at hand and confirmed its *prima face* jurisdiction in the case.[56]

Soon after the regular arbitral tribunal for this dispute was constituted pursuant to Annex VII of the UNCLOS, it had to deal with a novel procedural element. In 2003 the European Commission (EC) initiated an infringement procedure before the ECJ against Ireland for the failure to fulfil obligations under EU law and for ignoring the exclusive competence of the EU institutions in these areas. However, the arbitral tribunal built upon the reasoning of the ITLOS and confirmed its *prima facie* jurisdiction.[57] Nonetheless, it acknowledged that certain aspects of the case concern "the internal operation of a separate legal order" (*i.e.*, the EU legal order) and these questions should be decided by the ECJ.[58] Referring to mutual respect and comity between judicial institutions, the tribunal suspended the continuation of proceedings until the judgment of the ECJ.[59]

But the ECJ had a different understanding about jurisdiction in this case. In a judgment delivered in 2006 the ECJ held that it enjoys exclusive jurisdiction in disputes between member states concerning EU law even if these disputes overlap with other inter-

---

52 Ibid., para. 142. On the merits the arbitral tribunal rejected Ireland's claim explaining that obligation under Art. 9 falls within the domestic framework of state parties and is confined to inquiries by domestic natural and legal persons. (Ibid., paras. 159-182, 185.)

53 *The Mox Plant Case (Ireland v. United Kingdom)*, PCA, Case No. 2002-1, Order No. 3, 24 June 2003, para. 12.

54 *The Mox Plant Case (Ireland v. United Kingdom)*, ITLOS, No. 10, Order, 3 December 2001, paras. 39, 41.

55 Ibid., paras. 49-50.

56 Ibid. paras., 51-52. *See also* concurring separate opinions by Judge Wolfrum and Judge Treves.

57 *The Mox Plant Case (Ireland v. United Kingdom)*, PCA, Order No. 3, paras. 14, 41.

58 Ibid., paras. 24-26.

59 Ibid., para. 28 and Order No. 5, 14 November 2003.

national agreements.[60] The ECJ emphasized that an international agreement cannot affect the allocation of responsibilities defined in the EU Treaties and, consequently, the autonomy of the EU legal system.[61] According to the ECJ, the system for the resolution of disputes under the EU legal framework must in principle take precedence over those under other international agreements.[62] By asserting exclusive jurisdiction in cases touching upon EU law, the ECJ elevated itself above other international courts and tribunals. Commentators described the court's move in the MOX Plant case as a significant enlargement of its statutory judicial monopoly,[63] an extension of its constitutional monopoly on inter-state dispute resolution,[64] and as a "maximum extension of its exclusive jurisdiction".[65]

The jurisdictional rivalry between arbitral tribunals and the ECJ continued in the investment arbitration case of *Achmea (initially Eureko) v. Slovakia* under the applicable Dutch-Czechoslovak bilateral investment treaty (BIT). After the arbitral tribunal was constituted pursuant to UNCITRAL Arbitration Rules and chose Frankfurt as the seat of arbitration, Slovakia raised an objection that investment issues under the BIT overlap with EU law and that the arbitral tribunal had no jurisdiction in the case.[66] The arbitral tribunal made a comparison between rights granted to investors under EU law and under

60 Case C-459/03, *Commission v. Ireland*, ECJ, Grand Chamber, Judgment, 30 May 2006, paras. 121-123, 132, 154.

61 Ibid., para. 123. The above arguments were not new, but a restatement of the ones expressed in the court's opinions No. 1/91, 14 December 1991, para. 35 and No. 1/00, 18 April 2002, paras. 11-12, 21, 26. They were subsequently repeated in opinions No. 1/09, 8 March 2011, paras. 76, 89 and No. 2/13, 18 December 2014, paras. 183-184, 201, 205. Similarly determined was the ECJ with regard to other international regimes, such as the UN sanctions system or the WTO. (*See Kadi, Al Barakaat International Foundation v. Council, Commission, and UK*, ECJ, Grand Chamber, Joined Cases C-402/05 P and C-415/05 P, Judgment, 3 September 2008 and *Léon Van Parys NV v Belgisch Interventie- en Restitutiebureau (BIRB)*, ECJ, Grand Chamber, Case- C-377/02, Judgment, 1 March 2005, F. Casolari, 'The Acknowledgment of the Direct Effect of the EU International Agreements', *in* Rossi & Casolari, *The Principle of Equality in EU Law*, pp. 96-99; and C. Tietje, 'The Status of International Law in the European Legal Order: The Case of International Treaties and Non-binding International Instruments, pp. 60-61 and N. Lavranos, 'UN Sanctions and Judicial Review', pp. 185-204, both *in* Wouters *et al.*, *The Europeanisation of International Law*.)

62 *Commission v. Ireland*, paras. 123-125, 132.

63 Romano, 'Commission of the European Communities v. Ireland', p. 176.

64 Eicher, 'International Forum Shopping', pp. 391-392.

65 Lavranos, 'Protecting Its Exclusive Jurisdiction', p. 490.

66 *See Eureko B.V. v. The Slovak Republic*, PCA, Case No. 2008-13, Award on Jurisdiction, Arbitrability and Suspension, 26 October 2010. Although the arbitral tribunal was constituted under the international agreement and was competent to decide primarily on the basis of international law, the tribunal surprisingly considered itself not as an international, but a German arbitral tribunal. This qualification is somewhat contradictory since the tribunal referred to the BIT and international law, including the applicable EU law, as its relevant legal framework. (*See* ibid., paras. 224, 228.) Furthermore, arbitral tribunals under BITs are ordinarily considered as international tribunals. (S.P. Subedi, 'International Investment Law', *in* M. Evans (Ed.), *International Law*, OUP, Oxford, 2014, pp. 745-746.) By describing itself as a German tribunal (*i.e.*, the court of an EU member state) the arbitral tribunal presumably tried to downplay the potential jurisdictional conflict with the ECJ. Nonetheless, this qualification opened the way for regular German courts to seek a preliminary ruling of the ECJ concerning this case.)

the BIT. Although it identified a certain overlap, the tribunal held that the two regimes were not identical, as the scope of protection for investors was wider under the BIT.[67]

Replying to Slovakia's jurisdictional objection, the arbitral tribunal stated that while the ECJ had a monopoly on the final and authoritative interpretation of EU law, it did not have an 'interpretive monopoly' over EU law in general.[68] The tribunal acknowledged that the body of EU law may be applicable under the BIT. However, it emphasized that its own jurisdiction was confined merely to ruling on breaches of the BIT.[69] At the merits stage, the arbitral tribunal reaffirmed that its arbitral award did not refer to EU law and had no bearing on any issue of EU law.[70] From this argumentation it follows that the arbitral tribunal chose to follow a technique similar to the solution in the rivalry over the 'effective control' standard between the ICTY and the ICJ: the identical subject matter can be interpreted in distinct legal regimes within a normative framework proper of these regimes.

Nonetheless, after the case reached the ECJ through the request for a preliminary ruling by the German Federal Court,[71] the ECJ showed little understanding for the 'distinct but equally applicable regimes' approach envisaged by the arbitral tribunal. The ECJ repeated arguments from its previous case law that the interaction with another international court or tribunal must not affect the allocation of powers laid down in the EU treaties and, consequently, the autonomy of the EU legal system.[72] The arbitral tribunal may be called under the BIT to interpret fundamental provisions of EU law, including freedom of establishment and free movement of capital.[73] Furthermore, the arbitral tribunal is constituted under the international agreement and does not make part of the judicial system of the EU.[74] Consequently, disputes between an investor and a member state could be resolved in a manner that would jeopardize the full effectiveness of EU law.[75] The ECJ came to a conclusion that the judicial architecture under EU law precludes the existence of international investment legal regimes between EU member states.[76]

The Achmea judgment sent a shockwave through the international investment law community as it put under question the validity of 196 BITs that EU member states have concluded among themselves (so called intra-EU BITs). Additionally, the judgment instilled uncertainty about those BITs that EU member states have concluded with third

67 *See Eureko v. The Slovak Republic*, paras. 247-262.
68 Ibid., paras. 282-283.
69 Ibid., paras., 289-292.
70 *Achmea B.V. v. The Slovak Republic*, PCA, Case No. 2008-13, Final Award, 7 December 2012, paras. 275-276.
71 By virtue of TFEU Art. 267.
72 Case C-284/16, *Slowakische Republik v. Achmea B.V.*, Grand Chamber, 6 March 2018, para. 17. The ECJ here refers to Art. 344 of TFEU.
73 Ibid., para. 42.
74 Ibid., paras. 48, 58.
75 Ibid., para. 56.
76 Ibid., ruling.

countries (so called extra-EU BITs).[77] It seems that with the Achmea judgment the ECJ implicitly supported the EC's proposal for the creation of a European investment court that would be part of the EU architecture with the function to adjudicate on investment matters.[78] Even more importantly, the ECJ acted as a judicial hegemon in not allowing even the slightest possibility of incursion into EU law. In investment disputes among EU members, the ECJ is the exclusive and ultimate judicial authority to decide on questions of EU law.[79] Nonetheless, not all arbitral tribunals accepted the higher authority of the ECJ in international litigation and the judicial rivalry remains far from settled.[80]

Overall, in matters that fall under the competence of EU institutions and law, the ECJ exhibited a categorical stance. In the *Mox Plant* case, the ECJ stated that it has exclusive jurisdiction to deal with the protection of marine environment, which is regulated by the EU legal order. Similar was its reaction in the *Achmea* case that dealt with investment law that overlaps with EU law. The ECJ acted in this way to uphold its own 'constitutional order'.[81] Through these two cases the ECJ positioned itself as the only organ with the judicial power to consider disputes touching upon questions of EU law, and barred other international courts and tribunals from exercising any jurisdiction in these areas.[82]

10.4 Judicial Tension in the Context of the Judicial Dialogue on the Protection of Human Rights

The international protection of human rights represents one of the main features of global constitutionalism. Human rights agenda is at the forefront of many international courts and tribunals. The lead in the protection of human rights belongs to specialized

---

77 J.I. Blanck, 'Slovak Republic v. Achmea BV: The Death Knell for Intra-EU BITs?' 22 *ASIL Insights* 2018, 19 June 2018, www.asil.org/insights/volume/22/issue/8/slovak-republic-v-achmea-bv-death-knell-intra-eu-bits. *See also* J.H. Pohl, 'Intra-EU Investment Arbitration after the *Achmea* Case: Legal Autonomy Bounded by Mutual Trust?', 14 *European Constitutional Law Review* 2018, pp. 767-791.

78 *See* G. Nardell & R. Power, '*Slovak Republic v Achmea:* See you in Court', *20 Essex Street*, March 2018, https://www.20essexst.com/sites/default/files/Achmea%20judgement_Report_GN.pdf and A. Dimopoulos, 'Achmea: The Principle of Autonomy and Its Implications for Intra and Extra-EU BITs', EJIL: *Talk!*, 27 March 2018, www.ejiltalk.org/achmea-the-principle-of-autonomy-and-its-implications-for-intra-and-extra-eu-bits/

79 *Cf.* J. Lee, 'The Empire Strikes Back: Case Note on the CJEU Decision in *Slovak Republic v. Achmea B.V.*, March 6, 2018', 11 *Contemporary Asia Arbitration Journal* 2018, p. 145.

80 In the context of the Energy Charter Treaty litigation *see Vattenfall AB and Others v. Federal Republic of Germany*, ICSID, Case No. ARB/12/12, Decision, 31 August 2018, in particular paras. 169-232. *See also* K. Schwedt & H. Ingwersen, 'Intra-EU ECT Claims Post-Achmea: Vattenfall Decision Paves the Way', *Kluwer Arbitration Blog*, 13 December 2018, http://arbitrationblog.kluwerarbitration.com/2018/12/13/intra-eu-ect-claims-post-achmea-vattenfall-decision-paves-the-way/.

81 *Cf.* Bianchi, *International Law Theories*, p. 59.

82 The attitude of the ECJ to safeguard the distinct nature of EU law – despite its proclaimed 'friendliness' towards international law – is surveyed in more detail in J. Klabbers, '*Völkerrechtsfreundlich?* International Law and the Union Legal Order', *in* P. Koutrakos (Ed.), *European Foreign Policy: Legal and Political Perspectives*, Edward Elgar, Cheltenham, 2011, pp. 95-114.

international adjudicatory bodies, such as the ECtHR in the European context.[83] Additionally, human rights have become increasingly important in the context of EU law, including before the ECJ. A traditional follower of the ECtHR's jurisprudence, the ECJ has started to assert more independence concerning human rights protection in the EU legal framework, especially after the adoption of the *EU Charter of Fundamental Rights* in 2000. On the other hand, the ECtHR is reluctant to leave the ECJ unchecked when it comes to interpretation and application of human rights. Consequently, the two international courts developed a *modus vivendi* in which the ECtHR retains for itself a final say on the protection of human rights in the European context. In this way, the ECHR exercises a degree of control that can be labeled 'light hegemony'. Although the ECJ recognizes seniority to the ECtHR in the field of the protection of human rights,[84] it is less and less willing to tolerate its interference with EU law.[85] Instead of making references to the *corpus juris* under the ECHR, the ECJ is increasingly using the *EU Charter of Fundamental Rights* as the main legal source for human rights, which some commentators labeled as *Charter centrism*.[86]

The first model of hegemonic contestation and control by the ECtHR over the protection of human rights in the EU framework is the doctrine of equivalent protection.[87] According to it, the ECtHR recognizes the existence of an adequate level of human rights protection in the EU context, while retaining the prerogative to scrutinize it if needed.[88]

83 Other prominent international adjudicatory bodies are the Inter-American Court of Human Rights, the African Court on Human and Peoples' Rights and the UN Human Rights Committee.

84 *Cf.* K. Lenaerts, 'The ECHR and CJEU: Creating Synergies in the Field of Fundamental Rights Protection', Solemn hearing for the opening of the Judicial Year, European Court of Human Rights, 26 January 2018, p. 9, www.echr.coe.int/Documents/Speech_20180126_Lenaerts_JY_ENG.pdf.

85 *See* F. Fabbrini & J. Larik, 'The Past, Present and Future of the Relation between the European Court of Justice and the European Court of Human Rights', 35 *Yearbook of European Law* 2016, pp. 1-35 and G. de Búrca, 'After the EU Charter of Fundamental Rights: The Court of Justice as a Human Rights Adjudicator?', 20 *Maastricht Journal of European and Comparative Law* 2013, pp. 168-184.

86 L.R. Glas & J. Krommendijsk, 'From *Opinon 2/13* to *Avotiņš*: Recent Developments in the Relationship between the Luxembourg and Strasbourg Court', 17 *Human Rights Law Review* 2017, pp. 572-576.

87 For the interaction between the two courts, *see* Glas & Krommendijsk, 'From *Opinon 2/13* to *Avotiņš*', pp. 567-587 and J. Callewaert, '"Unionisation" and "Conventionisation" of Fundamental Rights in Europe: The Interplay between Union and Convention Law and its Impact on the Domestic Legal Systems of the Member States', *in* Wouters *et al.*, *The Europeanisation of International Law*, pp. 109-135.

88 It seems that the ECtHR took inspiration for this doctrine from the 'Solange' jurisprudence of the German Constitutional Court. For more on this influence *see* D.H. Sheuing, 'The Approach to European Law in German Jurisprudence', 5 *German Law Journal* 2004, pp. 707-710 and M. Rosenfeld, 'Rethinking Constitutional Ordering in an Era of Legal and Ideological Pluralism', 6 *International Journal of Constitutional Law* 2008, p. 419.

The equivalent protection doctrine crystallized through the adjudication of the Bosphorus case,[89] which at first came before the ECJ and later before the ECtHR.[90]

The airline charter company Bosphorus Airways leased two aircraft from the former Yugoslav airline company JAT, which remained a national carrier of the newly established FRY (Serbia and Montenegro). At the time (mid 90s), the UN put in place sanctions against the FRY with an aim to dissuade it from violating the integrity and security of Bosnia and Herzegovina. The EU incorporated these obligations in EU regulation No. 990/93. Bosphorus Airways sent one aircraft to Ireland for maintenance works. However, after repairs the Irish Ministry for transport decided that the airplane fell under the sanctions regime and halted its return to Turkey. In the litigation controversy that followed, Bosphorus Airways claimed that Irish authorities violated its right to property. In a decision pursuant to the preliminary ruling procedure, the ECJ ruled that the impoundment of the aircraft in question was neither inappropriate nor disproportionate.[91] Consequently, the general aims pursued by the sanctions regime prevailed over the rights of Bosphorus Airways.[92]

Subsequently, Bosphorus Airways brought a case against Ireland before the ECtHR for the violation of the right to property. The ECtHR found itself confronted with the delicate task of assessing compatibility between obligations of states (Ireland) under EU law and under ECHR. To respond to this challenge, the ECtHR constructed the equivalent protection doctrine, which presupposes that the ECtHR shall not scrutinize the legal regime of another international organization (in this case the EU and the ECJ as its judicial authority), subject to certain conditions.[93] The first condition is that interference into human rights by states in this international legal framework does not originate from their discretion, but amounts to compliance with obligations stemming from that legal regime (EU law).[94] The second condition is that the relevant system for the protection of human rights is comparable to the one under the ECHR. This means that the legal regime must afford the protection of substantive rights similar to the catalogue of ECHR as well

89 Even before the Bosphorus precedent, the ECtHR evaluated compatibility of primary EU law with human rights obligations in the case *Matthews v. the UK*, Grand Chamber, 18 February 1999.

90 For the doctrinal analysis of the Bosphorus case, *see* S. Douglas-Scott, 'Bosphorus Hava Yollari Turizm Ve Ticaret Anonim Sirketi v. Ireland', 43 *Common Market Law Review* 2006, pp. 243-254, C. Costello, 'The *Bosphorus* Ruling of the European Court of Human Rights: Fundamental Rights and Blurred Boundaries in Europe', 6 *Human Rights Law Review* 2006, pp. 87-130 and S. Peers, 'Bosphorus: European Court of Human Rights', 2 *European Constitutional Court Review* 2006, pp. 443-455.

91 Case C-84/95, *Bosphorus Hava Yollari Turizm v. Minister for Transport, Energy and Communications, Ireland and the Attorney General*, 30 July 1996, para. 26. It has to be added that the ECJ did not make a thorough consideration of this case from the perspective of human rights. However, in his opinion Advocate General Jacobs did make an extensive survey of applicable human rights standards. (*See Opinion of Advocate General Jacobs*, Case C-84/95, 30 April 1996. paras. 49-69.)

92 *See Opinion of Advocate General Jacobs*, paras. 62-67.

93 *See* Callewaert, '"Unionisation" and "Conventionisation" of Fundamental Rights in Europe', pp. 120-123.

94 *Bosphorus v. Ireland*, Grand Chamber, 30 June 2005, para. 148.

as a procedural machinery to ensure observance of these rights for individuals in practice.[95] A positive answer to these two conditions sets up a presumption that a state has not departed from its requirements under ECHR while implementing obligations of another international legal regime.[96] But this presumption can be lifted if the circumstances of a particular case demonstrate that the protection of ECHR rights was manifestly deficient. In such a case, the ECHR's role of a 'constitutional instrument of European public order' in the field of human rights would outweigh the interest of international cooperation.[97] Consequently, the ECtHR would be free to enter into a full consideration of the case.

However, when the ECtHR applied this doctrine to the circumstances of the Bosphorus case, it found that the interference originating from EU law left no discretion to state authorities, and that the protection of rights under the EU law was equivalent to the system under the ECHR. Furthermore, there was nothing to point to the fact that the protection of rights of the applicant in this case was manifestly deficient. Therefore, the ECtHR found no violation of ECHR.[98]

The second example of hegemonic contestation is interpretation by the ECtHR of the mutual trust principle. The ECJ considers it one of the fundamental principles of EU law and a device that instigates further integration in various areas of EU, including in the Area of Freedom, Security and Justice that covers asylum matters.[99] In the asylum case *M.S.S. v. Belgium and Greece*, the ECtHR provided a reading of the Dublin Regulation on the European asylum system that differs from the one until then established in the EU. According to the ECtHR, human rights obligations stemming from the ECHR require state parties to evaluate an asylum seeker's transfer under the Dublin procedure from one EU member state to another for compliance with human rights. Such a transfer is not automatic in the sense of mutual trust about adequate protection of human rights in EU countries. The Dublin procedure allows for a certain degree of discretion by EU member states when deciding about such transfers.[100] Therefore, states are obliged to take into account the human rights situation in the country of destination and make an individualized risk assessment concerning the asylum seeker. Since in the concrete case the asylum

95 Ibid., paras. 155, 159-160, 163.
96 Ibid., para. 156.
97 Id.
98 Ibid, paras. 164-167. For another important example of the equivalent protection doctrine, *see Michaud v. France*, Fifth Section, 6 December 2012.
99 *See* K. Lenaerts, 'The Principle of Mutual Recognition in the Area of Freedom, Security and Justice', The Fourth Annual Sir Jeremy Lever Lecture, All Souls College, University of Oxford, 30 January 2015, www.law.ox.ac.uk/sites/files/oxlaw/the_principle_of_mutual_recognition_in_the_area_of_freedom_judge_lenaerts.pdf.
100 *M.S.S. v. Belgium*, Grand Chamber, 21 January 2011, paras. 338-340.

system in Greece suffered systemic deficiencies that would affect human rights of the individual, the transfer was contrary to the ECHR.[101]

The ECJ tried to steer a middle course in the case *N.S. and Others* through relaxing the mutual trust principle. The ECJ reasoned that member states are under an obligation to take into account the situation of human rights in the country of transfer destination when they are aware of systemic deficiencies in the asylum procedure and in the reception conditions of asylum seekers that would put an individual under a real risk of being subjected to inhuman or degrading treatment.[102] However, that line of reasoning was focused more on the assessment of systemic deficiencies than on the individualized consideration of human rights.[103] The ECJ's approach did not satisfy the ECtHR. In a subsequent case *Tarakhel v. Switzerland*, the ECtHR made it clear that the transfer procedure under the Dublin asylum regime must include an individualized assessment whether a particular person would be subjected to treatment that would violate human rights in the context of the applicant's specific situation.[104]

If the ECJ has been somewhat stoic about light but persistent interferences by ECtHR's in various aspects of EU law, it gave a blunt statement about its competences in the opinion in which it forthrightly rejected a possible accession of the EU to the ECHR.[105] More than a rejection of the accession itself – which still remains a hypothetical possibility – the opinion is interesting for ECJ's red lines attempted to bar ECtHR's intrusions into the sphere of EU law. Two points are particularly interesting. First, the ECJ projected its stance about the autonomy of EU law also towards the ECtHR. The ECJ emphasized that an international agreement must not affect the powers of the ECJ since this might have adverse effects on the autonomy of the EU legal order.[106] Under EU treaties, the ECJ exercises control over primary and secondary EU law and if these powers are given to an external court such as the ECtHR, that would disrupt ECJ's exclusive jurisdiction over the definitive interpretation of EU law.[107]

Second, the ECJ defined mutual trust as the constitutional principle of EU law.[108] It stated that the principle of mutual trust between member states is of fundamental importance in EU law as it allows for the creating and maintaining of an area without

101 *See* ibid., paras. 344-368. As this decision is part of the discretionary assessment, it does not fall under the Bosphorus doctrine.

102 Cases C-411/10 and C-493/10, *N.S. and Others*, Grand Chamber, 21 December 2011, para. 2 of the ruling.

103 *See* ibid., paras. 83, 86, 100-106.

104 *See Tarakhel v. Switzerland*, Grand Chamber, 14 November 2014, paras. 104-105, 116-122. *Cf. also* T. Lock, 'The Future of the European Union's Accession to the European Convention on Human Rights after Opinion 2/13: Is It Still Possible and Is It Still Desirable?', 11 *European Constitutional Law Review* 2015, pp. 259-260 and P. Eeckhout, 'Opinion 2/13 on EU Accession to the ECHR and Judicial Dialogue: Autonomy or Autarky', 38 *Fordham International Law Journal* 2015, pp. 968-969.

105 *See Opinion 2/13 of the Court*, Full Court, 18 December 2014.

106 Ibid., para. 183.

107 Ibid., paras. 183-185, 244-246.

108 Lock, 'The Future of the European Union's Accession to the European Convention on Human Rights after Opinion 2/13', p. 258 and Glas & Krommendijsk, 'From *Opinon 2/13* to *Avotiņš*', p. 573.

international borders. That principle presupposes that when implementing EU law, member states may be required to presume that fundamental rights have been observed by other member states.[109] However, should the EU become a party to the ECHR, it would assume a role identical to that of a state party. Consequently, the EU law would lose its intrinsic nature and the ECtHR's control of EU legal relations, including an obligation of mutual trust between member states, would upset the underlying balance of the EU and undermine the autonomy of EU law.[110] Overall, the ECJ was clear that it was not ready to pass over the scrutiny of the EU constitutional order to the ECtHR.[111] Instead, the ECJ confirmed "its own position as the ultimate and, at least formally, unfettered authority on all EU law matters. It insists on having the last word."[112]

Nonetheless, the rhetorical pushback by the ECJ did not impress the ECtHR. The then President of the ECtHR, Dean Spielman, commented that the ECJ's opinion on non-accession to the ECHR may deprive some citizens of the right to have acts of the EU subjected to some external control as regards respect for human rights. Therefore, the burden of protecting citizens from the negative effects of such a situation remains to be on the ECtHR.[113]

Soon thereafter the ECtHR confirmed this stance in the *Avotiņš case.*[114] In it the Latvian applicant contested the validity of civil proceedings before Cypriot courts, as he had not been informed about them. Notwithstanding, the Cypriot debtor initiated a procedure for the execution of a Cypriot judgment in Latvia on the basis of the EU Regulation No. 1215/2012 (Brussels I *bis*) to collect his loan. Before Latvian courts and ultimately before the ECtHR, the applicant claimed that the recognition and execution of the Cypriot judgment in Latvia pursuant to the mentioned regulation would violate his rights of defense within Article 6 of ECHR.[115]

The ECtHR invoked the Bosphorus doctrine. In this case, there was no preliminary ruling of the ECJ as the applicant did not request it. But the ECtHR did not find that problematic under the equivalent protection doctrine.[116] The ECtHR went on to assess the seemingly automatic application of the EU regulation by the Latvian judicial system and estimated that it could 'in theory' lead to the unfairness in proceedings. Therefore,

109 *Opinion 2/13 of the Court*, paras. 191-192.

110 Ibid., paras. 193-194.

111 D. Halberstam, '"It's the Autonomy Stupid!" A Modest Defense of *Opinion 2/13* on EU Accession to the ECHR, and the Way Forward', 16 *German Law Journal* 2015, pp. 107-108.

112 Eeckhout, 'Opinion 2/13 on EU Accession to the ECHR and Judicial Dialogue', p. 989.

113 D. Spielmann, 'Preface', *in* ECtHR, *Annual Report 2014*, Registry of the European Court of Human Rights, Strasbourg, 2015, p. 6.

114 At the conceptual level, this case deals with the interaction between the Bosphorus doctrine and the EU principle of mutual trust. For an analysis, *see* P. Gragl, 'An Olive Branch from Strasbourg? Interpreting the European Court of Human Rights' Resurrection of *Bosphorus* and Reaction to *Opinion 2/13* in the *Avotiņš* Case', 13 *European Constitutional Law Review* 2017, pp. 551-567.

115 *Avotiņš v. Latvia*, Grand Chamber, 23 May 2016, paras. 13-35, 73-78.

116 Ibid., paras. 105-112.

the ECtHR lifted the presumption of 'equivalent protection' and opened the way for a more substantive consideration of the impact of the regulation on the right to defense.[117] However, in the end the decisive factor was that the applicant had had a realistic possibility to appeal the disputed judgment in Cyprus at the time but had failed to do so. Due to negligence on the applicant's part, the ECtHR found there was no violation of Article 6.[118]

The set of judgments in cases of Bosphorus, M.S.S. and Avotiņš demonstrate that the ECtHR does not shy away from exercising control whether application of EU obligations by states is compatible with their obligations under ECHR. However, this is not a straightforward judicial interference. The ECtHR imposes limitations on the ECJ when it comes to the interpretation of human rights on the basis of its case law. The ECtHR reserves for itself the final word on the question of the protection of human rights in Europe and acts as a light hegemon with regard to the EU legal framework.[119]

In the course of years, the ECHR has served as an inspiration for the EU and its organs, including the ECJ, on the standards of human rights protection. But it is becoming evident that the ECJ is getting increasingly reluctant to play the role of a junior judicial partner in the domain of human rights. In its Opinion 2/13, the ECJ sent a clear message that it would like to have the final say with regard to the EU legal order.[120] It is worth noting that while the Bosphorus case was decided before the ECJ's opinion, the judgment in the Avotiņš case came afterwards. The reasoning in the latter case, however, also sent a clear message that the ECtHR sees itself as the prime judicial organ for the protection of human rights in Europe.[121] It leaves no doubt that, if needed, the ECtHR will continue to exercise its control over implications of EU law on the legal space of ECHR and, implicitly, over the ECJ. Although judges of both courts tend to speak softly about the rivalry between them, it seems likely that judicial 'battles for meaning' on the substance of human rights in Europe will be continued.[122]

117 Ibid., paras. 117-121.

118 Ibid., paras. 122-127 and G. Biagioni, '*Avotinš v. Latvia.* The Uneasy Balance Between Mutual Recongition of Judgments and Protection of Fundamental Rights', 1 *European Papers* 2016, p. 585.

119 *Cf.* Biagioni, '*Avotinš v. Latvia*', pp. 593, 595-596.

120 For an in-depth overview of this opinion, *see* a special section in 16 *German Law Journal* 2015, Eeckhout, 'Opinion 2/13 on EU Accession to the ECHR and Judicial Dialogue', pp. 955-992 and I. Daukšienė & S. Grigons, 'Accession of the EU to the ECHR: Issues of the Co-respondent Mechanism', 1 *International Comparative Jurisprudence* 2015, pp. 98-105.

121 *Cf.* Glas & Krommendijsk, 'From *Opinon 2/13* to *Avotiņš*', p. 586.

122 *See* S. O'Leary, 'A Tale of Two Cities: Fundamental Rights Protection in Strasbourg and Luxembourg', 20 *Cambridge Yearbook of European Legal Studies* 2018, pp. 3-31, Lenaerts, 'The ECHR and the CJEU' and Gragl, 'An Olive Branch from Strasbourg?', pp. 552, 567.

10.5 Concluding Remarks on the Coexistence of Hegemony and Constitutionalism in International Adjudication

Insights from doctrine and examples from judicial practice confirm the existence of the hegemo-constitutional dialectic in international adjudication. The hegemonic contestation dynamic situates the judicial rivalry into a broader conceptual framework. It explains that each international judicial body seeks to expand its influence in accordance with its institutional framework, functional aims and jurisdictional preferences.

Judicial practice led to hegemonic contestation in three international constitutionalist domains: concerning the issue of state responsibility, regarding the exercise of judicial power (jurisdiction) and in the domain of the protection of human rights. With regard to state responsibility, the ICTY attempted to discredit the effective control test and 'export' its overall control test to general international law. But the ICJ retorted by giving an authoritative interpretation, confining the ICTY's interpretation to the former's functional domain in international criminal law. In a series of judgments vis-à-vis ad hoc sitting international tribunals (under the OSPAR Convention, the UNCLOS and the bilateral investment agreement) the ECJ asserted exclusive jurisdiction to decide on disputes touching upon EU law. The ECJ was resolute that foreign legal regimes can have no impact whatsoever on the allocation of powers in the EU and autonomy of EU law. The picture is somewhat different with regard to the dynamic between the ECJ and the ECtHR in the field of human rights. There, the ECtHR has a reputable role for the protection of human rights in Europe, while the ECJ has followed its lead as a junior partner. Nonetheless, the ECJ was eloquent in its Opinion 2/13 that it sees itself as the highest judicial authority in the EU legal space. But the ECtHR left no doubt that the prime judicial authority for the protection of human rights in Europe is bestowed upon the Strasbourg court. Consequently the ECtHR shall continue, if necessary, to exercise control over the compatibility between the EU and ECHR legal frameworks and implicitly also over the ECJ.

The examples analyzed in the preceding text are by no means exhaustive, but they give a vivid picture of the interplay between constitutional and hegemonic features in international adjudication. The reaction of the ECJ to draw lines in the sand with regard to ad hoc sitting tribunals, as well as an attempt of the ICTY to proffer a wider acknowledgement of the overall control test, are typical examples of a hegemonic attitude. Somewhat lighter, but still reflecting the dynamic of hegemonic contestation, were moves by the ICJ, some ad hoc tribunals and the ECtHR. Looking beyond the hegemo-constitutional reality, the pressing question remains if these relationships can be regulated in a more systemic manner in the future. The expansion of international normative frameworks is usually supplemented with the tendency for their institutional enhancement.[123] These

123 G. Abi-Saab, *Cours général de droit international public*, 207 *RCADI* 1996, pp. 95-96.

developments are related to the judicial function of international constitutionalism in the sense of the judicial epistemic community. Therefore, it is logical that international adjudicatory organs enhance their interaction through mutual cooperation and coordination, mostly through the development of adequate judicial techniques and doctrines.

However, with the increase of international courts and tribunals and their corresponding expansion of judicial functions, the danger of the fragmentation of international law is likely to increase.[124] In order to avoid the multiplication of judicial conflicts, more formalized solutions will have to be developed, either in the shape of a vertical hierarchy (*e.g.*, a greater role for the ICJ or creation of a world court), as an institutionalized horizontal cooperation (*e.g.*, formal judicial dialogue between courts and tribunals) or, possibly, as a combination of both.[125] These ideas go beyond the hegemo-constitutional dialectic and should be part of a deeper reflection on the future of the international legal system.

---

124 *See* Andenas, 'Reassertion and Transformation', pp. 685-734.

125 *See* Webb, *International Judicial Integration and Fragmentation*, pp. 209-228, Pauwelyn, 'Europe, America and the "Unity" of International Law', pp. 209-213, 224-225, Cohen, *Globalization and Sovereignty*, p. 312 and L. Boisson de Chazournes, 'Plurality in the Fabric of International Courts and Tribunals: The Threads of a Managerial Approach', 28 *EJIL* 2017, pp. 14-72.

Conclusion

Conclusion

This work analyzed the relevance of hegemony and constitutionalism for the world community. It finds inspiration in the approach according to which the world system "is in the first place power structure and, only secondly, functional structure."[1] Social power shows a tendency to form two international power structures: international hegemony and international constitutionalism. The hegemonic element resides in the existence of powerful, hegemonic centers dominating the rest of the world community. On the other hand, the constitutional element resides in a set of higher norms and mechanisms instituting an egalitarian framework for all international actors.[2] The constitutional element is important as it puts a check on the power structure and secures acquiescence of smaller entities to be active in such a system.

A quick look at hegemony and constitutionalism perceives them as obvious contradictions. However, the two phenomena do not necessarily exclude each other but, on the contrary, can go well together.[3] Upon a closer analysis the relationship between hegemony and constitutionalism represents the antinomy in that they exclude and confirm each other simultaneously. Dominance, as the central element of hegemony, is in opposition to equality and solidarity, which are at the core of international constitutionalism.[4] And yet, each phenomenon contains grains of the other. International hegemony can subsist as a stable framework only if it provides some concessions to other entities. This acknowledgment of the plurality of actors and identification of common interests for the benefit of stability of an international order amounts to constitutionalism.[5] Equally, international constitutionalism allows for the flow of power within the constitutional framework, which results in leadership of some entities. These entities inevitably rise over the egalitarian structure and perform hegemony.[6]

The phenomena of hegemony and constitutionalism also permeate international law. Understandably, hegemonic international law integrates values, preferences and interests of hegemonic actors and shapes the body of international law accordingly. On the other

1 Landheer, 'Contemporary Sociological Theories in International Law', p. 81.

2 *Cf.* Simpson, *Great Powers and Outlaw States*, p. 195.

3 *Cf.* M. Huber, *Die Soziologischen Grundlagen des Völkerrechts*, W. Rotschild, Berlin-Grunewald, 1928, p. 61 and M. Koskenniemi, 'The Politics of International Law – 20 Years Later', 20 *EJIL* 2009, p. 17.

4 Simpson speaks of the dialectic between hierarchical and egalitarian models of inter-state relations. (Simpson, *Great Powers and Outlaw States*, p. 9)

5 *Cf.* Triepel, *Egemonia*, p. 207. Triepel refers to Balfour's report that was presented at the Imperial conference in 1917, according to which Great Britain and the dominions are autonomous and equal entities within the British Empire. For more on the interplay between hegemony and constitutionalism in the British Empire, *see* Pitamic, *A Treatise on the State*, pp. 106-114.

6 *Cf.* Triepel, *Egemonia*, pp. 42-43, 149, 198.

hand, international constitutional law upholds legal relations on the basis of egalitarian plurality and puts limits on the exercise of power at the international level.

Hegemonic international law can be classified in three models. The nationalist model depicts a projection of hegemonic power to the international level on the basis of the national constitutional framework (the United States, China and Russia). The three hegemons succeeded in imposing their constitutional framework in the international context and influencing the meaning of international norms to their own benefit. The rational choice model surveys the international mobilization of a hegemon (the United States and China) that weighs between its national interests and the support to the international regime and its legal framework. As long as the cost benefit calculus is in favor of the hegemon, it continues to support the functioning of the international regime. However, the Trump administration in particular, uses the approach to tilt the balance to the maximalist position of a hegemon country, downplaying interests of the international regime and relevance of international law. Finally, in the internationalist model, hegemonic actors (the United States, the European Union and Russia) project their power on the international environment. In doing so they create, interpret or apply international legal rules in line with their strategies, preferences and national interests.

International constitutional law consists of five interconnected circles: the normative, the institutional, the judicial, the coordinative and the self-referential functions. The normative function consists of higher norms of the international community, such as concepts of *jus cogens* norms, *erga omnes* obligations, non-derogable human rights and other fundamental norms enshrined in international documents. The institutional component includes institutions of international organizations that elevated above the inter-state logic of international relations to exercise constitutional tasks through organs of international institutions (*e.g.*, the UN, the WTO, the EU and the Council of Europe). The growth of judicial powers in the shape of judicial review, *erga omnes* effects of judgments and remedies visibly strengthened the functioning of the international judicial function and positioned judicial bodies beyond the traditional role of peaceful resolution of inter-state disputes. Global processes prompt national power holders to meet through transgovernmental regulatory networks and exercise the coordinative function with regard to constitutional features of global governance. Finally, the self-referential function follows the dynamic of spontaneous sources of power, which pursue their own intrinsic logic and generate autonomous sources of law of constitutional importance at the global level.

The empirical approach to the deconstruction of antinomy presupposes instances of concrete and practical accommodations of the two contradicting premises in the form of a hybrid space in between. Therefore, a substantial part of this book focused on the interaction between hegemony and constitutionalism through encounters in the international reality. Examples of accommodations between both phenomena in the hegemo-constitutional space can be identified in areas of international organizations, the use of force on humanitarian grounds and international adjudication.

In the field of international organizations there is a dichotomy between the common interests of the international community and particularistic interests of leading countries. Nonetheless, this 'dialectic of the concrete' leads to the crystallizations of new functions, mechanisms and arrangements. In the UN, the Security Council agglomerated its power and assumed the role of the global legislator. The EU developed the mechanism of enhanced cooperation that allows for a further integration on the basis of convergence between communitarian interests and interests of leading EU countries. Paralyzed by the divisions between developing and developed countries, the WTO tries to follow a similar approach by resorting to the option of plurilateral agreements that can conciliate general interests of the WTO with those of progressive member states to deepen cooperation in specific sectors of world trade.

Massive atrocities that, sadly, keep occurring in the aftermath of the Cold War prompted developments concerning the international intervention for the protection of humanity. The hegemonic military intervention of NATO in Kosovo, widely considered as 'illegal but legitimate', opened the way for the development of the doctrine of Responsibility to Protect (R2P). The R2P doctrine recalibrated the constitutional tenets of the UN Charter and made the international intervention, including the use of force, permissible for the protection of human lives. Nonetheless, after R2P had been used in Sudan, Côte d'Ivoire and Libya, it was subjected to some criticism about its (in)efficiency and a possibility of hegemonic appropriation by great powers. It is clear that the standards and mechanisms of this concept should be further developed.

Finally, in the area of international adjudication there are numerous examples of the hegemo-constitutional dialectic as a mixture between hegemonic contestation of international adjudicatory bodies and the growth of international constitutionalism. In the area of state responsibility, the ICTY and ICJ disagreed on the meaning of the test of control over armed forces abroad. The expansive development of jurisdiction led to the judicial confrontation between the ECJ and ad hoc international tribunals in which the ECJ exercised the upper hand. In the context of the judicial dialogue on the protection of human rights in Europe, the rivalry between the ECtHR and the ECJ prompted the ECtHR to safeguard its seniority as to the protection of human rights in Europe.

The importance of these concrete hegemo-constitutional examples, however, goes beyond solutions that emerged to practical challenges in the international reality. Taken together these ad hocist developments embody a new logic transcending the horizontal architecture of inter-state relations. They represent incremental steps, giving some tonality about possible directions in which the world community should develop. In this sense, international organizations should adjust their functions so as to be capable of responding to global processes in the world community. Rules and practice on the use of force for the protection of humanity should likewise transcend the inter-state logic of decision-making in the United Nations. Whenever the danger of mass atrocities exists, the world community should be able to act quickly and effectively to prevent them. Likewise, international adjudicatory bodies should develop in the direction of a hierarchical world judicial system with adequate judicial powers.[7] These should include the prerogative to put limits on the exercise of political power in the world. Multiplication and subsequent aggregation of these hegemo-constitutional manifestations reflects a process of a further development of the world community beyond the confines of the inter-state architecture.

Another insight about the restructuring of the world community comes from the general approach to the deconstruction of antinomy. According to this approach, the accommodation of antinomy is to be found in the original premise. In case of antinomy between hegemony and constitutional, the common premise is power. Given that the purpose of the dialectical movement is to instigate historical development,[8] the accommodation of the hegemo-constitutional antinomy in this sense takes the form of a new paradigm based on the rearrangement of power in the world. As the new paradigm is oriented towards the future, a reflection about the shape of the future world community is inevitably an imaginative intellectual process.[9] Several outlines of the world community are possible, some of which are presented below.[10]

Under the influence of Hegel, the French philosopher Kojève developed the concept of a universal and homogeneous state.[11] As a starting point, he takes the dialectic between a master and a slave.[12] Through the process of mutual recognition, this dynamic leads to the relationship of equality, which, in terms of the bourgeois socio-economic relations, translates into the correlation of equivalence. The principle of equivalence stands at the

7 Useful insights may also come from other areas of international law, such as from international criminal justice, peace-building efforts and others.

8 *See* Hegel, *Logic*, p. 187 and R.C. Solomon, *In the Spirit of Hegel: A Study of G.W.F. Hegel's Phenomenology of Spirit*, OUP, New York-Oxford, 1983, pp. 22-23, 270, 277.

9 Domingo, *The New Global Law*, p. xv. For legal thinking as an imaginative and autonomous process *see* Bianchi, *International Law Theories*, pp. 3-11, Zupančič, *The Owl of Minerva*, pp. 158, 392 and Koskenniemi, *From Apology to Utopia*, p. 561.

10 That this is a topical issue is evident from a number of recent works that, from various angles, touch upon the idea of the new world order. (*See* Etzioni, *From Empire to Community*, E. Aksu (Ed.), *Early Notions of Global Governance: Selected Eighteenth-Century Proposals for 'Perpetual Peace'*, University of Wales Press, Cardiff, 2008, Mazower, *Governing the World*, A. Dynkin & N. Ivanova (Eds.), *Russia in a Polycentric World*, Izdatelstvo VESMIR, Moscow, 2012, O. Rosenboim, *The Emergence of Globalism: Visions of World Order in Britain and the United States, 1939-1950*, Princeton University Press, Princeton-Oxford, 2017, O. Haathaway & S.J Shapiro, *The Internationalists: How a Radical Plan to Outlaw War Remade the World*, Simon & Schuster, New York, 2017 and Q. Slobodian, *Globalists: The End of Empire and the Birth of Neoliberalism*, Harvard University Press, Cambridge (MA), 2018.)

11 For an overall presentation of Hegel's influence on Kojève, *see* M.S. Roth, 'A Problem of Recognition: Alexandre Kojève and the End of History', 24 *History and Theory* 1985, pp. 293-306.

12 This dialectic comes from Hegel. *See* G.W.F. Hegel, *Phenomenology of Spirit*, OUP, Oxford, 1977, trans. A.V. Millner, pp. 121-122 (§ 199-200).

heart of the nature of legal relationships.[13] In terms of a legal relationship this presupposes individuals A and B who engage in a reciprocal exchange. However, there is also the third actor – a neutral and powerful C – who is charged to intervene in case the legal transaction is not executed by one of the parties.[14]

Kojève applies this logic to international law. The main problem at the international level is the absence of a powerful C.[15] The only actors there are states (and possibly international organizations) which represent A-s and B-s. Therefore, international law is not a 'real' law. Instead of being law in actuality, as are national legal systems, international law is only law in potentiality.[16] However, international law may evolve to become fully actualized if it becomes 'domestic' public law of the supranational federal state.[17] Actualization of international law thus presupposes its transformation into global law. If such a supranational entity were to comprise all human beings then it would represent the universal and homogeneous state.[18] Kojève understood the end of classic state sovereignty as a result of constitutionalization, and not *vice versa*.[19]

But even Kojève presupposes a double track development for the attainment of the universal and homogeneous state. One way is through the creation of a legal federation on the basis of consensus between member states.[20] The other way is through legal expansion of one entity to all others, which can lead to the universal empire. In this context,

13 *See* Kojève, *Esquisse d'une phenomenologie du droit*, pp. 254-266 and R. Howse & B.-F. Frost, 'Introductory Essay: The Plausibility of the Universal and Homogenous State', *in* A. Kojève, *Outline of a Phenomenology of Right*, Rowman & Littlefield Publishers, Inc., Lanham, 2007, B.-P. Frost (Ed.), trans. B.-P. Frost & R. Howse, pp. 13-15.

14 *See* Kojève, *Esquisse d'une phenomenologie du droit*, pp. 28-90, D. Auffret, *Alexandre Kojève, La philosophie, l'État, la fin de l'Histoire*, Bernard Grasset, Paris, 1990, pp. 276-277 and Howse & Frost, 'Introductory Essay', pp. 18.

15 Kojève, *Esquisse d'une phenomenologie du droit*, pp. 116-117.

16 Ibid., pp. 376-377.

17 *Cf.* ibid., p. 389.

18 Ibid., pp. 90-92, 391-392. Subsequently the philosophical debate ensued between Kojève and Leo Strauss as to possible tyrannic metamorphoses of such a state. It seems that Strauss overlooked some fundamental features of the universal and homogeneous state, such as its reliance on the principle of justice and the controlling role of the judiciary. His argument in the debate seems unpersuasive. *See* T.W. Burns & B.-P. Frost (Eds.), *Philosophy, History and Tyranny: Reexamining the Debate between Leo Strauss and Alexandre Kojève*, SUNY Press, Alabany (NY), 2016, in particular B.-P. Frost, 'Who Won the Strauss-Kojève Debate? The Case for Alexandre Kojève in His Dispute with Leo Strauss', pp. 157-195. For a contemporary analysis of tyranny in the context of the international community, *see* A. O'Donoghue, 'Tyranny and Constitutionalism beyond the State', *in* Schütze, *Globalisation and Governance*, pp. 63-101.

19 Howse & Frost, 'Introductory Essay', p. 12.

20 *Cf.* Kojève, *Esquisse d'une phenomenologie du droit*, pp. 388-389, 391.

empire means the process of legal integration extending from one center to other areas.[21] The concept of the universal and homogeneous state is premised upon an inherent antinomy between hegemony and constitutionalism. A part of this solution is a realization that power is not something outside of law, but an intrinsic part of it. The universal and homogenous state is thus

> something to be achieved, not through tyranny or empire, but through legal integration between states that results in a kind of supranational constitutional order, informed and unified by a single, definitive concept of justice.[22]

Another perspective on the world community comes from the sociologist Immanuel Wallerstein. He contends that the contemporary era of European universalism has come to an end and the world is moving into a new era with a global structure. The looming structural crisis and subsequent transition years will be full of uncertainty, instability and random violence.[23] There are two alternatives of the new world order. The first alternative, according to Wallerstein, is a multiplicity of universalisms that would resemble a network of universal universalism.[24] This is a universalism without the superiority of the West.[25] The second alternative he describes as "a new hierarchical, inegalitarian world that will claim to be based on universal values, but in which racism and sexism will continue to dominate our practices".[26] This alternative amounts to the oppressive world system.

The entity composed of 'a network of universal universalism' has liberal flavor and is more acceptable as a vision of the future world community. However, given that universalism is not only an embodiment of values, but also likewise a power structure, a network of universal universalism presupposes a network of different power structures in which different powers carry different weights. Eventually, this downplays the character of universalism.[27] A closer structural look at the option of universal universalism reveals that at

---

21 *See* ibid., pp. 90-91, 390-391. This is also a presupposition of Kojève's outline for the world's reconstruction after World War II in which he gives a leading role to the so-called 'Latin Empire'. The idea of the Latin Empire eventually transformed into the project of the European integration. *See* A. Kojève, 'Outline of a Doctrine of French Policy', 126 *Policy Review* August & September 2004, trans. E. de Vries, available at: www.hoover.org/publications/policy-review. There Kojève states the following: "To be *politically* viable, the modern State must rest on a 'vast "imperial" union of affiliated Nations.' The modern State is only truly a State if it is an Empire."

22 Howse & Frost, 'Introductory Essay', p. 3.

23 Wallerstein, *European Universalism*, p. 84, I. Wallerstein, *After Liberalism*, The New Press, New York, 1995, p. 268. and I. Wallerstein, 'Structural Crises', 62 *New Left Review* 2010, pp. 137-138. *Similarly also* T. Volgy & A. Bailin, *International Politics and State Strength*, Lynne Rienner Publishers, Boulder, 2003, p. 122.

24 Wallerstein, *European Universalism*, p. 84.

25 S. Jonnson, 'The Ideology of Universalism', 63 *New Left Review* 2010, p. 117.

26 Id.

27 *Cf.* C. El-Ojeili, 'Reflections on Wallerstein: The Modern World-System, Four Decades on', 41 *Critical Sociology* 2014, p. 693.

its core it likewise presupposes the antinomy between hegemony (power) and constitutionalism (universal values), which is accommodated within a broader institutional structure. The problem with this model is that its framework is too permeable and would necessitate a stronger institutional structure, with necessary mechanisms attached to universal values, to put the check on the exercise of power.

Several authors advance the vision of the world community in the form of a global community with the new global law. In this sense the shaping of global law is an undertaking of prospection and construction.[28] Rafael Domingo put forward the most elaborate blueprint for global law. In a historically inspired account, he detects the use of international law for hegemony and constitutionalism through time and hints at their antinomic correlation.[29] But according to Domingo the time has now come "for a law that integrates the highest values of different legal traditions while acknowledging the living synthesis and often disparate cultures."[30] The approach to global law must employ new legal instruments, concepts and rubrics to regulate new social realities in accordance with the rule of law.[31] Global law is a world legal order that governs the ambit of justice in the sense that it affects humanity as a whole.[32] In this aspect, Domingo comes close to Kojève who likewise sees justice as the main generator for the existence and development of the world community.

The main idea behind Domingo's global vision is the organization of humanity in the form of 'anthroparchy' (*i.e.*, the global human community), which places the human being at the center of its concern.[33] This is a very flexible world structure based on legitimacy rather than on mere legality. It draws legitimacy from the fact that every organized community needs a just government. Humanity has become such a supreme community because globalization has allowed it to become conscious of itself, of its mission to protect the earth and solve common world issues.[34] In institutional terms, anthroparchy is constituted through the universal organization of 'United Humanity' and a network of institutions revolving around the Global Parliament as the main governing body. The Global Tribunal controls the legality of the functioning of the Global Parliament.[35] Thus, the global human community is a system of global governance and social

---

28 Walker, *Intimations of Global Law*, p. 171.

29 *See* Domingo, *The New Global Law*, pp. 35-37, 195.

30 Domingo, *The New Global Law*, p. xv.

31 Id.

32 Ibid., p. xvii.

33 R. Domingo, 'Gaius, Vattel, and the New Global Law Paradigm', 22 *EJIL* 2011, p. 641. It is worth observing that for Domingo international law, which grew into an autonomous body of law between the sixteenth and eighteenth centuries, serves mainly as a transitory stage to the new global law. (R. Lesaffer & R. Letschert, 'The Global Challenge to Public International Law: Some First Thoughts', 17 *Tilburg Law Review* 2012, pp. 258-259.)

34 Domingo, *The New Global Law*, pp. 118-119, 123-126. On the global human community, *see* R. Domingo, 'The New Global Human Community', 12 *Chicago Journal of International Law* 2012, pp. 580-587.

35 *See* Domingo, *The New Global Law*, pp. 119, 145-147.

cooperation set up by institutions and administered by a legal authority under the rule of law.[36]

The global legal order, according to Domingo, consists of three layers: the first layer is the individual dimension focused on the protection of human rights of individuals and other areas of individual activity; the second layer of the social dimension covers social interactions between individuals and the community, largely through the process of institutionalization; finally, the third dimension generates global law through its universal dimension and treats all humanity as the totality of members of the human species.[37] The three layers are interrelated as they all essentially deal with human persons, but are qualitatively distinct.[38] Global law is premised upon several fundamental principles. It shares three fundamental principles with international law, as they are indispensable to any legal order. These are justice (acquiescence about fundamental values as a consequence of man's social nature), reasonableness (rational articulation of justice) and coercion (application of justice). To these Domingo adds principles specific to global law: universality (acceptance by all the world's inhabitants and application everywhere), solidarity (concern for others), subsidiarity (self-governance of smaller entities) and horizontality or democratization (reliance on dialogue and consensus).[39] However, Domingo acknowledges that anthroparchy is currently more utopia than reality.[40]

Such is indeed the case with all three visions of the new world order presented by Kojève, Wallerstein and Domingo – currently they portray utopian concepts of the world community. This is understandable as it is impossible to predict the future. But given the present dynamic between hegemony and constitutionalism, it is highly likely than any account of the future world community will have to integrate – and adequately accommodate – antinomy between the two phenomena in its design. Until such a novel world community arises, we shall continue to live in the hegemo-constitutional dynamic of today.

36 Domingo, 'The New Global Human Community', p. 578.

37 Domingo, *The New Global Law*, pp. 150-151.

38 Domingo, 'Gaius, Vattel, and the New Global Law Paradigm', p. 644.

39 *See* Domingo, *The New Global Law*, pp. 157-185.

40 Ibid., p. 120.

Acknowledgments

This book started as a PhD project at the Institut de hautes études internationales et du Développement (IHEID) in Geneva more than a decade ago. The conceptual framework that culminated in the PhD in 2009 is nowadays getting increasing confirmation in the contemporaneous international reality. The original PhD text was substantially edited, updated and upgraded in the revising process, also with a view to reflect these developments. The book manuscript was finalized in May 2019.

I would like to express deep thanks to Professor Andrea Bianchi, my PhD mentor, for agreeing to supervise this challenging topic at the time when hegemony and constitutionalism were still exotic words in international legal scholarship. I warmly thank him for constant support during the writing and for many useful directions along the way. My sincere thanks goes to Professor Boštjan M. Zupančič who provided many inspiring insights from the jurisprudential perspective, and kindly accepted to sit as an external expert on the PhD defense committee. I would also like to thank Professor Andrew Clapham for his valuable supervisory input as second reader and chair of the PhD defense committee, as well as to Professor Cédric Dupont for expanding my knowledge in political science and international relations, which was a precondition for bringing international law, hegemony and constitutionalism together.

My heartfelt thanks goes to my family – mother Jožica, father Velimir, brother Gašper, aunt Pina and uncle Rajko – who supported me during all ups and downs of this intellectual journey, and to my wife Živa who kept encouraging me to finish the book, giving me helpful intellectual and practical insights and bringing the funny side to this enduring process.

I cannot thank enough Ms Selma Hoedt from Eleven International Publishing for accepting this book as part of the publishing program, as well as for her unwavering encouragement throughout the writing process and kind understanding at my prolonged extensions due to other obligations.

There are many who provided intellectual, moral or logistical support during the writing of this book and I would like to thank them in person: Pavle Adam, Vida Amirmokri, Alberto Aronovitz, Danièle Avanthay, Professor Peter Cain, Federico Casolari, Frances-Galatia Lanitou Williams, Melissa George, Ambassador Aljaž Gosnar, Iztok Grmek, Michelle Healy, Mélanie Jeanroy, Igor Jukič, Špela Lajmiš, Alejandro Lorite Escorihuela, Alenka Markov, Peter Pavlin, Chanu Peiris, Ivaylo and Kristina Petrov, Ana Polak Petrič, Marko Rakovec, Ignacio de la Rasilla y del Moral, Anna Riddell-Roberts, Deborah Ruiz Verduzco, Josef Skála, Georg Sommeregger, Martin Sychold, Tadej Vengušt, Jože and Nada Verginc, Professor Eric Wyler, Fuad Zarbiyev, Dušan Zidar and Jan van Zyl Smit.

The three-semester scholarship awarded by IHEID and the student loan by the Slovenian educational fund, Ad futura, were essential in enabling me to undertake research in Geneva and to finish the PhD, while being Visiting Researcher at the Department of Legal Studies at the University of Bologna (from autumn 2016 to spring 2017) helped me finalize a large portion of the book.

The topic of this book was presented in various academic fora: 'Global Public Policy Network' Student Conference, Lee Kuan Yew School of Public Policy at the National University of Singapore, 11-13 November 2009 (chaired by Ms Azul Ogazon Gomez), workshop 'Empire and International Law', University of Helsinki, 4-6 October 2011 (convened by Professors Martti Koskenniemi and Anne Orford), guest lecture in the course 'Global and Supranational Law', University of Bologna, 7 December 2016 (led by Professor Federico Casolari), workshop on 'Hegemony in the International Legal Order', University of Rome Tor Vergata and Institute 'Luigi Sturzo', 11-12 June 2018 (organized by Professor Claudio Corradetti) and guest lectures at the Faculty of Social Sciences of the University of Ljubljana (by invitation of Professors Milan Brglez, Petra Roter and Bojko Bučar). I thank all conveners for their kind invitations and participants for their useful questions, remarks and comments.

My research benefited from the kind assistance of library staff at the following libraries: IHEID, University of Geneva (Uni Mail and Uni Bastions), Bibliothèque cantonale et universitaire – Lausanne (Dorigny), Institut suisse de droit comparé (Lausanne), Institute of Advanced Legal Studies (London), European Inter-University Centre (Venice) and the Faculty of Law of the University of Ljubljana.

Last but not least, I am grateful to Dušan Zidar for a picturesque book cover, symbolizing the very idea of the book and to Chanu Peiris and the editorial department of Eleven International Publishing for undertaking a thorough and detailed editing of the book.

Naturally, the book is written in my personal capacity and the responsibility for any mistakes is my own.

Selected Bibliography

Monographs:

Abi-Saab, G., *Cours général de droit international public, in RCADI.*, vol. 207, Martinus Nijhoff Publishers, The Hague-Boston-London, 1996.

Alvarez, J. E., *International Organizations as Law-Makers*, OUP, Oxford, 2005.

Anderson, P., *The H-Word: The Peripeteia of Hegemony*, Verso, London-New York, 2017.

Anghie, A., *Imperialism, Sovereignty and the Making of International Law*, CUP, Cam bridge, 2005.

Arendt, H., *The Human Condition*, The University of Chicago Press, Chicago, 1958.

Arendt, H., *On Violence*, Allen Lane-The Penguin Press, New York-London, 1970.

Aristotle, *Metaphysics, Books I-IX*, The Loeb Classical Library, William Heinemann Ltd-Harvard University Press, London-Cambridge (MA), 1961, trans. H. Tredennick.

Aristotle, *Metaphysics*, Penguin Books, London, 2004, trans. H. Lawson-Tancred.

Aristotle, *Nicomachean Ethics*, Dover Publications Inc., Mineola (NY), 1998, trans. D.P. Chase.

Aristotle, *The Physics I, Books I-IV*, The Loeb Classical Library, William Heinemann Ltd-Harvard University Press, London-Cambridge (MA), 1962, trans. P.H. Wicksteed & F.M. Cornford.

Aristotle, *Politics*, The Loeb Classical Library, Harvard University Press, Cambridge (MA)-London, 1998, trans. H. Rackham.

Auffret, D., *Alexandre Kojève : La philosophie, l'Etat, la fin de l'Histoire*, Bernard Grasset, Paris, 1990.

Bannelier, K. *et al.* (Ed.), *L'intervention en Irak et le droit international*, CEDIN, Paris, 2004.

Bartelson, *Visions of World Community*, CUP, Cambridge, 2009.

Bellamy, A.J. & Dunne, T. (Eds.), *The Oxford Handbook of the Responsibility to Protect*, OUP, Oxford, 2016.

Benoît-Rohmer, F. & Klebes, H., *Council of Europe Law: Towards a Pan-European Legal Area*, Council of Europe Publishers, Strasbourg, 2005.

Bernhardt, R. (Ed.), *Encyclopedia of Public International Law*, Norht-Holland-Elsevier, London-Amsterdam, 1992-2003.

Bhandari, S., *Global Constitutionalism and the Path of International Law: Transformation of Law and State in the Globalized World*, Brill Nijhoff, Leiden-Boston, 2016.

Bianchi, A. *International Law Theories: An Inquiry into Different Ways of Thinking*, OUP, Oxford, 2016.

Bianchi, A. Peat, D., & Windsor, M. (Eds.), *Interpretation in International Law*, OUP, Oxford, 2015.

Bickel, A.M., *The Least Dangerous Branch: The Supreme Court at the Bar of Politics*, Yale University Press, New Haven (MA)-London, 1986.

Bingham, T., *The Rule of* Law, Penguin Books, London, 2011.

Black, H.C., *Black's Law Dictionary*, West Publishing Co., St. Paul (Minn.), 1990.

Bobbio, N., *Diritto e potere : Saggi su Kelsen*, Edizioni Scientifiche Italiane, Napoli-Roma, 1992.

Bobbitt, P., *The Shield of Achilles: War, Peace and the Course of History*, Penguin Books, London, 2002.

Bodin, J., *Les six livres de la République : livre premier*, Corpus des œuvres de philosophie en langue française, Fayard, Paris, 1986.

Böröcz, J. & Kovács, M. (Eds.), *Empire's New Clothes: Unveiling EU Enlargement*, Central Europe Review Ltd., 2001.

Bradley, C.A., *International Law in the U.S. Legal System*, OUP, Oxford, 2015.

Braillard, P. & de Senarclens, P., *L'impérialisme*, PUF, Paris, 1980.

Brownlie, I., *Principles of Public International Law*, OUP, Oxford, 2008.

Burdeau, G., *Traité de science politique, Présentation de l'univers politique: Le pouvoir politique*, Tome 1, vol. 2, L.G.D.J, Paris, 1980.

Burns, T.W. & Frost, B.-P. (Eds.), *Philosophy, History and Tyranny: Reexamining the Debate between Leo Strauss and Alexandre Kojève*, SUNY Press, Alabany (NY), 2016.

Butler, J., Laclau, E. & Žižek, S., *Contingency, Hegemony, Universality: Contemporary Dialogues on the Left*, Verso, London-New York (NY), 2000.

Byers, M., *Custom, Power and the Power of Rules: International Relations and Customary International Law*, CUP, Cambridge, 1999.

Byers, M. (Ed.), *The Role of Law in International Politics – Essays in International Relations and International Law*, OUP, Oxford-New York, 2000.

Byers, M. & Nolte, G. (Eds.), *United States Hegemony and the Foundations of International Law*, CUP, Cambridge, 2003.

Cass, D.Z., *The Constitutionalization of the World Trade Organization: Legitimacy, Democracy, and Community in the International Trading System*, OUP, Oxford-New York, 2005.

Chemain, R. & Pellet, A. (Eds.), *La Charte des Nations Unies, constitution mondiale ?*, Editions Pedone, Paris, 2006.

Cini, M. (Ed.), *European Union Politics*, OUP, Oxford, 2007.

Clapham, A., *Human Rights: A Very Short Introduction*, OUP, Oxford, 2007.

Clark, I., *Hegemony in International Society*, OUP, Oxford, 2011.

Clark, I., *Legitimacy in International Society*, OUP, Oxford, 2007.

Cohen B.J., *The Question of Imperialism – The Political Economy of Dominance and Dependence*, Basic Books, Inc., Publishers, New York.

Cohen, J.L, *Globalization and Sovereignty: Rethinking Legality, Legitimacy and Constitutionalism*, CUP, Cambridge, 2012.

Coicaud, J.-M. & Heiskanen, V. (Eds.), *The Legitimacy of International Organizations*, United Nations University Press, Tokyo-New York-Paris, 2001.

Conklin, W.E., *Hegel's Laws: The Legitimacy of a Modern Legal Order*, Stanford University Press, Stanford, 2008.

Cooper, R., *The Breaking of Nations: Order and Chaos in the Twenty-first Century*, Atlantic Monthly Press, New York, 2003.

Cooper, R., *The-Post Modern State and the World Order*, Demos-The Foreign Policy Centre, London, 2000.

Cooper, R.H. & Voïnov Kohler, J. (Eds.), *Responsibility to Protect: The Global Moral Compact for the 21st Century*, Palgrave Macmillan, Basingstoke-New York, 2009.

Cot, J.-P. & Pellet, A. (Eds.), *La Charte des Nations Unies : Commentaire article par article*, Economica, Paris, 1991.

Cot, J.-P., Pellet, A. & Forteau, M. (Eds.), *La Charte des Nations Unies*, Economica, Paris, 2005.

Craig, P. & de Búrca, G., *EU Law: Text, Cases, and Materials*, OUP, Oxford, 1998.

Craig, P. & de Búrca G. (Eds.), *The Evolution of EU Law*, OUP, Oxford, 1999.

Crawford, J., *State Responsibility: The General Part*, CUP, Cambridge, 2013.

Cronin, B., *Institutions for the Common Good: International Protection Regimes in International Society*, CUP, Cambridge, 2003.

Curtin, P.D. (Ed.), *Imperialism*, MacMillan, London-Basingstoke, 1972.

Dailler, P. & Pellet, A., *Droit International Public*, L.G.D.J., Paris, 1999.

De Búrca, G., *The EU Constitution: in Search of Europe's Identity*, Europa Law Publishing, Groningen, 2005.

De Jouvenel, B., *Du pouvoir: histoire naturelle de sa croissance*, Les éditions du cheval ailé, Genève, 1945.

De Senarclens, P., *Critique de la mondialisation*, Presses de Sciences Po, Paris, 2003.

De Visscher, C., *Theory and Reality in Public International Law*, Princeton University Press, Princeton (NJ), 1957, trans. P.E. Corbett.

Delević Đilas, M. & Đerić, V. (Eds.), *O međunarodnom I narodnom – eseji u čast Vojina Dimitrijevića/The International and the National – Essays in Honour of Vojin Dimitrijević*, Beogradski centar za ljudska prava, Beograd, 2003.

Diez, T. (Ed.), *A Different Kind of Power? The EU's Role in International Politics*, IDEBATE Press, New York, London & Amsterdam, 2014.

Dinan, D., *Ever Closer Union: An Introduction to European Integration*, Palgrave-MacMillan, Houndmills, 2005.

Disch, L.J., *Hannah Arendt and the Limits of Philosophy*, Cornell University Press, Ithaca-London, 1996.

Dobner, P. & Loughlin, M. (Eds.), *The Twilight of Constitutionalism?*, OUP, Oxford, 2010.
Domingo, *The New Global Law*, CUP, Cambridge, 2011.
Dominicé, C., *L'ordre juridique international entre tradition et innovation: Recueil d'études*, PUF, Paris, 1997.
Doyle, M.W., *Empires*, Cornell University Press, Ithaca-London, 1986.
Drolet, J.F., *American Neoconservatism: The Politics and Culture of A Reactionary Idealism*, Hurst & Company, London, 2011.
Duke, S., *Europe as a Stronger Global Actor: Challenges and Strategic Responses*, Palgrave Macmillan, London, 2017.
Dunoff, J.L. & Trachtman, J.P. (Eds.), *Ruling the World? Constitutionalism, International Law, and Global Governance*, CUP, Cambridge, 2009.
Dupuy, J.-P., *Pour un catastrophisme éclairé*, Editions du Seuil, Paris, 2002.
Dupuy, P.-M., *L'unité de l'ordre juridique international : Cours général de droit international public, in RCADI*, vol. 297, Martinus Nijhoff Publishers, Leiden-Boston, 2003.
Dupuy, R.-J., *La communauté internationale entre le mythe et l'histoire*, Economica-UNESCO, Paris, 1986.
Durkheim, E., *De la division du travail social*, PUF, Paris, 2004.
Duverger, M. (Ed.), *Le concept d'empire*, PUF, Paris, 1980.
Dyzenhaus, D., *Legality and Legitimacy: Carl Schmitt, Hans Kelsen and Hermann Heller in Weimar*, OUP, Oxford, 1999.
Dworkin, R., *Law's Empire*, Hart Publishing, Oxford and Portland (Oregon), 2003.
Etzioni, A., *From Empire to Community: A New Approach to International Relations*, Palgrave Macmillan, New York, 2004.
Evans, M. (Ed.), *International Law*, OUP, Oxford, 2006.
Falk, R., *Power Shift: On the New Global Order*, Zed Books, London, 2016.
Falk, R.A., Johansen, R.C. & Kim, S.S. (Eds.), *The Constitutional Foundations of World Peace*, State University of New York Press, Albany, 1993.
Fasulo, L., *An Insider's Guide to the UN*, Yale University Press, New Haven, 2015.
Fatoumata, J. & Kwa, A., *Behind the Scenes at the WTO: The Real World of International Trade Negotiations*, Zed Books, London, 2003.
Favoreu, L. *et al.*, *Droit Constitutionnel*, Editions Dalloz, Paris, 2001.
Femia, J.V., *Machiavelli Revisited*, University of Wales Press, Cardiff, 2004.
Fenby, J., *Will China Dominate the 21st Century?*, Polity, London, 2014.
Ferguson, N., *Colossus: The Rise and Fall of the American Empire*, Penguin Books, London-New York, 2005.
Ferguson, N., *Empire: The Rise and Demise of the British World Order and the Lessons for Global Power*, Basic Books, London-New York, 2002.
Fiott, D. & Koops, J. (Eds.), *The Responsibility to Protect and the Third Pillar: Legitimacy and Operationalization*, Palgrave Macmillan, Basingstoke, 2015.

Flauss, J.-F. (Ed.), *L'enseignement du droit constitutionnel*, Bruylant, Bruxelles, 2000.
Foley, M., *The Politics of the British Constitution*, Manchester University Press, Manchester-New York, 1999.
Foot, R., MacFarlane, N.S. & Mastanduno, M. (Eds.), *US Hegemony and International Organizations*, OUP, Oxford, 2003.
Forsyth, M., *Reason and Revolution: The Political Thought of the Abbé Sieyes*, Holmes & Meier Publishers Inc., New York, 1987.
Foucault, M., *Ethics: Subjectivity and Truth, Essential Works of Foucault 1954-1984*, The New Press, New York, 1997-2000.
Foucault, M., *Power/Knowledge: Selected Interviews and Other Writings 1972-1977*, Ed. C. Gordon, Harvester, London, 1980.
Fuller, L.L., *The Morality of Law*, Yale University Press, New Haven-London, 1969.
Fox, H. (Ed.), *The Changing Constitution of the United Nations*, BIICL, London, 1997.
Gauthier, R.A. & Jolif, J.Y., *L'éthique à Nicomaque – Introduction, Traduction et Commentaire*, vol. II, deuxième partie, Publications universitaires de Louvain-Publications Béatrice-Nauwelartes, Louvain-Paris, 1959.
Geiger, R. Khan, D.-E. & Kotzur, M. (Eds.), *European Union Treaties: Treaty on European Union, Treaty on the Functioning of the European Union*, C.H. Beck-Hart, 2015.
Gerth, H.H. & Wright Mills, C., *From Max Weber: Essays in Sociology*, Routledge, London, 1991.
Giddens, A., *Runaway World – How Globalisation is Reshaping our Lives*, Profile Books, London, 1999.
Gilpin, R., *War and Change in World Politics*, CUP, Cambridge, 1986.
Goldsmith, J.L. & Posner, E.A., *The Limits of International Law*, OUP, Oxford, 2005.
Goodrich, L.M., Hambro, E. & Simons, A.P., *Charter of the United Nations: Commentary and Documents*, Columbia University Press, New York-London, 1969.
Gordon, S., *Controlling the State: Constitutionalism from Ancient Athens to Today*, Harvard University Press, Cambridge (MA)-London, 1999.
Grabar (Hrabar), V.Z., *Nachalo ravensta gosudarstv' v' sovremennom' mezhdunarodnom' prave* [The Principle of the Equality of States in Contemporary International Law], Izvestiya Ministerstva Inostrannyh del' [Bulletin of the Ministry of Foreign Affairs], St. Petersburg, 1912, vol. 1.
Gramsci, A., *Cahiers de prison : Cahiers 10, 11, 12, 13*, Gallimard, Paris, 1978, R. Paris (Ed.), trans. P. Fulchignoni & N. Negri.
Gray, C., *Judicial Remedies in International Law*, OUP, Oxford, 1990.
Greenberg, K.J. & Dratel, J.L. (Eds.), *The Torture Papers: The Road to Abu Ghraib*, CUP, Cambridge, 2005.
Greene, J.P. (Ed.), *Exclusionary Empire: English Liberty Overseas, 1600-1900*, CUP, Cambridge, 2010.

Grewe, W., *The Epochs of International Law*, Walter de Gruyter, Berlin-New York, 2000, trans. & rev. M. Byers.

Grigas, A., *Beyond Crimea: The New Russian Empire*, Yale University Press, New Haven-London, 2016.

Grisoni, D. & Maggiori, R., *Lire Gramsci*, Editions Universitaires, 1973.

Halévy, E., *La formation du radicalisme philosophique*, Presses Universitaires de France, Paris, 1995.

Hall, K.L. (Ed.), *The Oxford Companion to the Supreme Court of the United States*, OUP, New York-Oxford, 1992.

Halperin, S. & Palan, R. (Eds.), *Legacies of Empire: Imperial Roots of the Contemporary Global Order*, CUP, Cambridge, 2015.

Hanhimäki, J.M., *The United Nations: A Very Short Introduction*, OUP, Oxford, 2015.

Hamilton, P. (Ed.), *MAX WEBER: Critical Assessments 2*, Routledge, London-New York, 1991.

Hanski, R. & Suksi, M. (Eds.), *An Introduction to the International Protection of Human Rights: A Textbook*, Institute for Human Rights, Åbo Akademi University, Turku-Åbo, 1998.

Hardin, R. *Liberalism, Constitutionalism, and Democracy*, OUP, Oxford, 1999.

Hardt, M. & Negri, A., *Empire*, Harvard University Press, Cambridge (MA)-London, 2000.

Harris, D. *et al.*, *Law of the European Convention on Human Rights*, OUP, Oxford, 2009.

Hart, H.L.A., *The Concept of Law*, Clarendon Press, Oxford, 1997.

Hauriou, M., *Aux sources du droit: Le pouvoir, l'ordre et la liberté*, Librairie Bloud & Gay, Paris, 1933.

Hegel, G.W.F., *The Encyclopaedia Logic (with the Zusätze)*, Hackett Publishing Company, Indianapolis-Cambridge, 1991, trans. T.F. Geraets, W.A. Suchting & H.S. Harris.

Hegel, *Hegel's Philosophy of Right*, Clarendon Press, Oxford, 1942, trans. T. M. Knox.

Hehir, A., *The Responsibility to Protect: Rhetoric, Reality, and the Future of the Humanitarian Intervention*, Palgrave Macmillan, Basingstoke-New York, 2012.

Held, D. & McGrew, A. (Eds.), *The Global Transformations Reader: An Introduction to the Globalization Debate*, Polity Press, Cambridge, 1999.

Hesse, J.J. & Johnson, N. (Eds.), *Constitutional Policy and Change in Europe*, OUP, Oxford, 1995.

Higgins, R., *Problems and Process: International Law and How We Use It*, Clarendon Press, Oxford, 1994.

Higgins, R. *et al.*, *Oppenheim's International Law – United Nations*, OUP, Oxford, 2017.

Hilpold, P. (Ed.), *Responsibility to Protect (R2P): A New Paradigm of International Law?*, Brill Nijhoff, Leiden-Boston, 2015.

Hirsch, M. *Invitation to the Sociology of International Law*, OUP, Oxford, 2015.

Hirsch, M. & Lang, A. (Eds.), *Research Handbook on the Sociology of International Law*, Edward Elgar, Cheltenham, 2018.

Hirschl, R., *Comparative Matters: The Renaissance of Comparative Constitutional Law*, OUP, Oxford, 2016.

Hirschl, R., *Towards Juristocracy: The Origins and Consequences of the New Constitutionalism*, Harvard University Press, Cambridge (MA)-London, 2007.

Hobbes, T., *Leviathan*, Penguin Books, London, 1985.

Hobbes, T., *The Elements of Law: Natural and Politic*, Frank Cass & Co. Ltd., London, 1969, F. Tönnies (Ed.).

Hobson, J.A., *Imperialism: A Study*, James Pott & Company, New York, 1902.

Huber, M., *Die Soziologischen Grundlagen des Völkerrechts*, W. Rotschild, Berlin-Grunewald, 1928.

Humbert, M., *Institutions politiques et sociales de l'Antiquité*, Dalloz, Paris, 1999.

Ikenberry, G.J., *After Victory: Institutions, Strategic Restraint, and the Rebuilding of Order after Major Wars*, Princetion University Press, Princeton (NJ)-Oxford, 2001.

Ikenberry, G.J., *Liberal Order and Imperial Ambition: Essays on American Power and World Politics*, Polity Press, Cambridge, 2006.

Ikenberry, G.J. (Ed.), *Power, Order and Change in World Politics*, CUP, Cambridge, 2014.

Jackson, J.H., *The World Trade Organization: Constitution and Jurisprudence*, The Royal Institute of International Affairs, London, 1998.

Jackson, V.C. & Tushnet, M., *Comparative Constitutional Law*, Foundation Press, New York, 2006.

Jacques, M., *When China Rules the World: The End of the Western World and the Birth of a New Global Order*, Penguin Books, London, 2012.

Jacob, A. & Auroux, S. (Eds.), *Encyclopédie philosophique universelle*, PUF, Paris, 1990.

Jacobsen, M. C., *Jean Bodin et le dilemme de la philosophie politique moderne*, Etudes Romanes, vol. 48, Museum Tusculanum Press-University of Copenhagen, Copenhagen, 2000.

Jayakumar, S. *et al.* (Eds.), *The South China Sea Disputes and Law of the Sea*, Edward Elgar, Cheltenham-Northampton (MA), 2014.

Jellinek, G., *L'état moderne et son droit: Théorie générale de l'Etat*, V. Giard & E. Brière, Paris, 1911, trans. G. Fardis.

Jellinek, G., *L'état moderne et son droit – Théorie juridique de l'État*, M. Giard & E. Brière, Paris, 1913, trans. G. Fardis.

Joerges, C., Sand, I.-J. & Teubner, G. (Eds.), *Transnational Governance and Constitutionalism*, Hart Publishing, Oxford, 2004.

Jouannet, E. & Ruiz Fabri, H. (Eds.), *Impérialisme et droit international en Europe et aux Etats-unis*, Société de législation comparé, Paris, 2007.

Jowell, J. & Oliver, D. (Eds.), *The Changing Constitution*, OUP, Oxford, 2011.

Judd, D., *The Lion and the Tiger: The Rise and Fall of the British Raj*, OUP, Oxford, 2003.

Kant, E., *Crtique de la raison pratique*, PUF, Paris, 2003, trans. F. Picavet.
Kant, E., *Crtique de la raison pure*, PUF, Paris, 2004, trans. A. Tremesaygues & B. Pacaud.
Kelsen, H., *General Theory of Law and State*, Lawbook Exchange, Union (NJ), 1999, trans. Anders Wedberg.
Kelsen, H., *The Law of the United Nations: A Critical Analysis of Its Fundamental Problems*, Stevens and Sons Limited, London, 1950.
Kelsen, H., *Pure Theory of Law*, Lawbook Exchange, Union (NJ), 2002, trans. Max Knight.
Keohane, R.O., *After Hegemony: Cooperation and Discord in the World Political Economy*, Princeton University Press, Princeton (NJ), 1984.
Keohane, R.O. & Nye, J.S. Jr., *Power and Interdependence: World Politics in Transition*, Little, Brown and Company, Boston (MA)-Toronto, 1977.
King, M. & Thornhill, C., *Niklas Luhmann's Theory of Politics and Law*, Palgrave Macmillan, Houndmills, 2003.
Klabbers, J., *An Introduction to International Institutional Law*, CUP, Cambridge, 2007.
Klabbers, J., Peters, A. & Ulfstein, G., *The Constitutionalization of International Law*, OUP, Oxford, 2009.
Kochenov, D. & Amtenbrink, F. (Eds.), *The European Union's Shaping of the International Legal Order*, CUP, Cambridge, 2014.
Koh, H.H., *The Trump Administration and International Law*, OUP, Oxford, 2019.
Kojève, A., Outline of a Phenomenology of Right, Rowman & Littlefield Publishers, Inc., Lanham, 2007, B.-P. Frost (Ed.), trans. B.-P. Frost & R. Howse.
Kojève, A., *Esquisse d'une phénoménologie du droit*, Gallimard, Paris, 1981.
Kojève, A., *Introduction à la lecture de Hegel*, Gallimard, Paris, 1997.
Kolb, R., *Théorie du* ius cogens *international : Essai de relecture du concept*, PUF, Paris, 2001.
Koskenniemi, M., *Fragmentation of International Law: Difficulties Arising from the Diversification and Expansion of International Law*, Report of the Study Group of the International Law Commission, UN Doc. A/CN.4/L.682, 4 April 2006.
Koskenniemi, M., *From Apology to Utopia: The Structure of International Legal Argument - Reissue with New Epilogue*, CUP, Cambridge, 2005.
Koskenniemi, M., *The Gentle Civilizer of Nations: The Rise and Fall of International Law 1870-1960*, CUP, Cambridge, 2005.
Kuhn, T., *La structure des révolutions scientifiques*, Flammarion, Paris, 1983, trans. Laure Meyer.
Kwa, A., *Power Politics in the WTO*, Focus on the Global South, Bangkok, 2003.
Laclau, E. & Mouffé, C., *Hegemony & Socialist Strategy: Towards a Radical Democratic Principles*, Verso, London-New York, 1985.
Laïdi, Z., *La grande perturbation*, Flammarion, Paris, 2004.
Laïdi, Z., *Un monde privé de sens*, Hachette, Paris, 2004.

Laïdi, Z., *La norme sans la force : l'énigme de la puissance européenne*, Presses de la fondation nationale des sciences politiques, Paris, 2005.

Lang, A.F. & Wiener, A. (Eds.), *Handbook on Global Constitutionalism*, Edward Elgar Publishing, Cheltenham-Northampton (MA), 2017.

Larsen, M.T. (Ed.), *Power and Propaganda: A Symposium on Ancient Empires*, Mesopotamia, Copenhagen Studies in Assyriology, vol. 7, Akademisk Forlag, Copenhagen, 1979.

Lasswell, H.D. & Kaplan, A., *Power and Society: A Framework for Political Inquiry*, Yale University Press, New Haven (CT)-London, 1969.

Latour, B., *Nous n'avons jamais été modernes: Essai d'anthropologie symétrique*, La Découverte, Paris, 1997.

Łazowski, A. (Ed.), *The Application of EU Law in the New Member States: Brave New World*, T.M.C. Asser Press, The Hague, 2010.

Leben, C. (Ed.), *Hans Kelsen – Écrits français de droit international*, PUF, Paris, 2001.

Lobba, P. & T. Mariniello, T. (Eds.), *Judicial Dialogue on Human Rights: The Practice of International Criminal Tribunals*, Brill-Nijhoff, Leiden-Boston, 2017.

Lorimer, J., *The Institutes of the Law of Nations*, William Blackwood and Sons, Edinburgh-London, 1883.

Luban, D., *Legal Ethics and Human Dignity*, CUP, Cambridge, 2007.

Luhmann, N., *Law as a Social System*, OUP, Oxford, 2004, trans. K.A. Ziegert.

Lukes, S. (Ed.), *Power*, Basil Blackwell, London, 1987.

Macdonald, R.St.J. & Johnston, D. (Eds.), *Towards World Constitutionalism: Issues in the Legal Ordering of the World Community*, Martinus Nijhoff, Leiden, 2005.

Machiavelli, N., *Discourses on Livy*, The University of Chicago Press, Chicago-London, 1996, trans. H.C. Mansfield and N. Tarcov.

Machiavelli, N., *The Prince*, CUP, Cambridge, 1988, Q. Skinner & R. Price (Eds.).

MacPherson, C.B., *The Political Theory of Possessive Individualism: Hobbes to Locke*, Clarendon Press, Oxford, 1964.

Madden, T.F., *Venice: A New History*, Viking, New York, 2012.

Madison, J., Hamilton, A. & Jay, J., *The Federalist Papers*, Penguin Books, Harmondsworth, 1987.

Marks, S. & Clapham, A., *International Human Rights Lexicon*, OUP, Oxford, 2005.

Mazower, M., *Governing the World: The History of an Idea*, The Penguin Press, New York, 2012

Mälksoo, L., *Russian Approaches to International Law*, OUP, Oxford, 2015.

McDougal, M. & Reisman, M.W., *International Law Essays: A Supplement to International Law in Contemporary Perspective*, The Foundation Press, Mineola (NY), 1981.

McIlwain, C.H., *Constitutionalism and the Changing World*, CUP, Cambridge, 1939.

McIlwain, C.H., *The Growth of Political Thought in the West: From Greeks to the End of the Middle Ages*, The MacMillan Company, New York, 1955.

McIlwan, C.H., *Constitutionalism: Ancient and Modern*, Great Seal Books, Ithaca (NY), 1958.

Mehta, U.S., *Liberalism and Empire: A Study in Nineteenth-Century British Liberal Thought*, The University of Chicago Press, Chicago-London, 1999.

Merton, R.K., *Social Theory and Social Structure*, The Free Press, Glencoe, 1962.

Miéville, C., *Between Equal Rights: A Marxist Theory of International Law*, Pluto Press, London, 2005.

Mill, J.S., *On Liberty*, Penguin Books, London, 1985.

Moir, M.I., Peers, D.M. & Zastoupil, L. (Eds.), *J.S. Mill's Encounter with India*, University of Toronto Press, Toronto-Buffalo-London, 1999.

Mommsen, W.J., *Theories of Imperialism*, The University of Chicago Press, Chicago, 1982, trans. P.S. Falla.

Mommsen, W. & Osterhammel, J. (Eds.), *Imperialism and After: Continuities and Discontinuities*, Allen & Unvwin, London-Boston-Sydney, 1986.

Montesquieu, De l'Esprit des Lois I, Garnier-Flammarion, Paris, 1979.

Mosler, H., *The International Society as a Legal Community, in RCADI*, 1974, IV, vol. 140, A.W. Sijthoff, Leyde, 1976.

Motyl, A.J., *Imperial Ends: The Decay, Collapse, and Revival of Empires*, Columbia University Press, New York, 2001.

Narlikar, A., Daunton, M. & Stern, R.M. (Eds.), *The Oxford Handbook on the World Trade Organization*, OUP, Oxford, 2014.

Nathan, A.J. & Scobell, A., *China's Search for Security*, Columbia University Press, New York, 2014.

Nicolaïdis, K. *et al.* (Eds.), *Echoes of Empire: Memory, Identity and Colonial Legacies*, I.B. Taurus, London-New York, 2015.

Niemeyer, G., *Law Without Force: The Function of Politics in International Law*, Transaction Publishers, New Brunswick (NJ)-London, 2001.

Nijman, J. & Nollkaemper, A. (Ed.), *New Perspectives on the Divide between National and International Law*, OUP, Oxford, 2007.

Nossova, I., *Russia's International Legal Claims in Its Adjacent Seas: The Realm of Sea as Extension of Sovereignty*, Tartu University Press, Tartu, 2013.

Nugent, N., *The Government and Politics of the European Union*, Duke University Press, Durham, 2003.

Nye, J.S. Jr., *Is the American Century Over?*, Polity, London, 2015.

O'Brien, P.K. & Clesse, A., *Two Hegemonies: Britain 1846-1914 and the United States 1941-2001*, Ashgate, Aldershot-Burlington (VT), 2002.

Orford, A., *International Authority and the Responsibility to Protect*, CUP, Cambridge, 2011.

Orrego Vicuña, F., *International Dispute Settlement in an Evolving Society: Constitutionalization, Accessibility, Privatization*, CUP, Cambridge, 2004.

Papisca, A. & Mascia, M., *Le relazioni internazionali nell'era dell'interdipendenza e dei diritti umani*, CEDAM, Padova, 1991.

Pashukanis, E.B., *The General Theory of Law and Marxism*, in Bierne, P. & Sharlet, R. (Eds.), *Pashukanis: Selected Writings on Marxism and Law*, Academic Press, London-New York, 1980, trans. Peter B. Maggs.

Peters, G.B., *Institutional Theory in Political Science: The 'New Institutionalism'*, Continuum, London-New York, 2005.

Pitamic, L., *A Treatise on the State*, Selected Works, vol. I, Ministry of Justice, Ljubljana, 2008 (reprint of the first edition published by J.H. Furst Company, Inc., Baltimore (MD), 1933).

Pocock, J.G.A., *The Machiavellian Moment: Florentine Political Thought and the Atlantic Republican Tradition*, Princeton University Press, Princeton-London, 1975.

Porter, B., *British Imperial: What the Empire Wasn't*, I.B. Tauris, London-New York, 2016.

Porter, B., *The Lion's Share: A History of British Imperialism 1850 to the Present*, Pearson, Harlow, 2012.

Popovski, V. & Fraser, T. (Eds.), *The Security Council as Global Legislator*, Routledge, London-New York, 2014.

Rabinow, P. (Ed.), *The Foucault Reader*, Penguin Books, London-New York (NY), 1984.

Rabkin, J., *Law without Nations? Why Constitutional Government Requires Sovereign States*, Princeton University Press, Princeton-Oxford, 2005.

Ramonet, I., *Géopolitique du chaos*, Galilée, Paris, 1997.

Reuter, P., *Introduction au droit des traités*, PUF, Paris, 1995.

Rivaud, *Le problème du devenir et la notion de la matière*, Félix Alcan, Paris, 1905.

Robson, J. M. (Ed.), *Essays on Politics and Society*, The Collected Works of John Stuart Mill, vols. 19 and 21, University of Toronto Press-Routledge & Kegal Paul, Toronto-London, 1963-1991.

Romano, C.P.R., Alter, K.J. & Shany, Y. (Eds.), *The Oxford Handbook of International Adjudication*, OUP, Oxford, 2014.

Romano, S., *L'ordre juridique*, Dalloz, Paris, 1975, trans. L. François & P. Gothot.

Rosenboim, O., *The Emergence of Globalism: Visions of World Order in Britain and the United States, 1939-1950*, Princeton University Press, Princeton-Oxford, 2017.

Rosenfeld, M. & Sajó, A. (Eds.), *Oxford Handbook of Comparative Constitutional Law*, OUP, Oxford, 2012.

Rosenthal, B., *Etude de l'oeuvre de Myers Smith McDougal en matière de droit international public*, Paris, L.G.D.J., 1970.

Ross, W.D., *Aristotle's Metaphysics: A Revised Text with Introduction and Commentary*, Clarendon Press, Oxford, 1924.

Rossi, L.S. & Casolari, F. (Eds.), *The Principle of Equality in EU Law*, Springer, Cham, 2017.

Rousseau, J.-J., *Du contrat social*, GF Flammarion, Paris, 2001.
Russell, B., *Power: A New Social Analysis*, George Allen & Unwin Ltd, London, 1938.
Sabine, G.H., *A History of Political Theory: Fourth Edition*, Dryden Press, Hinsdale (ILL), 1973, rev. T. Landon Thorson.
Said, E.W., *Culture & Imperialism*, Vintage, London, 1994.
Said, E.W., *Orientalism*, Pantheon Books, New York (NY), 1978.
Sancin, V. (Ed.), *Responsibility to Protect: Lessons Learned and the Way Forward*, University of Ljubljana, Ljubljana, 2019.
Sancin, V. (Ed.), *Responsibility to Protect: Where Do We Stand Ten Years After?*, University of Ljubljana, Ljubljana, 2015.
Sancin, V. & Kovič Dine, M. (Eds.), *Responsibility to Protect in Theory and Practice*, GV Založba, Ljubljana, 2013.
Schmitt, C., *Les trois types de pensée juridique*, PUF, Paris, 1995, trans. M. Köller and D. Séglard.
Schumpeter, J., *Impérialisme et classes sociales*, Flammarion, Paris, 1972, trans. S. de Segonzac & P. Bresson.
Schwarzenberger, G., *Power Politics: A Study of World History*, Steven & Sons Limited, London, 1964.
Schwöbel, C.E.J., *Global Constitutionalism in International Legal Perspective*, Martinus Nijhoff Publishers, Leiden, 2011.
Shaw, M., *International Law*, CUP, Cambridge, 2003, 2014.
Shelton, D., *Remedies in International Human Rights Law*, OUP, Oxford, 2001.
Simma, B. (Ed.), *The Charter of the United Nations: A Commentary*, OUP, Oxford, 1995.
Simma, B. (Ed.), *The Charter of the United Nations: A Commentary*, OUP, Oxford-New York, 2002.
Simpson, G., *Great Powers and Outlaw States: Unequal Sovereigns in the International Legal Order*, CUP, Cambridge, 2005.
Singh, R., *Barack Obama's Post-American Foreign Policy: The Limits of Engagement*, Bloomsbury Academic, London, 2012.
Skinner, Q., *The Foundations of Modern Political Thought*, CUP, Cambridge, 2000.
Skouteris, T., *The Notion of Progress in International Law Discourse*, T.M.C. Asser Press, The Hague, 2010.
Slaughter, A.-M., *A New World Order*, Princeton University Press, Princeton (NJ)-Oxford, 2005.
Slobodian, Q., *Globalists: The End of Empire and the Birth of Neoliberalism*, Harvard University Press, Cambridge (MA), 2018.
Souilhé, J., *Etude sur le terme dunamis dans les dialogues de Platon*, Librairie Félix Alcan, Paris, 1919.
Steinberger, H., *Models of Constitutional Jurisdiction*, European Commission for Democracy through Law, Council of Europe Press, Strasbourg, 1994.

Stokes, E., *The English Utilitarians and India*, OUP, Delhi, 1989.
Stone Sweet, A., *Governing with Judges: Constitutional Politics in Europe*, OUP, Oxford, 2000.
Strauss, L. & Cropsey, J., *History of Political Philosophy*, Rand McNally & Company, Chicago, 1966.
Sturzo, L., *Inner Laws of Society: A New Sociology*, P.J. Kennedy & Sons, New York, 1944.
Talmon, S. & Jia, B.B. (Eds.), *The South China Sea Arbitration: A Chinese Perspective*, Hart Publishing, Oxford-Portland (OR), 2014.
Terris, D., Romano C.P.R. & Swigart, L., *The International Judge: An Introduction to the Men and Women who Decide the World's Cases*, OUP, Oxford, 2007.
Teubner, G., *Constitutional Fragments: Societal Constitutionalism and Globalization*, OUP, Oxford, 2012, trans. G. Norbury.
Thakur, R. *The Responsibility to Protect: Norms, Laws and the Use of Force in International Politics*, Routledge, Abingdon-New York, 2011.
The Kosovo Report, The Independent International Commission for Kosovo, 2000.
The Responsibility to Protect, Report of the International Commission on Intervention and State Sovereignty, International Development Research Centre, Ottawa, 2001.
Timasheff, N., *An Introduction to the Sociology of Law*, Harvard University Committee on Research in the Social Sciences, Cambridge (MA), 1939.
Tomuschat, C., *International Law: Ensuring the Survival of Mankind on the Eve of a New Century. General Course on Public International Law, in RCADI*, 1999, vol. 281, Martinus Nijhoff Publishers, The Hague-Boston-London, 2001.
Tomuschat, C., *Human Rights: Between Idealism and Realism*, OUP, Oxford, 2008.
Tomuschat, C. & Thouvenin, J.-M. (Eds.), *The Fundamental Rules of the International Legal Order: Jus Cogens* and Obligations *Erga Omnes*, Martinus Nijhoff Publishers, Leiden-Boston, 2006.
Torfing, J., *New Theories of Discourse: Laclau, Mouffé and Žižek*, Blackwell Publishers, Oxford-Malden (MA), 1999.
Toynbee, A., *A Study of History*, 2 vols., OUP, Oxford-New York, 1956 and 1957, abridg. D.C. Somervell.
Tönnies, F., *Communauté et société : categories fondamentales de la sociologie pure*, PUF, Paris, 1946, trans. Joseph Leif.
Tønder, L. & Thomassen, L. (Eds.), *Radical Democracy: Politics between Abundance and Lack*, Manchester University Press, Manchester, 2014.
Trenin, D., *Post-imperium: A Eurasian Story*, Carnegie Endowment for International Peace, Washington (DC), 2011.
Triepel, H., *L'egemonia*, Casa editrice Sansoni, Firenze, 1949, trans. G. Battino.
Tsagourias, N. (Ed.), *Transnational Constitutionalism: International and European Models*, CUP, Cambridge, 2007.

Tully, J., *Public Philosophy in a New Key, Volume II: Imperialism and Civic Freedom*, CUP, Cambridge, 2008.

Tzanakopoulos, A., *Disobeying the Security Council: Countermeasures against Wrongful Sanctions*, OUP, Oxford, 2011.

Unger, R.M., *Knowledge and Politics*, Free Press, New York, 1984.

Vile, M.J.C., *Constitutionalism and the Separation of Powers*, Liberty Fund, Indianapolis, 1998.

Villalpando, S., *L'émergence de la communauté internationale dans la responsabilité des Etats*, PUF, Paris, 2005.

Virally, M., *Le droit international en devenir : Essais écrits au fil des ans*, PUF, Paris, 1990.

Von Bogdandy, A. & Bast, J. (Eds.), *Principles of European Constitutional Law*, Hart Publishing, Oxford-Portland (OR), 2006.

Von Ihering, R., *Law as a Means to an End*, The Lawbook Exchange, Union (NJ), 1999, trans. I. Husik.

Walker, N., *Intimations of Global Law*, CUP, Cambridge, 2015.

Wallersten, I., *After Liberalism*, The New Press, New York, 1995.

Wallerstein, I., *European Universalism: The Rhetoric of Power*, New York-London, New Press, 2006.

Wallerstein, I., *The Modern World-system I: Capitalist Agriculture and the Origins of the European World-Economy in the Sixteenth Century*, Academic Press, Inc., San Diego-London, 1974.

Wallerstein, I., *World-Systems Analysis: An Introduction*, Duke University Press, Durham-London, 2004.

Webb, P., *International Judicial Integration and Fragmentation*, OUP, Oxford, 2013.

Weber, M., *Basic Concepts in Sociology*, Greenwood Press Publishers, Westport (CT), 1977, trans. H.P. Secher.

Weiler, J.H.H., *The Constitution of Europe: "Do the New Cloths have an Emperor" and Other Essays on European Integration*, CUP, Cambridge, 1999.

Weiler, J.H.H. & Wind, M. (Eds.), *European Constitutionalism beyond the State*, CUP, Cambridge, 2003.

Weiss, T.G., *Humanitarian Intervention: Ideas in Action*, Polity Press, Cambridge, 2012.

White, R.C.A. & Ovey, C., *The European Convention on Human Rights*, OUP, Oxford, 2010.

Wolfrum, R. (Ed.), *Max Planck Encyclopedia of Public International Law*, OUP, Oxford, 2012.

Wormuth, F.D., *The Origins of Modern Constitutionalism*, Harper & Brothers Publishers, New York, 1949.

Wouters, J. *et al.* (Eds.), *The Europeanisation of International Law: The Status of International Law in the EU and its Member States*, T.M.C. Asser Press, The Hague, 2008.

Xue, H., *Chinese Contemporary Perspectives on International Law: History, Culture and International* Law, AIL-Pocket, The Hague, 2012.

Yemin, E., *Legislative Powers within the United Nations and Specialised Agencies*, A. W. Sijthoff, Leyden, 1969.

Young, M.A. (Ed.), *Regime Interaction in International Law: Facing Fragmentation*, CUP, Cambridge, 2015.

Zapperi, R. (Ed.), *Emmanuel-Joseph SIEYÈS : Ecrits politiques*, Editions des archives contemporaines, Paris-Montreux, 1985.

Zastoupil, L., *John Stuart Mill and India*, Stanford (CA), Stanford University Press, 1994.

Zielonka, J., *Europe as Empire: The Nature of the Enlarged European Union*, OUP, Oxford, 2006.

Zupančič, B.M., *Sur la Cour européenne des droits de l'homme : Rétrospective d'un initié (1998-2016)*, Harmattan, Paris, 2019.

Zupančič, B.M., *The Owl of Minerva: Essays on Human Rights*, Eleven International Publishing, Utrecht, 2008.

Zupančič, B.M., *Prvine (pravne) kulture [The Cultural Elements of the Rule of Law]*, FDV, Ljubljana, 1995.

Contributions to Periodicals and Collective Works, Reports:

Abi-Saab, Georges, 'A "New World Order"? Some Preliminary Reflections', 7 *Hague Yearbook of International Law* 1994.

Abi-Saab, G., 'Unused Charter Capacity', *in Issues in Global Governance: Papers Written for the Commission on Global Governance*, Kluwer Law International, London-The Hague-Boston, 1993.

Aggarwal, V.K. & Dupont, C. 'A Leader in Institutional Design? Europe and the Governance of Trade and Monetary Relations', *in* H. Kierzkowski (Ed.), *Europe and Globalization*, Palgrave Macmillan, Houndmills-New York (NY), 2002.

Akande, D., 'The International Court of Justice and the Security Council: Is there Room for Judicial Control of Decisions of the Political Organs of the United Nations?', 46 *ICLQ* 1997.

Akehurst, M., 'The Hierarchy of the Sources of International Law', 47 *BYIL* 1974-1975.

Alexidze, L. 'Kosovo and South Ossetia: Similar or Different? Consequences for International Law', 12 *BaYIL* 2012.

Allison, R., 'Russian "Deniable" Intervention in Ukraine: How and why Russia Broke the Rules', 6 *International Affairs* 2014.

Alvarez, J.E., 'Hegemonic International Law Revisited', 97 *AJIL* 2003.

Andenas, M., 'Reassertion and Transformation: From Fragmentation to Convergence in International Law', 46 *Georgetown Journal of International Law* 2015.

Anghie, A., 'Europe and International Law's Colonial Present', 6 *BaYIL* 2006.

Ansong, A., 'Single Undertaking, Different Speeds: Pliable Models for Decision-making in the WTO', 21 *Journal of International Economic Law* 2018.

Arangio-Ruiz, G., 'The "Federal Analogy" and UN Charter Interpretation: A Critical Issue', 8 *EJIL* 1997.

Arnardóttir, O.M., '*Res Interpretata, Erga Omnes* Effect and the Role of the Margin of Appreciation in Giving Domestic Effect to the Judgments of the European Court of Human Rights', 28 *EJIL* 2017.

Avbelj, M., 'Differentiated Integration—Farewell to the EU-27?', 14 *German Law Journal* 2013.

Avbelj, M., 'Questioning EU Constitutionalisms', 9 *German Law Journal* 2007.

Bahri, A., '"Appellate Body Held Hostage": Is Judicial Activism at Fair Trial?', 53 *Journal of World Trade* 2019.

Basedow, R. 'The WTO and the Rise of Plurilatelarism – What Lessons Can We Learn from the European Union's Experience with Differentiated Integration?', 21 *Journal of International Economic Law* 2018.

Bellamy, A.J. & Reike, R., 'The Responsibility to Protect and International Law', 2 *Global Responsibility to Protect* 2010.

Bermann, G.A., '*Marbury v. Madison* and European Union "Constitutional" Review', 36 *George Washington International Law Review* 2004.

Biagioni, G., '*Avotinš v. Latvia*. The Uneasy Balance Between Mutual Recongition of Judgments and Protection of Fundamental Rights', 1 *European Papers* 2016.

Bianchi, A., 'Ad-hocism and the Rule of Law', 13 *EJIL* 2002.

Bianchi, A., 'Assessing the Effectiveness of the UN Security Council's Anti-terrorism Measures: The Quest for Legitimacy and Cohesion', 17 *EJIL* 2007.

Bianchi, A., 'Enforcing International Law Norms against Terrorism: Achievements and Prospects', *in* Bianchi, A. (Ed.), *Enforcing International Law Norms against Terrorism*, Hart Publishing, Oxford-Portland (OR), 2004.

Bianchi, A., 'Extraterritoriality and Export Controls: Some Remarks on the Alleged Antinomy between European and U.S. Approaches', 35 *GYIL* 1992.

Bianchi, A., 'Immunity versus Human Rights: The *Pinochet* Case', 1 *EJIL* 1999.

Bianchi, A., 'International Law and US Courts: The Myth of Lohengrin Revisited', 15 *EJIL* 2004.

Bianchi, A., 'Human Rights and the Magic of *Jus Cogens*', 19 *EJIL* 2008.

Bianchi, A., 'Security Council's Anti-terror Resolutions and their Implementation by Member States', 4 *Journal of International Criminal Justice* 2006.

Bianchi, A., 'The International Regulation of the Use of Force: The Politics of Interpretive Method', 22 *LJIL* 2009.

Bobbitt, P., 'Better than Empire', *The Financial Times*, 13-14 March 2004.

Boission de Chazournes, L., 'Plurality in the Fabric of International Courts and Tribunals: The Threads of a Managerial Approach', 28 *EJIL* 2017.

Bolton, J.R., 'The Bush Administration's Forward Strategy for Nonproliferation', 5 *Chicago Journal of International Law* 2005.
Bolton, J., 'Is There Really "Law" in International Affairs?', 10 *Transnational Law & Contemporary Problems* 2000.
Bore Eveno, V., 'Le contrôle juridictionnel des resolutions du Conseil de securité : vers un constitutionnalisme international ?', 110 *RGDIP* 2006.
Borgen, C.J., 'Whose Public, whose Order? Imperium, Religion and Normative Friction', 32 *Yale Journal of International Law* 2007.
Borgen, C.J., 'Transnational Tribunals and the Transmission of Norms: The Hegemony of Process', 39 *George Washington International Law Review* 2007.
Bradley, C.A., 'Breard, Our Dualist Constitution, and the Internationalist Conception', 51 *Stanford Law Review* 1999.
Burke-White, W.W., 'Crimea and the International Legal Order', 56 *Survival* 2014.
Caflisch, L., 'Unequal Treaties', 35 *GYIL* 1992.
Cantore, C.M., 'We're One, but We're Not the Same: Enhanced Cooperation and the Tension between Unity and Asymmetry in the EU', 3 *Perspectives on Federalism* 2011.
Cappelletti, M., 'Judicial Review in Comparative Perspective' 58 *California Law Review*, 1970.
Carillo Salcedo, J.A., 'Reflections on the Existence of a Hierarchy of Norms in International Law', 8 *EJIL* 1997.
Casolari, F., 'The Janus-Faced New European Neighbourhood Policy: Normative (Hard) Power vs. the Pragmatic (Soft) Approach', Istituto Affari Internazionali, Documenti IAI 13/08, November 2013.
Cass, D., 'The "Constitutionalization" of International Trade Law: Judicial Norm-Generation as the Engine of Constitutional Development in International Trade', 12 *EJIL* 2001.
Cassese, A. 'The Nicaragua and Tadić Tests Revisited in Light of the ICJ Judgment on Genocide in Bosnia', 18 *EJIL* 2007.
Charney, J.I., 'The Impact on the International Legal System of the Growth of International Courts and Tribunals', 31 *N.Y.U. Journal of International Law and Politics* 1999.
Chen, C.-H., 'Different Meanings of the Term Energeia in the Philosophy of Aristotle', 17 *Philosophy and Phenomenological Research* 1956.
Chen, C.-H., 'The Relation between the Terms energeia and entelexeia in the Philosophy of Aristotle', 8 *The Classical Quarterly* 1958.
Chen, L., 'Taiwan's Current International Legal Status', 32 *New England Law Review* 1998.
Chevallier-Govers, C., 'Actes constitutifs des organisations internationales et constitutions nationales ', 105 *RGDIP* 2001.

Chimni, B. S., 'International Institutions Today: An Imperial Global State in the Making', 15 *EJIL* 2004.
Chua, A., 'The Precedential Effect of WTO Panel and Appellate Body Reports', 11 *LJIL* 1998.
Colandrea, V., 'On the Power of the European Court of Human Rights to Order Specific Non-Monetary Measures: Some Remarks in Light of the *Assanidze, Broniowski* and *Sejdovic* Cases', 7 *Human Rights Law Review* 2007.
Conklin, W.E., 'The Peremptory Norms of the International Community', 23 *EJIL* 2012.
Cooper, R., 'The New Liberal Imperialism', *The Observer*, 7 April 2002.
Corten, O., 'The Controversies over the Customary Prohibition on the Use of Force', 16 *EJIL* 2006.
Costello, C., 'The *Bosphorus* Ruling of the European Court of Human Rights: Fundamental Rights and Blurred Boundaries in Europe', 6 *Human Rights Law Review* 2006.
Cot, J.-P., 'Tableau de la pensée juridique américaine', 110 *RGDIP* 2006.
Cottier, T., 'John H. Jackson, Sovereigny-Modern and the Constitutional Approach to International Law', 19 *Journal of International Economic Law* 2016.
Cottier, T. & Hertig, M., 'The Prospects of 21st Century Constitutionalism', *in* Cottier, T., *The Challenge of WTO Law: Collected Essays*, Cameron May, London, 2007.
Crawford, J., '*Marbury v. Madison* at the International Level', 36 *George Washington International Law Review* 2004.
Cremona, M., 'Values in EU Foreign Policy', *in* M. Evans & P. Koutrakos (Eds.), *Beyond the Established Legal Orders*, Hart Publishing, Oxford-Portland (OR), 2011.
D'Amato, A., 'It's a Bird, It's a Plane, It's Jus Cogens!', 6 *Connecticut Journal of International Law* 1990.
De Búrca, G. 'After the EU Charter of Fundamental Rights: The Court of Justice as a Human Rights Adjudicator?', 20 *Maastricht Journal of European and Comparative Law* 2013.
De la Mare, T., 'Article 177 in Social and Political Context', *in* Craig, P. & de Búrca, G. (Eds.), *The Evolution of EU Law*, OUP, Oxford, 1999.
De la Rasilla del Moral, I., 'All Roads Lead to Rome, or the Liberal Cosmopolitan Agenda as a Blueprint for a Neo-Conservative Legal Order', 7 *Global Jurist* 2007, Article 2.
De la Rasilla y del Moral, I., 'Review Essay – Remarks on Post-Sovereignty and International Legal Neo-conservatism: Reading Jeremy Rabkin', 8 *German Law Journal* 2007.
De Wet, E., 'The Emergence of International and Regional Value Systems as a Manifestation of the Emerging International Constitutional Order', 19 *LJIL* 2006.
De Wet, E., 'The International Constitutional Order', 55 *ICLQ* 2006.
De Zwaan, J.W., *Stability and Differentiation in the European Union*, Eleven International Publishing, The Hague, 2017.
Delbrück, J., 'Max Huber's Sociological Approach to International Law Revisited', 18 *EJIL* 2007.

Delcourt, B., 'The Normative Underpinnings of the Use of Force. Doctrinal Foundations and Ambiguities in the CFSP/ESDP Discourse', 6 *BaYIL* 2006.

Devuyst, Y., 'The European Union's Constitutional Order? Between Community Method and *Ad-hoc* Compromise', 18 *Berkeley Journal of International Law* 2000.

Domingo, R., 'Gaius, Vattel, and the New Global Law Paradigm', 22 *EJIL* 2011.

Domingo, R., 'The New Global Human Community', 12 *Chicago Journal of International Law* 2012.

Donald, A. & Speck, A.-K., 'The European Court of Human Rights' Remedial Practice and its Impact on the Execution of Judgments', 19 *Human Rights Law Review* 2019.

Douglas-Scott, S., 'Bosphorus Hava Yollari Turizm Ve Ticaret Anonim Sirketi v. Ireland', 43 *Common Market Law Review* 2006.

Drabkin, I.E., 'Notes of the Laws of Motion in Aristotle', 59 *The American Journal of Philology* 1938.

Drzemczewski, A. & Tavernier, P., 'L'exécution des 'décisions' des instances internationales de contrôle dans le domaine des droits de l'homme', *in La protection des droits de l'homme et l'évolution du droit international, Colloque de Strasbourg*, Société Française pour le Droit International, Editions A. Pédone, Paris, 1998.

Dupuy, F. & Dupuy, P.-M., 'A Legal Analysis of China's Historic Rights Claim in the South China Sea', 107 *AJIL* 2013.

Dupuy, P.-M., 'The Constitutional Dimension of the Charter of the United Nations Revisited', 1 *Max Planck Yearbook of United Nations Law* 1997.

Dutheil de la Rochère, J., 'The EU and the Individual: Fundamental Rights in the Draft Constitutional Treaty', 41 *Common Market Law Review* 2004.

Dutton, P.A., 'Caelum Liberam: Air Defense Identification Zone Outside Sovereign Airspace', 103 *AJIL* 2009.

Eeckhout, P., 'Opinion 2/13 on EU Accession to the ECHR and Judicial Dialogue: Autonomy or Autarky', 38 *Fordham International Law Journal* 2015.

Ehlermann, C.D., 'Reflections on the Appellate Body of the WTO', 6 *Journal of International Economic Law* 2003.

Eicher, P.T., 'International Forum Shopping: The Mox Plant Case and the ECJ', 30 *Dublin University Law Journal* 2006.

Eitel, T., 'The UN Security Council and its Future Contribution in the Field of International Law: What May We Expect?', 4 *Max Planck Yearbook of United Nations Law* 2000.

El-Ojeili, C., 'Reflections on Wallerstein: The Modern World-System, Four Decades on', 41 *Critical Sociology* 2014.

Esty, D., 'The World Trade Organization's Legitimacy Crisis', 1 *World Trade Review* 2002.

EU, *Shared Vision, Common Action: A Stronger Europe, A Global Strategy for the European Union's Foreign And Security Policy*, June 2016.

European Commission, *White Paper on the Future of Europe: Reflections and Scenarios for the EU27 by 2025*, 1 March 2017, COM(2017)2025.

Fabbrini, F., 'Enhanced Cooperation under Scrutiny: Revisiting the Law and Practice of Multi-Speed Integration in Light of the First Involvement of the EU Judiciary', 40 *Legal Issues of Economic Integration* 2013.

Fabbrini, F. & Larik, J., 'The Past, Present and Future of the Relation between the European Court of Justice and the European Court of Human Rights', 35 *Yearbook of European Law* 2016.

Fassbender, B., 'The United Nations Charter as Constitution of the International Community', 36 *Columbia Journal of Transnational Law* 1998.

Fastenrath, U., 'Relative Normativity in International Law', 4 *EJIL* 1993.

Feinstein, L. & Slaughter, A.-M., 'A Duty to Prevent', 83 *Foreign Affairs* 2004.

Flauss, J.-F., 'La Cour européenne des droits de l'homme est-elle une Cour constitutionnelle?', 36 *Revue française de Droit constitutionnel* 1998.

Fleig-Goldstein, R.M., 'The Russian Constitutional Court versus the European Court of Human Rights: How the Strasbourg Court Should Respond to Russia's Refusal to Execute ECtHR Judgments', 56 *Columbia Journal of Transnational Law* 2017.

Flexible Integration: Towards a More Effective and Democratic Europe, Monitoring European Integration 6, Center for Economic Policy Research, London, 1995.

Forcese, C., 'Hegemonic Federalism: The Democratic Implications of the UN Security Council's "Legislative" Phase', 38 *Victoria University Wellington Law Review* 2007.

Franck, T.M., 'Legitimacy in the International System', 82 *AJIL* 1988.

Franck, T.M., 'The Power of Legitimacy and the Legitimacy of Power: International Law in an Age of Power Disequilibrium', 100 *AJIL* 2006.

Franck, T.M., 'Why a Quest for Legitimacy?', 21 *UC Davis Law Review* 1988.

Gallagher, J. & Robinson, R., 'The Imperialism of Free Trade', 6 *The Economic History Review, New Series* 1953.

Galtung, J., 'A Structural Theory of Imperialism', 8 *Journal of Peace Research* 1971.

Gao, J. 'Comments on *Commission of the European Communities v. Ireland*', 7 *Chinese Journal of International Law* 2008.

Gao, Z. & Jia, B.B., 'The Nine-Dash Line in the South China Sea: History, Status and Implications', 107 *AJIL* 2013.

Garwood-Gowers, A., 'China's "Responsible Protection" Concept: Reinterpreting the Responsibility to Protect (R2P) and Military Intervention for Humanitarian Purposes', 6 *Asian Journal of International Law* 2016.

Garwood-Gowers, A., 'The Responsibility to Protect and the Arab Spring: Libya as the Exception, Syria as the Norm?', 36 *UNSW Law Journal* 2013.

Gill, T.F., 'Legal and Some Political Limitations on the Power of the UN Security Council to Exercise its Enforcement Powers under Chapter VII of the Charter', 26 *Netherlands Yearbook of International Law* 1995.

Ginther, K., 'Hegemony', *in* Bernhardt, R. (Ed.), *Encyclopedia of Public International Law*, vol. II, 1995.

Glas, L.R. & Krommendijsk, J., 'From *Opinon 2/13* to *Avotiņš*: Recent Developments in the Relationship between the Luxembourg and Strasbourg Court', 17 *Human Rights Law Review* 2017.

Goldstone, R.J. & Hamilton, J., '*Bosnia* v. *Serbia*: Lessons from the Encounter of the International Court of Justice with the International Criminal Tribunal for the Former Yugoslavia', 21 *EJIL* 2008.

Gottlieb, Y., 'The Security Council's Maritime Piracy Resolutions: A Critical Assessment', 24 *Minnesota Journal of International Law* 2015.

Gowlland Debbas, V., 'The Limits of Unilateral Enforcement of Community Objectives in the Framework of UN Peace Maintenance', 11 *EJIL* 2000.

Gowlland-Debbas, V., 'Security Council Enforcement Action and Issues of States Responsibility', 43 *ICLQ* 1994.

Gragl, P., 'An Olive Branch from Strasbourg? Interpreting the European Court of Human Rights' Resurrection of *Bosphorus* and Reaction to *Opinion 2/13* in the *Avotiņš* Case', 13 *European Constitutional Law Review* 2017.

Grané, P., 'Remedies under WTO Law', 4 *Journal of International Economic Law* 2001.

Guillaume, G., 'The Use of Precedent by International Judges and Arbitrators', 2 *Journal of International Dispute Settlement* 2011.

Haas, P.M., 'Introduction: Epistemic Communities and International Policy Coordination', 46 *International Organization* 1992, Knowledge, Power, and International Policy Coordination.

Haass, R., 'How a World Order Ends: And What Comes in Its Wake', 98 *Foreign Affairs* 2019.

Halberstam, D., '"It's the Autonomy Stupid!" A Modest Defense of *Opinion 2/13* on EU Accession to the ECHR, and the Way Forward', 16 *German Law Journal* 2015.

Hébié, M., 'Was There Something Missing in the Decolonization Process in Africa?: The Territorial Dimension', 28 *LJIL* 2015.

Helfer, L.R., 'Exiting Treaties', 91 *Virginia Law Review* 2005.

Helfer, L.R., 'Redesigning the European Court of Human Rights: Embeddedness as a Deep Structural Principle of the European Human Rights Regime', 19 *EJIL* 2008.

Hettne, B. & Söderbaum, F., 'Civilian Power of Soft Imperialism? The EU as a Global Actor and the Role of Interregionalism', 10 *European Foreign Affairs Review* 2005.

Higgins, R., 'The ICJ, the ECJ, and the Integrity of International Law', 52 *ICLQ* 2003.

Hirschl, R., 'Preserving Hegemony? Assessing the Political Origins of the EU Constitution', 3 *International Journal of Constitutional Law* 2005.

Hirschl, R., 'The Struggle for Hegemony: Understanding Judicial Empowerment through Constitutionalisation in Culturally Divided Polities', 36 *Stanford Journal of International Law* 2000.

Hoekman, B.M. & Mavroidis, P.C., 'Embracing Diversity: Plurilateral Agreements and the Trading System', 14 *World Trade Review* 2015.

Hoekman, B.M. & Mavroidis, P.C., 'Variable Geometry in the WTO', *in* R. Schütze (Ed.), *Globalisation and Governance: International Problems, European Solutions*, CUP, Cambridge, 2018.

Hoekman, B.M. & Mavroidis, P.C., 'WTO "à la carte" or "menu du jour"? Assessing the Case for More Plurilateral Agreements", 26 *EJIL* 2015.

Holzinger, K. & Schimmelfennig, F., 'Differentiated Integration in the European Union: Many Concepts, Sparse Theory, Few Data', 19 *Journal of European Public Policy* 2012.

Howse, R., 'The World Trade Organization 20 Years On: Global Governance by Judiciary', 27 *EJIL* 2016.

Hsiao, A.H., 'Is China's Policy to Use Force against Taiwan a Violation of the Principle of Non-Use of Force under International Law?', 32 *New England Law Review* 1998.

Hyde-Price, A., '"Normative Power" Europe: A Realist Critique', 13 *Journal of European Public Policy* 2006.

Iglesias Sánchez, S., 'The Court and the Charter: The Impact of the Entry of the Lisbon Treaty on the ECJ's Approach to Fundamental Rights', 49 *Common Market Law Review* 2012.

ILC, 'Fourth Report on Peremptory Norms of General International Law (Jus Cogens) by Dire Tladi, Special Rapporteur', 31 January 2019, A/CN.4/727.

Lesaffer, R. & Letschert, R., 'The Global Challenge to Public International Law: Some First Thoughts', 17 *Tilburg Law Review* 2012.

Jackson, J.H., 'The WTO "Constitution" and Proposed Reforms: Seven "Mantras" Revisited', 4 *Journal of International Economic Law* 2001.

Jackson, J.L., '*Broniowski v. Poland*: A Recipe for Increased Legitimacy of the European Court of Human Rights as a Supranational Constitutional Court', 39 *Connecticut Law Review* 2006.

Jenks, W.C., 'The Will of the World Community as the Basis of Obligation in International Law', *in Hommage d'une generation de jurists au Président Basdevant*, Editions A. Pedone, Paris, 1960.

Jia, B.B., 'China and the International Criminal Court: Current Situation', 10 *Singapore Year Book of International Law* 2006.

Jonnson, S., 'The Ideology of Universalism', 63 *New Left Review* 2010.

Jouannet, E., 'Universalism and Imperialism: The True-False Paradox of International Law', 18 *EJIL* 2007.

Kelly, P.J., 'Judicial Activism at the World Trade Organization: Developing Principles of Self-Restraint', 22 *Northwestern Journal of International Law & Business* 2002.

Kirchner, S., 'Relative Normativity and the Constitutional Dimension of International Law: A Place for Values in the International Legal System?', 5 *German Law Journal* 2004.

Klabbers, J., 'Constitutionalism Lite', 1 *International Organizations Law Review* 2004.

Klabbers, J., 'The Sociological Jurisprudence of Max Huber: An Introduction', 43 *Austrian Journal of Public International Law* 1992.

Klamberg, M., *Power and Law in International Society: International Relations as the Sociology of International Law*, Routledge, London & New York, 2015.

Kubin, T., 'Enhanced Cooperation, EMU Reforms and Their Implications for Differentiation in the European Union', 7 *Baltic Journal of European Studies* 2017.

Kuijper, P.J. 'The US Attack on the WTO Appellate Body', 45 *Legal Issues of Economic Integration* 2018.

Knox, R., 'Hegemony', *in* D'Aspremont, J., Sing, S. & McBain, G.C. (Eds.), *Concepts for International Law: Contributions to Disciplinary Thought*, Edward Elgar Publishing, Cheltenham-Northampton (MA), 2019.

Koh, H.H., 'On American Exceptionalism', 55 *Stanford Law Review* 2003.

Kojève, A., 'Outline of a Doctrine of French Policy', 126 *Policy Review* August & September 2004, trans. Erik de Vries.

Koskenniemi, M., 'Constitutionalism as Mindset: Reflections on Kantian Themes about International Law and Globalization', 8 *Theoretical Inquires in Law* 2007, Article 2.

Koskenniemi, M., 'International Law and Hegemony: A Reconfiguration', 17 *Cambridge Review f International Affairs* 2004.

Koskenniemi, M., 'International Legal Theory and Doctrine', *in Max Planck Encyclopedia of Public International Law*, On-line edition, 2007.

Koskenniemi, M., 'Letter to the Editors of the Symposium', *in* Ratner, S.R. & Slaughter, A.-M. (Eds.), *The Methods of International Law*, The American Society of International Law, Washington (DC), 2004.

Koskenniemi, M., 'Methodology of International Law', *in Max Planck Encyclopedia of Public International Law*, On-line edition, 2007.

Koskenniemi, M., 'The Place of Law in Collective Security', 17 *Michigan Journal of International Law* 1996.

Koskenniemi, M., 'The Police in the Temple – Order, Justice and the UN: A Dialectical View', 6 *EJIL* 1995.

Koskenniemi, M. & Leino, P., 'Fragmentation of International Law? Postmodern Anxieties', 15 *LJIL* 2002.

Kozyrev, A.V., 'Politika gegemonizma – ugroza miru i mezhdunarodnomu pravoporyadku' [The Policy of Hegemony – A Threat to Peace and International Legal Order], 1982 *Sovetskoe gosudarstvo i pravo* [*Soviet State and Law*].

Krähenmann, S., 'Foreign Fighters under International and National Law', 20 *Recueils de la Société Internationale de Droit Pénal Militaire et de Droit de la Guerre* 2015.

Krisch, N., *Imperial International Law*, Global Working Paper 01/04, New York University School of Law.

Krisch, N., 'International Law in Times of Hegemony: Unequal Power and the Shaping of the International Legal Order', 16 *EJIL* 2005.

Krisch, N., 'Unilateral Enforcement of the Collective Will: Kosovo, Iraq, and the Security Council', 3 *Max Planck Yearbook of United Nations Law* 1999.

Kroll, D.A. & Leuffen, D., 'Enhanced Cooperation in Practice. An Analysis of Differentiated Integration in EU Secondary Law', 22 *Journal of European Public Policy* 2015.

Ku, J., 'Treaties as Laws: A Defense of the Last-in-Time Rule for Treaties and Federal Statutes', 80 *Indiana Law Journal* 2005.

Kurtz, S., 'Democratic Imperialism: A Blueprint', 118 *Policy Review* April-May 2003.

Lamy, P., 'The Place of the WTO and its Law in the International Legal Order', 17 *EJIL* 2007.

Landheer, B., 'Contemporary Sociological Theories and International Law', *in RCADI*, vol. 91, 1957-I, A. W. Sijthoff, Leyde, 1958.

Lavranos, N., 'MOX Plant Dispute: Court of Justice of the European Communities', 2 *European Constitutional Law Review* 2006.

Lavranos, N., 'Protecting the Exclusive Jurisdiction: The *MOX Plant*-Judgment of the ECJ', 5 *The Law and Practice of International Courts and Tribunals* 2006.

Lawless, R., 'A State of Complicity: How Russia's Persistent and Public Denial of Syrian Battlefield Atrocities Violates International Law', 9 *Harvard National Security Journal* 2018.

Lawrence, R.Z., 'Rulemaking amidst Growing Diversity: A Club-of-Club Approach to WTO Reform and New Issue Selection', 9 *Journal of International Economic Law* 2006.

Lee, J., 'The Empire Strikes Back: Case Note on the CJEU Decision in *Slovak Republic v. Achmea BV*, March 6, 2018', 11 *Contemporary Asia Arbitration Journal* 2018.

Lenin, V.I., 'Imperialism, the Highest Stage of Capitalism: A Popular Outline', *in* Lenin, V.I., *Selected Works in Three Volumes*, Progress Publishers, Moscow, 1970, vol. 1.

Lipkin, R.J., 'The Quest for the Common Good: Neutrality and Deliberative Democracy in Sunstein's Conception of American Constitutionalism', 26 *Connecticut Law Review* 1994.

Llewellyn, K.N., 'The Constitution as an Institution', 34 *Columbia Law Review* 1934.

Lock, T., 'The Future of the European Union's Accession to the European Convention on Human Rights after Opinion 2/13: Is It Still Possible and Is It Still Desirable?', 11 *European Constitutional Law Review* 2015.

Loja, M.H., 'Status Quo Post Bellum and the Legal Resolution of the Territorial Dispute between China and Japan over the Senkaku/Diaoyu Islands', 27 *EJIL* 2016.

Lorite Escorihuela, A., 'Cultural Relativism the American Way: The Nationalist School of International Law in the United States', 5 *Global Jurist* 2005, Article 2.

Mabee, B., 'Discourses of Empire: The US 'Empire', Globalisation and International Relations', 8 *Third World Quarterly* 2004.

Magnette, P. & Nicolaïdis, K., 'Coping with the Lilliput Syndrome: Large vs. Small Member States in the European Convention', 11 *European Public Law* 2005.
Mälksoo, L., 'Russia's Constitutional Court Defies the European Court of Human Rights', 12 *European Constitutional Law Review* 2016.
Mälksoo, L., 'The Science of International Law and the Concept of Politics: The Arguments and Lives of the International Law Professors at the University of Dorpat/Iur'-ev/ Tartu 1855-1985', 76 *BYIL* 2005.
Manners, I., 'Normative Power Europe: A Contradiction in Terms?', 40 *Journal of Common Market Studies* 2002.
Maspetiol, R., 'Le droit et la politique : deux visions partielles et fragmentaires d'une même réalité sociale', 16 *Archives de philosophie du droit* 1971.
Matheson, M.J., 'ICJ Review of Security Council Decisions', 36 *George Washington International Law Review* 2004.
Mavroidis, P.C., 'Remedies in the WTO Legal System: Between a Rock and a Hard Place', 11 *EJIL* 2000.
McDougal, M.S. & Reisman, M.W., 'The Prescribing Function in World Constitutive Process: How International Law Is Made', 6 *Yale Studies in World Public Order* 1980.
McDougal, M.S., Reisman, W.M. & Willard, A.R., 'The World Process of Effective Power, The Global War System', *in* McDougal, M.S. & Reisman, W.M., *Power and Policy in Quest of Law: Essays in Honor of Eugene Victor Rostow*, Martinus Nijhoff Publishers, Dordrecht-Boston-Lancaster, 1985.
Monaco, R., 'Le caractère constitutionnel des actes institutifs d'organisations internationales', *in Mélanges offerts à Charles Rousseau – La communauté internationale*, Editions A. Pedone, Paris, 1974.
Mühlfried, F., 'Citizenship at War: Passports and Nationality in the 2008 Russian-Georgian Conflict', 26 *Anthropology Today* 2010.
Müllerson, R., 'International Law between Anarchy and Hegemony', *in* Petman, J. & Klabbers, J. (Eds.), *Nordic Cosmopolitanism: Essays in International Law for Martti Koskenniemi*, Martinus Nijhoff Publishers, Leiden-Boston, 2003.
Narlikar, A. & Wilkinson, R., 'Collapse at the WTO: A Cancun Post-Mortem', 25 *Third World Quarterly* 2004.
National Security Strategy of the United States of America, September 2002, The White House, Washington (DC).
National Security Strategy of the United States of America, March 2006, The White House, Washington (DC).
National Security Strategy of the United States of America, May 2010, The White House, Washington (DC).
National Security Strategy of the United States of America, December 2017, The White House, Washington (DC).

Nicolaïdis, K. & Howse, R., '"This is my EUtopia …": Narrative as Power', 40 *Journal of Common Market Studies* 2002.
Nollkaemper, A., 'Concurrence between Individual and State Responsibility in International Law', 52 *ICLQ* 2003.
Nollkaemper, A., 'Constitutionalization and Unity of the Law of International Responsibility', 16 *Indiana Journal of Global Legal Studies* 2009.
O'Donoghue, A., 'International Constitutionalism and the State', 11 *International Journal of Constitutional Law* 2013.
O'Leary, S., 'A Tale of Two Cities: Fundamental Rights Protection in Strasbourg and Luxembourg', 20 *Cambridge Yearbook of European Legal Studies* 2018.
Orford, A. 'From Promise to Practice? The Legal Significance of the Responsibility to Protect Concept', 3 *Global Responsibility to Protect* 2011.
Orford, A., 'Jurisdiction without Territory: From the Holy Roman Empire to the Responsibility to Protect', 30 *Michigan Journal of International Law* 2009.
Paulus, A., 'The War against Iraq and the Future of International Law: Hegemony or Pluralism?', 25 *Michigan Journal of International Law* 2004.
Paulus, A., '*Jus cogens* in a Time of Hegemony and Fragmentation – An Attempt at a Reappraisal', 74 *Nordic Journal of International Law* 2005.
Pauwleyn, J., 'Bridging Fragmentation and Unity: International Law as a Universe of Inter-connected Islands', 25 *Michigan Journal of International Law* 2004.
Peers, S., 'Bosphorus: European Court of Human Rights', 2 *European Constitutional Court Review* 2006.
Peers, S., 'Divorce, European Style: The First Authorization of Enhanced Cooperation', 6 *European Constitutional Law Review* 2010.
Pernice, I., 'The Global Dimension of Multilevel Constitutionalism: A Legal Response to the Challenges of Globalisation', *in* Dupuy, P.-M. (Ed.), *Völkerrecht als Wertordnung: Festschrift für Christian Tomuschat*, N.P. Engel, Kehl, 2006.
Pernice, I. & Mayer, F.C., 'De la constitution composée de l'Europe', 36 *Revue trimestrielle de droit européen* 2000.
Persaud, R.B., 'Shades of American Hegemony: The Primitive, the Enlightened, and the Benevolent', 19 *Connecticut Journal of International Law* 2004.
Peters, A., 'Global Constitutionalism in a Nutshell', *in* von Dicke, K. (Ed.), *Weltinnenrecht: Liber amicorum Jost Delbrück*, Duncker & Humblot, Berlin, 2005.
Peters, A., 'Compensatory Constitutionalism: The Function and Potential of Fundamental International Norms and Structures', 19 *LJIL* 2006.
Peters, A., 'Humanity as the A and Ω of Sovereignty', 20 *EJIL* 2009.
Peters, A., 'The Growth of International Law between Globalization and the Great Power', 8 *Austrian Review of International and European Law* 2003.
Peters, A., 'There is Nothing more Practical than a Good Theory: An Overview of Contemporary Approaches to International Law', 44 *GYIL* 2001.

Petersmann, E.-U., 'Human Rights, Constitutionalism and the World Trade Organization: Challenges for World Trade Organization Jurisprudence and Civil Society', 19 *LJIL* 2006.

Petersmann, E.-U, 'The WTO Constitution and Human Rights', 3 *Journal of International Economic Law* 2000.

Pitamic, L., 'Some Aspects of the Problem of Interpretation', 19 *American Bar Association Journal* 1933.

Pohl, J.H., 'Intra-EU Investment Arbitration after the *Achmea* Case: Legal Autonomy Bounded by Mutual Trust?', 14 *European Constitutional Law Review* 2018.

Pollack, M.A., 'Who Supports International Law, and Why? The United States, the European Union and the International Legal Order', 13 *EJIL* 2016.

Powell, C., 'Libya: A Multilateral Constitutional Moment', 106 *AJIL* 2012.

Puder, M.G., 'Supremacy of the Law and Judicial Review in the European Union: Celebrating *Marbury v. Madison* with *Costa v. Enel*', 36 *George Washington International Law Review* 2004.

Rabkin, J., 'Is the EU Policy Eroding the Sovereignty of the Non-Member States?', 1 *Chicago Journal of International Law* 2000.

Ramiro Brotóns, A., 'New Imperial Order or (Hegemonic) International Law?', 8 *Austrian Review of International and Comparative Law* 2003.

Ramos-Mrosovsky, C., 'International Law's Unhelpful Role in the Senkaku Islands', 29 *University of Pennsylvania Journal of International Law* 2008.

Reale, M., 'Law and Power and Their Correlation', *in* Newman, R.A. (Ed.), *Essays in Jurisprudence in Honor of Roscoe Pound*, The Bobbs-Merrill Co., Indianapolis, 1962.

Roberts, A., 'NATO's "Humanitarian War" over Kosovo', 41 *Survival* 1999.

Romano, C.P.R., 'Commission of the European Communities v. Ireland', 101 *AJIL* 2007.

Rosand, E., 'The Security Council as 'Global Legislator': Ultra Vires or Ultra Innovative?', 28 *Fordham International Law Journal* 2005.

Rosenau, J.N., 'Governance, Order, and Change in World Politics', *in* Rosenau, J.N. & Czempiel, E.-O. (Eds.), *Governance without Government: Order and Change in World Politics*, CUP, Cambridge, 1992.

Rosenfeld, M., 'Is Global Constitutionalism Meaningful or Desirable?', 25 *EJIL* 2014.

Ruffert, M., 'Rights and Remedies in European Community Law: A Comparative View', 34 *Common Market Law Review* 1997.

Sabel, C.F. & Gerstenberg, O., 'Constitutionalising an Overlapping Consensus: The ECJ and the Emergence of a Coordinate Constitutional Order', 16 *European Law Journal* 2010.

Scelle, G., 'Le droit constitutionnel international', *in Mélanges Raymond Carré de Malberg*, Librairie du recueil Sirey, Paris, 1933, pp. 503-515.

Schachter, O., 'The Role of Power in International Law', 93 *ASILP* 1999.

Schnetter, M., 'Remedies at the International Court of Justice: A New Analytical Approach', No. 1 *Bucerius Law Journal* 2017.

Schwarzenberger, G., 'Power Politics', *in* Bernhardt, R. (Ed.), *Encyclopedia of Public International Law*, vol. III, 1997.

Schwarzenberger, G. 'The Inductive Approach to International Law', 60 *Harvard Law Review* 1947.

Sellers, M.N.S, 'Niccolò Machiavelli: Father of Modern Constitutionalism', 28 *Ratio Juris* 2015.

Shaffer, G., 'The New Legal Realist Approach to International Law', 28 *LJIL* 2015.

Shin, W. & Ahn, D., 'Trade Gains from Legal Rulings in the WTO Dispute Settlement System', 18 *World Trade Review* 2019.

Simma, B., 'From Bilateralism to Community Interest in International Law', *in RCADI*, 1994, VI, vol. 250, Martinus Nijhoff Publishers, The Hague-Boston-London, 1994.

Simpson, G., 'Imagined Consent: Democratic Liberalism in International Legal Theory', 15 *Australian Yearbook of International Law* 1994.

Simpson, G., 'Two Liberalisms', 12 *EJIL* 2001.

Skach, C., 'We, the Peoples? Constitutionalizing the European Union', 43 *Journal of Common Market Studies* 2005.

Slaughter, A.-M., 'Global Government Networks, Global Information Agencies, and Disaggregated Democracy', *in* Ladeur, K.-H. (Ed.), *Public Governance in the Age of Globalization*, Ashgate, 2004.

Slaughter, A.-M., 'Government Networks: The Heart of the Liberal Democratic Order', *in* G.H. Fox & B.R. Roth (Ed.), *Democratic Governance and International Law*, CUP, Cambridge, 2000.

Slaughter, A.-M., 'International Law in a World of Liberal States', 6 *EJIL* 1995.

Stahn, C., 'Responsibility to Protect: Political Rhetoric or Emerging Legal Norm?', 101 *AJIL* 2007.

Steinberger, H., 'Decisions of the Constitutional Court and their Effects', *in The Role of the Constitutional Court in the Consolidation of the Rule of Law*, Proceedings of the UniDem seminar organised in Bucharest on 8-10 June 1994, Collection science and technique of democracy, No. 10, Council of Europe Press, Strasbourg, 1994, pp. 72-101.

Stemplowski, R., 'Hegemony in the European Union?', 4 *Polish Foreign Affairs Digest* 2004.

Stern, B., 'Custom at the Heart of International Law', 89 *Duke Journal of Comparative and International Law* 2001, pp. 89-108.

Stern, B., 'Vers la mondialisation juridique ? Les lois Helms-Burton et D'Amato-Kennedy', 100 *RGDIP* 1996.

Stubb, A., 'A Categorization of Differentiated Integration', 34 *Journal of Common Market Studies* 1996.

Sullivan, E.P., 'Liberalism and Imperialism: J. S. Mill's Defense of the British Empire', 44 *Journal of the History of Ideas* 1983.

Stein, E., 'Lawyers, Judges and the Making of a Transnational Constitution', 75 *AJIL* 1981.

Sur, S., 'La resolution 1540 du Conseil de Securité (28 avril 2004) : entre la proliferation des armes de destruction massive, le terrorisme et les acteurs non étatiques', 108 *RGDIP* 2004.

Szasz, P.C., 'The Security Council Starts Legislating', 96 *AJIL* 2002.

Talmon, S., 'Determining Customary International Law: The ICJ's Methodology between Induction, Deduction and Assertion', 26 *EJIL* 2015.

Talmon, S., 'The Security Council as World Legislature', 99 *AJIL* 2005.

Tacheva, B. & Wallace Brown, G., 'Global Constitutionalism and the Responsibility to Protect', 4 *Global Constitutionalism* 2015.

Tanzi, A., 'Remarks on Sovereignty in the Evolving Constitutional Features of the International Community', *in* Arsanjani, M.H. *et al.* (Eds.), *Looking to the Future: Essays on International Law in Honor of W. Michael Reisman*, Martinus Nijhoff, Leiden-Boston, 2011.

Teubner, G., 'Constitutionnalisme sociétal et globalisation : alternatives à la théorie constitutionnelle centre sur l'État', 3 *Revue Juridique Themis* 2005.

Teubner, G., '"Global Bukowina": Legal Pluralism in the World Society', *in* Teubner, G. (Ed.), *Global Law without a State*, Dartmouth, Aldershot-Brookfield-Singapore-Sidney, 1997.

Teubner, G., 'Global Private Regimes: Neo-spontaneous Law and Dual Constitutions of Autonomous Sectors in World Society', *in* Ladeur, K.-H. (Ed.), *Globalization and Public Governance*, CUP, Cambridge, 2000.

Teubner, G. & Fischer-Lescano, A., 'Regime Collisions: the Vain Search for Legal Unity in the Fragmentation of Global Law', 25 *Michigan Journal of International Law* 2004.

Thym, D., 'Competing Models for Understanding Differentiated Integration', *in* de Witte, B., Ott, A. & Vos, E. (Eds.), *Between Flexibility and Disintegration: The Trajectory of Differentiation in EU Law*, Edward Elgar, Cheltenham-Northampton, 2017.

Thürer, D., 'Hegemony', *in* R. Wolfrum (Ed.), *Max Planck Encyclopedia of Public International Law*, OUP, Oxford, 2012, vol. IV.

Tomuschat, C., 'Obligations Arising for States without or against their Will', *in RCADI*, 1993, IV, vol. 241, Martinus Nijhoff Publishers, Dordrecht-Boston-London, 1994.

Tuori, K., 'Law, Power and Critique', *in* Tuori, K., Bankowski, Z. & Uusitalo, J. (Eds.), *Law and Power: Critical and Socio-Legal Essays*, Deborah Charles Publications, Liverpool, 1997.

Tuzmukhamedov, B., 'Legislative Regulation of Trans-boundary Use of Armed Force: Russian Case Study', 12 *BaYIL* 2012.

UN GA, *A More Secure World: Our Shared Responsibility*, 2 December 2004, A/59/565.

UN SG, *Implementing the Responsibility to Protect*, Report of the Secretary-General, 12 January 2009, A/63/677.

UN SG, *In Larger Freedom: Towards Development, Security and Human Rights for All*, Report of the Secretary General, 21 March 2005, A/59/2005.

UN SG, *Mobilizing Collective Action: The Next Decade of the Responsibility to Protect*, Report of the Secretary-General, 22 July 2016, A/70/999-S/2016/620.

UN SG, *One Humanity: Shared Responsibility*, Report of the Secretary-General for the World Humanitarian Summit, 2 February 2016, A/70/709.

Vagts, D., 'Hegemonic International Law', 95 *AJIL* 2001.

Vagts, D., 'The United States and Its Treaties: Observance and Breach', 95 *AJIL* 2001.

Vagts, D., 'Treaty Interpretation and the New American Ways of Law Reading', 4 *EJIL* 1993.

Vázques, C.M., 'Judicial Review in the United States and in the WTO: Some Similarities and Differences', 36 *George Washington International Law Review* 2004.

Venice Commission, 'Opinion on the Federal Law on the Amendments to the Federal Law on Defence of the Russian Federation', 21 December 2010, CDL-AD(2010)052.

Venice Commission, 'Report on the Rule of Law', 4 April 2011, CDL-AD(2011)003rev.

Venice Commission, 'Rule of Law Checklist', 18 March 2016, CDL-AD(2016)007.

Venice Commission, 'Russian Federation - Final Opinion on the Amendments to the Federal Constitutional Law on the Constitutional Court', 13 June 2016, CDL-AD (2016)016.

Verdross, A., 'Forbidden Treaties in International Law: Comments on Professor Garner's Report on "The Law of Treaties"', 31 *AJIL* 1937.

Von Bogdandy, A., 'Law and Politics in the WTO – Strategies to Cope with a Deficient Relationship', 5 *Max Planck Yearbook of United Nations Law* 2001.

Von Bogdandy, A. & I. Venzke, 'On the Function of International Courts: An Appraisal in Light of Their Burgeoning Public Authority', 26 *LJIL* 2013.

Watson, G.R., 'Constitutionalism, Judicial Review, and the World Court', 34 *Harvard International Law Journal* 1993.

Weil, P., 'Towards Relative Normativity in International Law?', 77 *AJIL* 1983.

Weiler, J.H.H., *The Rule of Lawyers and the Ethos of Diplomats: Reflections on the Internal and External Legitimacy of WTO Dispute Settlement*, Harvard Jean Monnet Working Paper 9/00, Cambridge (MA), 2000.

Welsh, J.M., 'Norm Contestation and the Responsibility to Protect', 5 *Global Responsibility to Protect* 2013.

Wiener, A., *Towards a Transnational Nomos: The Role of Institutions in the Process of Constitutionalization*, Jean Monnet Working Paper 9/03, Heidelberg, 2003.

Wildhaber, L., 'A Constitutional Future for the European Court of Human Rights', 23 *Human Rights Law Journal* 2002.

Wildhaber, L., 'The European Court of Human Rights in Action', 21 *Ritsumeikan Law Review* 2004.
Worster, W.T., 'The Inductive and Deductive Methods in Customary Law Analysis: Traditional and Modern Approaches', 45 *Georgetown Journal of International Law* 2014.
Xue, H., 'Chinese Observations on International Law', 6 *Chinese Journal of International Law* 2007.
Yee, S., 'Towards a Harmonious World: The Roles of the International Law of Co-progressiveness and Leader States', 7 *Chinese Journal of International Law* 2008.
Zidar, A., 'The European Court of Human Rights and the Question of Remedies', *in* Creta, A. *et al., European Master's Degree in Human Rights and Democratization Awarded Theses of the Academic Year 1998/1999*, Marsilio, Venice, 2001.
Zidar, A., 'Legal Imperialism through Decisions of International Organs', *in Imperialism and Chauvinism in the Law, Reports Presented to a Colloquium on the Occasion of the 20th Anniversary of the Swiss Institute of Comparative Law*, Lausanne, 3-4 octobre 2002, Schulthess, Genève-Zurich-Basle, 2004.
Zou, K., 'Governing the Taiwan Issue in Accordance with Law: An Essay on China's Anti-Secession Law', 4 *Chinese Journal of International Law* 2005.
Zupančič, B.M., 'Adjudication and the Rule of Law', 5 *European Journal of Law Reform* 2003.
Zupančič, B.M., 'Criminal Law and Its Influence upon Normative Integration', 7 *Acta Criminologica* 1974, http://id.erudit.org/iderudit/017031ar.
Zupančič, B.M. 'From Combat to Contract: "What Does the Constitution Constitute?"', 1 *European Journal of Law Reform* 1998/1999.
Zupančič, B.M., 'Constitutional Law and the Jurisprudence of the European Court of Human Rights: An Attempt at a Synthesis', 2 *German Law Journal* 2001.

LEGAL SOURCES:

Documents:

United Nations

The Charter of the United Nations and Statute of the International Court of Justice, signed on 26 June 1945, entered into force on 24 October 1945.
Universal Declaration of Human Rights, adopted and proclaimed by the resolution of the General Assembly No. 217 A (III) on 10 December 1948.
Convention against Torture and Other Cruel, Inhuman or Degrading Treatment or Punishment, adopted by the General Assembly resolution 39/46 of 10 December 1984, entered into force on 26 June 1987.

Vienna Convention on Consular Relations, 24 April 1963, entered into force on 19 March 1967, UNTS, vol. 596, p. 261.

Vienna Convention on the Law of Treaties, 23 May 1969, entered into force on 27 January 1980, UNTS, vol. 1155, p. 18.

United Nations Convention on the Law of the Sea, opened for signature on 10 December 1982, entered into force on 16 November 1994.

Declaration on Principles of International Law concerning Friendly Relations and Co-operation among States in accordance with the Charter of the United Nations, No. 2625 (XXV), adopted on 24 October 1970.

Declaration on the Establishment of a New International Economic Order (A/RES/S-6/3201), adopted on 1 May 1974.

Resolution A/34/103, adopted on 14 December 1979.

Resolution A/ES-6/2, adopted on 14 January 1980.

Resolution '60/1. 2005 World Summit Outcome', 24 October 2005, A/RES/60/1.

Text of the Draft Articles on Responsibility of States for Internationally Wrongful Acts, in Report of the International Law Commission, Fifty-third session (23 April-1 June and 2 July-10 August 2001), General Assembly, Official Records, Fifty-sixth session, Supplement No. 10 (A/56/10), United Nations, New York, 2001.

Resolutions of the Security Council:

Res. 678 (1990), Res. 687 (1991), Res. 1160 (1998), Res. 1199 (1998), Res. 1203 (1998), Res. 1244 (1999), Res. 1373 (2001), Res. 1441 (2002), Res. 1422 (2002), Res. 1487 (2003), Res. 1540 (2004), Res. 1564 (2004), Res. 1653 (2006), Res. 1674 (2006), Res, 1706 (2006), Res. 1816 (2008), Res. 1851 (2008), Res. 1894 (2009), Res. 1970 (2011), Res. 1975 (2011), Res. 2015 (2011), Res. 2178 (2014).

WTO

Agreement Establishing the World Trade Organization, adopted on 15 April 1994, entered into force 1 January 1995.

Council of Europe

European Convention on Human Rights as Amended by Protocol No. 11, Council of Europe, Strasbourg, 1998.

European Union

Charter of Fundamental Rights of the European Union, No. 2000/C 364/01, Official Journal of the European Communities, 18 December 2000.

Consolidated version of the Treaty on European Union, Official Journal C 326, 26 October 2012.

Consolidated version of the Treaty on the Functioning of the European Union, Official Journal C 326, 26 October 2012.

Judicial decisions:

Permanent Court of International Justice

Case concerning the Factory at Chorzów (Claim for Indemnity), Merits, 13 September 1928, Permanent Court of International Justice, Series A, No. 17.

International Court of Justice

Certain Expenses of the United Nations, Advisory Opinion, 20 July 1962 (ICJ Reports 1962, p. 151).
North Sea Continental Shelf Cases, Judgment, 20 February 1969, (ICJ Reports 1969, p. 3).
Barcelona Traction, Light and Power Company, Limited, Judgment, 5 February 1970, (ICJ Reports 1970, p. 3).
Legal Consequences for States of the Continued Presence of South Africa in Namibia (South West Africa) notwithstanding Security Council Resolution 276 (1970), Advisory Opinion, 21 June 1971 (ICJ Reports 1971, p. 16).
Fisheries Jurisdiction Case (United Kingdom v. Iceland), Jurisdiction of the Court, 2 February 1973 (ICJ Reports 1973, p. 3).
Military and Paramilitary Activities in and against Nicaragua (Nicaragua v. United States of America), Merits, Judgment, ICJ Rep. 1986.
Questions of Interpretation and Application of the 1971 Montreal Convention arising from the Aerial Incident at Lockerbie (Lybian Arab Jamahiriya v. United Kingdom), Provisional Measures, Order of 14 April 1992, (ICJ Reports, 1992).
Application of the Convention on the Prevention and Punishment of the Crime of Genocide (Preliminary Objections), 11 July 1996 (ICJ Reports 1996, p. 595).
Case concerning the Vienna Convention on Consular Relations (Paraguay v. United States of America), Provisional Measures, Order of 9 April 1998 (ICJ Reports 1998, p. 248).
LaGrand (Germany v. United States of America), Provisional Measures, Order of 3 March 1999 (ICJ Reports 1999, p. 9).
LaGrand (Germany v. United States of America), Judgement, 27 June 2001, (ICJ Reports 2001, p. 466).
Avena and Other Mexican Nationals (Mexico v. United States of America), Provisional Measures, Order of 5 February 2003 (ICJ Reports 2003, p. 77).
Avena and Other Mexican Nationals (Mexico v. United States of America), Judgement, 31 March 2004 (ICJ Reports 2004, p. 12).
Case concerning Armed Activities on the Territory of Congo (Democratic Republic of the Congo v. Uganda), Judgment, ICJ Reports 2005.

Case concerning Armed Activities on the Territory of the Congo (New Application: 2002) (Democratic Republic of the Congo v. Rwanda), Jurisdiction of the Court and Admissibility of the Application, 3 February 2006, (General List No. 126).
Application of the Convention on the Prevention and Punishment of the Crime of Genocide (Bosnia and Herzegovina v. Serbia and Montenegro), Judgment, 26 February 2007 (General list No. 91).
Request for Interpretation of the Judgment of 31 March 2004 in the Case concerning Avena and Other Mexican Nationals (Mexico v. United States of America), Judgment, 19 January 2009.
Legal Consequences of the Separation of the Chagos Archipelago from Mauritius in 1965, Advisory Opinion, 25 February 2019 (General List No. 169).

Permanent Court of Arbitration
The Mox Plant Case (Ireland v. United Kingdom), PCA, Case No. 2002-1, Order No. 3, 24 June 2003.
The Mox Plant Case (Ireland v. United Kingdom), PCA, Case No. 2002-1, Order No. 5, 14 November 2003.
Dispute concerning Access to Information under Article 9 of the OSPAR Convention (Ireland v. UK), Case No. 2001-3, PCA arbitral tribunal, Final Award, 2 July 2003.
Eureko B.V v. The Slovak Republic, PCA, Case No. 2008-13, Award on Jurisdiction, Arbitrability and Suspension, 26 October 2010.
Achmea B.V. v. The Slovak Republic, PCA, Case No. 2008-13, Final Award, 7 December 2012.

ITLOS
The Mox Plant Case (Ireland v. United Kingdom), ITLOS, No. 10, Order, 3 December 2001.

WTO Appellate Body
United States – Standards for Reformulated and Conventional Gasoline, WT/DS2/AB/R, 29 April 1996.
United States – Import Prohibition of Certain Shrimp and Shrimp Products, WT/DS58/AB/R, 12 October 1998.

International Criminal Tribunal for Former Yugoslavia
Prosecutor v. Duško Tadić a/k/a "Dule", Decision on the Defence Motion for Interlocutory Appeal on Jurisdiction, 2 October 1995.
Prosecutor v. Anto Furundžija, Judgment, 10 December 1998.
Prosecutor v. Duško Tadić, Appeals Chamber, Case No. IT-94-1-A, Judgment, 15 July 1999.

European Court of Human Rights

Loizidou v. Turkey (Preliminary Objections), 23 March 1995.
Cable and Others v. United Kingdom, 18 February 1999.
Scozzari and Giunta v. Italy, 13 July 2000.
Lucà v. Italy, 27 February 2001.
Al-Adsani v. the United Kingdom, 21 November 2001.
Assanidze v. Georgia, 8 April 2004.
Broniowski v. Poland, 22 June 2004.
Ilaşcu and Others v. Moldova and Russia, 8 July 2004.
Bosphorus v. Ireland, 30 June 2005.
Broniowski v. Poland (friendly settlement), 28 September 2005.
Lukenda v. Slovenia, 6 October 2005.
Sejdović v. Italy, 1 March 2006.
M.S.S. v. Belgium, Grand Chamber, 21 January 2011.
Tarakhel v. Switzerland, Grand Chamber, 14 November 2014.
Avotiņš v. Latvia, Grand Chamber, 23 May 2016.
Advisory Opinion concerning the recognition in domestic law of a legal parent-child relationship between a child born through a gestational surrogacy arrangement abroad and the intended mother, Requested by the French Court of Cassation, Grand Chamber, 10 April 2019.

EU Courts

Court of First Instance
Case T-306/01, Yusuf and Al Barakaat International Foundation v. Council and Commission, 21 September 2005.
Case T-315/01, Kadi v. Council and Commission, 21 September 2005.

European Court of Justice
Case 26-62, *NV Algemene Transport-en Expeditie Onderneming van Gend & Loos v. Netherlands Inland Revenue Administration*, 5 February 1963, Sect. II/B (ECR 1963, p. 1).
Case 6/64, *Flaminio Costa v E.N.E.L.*, 15 July 1964 (ECR 1964, p. 585).
Case 33/76, *Rewe-Zentrafinanz and Rewe-Zentral AG v. Landwirtschaftskammer für das Saarland*, 16 December 1976 (ECR 1976, p. 1989).
Case 45/76, *Comet BV v Produktschap voor Siergewassen*, 16 December 1976 (ECR 1976, p. 2043).
Case 14/83, *Sabine von Colson and Elisabeth Kamann v. Land Nordrhein-Westfalen*, 10 April 1984 (ECR 1984, p. 1891).
Case C-213, *The Queen v. Secretary of State for Transport, ex parte: Factortame Ltd and Others*, 19 June 1990 (ECR 1990, p. I-2433).

Joined Cases C-6/90 and C-9/90, *Andrea Francovich and Danila Bonifaci and Others v. Italian Republic*, 19 November 1991 (ECR 1991, p. I-5357).
Case C-271/92, *M. Hellen Marshall v Southampton and South West Hampshire Area Health Authority*, 2 August 1993 (ECR 1993, p. I-04357).
Case C-312/93, *Peterbtroeck, Van Campenhout & Cie SCS v Belgian State*, 14 December 1995 (ECR 1995, p. I-4599).
Case C-430/93, *Jeroen van Schijndel and Johannes Nicolaas Cornelis van Veen v Stichting Pensioenfonds voor Fysiotherapeuten*, 14 December 1995 (ECR 1995, p. I-4705).
Case C-84/95, *Bosphorus Hava Yollari Turizm v. Minister for Transport, Energy and Communications, Ireland and the Attorney General*, 30 July 1996.
Case C-376/98, *Germany v. Parliament and Council, Directive 98/43/EC - Advertising and sponsorship of tobacco products*, 5 October 2000.
Case- C-377/02, *Léon Van Parys NV v Belgisch Interventie- en Restitutiebureau (BIRB)*, 1 March 2005.
Case C-459/03, *Commission of the European Communities v. Ireland*, 30 May 2006.
Joined Cases C-402/05 P and C-415/05 P, *Kadi, Al Barakaat International Foundation v. Council, Commission, and UK*, 3 September 2008.
Cases C-411/10 and C-493/10, *N.S. and Others*, Grand Chamber, 21 December 2011.
Joined Cases C-274/11 and C-295/11, *Kingdom of Spain and Italian Republic v. Council of the European Union*, Grand Chamber, 16 April 2013.
Case C-284/16, *Slowakische Republik v. Achmea BV*, Grand Chamber, 6 March 2018.
Opinion 2/13 on EU Accession to the ECHR, Full Court, 18 December 2014.

National Courts

Russia
Judgment of the Russian Constitutional Court on the case concerning the review of constitutionality of Art. 1 of the Convention for the Protection of Human Rights and Fundamental Freedoms and Protocols thereto, 14 July 2015, No. 21-P/2015.
Judgment of the Russian Constitutional Court on the case concerning the resolution of the question of possibility to execute the judgment of the European Court of Human Rights of 4 July 2013 in the case of Anchugov and Gladkov v. Russia, 14 April 2016, No. 12-P/2016.

United States of America
Marbury v. Madison, US Supreme Court, February 1803, 5 U.S. 137 (Cranch).
The Chinese Exclusion Case/Chae Chan Ping v. United States, US Supreme Court, 13 May 1889, 130 U.S. 581 (1889).
Breard v. Greene, Warden, US Supreme Court, 14 April 1998, 523 U.S. 371.
Medellin v. Texas, US Supreme Court, 25 March 2008, No. 06-984, 552 U.S. (2008).

Internet sources:

ASIL Insights, https://www.asil.org/insights.
Avalon Project at the Yale School of Law, http://avalon.law.yale.edu.
EJIL: *Talk!*, www.ejiltalk.org.
European Court of Human Rights, www.echr.coe.int.
Gallica, la bibliothèque numérique, https://gallica.bnf.fr/.
German Law Journal, www.germanlawjournal.com.
International Court of Justice, www.icj-cij.org.
International Criminal Tribunal for the Former Yugoslavia, www.un.org/icty/.
Just Security, www.justsecurity.org.
Lawfare, www.lawfareblog.com.
Max Planck Encyclopedia of Public International Law On-Line, https://opil.ouplaw.com/home/EPIL.
Merriam-Webster Online Dictionary, https://www.merriam-webster.com/.
Permanent Court of International Justice, https://www.icj-cij.org/en/pcij.
Policy Review, https://www.hoover.org/publications/policy-review.
The Constitution Society, www.constitution.org.
The Online Library of Liberty, https://oll.libertyfund.org/.
The Stanford Encyclopaedia of Philosophy, https://plato.stanford.edu/index.html.
US Supreme Court, https://supreme.justia.com/.

INDEX

U

V

W

Z

Printed by Libri Plureos GmbH in Hamburg,
Germany

9 789462 369245